Voluntary Assignments for the Benefit of Creditors

VOLUME I

Voluntary Assignments for the Benefit of Creditors

BY

JAMES AVERY WEBB

VOLUME I

BeardBooks
Washington, D.C.

Copyright 1858 by Alexander M. Burrill,

1894 by James Avery Webb

Reprinted 1999 by Beard Books, Washington, D.C.

ISBN 1-893122-28-X

Printed in the United States of America

A TREATISE

ON THE

LAW AND PRACTICE

OF

VOLUNTARY ASSIGNMENTS

FOR THE

BENEFIT OF CREDITORS,

ADAPTED TO THE

LAWS OF THE VARIOUS STATES,

WITH AN

APPENDIX OF FORMS.

BY

ALEXANDER M. BURRILL,

AUTHOR OF A LAW DICTIONARY AND GLOSSARY, A TREATISE ON CIR-
CUMSTANTIAL EVIDENCE, A TREATISE ON PRACTICE, ETC.

REVISED AND ENLARGED

BY

JAMES L. BISHOP.

SIXTH EDITION REVISED AND ENLARGED AND AN
APPENDIX OF STATE STATUTES ADDED

BY

JAMES AVERY WEBB,

OF THE MEMPHIS, TENN., BAR.

Entered, according to Act of Congress, in the year eighteen hundred and fifty-eight, by
ALEXANDER M. BURRILL,
In the Clerk's Office of the District Court of the United States for the Southern District of New York.

PREFACE TO THE (REVISED) SIXTH EDITION.

IN the preparation of the sixth edition of this book I have endeavored to better adapt it to the use of lawyers by some material changes which I have made in both its composition and arrangement. I have eliminated from the text all quotations from or references to state statutes, except where their retention either as illustrations or as the leading point in decisions of importance was deemed advisable, and have prepared, instead, a synopsis of the statutes of the several states and territories regulating voluntary assignments for the benefit of creditors, which is added to the text as Appendix I. The increased number and importance of such statutes in many of the states, and the fact that frequent calls are made upon counsel relative to the assignment laws of foreign states, suggested this change, which, with the balance of the work, I have undertaken to perform as best I could amid the usual interruptions of the practitioner. I have revised the forms, and eliminated all the repealed statutes, the cases construing them, and overruled cases. I have examined and cited practically all the American and English cases decided since 1877, adding nearly one thousand in number to those cited in the fifth edition. This frequently necessitated the rewriting of the text to make it include and conform to the law as announced in the late cases, and a revision of the notes. The section names or paragraph head-lines have been increased in number and so arranged that the contents of each section or paragraph is indicated by its head-line, and the contents of each chapter by a table at its beginning.

J. A. W.

MEMPHIS, TENN., July 27, 1893.

PREFACE TO THE FIFTH EDITION.

My work in preparing this edition has been confined principally to an examination of the cases which have been reported since the publication of the fourth edition, and to preparing notes referring to them.

In a few instances additions have been made to the text, so that, with the notes, the number of pages in the volume has been increased by forty-one.

About six hundred new cases have been cited.

G. L. STERLING.

NEW YORK, February 18, 1887.

PREFACE TO THE FOURTH EDITION.

SINCE the publication of the previous edition of this work, the Bankrupt Act has been repealed, and the system of voluntary assignments, with various modifications, now prevails to a greater extent than before throughout the United States. One may almost say that every new volume of reports contains at least some case bearing upon the questions treated in this book.

In preparing the fourth edition, no alterations have been made in the arrangement of the matter, and none of importance in the text except where statutes have rendered a change necessary. About seventy-five pages of new matter, scattered through the volume, have been added, however, and nearly eight hundred new cases.

The various state statutes, many of them recent and lengthy, have not been set out in full from lack of space, but it is hoped that enough has been given to furnish a reliable guide, and suggest to the reader the points to be observed and looked for in the statutory regulations affecting voluntary assignments.

G. L. STERLING.

NEW YORK, November 1, 1882.

PREFACE TO THE (REVISED) THIRD EDITION.

Mr. Burrill's "Treatise on Assignments" is well known to the profession as a work of high order of merit, and requires at this time no formal introduction. The present edition, however, in which some changes have been made in the structure as well as in the substance of the work, may properly call for a few words of explanation. During the period which has elapsed since the appearance of the last edition — now nearly twenty years — the bankrupt law has been enacted, many statutes relating to voluntary assignments have been passed in the several states, and upwards of a thousand cases illustrating the questions discussed have been reported. The matter available in preparing a new edition was therefore extensive as well as important. The plan upon which the work was originally prepared by the learned author included, in some instances, a very full discussion of the cases, with copious extracts from statutes, many of which have since been repealed or amended. Hence it was feared that mere notes of reference to the modifications and changes which have taken place in the law might prove unsatisfactory. The editor has therefore undertaken the delicate task of revising as well as annotating the text.

The design has been to make as few alterations in the language of the original work as possible, although in some instances, for the sake of brevity, the order of chapters, paragraphs and sentences has been changed. Thus the first, third and twelfth chapters, which treated respectively of "assignments in general," "assignments distinguished from other modes and instruments of transfer," and "assignments directly to creditors," have been condensed into the first chapter. In like manner the fourth, sixteenth and twenty-ninth chapters of the original, treating of "what may be assigned," "the amount assigned," and "what passes by an assignment," are here found under the sixth chapter, entitled "of the assigned property." So the ninth, eighteenth and nineteenth are here condensed into one chapter, treating of the "form of the assignment."

A new chapter, on voluntary assignments considered in connection with the bankrupt law, has been added, and it should here be remarked that several important cases touching upon the questions discussed in that chapter, but which have been reported since it was put in print, are to be found in the addenda of cases, at page 719. The chapter on the *lex loci* has been partially rewritten, in accordance with the intention of the learned author, and partly from notes left by him.

The perplexing questions which formerly arose in relation to preferences and releases are now of little or no interest, and the portions of the work which treat of these subjects have received the least attention, while the chapters which refer to the creation of the trust, and the duties of the trustees, have been more carefully considered.

The work has been, throughout, divided into sections with catchwords for convenience of reference.

The forms which are annexed are not expected to supply the wants of practitioners under the various state statutes, but are inserted rather as general guides. They have been selected, in every instance, from instruments which have stood the test of judicial criticism.

It was the desire of the editor to distinguish, in some suitable manner, the additions and alterations which have been made in this edition, lest any error or failure on his part should seem to mar the well-deserved reputation of the distinguished author for thorough accuracy and reliability; but the changes were necessarily so numerous, and of such a character, that no acceptable plan suggested itself, and the purpose was reluctantly abandoned. In presenting the edition in this form, therefore, the editor must justly be held responsible for any errors or shortcomings which appear in the following pages. The difficulties of the task will be apparent to the reader, and need not be dwelt upon. If the result shall prove in any degree serviceable at a time when attention is being universally recalled to the subject of voluntary assignments, all that was anticipated will have been accomplished.

J. L. B.

NEW YORK, January, 1877.

PREFACE TO THE FIRST EDITION.

THE importance of the subject of voluntary assignments for the benefit of creditors, in a mercantile community like the United States, will hardly need any special remark by way of introduction to the following work. The frequency with which these transfers are resorted to, and the magnitude of the consequences which they often involve, render them matters of constant practical interest to the merchant and trader; while the importance of the principles by which they are regulated, and the great variety of questions to which they have given rise, impart to them a peculiar prominence as objects of professional attention and study. Of the law of voluntary assignments it may indeed be said that it has been subjected in this country to so much modification, by legislative enactment and otherwise, as to have assumed, in many respects, a distinctively American character. Several of its leading principles, it is true (including some very important statutory provisions), have been borrowed from the law of England, and occasional illustrations and analogies have been and still are derived from the same source; but the great body of its rules, and much of what may be called its practice, have been established on quite independent grounds.

The difficulties by which the subject is or has been distinguished claim a further word of remark in this place. The leading doctrines of this branch of the law of transfer have not been established without severe and repeated contests between the interests of debtor and creditor, which they so largely affect. In some of these contests, the considerations addressed to the courts have been so nearly balanced as to lead to conflicting decisions, even in the same state, leaving eminent judges sometimes at a loss to determine on which side lay the preponderance. In other states, the current of decisions, after having been for some time uniform in one direction, has gradually inclined in another, leading ultimately to quite opposite conclusions. The difficulties arising from these sources have been increased by the diversities always inseparable from the administration even of the same general system of laws by numerous independent tribunals; and still further, by sectional differences growing out of long-established modes of transfer peculiar to certain states. The right of a debtor to give preferences to certain creditors over others, in an assignment of his property; his right to annex conditions to the assignment; to reserve benefits to himself or his family, or to reserve any control over the assignment, the assignee or the property itself; the necessity of the assent of creditors to the validity of the transfer; the necessity of a delivery of possession of the assigned property — all prominent points in the law of assignments, together with the great question which may be said to comprise them all — what renders an assignment fraudulent and void against creditors? — have been, in a most emphatic sense, "vexed questions;" and some of them, to a considerable extent, still remain so.

The only work in which the principles of this branch of American law have been professedly treated and reduced to anything like a system[1] is the "Summary" of Mr. Angell, which appeared in 1835. This was a very acceptable manual to the profession, comprehending, within a small compass, much valuable matter conveniently arranged. Since the date of its publication, however, the law of assignments has not only spread itself over a vastly wider field, but has assumed in many respects a new character. The very numerous decisions which have been made in the state and federal courts have not only established many new rules, but have materially modified some that had been previously settled. Another and more obvious feature of difference is presented in the *statutes* which have been enacted in several of the states, with express reference to voluntary assignments; settling some important principles of law affecting their form and operation, and regulating, often with minuteness, the practical course of proceedings under them.

Under these circumstances, a new work being called for, the present treatise was undertaken, not without hesitation on the part of the author, in view of the difficulties which have been mentioned. The subject seemed to require a mode of treatment which should present a view, first, of the principles constituting what may be denominated the general American law of voluntary assignments, combined with adequate references to the local law of the states; and, secondly, of the practice under these transfers — both being reduced, so far as the multifarious character of the ma-

---

[1] The author does not here overlook the valuable note to the case of Thomas v. Jenks and Grover v. Wakeman, contained in the first volume of the American Leading Cases, in which the latest law on the subject is digested in a clear and able manner.

terials would permit, to something like a uniform system possessing both general and local utility. The latter branch of the subject was wholly untouched by Mr. Angell, and has not hitherto been illustrated by any American writer. It has been found, however, to possess so much importance that it has been principally had in view in the arrangement of the whole work.

The following pages present, it will be seen, not only a summary of the *principles* upon which voluntary assignments are constructed, and by which their operation is regulated, but also a historical view of the *proceedings*, in the order in which they occur in practice, from the first drafting of the instrument to the close of the trust created by it; thus placing before the reader, successively, first, the acts of the debtor in making and completing the assignment; secondly, the acts of the assignee in carrying it into effect; and lastly, the acts of the creditors in acceptance or rejection of the provisions made by it.

In the treatment of the subject according to the plan here indicated, regard has been had not only to the convenience of practiced and professional readers, but to the wants of students and such non-professional persons as may consult the work. This will serve to explain what perhaps might otherwise be considered a too frequent reference to familiar rules, and repetitions of matter which might have been dispensed with. As to any omissions or misstatements which may be discovered, particularly in reference to the statute law of the states, the author relies on the indulgence of those whose familiarity with the subject best enables them to appreciate the difficulty of attaining at once entire fullness and accuracy where the sources of information are numerous and not always conveniently accessible.

The forms presented in the Appendix embrace examples of the principal varieties of assignments in most frequent use; and, it is hoped, will be found convenient as general guides to the draftsman, or as illustrations to the reader. They are not intended, however, to dispense with a constant reference to the rules laid down in the body of the work; and are, of course, always to be taken subject to modification by local law or usage. The collection might have been considerably extended; and it was the author's design, had time permitted, to have included examples of all the most important varieties of assignments in use throughout the United States. These will be supplied on a future occasion, should a revision of the work be found necessary.

NEW YORK, June 18, 1853.

CONTENTS.

	PAGE.
TABLE OF CASES CITED	xvii

CHAPTER I.

Assignments in general — Voluntary assignments for the benefit of creditors defined and distinguished from other modes and instruments of transfer 1

CHAPTER II.

The right to assign — Statutory provisions restricting the right to assign, and regulating the operation of assignments 19

CHAPTER III.

Voluntary assignments considered in connection with the bankrupt law . 25

CHAPTER IV.

Who may make an assignment 58

CHAPTER V.

To whom an assignment may be made — Qualifications of assignees . . 92

CHAPTER VI.

The assigned property; the amount assigned; what may be assigned; what passes by the assignment 97

CHAPTER VII.

For whose benefit an assignment may be made 115

CHAPTER VIII.

Form of the assignment 122

CHAPTER IX.

Partial assignment 157

CHAPTER X.
Assignments with preferences 162

CHAPTER XI.
Assignments with special provisions 193
    1. Stipulations for the release of the debtor as a condition of the assignment 197
    2. Reservations of benefit to the debtor 217
    3. Appropriations of assets in assignments by firms and their members 234
    4. Stipulations for the continuance of assignor's business . . . 243
    5. Provisions respecting the time for executing the trust . . . 245
    6. Limitation of time for creditors to become parties, or assent . 249
    7. Provisions respecting the sale of the property assigned . . . 251
    8. Special powers and directions to assignees 266
    9. Stipulations for the benefit of assignees 272
    10. Reservations of powers to assignors 273

CHAPTER XII.
Consideration of assignments 277

CHAPTER XIII.
Trusts of assignments 280

CHAPTER XIV.
Execution of the assignment 285

CHAPTER XV.
Record or registry of the assignment 292

CHAPTER XVI.
Delivery of the assignment 301

CHAPTER XVII.
Amendments and additions to assignments 304

CHAPTER XVIII.
Acceptance by the assignee 309

CHAPTER XIX.
Delivery of possession of the property assigned 315

CHAPTER XX.
Assent of creditors 332

CHAPTER XXI.
Time when the assignment takes effect 349

CHAPTER XXII.
Operation of an assignment 352

CHAPTER XXIII.
The *lex loci* in its application to assignments 357

CHAPTER XXIV.
Construction of assignments 381

CHAPTER XXV.
Fraudulent and void assignments 399

CHAPTER XXVI.
Assignments considered in connection with other transfers by the assignor 450

CHAPTER XXVII.
Revocation and cancellation of assignments 459

CHAPTER XXVIII.
Proceedings by the assignee in execution of the trust — General outline of the proceedings, and of the duties, powers and liability of assignees 463

CHAPTER XXIX.
Notice of the assignment 466

CHAPTER XXX.
Taking possession of the property assigned 468

CHAPTER XXXI.
Inventory and appraisement of the property — Bond by the assignee . 476

CHAPTER XXXII.
Rights, duties and powers of the assignee 478

CHAPTER XXXIII.
To what extent the assignor's business may be continued by the assignee . 490

CHAPTER XXXIV.

Collection of debts and recovery of property — Actions by the assignee . 494

CHAPTER XXXV.

Sale of the assigned property 505

CHAPTER XXXVI.

Expenses of the trust and compensation to the assignee 518

CHAPTER XXXVII.

Distribution among creditors 528

CHAPTER XXXVIII.

Disposition of the surplus remaining after distribution 551

CHAPTER XXXIX.

Final accounting and close of the trust by the assignee 554

CHAPTER XL.

Liability of assignees 561

CHAPTER XLI.

Proceedings in case of the death, removal, non-acceptance, resignation, misconduct, insolvency or incapacity of an assignee 574

CHAPTER XLII.

Proceedings of creditors — Coming in under the assignment . . . 580

CHAPTER XLIII.

Release by creditors 588

CHAPTER XLIV.

Proceedings by creditors to enforce the trust — Suits against assignee . 593

CHAPTER XLV.

Proceedings of creditors in opposition to the assignment and in avoidance of it 599

APPENDIX I.

SYNOPSIS OF THE STATUTE LAWS OF THE SEVERAL STATES AND TERRITORIES REGULATING VOLUNTARY ASSIGNMENTS FOR THE BENEFIT OF CREDITORS.

Alabama	609
Arizona	609
Arkansas	612
California	613
Colorado	615
Connecticut	617
Delaware	619
District of Columbia	619
Florida	620
Georgia	621
Idaho	622
Illinois	622
Indiana	624
Indian Territory	627
Iowa	627
Kansas	629
Kentucky	633
Louisiana	634
Maine	634
Maryland	634
Massachusetts	635
Michigan	635
Minnesota	638
Mississippi	641
Missouri	642
Montana	646
Nebraska	646
Nevada	651
New Hampshire	651
New Jersey	654
New Mexico	656
New York	660
North Carolina	665
North Dakota	665
Ohio	667
Oklahoma	671
Oregon	673
Pennsylvania	675
Rhode Island	678
South Carolina	679
South Dakota	680
Tennessee	681
Texas	682
Utah	685
Vermont	685
Virginia	686
Washington	686
West Virginia	687
Wisconsin	688
Wyoming	692

APPENDIX II.

FORMS AND PRECEDENTS.

ASSIGNMENTS BY INDENTURE BIPARTITE 695
   1. A general assignment of real and personal property for the benefit of creditors ratably 695
   2. Assignments bipartite, with preferences 696
   3. A general assignment of real and personal property, giving preferences, without schedules 699
   4. A general assignment, with stipulations for a release, . . 701
   5. Copartnership assignment — Assignment by copartners without preference 701
   6. Assignment by copartnership (shorter form) . . . 704
   7. An assignment with special provisions as to the employment of agents, hiring of store, insurance of property, and correction of schedules 705
   8. An assignment by a bank for the payment of its depositors and the holders of its notes, with special provisions as to dividends 706
   9. An assignment by a married woman 708

ASSIGNMENT BY DEED POLL 709
   10. A general assignment for the benefit of creditors, ratably, with schedules 709

ASSIGNMENTS BY INDENTURE TRIPARTITE 710
   11. A general assignment for the benefit of creditors, with preferences to such as become parties, and with covenant of release by creditors 710

INVENTORY, BOND AND NOTICE TO CREDITORS 712
   12. Title to inventory 712
   13. Inventory 713
   14. Schedules 714
   15. Classification 715
   16. Affidavit to inventory and schedules 716
   17. Assignee's bond on assignment 716
   18. Affidavit to obtain order authorizing assignee to advertise for claims 717
   19. Order of publication of notice to creditors . . . 718
   20. Notice to creditors 718
   21. Proof of debt 719
   22. Petition for citation for final accounting . . . 719
   23. Order for citation 720
   24. Citation for accounting 721
   25. Order of reference 721
   26. Referee's report 722
   27. Final decree 724

INDEX 729

TABLE OF CASES.

References are to pages.

Aaronson v. Deutsch, 442, 612.
Abbot v. Burbage, 32.
Abbott v. Am. Hard Rub. Co., 65, 512, 513.
Abbott v. Chaffee, 476.
Abbott v. Stearns, 487.
Abbott v. Treatt, 427.
Abercrombie v. Bradford, 226, 255, 259, 325, 333, 335, 421.
Aberdeen R. R. Co. v. Blaklie Bros., 510.
Abraham v. Plestoro, 361.
Acker v. Leland, 605.
Ackers v. Rowan, 62.
Acton v. Woodgate, 128, 279, 340, 583.
Adams, Matter of, 531, 581.
Adams v. Alexander, 182.
Adams v. Blodgett, 7, 103, 279, 344.
Adams v. Bradey, 503.
Adams v. Davidson, 442, 469, 502.
Adams v. Houghton, 285, 286, 290.
Adams v. Humes, 517.
Adams v. Hyams, 53.
Adams v. Lewis, 480.
Adams v. Ryan, 95.
Adams v. Thornton, 85.
Adams v. Woods, 132.
Addison v. Burckmyer, 478, 482.
Adee v. Cornell, 67, 85, 86.
Adler v. Ecker, 421.
Adlum v. Yard, 215, 246, 254, 536, 559, 586, 602.
Agnew v. Dorr, 590.
Ahl's Appeal, 6, 527.
Ahl v. Rhoads, 65, 355, 501.
Aiken v. Price, 207.
Ainslee v. Boynton, 479, 500.
Akers v. Rowan, 518, 680.
Albany, etc., Co. v. Southern Ag. Works, 621.

Alderson v. Temple, 30, 32, 64.
Alexander v. Cana, 502.
Aldrich v. Arnold, 678.
Allen, Matter of, 57.
Allen v. Brown, 496.
Allen v. Gardner, 172, 188, 206, 212.
Allen v. Montgomery, 54, 335.
Allen v. Massey, 52.
Allen v. Wheeler, 319.
Allemand v. Russell, 149, 172, 530, 533.
Alnutt v. Leper, 602.
Alpaugh v. Roberson, 460, 576.
Alsop, Ex parte, 34.
American v. Frank, 297, 303, 349, 627.
American Bank v. Doolittle, 200.
Am. Exchange Bank v. Inloes, 176, 261, 492.
Am. Ice Machine Co. v. Patterson St. Fire Eng. & Mach. Co., 185.
Ames v. Blunt, 444, 448, 567, 581, 607.
Ames v. Downing, 513.
Amory v. Francis, 549.
Anderson v. Fuller, 284, 318.
Anderson v. Hook, 118, 445, 447.
Anderson v. Lachs, 260.
Anderson v. Tompkins, 68, 72, 73, 80, 81, 84–88, 105, 286, 355.
Anderson v. Tydings, 167, 428.
Anderson v. Wilson, 54.
Andress v. Miller, 239.
Andrews v. Carr, 3.
Andrews v. His Creditors, 378.
Andrews v. Hobson's Adm'r, 514.
Andrews v. Herriot, 367.
Andrews v. Ludlow, 147, 200, 520, 526.
Angel v. Rosenbury, 60, 93, 94.
Anon. v. Gelpcke, 498, 532, 566.
Ansley v. Patterson, 54.
Ansted v. Bentley, 688.

TABLE OF CASES.

References are to pages.

Antignance v. Central Bank of Georgia, 600.
Archer v. O'Brien, 22, 165.
Archer v. Long, 95.
Arledge, In re, 44, 51, 52.
Armstrong v. Byrne, 203, 213.
Armstrong v. Campbell, 514.
Armstrong v. Fahnstock, 89.
Armstrong v. Morrill, 309.
Armstrong v. Pratt, 594.
Armitage v. Rector, 526.
Arnold v. Bailey, 460.
Arnold v. Brown, 68, 513.
Arnold v. Grimes, 478.
Arnold v. Hagerman, 410.
Arnold v. Maynard, 37.
Arthur v. The Commercial, etc. Bank, 65, 228, 246, 249, 415, 419.
Ash v. Savage, 319.
Ashley v. Robinson, 53, 337, 460.
Ashton v. The Atlantic Bank, 503.
Ashurst v. Martin, 150, 198, 217, 250, 255, 259, 270, 335, 397.
Askew v. La Cygne Bank, 359, 375.
Aspinwall v. Jones, 600.
Association, etc. v. Beekman's Adm'r, 503.
Astor v. Lent, 110.
Atherton Co. v. Ives, 372.
Atkinson v. The Farmers' Bank, 165.
Atkinson v. Brindall, 32.
Atkinson v. Jordan, 164, 168, 170, 207, 209, 210, 606.
Atkinson v. Tomlinson, 179.
Attorney-General v. Lord Dudley, 511.
Atwood v. Protection Ins. Co., 295, 377.
Aubrey v. Osterman, 67, 85, 135, 234.
Aultman v. Seiberling, 669.
Austin v. Bell, 159, 201, 205, 232, 444.
Austin v. Morris, 602, 680.
Averill v. Longfellow, 109.
Averill v. Loucks, 151, 155, 188, 190, 274, 281, 443, 567.
Avery v. Fisher, 58.

Babb v. Clemson, 317.
Babcock v. Dill, 586.
Backer, In re, 460.
Backer, Matter of, 40, 57.
Backhaus v. Sleeper, 691.

Backrack v. Norton, 92.
Bagley v. Bowe, 269, 382, 429, 431, 433.
Bholen v. Cleveland, 327, 474.
Bailey, Matter of, 538.
Bailey v. Bergen, 562.
Bailey v. Kansas Mfg. Co., 135.
Bailey v. Mills, 172, 230, 412.
Baker, In re, 555, 623, 690.
Baker v. Crookshank, 224.
Balderston v. Mauro, 328.
Baldwin v. Buckland, 60, 63, 95, 442.
Baldwin v. Ely, 105.
Baldwin v. Patton, 467.
Baldwin v. Peet, 98, 101, 158, 208, 212, 272, 420-422.
Baldwin v. Short, 443.
Baldwin v. Tynes, 67, 84, 286, 290.
Ball v. Bowe, 689.
Ball v. Dunsterville, 345.
Ball v. Loomis, 322, 469.
Ball v. Slafter, 112, 488.
Balt. & Ohio R. R. Co. v. Glenn, 228, 357.
Ballou, Petition of, 678.
Bamberger v. Halberg, 593.
Bamford v. Baron, 32, 51.
Bancroft v. Blizzard, 421.
Bancroft v. Snodgrass, 92.
Bank v. Cox, 115.
Bank v. Hackett, 689.
Bank v. Holmes, 312, 351.
Bank v. Knox, 499.
Bank v. Newton, 164.
Bank v. Noe, 124, 681.
Bank v. Partee, 346.
Bank v. Versailles Woolen Co., 617.
Bank of Alexandria v. Payne, 111.
Bank of Bellows Falls v. Derring, 342.
Bank of Beloit v. Beale, 498.
Bank of Commerce v. Payne, 99, 412, 477, 586.
Bank of Harlem v. Bayonne, 332.
Bank of Marietta v. Pindall, 3.
Bank of Metropolis v. Guttschlick, 309.
Bank of Mobile v. Dunn, 382, 389.
Bank of Montreal v. Salt & Lumber Co., 13.
Bank of Newberry v. Walker, 586.
Bank of New Brunswick v. Hassert, 319.

TABLE OF CASES. xix

References are to pages.

Bank of Orange Co. v. Fink, 323.
Bank of Pennsylvania v. Gratz, 589, 597.
Bank of Pennsylvania v. McCalmont, 387, 548.
Bank of Silver Creek v. Talcott, 115, 150, 393, 410, 441.
Bank of United States v. Huth, 65.
Bankmay-Fouche v. Brower, 65.
Banks v. Barb Wire Co., 453.
Banks v. Clapp, 103, 221.
Banks v. Wilkes, 569.
Banning v. Sibley, 5, 11, 230.
Barber v. Buffalo, 98.
Barber v. Rogers, 39.
Barber v. Spencer, 500.
Barbour v. Conn. Mut. Life Ins. Co., 400.
Barbour v. Everson, 151.
Barcroft v. Snodgrass, 85, 254, 309, 311, 313, 575.
Barhydt v. Perry, 426.
Barings v. Dabney, 51.
Barker v. Hall, 7, 14, 169, 171.
Barker v. Harlan, 462.
Barker v. Smith, 480.
Barkman v. Simmons, 145.
Barnard v. Duncan, 516.
Barnes v. Fisher, 479.
Barnes v. Rettew, 27, 29, 40, 44, 51.
Barnewell v. Dunn, 52.
Barney v. Griffin, 148, 175, 180, 195, 223, 229, 230, 256, 257, 259, 419, 430, 438, 440, 568.
Barney v. Saunders, 523, 527.
Barnitz v. Rice, 157, 159, 199, 216.
Barnum v. Hempstead, 116, 186, 188, 189, 268, 283, 387, 444.
Barr v. Boyles, 428.
Barr v. Hatch, 319, 326.
Bartlett v. Reids, 207, 606.
Barroilbet v. Fisch, 615.
Bartholomew v. Leach, 513.
Bartlett v. Blake, 319, 427.
Bartlett v. Pearson, 105.
Bartlett v. Teah, 3, 255, 612.
Bartlett v. Williams, 326.
Barton v. Brent, 23, 24, 164.
Bascom v. Rainwater, 23.
Bason v. Harden, 530, 563.

Bassett v. Parsons, 105.
Bate v. Graham, 603.
Bateman v. Conner, 501.
Bates v. Ableman, 60, 64, 101, 152, 158, 442.
Bates v. Bradley, 54.
Bates v. Coe, 15, 17, 167, 169, 178, 452, 453.
Bates v. Simmons, 139, 146, 472, 688.
Batesville Institute v. Kauffman, 575.
Batten v. Smith, 443.
Battles v. Forbes, 287, 582.
Baum v. Pearce, 382.
Baxter v. Wheeler, 225.
Bay v. Cook, 318.
Bayles v. Staats, 578.
Baylor County v. Craig, 208.
Bayly v. Scofield, 61.
Bayne v. Denny, 208.
Bayne v. Wylie, 205, 217, 271, 282.
Beach v. Beston, 5, 10.
Beach v. The Fulton Bank, 534, 535.
Beadle, In re, 41.
Beamish v. Conant, 472.
Bean v. Amsink, 41, 52, 53.
Bean v. Brookmire, 52.
Beans v. Bullitt, 5, 131.
Beard v. Kimball, 143.
Beaston v. Farmers' Bank of Delaware, 65, 354, 541.
Beattie v. Robins, 318.
Beatty v. Davis, 172, 173, 267.
Bebb v. Preston, 10.
Beck v. Barker, 39.
Beck v. Burdett, 102, 230, 231.
Beck v. Burns, 108.
Beck v. Parker, 24, 441.
Becker v. Rardin, 9.
Becker v. Shayne, 684.
Beckwith v. Brown, 172, 206, 395.
Beckwith v. Union Bank, 111, 461, 479, 499.
Becton v. Ferguson, 107.
Bedell v. Janney, 597.
Bedell v. Scruton, 363.
Bedford v. Penney, 353.
Beers v. Lyon, 8, 171.
Beeson v. Beeson, 513.
Beisenthal, In re, 41, 47, 53, 56.
Beidler v. Crane, 231.

TABLE OF CASES.

References are to pages.

Bell v. Wilson, 448.
Belden v. Smith, 41, 51.
Belding v. Franckland, 142, 386, 681.
Belk v. Massey, 427.
Bell v. Dudnit, 669.
Bell v. Fleming's Ex'rs, 545.
Bell v. Holford, 307.
Bell v. Lond. & N. W. Railway Co., 105.
Bell v. Thompson, 172.
Bellamy v. Bellamy's Adm'r, 104, 127, 139, 172, 382, 386, 448, 485, 514, 592.
Bellingsley's Adm'r v. Bunce, 227.
Bellows v. Partridge, 187, 252, 263, 264, 269.
Belmont v. O'Brien, 574.
Benedict v. Huntington, 253, 265, 428.
Benedict v. Morse, 146, 516.
Benedict v. Parmenter, 369.
Benne v. Schencko, 435.
Bennett, Ex parte, 511, 512, 515.
Bennett v. Cocks, 299.
Bennett v. Denny, 640.
Bennett v. Ellison, 191, 259, 270, 481, 482.
Bennett v. Union Bank, 246, 247.
Benning v. Nelson, 337.
Bentley v. Shreve, 522.
Bentley v. Thrasher, 24.
Bentley v. Whittmore, 375.
Benton v. Snyder, 259.
Benss v. Shaughnessy, 266.
Bernheim v. Christal, 435.
Berry v. Cutts, 133, 453.
Berry v. Hayden, 266.
Berry v. Matthews, 260.
Berry v. Riley, 159, 232, 245.
Berryman v. Sullivan, 601.
Besley v. Lawrence, 187, 543, 549, 587.
Beste v. Burger, 90.
Bethune v. Dougherty, 309, 312, 314, 576.
Bettis v. Weir Plow Co., 685.
Betton v. Valentine, 604.
Betts' Estate, 506.
Bidwell v. Bidwell, 57.
Bigelow v. Baldwin, 400, 448.
Bigelow v. Stringer, 230, 431.
Bigelow v. Wilson, 103, 106.
Bigler v. National Bank, 40, 57.

Billings v. Billings, 260, 426, 432.
Billings v. Russell, 421.
Billingsley's Adm'r v. Bunce, 431.
Bills v. Smith, 32.
Billups v. Sears, 17, 446, 605.
Bingham v. Claflin, 54.
Bingham v. Tillinghast, 432.
Birchell v. Strauss, 144.
Birdsey v. Vansands, 617.
Birdseye v. Ray, 167.
Birdwell v. Cain, 103.
Biscoe v. Royston, 352.
Bishop v. Chamberlin, 568.
Bishop v. Hart's Trustees, 124, 125, 519, 568, 600.
Bishop v. Houghton, 561, 593.
Bissell v. Besson, 65, 164.
Bittenger v. Railroad Co., 132.
Black, Matter of, 513.
Black's Appeal, 240.
Black v. Terrin, 52.
Black v. Weathers, 153, 624.
Black v. Zacharie, 365.
Blackburne's Appeal, 563, 676.
Blackford v. Hurst, 296.
Blackington v. Goldsmith, 186.
Blain v. Pool, 441.
Blake v. Hubbard, 347, 448, 601.
Blake v. Williams, 361, 367.
Blakey's Appeal, 22, 132, 163, 167, 168, 169.
Blalock v. Kernersville Mfg. Co., 188.
Blanchard v. Russell, 359.
Blank v. German, 10, 133.
Blank, etc. Co. v. Walker, 67.
Blauvelt v. Ackerman, 511, 513, 514, 564.
Blennerhassett v. Sherman, 10.
Blight v. Schenck, 515.
Bliss v. Cottle, 497.
Block v. Peter, 278.
Bloom v. Noggle, 13, 16, 179.
Bloomingdale v. Stein, 667.
Blount v. Davis, 106.
Blow v. Gage, 62, 63, 147, 148, 427, 472, 518.
Blum v. Welborne, 421.
Boardman v. Halliday, 174, 188, 189.
Boardman v. Keeler, 318.
Boardman v. Mosman, 571.

TABLE OF CASES.

References are to pages.

Boardman v. Willard, 311.
Bobbitt v. Rodwell, 99.
Bock v. Perkins, 138, 142.
Bodenhamer v. Welch, 106.
Bodley v. Goodrich, 129, 147, 200, 249, 400, 448, 525.
Boedefeld v. Reed, 39.
Boegler v. Eppley, 525.
Boeppler v. Menown, 108, 482.
Boese v. King, 40.
Bogert v. Haight, 229, 427, 428, 458, 605.
Bohart v. Atkinson, 513.
Bohlen v. Cleveland, 377.
Boker v. Crookshank, 100, 143.
Boland, Ex parte, 165.
Boling v. Howell, 22, 166.
Bolling v. Munchus, 52.
Bones v. Booth, 413.
Bonner v. Hodges, 434.
Booker v. Crookshank, 676.
Boone v. Hall, 53.
Boos v. Marion, 236.
Booth v. Conn. Mut. Ins. Co., 566.
Booth v. Grant, 227.
Booth v. McNair, 266.
Boston Iron Co. v. Boston Locomotive Works, 361.
Bostwick v. Berger, 567.
Bostwick v. Burnett, 40, 41, 477.
Bostwick v. Menck, 607.
Boswell v. Green, 68.
Botcherly v. Lancaster, 28, 33.
Bothick v. Purdy, 104.
Bouchaud v. Dias, 124, 541, 543.
Boughton v. Bradley, 359.
Boughton v. Crosby, 89, 383, 480.
Bourdilon v. Dalton, 475.
Bourne, Ex parte, 32, 33, 50.
Bousman's Appeal, 100.
Bouton v. Dement, 112.
Bowe v. Arnold, 600.
Bowen v. Brainridge, 420.
Bowen v. Hadden Blue Stone Co., 130.
Bowen v. Lease, 355.
Bowen v. Parkhurst, 259.
Bowker v. Burdekin, 155, 302.
Bowles v. Bowles' Ex'r, 478.
Bowman v. Draughan, 414.
Bowman v. Rainteaux, 571, 575.
Box v. Goodbar, 13.

Boyce, Matter of, 557.
Boyd v. Boyd, 569.
Boyd v. Dunlop, 347.
Boyd v. Hawkins, 514, 523.
Boyd v. Haynie, 208.
Boyd v. Meyers, 518, 567.
Boyd v. Rockford Mills, 368.
Boyden v. Moore, 129, 281, 319.
Boyden v. Partridge, 503.
Boynton Furnace Co. v. Lorensen, 688.
Brackenridge v. Holland, 513.
Brackett v. Barney, 301.
Bradford v. Tappan, 448.
Braddock v. Watson, 411.
Bradley v. Bischel, 67, 99.
Bradley Fertilizer Co. v. Fuller, 497.
Bradley v. Kroft, 688, 689.
Bradshaw v. Klein, 52, 53.
Bradley v. Norton, 106.
Brahe v. Eldridge, 28, 307, 461, 689.
Brahmstadt v. McWhirter, 92, 266, 427.
Brainard v. Dunning, 116, 117.
Branch Bank v. Robertson, 548.
Brandon v. Rogers, 182.
Brannock v. Brannock, 118, 120.
Brashear v. West, 123, 141, 152, 163, 172, 205, 210, 212, 315, 332, 334, 346, 552.
Breck v. Cole, 191.
Breedlove v. Stump, 337, 576.
Brennan v. Wilson, 92, 311, 314, 516.
Brenneman, Ex parte, 36, 168, 181, 401.
Brent v. The Bank of Washington, 541.
Brent v. Shouse, 367.
Bresson v. Musselman, 9.
Brevard v. Neely, 298, 302, 303, 312, 313, 337, 460, 461.
Brice's Appeal, 522.
Brice v. Stokes, 569, 570, 571.
Brichta v. New York Lafayette Ins. Co., 105.
Bridges v. Hindes, 133.
Bridges v. Miles, 63.
Bridges v. Wood, 159, 199, 212, 443.
Bridgford v. Barbour, 482.
Brigee v. Starbuck, 504, 667, 668.
Briggs v. Davis, 10, 13, 15, 228, 484, 486, 517, 551.
Briggs v. Palmer, 352, 486, 551.
Brigham v. Jones, 382.

TABLE OF CASES.

References are to pages.

Brigham v. Tillinghast, 137, 172, 175, 252, 253, 256, 264, 239, 382, 427, 441.
Brinkerhoff v. Wernple, 503.
Brinks v. Heise, 428.
Brinley v. Springs, 319.
Brittenbender v. Sunbury & Erie Railroad Co., 111.
Brittlestone v. Cook, 31.
Britton v. Boyer, 164.
Britton v. Hughes, 190.
Britton v. Lorenz, 131, 281, 290.
Broach v. Powell, 53.
Broadbent v. Thornton, 343, 583.
Brockley v. Brockley 205.
Brock v. Headen, 255, 508.
Brodhead, In re, 44, 57.
Bromberg v. Heyer, 602.
Brooks v. Brooks, 106, 110, 313, 680.
Brooks v. Marbury, 126, 172, 297, 311, 326, 334, 342, 349.
Brooks v. Nichols, 98.
Brooks v. Peck, 594.
Brooks v. Stanton, 5.
Brooks v. Sullivan, 81.
Brooks v. Wilson, 443.
Brooks v. Wimer, 227, 431.
Brough's Estate, 549.
Broughton v. Broughton, 511.
Brouwer v. Harbeck, 183.
Brower v. Goodyer, 114.
Brown, Matter of, 120.
Brown v. Agnew, 356.
Brown v. Bartee, 172, 278, 427.
Brown v. Brabb, 478.
Brown v. Brittain, 499.
Brown v. Cavendish, 128.
Brown v. Chamberlain, 127, 131, 460.
Brown v. Chambers, 104.
Brown v. Foster, 22, 169, 177, 453, 455.
Brown v. Guthrie, 124, 268, 275, 450, 480.
Brown v. Holcomb, 131, 654.
Brown v. Kempton, 32, 164.
Brown v. Knox, 148, 154, 208, 377.
Brown v. Lee, 179.
Brown v. Lyon, 140, 152, 229, 233, 250, 335, 341, 343, 351.
Brown v. Maine Bank, 105, 107.
Brown v. May, 606.
Brown v. Merchants' Bank, 549.

Brown v. Minturn, 23, 312, 327, 342.
Brown v. Rickets, 511.
Brown v. Smart, 380.
Brown v. Vanlier, 337.
Brown v. Warren, 341.
Brown v. Webb, 13, 16.
Brown v. Wier, 149.
Brownwell v. Curtis, 104, 111, 486.
Browning v. Hart, 94, 104, 111, 322, 353, 441, 472.
Bruce's Adm'rs v. Smith, 166.
Bruen v. Gillet, 563, 572.
Bruen v. Marquard, 345, 394.
Bryan v. Brisbin, 380.
Bryant v. Bryant, 603.
Bryant v. Kelten, 320.
Bryant v. Russell, 550, 594.
Bryant v. Young, 284.
Bryce, Matter of, 577.
Bryce v. Foot, 23.
Buck v. Pennybacker, 595.
Buck v. Sherman, 415, 427.
Buckley v. Dunn, 167.
Buckner v. Sayre, 111.
Buell v. Buckingham, 65, 66, 179.
Buffum v. Green, 165, 172.
Bulger v. Roche, 359.
Bulger v. Rosa, 89.
Bulkley v. Dayton, 345.
Bull v. Bray, 400.
Bull v. Harris, 85.
Bull v. Loveland, 244.
Bullis v. Borden, 320.
Bullis v. Montgomery, 329, 442, 469, 502.
Bullitt v. Methodist Ep. Church, 483.
Bump v. Van Orsdale, 3.
Bumpas v. Dotson, 95, 118.
Burbank, Matter of, 524.
Burckmyer v. Beach, 523.
Burd v. Fitzsimmons, 204, 205.
Burd v. Smith, 93, 152, 170–172, 205, 210, 217, 230, 232, 250, 277, 282, 301.
Burdick, Matter of, 582.
Burdick v. Huntting, 259.
Burdick v. Post, 180, 256, 258, 259, 260, 508.
Burgaman v. Hickman, 268.
Burgett v. Paxton, 53.
Burghard v. Sondheim, 144.

TABLE OF CASES.

xxiii

References are to pages.

Burgin v. Burgin, 17, 102, 229, 230, 255, 296, 350, 507.
Burke's Estate, 346.
Burke v. Murphy, 443.
Burke v. Railroad Co., 518.
Burkholder's Appeal, 509, 522, 525.
Burkholder v. Stump, 44, 55, 56.
Burley v. Hartson, 186.
Burlingame v. Bell, 144.
Burlock v. Taylor, 339, 377.
Burnell, Ex parte, 512.
Burnett, Matter of, 577.
Burney v. Spear, 523.
Burnham v. Haskins, 636.
Burns v. Bangert, 601.
Burr's Ex'r v. McDonald, 65, 275, 296.
Burrall v. Leslie, 204.
Burrows v. Heter, 536, 602.
Burrows v. Keays, 108, 384.
Burrows v. Lehndorff, 6, 93, 125, 133, 135, 452.
Burt, In re, 44.
Burtnett, Matter of, 557.
Busby v. Firm, 120.
Bush v. Moore, 178.
Bush v. Roberts, 400.
Busley v. Finn, 536.
Butcher v. Easto, 31.
Butler's Appeal, 512.
Butler v. Haskell, 514.
Butler v. Jaffray, 208, 212, 568.
Butler v. New York & Erie R. R. Co., 107.
Butler v. Stoddard, 102, 321, 469.
Butler v. Thompson, 353.
Butler v. Wendell, 379.
Butt v. Peck, 147, 148, 273.
Byrd v. Bradley, 218.
Byrne v. Becker, 421.

Cabot Bank v. Bodman, 549.
Cadagan v. Kennett, 4, 20, 326, 400, 401, 404, 413.
Cadwell's Bank v. Crittenden, 15.
Cady v. Sanford, 53.
Calder v. Moran, 129.
Caldwell v. Bruggerman, 126.
Caldwell v. Coates, 561.
Caldwell v. Rose, 95, 319, 329.
Caldwell v. Williams, 95, 284, 319, 329, 347, 443, 470, 484, 502.

Calhoun v. Richards, 489.
Calkins v. Packer, 3.
Callan v. Thompson, 320.
Cameron v. Montgomery, 172.
Cameron v. Scudder, 172, 179.
Camp v. Camp, 348.
Camp v. Marshall, 151.
Camp v. Mayer, 341.
Campbell v. Bruen, 557.
Campbell v. Colorado Coal Co., 358.
Campbell v. James, 106.
Campbell v. Johnson, 513.
Campbell v. Pa. Life Ins. Co., 513.
Campbell v. Walker, 511, 513, 515.
Campbell v. Woodworth, 148, 446.
Campfield v. Lang, 186.
Canaday v. Paschall, 149.
Canal Bank v. Cox, 100, 115, 147, 172, 198.
Cannon v. Kelly, 487.
Cannon v. Peebles, 195, 254, 274-276, 431.
Cannon v. Young, 567.
Canton v. Mosely, 148.
Carlton v. Baldwin, 26, 208, 212, 260, 268, 270, 412.
Carnahan v. Schwab, 164.
Carnegie v. Morrison, 359.
Carpenter, Matter of, 112, 494, 563.
Carpenter v. Dick, 669.
Carpenter v. Mayer, 317, 327.
Carpenter v. Underwood, 101, 158, 181, 196, 224, 261.
Carr v. Dole, 128.
Carr v. Gale, 53.
Carr v. Hilton, 37, 52, 53.
Carr v. Van Hoesen, 600.
Carroll v. Boston Marine Ins. Co., 105.
Carroll v. Else, 99.
Carson v. Byres, 13.
Carson v. Marshall, 515.
Carter v. Connell, 591.
Carter v. Hammett, 475.
Carter v. Rewey, 14, 22, 164.
Carter v. Stanfield, 320.
Cartwright v. Dickinson, 65, 108.
Cary v. Brown, 503.
Cary v. Hess, 191.
Caryl v. Russell, 181.
Case v. Beauregard, 241.
Case v. Edney, 517.

TABLE OF CASES.

References are to pages.

Case v. Gerrish, 191.
Case v. Ingersoll, 352, 630.
Casey v. Jones, 268, 472.
Caskie v. Webster, 108, 358, 368, 374.
Cason v. Murray, 166, 169, 172, 419.
Cassady v. Wallace, 268.
Cassel, Ex parte, 554.
Caswell, Ex parte, 519.
Caswell v. Caswell, 601, 603.
Catlin v. Hoffman, 48.
Catlin v. The Eagle Bank of Maryland, 64.
Catlin v. Eagle Bank of New Haven, 65.
Caton v. Moseley, 281.
Cavanaugh v. Morrow, 583, 602.
Cavin v. Gleason, 164.
Cawkwell, Ex parte, 33, 51.
Cecil v. Sowards, 634.
Central Nat. Bank v. Seligman, 134.
Central R. Co. v. B. & W. R. R. Co., 109.
Chace v. Chapin, 483.
Chadbourne v. Harding, 235.
Chadwick v. Burrows, 80, 85, 204, 417.
Chadwick v. Carson, 41.
Chafee v. Fourth Nat. Bank, 373, 377, 342, 347, 367.
Chaffee v. Risk, 5, 293.
Chamberlain v. Bromberg, 66.
Chambers v. Meant, 94.
Chambers v. Smith, 457.
Chambersburg Association's Appeal, 564.
Chandler v. Jenks, 98.
Chandler v. Powers, 604.
Chapin v. Thompson, 120, 536.
Chaplin, Ex parte, 400.
Chase v. Tuttle, 66.
Chatfield v. Boyle, 607.
Chattanooga Stove Co. v. Adams, 567.
Cheatham v. Hawkins, 218, 431.
Cheever v. Imlay, 205, 394.
Cherry, In re, 165.
Chesley v. Chesley, 506.
Chesterfield v. Janssen, 190, 191.
Chertsey Market, In re, 571.
Chew v. Ellingwood, 65.
Chilcoat's Appeal, 99.
Child's Estate, 676.

Childs v. Kendall, 488.
Childs v. Mouseley, 93.
Chipman v Bank, 500.
Chipman v. Montgomery, 557.
Chippendale, Ex parte, 518.
Chittenden v. Brewster, 565.
Chittenden v. Davidson, 488.
Christ's Church in Londonderry, In re, 532.
Christian's Appeal, 121.
Christmas v. Mitchell, 516.
Christopher v. Covington, 247, 254, 320, 325, 412.
Church v. Drummond, 409.
Churchill v. Whipple, 688.
Citizens' Bank v. Patterson, 549.
City Bank v. Sherlock, 479.
City of Richmond v. Davis, 267.
Claflin v. Hirsch, 192, 236.
Claflin v. Houseman, 54.
Claflin v. Iseman, 191, 207, 216, 218, 606, 680.
Claflin v. Maglaughlin, 5, 10, 14.
Claflin v. Rosenberg, 320.
Claflin v. Smith, 606.
Claflin v. Sylvester, 168.
Clap v. Smith, 139, 305.
Clapp v. Ditman, 12, 642.
Clapp v. Nordemeyer, 135.
Clapp v. Sherman, 678.
Clark v. Bartlett, 114.
Clark v. Chambers, 549.
Clark v. Craig, 472, 506, 507, 564, 597.
Clark v. Few, 138, 144.
Clark v. Figgins, 207.
Clark v. Flint, 482.
Clark v. Fuller, 255, 263, 396.
Clark v. Gibboney, 562, 564.
Clark v. Hoyt, 525.
Clark v. Iselin, 21.
Clark v. Lamoreux, 688.
Clark v. McClelland's Assignee, 89.
Clark v. McDonald, 416.
Clark v. Marx, 56, 140, 145, 151, 285.
Clark v. Robbins, 221, 275.
Clark v. Sawyer, 526.
Clark v. Stanton, 483, 554.
Clark v. Taylor, 420.
Clark v. Trust Co., 510.
Clark v. White, 165, 172, 191.

TABLE OF CASES. XXV

References are to pages.

Clark v. Wilson, 89, 513, 579, 593.
Clarke v. Booth, 361.
Clarke v. Hume, 475.
Clay v. Severance, 57.
Clayton v. Brown, 4.
Clayton v. Johnson, 198, 210, 215, 351, 612.
Cleaver v. Brenzel, 85.
Cleveland v. Clap, 105.
Close v. Sinclair, 99.
Clow v. Woods, 317, 326.
Clute v. Barrow, 514.
Clute v. Newkirk, 323.
Coakley v. Weil, 199, 216.
Coate v. Williams, 223, 224, 242.
Coates' Estate, 559.
Coates' Ex'r v. Muse's Adm'rs, 108.
Coates v. First Nat. Bank, 47, 53, 111.
Coburn v. Pickering, 319.
Cochran v. Paris, 104, 246.
Cock v. Goodfellow, 164, 171.
Cocke v. Chapman, 319.
Cockshott v. Bennett, 191.
Coddington v. Davis, 398, 457.
Codwise v. Gelston, 532.
Cody v. Quarterman, 104.
Coe v. Hutton, 589.
Coffee v. Pleasants, 585.
Coffin, Matter of, 513, 527.
Coffin v. Douglass, 67, 234, 382, 383.
Coffin v. McLean, 109, 500.
Coflin v. Kelling, 359.
Coggill v. Botsford, 234, 295, 383, 617.
Cogar v. Stewart, 297, 634.
Cohen, In re, 56, 662.
Cohen v. Morris, 563, 577, 592, 602.
Cohen v. Plousky, 423.
Cohen v. State Bank of Florida, 544.
Cohen v. Summers, 208, 305.
Colburn v. Morton, 513.
Colburne v. Shay, 623.
Colby v. O'Donnell, 623.
Cole v. Albers, 172.
Cole v. Dealham, 452, 627.
Cole v. Dealman, 179, 180.
Coleman v. Darling, 67, 81, 85.
Coleman v. Rosenfeld, 85.
Coles v. Trecothick, 512.
Colgin v. Redman, 155, 392, 595, 609.
Collateral Bank v. Fowler, 54.

Collier v. Bickley, 353.
Collier v. Davis, 198.
Collier v. Munn, 519.
Collins, In re, 18, 480.
Collins, Matter of, 488.
Collins v. Blantern, 446.
Collins v. Brush, 330.
Collins v. Cronin, 95.
Collins v. Knapp, 3.
Collomb v. Read, 239, 607.
Collumb v. Bloodgood, 68.
Collumb v. Coldwell, 88, 222, 229, 237, 239, 440.
Combs v. Watson, 602.
Comegys v. Vasse, 105, 106, 109.
Comer v. Constantine, 18.
Commercial Bank's Appeal, 617.
Commercial Bank v. Brewer, 221, 226, 244, 431.
Commercial Bank v. Cunningham, 586.
Commercial Nat. Bank of Detroit v. Mosser, 310.
Compton v. Bedford, 31.
Commissioners v. Bank of Brest, 65.
Comstock v. Rayford, 320, 324.
Conard v. Atlantic Ins. Co., 161, 323, 324, 327, 328, 540, 541.
Cones v. Wilson, 545.
Conkling v. Carson, 208, 212, 230, 234, 461.
Conkling v. Conrad, 260, 270, 308, 461, 508.
Conlee Lumber Co. v. Meyer, 537.
Conlee Lumber Co. v. Ripon L. & M. Co., 92, 94, 186, 689.
Connah v. Sedgwick, 94, 95, 321, 469, 492, 578.
Connaughey v. Chambers, 479.
Connell, In re, 664.
Connor, Matter of, 557.
Conrad v. Burke, 89.
Conrad v. Marcotte, 129.
Constantine v. Twelves, 223, 320, 470.
Converseville Co. v. Chambersburg Wool Co., 663.
Conway, Ex parte, 65, 165, 172.
Cook v. Fountain, 281.
Cook v. Kelly, 285, 290.
Cook v. Morley, 29.
Cook v. Pritchard, 164.

TABLE OF CASES.

References are to pages.

Cook v. Rogers, 10, 24, 40.
Cook v. Smith, 312, 456.
Cook v. Van Horn, 359.
Cook v. Whipple, 54.
Cook County Nat. Bank v. United States, 539.
Cooke v. Smith, 442.
Cooley's Appeal, 544.
Coope v. Bowles, 79, 85, 601.
Cooper v. Davidson, 320, 434.
Cooper v. Day, 564.
Cooper v. Douglass, 106.
Cooper v. Kramer, 529.
Cooper v. McClun, 166.
Coots v. Chamberlain, 152, 441, 457.
Coots v. McConnell, 354.
Coots v. Radford, 477.
Coots v. Topping, 111.
Copeland v. Mercantile Ins. Co., 513.
Copeland v. Stevens, 475.
Copeland v. Weld, 115, 341.
Copper Mining Co. v. Beach, 516.
Corder v. Corder, 282.
Corgan v. Frew, 318.
Corn v. Saus, 478, 479.
Corn Ex. Nat. Bank v. Philadelphia Trust, etc. Co., 5, 131.
Cornell, In re, 485, 563.
Corning v. White, 479.
Cornish v. Dews, 17, 352, 353, 421.
Cornwell's Appeal, 37, 54.
Corprew v. Arthur, 414.
Corser v. Craig, 105.
Coster v. Lorillard, 445.
Couch v. Delaplaine, 108, 110, 385.
Coursey v. Morton, 317.
Covanhovan v. Hart, 166.
Coverdale v. Aldrich, 104, 111.
Coverdale v. Wilder, 382, 391.
Covert v. Rhodes, 111.
Covert v. Rogers, 65, 92, 442.
Cowles v. Ricketts, 1, 5.
Cowing, Matter of, 557.
Cox v. Adams, 367.
Cox v. Palmer, 260.
Cox v. Platt, 236, 241, 441.
Coyne v. Weaver, 270, 428, 442.
Craddock v. Orand, 552.
Craft v. Bloom, 421, 526.
Cragin v. Carmichael, 52, 53.

Cragin v. Thompson, 55.
Craig's Appeal, 65, 495.
Cram v. Mitchell, 93-95, 175, 322, 476.
Crane v. Rosa, 89, 241.
Cranston v. Crane, 516.
Crapo v. Kelly, 360, 361, 363.
Craven, Ex parte, 165.
Cravens v. Chambers, 504, 626.
Crawford v. Kirksey, 11, 15, 23.
Creswell v. Jones, 485.
Crevelling v. Fritts, 484, 512.
Cribben v. Ellis, 99, 690.
Criswell's Appeal, 586.
Crittenden v. Coleman, 621.
Crocker v. Whitney, 104, 105.
Croft, In re, 47, 57.
Cromie v. Bull, 578.
Cromien, Matter of, 558.
Crook v. Rindskopf, 240, 382, 431, 444.
Cropsey v. McKenney, 601.
Crosbie v. Leary, 495.
Crosby v. Hillyer, 309, 310, 349.
Crosby v. Huston, 17.
Cross v. Bryant, 172.
Crossley v. Moore, 191.
Croswell v. Allis, 409.
Croughwell, In re, 47.
Croughwell, Matter of, 660.
Crouse v. Frothingham, 110, 496, 577, 594.
Crow v. Beardsley, 12, 17, 412, 642.
Crow v. Colton, 114.
Crow v. Ruby, 138.
Crowe v. Ballard, 510, 511.
Crowninshield v. Kittredge, 567.
Cruger v. Halliday, 576.
Crutchfield v. Hudson, 586, 603.
Cullum v. Bloodgood, 86.
Cullum v. Branch Bank at Mobile, 575.
Cumberland Bank v. Hann, 319.
Cummings v. McCullough, 227, 453, 469.
Cunningham v. Butler, 364.
Cunningham v. Freeborn, 6, 115, 123, 128, 150-153, 164, 168, 170, 186, 242, 248, 277, 287, 333, 335, 339, 342, 381, 415, 422-425, 432, 434, 435, 559, 605, 606.
Cunningham v. McGregor, 499.
Cunningham v. Neville, 317, 329.

TABLE OF CASES. xxvii

References are to pages.

Cunningham v. Norton, 63, 138, 382.
Curd v. Miller's Ex'rs, 320.
Currie v. Hart, 94, 95, 116, 220, 469.
Currier, Matter of, 538, 558, 662.
Curtis v. Leavitt, 13, 61, 63, 166, 167, 180, 183, 184, 221-223, 229, 283, 284, 322, 407, 416, 437-440, 446, 520.
Cushing v. Gore, 116.
Cushman v. Gephart, 624.
Cushwa v. Cushwa, 448.
Cutler v. Copeland, 319.
Cutler v. Reilly, 499.
Cuyler v. McCartney, 421, 441, 442, 502, 503.

Da Costa v. Guien, 387.
Daggett, etc. Co. v. Herman, 616.
Daily's Ex'r v. Warren, 502.
Dakin v. Pomeroy, 367.
Dale v. Olmstead, 129.
Dallam v. Fitler, 317, 477.
Dalton v. Currier, 361.
Dana v. Bank of the United States, 65, 247, 286, 442, 558.
Dana v. Lull, 4, 75, 85-87, 157, 175, 230, 282.
Dana v. Stamfords, 8, 12.
Dance v. Seaman, 104, 115, 134, 172, 173, 220, 223, 225, 246, 254, 260, 408.
Danford v. Denny, 14, 169, 177.
Daniel v. Fain, 526.
Daniels, Petition of, 85, 86.
Daniels v. Willard, 338, 376.
Danley v. Rector, 319.
Danner v. Brewer, 10, 15, 130, 135, 364, 609.
Dansby v. Frieberg, 191.
Darbour v. Duncanson, 502.
Dargan v. Richardson, 350.
Darling v. Rogers, 126, 256, 258, 267, 283, 381, 382, 444, 446.
Darrow, Matter of, 559.
Darrow v. Bruff, 90, 91, 286.
Darwin v. Hundley, 228, 320.
Davenport, In re, 519.
Davenport v. Gentry's Adm'r, 105.
Davenport v. McCole, 561.
Davenport v. Thornton, 371.
Davidson v. Cowan, 296.
Davidson v. Robinson, 82.

Davis v. Anderson, 167, 179.
Davis v. Chicago Dock Co., 478.
Davis v. Gibbon, 179, 627.
Davis v. Gibson, 160, 169.
Davis v. Harman, 563, 564.
Davis v. Harrington, 433.
Davis v. Howell, 235.
Davis v. Newcomb, 484.
Davis v. Simpson, 514.
Davis v. Turner, 49, 320.
Davis & Desauque, Estate of, 508.
Davoue v. Fanning, 513, 514.
Dawes v. Cope, 316, 326, 327, 474.
Dawson v. Coffey, 600, 601.
Dawson v. Crossen, 152, 298, 476, 673, 674.
Dawson v. Dawson, 313, 314.
Day v. Bardwell, 39.
Dean, Matter of, 491, 524, 554.
Dearing v. Watkins, 320.
Dearman v. Radcliffe, 448.
Deaver v. Savage, 151, 153.
Debee v. De Baun, 508, 509.
De Brodleben v. Beekman, 318.
De Caters v. Le Ray de Chaumont, 343, 346, 582, 583.
Deckard v. Case, 73, 74, 79, 85-87, 286, 472.
Deckert v. Filbert, 74, 86.
Dedham Bank v. Richards, 149, 154, 250, 287, 307, 582.
Deering v. Cox, 343.
De Forest v. Bacon, 172, 243, 341.
De Graw v. King, 291.
Dehner v. Helmbacher, 24, 104, 353.
Deisbach v. Merritt, 615.
Delaware, etc. Co. v. Scranton, 353.
Dell v. King, 35.
Demarest v. Willard, 103.
Deming v. Colt, 76, 77, 85.
Den v. McKnight, 513, 514.
Den v. Wright, 513, 514.
Dennistown v. Hubbell, 474.
Denzer v. Mundy, 299.
Depeyster v. Ferrers, 523.
Derry Bank v. Davis, 286, 334.
De Rouge v. Elliott, 105.
De Ruyter v. St. Peter's Church, 11, 64, 95, 355.
Dessar v. Field, 166.

TABLE OF CASES.

References are to pages.

Desch v. Nette, 400.
Descombes v. Wood, 66.
Demmick v. Register, 9.
De Sobry v. De Laistre, 358, 359, 367.
Dessar v. Field, 10, 15, 22.
De Tastet v. Le Tavernier, 61.
Detroit Stove Works v. Osmun, 353.
Detwiler's Appeal, 475, 485, 563.
Devey v. Thornton, 519.
Dewey v. Adams, 322, 323, 329.
Dewey v. Littlejohn, 115, 116, 296, 300, 319, 325, 507.
De Wolf v. Johnson, 535.
De Wolf v. Sprague Mfg. Co., 18, 243, 272, 605.
Dews v. Olwill, 334, 345.
Dexter v. Parkins, 318.
Dey v. Dunham, 23, 277, 480.
Dias v. Bouchaud, 8, 15, 123, 161, 540.
Dick v. Pitchford, 314.
Dickerson v. Benham, 420.
Dickinson, Ex parte, 359, 486.
Dickinson v. Burrill, 488.
Dickinson v. Legare, 69, 72.
Dickinson v. Metacomet Nat. Bank, 389, 394.
Dickson v. Chorm, 545.
Dickson v. Rawson, 5, 115, 179, 230, 606.
Diefendorf v. Spraker, 314.
Dieffenderffer v. Winder, 568.
Diesbach v. Becker, 14.
Dimmock v. Bixby, 532, 566, 597.
Dimon v. Delmonico, 117, 121.
Dimon v. Hazard, 89, 241.
Dinsmore v. Boyd, 108.
D'Ivernois v. Leavitt, 221, 248, 366, 454, 455.
Dix v. Cobb, 105.
Dobbin v. Walton, 65.
Dobbs v. Prescott, 298.
Dobyns v. Dobyns, 634.
Dobyns v. McGovern, 105.
Dockray v. Dockray, 172, 206, 212.
Dodd v. Hills, 101, 167, 427.
Dodd v. Martin, 145, 198, 215.
Dodge v. Doub, 548.
Dodge v. Sheldon, 54.
Doe v. Pitcher, 446.
Doe v. Rutledge, 4.
Doe v. Scribner, 591.

Dohlman v. Jacobs, 601.
Dolson v. Kerr, 40, 41, 98, 323, 469.
Donaho v. Fish, 67, 682.
Donelson's Adm'rs v. Posey, 520, 525.
Donohue v. Ladd, 352, 640.
Doolittle v. Cook, 453.
Doolittle v. Southworth, 389.
Doremus v. Lewis, 231.
Doremus v. O'Hara, 179.
Dorr v. Gibboney, 562, 564, 594, 598.
Dorrance v. Jones, 475.
Doub v. Barnes, 602.
Dougherty v. Bethune, 309.
Dougherty v. Daraach, 294.
Douglass v. Cissna, 92, 93, 229.
Douglass v. Simpson, 279, 553.
Dow v. Platner, 98, 221.
Dowdell v. Hamm, 384, 398.
Downes v. Grazebrook, 511.
Downing v. Kentzing, 134.
Downs v. Grazebrook, 506.
Doyle v. Peckham, 486.
Doyle v. Smith, 245, 491.
Drain v. Mickel, 24, 477.
Drake v. Ellman, 633.
Drake v. Rogers, 75, 85, 128, 208, 288.
Drake v. Rollo, 501.
Drakeley v. De Forest, 139, 152.
Drane v. Gunter, 576.
Drew v. Drum, 478.
Drew Glass Co. v. Baldwin, 310, 642.
Drewson v. The American Surety Co., 496.
Driesach v. Price, 675.
Driggs & Co.'s Bank v. Norwood, 59.
Driscoll v. Fiske, 143.
Drucker v. Wellhouse, 67.
Dryer, Matter of, 557, 579.
Dube v. Fire Ins. Co., 105.
Dubose v. Dubose, 253, 335, 507.
Du Bose v. Carlisle, 102, 124, 160, 609.
Dudley v. Danforth, 421.
Dudley v. Whiting, 630.
Dufford v. Smith, 527.
Duffy v. Duncan, 148, 492, 501, 519, 521, 524.
Duggan v. Bliss, 198, 616.
Dumahaut, In re, 56, 57.
Duncan, Matter of, 240, 558.
Duncan v. Miller, 453.

TABLE OF CASES. xxix

References are to pages.

Duncan v. Stanton, 499.
Duncan v. Taylor, 682, 685.
Dundas v. Bowler, 364, 366, 367, 379.
Dunham, Ex parte, 507.
Dunham v. Gates, 427, 605.
Dunham v. Pettee, 329.
Dunham v. Waterman, 159, 175, 196, 204, 242, 425, 455, 492.
Dunham v. Whitehead, 12, 15.
Dunkee v. Chambers, 442.
Dunklin v. Kimball, 85.
Dunlap v. Beckes, 514.
Dunlap v. Bournonville, 95, 317, 473.
Dunn v. Snell, 107.
Dunsmore v. Furstenfeldt, 479.
Dupuy v. Ullman, 474.
Durant v. Pierson, 90.
Durfee, In re, 565.
Durham v. Hall, 592, 594.
Dutchess Co. v. Van Wagonen, 660.
Dutton v. Morrison, 33.
Duvall v. Raisin, 115, 128, 151, 186, 332, 643.
Dwight v. Lumber Co., 164.
Dwight v. Overton, 10, 17, 352, 461, 462.
D'Wolf v. Harris, 327, 328.
Dwyer v. Garlough, 109, 669.
Dye v. Dye, 582, 669.
Dyer v. Burnham, 104.

Eagle v. Eichelberger, 327.
Eames, Ex parte, 39.
Eames v. Mayo, 479, 546.
Earle v. N. Y. Life Ins. Co., 560.
Eastman v. McAlpin, 22, 166, 172, 179.
Eastman v. Wright, 105.
Easton Nat. Bank v. Halshizer, 380.
Eaton, Matter of, 660.
Ebersole v. Adams, 40, 634.
Eckhardt v. Wilson, 32.
Eddy v. Winchester, 359.
Eden v. Everson, 297, 333, 347, 604.
Edgell v. Hart, 321.
Edison v. Frazier, 3, 129.
Edmonson v. Harris, 575.
Edrington v. Rogers, 164-166, 172, 191, 284.
Edwards v. Glyn, 32.
Edwards v. Mitchell, 400.
Edwards v. Peterson, 108.

Egbert v. Baker, 379.
Egbert v. Brooks, 518, 522.
Egbert v. Wood, 69, 72, 84, 85, 87, 89, 181, 237.
Eicks v. Copeland, 248, 260, 330, 435, 441.
Einstein v. Chapman, 322.
Einstein v. Shouse, 620.
Eldridge v. Post, 297.
Ellenberger v. Milligan, 625.
Elliott v. Carter, 568.
Elliott v. Pool, 501.
Ellison v. Ellison, 578.
Ellison v. Lindsley, 582.
Elmes v. Sutherland, 17, 228, 246, 335, 336, 341.
Ely v. Cook, 60, 64, 229.
Ely v. Hair, 67, 84, 152, 230, 255.
Emerick v. Coakley, 105.
Emerson v. Knower, 138, 151-153, 345.
Emerson v. Senter, 89, 141, 412, 421, 441.
Emigrant Industrial Savings Bank v. Roche, 107, 382, 386.
Emmons v. Cairns, 103, 106.
Empey v. Sherwood, 462, 581.
Empire City Bank, Matter of, 183.
England v. Reynolds, 148, 260, 337.
Englebert v. Blaujot, 292, 486, 676.
Ennis v. Leach, 516.
Ensign v. Kellogg, 104.
Epperson v. Young, 448.
Eppright v. Nickerson, 66, 108, 291.
Equitable Trust Co. v. Fisher, 506.
Eshelman v. Shuman, 109.
Estabrook v. Messersmith, 112.
Estwick v. Caillaud, 22, 155, 160, 171, 230, 340, 423.
Evans v. Chapin, 151.
Evans v. Dunkelberger, 295.
Evans v. Greenhow, 278.
Evans v. Lamar, 253, 255, 260.
Everett v. Stone, 37.
Everett v. Walcott, 279, 339, 341, 344.
Everitt, Matter of, 557.
Everitt v. Strong, 68, 286.
Everson v. Gehrman, 76.
Evertson v. Tappan, 511.
Every v. Edgerton, 323, 326.
Ewing v. Gargill, 516.

TABLE OF CASES.

References are to pages.

Exchange Bank v. Knox, 277, 278.
Executors of Luce v. Park, 110.
Eyre v. Beebe, 148, 237, 240, 241, 268, 273, 524.
Ezekiel v. Dixon, 179.

Fahey v. Clarke, 192, 522.
Fahnestock v. Bailey, 567.
Fairbanks v. Haynes, 177, 451.
Fairchild v. Gwinne, 151, 290.
Falconer v. Hunt, 612.
Fall River Iron Works v. Croade, 278, 339, 343, 344, 368.
Fallon v. McCunn, 495.
Fanshawe v. Lane, 91.
Farmers' Bank v. Douglass, 17, 246, 247, 407, 559.
Farmers' Bank v. Gilpin, 529.
Farmers' Bank v. Willis, 499.
Farmers' Dep. Nat. Bank v. Pennsylvania Bank, 500.
Farnham, Matter of, 556.
Farnsworth v. Shephard, 318.
Farquharson v. Eichelberger, 146, 199, 216, 240, 260, 267, 297.
Farquharson v. McDonald, 98, 229, 254, 255, 337.
Farrall v. Howard, 179.
Farrell v. Farnen, 421, 482.
Farrin v. Crawford, 26, 43, 53.
Farrington v. Sexton, 98, 433.
Farrow v. Hayes, 212, 305, 431.
Farwell v. Bohen, 3.
Farwell v. Gundry, 140.
Farwell v. Howard, 160, 169, 627.
Farwell v. Jones, 192, 453.
Farwell v. Nilsoon, 164.
Farwell v. Webster, 67, 86, 688.
Fassett v. Phillips, 206, 224.
Fassett v. Traber, 167.
Faulkner v. Hyman, 278, 339, 368, 378.
Faunce v. Lesley, 219.
Faust v. Levy, 527.
Faut v. Elsbury, 683.
Faxon v. Durant, 331.
Fay v. Grant, 101, 218.
Fay v. Jenks, 359.
Fayette Nat. Bank v. Kenney, 547.
Fecheimer v. Robertson, 5.
Feimester v. McRorie, 277.

Feimster v. Smith, 3.
Felch v. Bugbee, 361.
Fellows v. Commercial Bank, 228, 249.
Fellows v. Greenleaf, 88, 89, 112, 127, 334.
Fellows v. Vicksburg R. R. & B. Co., 337.
Felt v. Dorr, 499.
Fera v. Wickham, 499, 500.
Ferebee v. Doxey, 107.
Ferris v. American Ins. Co., 498.
Fermor's Case, 413.
Fiedler v. Day, 119, 443, 447, 456.
Field v. Arrowsmith, 313, 337.
Field v. Flanders, 281, 484.
Field v. Ridgley, 623.
Field v. Simco, 319.
Fieley v. King, 489, 617.
Finlay v. Dickerson, 229, 230, 234, 266, 273.
First Con. Soc. of Raynham v. Trustees, etc., 592.
First Nat. Bank v. Central Nat. Bank, 462.
First Nat. Bank v. Coates, 111.
First Nat. Bank v. Hackett, 81, 99, 101.
First Nat. Bank v. Hartman Co., 109.
First Nat. Bank v. Hughes, 60, 367, 377, 431, 449, 460, 481.
First Nat. Bank v. Kennedy, 427.
First Nat. Bank v. Kimberlands, 106.
First Nat. Bank v. Mastin Bank, 479.
First Nat. Bank v. Smith, 339.
First Nat. Bank of Bath v. Warner, 433.
First Nat. Bank of Dubuque v. Baker, 441.
First Nat. Bank of Fargo v. Briggs, 640.
Fisher v. Dinwiddie, 160.
Fisher v. Johnson, 104.
Fisher v. Murray, 77.
Fisher v. Shelver, 400.
Fiske v. Carr, 114, 350, 586.
Fitch v. Workman, 592, 593, 597.
Fitler v. Maitland, 317, 472.
Fitzgerald v. Vestal, 106.
Fitzherbert's Case, 413.
Fitzpatrick v. Flannagan, 241.
Flagg v. Mann, 527.
Flagler v. Schoeffel, 146, 442, 502.

TABLE OF CASES. xxxi

References are to pages.

Flagler v. Wheeler, 442, 502.
Flanagan v. Wetherill, 293, 307.
Flanigan v. Lampman, 442, 470.
Flannigan v. Althouse, 453.
Flash v. Wilkerson, 681.
Fleming v. Townsend, 320.
Fletcher v. Piatt, 105.
Fletcher v. Willard, 319.
Flickey v. Looney, 105.
Flint v. Bell, 593.
Flint v. Clinton Co., 64, 126, 287.
Flower v. Cornish, 112, 481.
Floyd v. Smith, 230.
Flynn v. Ledger, 478.
Foakes v. Beer, 192.
Focke v. Blum, 67.
Fogerty v. Phila. Trust, etc. Co., 499.
Foley, Matter of, 600.
Follweiler v. Lutz, 294.
Foot v. Goldman, 58.
Foote v. Cobb, 115, 414.
Forbes v. Limond, 197.
Forbes v. Scannell, 23, 77, 86, 93, 127, 132, 146, 152, 240, 282, 333, 373, 379, 441, 484.
Forbes v. Waller, 432.
Ford v. Cook, 522.
Ford v. Williams, 165, 166.
Fordyce v. Pipher, 297.
Foreman v. Burnette, 13.
Forepaugh v. Appold, 105, 467.
Forkner v. Schafer, 297.
Forkner v. Stuart, 68.
Fort v. Martin Tobacco Co., 621.
Fort Stanwix Bank v. Leggett, 603.
Fosdyke v. Nixon, 530.
Foster v. Beals, 502.
Foster v. Brown, 297, 427.
Foster v. Deming, 555.
Foster v. Libby, 100, 101.
Foster v. Lowell, 129.
Foster v. Saco Manufacturing Co., 8, 103, 136, 172, 244, 284.
Foster v. Woodfin, 423.
Fouche, Assignee, v. Brower, 579.
Fouke v. Fleming, 17.
Fournier v. Ingraham, 576, 577.
Fox v. Adams, 198, 217, 249, 350, 368.
Fox v. Hanbury, 68.
Fox v. Heath, 58, 237, 600.

Fox v. Mackreth, 510
Fox v. Willis, 601.
Foy v. Troy & Boston R. R. Co., 107.
Francis v. Burnett, 109.
Francis v. Evans, 595.
Francis v. Herz, 208.
Francisco v. Aguirre, 479.
Francklyn v. Sprague, 482.
Franco v. Franco, 571.
Franey v. Smith, 477, 661.
Frank v. Cruthers, 429.
Frank v. Moses, 623.
Frankell v. Coats, 442, 502.
Franklin v. Menown, 108.
Frazer v. Thatcher, 167.
Frazer v. Thompson, 31.
Frazier v. Fredericks, 359.
Frazier v. Truax, 119, 155.
Freeman v. Cook, 532, 562, 566.
Freeman v. Deming, 21, 36, 54.
French v. Lovejoy, 236.
French v. Townes, 133, 548.
Freund v. Jaegerman, 135, 642.
Freydendall v. Baldwin, 623.
Friend v. Michaelis, 236, 431, 600.
Frierson v. Branch, 342, 545, 581, 584, 586, 602.
Frink v. Buss, 92, 100.
Frisbee, In re, 47.
Fromme v. Jones, 12, 160, 169, 179, 627.
Frost v. Citizens' Nat. Bank, 112.
Frost v. Wilson, 479.
Frow v. Downman, 482.
Fry v. Boyd, 104, 479.
Fry v. Soper, 601.
Fuhrman v. Jones, 688.
Fuller, In re, 484.
Fuller v. Davis, 579.
Fuller v. Hasbrouck, 477.
Fuller v. Steiglitz, 375, 379, 499.
Fulton, Matter of, 524.
Furman v. Fisher, 245, 309, 311, 313, 337, 460, 461, 575.

Gable v. Williams, 89.
Gage v. Chesebro, 15.
Gaither v. Mumford, 319.
Gale v. Hubbel, 688.
Gale v. Mensing, 128, 288, 338, 341.
Gallagher, Matter of, 147, 676.

xxxii   TABLE OF CASES.

References are to pages.

Galt v. Calland, 89.
Galt v. Dibrell, 176, 225, 312, 460, 461.
Gamble v. Railroad Co., 109.
Gammons v. Coleman, 478.
Gammons v. Holman, 114.
Gardner v. Adams, 106.
Gardner v. Commercial Bank of America, 678.
Gardner v. Commercial Nat. Bank, 60, 245, 259, 267, 366, 409, 430, 449, 458, 461.
Gardner v. Diedrichs, 545.
Gardner v. Hoeg, 106.
Gardner v. Howland, 327, 328, 474.
Gardner v. National City Bank, 478.
Gardner v. Pike, 149.
Garner v. Frederick, 98, 99.
Garr v. Hill, 166, 167, 169, 178.
Garrard v. Lauderdale, 127, 340, 341, 583.
Garret v. Burlington Plow Co., 135.
Garretson v. Brown, 178, 655.
Garwood, Ex parte, 165.
Gasherie v. Apple, 420.
Gasper v. Bennett, 605.
Gassett v. Wilson, 164, 166.
Gates v. Andrews, 259, 307.
Gates v. Labaume, 9, 234, 260, 271, 278, 421, 441, 481, 496, 529.
Gathercole v. Bedel, 342.
Gayden v. Tufts, 114.
Gayle v. Randall, 54.
Gaylord v. City of Lafayette, 461.
Gazzam v. Poyntz, 188, 198, 218, 227, 335, 430, 431.
Geery's Appeal, 40, 52.
Geilinger v. Philippi, 102.
Geisse v. Beal, 346, 400, 448, 484, 505, 514, 524, 536, 537, 580, 581, 594, 595.
Geist's Appeal, 105, 531, 581.
George v. Norris, 319.
George v. Williamson, 448.
Gere v. Murray, 421.
German Bank v. Schloth, 106.
German Ins. Bank v. Nunes, 412.
Germantown Pass. R. Co. v. Fitler, 355, 495.
German Sav. Institution v. Adae, 478.
German Security Bank v. Jefferson, 634.

Gibbs v. Cunningham, 548.
Gibbs v. Thompson, 118.
Gibson v. Chedic, 460.
Gibson v. Cook, 104.
Gibson v. Courthope, 475.
Gibson v. Jeyes, 511.
Gibson v. Love, 416, 426.
Gibson v. Muskett, 32, 184.
Gibson v. Rees, 127, 304, 333, 340, 346, 460, 461, 559.
Giddings v. Eastman, 513.
Giddings v. Sears, 167.
Gilbert, Matter of, 582, 662.
Gilbert v. McCorkel, 453.
Gilbert v. Sutliff, 522, 524, 527, 566.
Gilchrist v. Gilmer, 388.
Gilchrist v. Stevenson, 314.
Giles v. Ash, 108.
Gilkerson-Sloss Com. Co. v. London, 612.
Gill v. Carmine, 566.
Gillespie v. Smith, 516.
Gilmer v. Earnhardt, 254.
Gillet v. Phillips, 67, 183, 184.
Gilson v. Boutts, 32.
Gimble v. Ferguson, 104.
Ginther v. Richmond, 125, 270.
Givens v. Taylor, 299.
Gitt's Estate, 186.
Gladsden v. Carson, 237.
Glen v. Grover, 166.
Glenn v. Busey, 364, 579.
Glenn v. Howard & Savage, 54.
Glenn v. McKim, 569.
Glenn v. McNeal, 400.
Glenn v. Mickey, 507.
Glenn v. Randall, 400.
Glenny v. Langdon, 54, 604.
Globe Ins. Co. v. Cleveland Ins. Co., 35, 37, 40, 43-45.
Gloucester Bank v. Worcester, 200, 394.
Goar v. McCanless, 164.
Goddard v. Hapgood, 230.
Goddard v. Winthrop, 869.
Godden, Ex parte, 35.
Godfrey v. Poole, 400.
Goding, Ex parte, 507.
Goepper v. Heckle, 594.
Golden's Appeal, 284, 301, 460, 575, 577.

TABLE OF CASES. xxxiii

References are to pages.

Golden v. Musgrove, 460.
Goldschmidt, In re, 44, 45, 57, 675.
Goll v. Hubbell, 99, 101.
Goncilier v. Frost, 593.
Goodbar v. Mears, 612.
Goodman v. Niblack, 108.
Goodrich v. Downs, 180, 218, 221–223, 229, 230, 257, 283, 425, 430, 432, 437–440, 443, 444.
Goodrich v. Proctor, 281, 505.
Goodrich v. Wilson, 54.
Googins v. Gilmore, 319.
Goodsell v. Benson, 362.
Goodwin v. Kerr, 320, 441, 460.
Goodwin v. Mix, 478, 563, 568.
Goodwin v. Sharkey, 54, 546.
Goodwin v. Wertheimer, 479.
Gordon, Matter of, 160.
Gordon v. Cannon, 85, 92, 152, 159, 172, 207, 212, 217, 241, 272, 472.
Gordon v. Coolidge, 310.
Gordon v. Freeman, 356, 466.
Gordon v. Green, 129, 131.
Gordon v. Worthley, 62.
Gore v. Clesby, 507.
Gorham v. Innis, 164.
Gorham v. Reeves, 482.
Gorsuch v. Briscoe, 575.
Goss v. Neale, 22, 160.
Gott v. Hoschina, 489.
Gough v. Clift, 268, 485.
Gould v. Hayes, 523, 525.
Gould v. Keer, 547.
Gould v. Lamb, 281, 505.
Gouldy v. Metcalf, 58.
Gourdon v. Ins. Co. of North America, 105.
Governor, use, etc. v. Campbell, 333, 335, 421, 441.
Grady v. Bowe, 361.
Graeff's Appeal, 543.
Graff's Estate, 486.
Graham v. Candy, 32.
Graham v. Davidson, 520.
Graham v. Evans, 639.
Graham v. Henry, 106.
Graham v. Lockhart, 136, 226, 254, 336.
Graham v. Newman, 104.
Graham v. Railroad Co., 10.
Grangers, etc. Co. v. Kamper, 482.

Grant v. Chapman, 117, 188, 196, 261.
Graser v. Stillwagen, 68, 84.
Graves v. Alden, 179.
Graves v. Blondwell, 220.
Graves v. Hull, 78, 85.
Graves v. Long, 483, 516.
Graves v. McFarlane, 103.
Gray, Matter of, 557.
Gray v. Bell, 593, 597.
Gray v. Hill, 126.
Gray v. Lynch, 565.
Gray v. McCallister, 179, 180, 627.
Gray v. Rollo, 501.
Gray v. Thompson, 597.
Grayson v. Sandford, 106.
Greeley v. Dixon, 208.
Green v. Banks, 59, 338, 434.
Green v. Bradfield, 164.
Green v. Demoss, 337.
Green v. Gross, 363, 364.
Green v. Morse, 535, 536, 584, 603.
Green v. Trieber, 159, 199, 215, 216, 218, 221, 230, 232, 249, 251, 268, 274, 431, 432.
Green v. Van Buskirk, 318, 370, 371.
Green v. Winter, 511, 519, 554.
Greene v. Breck, 90.
Greene v. Mowry, 350.
Greene v. Sprague Mfg. Co., 347, 365.
Greene & Button Co. v. Van Vechten, 457.
Greenfield's Estate, 388.
Greenleaf v. Edes, 259.
Greenleaf v. Mumford, 602.
Greenleaf v. Queen, 508.
Greenwood v. Marvin, 356.
Gregory v. Gregory, 512.
Gresham v. Crossland, 602.
Griffin v. Alsop, 474.
Griffin v. Doe, 252.
Griffin v. Rogers, 5, 178.
Griffin v. Wallace, 479.
Griffin's Ex'r v. Macaulay's Adm'r, 108, 113, 115, 137, 252, 421, 432, 478, 482, 533, 571.
Griffith v. Cox, 60, 602.
Grimes v. Farrington, 423.
Grimshaw v. Walker, 198, 227, 233.
Grimsley v. Hooke, 567.
Griswold v. Watkins, 54.

TABLE OF CASES.

References are to pages.

Grocers' Nat. Bank v. Clark, 105.
Grocery Co. v. Records, 221.
Groencke, Matter of, 582.
Gross v. Bunn, 585, 586.
Grover v. Grover, 400, 427.
Grover v. Wakeman 5, 159, 163, 168, 172, 174–176, 180. 187, 188, 200, 202, 204, 209, 210, 213, 216, 245, 268, 382, 427. 428. 431, 438, 444.
Grubbs v. Morris, 160, 170, 181, 624.
Gruce v. Sanders, 320.
Gryder v. Payne, 514.
Guerin v. Hunt, 93, 142, 441.
Guggenheimer v. Groeschel, 191.
Guilford v. Childs, 296, 299.
Guillander v. Howell, 108, 358, 370, 372–374, 379.
Guittard v. Robinson, 531.
Gulick v. Lodor, 367.
Gump, Matter of, 505.
Gundry v. Vivian, 530.
Gunnell v. Adams, 260.
Gutman v. McNulty, 89, 241, 454.
Gutzweiler v. Lackman, 536.
Guy v. McIlree, 167, 109, 294.
Guyer, Assignment of, 192.

Haas v. O'Brien, 47.
Hackers v. Perkins, 390.
Hadden v. Knickerbocker, 546.
Haenssler v. Teichman, 432.
Hafner v. Irwin, 17, 163, 166, 172, 175, 207, 216, 228, 245, 254, 408, 419, 443.
Hagen's Appeal, 190.
Haggard v. Lehman, 585.
Haggarty v. Pittman, 94.
Haggerty v. Granger, 85, 88.
Haggerty v. Palmer, 473, 479, 480, 482.
Hahn v. Salmon, 454, 478.
Haile v. Brewster, 320.
Haines v. Campbell, 259, 307.
Hairgrove v. Millington, 348, 421, 502.
Halbert v. Deering, 103, 105.
Hale v. Allnutt, 164.
Hall v. Arnold, 167.
Hall v. Crane Co., 11.
Hall v. Denison, 23, 127, 128, 166, 172, 180, 207, 229, 277, 352, 353.
Hall v. Hallett, 510, 511.
Hall v. Harrell, 110.

Hall v. Harris, 592.
Hall v. Howell, 625.
Hall v. Kellogg, 168.
Hall v. Marston, 130.
Hall v. Mullen, 358.
Hall v. Noyes, 511.
Hall v. Parsons, 318, 329.
Hall v. Robinson, 106.
Hall v. Wheeler, 319, 330, 472.
Halm v. Salmon, 673.
Halsey v. Whitney, 23, 104, 115, 126, 148, 151, 152, 154, 157, 158, 168, 172, 200, 209–213, 217, 229, 233, 249, 250, 270, 282, 307, 334, 341, 343, 345, 347, 443, 551, 552, 583.
Halstead v. Gordon, 254, 273.
Halsted v. Halsted, 488.
Hastings v. Belknap, 602.
Hamilton v. Colt, 678.
Hamilton v. Russell, 20, 323, 324.
Hamilton v. Wright, 485, 510.
Hammond v. Stanton, 596.
Hampton v. Morris, 59.
Hanbury v. Kirkland, 569.
Hanchett v. Waterbury, 623.
Hancock v. Horan, 166, 167, 191.
Hancock v. Wooten, 605.
Hanes v. Tiffany, 112, 481.
Hanford v. Paine, 318, 358, 372, 685.
Hanford Oil Co. v. First Nat. Bank of Chicago, 164, 483.
Hannah v. Carrington, 17, 228, 574.
Hanscom v. Buffum, 163.
Hansell v. Lutz, 544.
Hauselt v. Vilmar, 23.
Hanson v. Dunn, 689.
Hanson v. Stephenson, 475.
Hard v. Milligan, 488.
Hardcastle v. Fisher, 9, 118, 151, 476, 482, 600, 643.
Hardin v. Osborne, 208, 250, 252.
Harding v. Crosby, 47.
Hargdime v. Henderson, 18, 642.
Hardy v. Clarke, 48.
Hardy v. Simpson, 59.
Hardy v. Skinner, 59, 225, 228, 245, 246, 319.
Hargrooves v. Chambers, 562.
Hargrove v. Millington, 442.
Harkins v. Bailey, 5, 166, 169.

TABLE OF CASES. XXXV

References are to pages.

Harkist v. Alexander, 511.
Harkrader v. Leiby, 13, 16, 179.
Harman v. Fisher, 30, 151, 290, 441.
Harman v. Hoskins, 431.
Harmon v. McRae, 10.
Harrington v. Brown, 514.
Harris v. Bratton, 281.
Harris v. De Graffenreid, 17, 118, 447.
Harris v. D'Wolf, 327.
Harris v. Exchange Nat. Bank, 41.
Harris v. Rickett, 31.
Harris v. Rucker, 313.
Harris v. Sumner, 200, 218, 230, 347, 430, 443.
Harris v. Thompson, 66.
Harris v. Visher, 67.
Harrison v. Farmers' Bank, 108, 352.
Harrison v. Mack, 312, 484, 563, 596.
Harrison v. Sterry, 68, 71, 72, 86, 87, 361, 367.
Harrison v. Winston, 584.
Harrison Nat. Bank v. Ellicott, 479.
Hart v. Acker, 322.
Hart v. Blum, 6.
Hart v. Bulkley, 570, 574.
Hart v. Crane, 251, 255, 492, 506, 507, 509.
Hart v. McFarland, 275, 416.
Hart v. Rust, 516.
Harvey, Ex parte, 18.
Harvey v. Cubbedge, 65.
Harvey's Adm'r v. Steptoe's Adm'r, 119, 506, 551, 556.
Haskell v. Ingalls, 48.
Haskins v. Alcott, 113, 342, 582, 586, 669.
Hasseld v. Seyforth, 141, 625.
Hastings v. Baldwin, 103, 144, 200, 231, 341, 344.
Hastings v. Belknap, 204, 601.
Hastings Matting Co. v. Heller, 118.
Hastings v. Spencer, 527.
Haswell v. Simpson, 31.
Hatch v. Smith, 138, 165, 172, 200, 345.
Hatcher v. Winters, 227, 329, 352, 577, 581, 593, 603, 605.
Hatchett v. Blanton, 580, 584.
Hathaway v. Fall River Nat. Bank, 479, 483.
Hauselt v. Vilmar, 165, 172, 175, 420, 422.

Havemeyer v. Loeb, 607.
Haven v. Law, 319.
Haven v. Richardson, 152, 172, 207, 277.
Havens v. Hussey, 68, 72, 75, 76, 84, 86, 87, 286.
Hawkins' Appeal, 40.
Hawkins, In re, 44.
Hawkins v. Alston, 507.
Hawkins v. Bailey, 10.
Hawks v. Pritzlaff, 112, 481.
Hawley v. Cramer, 513.
Hawley v. James, 445, 515, 519, 567.
Hawley v. Muncius, 511.
Haxum v. Bishop, 65, 66.
Haydock v. Coope, 175, 188.
Haydock v. Stanhope, 206.
Haydock Carriage Co. v. Pier, 92, 519, 567.
Hayes v. Heyer, 75-77, 90.
Hayer v. Hellman, 172.
Hayner v. Fowler, 604.
Haynes' Assignment, In re, 362.
Haynes v. Brooks, 90, 236.
Haynes v. Crutchfield, 507, 510.
Haynes v. Thompson, 108.
Hays v. Doane, 141, 509.
Hays v. Drake, 654.
Hays v. Hostetter, 229.
Haywood v. McNair, 479.
Hazel v. Bank, 410.
Heacock v. Durand, 273, 526, 601.
Head v. Miller, 478.
Hecht v. Green, 600, 615.
Heckerts' Appeal, 522, 524.
Heckley v. Hendrickson, 427.
Heckman v. Messenger, 98, 100, 240, 477.
Hedges v. Sealy, 3.
Heelan v. Hoagland, 291, 298.
Hefner v. Metcalf, 412.
Hegeman v. Hyslop, 499.
Hegeman v. Hegeman, 106.
Heilner v. Imbrie, 186, 389, 390.
Heineman v. Hart, 489.
Heinrichs v. Woods, 112, 482.
Helfrich v. Obermyer, 109, 126.
Helm v. Gilroy, 478.
Hemphill v. Haas, 99.
Hempstead v. Johnson, 118, 172, 228, 246, 315, 319, 324, 338, 421, 427, 441.

TABLE OF CASES.

References are to pages.

Henckley v. Hendrickson, 428.
Henderson's Appeal, 5, 293.
Henderson v. Bliss, 159, 208, 212, 214, 215, 217, 251.
Henderson v. Dodd, 516.
Henderson v. Downing, 218, 220, 246, 300, 350, 430.
Henderson v. Hudden, 236, 446.
Henderson v. Pierce, 624.
Hendricks v. Mount, 163, 319.
Hendricks v. Robinson, 17, 115, 116, 172, 186.
Hennessy v. The Western Bank, 74, 85, 125, 206, 215, 268, 272.
Henriques v. Houe, 601, 606.
Henry v. Hughes, 104, 105.
Henry v. Murphy, 529.
Henry v. Root, 102, 158, 426, 432.
Henshaw v. Sumner, 7, 14, 169, 177, 453.
Herbert v. Bronson, 108.
Herman, Matter of, 57.
Herrick v. Borst, 61–63.
Hershiser v. Higman, 12.
Hertle v. McDonald, 129.
Herver v. Rhode I. L. Works, 369.
Hess' Estate, 549.
Hess v. Blakeslee, 146.
Hessing v. McCloskey, 22.
Hewitt v. Hullins, 14.
Hext v. Porcher, 562, 564, 565.
Hexter v. Loughry, 593.
Heydock v. Stanhope, 166, 212, 420.
Heye v. Bolles, 89, 236, 241, 602.
Heyer v. Alexander, 363.
Hibbard v. Lamb, 578.
Hickley v. Farmers' & Merchants' Bank, 166, 172.
Hickman v. Cox, 242.
Hickman v. Messenger, 224.
Hickman's Ex'r v. Trout, 435.
Hicks v. McGrorty, 499.
Higginbottom v. Peyton, 129.
Higgins v. Whitson, 505.
Hildebrand v. Bowman, 100, 101.
Hill v. Agnew, 244, 272, 273, 430.
Hill v. Alexander, 681.
Hill v. Manser, 17.
Hill v. Morgan, 518.
Hill v. Reed, 65, 185.

Hill v. W. & A. R. R. Co., 486, 576.
Hill's Estate, 505.
Hills v. Elliott, 284.
Hindman v. Dill, 172, 227, 229, 247.
Hine v. Bowe, 10.
Hinson v. Williamson, 569.
Hitchcock v. Cadmus, 243, 395, 485.
Hitchcock v. St. John, 68, 83, 85–87, 323, 329, 330, 472, 473.
Hoagland v. See, 596.
Hoagland v. Trask, 503.
Hobart v. Andrews, 575.
Hobson, In re Assignment of, 531, 545.
Hobson v. Markson, 44.
Hodge v. Wyatt, 226.
Hodges v. Blagrave, 516.
Hodges v. Harris, 68, 87, 327.
Hodges v. Wyatt, 336, 337.
Hodgman v. Western R. R. Co., 107.
Hodgson v. Barrett, 478.
Hodgson v. Macey, 484.
Hoey v. Pierron, 13.
Hoff v. Roane, 172.
Hoffman v. Mackall, 18, 23, 230, 256, 409, 420.
Hoge v. Hollister, 99.
Hogg's Appeal, 388.
Holbird v. Anderson, 22, 167.
Holbrook, Matter of, 557.
Holbrook v. Allen, 172.
Holbrook v. Baker, 319.
Holcomb's Ex'rs v. Bridge Co., 185.
Holland v. Croft, 603, 607.
Holland v. Drake, 80, 85, 86.
Hollingsworth v. Napier, 329.
Hollins v. Mayer, 199, 212, 354.
Hollister v. Loud, 8, 98, 152, 165, 172, 173, 229, 240, 248, 278, 321, 408, 415, 420, 427, 429, 471.
Hollister v. Noyes, 252.
Holmberg v. Dean, 24, 60, 94.
Holmes v. Marshall, 245, 430.
Holmes v. Remsen, 108, 361.
Holmes v. Winchester, 113.
Holridge v. Gillespie, 511.
Holt, Matter of, 537.
Holt v. Bancroft, 135, 158, 160, 453, 609.
Hombeck v. Van Metre, 319.
Hon v. Hon, 281.
Hone v. Henriquez, 204, 400, 448.

TABLE OF CASES. xxxvii

References are to pages.

Hone v. Woolsey, 459-461.
Hook v. Lowry, 527.
Hook v. Stone, 75, 85.
Hooker v. Baillie, 67.
Hooper v. Smith, 30, 31.
Hooper v. Tuckerman, 231, 282, 603.
Hoopes v. Knell, 129, 221, 277, 297, 446.
Hopkins, Ex parte, 67, 99, 101, 234.
Hopkins v. Beebe, 165, 178.
Hopkins v. Gallatin, 65.
Hopkins v. Lacontre, 17.
Hopkins v. Ray, 164, 255, 503.
Hopkins v. Scott, 116, 325.
Horbach v. Hill, 427.
Horsely v. Fawcett, 503.
Horsey v. Chew, 602.
Horsfall, Matter of, 556.
Horton's Appeal, 88, 89, 356.
Hotop v. Durant, 441.
Hotop v. Neidig, 144, 151.
Houghton v. Davis, 575, 5C4.
Housatonic Bank v. Martin, 451.
Housel v. Cremer, 479.
Houston v. Nowland, 297, 333, 365.
Hovarty v. Davis, 475.
Hovey v. Home Ins. Co., 501.
How v. Camp, 172.
Howard v. Snelling, 442.
Howard v. Teel, 235.
Howard Nat. Bank v. King, 372, 374.
Howe v. Newbegin, 307.
Howell v. Bell, 320.
Howell v. Edgar, 172, 208, 250, 444.
Howell v. Moore, 484, 525.
Hower v. Geesaman, 152, 248, 316, 494.
Howerton v. Holt, 320.
Howitt v. Blodgett, 688.
Howland v. Knox, 605.
Hoyt v. Sprague, 547.
Hoyt v. Thompson, 67, 361.
Hubbard v. Fisher, 522.
Hubbard v. McNaughton, 209, 342, 416, 431, 433.
Hudson v. Maze, 269, 277, 469.
Hudson v. Ravett, 148.
Huger v. Huger, 507.
Huggins v. Perrine, 414.
Hughes, Ex parte, 511.
Hughes v. Brown, 313.
Hughes v. Ellison, 75, 85, 351.

Huiscamp v. Albert, 545.
Hulan v. Hoagland, 647.
Hulbert, Matter of, 524.
Hulbert v. Dean, 604.
Hull v. Roane, 171.
Hull v. Sigsworth, 617.
Hulls v. Jeffrey, 169, 179.
Hulse v. Marshall, 338, 484, 597.
Humphries v. Freeman, 284.
Hunker v. Bing, 524.
Hunt v. Bass, 506, 514.
Hunt v. Weiner, 421, 519, 527, 567, 594, 601, 604, 607.
Hunter v. Hubbard, 559.
Hunter v. United States, 542.
Hurd v. Silsby, 207.
Hurlbert v. Dean, 236, 240.
Hurlbut v. Carter, 65, 185, 355, 356.
Hurley, Ex parte, 507.
Hurth v. Bower, 558, 663.
Hurtt v. Fisher, 562.
Huse v. Ames, 500.
Huston v. Worthly, 504.
Hutcheson v. Peshine, 361, 363.
Hutchings v. Low, 129.
Hutchins v. Hutchins, 565.
Hutchins v. Sprague, 567.
Hutchins v. Taylor, 37.
Hutchinson v. Brown, 688.
Hutchinson v. Green, 66, 604.
Hutchinson v. Lord, 259, 265, 273, 396, 398, 600.
Hutchinson v. McClure, 169, 178.
Hutchinson v. Smith, 90, 237.
Hutchinson v. Watkins, 627.
Hutton v. Crutwell, 30, 31.
Hyde v. Olds, 338, 460.
Hyde v. Sontag, 41, 52.
Hyde v. Weitzner, 23.
Hyde v. Zacharie, 39.
Hyslop v. Clarke, 172, 187, 201, 202, 444.

Iddings v. Bruen, 512.
Ingersoll v. Kendall, 324.
Ingham v. Burnell, 130, 281.
Ingham v. Lindeman, 104, 480, 519, 522.
Inglehart v. Armiger, 104.
Inglis v. Floyd, 485.
Ingliss v. Grant, 22, 133, 155, 340.

TABLE OF CASES.

References are to pages.

Ingraham v. Geyer, 200, 339, 365, 368, 378, 379.
Ingraham v. Grigg, 65, 100, 147, 157, 159, 160, 218, 271, 302, 408, 525, 550.
Ingraham v. Wheeler, 172, 208, 306, 327, 457.
Ingram v. Kirkpatrick, 115, 127, 323, 325, 335, 340, 352, 353, 460, 581.
Ingram v. Osborn, 688.
Inloes v. American Ex. Bank, 245, 261, 431, 507.
Innis v. Lansing, 91, 558.
Insurance Co. v. Jones, 495.
Insurance Co. v. Wallace, 216.
Insurance Co. v. Wallis, 199, 304.
International Trust Co. v. Boardman, 487.
Iowa Seed Co. v. Door, 112, 516.
Irvine v. Dunham, 575, 578.
Irwin v. Keen, 443, 494, 600.
Irwin v. Tabb, 536.
Iselin v. Dalrymple, 147.
Iselin v. Henlein, 434.
Isidor, Matter of, 577.
Isles v. Martin, 505.
Ivison v. Grassiot, 106, 387.

Jack v. Wiennett, 545.
Jackson v. Cornell, 93, 187, 204, 213, 236, 237, 239, 323, 326, 420, 448, 472.
Jackson v. Dean, 320.
Jackson v. Harby, 427, 435, 502.
Jackson v. Heath, 3.
Jackson v. Irvine, 51.
Jackson v. Lewis, 417.
Jackson v. Lomas, 190, 191, 197.
Jackson v. Losee, 106, 109, 398.
Jackson v. Mather, 424.
Jackson v. McCullough, 41, 48, 53.
Jackson v. Mitchell, 190, 191.
Jackson v. Parker, 218.
Jackson v. Peek, 424.
Jackson v. Rounds, 624, 626.
Jackson v. Sheldon, 90, 91.
Jackson v. Zimmerman, 424.
Jacobs v. Allen, 150, 272.
Jacobs v. McCally, 673.
Jacobs v. Remsen, 118, 119, 172, 175, 229, 322.
Jacot v. Corbett, 207, 216, 233.

Jacques v. Greenwood, 420.
Jaeger v. Kelly, 421.
Jaffray v. Greenbaum, 15.
Jaffray v. McGahee, 507.
Jaffray v. Steedman, 191.
Jagoe v. Alleyn, 3.
James, Ex parte, 511, 518.
James v. Fulcrod, 130.
James v. Mechanics' Nat. Bank, 478, 678.
James v. Whitbread, 23, 155, 197, 224, 242, 255, 256, 415.
Jamison v. McNally, 606.
January v. Powell, 585.
Jayne v. Dillon, 320.
Jefferie's Appeal, 581, 593.
Jeffries v. Bleckman, 208, 642.
Jellenik v. May, 442.
Jenkins v. Eldridge, 523, 527.
Jenkins v. Pierce, 53.
Jenness v. Doe, 432.
Jennings v. Prentice, 93, 94.
Jermain v. Pattison, 475, 494.
Jessup v. Herzfeld, 270.
Jessup v. Hulse, 221, 252, 264, 281, 446.
Jessup v. Johnson, 426, 432.
Jewett v. Tucker, 482.
Jewett v. Woodward, 395, 519, 525, 529, 536, 581, 583, 584.
John's Estate, In re, 505.
Johns v. Bolton, 100, 676.
Johns v. Erb, 534.
John Shilleto Co. v. McConnell, 453.
Johns v. James, 450.
Johnson's Appeal, 14.
Johnson, Matter of, 524.
Johnson v. Baker, 302.
Johnson v. Bloodgood, 499.
Johnson v. Bray, 640.
Johnson v. Bush, 183.
Johnson v. Candage, 503, 595.
Johnson v. Farnam, 208, 601.
Johnson v. Herring, 292, 575.
Johnson v. McAllister's Assignee, 160, 169, 230, 234, 260, 426.
Johnson v. McGraw, 5, 179.
Johnson v. Merritt, 475.
Johnson v. Osenton, 420.
Johnson v. Rogers, 41, 52, 584.
Johnson v. Roberson, 12, 81, 84, 86.

TABLE OF CASES. xxxix

References are to pages.

Johnson v. Sharp, 302, 350, 369.
Johnson v. Whitwell, 130, 133, 158, 165, 167, 168, 296, 400, 458.
Johnson v. Thweatt, 103, 125, 220, 246, 432–434.
Johnston v. Eason, 506, 509.
Johnston v. Zane's Trustees, 92, 260, 278, 332.
Johnston's Heirs v. Harvey, 215, 219.
Joiner v. Van Alstyne, 59.
Jones, Matter of, 576.
Jones v. Bartlett, 239.
Jones v. Beach, 290.
Jones v. Dougherty, 127, 278, 333, 337, 422, 460, 462, 592.
Jones v. Hamblet, 389.
Jones v. Housman, 474.
Jones v. Jones, 359, 367.
Jones v. Kinney, 56.
Jones v. Sleeper, 21, 37.
Jones v. Stockett, 314, 566, 576.
Jones v. Syer, 244, 431.
Jones v. Tilton, 339.
Jones v. Whitbread, 270.
Jones v. Yates, 112.
Jordan's Appeal, 531, 556.
Jordan v. Gellen, 107, 109.
Jordan v. Sherlock, 500.
Joseph v. Levi, 431.
Journeay v. Brackley, 475.
Judd v. Langdon, 318.
Judson v. Abeel, 259.
Juliand v. Rathbone, 151, 307.
Julliard v. May, 361.
Jung, Matter of, 557.

Kaine v. Weigley, 427, 428.
Kalkman v. McElderry, 23, 131, 338.
Kallman v. Creditors, 166.
Kane v. Drake, 319.
Kane v. Roberts, 602.
Kasson, In re, 47.
Kavanagh v. Beckwith, 119, 422, 432, 533.
Kayser v. Heavenrich, 118, 221, 421.
Keating v. Vaughn, 421, 577, 682.
Keeley v. Cassidy, 546.
Keen v. Hall, 453.
Keen v. Preston, 5, 10.
Keep v. Lord, 499.

Keep v. Sanderson, 143, 265, 273, 396.
Keevil v. Donaldson, 269, 432.
Kehoe v. Taylor, 483.
Keiley v. Dusenberry, 576.
Keim's Appeal, 543, 556.
Keith v. Fink, 236, 241.
Keith v. Ham, 89.
Keller v. Blanchard, 320.
Keller v. Smalley, 481, 482, 682.
Kellogg v. Miller, 436, 543.
Kellogg v. Root, 135, 450.
Kellogg v. Slawson, 60, 64, 136, 140, 145, 151–153, 256, 261, 263, 265, 277, 427.
Kelly v. Baker, 79, 84, 85.
Kelly v. Crapo, 358, 474.
Kelly v. Duffy, 99.
Kelstadt v. Reilly, 358.
Kemp v. Carnley, 77, 79, 85, 239, 241.
Kemp v. Porter, 336.
Kendall v. Bishop, 65, 124.
Kendall v. Fitts, 319.
Kendall B. & S. Co. v. Bain, 103.
Kendall v. New England Carpet Co., 243, 522.
Kendall v. Rider, 500.
Kendrick v. Glover, 105.
Kenefick v. Perry, 10.
Kennear v. Johnson, 82.
Kennedy v. Rose, 318.
Kennedy v. Winn, 287, 312.
Kennedy v. Wood, 433.
Kent's Appeal, 507.
Kepler v. Erie Dime Sav. etc. Co., 478.
Kerbs v. Ewing, 12, 642.
Kercheis v. Schloss, 151, 152, 155, 188, 190, 268, 281.
Kerr v. Blodgett, 538, 558.
Kern v. Powell, 295.
Ketchum v. Watson, 318.
Keteltas v. Wilson, 115, 147, 415, 521, 524.
Kettle v. Hammond, 32.
Kettlewell v. Stewart, 199.
Kevan v. Branch, 140, 207, 225.
Keyes v. Brush, 145, 151, 153, 350, 578, 592, 597.
Kidder v. Horrowbin, 54.
Kilbee v. Sneyd, 511.
Kilbourne v. Fay, 481.
Killick v. Flexney, 510.

TABLE OF CASES.

References are to pages.

Kilpatrick v. Dean, 660.
Kimball, In re, 40, 152.
Kimball v. Hamilton Fire Ins. Co., 69.
Kingston v. Koch, 421.
King v. Donnelly, 310, 312, 575.
King v. Glass, 24, 358, 363.
King v. Gustafson, 164.
King v. Kenan, 227, 245.
King v. Mitchell, 398.
King v. Moore, 289, 312.
King v. Trice, 166.
King v. Watson, 197, 209, 210.
Kingman v. Barton, 477, 689.
Kingston v. Koch, 301.
Kinnard v. Thompson, 126, 335, 336, 352.
Kintner v. Jones, 396.
Kintzing, In re, 44.
Kirby v. Goodykoontz, 564.
Kirby v. Ingersoll, 68, 74, 85-87.
Kirby v. Schoonmaker, 88, 235-237, 239.
Kircheis v. Schloss, 144, 145.
Kirkland v. Brune, 296.
Kirtland v. Snow, 319.
Kiser v. Dannenburg, 453.
Kissam v. Edmonston, 220, 443.
Kittell v. Osborne, 283.
Kitchen v. Reinsky, 380.
Klapp's Assignees v. Shirk, 227, 317, 325, 338, 349, 352, 441.
Klauber v. Charlton, 94, 688.
Kleine v. Nie, 434.
Kloeckner v. Bergstrom, 112.
Klump v. Gardner, 67.
Knapp v. McGowan, 60, 229, 660.
Knauth v. Bassett, 236, 240, 601.
Knefler v. Shreve, 138, 144, 386.
Kneeland v. Cowles, 230.
Knevals v. Blauvelt, 104.
Knight v. Haynie, 569.
Knight v. Hunt, 191.
Knight v. Packer, 227, 246.
Knight v. Waterman, 100, 158, 224, 676.
Knighton v. Tufli, 105.
Knower v. Central Nat. Bank, 400, 480.
Knowles, Petition of, 549.
Knowles v. Lord, 482.
Knowlton v. Mosely, 52, 53.
Knox, Matter of, 106.
Knoxville Nat. Bank v. Hanirick, 548.

Kobbe, Matter of, 583.
Kohlsaat v. Hoguet, 21.
Kohn v. Clement, 15.
Koontz, Matter of, 577.
Koster v. Merritt, 372.
Kraft, In re, 47.
Kraft v. Dalles, 497.
Kreider's Estate, 443.
Krug v. McGilliard, 98, 124, 308.
Kruse v. Prindle, 135, 187.
Kuhn v. Nieberg, 99.
Kuykendall v. McDonald, 164, 166, 320.
Kyle v. Harveys, 254, 255.
Kyle v. O'Neil, 602.
Kynaston v. Crouch, 164.

La Belle Wagon Works v. Tidball, 682.
Lacey, Ex parte, 511.
Lacker v. Rhoads, 114.
Lafferty v. Rutherford, 105.
Lahm v. Johnson, 553, 573, 595, 669.
Lains, In re, 56.
Laird v. Campbell, 191.
Lake v. De Lambert, 578.
Lamar v. Pool, 680.
Lamb v. Cecil, 65, 66.
Lamb v. Durant, 68, 87, 165.
Lamb v. Goodwin, 510, 516.
Lamb v. Johnson, 529.
Lamb v. Laughlin, 65.
Lampson v. Arnold, 169, 179, 421, 452, 453.
Lanahan v. Latrobe, 342, 536, 585, 602, 603.
Lancaster v. Elce, 583, 585.
Lanckton v. Wolcott, 549.
Land v. Jeffries, 324, 326.
Landaur, Matter of, 557.
Lane's Appeal, 292, 600.
Lane v. Bailey, 499.
Lane v. Coleman, 522.
Lane v. Nickerson, 54.
Laner, In re, 51.
Laney v. Laney, 448.
Lanfear v. Sumner, 361.
Lang v. Simmons, 186.
Langdon v. Horton, 327, 328.
Langdon v. Thompson, 268, 496, 503.
Langley, In re, 42, 51.
Langley v. Perry, 42, 45, 46.

TABLE OF CASES. xli

References are to pages.

Lanier v. Driver, 17, 226, 335.
Lansing v. Woodnorth, 116, 132, 186, 229, 454.
Lanson v. De Bolt, 624, 625.
Lassell v. Tucker, 85, 241.
Latham, Trustee, v. Simmons, 495.
Latimer, Estate of, 557.
Latrobe v. Tiernan, 569.
Lavender v. Blackstone, 274.
Lavender v. Thomas, 15, 179.
Law v. Mills, 358.
Law v. Wyman, 7, 169.
Lawrence, In re, 47.
Lawrence v. Bayard, 106.
Lawrence v. Davis, 166, 172, 173, 277, 309, 334, 341, 342.
Lawrence v. Martin, 107, 109.
Lawrence v. McVeagh, 624.
Lawrence v. Nuff, 12.
Lawson v. De Bolt, 508.
Lawton v. Levy, 601.
Lay v. Seago, 172, 208.
Layson v. Rowan, 92, 126, 148, 187, 324.
Lazarus v. Bryson, 513.
Lazarus v. Commonwealth Ins. Co., 105, 551.
Leach v. Kelsey, 111, 353, 457.
Leadman v. Harris, 218.
Leahy, Matter of, 660.
Leavitt v. Yates, 520.
Lee's Appeal, 206, 529.
Lee v. Brown, 179.
Lee v. Green, 420.
Lee v. Huntoon, 330.
Lee v. Tabor, 600.
Leeds v. Commonwealth, 303, 441.
Leger v. Bonaffe, 478.
Legg v. Willard, 329.
Leggett v. Hunter, 576.
Lehman v. Rosengarten, 489.
Lehman v. Tallassee Mfg. Co., 337, 609.
Leicester v. Rose, 190.
Leitch v. Hollister, 7, 13, 62, 107, 123, 167, 229, 230, 234, 415, 438.
Leitensdorfer v. Webb, 160, 338.
Lent v. Flint, 482.
Lentilhon v. Moffatt, 147, 157, 159, 203, 605.
Leon v. Welborne, 62, 682.
Leon v. Wittermark, 597.

Leonard v. Claflin, 112.
Leonard v. Clinton, 488.
Le Prince v. Guillemot, 160, 207.
Lerry v. Bibeau, 536.
Lester v. Abbott, 236, 240, 241.
Lester v. Pollock, 241.
Letson v. Kenyon, 549.
Leverenz v. Haines, 329.
Levy's Accounting, 271, 273, 492, 519, 557.
Levy v. Adler, 421.
Levy v. James, 347.
Lewenthal, Matter of, 557, 579, 582.
Lewis, Matter of, 480, 545.
Lewis, In re, 483, 484.
Lewis v. Bank of Penn. Township, 591.
Lewis v. Caperton's Ex'r, 152, 246.
Lewis v. County Clerk, 39.
Lewis v. Hake, 554.
Lewis v. Miller, 4.
Lewis v. Simon, 417, 601.
Lewis v. Whitemore, 319.
Lewis v. Ziegler, 281.
Lill v. Brant, 14, 115, 130, 135, 230.
Lincoln v. Field, 301, 382.
Lindemann v. Ingham, 480, 517.
Linden v. Sharpe, 50, 93.
Linder v. Lewis, 41, 47, 53.
Lindsay v. Jackson, 500.
Lindsey v. Platner, 597.
Lininger v. Raymond, 140, 229, 270, 512.
Linn v. Wright, 152.
Linthecum v. Fenley, 634.
Lionberger v. Broadway Savings Bank, 65, 108, 482, 495.
Lippincott v. Barker, 172, 205, 209, 210, 211.
Lister v. Lister, 511.
Litchfield v. Cudworth, 513.
Litchfield v. White, 150, 196, 272, 397, 464, 485, 563, 583.
Little v. Commonwealth, 573.
Little v. Eddy, 166.
Littlejohn v. Turner, 342.
Livermore v. Jenckes, 208, 212, 359.
Livermore v. McNair, 167, 319, 455, 654, 655.
Livermore v. Northop, 4, 119, 120, 422.
Livermore v. Rhodes, 420.
Livingston v. Bell, 205, 230, 233.

TABLE OF CASES.

References are to pages.

Lloyd v. Williams, 166.
Loan Co. v. Turner, 359.
Locke v. Winning, 21.
Lockhard v. Brodie, 118, 137, 176.
Lockhart v. Stevenson, 7.
Lockhart v. Wyatt, 226, 336.
Lockwood v. Beckwith, 499.
Lockwood v. Canfield, 129.
Lockwood v. Nelson, 336.
Lockwood v. Slevin, 566.
Loeb v. Pierpont, 80, 85.
Loeschick v. Baldwin, 456.
Loeschigk v. Addison, 90.
Loeschigk v. Hatfield, 90.
Loeschigk v. Jacobson, 115, 117.
Loftin v. Lyon, 129.
Loller v. Croft, 523.
Lomax v. Buxton, 30, 31, 33.
Lomax v. Pendleton, 597.
Loney v. Bayly, 181, 199, 216.
Long v. Girdwood, 379, 676.
Longmire v. Goode, 4, 102, 609.
London v. Parsley, 60.
Loomis v. Griffin, 347, 386.
Loomis v. Stewart, 627.
Loos v. Wilkinson, 421, 443.
Lord v. Brig Watchman, 209, 210.
Lord v. Devendorf, 236, 259, 296.
Lord v. Fisher, 453.
Lord v. Meachen, 640.
Lorenz v. Orlady, 113.
Loring v. Palmer, 133.
Lothrop v. Highland Foundry Co., 39.
Loveman v. Taylor, 527.
Loving v. Pairo, 365, 601.
Low v. Graydon, 187, 204.
Low v. Welch, 113.
Low v. Wyman, 14, 177.
Lowe v. Morris, 518, 523.
Lowenstein v. Flamand, 84, 286, 290, 660.
Lowenstein v. Love, 219, 246.
Lowery v. Clinton, 105, 604.
Lowry v. Hall, 360.
Lucas v. The Sunbury Erie Railroad Co., 5, 132.
Luce v. Barnum, 99.
Luce's Ex'rs v. Park, 106.
Luckemeyer v. Seltz, 101, 223.
Luckenbach v. Brickenstein, 478.

Luckes, Ex parte, 34, 35, 49.
Ludington's Petition, 5, 556, 582.
Ludwig v. Highley, 113, 216, 591.
Ludwig v. Iglehart, 394.
Lundecke, Petition of, 640.
Lupton v. Cutter, 200.
Lycoming Ins. Co. v. Storrs, 478.
Lyman v. Bond, 39.
Lyon v. McIlvaine, 453, 627.
Lyon v. Platner, 262.
Lyon v. Receiver of Taxes, 545.
Lyons v. Field, 17.

Maack v. Maack, 164.
Maas v. Goodman, 478, 482.
Mabbett v. White, 68, 84.
Maberry v. Shisler, 379.
Maccubbin v. Cromwell, 568, 572.
Macdonald v. First Nat. Bank, 380.
Macdonald v. Moore, 41, 47, 56.
Mackay v. Bloodgood, 345.
Mackie v. Cairns, 163, 166, 172, 217, 218, 221, 430, 438, 443, 448, 454.
Mackintosh v. Comer, 118, 277, 317, 348, 447, 468, 536.
Macomber v. Parker, 319.
Macomber v. Weeks, 455.
Maennel v. Murdock, 172, 199, 216, 251.
Magee v. Carpenter, 17.
Magnus v. Sleeper, 690.
Magovern v. Richard, 680.
Maguire v. Pingree, 359.
Main v. Lynch, 421, 442, 455.
Maitland v. Newton, 108.
Major v. Hill, 338, 346.
Malcolm v. Hall, 23.
Malcolm v. Hodges, 157, 199, 200, 212, 232, 244, 281, 282, 383, 431.
Maltbie v. Hotchkiss, 39, 40, 52.
Malvin v. West, 60, 62.
Manahan, In re, 54.
Mandel v. Peay, 241, 577, 594.
Maney v. Killough, 320.
Manhattan Co. v. Greenwich Bank, 397.
Mann, In re, 233, 640.
Mann v. Flower, 52-54, 481.
Mann v. Huston, 329, 474.
Mann v. Whitbeck, 264, 268, 271.
Manning v. Beck, 660.
Manning v. Manning, 520.

TABLE OF CASES. xliii

References are to pages.

Manning v. Stern, 577.
Manny v. Logan, 4, 160.
Manufacturers' & Mechanics' Bank v. Bank of Pennsylvania, 14.
Marbury v. Brooks, 8, 172, 192, 312, 421, 467.
Marcum v. Hereford, 105.
Marden v. Babcock, 14.
Marder v. Wright, 537.
Marenthal v. Moster, 549.
Market Nat. Bank v. Hofheimer, 446, 603.
Marklin, Matter of, 491.
Marks' Appeal, 295, 303, 313, 486, 676.
Marks v. Bradley, 89, 118, 426.
Marks v. Hill, 228, 245, 472.
Marquand, Matter of, 485.
Marsalis v. Oglesby, 277.
Marsh v. Bennett, 89, 90, 188, 209, 211, 420, 431.
Marsh v. Vawter, 353, 626.
Marshall v. Barkworth, 51.
Marshall v. Hutchinson, 172.
Marshall v. Livingston Nat. Bank, 16, 92.
Marshall v. Means, 107.
Marshall v. Shibley, 285, 630.
Marston v. Coburn, 155, 287, 301, 339, 371.
Marter, In re, 44.
Martin v. Hall, 120.
Martin v. Hauseman, 12, 14.
Martin v. Kennedy, 95.
Martin v. Kunzmuller, 499, 500.
Martin v. Martin, 359.
Martin v. Mathiot, 317.
Martin v. Pewtress, 30.
Martin v. Pillsbury, 500.
Martin v. Potter, 369.
Martin v. Price, 593.
Martine v. Willis, 499.
Mason v. Martin, 514.
Mason v. Stricker, 380.
Mass v. Goodman, 500.
Massey v. Allen, 52, 53.
Massey v. Noyes, 600.
Masson v. Anderson, 605.
Mather v. Nesbit, 361.
Mather v. Pratt, 588, 597.
Mathew, Ex parte, 165.

Mathews v. Dragand, 511.
Mathews v. Poultney, 151, 421, 441.
Matison v. Demarest, 241.
Matlack's Appeal, 394, 591.
Matthews v. Stewart, 41.
Matthie v. Edwards, 506.
Mattison v. Judd, 245, 260, 273, 382, 526.
Maughlin v. Tyler, 85, 181, 199, 216, 251.
Maulden v. Armstead, 335, 336, 344.
Mawson v. Stock, 190.
Maxwell, Matter of, 526.
Maxwell v. Evans, 39.
Maxwell v. Simonton, 16.
May v. First Nat. Bank, 369.
May v. Walker, 157, 233, 234, 339, 341, 342, 344, 368, 640.
Mayer, Matter of, 577.
Mayer v. Bernstein, 68.
Mayer v. Galluchat, 526.
Mayer v. Hazard, 519.
Mayer v. Hellman, 23, 40, 44, 46, 49, 51, 52.
Mayer v. Shields, 208.
Mayeski v. Creditors, 428.
Maynard v. Maynard, 536.
Mayo v. Sneed, 382, 384.
Mays v. Fritton, 21, 165.
McAllister v. Marshall, 22, 215, 284.
McAllister v. Richards, 21, 37.
McArthur v. Chase, 62, 91.
McBlain v. Spelman, 299, 302, 350.
McBride v. Bohanan, 208, 337.
McBride v. Clelland, 317.
McBride v. Dorman, 502.
McBride v. Hagan, 345.
McBroom v. Turner, 455.
McBroom & Wood's Appeal, 12, 14.
McCabe's Account, 556.
McCabe's Appeal, 113.
McCahill v. Hamilton, 559.
McCain v. Pickens, 338.
McCall v. Hinckley, 172, 199, 210, 232.
McCallie v. Walton, 65, 264, 266.
McCart v. Maddox, 682.
McCartney v. Bostwick, 593.
McCartney v. Welch, 121.
McCleery v. Allen, 266.
McClelland v. Remsen, 12, 15, 68, 181, 223.
McClure v. Campbell, 26, 212.

TABLE OF CASES.

References are to pages.

McClure v. Miller, 515.
McClurg v. Lecky, 215, 218, 219, 222, 443, 600.
McColgan v. Hopkins, 172, 181.
McConnaughey v. Chambers, 500.
McConnell v. Sherwood, 269, 431.
McCormick v. Sullivan, 364.
McCracken v. Milhous, 496, 623.
McCrea v. Purmont, 592, 597.
McCullough v. Hutchinson, 234, 284.
McCullough v. Roderick, 361, 365.
McCullough v. Somerville, 73, 85, 86, 88, 172, 239, 241, 286, 576.
McCullum, Matter of, 530.
McDaniel v. Baca, 428, 429.
McDonald v. Kelly, 106.
McDonald v. McDonald, 106.
McDougal v. Dougherty, 594.
McDowell v. Caldwell, 519, 554.
McElroy v. Seery, 104.
McFarland v. Bate, 67, 99.
McFarland v. Birdsall, 208, 230, 232, 234.
McFerran v. Davis, 181, 462, 576.
McGee v. Carpenter, 325.
McGoon v. Scales, 365.
McGready v. Harris, 51.
McGregor v. Chase, 15.
McGregor v. Ellis, 78, 85, 86.
McGuire v. Faber, 441.
McHose v. Dutton, 11.
McIlhargy v. Chambers, 301, 350, 660.
McIlhenny v. Todd, 549, 578, 683.
McIntire v. Benson, 273, 400.
McIntyre v. McClenaghan, 537, 554, 581, 680.
McKee v. Coffin, 58.
McKee v. Judd, 106, 109.
McKee v. Scober, 634.
McKelvy v. Blair, 356.
McKenzie v. Garrison, 182.
McKesson's Estate, 509.
McKindley v. Nourse, 627.
McKinley v. Combe, 460.
McKinley v. Irwin, 514.
McKinney v. Rhoads, 301, 302, 350.
McKinnon v. Stewart, 127.
McKissick v. McKissick, 367.
McLain v. Simington, 519, 522, 554.
McLean v. Britton, 440.
McLean v. Johnson, 37, 42.
McLean v. Meline, 37, 42.
McLean v. Prentice, 607.
McLellan's Appeal, 483, 495, 519, 557.
McLemore v. Nuckolls, 597.
McLeod v. Latimar, 54..
McMahon v. Allen, 112, 488.
McMahon v. Morrison, 22.
McMenomy v. Ferrers, 172.
McMillen v. Scott, 522.
McNair v. Rewey, 99, 101.
McNeeley v. Hart, 106.
McNutt v. Strayhow, 68, 86.
McPike v. Atwell, 427.
McQueen v. Babcock, 494.
McQuinnay v. Hitchcock, 172, 320.
Meacham v. Stevens, 148, 257, 258, 261, 263, 396, 492, 520, 523, 524, 534, 562, 567.
Mead v. Dayton, 372.
Mead v. Phillips, 271, 310, 322, 323, 331, 420, 421.
Means v. Dowd, 218.
Means v. Hapgood, 358.
Means v. Montgomery, 151, 152, 325, 423, 430.
Mears v. Commonwealth, 477.
Mechanics' Bank v. Gorman, 205, 230, 233.
Mechanics' & Traders' Bank v. Dakin, 602.
Meeker v. Felts, 110.
Meeker v. Saunders, 152, 266, 277, 297, 441.
Meeker v. Wilson, 20, 323, 326, 327, 474.
Mehaffy v. Share, 114.
Meinhard v. Strickland, 680.
Melick v. Voorhies, 506, 513, 565.
Mellon's Appeal, 178, 478, 559.
Mendelsohn, In re, 44, 46.
Menown v. Crawford, 108.
Meredith Man. Co. v. Smith, 22, 169, 177.
Merrick's Estate, 551, 597.
Merrill v. Englesby, 230, 306, 346, 400, 461.
Merrill v. Neill, 239.
Merrill v. Wilson, 100, 112, 141.
Merrils v. Swift, 350.

TABLE OF CASES. xlv

References are to pages.

Merwin, Matter of, 557, 579.
Merwin v. Richardson, 594.
Messinger v. Yager, 623.
Messonier v. Kauman, 461.
Metcalf v. Van Brunt, 273, 307, 308, 460.
Metropolitan Nat. Bank v. Morehead, 537, 538.
Metzger, In re, 53.
Meux v. Anthony, 601.
Meux v. Howell, 23, 132, 407, 410, 412.
Meyer's Appeal, 529.
Meyer v. Davis, 499.
Meyer v. Evans, 453, 481.
Meyer v. Pulliam, 250.
Meyers v. Briggs, 503.
Meyers v. Conway, 99.
Myers, In re, 53, 54.
Mezesheimer v. Kennedy, 688.
Michelstetter v. Weiner, 16.
Michoud v. Girod, 513-515.
Middleton v. Onslow, 190.
Midgeley v. Slocum, 545.
Mifflin v. Rasey, 548.
Milburn v. Waugh, 320.
Miles v. Bacon, 149, 522.
Miles v. Blakeman, 518.
Miles v. Parkhurst, 333.
Millard v. Hall, 320.
Millard v. Webster, 61, 63.
Miller's Appeal, 110, 544.
Miller's Estate, 549.
Miller v. Cherry, 149.
Miller v. Conklin, 179, 208, 210, 212, 214.
Miller v. Crawford, 186, 536, 548.
Miller v. Ewtell, 241.
Miller v. Halsey, 112, 469, 488.
Miller v. Holcomb's Ex'r, 190, 564, 568, 572.
Miller v. Kernaghan, 361.
Miller v. Lockwood, 322.
Miller v. Mulford, 490, 538.
Miller v. O'Bannon, 298, 353.
Miller v. Pancoast, 319.
Miller v. Sherry, 501.
Miller v. Sligh, 569.
Miller v. Stetson, 229, 260.
Miller v. Whittier, 554.
Milliken v. Dart, 106, 600.
Milliken v. Steiner, 66.

Mills v. Argall, 90, 91, 182, 448, 458, 459, 581.
Mills v. Barber, 68, 72, 74, 84, 87, 88.
Mills v. Goodsell, 513.
Mills v. Haines, 337.
Mills v. Harris, 460.
Mills v. Levy, 203, 204.
Mills v. Warner, 318.
Mills v. Williams, 18.
Milne v. Henry, 317.
Mims v. Armstrong, 142.
Miners' Bank Appeal, 178.
Miners' National Bank Appeal, 159, 169, 215.
Minor v. Edwards, 105.
Minuse v. Cox, 509, 597.
Missimer v. Curtis, 353.
Mitchell v. Beal, 246, 247, 320.
Mitchell v. Gazzam, 179.
Mitchell v. Glendell, 454.
Mitchell v. Kendall, 561.
Mitchell v. Stiles, 188, 276, 414, 416, 432, 434, 435, 600.
Mitchell v. Willock, 325.
Mitchell v. Winslow, 106, 317.
Moale v. Buchanan, 305.
Mobile Bank v. McDonnell, 427.
Moddewell v. Keever, 112, 486.
Moennel v. Murdock, 701.
Moffat v. Ingham, 469.
Moffat v. McDowall, 172.
Mohawk Bank v. Atwater, 601.
Moir v. Brown, 92, 143, 145, 151-153, 262, 303, 305, 310.
Moise v. Chapman, 579.
Monell v. Monell, 569-571.
Monteith v. Hogg, 353.
Montgomery v. Commercial Bank of Rodney, 65.
Montgomery v. Galbraith, 267.
Montgomery v. Goodbar, 220.
Montgomery's Ex'rs v. Kirksey, 95, 104, 227.
Moody v. Carroll, 551, 601.
Moody v. Litton, 478.
Moody v. Paschal, 133, 189, 268.
Moore v. Bonnell, 376.
Moore v. Church, 135, 366, 369.
Moore v. Collins, 172, 231, 350.
Moore v. Hinnant, 335, 408, 430.

TABLE OF CASES.

References are to pages.

Moore v. Ireland, 108.
Moore v. McKinstry, 107.
Moore v. Willett, 358, 360, 474.
Moore v. Wyman, 523.
Morehead v. Bank, 530.
Morey v. Crocker, 466.
Morgan's Appeal, 178.
Morgan, Ex parte, 28, 33, 34, 35, 529, 557.
Morgan v. Bogue, 230, 320, 412, 601.
Morgan v. Brundrett, 32.
Morgan v. Kinney, 479.
Morgan v. United States, 108.
Morgentham v. Harris, 59, 64.
Morrill v. Richardson, 573.
Morris' Appeal, 478.
Morris v. Mowatt, 587.
Morris v. Olwine, 543.
Morris v. Parker, 546, 547.
Morris v. Rexford, 498.
Morris, etc. Co. v. Reeder, 676.
Morrison v. Atwell, 240, 241, 601.
Morrison v. Brand, 259, 448, 559.
Morrison v. Morrison, 518.
Morrison v. Shuster, 308, 457.
Morrow v. Bright, 500.
Morse v. Cohannet Bank, 37.
Morse v. Royal, 511.
Morse v. Slason, 189.
Moses, Matter of, 53.
Moses v. Murgatroyd, 311.
Moses v. Thomas, 98, 178, 654.
Moss v. Humphrey, 101.
Motley v. Harris, 529.
Mott v. Morris' Assignees, 540.
Mott v. McNeil, 318.
Moule v. Buchanan, 342, 536, 586.
Mower v. Hanford, 259, 453.
Mowry's Appeal, 552.
Mowry v. Crocker, 373.
Mowson v. Mendenhall, 68.
Muhr v. Pinover, 99.
Muir v. Glinsman, 475.
Mulford v. Shirk, 98.
Muller v. Norton, 396.
Murray v. De Rottenham, 545.
Murray v. Judson, 119, 535.
Murray v. McNealy, 10.
Murray v. Riggs, 171, 172, 201.
Murray v. Roberts, 362.
Murrill v. Neill, 392.

Mumford v. Murray, 570.
Mumper v. Rushmore, 322, 479.
Munsell v. Lewis, 106.
Munson v. Ellis, 60, 477.
Munson v. Frazer, 358, 627.
Munzeheimer v. Mayer, 428.
Murphy's Assignment, 292.
Murphy v. Bell, 262, 270.
Murphy v. Caldwell, 6, 609.
Muscogee Lumber Co. v. Hyer, 522.
Mussey v. Noyes, 4, 7, 123–125, 133, 157, 167, 172, 173, 252, 258, 261, 265, 266, 443, 444, 483, 508, 509, 685.
Myer's Appeal, 100, 354.
Myer v. Fales' Sons & Co., 349.
Myers v. Kinzie, 412.

Nack v. Meisen, 688.
Nailer v. Young, 311, 313, 337.
Nash v. Simpson, 53.
Nashville Trust Co. v. Bank, 500.
National Bank v. Chase, 105.
National Bank v. Cohn, 236.
National Bank v. Lanahan, 200, 212.
National Bank v. Lorenberg, 682, 685.
National Bank v. Morris, 163.
National Bank v. Printup, 596.
National Bank v. Ridenour, 312.
National Bank v. Sackett, 79, 85, 285.
National Bank v. Scriven, 67.
National Mech. & Trad. Bank v. Eagle Sugar Refinery, 339.
National Park Bank v. Lanihan, 600.
National Park Bank v. Whitmore, 192.
National Union Bank v. Copeland, 339.
Nave v. Britton, 138.
Neal v. Lea, 479, 500.
Neally v. Ambrose, 255, 263, 396, 508.
Needles v. Needles, 106.
Neill v. Jackson, 55, 567.
Nelson v. Dunn, 336.
Nelson v. Garey, 135.
Nelson v. Tenney, 89.
Nesbit, Matter of, 640.
Nesbitt v. Digby, 95, 284.
Neuffer v. Pardue, 116.
Neustadt v. Joll, 601.
New v. Reissner, 297, 625, 626.
New Albany & S. R. R. Co. v. Huff, 230, 234, 248.
Newby v. Hill, 129.

TABLE OF CASES. xlvii

References are to pages.

Newell v. Martin, 236.
New England Bank v. Lewis, 311, 341, 581.
New England Iron Co. v. Gibert Elevated R. Co., 353.
Newlin v. Lyon, 502.
Newman v. Bagley, 237.
Newman v. Mineral Co., 160, 636.
Newman v. Vickery, 105.
Newton v. Chandler, 30.
New York County Bank v. Carter, 22.
New York Ins. Co. v. Roulet, 592, 597.
Niagara County Nat. Bank v. Lord, 557.
Niblack v. Goodman, 354.
Nichol v. Spowers, 660.
Nichols v. Cass, 652.
Nichols v. Ellis, 168.
Nichols v. Kribs, 486.
Nichols v. McEwen, 171, 221, 263, 446, 526.
Nichols v. Wellings, 164, 191.
Nicholson v. Leavitt, 158, 173, 175, 238, 239, 253, 255, 260, 273, 407, 410, 419, 424, 426, 432, 472, 508.
Nicholson v. Tutin, 343, 346, 583.
Nicoll v. Mumford, 23, 125, 311, 312, 333, 335, 342.
Nightingale v. Harris, 172, 188, 206, 212, 216.
Nimmo v. Davis, 106.
Nimmo v. Kuykendall, 423.
Niolon v. Douglass, 172, 207.
Noble v. Coleman, 315, 320.
Noble v. Smith, 373.
Norris v. Douglass, 105.
Norris v. Norris' Adm'r, 448.
North v. Turner, 107, 334, 341.
North River Bank v. Schumann, 255.
Northrup v. Livermore, 60.
North Star Boot & Shoe Co. v. Lovejoy, 640.
Norton v. Kearney, 133, 265, 442.
Norton v. Simmes, 446.
Norwich Yarn Co., Ex parte, 518.
Nostrand v. Atwood, 165, 168, 172, 200, 215.
Noyes, In re, 519.
Noyes v. Hickok, 124, 125, 685.
Noyes v. Beaupre, 493.

Noyes v. Blakeman, 518, 519.
Noyes v. Johnson, 678.
Noyes v. Wernberg, 311, 558.
Nuckolls v. Tomlin, 593.
Nueffer v. Pardue, 137, 138.
Numbers v. Shelly, 100.
Nunn v. Wilsmore, 4, 22, 171, 242.
Nutter v. Harris, 277.
Nutter v. King, 343.
Nye v. Van Husan, 152, 241, 268, 427.

Oakley, Matter of, 131.
Oatman v. Bank, 500.
O'Brien, Matter of, 557.
O'Brien v. Greenbaum, 192.
Oberholser v. Keefer, 601.
Ockerman v. Cross, 367, 372.
Ocean Nat. Bank v. Olcott, 593.
O'Connell v. Ackerman, 199.
O'Fallen v. Tucker, 272.
Ogden v. Arnot, 89.
Ogden v. Jackson, 21, 165.
Ogden v. Peters, 4, 60, 63, 64, 196, 252, 281, 457, 472.
Ogden v. Prentice, 448, 494, 495, 500, 503, 601.
Ogden v. Saunders, 39, 361.
Ogden v. Stone, 164.
O'Hara v. Jones, 478, 546.
Ohio Life & Trust Co. v. Merchants' Ins. & Trust Co., 65, 355, 495.
Okie v. Kelley, 516, 568.
Olcott v. MacLean, 54.
Old Nat. Bank v. Joslin, 636.
Oliver v. Court, 571.
Oliver v. King, 51.
Oliver Lee & Co. Bank v. Talcott, 231, 432.
Olivier v. Townes, 367, 378.
Olmstead v. Herrick, 273, 563, 584.
Olney v. Tanner, 52, 54, 427, 441, 472, 604.
Olson v. Scott, 427.
Oneida Bank v. Ontario Bank, 488.
O'Neil v. Beck, 99, 625, 626.
O'Neill v. Salman, 235, 237, 239.
Onslow v. Londesborough, 516.
Ontario Bank v. Root, 603.
Oppenheimer v. Holff, 167.
Ord v. Noel, 506.

TABLE OF CASES.

References are to pages.

Ordway v. Montgomery, 681.
Oriental Banking Co. v. Coleman, 80.
Orser, Matter of, 491, 548.
Osborn v. Adams, 361, 363-365.
Osborn v. Tuller, 319.
Osborne's Estate, 546.
Osborne v. Moss, 448.
Oschwend v. Estes, 562.
Osgood v. Franklin, 506.
O'Shea v. Collier White Lead & Oil Co., 191.
Ostrander v. Meunch, 51.
Otis v. Maguire, 10, 15.
Outcalt v. Van Winkle, 104, 109.
Owen v. Body, 242.
Owen v. Foulkes, 511.
Owens v. Ramsdell, 537, 582, 669.
Owings v. Rhodes, 563.
Ownby v. Ely, 514.

Paddock, In re, 94.
Paddock v. Bates, 544.
Page v. Broom, 516.
Page v. Olcott, 258, 266, 484, 485, 505, 509, 554, 564, 568, 592, 594, 595.
Page v. Smith, 6.
Page v. Weymouth, 130.
Page-Sexsmith Lumber Co., In re, 638.
Paget's Case, 279.
P. & H. Manuf. Co. v. Caldwell, 163.
Paige, In re, 359.
Paige's Estate, Matter of, 282.
Paige v. Broom, 340.
Paige v. Cagwin, 502.
Paine v. Lester, 375, 377.
Painter v. Henderson, 513, 514.
Palmer v. Cross, 298.
Palmer v. Giles, 187, 516.
Palmer v. Hussey, 39.
Palmer v. Mason, 12, 230, 366, 427.
Palmer v. Myers, 78, 79, 85.
Palmer v. Thayer, 112, 489.
Palmer v. Woodward, 480.
Palmer v. Yarborough, 458.
P. & M. Bank of Mobile v. Clarke, 223.
Pancoast v. Spowers, 299, 302.
Park v. Glover, 93.
Park v. Snyder, 400.
Parker, Matter of, 579.
Parker v. Grout, 105.

Parker v. Jervis, 469, 473.
Parker v. Sraat, 563.
Parkhurst v. McGraw, 427-429.
Parks v. Parks, 445.
Parmelee v. Egan, 587.
Perrot v. Wells, 345.
Parsell v. Patterson, 320, 330, 433, 470, 471.
Parsell v. Thayer, 12.
Parsons v. Clark, 353, 354, 549.
Parsons v. Gloucester Bank, 288.
Parsons v. Powder Works, 355.
Passmore v. Eldridge, 140, 215, 284.
Passumpsic Bank v. Strong, 685.
Paton v. Wright, 85, 241.
Patten's Appeal, 544.
Patten's Estate, 490, 492.
Patten v. Wilson, 107, 109.
Patterson's Appeal, 572.
Patterson v. Jenks, 446.
Patterson v. Johnson, 268, 310.
Patton v. Bencini, 594.
Patton v. Cone, 523.
Patton v. Royal B. P. Co., 500, 564.
Patton v. Thompson, 514.
Paul v. Baugh, 427.
Paul v. Cullum, 67.
Paul v. Loganport, 338.
Payne v. Matthews, 237.
Payne v. Smith, 356.
Peabody v. Knapp, 63.
Peacock v. Thompkins, 118, 607.
Peak v. Ellicott, 479.
Pearce v. Beach, 94.
Pearce v. Jackson, 157, 160, 188.
Pearpoint v. Graham, 70, 72, 84, 87, 151, 153, 172, 205, 207, 209, 211, 212, 217, 588, 589.
Pearpoint v. Lord, 70.
Pearsall v. Kingsland, 535.
Pearson v. Crosby, 199, 586.
Pearson v. Rockhill, 172, 311, 472, 587.
Pearson v. Talbot, 107.
Pechell v. Fowler, 506.
Peck v. Crouse, 421.
Peck v. Ingraham, 574.
Peck v. Whiting, 473.
Peck & Co. v. Merrill, 7, 15, 125, 133, 167, 171, 266.
Peckham v. Mattison, 236.

TABLE OF CASES. xlix

References are to pages.

Peeler v. Peeler, 400.
Peet v. Spencer, 478.
Peninsular Stove Works v. Sackett, 400.
Penn's Ex'rs v. Penn, 112.
Pennebaker v. Tomlinson, 533.
Pennell v. Heading, 32.
Pennington v. Woodall, 149, 601, 605.
Penzel Grocer Co. v. Williams, 330.
People v. Chalmers, 573.
People v. Hudson R. R. R. Co., 107.
People v. Norton, 577.
People v. Soper, 532.
People v. White, 573.
People ex rel. Short v. Bacon, 352.
Perit v. Pittfield, 548.
Perkes, Ex parte, 515.
Perkins v. Zarracher, 476.
Perry v. Colby, 12, 642.
Perry v. Dixon, 514.
Perry v. Holden, 450.
Perry v. Murray, 548.
Perry v. Stevens, 684.
Perry v. Vezina, 101, 135.
Perry Ins. & Trust Co. v. Foster, 4, 15, 117, 118, 221, 242, 246, 247, 253, 320.
Person v. Oberteuffer, 482.
Petchell, Matter of, 491.
Peters v. Bain, 235, 443.
Peters v. Cunningham, 199.
Peters v. Light, 245, 561.
Peters S. & H. Co. v. Schollkoff, 435.
Peterson v. Chemical Bank, 362.
Petrie v. Lansing, 558.
Petrie v. Petrie, 558.
Petrikin v. Davis, 460, 461, 508.
Petry v. Randolph, 477.
Pettee v. Orser, 78, 85.
Pettit v. Johnson, 17, 352.
Pettus v. Wallace, 545.
Peyser v. Myers, 550.
Pfeifer v. Dargan, 207, 537, 552.
Phelps v. Curtis, 245, 251, 276.
Phelps v. McNeely, 241, 547.
Phettiplace v. Sayles, 315, 326.
Philips v. Wooster, 41.
Phillips v. Bustard, 522.
Phillips v. Evarard, 516.
Phillips v. Ross, 477.
Phillips v. Zerbe Run, etc. Co., 247.
Philson v. Barnes, 295, 373.

Phippen v. Durham, 172, 207, 224, 230, 232, 233. 250, 332.
Phœnix v. Ingraham's Assignees, 165.
Phœnix Bank v. Sullivan, 287, 343, 345, 582.
Pickersgill v. Riker, 477, 597.
Pickett v. King, 549.
Pickett v. Leonard, 549.
Pickstock v. Lyster, 26, 34, 405, 406, 411.
Pickstock v. McNair, 420.
Pierce v. Brewster, 255, 259, 304.
Pierce v. Crompton, 377, 678.
Pierce v. Jackson, 101, 172, 441.
Pierce v. O'Brien, 339, 342, 368, 369.
Pierce v. Holbrook, In re, 51, 55, 57.
Pierpoint v. Graham, 393.
Pierpont v. Lord, 209, 210.
Pierson v. Hooker, 345.
Pierson v. Manning, 171, 230, 251, 276, 309, 416, 426, 432, 433, 443.
Piggott v. Schram, 298, 441, 446.
Pike v. Bacon, 330, 385, 420, 496.
Pillsbury v. Kingon, 24, 60, 487.
Pinckney v. Lanahan, 362, 363.
Pine v. Rickert, 322, 428, 469, 517.
Pingree v. Comstock, 127, 139, 170, 311, 563, 581.
Pinkston v. Brewster, 565.
Pinneo v. Hart, 118, 536, 577.
Piper's Appeal, 577.
Pitkins v. Thompson, 359, 367.
Pitt v. Petway, 514.
Pitts v. Steubenville R. R. Co., 531, 536.
Pitts v. Viley, 273, 460.
Place v. Miller, 420.
Planck v. Schermerhorn, 60, 96, 271, 275, 282, 314, 420.
Planters' Bank v. Whittle, 65, 686.
Planters' & M. Bank of Mobile v. Clarke, 244.
Planters' & Merchants' Bank v. Clark, 227, 252.
Platt v. Adams, 444, 531.
Platt v. Archer, 607.
Platt v. Hodge, 148, 149.
Platt v. Hunter, 89, 236, 431.
Platt v. Preston, 47, 144, 151.
Platt v. Sheriffs of London, 413.
Platt v. Stewart, 480.

TABLE OF CASES.

References are to pages.

Plume & Atwood Mfg. Co. v. Caldwell, 479.
Plunkett v. Carew, 478.
Poehlmann v. Kennedy, 152.
Poland v. Glyn, 32.
Polkinghorne v. Martinez, 396.
Pollock v. Okolona Sav. Inst., 606.
Pomeroy v. Ainsworth, 359.
Pomeroy v. Manin, 167, 169.
Pond v. Comstock, 567.
Pond v. Sweetzer, 382.
Pond v. Williams, 589.
Pool v. Ellison, 441.
Pool v. McDonald, 54, 57.
Pope v. Brandon, 66, 92, 140.
Porter v. Lazear, 109.
Porter v. Walker, 33.
Porter v. West, 579.
Porter v. Williams, 256, 259, 307, 458, 604.
Portland Bank v. Stacy, 327.
Posey v. Decatur Bank, 149, 533.
Postlewait v. Howes, 62.
Potter's Estate, 677.
Potter, In re, 10, 551.
Potter v. McDowell, 8, 412.
Potter v. Paige, 229.
Potter & Paige, Estate of, In re, 559.
Potts, Ex parte, 165.
Potts v. The Thames Haven & Dock Co., 503.
Potts & Garwood, Ex parte, 37.
Powell v. Kelly, 9.
Power v. Alger, 531.
Power v. Kirk, 89.
Powers v. Carpenter, 110, 475.
Powers v. Graydon, 187, 204, 440, 458.
Powers v. Green, 166, 473.
Powles v. Dilley, 165, 166.
Pratt v. Adams, 119, 390, 566, 584, 603.
Pratt v. Curtis, 53.
Pratt v. Levan, 111, 474, 485, 547.
Pratt v. Rathbun, 587.
Pratt v. Stevens, 660.
Pratt v. Thornton, 513.
Presley v. Rogers, 298.
Pressley v. Lamb, 624, 625.
Preston v. Spaulding, 135, 623.
Prevost v. Gratz, 484, 514, 522.
Prewett v. Dobbs, 297.

Prewit v. Wilson, 400.
Price v. De Ford, 89.
Price v. Ford, 181, 241, 270.
Price v. Haynes, 102, 103, 142, **385.**
Price v. Mazange, 244, 609.
Price v. Moses, 115.
Price v. Parker, 310, 333, 334, 476, **477,** 627.
Price v. Pitzer, 244, 274, 318, 431.
Price v. Thompson, 514.
Prince v. Shepard, 447.
Princeton Mfg. Co. v. White, **181.**
Prindle v. Carruthers, 105.
Probst v. Welden, 434.
Produce Bank v. Morton, 606.
Prosser v. Hartley, 639.
Pulliam v. Newberry, 166, 169, **414.**
Pulling v. Tucker, 31.
Pulver v. Harris, 106.
Putnam v. Hubbell, 172, 421.
Putnam v. Reynolds, 481.
Putney v. Friesleben, 680.
Purdy v. Whitney, 281, 505.
Pusey v. Clemson, 522.

Quackenboss, In re, 57.
Quackenbush v. Leonard, 506.
Quarles v. Kerr, 254.
Quinnebaug Bank v. Brewster, **64.**

Rabel v. Griffin, 479.
Radtke, Matter of, 557.
Ragan v. Kennedy, 320.
Rahn v. McElrath, 231, 234.
Railroad Co. v. Barron, 367.
Railroad Co. v. Packet Co., 369.
Railroad Co. v. Woodring, 108.
Rainwater v. Stevens, 101.
Raleigh v. Griffith, 255, 612, **613.**
Ramsdell v. Edgarton, 288.
Ramsdell v. Sigerson, 172, **208, 307,** 600.
Ramsey v. Hurley, 457.
Randall v. Cook, 330.
Randall v. Dusenbury, 290.
Randall v. Errington, 511.
Randall & Sunderland, In re, 41, **44, 45,** 53, 62.
Randolph v. Quidnick Co., 367.
Rankin v. Holloway, 320.

TABLE OF CASES.

References are to pages.

Rankin v. Loder, 172, 176, 180, 198, 272, 333, 334, 344.
Ransom, Matter of, 270, 498, 664.
Ransom v. Jones, 104.
Rapalee v. Stewart, 259, 263, 265, 602.
Rapelye v. Cummins, 344.
Rapier v. Gulf City Paper Co., 609.
Rasmussen v. State Nat. Bank, 198.
Ratcliffe v. Sangston, 575.
Rathbun v. Platner, 60, 180, 421.
Rauth, Matter of, 491, 524.
Ravisies v. Alston, 244, 324.
Rawlings, Ex parte, 35.
Raworth v. Parker, 343, 345, 583.
Ray v. Hiller, 616.
Ray v. Raymond, 319.
Raymond's Appeal, 98.
Raymond, Matter of, 557.
Raynolds v. Ray, 152.
Raynor v. Raynor, 139.
Read v. Baylis, 241.
Read v. Mosby, 106.
Read v. Pelletier, 431.
Read v. Robinson, 295, 303, 312, 349, 350, 376.
Read v. Worthington, 151.
Reading Iron Works, 531.
Reamer v. Lamberton, 93.
Reavis v. Garner, 212.
Redmond v. Wemple, 519, 606.
Redpath v. Tutewiler, 624.
Reed v. Bigelow, 103.
Reed v. Emery, 94, 95, 578.
Reed v. Jewett, 319.
Reed v. McIntyre, 41, 51, 172, 406, 420.
Reed v. Newcomb, 686.
Reed v. Noxon, 427.
Reed v. Pellestier, 227.
Reed v. Sands, 478.
Reed v. Worthington, 117.
Reehling v. Byers, 167.
Regenstein v. Pearlstein, 680.
Reichenbach v. Winkhaus, 274, 303, 431.
Reid v. Sands, 482.
Reiff v. Eshleman, 125, 186, 348, 447, 536.
Reiff v. Horst, 186.
Reigart's Appeal, 130.
Reinhard v. Bank of Kentucky, 136, 332, 333, 337, 341, 443.

Relfe v. Commercial Ins. Co., 67.
Renard v. Graydon, 204, 458.
Rendleman v. Willard, 291, 297, 309, 477.
Renenheim v. Morgan, 505.
Rennie v. Bean, 290, 299, 311, 660.
Renton v. Kelly, 243.
Rettew v. Barnes, 44.
Reubens v. Joel, 601.
Reves v. Walthal, 414.
Reynolds, In re, 39.
Reynolds v. Bank of Virginia, 17, 125, 313.
Reynolds v. Collins, 108.
Reynolds v. Cook, 227.
Rhawn v. Pearce, 363.
Rhines v. Phelps, 318.
Rhoads v. Blatt, 139, 385, 398.
Rice, Matter of, 491.
Rice v. Courtis, 318, 372.
Rice v. Frayser, 509, 612.
Richards v. Hazard, 172, 218.
Richards v. La Tourette, 500.
Richards v. Levin, 163, 165, 172, 229, 230.
Richards v. White, 602.
Richardson, Ex parte, 33.
Richardson v. Coe, 314.
Richardson v. Haney, 282.
Richardson v. Herron, 186, 600.
Richardson v. Jones, 514.
Richardson v. Leavitt, 377.
Richardson v. Marqueze, 176, 260, 268, 419, 430.
Richardson v. Mead, 496.
Richardson v. Rogers, 66, 378, 448.
Richardson v. Stapleton, 247.
Richardson v. Thurber, 660.
Richardville v. Cummins, 108.
Riches v. Evans, 420.
Richmond v. Mississippi Mills, 6.
Riddle v. Norris, 112.
Rider, Matter of, 506.
Ridgway v. Stewart, 14, 294.
Riggs v. Murray, 170, 174, 274, 275.
Rindskoff v. Guggenheim, 223, 245, 254, 412.
Rindskopf, Matter of, 557.
Ring v. Ring, 229.
Ringer v. Cann, 110.

TABLE OF CASES.

References are to pages.

Ringgold v. Ringgold, 506, 522.
Ringo v. Real Estate Bank, 65.
Risley, Matter of, 531.
Roan v. Winn, 421.
Roane v. Bank of Nashville, 120.
Robb v. Van Horn, 600.
Robbins v. Magee, 125, 242, 333, 338, 626
Roberts v. Corbin, 428.
Roberts v. Guernsey, 427.
Roberts v. Lewald, 533.
Roberts v. Phillips, 634.
Roberts v. Shepherd, 79, 84.
Roberts v. Victor, 416, 661.
Robertson, State ex rel., 443.
Robertson v. Burnell, 371.
Robertson v. Sublett, 127, 311, 460, 581.
Robertson v. Todd, 112, 489.
Robins v. Embry, 23, 65, 140, 151, 152, 208, 228, 245, 249.
Robinson v. Crowder, 69, 71, 72, 82, 85, 86, 286.
Robinson v. Frankell, 435.
Robinson v. Gregory, 78, 79, 85.
Robinson v. Macdonnell, 106.
Robinson v. Mauldin, 104.
Robinson v. McIntosh, 77, 90, 91.
Robinson v. Nix, 620.
Robinson v. Rapelye, 140, 172, 198, 335.
Roby v. Meyer, 486.
Rochester v. Armour, 168.
Rodman v. Nathan, 562.
Rogers v. Allen, 361, 365.
Rogers v. De Forest, 256–259, 267, 283, 444, 446.
Rogers v. Dibrell, 104.
Rogers v. Palmer, 48.
Rogers v. Rogers, 594, 604.
Rogers v. Spence, 107, 109.
Rogers v. Vail, 318.
Rohrbough v. Leopold, 497.
Rohrer v. Turrell, 495.
Rokenbanugh v. Hubbell, 62.
Rollins v. Van Baalen, 135, 636.
Roller Wheel Co. v. Fielding, 68, 181.
Rome Exch. Bank v. Eames, 440, 446, 531.
Roosevelt v. Mark, 549.
Root v. Hare, 167, 453.
Root v. Potter, 489.

Root v. Stuyvesant, 445.
Rose v. Meldrum, 422.
Rosenbaum v. Moller, 681.
Rosenberg v. Moore, 157, 159, 199, 216, 232, 431, 597.
Rosenburg v. Shaper, 546.
Rosenthal v. Frank, 9.
Rosenthal v. Scott, 98.
Rossett v. Fisher, 146.
Rossman v. McFarland, 447.
Rothell v. Grimes, 22.
Rothschild v. Saloman, 101, 218.
Rouse v. Bowers, 112, 400, 519.
Rowe v. Page, 39.
Rowland v. Coleman, 172.
Rowland v. Hewitt, 310.
Royal's Adm'r v. McKenzie, 494, 563, 564, 572.
Royer Wheel Co. v. Fielding, 125, 237, 309, 431, 660.
Rubey v. Watson, 479, 499.
Ruble v. McDonald, 421.
Ruckman v. Ruckman, 448.
Rugeley v. Harrison, 227.
Ruhl v. Phillips, 421.
Rumery v. McCulloch, 80, 81, 85, 88, 308, 448, 449.
Rumsey v. Town, 481, 482, 623.
Rundlett v. Dole, 143, 151, 245, 451.
Rush v. Good, 561, 597.
Russell v. Filmore, 105.
Russell v. Lasher, 604, 607.
Russell v. Rogers, 191.
Russell v. Woodward, 103, 172, 225, 279, 284, 339, 341, 344.
Rust v. Cooper, 80.
Ryerson v. Eldred, 291.
Ryhiner v. Ruegger, 304.

Sackett, In re, 186.
Sackett v. Mansfield, 254, 266, 696.
Sadler v. Immel, 39, 40, 141, 344.
Sadler & Jackson, Ex parte, 190.
Sadlier v. Fallon, 188, 206, 333, 338.
Sale v. Dishman's Ex'rs, 286.
Salisbury v. Ellison, 89.
Salmon v. Davis, 345.
Salmon v. Stuyvesant, 445.
Salter v. Salter, 310.
Saltmarsh v. Beene, 514.

TABLE OF CASES. liii

References are to pages.

Sampson v. Shaw, 642.
Sams v. Binns, 631.
Samson v. Arnold, 160, 627.
Sanborn v. Norton, 338, 683.
Sanders, In re, 51.
Sanderson v. Bradford, 377.
Sanderson v. Stockdale, 17, 602.
Sands v. Church, 535.
Sands v. Hildreth, 20, 421.
Sandwich Mfg. Co. v. Wright, 482.
Sanford v. Conant, 141.
Sangston v. Gaither, 159, 172, 180, 199, 212, 215, 216, 232.
Sargent v. Webster, 7.
Sattler v. Marino, 95.
Saunders v. Harris, 337.
Saunders v. Lee, 448.
Saunders v. Mitchell, 26.
Saunders v. Reilly, 237, 602.
Saunders v. Waggoner, 503.
Saunders v. Williams, 361.
Savage v. Knight, 408, 421, 423, 443.
Savery v. Spaulding, 63, 441, 442, 472, 502.
Savings Bank v. Ela, 154.
Sawyer v. Hoag, 501.
Sawyer v. McAdie, 342.
Scanlan v. Scanlan, 513, 562.
Schaller, Matter of, 524, 557, 582.
Schaller v. Wright, 486, 497.
Scheibler v. Mundinger, 138, 142, 144, 477.
Schell, Matter of, 524.
Schieffelin v. Stewart, 511.
Schiele v. Healy, 89, 235, 236, 431.
Schisster v. Rader, 237.
Schlang, Matter of, 527.
Schleicher v. Walker, 427.
Schlenck v. Hart, 448.
Schlueter v. Raymond, 352.
Schlussel v. Willett, 243.
Schneider v. Altman, 557.
Schneider v. Bullard, 682.
Schnell v. Reiman, 557.
Schnitzler v. Andrews, 479.
Scholefield v. Hull, 322.
Schooher v. Hutchins, 382, 682.
Schoolfield v. Johnson, 133.
Schuehle v. Reiman, 558.
Schufeldt v. Abernethy, 262.

Schuler v. Israel, 358.
Schultz v. Christman, 107.
Schultz v. Hoagland, 661.
Schultz v. McNaughton, 433.
Schumann v. Peddicord, 58, 125, 416, 431, 433, 448.
Schuylkill Bank v. Reigart, 130, 292, 293.
Schwab v. Lemon, 624.
Schwartz v. Soutter, 311, 660.
Schwartz v. Wendell, 522.
Scott, Matter of, 519, 524.
Scott v. Edes, 342, 536, 586, 602.
Scott v. Freeland, 514.
Scott v. Guthrie, 237, 239, 299, 440.
Scott v. Mills, 660.
Scott v. Morris, 549.
Scott v. Porter, 39.
Scott v. Seaver, 310, 688.
Scruggs v. Burruss, 88.
Seal v. Duffy, 206, 294, 312, 314, 349, 352, 447, 458, 576, 600.
Seale v. Vaiden, 208, 344.
Seals v. Robinson, 435.
Seaman v. Stoughton, 54, 595.
Seattle Coal Co. v. Thomas, 39.
Seaver v. Spink, 52, 53.
Seavey v. Maples, 54.
Seaving v. Brinkerhoff, 157, 159, 202, 215.
Seavis v. Garner, 233.
Seay v. Bank of Rome, 65, 545.
Second Nat. Bank v. Schranck, 601.
Sedgwick v. Place, 43, 45, 46.
See v. Zabriskie, 106, 111, 655.
Seeley, In re, 47.
Seers v. Conover, 105.
Seibert v. Milligan, 625.
Seibert v. Spooner, 30.
Seibert v. Thompson, 60.
Seifreid v. People's Bank, 385.
Seiz v. Evans, 230.
Selden v. Vermilya, 560.
Selleck v. Pollock, 453, 526.
Seuter v. Turner, 315.
Severson v. Porter, 235, 692.
Sevier v. McWhorter, 352, 460.
Sewall v. Henry, 118.
Sexton v. Wheaton, 19, 407.
Seymour v. Wilson, 22, 604.

TABLE OF CASES.

References are to pages.

Shaeffer's Appeal, 100.
Shafer v. Alden, 602.
Shaffer v. Watkins, 221.
Shakelford v. P. & M. Bank of Mobile, 63, 137, 152, 180, 226, 251, 255, 260, 432, 434.
Shakeman v. Schleuter, 689.
Shanks v. Lancaster, 296.
Shapleigh v. Baird, 160.
Sharp v. Goodwin, 579.
Shattuck v. Chandler, 85.
Shattuck v. Freeman, 288, 339, 441, 472.
Shattuck v. Knight, 223, 246, 254, 470.
Shaw, Matter of, 524.
Shaw v. Glen, 479, 482, 487.
Shaw v. Lowry, 104, 319.
Shaw v. Smith, 489, 617.
Shawano County Bank v. Koeppen, 99.
Shawhan v. Wherritt, 42.
Shearer v. Loftin, 125, 287, 288, 337, 341, 344.
Sheepshanks v. Cohen, 205, 395, 589.
Sheerer v. Lautzerheizer, 247, 254, 276.
Sheffy's Appeal, 513.
Sheldon v. Dodge, 113, 188, 189, 268, 281, 381, 416, 432.
Sheldon v. Mann, 16, 163.
Sheldon v. Smith, 460, 531.
Sheldon v. Stryker, 323, 516.
Shelley v. Boothe, 167.
Shepherd v. McEvers, 311, 576, 581.
Sheppards v. Turpin, 218, 494.
Sheridan v. Mayor, 496.
Sherman v. Elder, 428.
Sherrill v. Hopkins, 359.
Sherrill v. Shuford, 148, 523.
Sherwood v. His Creditors, 236.
Shettle, In re, 35.
Shipman's Petition, 498.
Shipman v. Ætna Ins. Co., 112.
Shipman v. Graves, 113.
Shirly v. Teal, 13, 15, 131, 609.
Shober v. Hanser, 120.
Shockley v. Fisher, 65, 66, 310, 575.
Shone v. Lucas, 61.
Shook v. Shook, 574.
Shotwell, In re, 101, 220.
Shotwell v. Webb, 108.
Showning v. Cox, 15.
Shroeder v. Babbitt, 168.

Shropshire v. Behrens, 67.
Shryock v. Bashore, 39, 51, 65, 355, 495.
Shryock v. Waggoner, 94.
Shubar v. Winding, 130.
Shufeld v. Jenkins, 420.
Shultz v. Christman, 482.
Shultz v. Hoagland, 95, 141, 428, 429, 441.
Shultz v. Sutter, 65, 108, 642.
Shumos v. Caig, 116.
Shyer v. Lockard, 310, 314, 592, 594.
Sibbald's Estate, 107, 109, 384.
Sibley v. Hood, 165, 172.
Sibley v. Killom, 153.
Sibley v. Prescott Ins. Co., 477.
Sickman v. Abernathy, 347.
Siebert v. Spooner, 28.
Siggers v. Evans, 128, 309, 340.
Silverman, In re, 48.
Simmons v. Curtis, 102.
Simmons Hdw. Co. v. Kaufman, 683.
Simon v. Kaliske, 299, 467.
Simon v. Mann, 640.
Simon v. Sevier Ass'n, 66.
Simonton v. First Nat. Bank, 111, 354.
Simpkinson v. McGee, 298.
Simpson, Ex parte, 32.
Simpson v. Ætna Ins. Co., 489.
Simpson v. Gowdy, 563.
Simpson v. Roberts, 98.
Simpson v. Shaw, 642.
Simpson v. Warren, 488.
Singer v. Armstrong, 310, 311.
Singmaster's Appeal, 504.
Sininger v. Herron, 95.
Sipe v. Earman, 225, 228, 276, 421.
Sirlott v. Tandy, 105.
Sisson v. Roath, 112.
Sixth Ward Bank v. Wilson, 536.
Sixth Ward Building Ass'n v. Wilson, 486.
Skinner's Appeal, 113.
Skipwith's Ex'r v. Cunningham, 159, 172, 207, 212, 215, 223, 224, 230, 232, 233, 332, 349.
Skoll, In re, 47.
Slade v. Van Vechten, 480, 483, 513.
Slatter v. Carroll, 366.
Sleeper v. Iselin, 311.

TABLE OF CASES.

References are to pages.

Slicker v. Fisher, 525.
Slinkard v. State, 54.
Sloan v. Moore, 85.
Slocum v. Hooker, 58.
Small v. Ludlow, 485.
Small v. Marwood, 312.
Small v. Oudley, 27, 171.
Small v. Sproat, 459, 462.
Smith's Appeal, 358, 361, 576, 584.
Smith, Ex parte, 33.
Smith, In re, 44, 45.
Smith v. Atwood, 367.
Smith v. Bank of Washington, 676.
Smith v. Bowen, 688, 689.
Smith v. Bowdre, 96.
Smith v. Boyd, 290.
Smith v. Brinckerhoff, 499.
Smith v. Buchanan, 48.
Smith v. Cannan, 33, 172.
Smith v. Chicago & N. W. R. R. Co., 373.
Smith v. Craft, 192, 268.
Smith v. Cunningham, 533.
Smith v. Ely, 53, 57.
Smith v. Felton, 500.
Smith v. Fox, 500.
Smith v. Hartwell, 186.
Smith v. Henry, 318.
Smith v. Howard, 89, 235, 236, 240, 241, 448, 606.
Smith v. Hurst, 128.
Smith v. Isaac, 514.
Smith v. Keating, 279, 339, 340, 495.
Smith v. Leavitts, 198, 224, 336, 469.
Smith v. Longmire, 600.
Smith v. Lowell, 234.
Smith v. McCulloch, 688.
Smith v. Millett, 207, 338, 345, 352, 553, 561, 596.
Smith v. Mitchell, 98, 181, 442, 470.
Smith v. Mobile Bank, 429.
Smith v. New York Consolidated Stage Co., 65.
Smith v. N. Y. & N. H. R. R. Co., 105.
Smith v. Smith, 234.
Smith v. Spengler, 479, 500.
Smith v. Spinola, 367.
Smith v. Stokes, 140, 151, 152.
Smith v. Stone, 191.
Smith v. Teutonia Ins. Co., 44.

Smith v. Timms, 32, 33.
Smith v. Tinn, 290.
Smith v. Turrentine, 126, 594.
Smith v. Welch, 320.
Smith v. Wheeler, 312.
Smith v. Whitfield, 168.
Smith v. Woodruff, 4.
Smith & Wolf's Appeal, 110.
Smythe v. Sprague, 113.
Snell v. Harrison, 435.
Solinsky v. Lincoln Sav. Bank, 448, 526.
Solomon v. Sparks, 8, 15.
Soper v. Fry, 58.
Southard v. Benner, 112, 488.
Southern Bank v. Wood, 360.
Southworth v. Casey, 10.
Southworth v. Sheldon, 262.
Spangler's Estate, 522.
Spaulding v. Strong, 187, 204, 458.
Spear v. Wardell, 168, 182, 601.
Speed v. May, 108, 367, 373.
Spelman v. Freedman, 455, 602, 660.
Spence v. Bagwell, 220, 225, 276, 420.
Spencer v. Slater, 400.
Sperritt v. Willows, 33.
Sperry v. Gallagher, 208.
Spicer v. Ayres, 593.
Spicer & Peckham, In re, 44.
Spies v. Boyd, 440.
Spies v. Joel, 231.
Spindler v. Atkinson, 514.
Spinney v. Portsmouth Co., 341.
Sprenkle's Appeal, 522.
Spring v. Short, 488, 602.
Spring v. S. Carolina Ins. Co., 104, 105, 172, 212.
Springfield Homestead Ass'n v. Roll, 112.
Spurrett v. Spiller, 190, 191.
Spyer, Ex parte, 35.
Stadhman v. Loehr, 80, 85.
Stafford v. Merrill, 432.
Stamets v. Guinn, 167.
Stamford Bank v. Benedict, 529.
Stamp v. Case, 145, 152, 302, 310.
Standard Wagon Co. v. Nichols, 479.
Stanford v. Lockwood, 108, 559.
Stanley v. Bunce, 227, 431.
Stanley v. Nat. Union Bank, 166.

TABLE OF CASES.

References are to pages.

Stanley v. Robbins, 685.
Starr v. Dugan, 536.
State v. Bank of Maryland, 43, 65, 172.
State v. Benoist, 12, 158, 160, 169, 412, 430.
State v. Evans, 320.
State v. Grover, 545.
State v. Guilford, 589.
State v. Hart, 573.
State v. Hemingway, 16.
State v. Kansas Ins. Co., 537 631.
State v. Keeler, 138, 421.
State v. Krug, 496.
State v. Platt, 522.
State v. Real Estate Bank, 356.
State v. Rogers, 522.
State v. Smith, 320.
State v. Tasker, 320.
State Bank v. Chapelle, 12.
State for Use v. Hunt, 526.
State of Ohio v. Guilford, 571.
Stedger v. Evans, 508.
Stedman v. Davis, 369.
Steel v. Brown, 41, 326.
Steel v. Tuttle, 590.
Steele v. Frierson, 106.
Steele v. Goodwin, 358.
Stehman's Appeal, 527.
Stein v. La Dow, 79, 85, 86.
Stein v. Wilkson, 509.
Steinhart v. Fyhrie, 85.
Steinlein v. Halstead, 152, 310, 691.
Stell's Appeal, 556, 569.
Stelle, In re, 573.
Stephens v. Hotham, 516.
Stephens v. Regenstein, 400.
Stephenson v. Hayward, 277.
Sterling v. Van Cleve, 319.
Stern v. Fisher, 117, 261.
Stetson v. Miller, 102, 160, 609.
Stevens v. Bell, 115, 151, 152, 168, 248, 339, 559.
Stevenson's Assignees, 530.
Stevenson, Matter of, 310.
Stevenson v. Crapnell, 282.
Stewart v. Ackley, 448.
Stewart v. English, 420.
Stewart v. Hall, 337.
Stewart v. Isidor, 54.
Stewart v. Jackson, 418.

Stewart v. McMinn, 292, 519, 567.
Stewart v. Moody, 33.
Stewart v. Pettus, 574.
Stewart v. Platt, 49.
Stewart v. Railway Co., 109.
Stewart v. Spencer, 158, 160, 163, 172, 207, 211, 215, 312, 347, 430, 434.
St. Helen's Mills Co., In re, 52.
Stidger v. Evans, 110, 421.
Stiffel v. Barton, 635.
Stiles v. Hill, 14.
Still v. Fock, 67.
Stimpson v. Fries, 17, 123, 127, 131, 133, 268, 275, 340.
Stine v. Wilson, 17.
Stiness v. Pierce, 383.
Stites v. Champion, 9.
Stix v. Sadler, 167.
St. Louis v. Clemens, 105.
Stobaugh v. Mills, 41, 56.
Stockbridge, Matter of, 557.
Stockett v. Goodman, 479.
Stoddard v. Doane, 549.
Stoddard v. Tomlinson, 115.
Stokes v. Jones, 218.
Stone v. Frost, 496.
Stone v. Miller, 532.
Stone v. Waggoner, 319.
Storm v. Davenport, 254, 271, 419, 448.
Story v. Livingston's Ex'rs, 503.
Story v. Palmer, 92.
Stout v. Higbee's Ex'rs, 605.
Stout v. Rapp, 647.
Stout v. Watson, 6, 673.
Stover v. Harrington, 165, 166.
Stow v. Yarwood, 478.
Stowell, Matter of, 57.
Strachan v. Barton, 32.
Strang, Ex parte, 51.
Strang v. Spaulding, 204.
Stray, Ex parte, 51.
Stricker v. Tinkham, 380.
Strickler's Estate, Matter of, 505.
Stratton v. Tabb, 236, 547.
Straus, Matter of, 57, 577.
Straus v. Rose, 427.
Strawn v. Jones, 371.
Streatfield v. Streatfield, 536.
Strong v. Carrier, 135, 139, 295, 819, 826, 471.

TABLE OF CASES.   lvii

References are to pages.

Strong v. Goldbaum, 623.
Strong v. Lynn, 151, 639.
Strong v. Skinner, 117, 187, 188, 229, 268, 548, 587.
Strong v. Willis, 314, 603.
Stubbs, In re, 44.
Stuchert v. Harvey, 110, 384.
Stultz v. Fleming, 522, 621.
Sturgis v. Crowninshield, 39.
Sturtevant v. Ballard, 432.
Suarez v. Pumpelly, 578.
Sugg v. Tillman, 98.
Sullivan v. Miller, 480.
Sullivan v. Smith, 85, 329, 441, 469.
Summers v. Rose, 320.
Suppiger v. Gruaz, 531.
Surget v. Boyd, 164.
Sutherland v. Bradner, 229, 307, 458.
Sutton v. Dana, 164.
Sutton v. Hanford, 259.
Suydam v. Dequindre, 337.
Swan v. Crafts, 278, 339.
Swan v. Dent, 602.
Swanson v. Tarkington, 536.
Swearingen v. Slicer, 128, 288, 341, 593.
Sweeney v. Conley, 10.
Sweet v. Tinslar, 448.
Sweetser v. Camp, 489, 603.
Sweetzer v. Higby, 167, 453.
Sweezy, Matter of, 557.
Swift v. Hart, 430, 488, 593.
Swift v. Stebbins, 503.
Switzner v. Miller, 297, 466, 625.
Swoyer's Appeal, 110, 479, 503.

Talcott v. Harder, 41.
Talcott v. Hess, 119, 141, 428.
Talcott v. Rosenthal, 441.
Tapley v. Butterfield, 68, 88, 286.
Tappan v. Whittemore, 53.
Tappenden v. Burgess, 32.
Tarrin v. Crawford, 41.
Tarver v. Roffe, 140, 252.
Taylor v. Atwood, 310, 489, 496.
Taylor v. Bonham, 569.
Taylor v. Columbian Ins. Co., 368.
Taylor v. Davis, 11.
Taylor v. Palmer, 105.
Taylor v. Roberts, 569.
Taylor v. Taylor, 483.

Tate v. McCormick, 322.
Tatum v. Hunter, 118, 414.
Teah v. Roth, 507, 613.
Teed v. Johnson, 288.
Telford v. Barney, 515.
Tempest, Ex parte, 165.
Temple, In re, 47, 51, 52, 613.
Tennant v. Battey, 601.
Tennant v. Stoney, 288.
Tenney v. Johnson, 547.
Tenney v. Simpson, 133.
Tennor's Case, 444.
Terry v. Butler, 118, 151, 153, 322, 414, 533, 606.
Thatcher v. Candee, 314, 503, 576.
Thatcher v. Franklin, 298, 301, 311, 349, 612.
Thatcher v. Rockwell, 54.
Thelluson v. Smith, 539.
Therasson v. Hickok, 230, 567, 602.
Third Nat. Bank v. Guenther, 58, 164.
Third Nat. Bank v. Hang, 544.
Third Nat. Bank v. Lanahan, 545.
Thomas, Matter of, 519.
Thomas v. Beales, 510.
Thomas v. Beck, 112, 489.
Thomas v. Chapman, 338.
Thomas v. Clark, 277.
Thomas v. Goodwin, 567.
Thomas v. Jenks, 24, 158, 159, 176, 187, 206, 214-216.
Thomas v. Merry, 281.
Thomas v. Penrich, 236, 486, 498, 547.
Thomas v. Talmadge, 254, 421, 495, 577.
Thomkins v. Wheeler, 302, 472.
Thompkins v. Hunter, 191.
Thompson, Matter of, 120, 536, 557, 601.
Thompson v. Blanchard, 322.
Thompson v. Bowman, 88.
Thompson v. Childress, 273, 551, 554, 573, 575, 681.
Thompson v. Dougherty, 486.
Thompson v. Fry, 347.
Thompson v. Heffner, 634.
Thompson v. Hooker, 499.
Thompson v. Ketchum, 359.
Thompson v. Parker, 230, 624.
Thompson v. Sweet, 54.
Thornton v. Davenport, 318.
Thornton v. Hook, 427.

TABLE OF CASES.

References are to pages.

Thorp v. McCallum, 513.
Thorpe v. Dunlap, 478, 479.
Thrasher v. Bentley, 40.
Thurber v. Blanck, 600, 602.
Thurmond v. Andrews, 54.
Thurston v. Rosenfield, 377, 380.
Thus v. Davidson, 400.
Tibbetts v. Weaver, 466, 479.
Tichenor v. Coggins, 673.
Ticknor v. Wiswall, 443.
Tieman v. Molliter, 88, 89, 112.
Tiemeyer v. Turnquist, 124.
Tiffany v. Lucas, 47.
Tillou v. Britton, 22, 163, 165, 168, 169, 172, 178, 654.
Titley v. Taylor, 28.
Todd v. Buckman, 198, 341.
Tomlinson v. Matthews, 22, 121, 172.
Tomlinson v. Smallwood, 564.
Tompkins v. Adams, 366.
Tompkins v. Wheeler, 7, 8, 13, 95, 165, 172, 315, 322, 326, 334.
Toof v. Martin, 62.
Tootle v. Caldwell, 167, 629.
Torrens v. Hammond, 39, 363.
Totten v. Brady, 163.
Towle v. Ambs, 527.
Towle v. Mack, 519.
Town v. Bank of River Raisin, 65, 355.
Towne v. Rublee, 344.
Townsend v. Harwell, 335, 337.
Townsend v. Stearns, 248, 252, 265, 428.
Towsley v. McDonald, 22.
Tracy v. Railroad Co., 523.
Tracy v. Talmadge, 488.
Tracy v. Tuffly, 91.
Train v. Kendall, 379.
Trapp v. Moore, 305.
Traver v. Rogers, 623.
Travis v. Meyers, 558.
Treadwell v. Sackett, 290.
Trenton Bank v. Woodruff, 511.
Trevitt v. Converse, 516.
Troth, Matter of, 40.
Trott v. Dawson, 518.
Trotter v. Blocker, 566.
Troustine v. Lask, 447.
Truax v. Slater, 502.
True v. Congdon, 273, 412.
Truitt, Estate of, 426, 564.

Truitt v. Caldwell, 6, 131, 230, 259, 261.
Truss v. Davidson, 301, 337.
Tua v. Carriere, 39.
Tucker v. Beacham, 530, 652.
Tucker v. Clesby, 113.
Tucker v. Parks, 92.
Tucker v. Tucker, 557.
Tully, In re, 519.
Tully v. Nash, 481.
Tunner v. Richardson, 475.
Turbuck v. Marbury, 274.
Turner v. Douglass, 208.
Turner v. Hardcastle, 33.
Turner v. Jaycox, 144, 151, 240.
Turnipseed v. Schaefer, 176, 621.
Tuttle v. Gilmore, 397.
Twelves v. Williams, 479.
Twyne's Case, 404, 435.
Tyler v. Abergh, 482.
Tyler v. Herring, 487.
Tyler v. Tyler, 433.
Tyler v. Wing, 54.
Tyson v. Dorr, 590.

Uglow, Matter of, 557.
Uhler v. Maulfair, 163, 166, 169, 178.
Uhrig Brewing Co., Matter of, 583.
Ulmer v. Hills, 319.
Union Bank v. Bell, 535.
Union Banking Co., Matter of, 66, 576.
Union Bank of Chicago v. K. C. Bank, 383.
Union Bank of Tennessee v. Ellicott, 64, 65.
Union Nat. Bank v. Bank of Commerce, 305, 386.
Union Pacific R. R. Co., In re, 44, 46, 47.
Union Trust Co. v. Trumbull, 419.
United States v. Bank of the United States, 20, 23, 65, 124, 134, 158, 161, 166, 270, 277, 328, 333, 338, 342, 379, 400, 407, 427, 434, 538, 540, 634.
United States v. Clark, 124, 153, 161, 540.
United States v. Fisher, 539, 541.
United States v. Griswold, 161.
United States v. Hooe, 124, 161, 323, 400, 418, 540, 541.
United States v. Howe, 116.
United States v. Howland, 141, 540.

TABLE OF CASES. lix

References are to pages.

United States v. Hoyt, 116, 281, 340, 842.
United States v. Hunter, 108, 540, 542.
United States v. King, 166, 172, 173.
United States v. Langton, 142, 540.
United States v. McLellan, 4, 8, 123, 161, 540.
United States v. Mott, 124, 540, 542.
United States v. Munroe, 540.
United States v. Murphy, 539, 543.
United States v. The State Bank of N. C., 539, 540.
United States Bank v. Huth, 92, 148, 270, 277.
Upson v. Milwaukee Nat. Bank, 546.

Vail v. Pecks, 685.
Valentine v. Decker, 333, 593, 602.
Vallance v. Miners' Life Ins. Co., 5, 14.
Van Alstyne v. Cook, 90.
Van Arsdale v. Richards, 593, 597.
Van Buskirk v. Warren, 12, 15, 322, 370.
Vance v. Phillips, 321, 423.
Van Cott v. Prentice, 133.
Vandeveer v. Conover, 582, 585.
Van Dine v. Willett, 105, 268, 545.
Van Dyke v. Christ, 111.
Van Hensen v. Radcliffe, 112, 478, 480, 486.
Van Hook v. Walton, 148, 229, 299, 301, 320, 472.
Van Horn v. Smith, 135.
Van Horne v. Fonda, 513.
Vanhouten v. Reily, 107.
Van Keuren v. McLaughlin, 487, 537, 553.
Van Kleeck v. Miller, 41, 53.
Van Nest v. Yoe, 44, 60, 136, 152, 188, 240, 267, 269, 271, 272, 322, 419, 469, 603.
Van Patten v. Burr, 135, 169, 627.
Van Patten v. Thompson, 13.
Van Rossum v. Walker, 195, 229, 237, 238, 261.
Vansands v. Miller, 275, 617.
Van Slyke v. Bush, 529, 662.
Vanslyke v. Shryer, 52.
Van Valkenberg v. Elmendorf, 503.
Van Vleet v. Slauson, 133, 135, 151.

Van Waggoner v. Moses, 98, 178, 654.
Van Winkle v. McKee, 448.
Varnum v. Camp, 359, 654.
Varnum v. Evans, 586.
Vaughan v. Evans, 115.
Vaughan v. West, 212.
Vernon v. Morton, 23, 104, 107, 137, 147, 172, 212, 268, 270, 297, 320, 325, 345, 414, 419, 427, 457, 459, 472, 487, 520, 525, 552, 605, 607.
Vernon v. Upson, 236, 443.
Vidvard v. Powers, 502.
Vietor v. Henlien, 430, 431.
Von Heim v. Elkus, 47, 578.
Von Wettberg v. Carson, 284, 283, 480, 617.
Voorhees v. Frisbie, 54.
Vose v. Holcombe, 199, 586.
Vosper v. Kramer, 89, 241, 603.
Vredenburg v. White, 469.

Waddingham v. Laker, 427.
Wade v. Pettibone, 513.
Wadleigh v. Merkle, 301, 310, 688.
Wagener v. Boynston, 680.
Waggoner v. Smith, 428.
Wagner v. Hodge, 299.
Wagner v. Jaffray, 368.
Waite's Accounting, Matter of, 862.
Wakefield v. Martin, 105.
Wakeman v. Barrows, 481.
Wakeman v. Dalley, 425, 432.
Wakeman v. Grover, 164, 189, 203, 204, 205, 210, 214, 268, 341, 444, 567, 594, 604, 607.
Wald v. Wehl, 55, 56.
Waldron v. Wilcox, 218, 255, 267.
Waldron v. Willard, 488.
Wales v. Chase, 475.
Walker, In re, 41, 260.
Walker v. Crowder, 460.
Walker v. Miller, 353, 479, 482, 503.
Walker v. Newlin, 140, 141, 349.
Walker v. Smyer's Ex'rs, 578.
Walker v. Stone, 578.
Walker v. Symonds, 571.
Walkins v. Jenks, 103.
Wall v. Lakin, 165.
Wallace v. Burdell, 301.
Wallace v. Cumming, 583, 586.

TABLE OF CASES.

References are to pages.

Wallace v. Wainright, 6, 131, 293.
Wallis v. Rhea, 296.
Wallon v. Scott, 115.
Wallwyn v. Coutts, 340.
Walter v. Whitbeck, 105.
Walters v. Whitlock, 361, 466.
Walworth v. Readsboro, 318.
Wandel v. Peay, 421.
Ward, Matter of, 484, 488, 530.
Ward v. Lamson, 343.
Ward v. Lewis, 127, 186, 302, 303, 311, 341, 350, 389, 459, 460, 529, 565, 570, 581, 592, 597.
Ward v. Tingley, 149, 188, 190, 270, 441.
Ward v. Trotter, 137, 246.
Ward v. Webster, 114.
Ward v. Wooten, 516.
Waring v. Buchanan, 53.
Warner v. Jaffray, 299, 302, 350, 361, 371.
Warner v. Jameson, 479, 482.
Warner v. Littlefield, 12, 16.
Warner v. Mower, 64.
Warren v. Dwyer, 13.
Warren v. Fenn, 478.
Warren v. Lee, 17.
Warren v. Tenth Nat. Bank, 48.
Warren v. Warren Thread Co., 106.
Warshing, In re, 519.
Washer v. Everhart, 358.
Washington v. Ryan, 337, 427.
Wasson v. English, 514.
Wasson v. Garrett, 566.
Waterbury v. Sturtevant, 421.
Waterbury v. Westervelt, 448, 495.
Waters v. Comly, 167.
Watkins v. Jenkins, 102.
Watkins v. Wallace, 270, 429.
Watson v. Bagaley, 11, 131, 293.
Watson v. Bailey, 3.
Watson v. Brewster, 359.
Watson v. Butcher, 242, 492.
Watson v. Hankins, 105.
Watson v. Orr, 359.
Watts v. Eufaula Nat. Bank, 13, 132, 580, 584.
Watts v. Shipman, 111, 113.
Waugh v. Wyche, 314.
Wear, In re, 556.
Weatherly v. Strauss, 427.

Weaver v. Leiman, 60, 282.
Webb v. Armistead, 244.
Webb v. Daggett, 93, 163, 172, 173, 175, 415, 425.
Webb v. Dean, 302, 312, 313.
Webb v. Ingham, 435.
Weber v. Mick, 3, 12.
Weber v. Samuel, 160, 216, 293, 294, 586, 676.
Webster v. Harkness, 334.
Webster v. Vanderventer, 314.
Weeks v. Millardet, 153.
Weeks v. Wead, 318.
Wehl v. Wald, 52, 54, 55.
Weide v. Porter, 352.
Weider v. Maddox, 24.
Weil v. McDonald, 475.
Weinhaus, Matter of, 557.
Weir v. Tannehille, 127, 311, 594.
Weiskettle's Appeal, 368.
Welch v. Mandeville, 105.
Welch v. Myers, 475.
Welckler v. Staples, 514.
Welles v. March, 67, 78, 79, 85, 420.
Wells, In re, 44, 45.
Wells v. Lamb, 298.
Wells v. Treadwell, 4.
Welsh v. Britton, 236.
Wensley, Ex parte, 33.
Wente v. Young, 54.
West v. Schneider, 507.
West v. Snodgrass, 198, 230, 609.
West v. Steward, 110, 145, 148, 153, 155.
West v. Tupper, 350.
Westbrook v. McDowell, 104.
Westcott v. Potter, 105.
Weston v. Barker, 312.
Weston v. Loyhed, 640.
Wetter v. Schlieper, 85.
Whallon v. Scott, 116, 195, 276, 492.
Wharton v. Fisher, 383.
Wharton v. Hopkins, 479.
Whatton v. Toone, 510.
Whedbee v. Stewart, 159, 200, 212, 233, 415.
Wheeler v. Evans, 199.
Wheeler v. Hawkins, 297.
Wheeler v. Kerkendall, 15.
Wheeler v. Perry, 532.

TABLE OF CASES. lxi

References are to pages.

Wheeler v. Sumner, 212, 327, 341, 343, 474.
Wheeler v. Wheeler, 105.
Wheelock v. Kost, 62.
Whelpdale v. Cookson, 511.
Whichcote v. Lawrence, 511, 513.
Whipple v. Pope, 273.
Whipple v. Stebbin, 164.
Whipple v. Thayer, 376.
Whitaker v. Gavit, 106, 109, 306.
Whitaker v. Lindley, 179, 627.
Whitcomb v. Fowle, 182, 460.
Whitcomb v. Minchin, 512.
White v. Banks, 346, 400.
White v. Buck, 105.
White v. Cotzhausen, 134.
White v. Davis, 428.
White v. Fagan, 141.
White v. Folgambe, 516.
White v. Griffin, 54.
White v. Hill, 519.
White v. Monsarrat, 269.
White v. Thomas, 547.
White v. Union Insurance Co., 89.
White v. Winn, 210, 213.
Whitehead v. Woodruff, 634.
Whiteley v. May, 237.
Whitewright v. Stimpson, 90, 91.
Whitney's Appeal, 477, 556, 596.
Whitney v. Brunnette, 320.
Whitney v. Freeland, 448.
Whitney v. Hirsch, 236.
Whitney v. Kelley, 128.
Whitney v. Krows, 195, 258, 262, 264, 268, 485.
Whittaker v. Williams, 135, 306.
Whittemore v. Gibbs, 104.
Whitten v. Fitzwater, 114.
Whitton v. Smith, 68.
Whitwell v. Thompson, 30, 31.
Whitworth v. Benbow, 241.
Whitworth v. Patterson, 85.
Whorter v. Wright, 179.
Wickham v. Green, 140, 247.
Wickham v. Martin, 278, 497.
Wickliffe v. The City of Lexington, 559.
Wicks v. Wescott, 517.
Widdall v. Garsed, 326.
Widgery v. Haskell, 165, 166, 172, 200, 214, 339.

Wieder v. Maddox, 361.
Wiener v. Davis, 3, 159.
Wiesenfeld v. Stevens, 419, 423.
Wilbur v. Fradenburgh, 472.
Wilcox v. Bates, 569.
Wilcox v. Jackson, 85.
Wilcox v. Kellogg, 22, 169, 179.
Wilcoxson v. Annesley, 10, 624.
Wilde v. Rawlings, 208, 212, 233.
Wilder v. Fondey, 407.
Wilder v. Keeler, 237.
Wilder v. Winne, 167, 407, 410.
Wiley's Appeal, 100.
Wiley v. Collins, 342.
Wiley v. Knight, 167.
Wilhelm v. Byles, 353, 491.
Wilkes v. Ferris, 142–144, 172, 229, 231, 282.
Wilkins v. Davis, 480.
Wilkinson, Matter of, 557.
Wilkinson v. Wilkinson, 517.
Wilks v. Walker, 680.
Willard v. Tillman, 103.
Willets v. Waite, 361.
Williams' Appeal, 531, 581.
Williams v. Brown, 167.
Williams v. Frost, 79, 638.
Williams v. Galt, 105.
Williams v. Gartrell, 627.
Williams v. Hadley, 383.
Williams v. Jones, 172, 434, 435.
Williams v. Lowdnes, 321.
Williams v. Otey, 146, 500, 562.
Williams v. Whedon, 90.
Williams v. Winsor, 479.
Williamson v. Berry, 9.
Williamson v. Croft, 523.
Williamson v. Nealy, 478.
Williamson v. Richardson, 111.
Williamson v. Wilkins, 523.
Willis v. Bremner, 236, 691.
Willis v. Farley, 502.
Willis v. Henderson, 478, 482.
Willis v. Stewart, 499.
Williston v. Camp, 356.
Wilmer v. Thomas, 106.
Wilson, In re, 88, 154, 159, 205, 206, 210, 215, 285, 307, 519, 556, 567, 600.
Wilson v. Berg, 169, 172, 441, 442.
Wilson v. Britton, 420.
Wilson v. Brown, 566.

TABLE OF CASES.

References are to pages.

Wilson v. City Bank, 48, 165.
Wilson v. Day, 30.
Wilson v. Eifler, 421.
Wilson v. Esten, 481.
Wilson v. Ferguson, 469.
Wilson v. Forsyth, 181, 322, 330, 331, 421, 602.
Wilson v. Hanson, 387.
Wilson v. Hooper, 318.
Wilson v. Kneppley, 205, 394.
Wilson v. Lott, 427.
Wilson v. Pearson, 304, 318, 349.
Wilson v. Robertson, 235-237, 240, 241, 253, 264, 283, 431, 440.
Wilson v. Russell, 17.
Wilson v. Staats, 581.
Wilson Bros. Co. v. Daggett, 583, 586, 602.
Wilt v. Franklin, 92, 93, 152, 153, 172, 205, 248, 277, 317, 349, 420, 435.
Wilt v. Wheeler, 327.
Wimbish v. Talbois, 413.
Winder v. Diffenderffer, 522.
Windham v. Patty, 338, 476, 683.
Winebrener's Appeal, 513.
Winn v. Crosby, 494, 520, 526, 562, 563.
Winn v. Madden, 151, 297, 477.
Winner v. Hoyt, 13, 92, 135.
Winslett v. Randle, 682.
Winslow v. Assignees of Ancrum, 155.
Wintringham v. Lafoy, 172, 229.
Wise v. Wimer, 9, 482.
Wiswall v. Potts, 115.
Wiswall v. Ross, 335.
Wiswall v. Ticknor, 198, 227.
Witner, Matter of, 558.
Wolf's Appeal, 547.
Wolf, Matter of, 524, 527.
Wolf v. Gray, 612.
Wolf v. O'Conner, 155.
Wolverhampton Bank v. Marshton, 420.
Wood, In re, 34, 35, 49.
Wood v. Augustine, 516.
Wood v. Bolard, 168, 182.
Wood v. Radcliffe, 142, 143.
Wood v. White, 505.
Woodbridge v. Perkins, 105.
Woodburn v. Mosher, 253, 263, 270.
Woodhouse, In re, 28, 33-35.
Woodley v. Hassell, 417.

Woodruff v. Bowles, 408.
Woodruff v. Railroad Co., 526.
Woodruff v. Robb, 18.
Woods v. Timmerman, 160.
Woodward v. Baynard, 115.
Woodward v. Brooks, 358, 369.
Woodward v. Marshall, 145, 153, 244, 456, 464, 485, 490.
Woodworth v. Sweet, 121.
Wooldridge v. Irving, 84, 99-101.
Woolsey v. Urner, 207.
Woolson v. Pipher, 319.
Wooster v. Stanfield, 92, 251, 476.
Wooten v. Clark, 315.
Work v. Ellis, 196, 254, 415, 421, 429.
Worley v. Frampton, 516.
Worman v. Wolfersberger's Ex'rs, 132, 169, 178.
Worseley v. De Mattos, 30, 31.
Worth v. McAden, 569.
Worthington v. Greer, 113.
Worthley, Matter of, 526.
Wright v. Bundy, 484.
Wright v. Clapp, 120, 536.
Wright v. Gay, 281.
Wright v. Gelvin, 109, 624, 625.
Wright v. Henderson, 592, 593.
Wright v. Linn, 166, 172, 221, 284, 400, 428, 470.
Wright v. Mack, 594.
Wright v. McCormick, 495.
Wright v. Thomas, 260, 275, 626.
Wright v. Wigton, 480, 545.
Wright v. Williamson, 105.
Wright v. Zeigler, 503.
Wurtz v. Hart, 117, 545, 549.
Wyeth Hdw. Co. v. Standard Implement Co., 453.
Wykoff v. Carr, 442.
Wyles v. Beals, 101.
Wylie's Appeal, 532.
Wynkoop v. Shardlow, 148, 453, 524.
Wynne, In re, 52, 53.
Wynne v. Glidewell, 502.
Wynne v. Simmons Hdw. Co., 397, 480, 485, 491.

Yargin v. Shriner, 508.
Yates v. Lyon, 53.
Yeager, Matter of, 579.

TABLE OF CASES. lxiii

References are to pages.

Yeager v. Scranton Trust Co., 108.
Yelverton v. Sheldon, 387.
York County Bank v. Carter, 165, 169, 178.
Young v. Booe, 254.
Young v. Cardwell, 313.
Young v. Dumas, 166, 169.
Young v. Gillespie, 152.
Young v. Hail, 246.
Young v. Harris, 359.
Young v. Keighley, 68.
Young v. McClure, 317, 329.
Youngs, Master of, 270.
Youngs v. Hannas, 506.

Zacharie v. Kirk, 320.
Zaring v. Cox, 297, 342, 529.
Zeigler's Appeals, 121, 529, 581.
Zeigler v. Maddox, 430.
Zergenfuss, Ex parte, 39.
Zimmer v. Miller, 434.
Zimmerman v. Harman, 514.
Zimmerman v. Willard, 291, 622.
Zipcey v. Thompson, 361, 379, 380.
Zoebisch v. Von Minden, 192.
Zuppann v. Bauer, 375.
Zuver v. Clark, 581.
Zwang, In re, 18.
Zwelchenbart, Ex parte, 33.

VOLUNTARY ASSIGNMENTS.

CHAPTER I.

ASSIGNMENTS IN GENERAL — VOLUNTARY ASSIGNMENTS FOR THE BENEFIT OF CREDITORS DEFINED AND DISTINGUISHED FROM OTHER MODES AND INSTRUMENTS OF TRANSFER.

§ 1. Assignments in General.
2. Voluntary Assignments for the Benefit of Creditors Defined.
3. Assignments Distinguished — Conveyances Directly to Creditors.
4. Distinguished from Sales.
5. Distinguished from Agencies.
6. Distinguished from Mortgages.
7. Distinguished from Mortgages — Illustrations.
8. Distinguished from Deeds of Trust in the Nature of Mortgage.

§ 1. **Assignments in General.**— An *assignment* is a transfer or setting over of property, or of some right or interest therein, from one person to another; the term denoting not only the *act* of transfer, but also the *instrument* by which it is effected.[1] In these senses the word is variously applied in law.[2] As applied to *real* estate, an assignment is properly a transfer, or making over to another, of one's whole interest in lands or tenements, whatever that interest may be;[3] but in England it is usually applied to express the trans-

---

[1] These appear to be secondary senses of the term, the primary meanings being those of *appointment, allotment, specification* or *designation;* all which are still retained. In the Latin of the old books it is termed *assignatio*, from which the Scotch *assignation* has been formed; but the word *assignment* itself is obviously taken from the Law French. Britt., chs. 34, 83, 103.

[2] An assignment is properly the transfer of one's whole interest in any estate; but it is now generally appropriated to the transfer of chattels, either real or personal, or of equitable interests. Watkins on Conv., b. 2, ch. 9, p. 227. The common-law definition of an assignment is, "the transferring and setting over to another of some right, title or interest in things in which a third party, not a party to the assignment, has a concern and interest." 1 Bac. Abr. 329. See Mr. Justice Isbell, in Cowles v. Ricketts, 1 Iowa, 582.

[3] The introduction of the word *assigns* into the old instruments of feudal conveyance had the effect of conferring on the purchaser the power of alienation. Britt., ch. 35; Mirr., ch. 1, § 3; 2 Bl. Com. 289. Hence the proper sense of assign-

1

fer of an estate for life or years.¹ Considered as an instrument, an assignment at common law is a species of deed, and is classed, by Blackstone and other writers, among common-law conveyances of a secondary or derivative character, which also presupposes a conveyance precedent.² As applied to *personal* estate the term *assignment* has the same double sense of the act and instrument of transfer. Where an article of merchandise or personal chattel is the subject of it, the act is more commonly termed a *sale*, and the instrument used to express and authenticate it, a *bill of sale*.³ But in other cases of transfer the term is usually employed to denote both the act and the instrument; the latter being either separately drawn in the form of a deed, or indorsed upon other instruments (such as bonds, policies, etc.), in shorter form; and in cases of transfer of bills of exchange and promissory notes, the assignment is still more compendiously expressed by the indorsement of the assignor's name.⁴ In many cases, however, no instrument or

---

ment, in ancient conveyancing, seems to have been *alienation by virtue of a previous instrument.* This serves to account for the restriction of the term, which has so long prevailed in England, to the sense of the transfer of an *interest held under a previous conveyance;* the assignor creating no new estate by the assignment, but merely passing or setting over an estate already created, to be held as the assignor himself held it; the assignee being put in his place, or (in the ancient sense of the latter word) *deputed* for that purpose. See the next note.

¹ 1 Steph. Com. 485. Sir William Blackstone defines an assignment to be "properly a transfer, or making over to another, of the right one has in any estate; but it is usually applied to an estate for *life or years.*" 2 Bl. Com. 326. Dr. Wooddesson restricts the proper meaning of the term to "the transfer of the interest which any one has in the unexpired residue of a term or estate *for years.*" 2 Woodd. Lect. 170, 171. In Cruise's Digest an assignment is said to be "properly a transfer of some particular estate or interest in lands, but it is usually applied to the transfer of a term *for years.*" Cruise Dig., tit. xxxii (Deed), ch. vii, sec. 15. The reason of this peculiar restriction of the term to estates for years is to be found in the nature of those estates, which could not be adequately conveyed by a *new* instrument of the *same* kind (that is, the lessee or tenant for years could not convey or divest himself of the whole of his estate at once, by a new lease, as a feoffee might by a new feoffment, the idea of a lease implying a reversion of some kind to the lessor on its termination, and of course a continuing interest in the lessor to that extent), but only by setting over the *same* instrument, and the estate held under it. Hence the distinction, which has become so well established in modern law, between an assignment and a derivative or under lease. In American law the term *assignment*, though constantly employed to denote the transfer of a leasehold interest, is not so frequently restricted to that particular sense.

² See 2 Bl. Com. 310, 324, 326.

³ See 2 Steph. Com. 104; 1 Tucker's Com. (Laws of Virginia), [333] 323, note (a). The resemblances and distinctions between an assignment and a sale will be more fully noticed in § 4.

⁴ The term *assignment* is here used in the larger sense of transfer in general. Chitty on Bills (Perk. ed., 1854), [5, 6] 8, [8] 11, 12, [196] 225; Story on Bills, § 17. In practice, however, the term, as applied to the transfer of bills and notes, is generally restricted to such as are not negotiable, as distinguished from the in-

writing is used, the title to the property passing by mere delivery.[1] In mercantile transactions, the term *assignment* is not used in the sense of *sale*, but rather in contradistinction from it; being confined in its application either to transfers of a special kind, auxiliary to sales, or in completion of them (such as assignments of bills of lading, of policies of insurance, etc.), or to transfers by way of security for or in payment of *debts*. Indeed, in most of its applications, the term seems to imply the existence of the relation of *debtor and creditor;* and it is in this latter sense only that these modes and instruments of conveyance are now proposed to be considered.

§ 2. **Voluntary Assignments for the Benefit of Creditors Defined.**— Voluntary assignments for the benefit of creditors are transfers, without compulsion of law, by debtors, of some or all of their property to an assignee or assignees, in trust to apply the same, or the proceeds thereof, to the payment of some or all of their debts, and to return the surplus, if any, to the debtor.[2]

Assignments, in this restricted sense, are distinguished with reference to their subject-matter, as being of all or of part of the debt-

---

dorsement of negotiable paper. Shankland, J., in Bump v. Van Orsdale, 11 Barb. 634, 639; Bank of Marietta v. Pindall, 2 Rand. 465. See, also, on this point, Jagoe v. Alleyn, 16 Barb. 580; Watson v. Bailey, 2 Duer, 509.

[1] The term *assignment* is frequently used in the books to express the transfer of a promissory note by delivery. Edison v. Frazier, 4 Eng. (Ark.) 219, 220; Jackson v. Heath, 1 Bailey, 355; Chitty on Bills (Perk. ed. 1854), 259, note 3, and cases cited ibid.; Hedges v. Sealy, 9 Barb. 214; Bump v. Van Orsdale, 11 id. 634: Collins v. Knapp, 18 id. 532. But see Calkins v. Packer, 21 id. 275. And see Andrews v. Carr, 26 Miss. 577. In Feimster v. Smith, 5 Eng. (Ark.) 494, the term, applied to a bond in pleading, was held to import delivery, *ex vi termini*. In Andrews v. Carr (*ub sup.*), it was held that the words *transfer* and *assign* mean, in legal proceedings, a transfer by *writing;* and that when a party, in pleading, says that he acquired title to a note by assignment, he is understood to mean *written* assignment, unless he qualifies the meaning of the words.

[2] The definition given in the text is approved in Bartlett v. Teah, 1 McCrary, 176, 178. A "voluntary assignment" means, presumably, an assignment of all the debtor's property in trust to pay debts; as contradistinguished from a sale to a creditor in payment of his claim and from a pledge or hypothecation as a security in the nature of a mortgage. Anderson's Dic. of Law, p. 83. In the case of Weber v. Mick, 131 Ill. 521; 23 N. E. Rep. 646, Mr. Justice Bailey said: "A voluntary assignment is an instrument in writing executed by a failing debtor by which he assigns or transfers to some third person, as assignee or trustee, the whole, or sometimes the bulk, of his property, to be by such trustee distributed among the assignor's creditors in satisfaction of their demands." Under the Pennsylvania statute an assignment has been defined to be "a transfer by a debtor of the whole or a part of his effects to some person in trust to pay all of his creditors in like proportion, and to return the surplus, if any, to the debtor." Mr. Justice Lowrie, in Wiener v. Davis, 18 Pa. St. 332. See, also, Farwell v. Bohen, 138 Ill. 216. "An assignment whereby a debtor, generally an insolvent, transfers to another his property, in trust to pay his debts or apply the property upon their payment." Black's Law Dic., p. 98.

or's property.[1] The former are known as *general*[2] assignments, in distinction from *partial* assignments, by which term the latter are defined.

Such assignments are termed voluntary,[3] to distinguish them from such as are made by compulsion of law, as under statutes of bankruptcy and insolvency (the latter being sometimes termed *statutory* assignments), or by order of some competent court. Assignments, in the sense in which they are here employed, are usually resorted to by debtors who find themselves unable to pay their creditors in full, or the embarrassed state of whose affairs has compelled them to discontinue the transaction of business, and, in some instances, the provisions of the statutes[4] which have been passed by the state legislature, regulating and restricting the operation of such assignments, are confined exclusively to assignments made by insolvents or by persons in contemplation of insolvency; but the solvency of the debtor, in his own estimation or in fact, will not, apart from statutory provisions, unless connected with other evidence of fraud, invalidate an assignment.[5]

[1] This division of the subject will be found more precisely stated in ch. VIII. "An assignment of all one's property for the benefit of all one's creditors is clearly a general assignment." Mr. Justice Bennett, in Dana v. Lull, 17 Vt. 390. "A general assignment must include substantially *all* a man's property; and a partial assignment must omit some substantial portion of the property; and cannot be made to rest upon a mere colorable omission." Mr. Chief Justice Redfield, in Mussey v. Noyes, 27 Vt. 474; Longmire v. Goode, 38 Ala. 577.

[2] In the case of The United States v. M'Lellan, 3 Sum. 345, the designation of voluntary assignments, as being "for the benefit of creditors," was held to imply a conveyance to trustees for the benefit either of the creditors at large, or of some other creditors than the immediate grantees. Id. 354, 355. And see Smith v. Woodruff, 1 Hilt. 469.

[3] Manny v. Logan, 27 Mo. 528. This is quite a different application of the word *voluntary* from the technical sense in which it is frequently employed, viz., that of being *without consideration*, or without valuable consideration. In the latter sense *voluntary* is sometimes used as synonymous with *fraudulent*, though in other instances it is distinguished. See Nunn v. Wilsmore, 8 Term R. 521, 528, 529. Lord Mansfield, in Cadagan v. Kennett, Cowp. 432, 434, and in Doe v. Rutledge, id. 705, 711; 4 Kent's Com. [463] 510; 1 Story's Eq. Jur., § 353; 3 N. Y. Rev. Stat. (6th ed.) p. 145, § 4. And see Wells v. Treadwell, 28 Miss. 717; Lumpkin, J., Clayton v. Brown, 17 Ga. 217, 222. Mr. Roberts has alluded to the unsettled meaning of the term *voluntary* in this application. Roberts on Fraud. Conv. 63, 65, 70, 71, 72, 400. Whatever may be the form or character of the instrument, to operate as a general assignment it must proceed from the will and be the act of the debtor. Hence the transfer is defined as voluntary. Perry Ins. & Trust Co. v. Foster, 58 Ala. 502, 521. In Lewis v. Miller, 23 N. Y. Weekly Dig. 495, a deed and trust declaration were held not to be a general assignment for the benefit of creditors because not voluntary in character, each of them being based on good consideration passing to and from the various parties in interest.

[4] See these statutes in Appendix I.

[5] Ogden v. Peters, 21 N. Y. 23. See Livermore v. Northop, 44 N. Y. 107. As to what constitutes insolvency, and the effect of solvency upon the right to make assignments, see chapter IV.

Voluntary assignments for the benefit of creditors are in many respects peculiar to American law and practice,[1] and have in this country acquired a technical signification. They are frequently referred to by name in statutory enactments as well as in judicial discussions, and a somewhat more careful illustration of their characteristic features may be necessary to distinguish them from other instruments and modes of transfer, to which they are in some respects analogous.

§ 3. **Assignments Distinguished — Conveyances Directly to Creditors.**— A voluntary assignment for the benefit of creditors implies a trust and contemplates the intervention of a trustee.[2] Assignments directly to creditors, and not upon trust, are not voluntary assignments for the benefit of creditors.[3] Assignments may be made either to the whole body of the creditors or to particular creditors, or they may be of all or of a part of the debtor's property; but unless a trust is thereby created by the assignor in favor of creditors, such conveyances are not within the class of instruments known as assignments for creditors.[4]

[1] Grover v. Wakeman, 11 Wend. 187. For a history of the law of voluntary assignments, see Ludington's Petition, 5 Abb. N. C. 307.

[2] Cowles v. Rickett, 1 Iowa, 382; Dickson v. Rawson, 5 Ohio St. 218. And where a railroad company executed a lease of its property for a term of years, providing that the net earnings should be apportioned one half to the lessee and the other half to the payment of certain debts of the lessor, this was regarded as an assignment for creditors within the Pennsylvania statute. Mr. Justice Read, in delivering the opinion of the court, said: "We have here property, a trustee, a trust, and creditors of an insolvent company, who are to take under it." Mr. Justice Hare, in the same case, said: "The means employed would seem to me immaterial if the result were a transfer in trust, or a trust bottomed on a transfer; if, in short, the property ceased to be the debtor's without vesting directly and absolutely in his creditors, and remaining outstanding in the hands of a third person, who could not be compelled to render an account or to fulfill the duties imposed on him without recourse to the aid of equity." Lucas v. The Sunbury & Erie Railroad Co., 32 Pa. St. 458. If a conveyance places the property transferred beyond the reach of an execution and creates a trust for the benefit of creditors, it is an assignment within the meaning of the Pennsylvania statutes, without regard to its form. Corn Ex. Nat. Bank v. Philadelphia Trust, etc. Co., 11 Phila. 510.

[3] Claflin v. Maglaughlin, 65 Pa. St. 492; Beach v. Beston, 47 Ill. 521; Keen v. Preston, 24 Ind. 395; Harkins v. Bailey, 48 Ala. 377; Johnson v. McGraw, 11 Iowa, 151; Beans v. Bullitt, 57 Pa. St. 221; Henderson's Appeal, 31 id. 502; Banning v. Sibley, 3 Minn. 389; Griffin v. Rogers, 38 Pa. St. 382; Chaffees v. Risk, 24 id. 432; Vallance v. Miners' Life Ins. Co., 42 id. 441; Brooks v. Stanton, 11 Rep. 260; Fecheimer v. Robertson, 53 Ark. 101; 13 S. W. Rep. 423.

[4] Whether it is so in trust, and the assignee or grantee such trustee, depends upon the question whether, by the terms of the instrument or by necessary implication, he is liable to account to the creditors for the property in his hands and for the manner in which he disposes of it. If a court of chancery at the instance of the creditor would compel him thus to account, the character of the

It is not essential, however, that a trustee should be named as such in the instrument.[1] And when the creditor undertakes, under an agreement with the assignor, to sell the property and apply the proceeds to the payment of his own and other debts of the assignor, and refund the surplus, he becomes a trustee, and the transaction amounts to a voluntary assignment.[2]

Assignments of the whole of a debtor's property directly to the whole body of the creditors are rare in practice, although mentioned with approval in some judicial opinions.[3] The acts of taking

---

transfer and his own possession are thereby determined. Dickson v. Rawson, 5 Ohio St. 218. An instrument executed by a debtor with the intention that it shall operate as an assignment, and that the property thereby conveyed shall pass absolutely to the trustee for the purpose of raising a fund to pay debts, is an assignment for the benefit of creditors. Richmond v. Mississippi Mills, 52 Ark. 30; 11 S. W. Rep. 960. In Wallace v. Wainwright, 87 Pa. St. 263, an instrument reciting the indebtedness of the subscribers to certain parties, and assigning certain claims, etc., to third persons *in payment* of the creditors named, was held to be an assignment for the benefit of creditors. The intervention of the third persons in whom the legal title to the property was vested was held to create a trust for the creditors named.

[1] Burrows v. Lehndorff, 8 Iowa, 96. Mr. Chief Justice Wright, in that case, remarked: "The fact that he (the debtor) appoints a trustee seems, perhaps, in most instances, to fix conclusively the character of the transaction as a general assignment." In that case the instruments by which the assignment was made were all mortgages, and therefore there was no trustee named; but this was not taken to be the reason why the instruments should not be regarded as an assignment. And see Dickson v. Rawson, 5 Ohio St. 218.

[2] Truitt v. Caldwell, 3 Minn. 364; Page v. Smith, 24 Wis. 368. And where a debtor made an absolute conveyance of all his property to one of his creditors in consideration of the grantees paying certain other creditors, this was held to be a general assignment. Murphy v. Caldwell, 50 Ala. 461. If an assignment of real and personal property be made to another, who agrees to hold the property and apply the income thereof to the debts of the assignor, and the assignors at the same time sell and convey to the assignee other property, the assignee to hold the purchase-money and apply it to the same object, the assignee is liable to account, as trustee, for all the funds that come into his hands from the property of the assignor. Ahl's Appeal, 129 Pa. St. 26. And in the Oregon case of Stout v. Watson, 19 Oreg. 251; s. c., 24 Pac. Rep. 230, it was held substantially that when a creditor enters into an agreement with the assignor to sell the property and refund the surplus, he becomes a trustee, and the transaction amounts to a voluntary assignment; so a transfer by a debtor to one of his creditors to satisfy his claim, and the balance to be distributed *pro rata* among other creditors named, was held to be an assignment and not a mortgage. Hart v. Blum, 76 Tex. 113; s. c., 13 S. W. Rep. 181.

[3] This is the form of assignment for which Mr. Justice Nelson expressed his preference in the case of Cunningham v. Freeborn, 11 Wend. 240, 256, 257, in the following language: "I would hold a debtor in failing circumstances to pay or give security to his creditor or creditors directly, without the intervention of a trustee, who is often the creature of the debtor, without interest or sympathy on behalf of the creditor. In this way the creditors would obtain the control of the fund the moment the debtor parted with it; and if favored creditors were preferred, they would be obliged to see to it that they took no more than was a fair security for their debts. They should not be permitted to justify their pos-

possession of the property assigned, and applying it in satisfaction of the debts provided for, are such as cannot always be performed by the creditors personally, where they are at all numerous, but requires the intervention of an agent, who thereby becomes, in most instances, a trustee for the creditors. In some cases the assignment itself expressly directs or authorizes the appointment of such agent or trustee by the creditors.[1] In others, the creditors agreed among themselves that one of their number should act for the others.[2] A trust also would result for the debtor in the event of a surplus remaining after full satisfaction of the debts.

But provision by the method of direct transfer is more commonly made in favor either of a single creditor, or of a few selected creditors; and a debtor may, in this way, transfer all his property,[3] or a specific portion of it, or some single article or item.[4] Where the assignment is to a single creditor, or to a few selected creditors, and is made absolutely, and by way of full payment or satisfaction, it is, of course, wholly divested of the character of a trust,

---

session under the cover of trusteeship for others. Each creditor should be his own trustee. If inconvenient for creditors personally to execute the trust, they could appoint a trustee in their place. This modification would have the effect to give the possession and control of the fund, in the first instance, to the creditors or to a person appointed by them." In the case of Mussey v. Noyes, in the supreme court of Vermont (20 Vt. 462, 471), it was said by Chief Judge Redfield, that "assignments made directly to the creditors, so far as to require them to name the trustee, and thus make him their man, instead of his being, as is too often the case, the mere creature of the assignor, are certainly entitled to the most favorable consideration of the courts."

[1] This was the case in Tompkins v. Wheeler, 16 Pet. 106, the assignment giving to the creditors, or a majority of them, power to nominate and appoint an agent, attorney, or trustee, to carry the purposes of the instrument into full effect. It is to be observed, however, that the assignment in this case, though made directly to the creditors of certain specified classes, was expressly declared to be *in trust* for the payment of the debts.

[2] This was the case in Adams v. Blodgett, 2 Woodb. & Min. 233. The creditors agreed that one of them, in behalf of all, should go and take possession of the property which the debtor had agreed to assign. O. L. was selected for that purpose, and received from the debtor a written order to have the charge of all his property, books, and notes, etc., and to dispose of them for the benefit of all his creditors. O. L. went accordingly and took possession. The court treated O. L. as a trustee for the creditors. In Lockhart v. Stevenson, 61 Pa. St. 64, where a debtor in failing circumstances transferred his stock of goods to certain of his creditors who had previously made an arrangement to divide the proceeds among themselves, this was not regarded as an assignment for the benefit of creditors. The fact that there may have been a trust created among the creditors as to the distribution of the proceeds was not deemed material; the trust was not constituted by the assignor.

[3] Law v. Wyman, 8 N. H. 536; Barker v. Hall, 13 id. 298; Henshaw v. Sumner, 23 Pick. 446; Sargent v. Webster, 13 Metc. 497; Peck & Co. v. Merrill, 26 Vt. 686.

[4] Leitch v. Hollister, 4 N. Y. 211.

and is in the nature of an ordinary conveyance or sale for valuable consideration.[1] But where it is made by way of security only, or where a larger amount of property is assigned than is supposed necessary to satisfy the debts to which it is applied, a trust as to any remaining surplus results from the nature of the security,[2] although no express provision to that effect is contained in the transfer. Indeed, the transaction in such case is regarded by the courts, whatever may be its form, as in legal effect only a mortgage, creating but a specific lien on the property assigned.[3]

§ 4. **Distinguished from Sales.**— A sale, as we have seen,[4] is in law a species of assignment (taking the latter word in its broadest sense), and the affinity between the two modes of conveyance is shown by the circumstance that the instruments by which both are evidenced have usually the same formal words of transfer, "assign, transfer and set over." In some cases assignments have been drawn in nearly the exact form of a bill of sale, with the feature of a trust superadded.[5] Assignments have been spoken of in judicial opinions as sales, the assignors as vendors,[6] and the assignees as purchasers;[7] and the terms *sale* and *assignment* are frequently

---

[1] In the case of Dias v. Bouchaud, 10 Paige, 445, 448, 461, the words "voluntary assignment" in the act of congress of March 2, 1799, section 65, giving priorities to the United States in cases of insolvency, were held by the chancellor to mean an assignment of all the debtor's property, in trust, to pay debts, as contradistinguished from a mere *sale* of the property to a creditor in payment of his debt, or the pledge or hypothecation of the property to a particular creditor, as a mere security in the nature of a *mortgage*. In the same case on appeal (Bouchaud v. Dias, 1 N. Y. 201, 204), the act was further held to have intended an assignment for the benefit of creditors in general, as distinguished from an assignment for the benefit of a single creditor. In the case of The United States v. M'Lellan, 3 Sum. 345, it had been previously held by Mr. Justice Story that a conveyance by a debtor, known to be insolvent, of all his property to one or more creditors, in discharge of their own debts and liabilities, not exceeding the amount due to and payable by them, and not for the benefit of the creditors at large, or of any other creditors than the immediate grantees, is not a "voluntary assignment" for the benefit of creditors within the purview of the act of 1799, so as to be affected by the priority of the United States, unless it appear that it was made with the intent to evade the priority given by the act.

[2] Gardiner, J., in Leitch v. Hollister, 4 N. Y. 211, 216.

[3] Leitch v. Hollister, 4 N. Y. 211; Tompkins v. Wheeler, 16 Pet. 106; Peck & Co. v. Merrill, 26 Vt. 686, 691, where the cases are reviewed; Solomon v. Sparks, 27 Ga. 335; Potter v. McDowell, 31 Mo. 62; Dana v. Stamfords, 10 Cal. 269.

[4] *Ante*, p. 2.

[5] See Marbury v. Brooks, 7 Wheat. 556. An absolute bill of sale was called and treated as an assignment in Beers v. Lyon, 21 Conn. 604; so, also, in Truitt v. Caldwell, 3 Minn. 364.

[6] See Foster v. Saco Manufacturing Co., 12 Pick. 451, 453.

[7] See the opinion of Story, J., in United States v. M'Lellan, 3 Sum. 345, 355; and see Hollister v. Loud, 2 Mich. 309. In this case an assignee was considered

§ 4.] DISTINGUISHED FROM SALES. 9

applied indifferently to the transfer of choses in action.[1] But *assignments*, in the sense in which they will be considered in the present work, are clearly distinguishable from *sales*, not only in their occasion and object, but in their essential legal qualities and operation. Sales are transfers in the ordinary course of business; assignments commonly grow out of the embarrassments or suspension of business.[2] A sale is usually for a consideration actually paid, or agreed to be paid, and created or passing simultaneously;[3] an assignment is in most cases for a consideration already executed, as for a precedent or subsisting debt.[4] An important distinction between the two modes of transfer arises out of the character of a *trust*, which belongs to an assignment.[5] A sale (in cases free from fraud) is, on delivery of the thing sold and receipt of the consideration, a complete transaction, passing absolutely and irrevocably all the seller's interest in the subject of it, without reversion or return under any circumstances. An assignment is likewise an absolute conveyance by which both the legal and equitable estate is divested out of the grantor, but the title vested in the assignee is subject to

---

by the court as a purchaser for a valuable consideration. See, also, Gates v. Lebaume, 19 Mo. 17; Wise v. Winer, 23 id. 237; Hardcastle v. Fisher, 24 id. 70; but see Pierson v. Manning, 2 Mich. 445, 453, *contra*.

[1] Hilliard on Sales, 338, 339.

[2] Stout v. Watson, 19 Oreg. 251; 24 Pac. Rep. 230.

[3] A sale is a transferring of property from one person to another in consideration of a sum of *money to be paid* by the vendee to the vendor. Long on Sales, 1. A sale has been defined to be "a contract between parties to give and to pass rights of property for *money*, which the buyer pays, or promises to pay, to the seller for the thing bought and sold." Wayne, J. in Williamson v. Berry, 8 How. 495, 544. A sale may be defined to be a transfer of the absolute or general property in a thing for a price in money. Benjamin on Sales (1st Am. ed.), p. 1. But the fact that a consideration is paid will not necessarily change the character of the transaction. Truitt v. Caldwell, 3 Minn. 364.

[4] To constitute a bill of sale there must be either a consideration actually paid or agreed to be paid for the property, or it must appear that the assignment was received at a fixed sum in payment or part payment of a debt and subject to no conditions or trusts. A deed of assignment is an absolute transfer of property to an assignee in trust for the purpose of raising funds by a sale of the property to pay debts, and by which the grantor parted with dominion over the property. Rosenthal v. Frank, 37 Mo. App. 278.

[5] While the form and words of an assignment and bill of sale are generally the same, the element of trust, either express, implied or secret, distinguishes an assignment from a sale. Powell v. Kelly, 82 Ga. 1. A voluntary assignment for the benefit of creditors implies a trust and contemplates the intervention of a trustee. Stout v. Watson, 19 Oreg. 251; 24 Pac. Rep. 230, *supra*. A bill of sale is distinguished from an assignment for the benefit of creditors in that in the former there is a fixed price and no trust, while in the latter there is a mere trust and no fixed value given to the property. Becker v. Rardin, 107 Mo. 11; 17 S. W. Rep. 892. See Demmick v. Register, 92 Ala. 458; 9 So. Rep. 79; Bresson v. Musselman, 86 Mich. 186; 49 N. W. Rep. 39; Stites v. Champion, 49 N. J. Eq. 446.

the uses and trusts in favor of the creditors,[1] and upon their satisfaction a trust results in favor of the assignor in the residue of the unappropriated property or its proceeds.[2] A transfer of specific property to a creditor in discharge of a pre-existing debt is in effect a sale.[3] An assignment of itself does not satisfy the claims of the creditors to any extent, but provides a method for raising the means with which to pay them.[4] Sales are often subject to covenants on the part of buyer and seller, from which assignments are free. An assignee is not liable to the payment of incumbrances to the same extent as a purchaser. The distinction between a *sale* and an *assignment*, in this particular, has been judicially declared in Pennsylvania. Thus, a conveyance of property by a debtor to two of his creditors, for the use of them and others, in consideration that they would release him, was held to be not a *sale*, but an ordinary *assignment* for the benefit of creditors, the debtor having a resulting interest in the surplus; and the creditors were held to be not liable to pay off a subsisting incumbrance beyond the amount realized from the property assigned.[5] In a case in the court of

---

[1] Dwight v. Overton, 35 Tex. 390; Dessar v. Field, 99 Ind. 548; Danner v. Brewer, 69 Ala. 191. An absolute unconditional sale and conveyance of his property by a debtor, free from all reservation, in payment and satisfaction of antecedent debts, cannot be declared a general assignment, although it may embrace all the debtor's property and he be insolvent. Otis v. Maguire, 76 Ala. 295. The assignor and those claiming under him have no right, legal or equitable, in the assigned property until the purposes of the trust are satisfied. Briggs v. Davis, 21 N. Y. 574; s. c., 20 N. Y. 15. In this application the word has its full original meaning already noticed. See *ante*, p. 1, note 1.

[2] In re Potter, 54 Pa. St. 465.

[3] Johnson v. McGraw, 11 Iowa, 151; Hawkins v. Bailey, 48 Ala. 377; Claflin v. Maglaughlin, 65 Pa. St. 492; Lockhart v. Stevenson, 61 id. 64; Keen v. Preston, 24 Ind. 395; and see Beach v. Bestor, 47 Ill. 521. The fact that the consideration of the sale is to be applied in part to the payment of other debts than those of the vendee does not render the transaction an assignment for the benefit of creditors. Johnson v. McGraw, *supra;* Beach v. Bestor, *supra;* Beans v. Bullitt, 57 Pa. St. 221; Wilcoxson v. Annesley, 23 Ind. 285. See Murphy v. Caldwell, 50 Ala. 461. Where the partners of an insolvent firm by an instrument under seal assign all the partnership property and assets to a creditor as agent of and in trust for all other creditors whose names are or shall be signed to an agreement thereto annexed, accepting the property in full satisfaction of their respective debts, the conveyance, in the absence of fraud, is to be regarded as an ordinary sale upon a valuable consideration and not an assignment. Kenefick v. Perry, 61 N. H. 362. See Hine v. Bowe, 46 Hun, 196; Dessar v. Field, 99 Ind. 548; Sweeney v. Conley, 71 Tex. 543; 9 S. W. Rep. 548; Blennerhassett v. Sherman, 105 U. S. 100; Murray v. McNealy, 86 Ala. 234; s. c., 5 So. Rep., 565; Graham v. Railroad Co., 102 U. S. 148; Harmon v. McRae, 91 Ala. 401; Southworth v. Casey, 78 Ky. 395.

[4] Bebb v. Preston, 3 Clark (Iowa,) 460.

[5] Blank v. German, 5 Watts & Serg. 36. The conveyance in this case was in the form of an ordinary deed, but it was executed in pursuance of a prior written agreement on the part of the debtor to convey the property, subject to a full

appeals of New York,[1] an assignment of real estate by a religious corporation was construed to signify a *sale*, within the meaning of the charter, although the court seem to have been willing to concede that the assignment was not, strictly speaking, a sale, in consequence of the equitable interest which the assignors still retained in the application of the avails of the lands.

§ 5. **Distinguished from Agencies.**— It is a general rule of law that an agent represents and acts for his principal, and his contracts bind his principal only; a trustee in general is a person in whom some estate, interest or power in or affecting property is vested for the benefit of another, and his contracts are binding only upon himself.[2] A revocable power of attorney to collect debts and apply the proceeds does not amount to an assignment for the benefit of creditors, for the reason that there is no transfer of the title of the property.[3] Something more than a mere transmission of the custody and management of the assigned property is essential to constitute such an assignment. Thus, where a railroad company, having received certain state aid bonds, transferred them to a trustee to be distributed among such of its creditors as would accept them in payment at ninety-five cents on the dollar, and provided for the return to the company of such of the bonds as should not be disposed of before a specified time, this did not create an assignment for the benefit of creditors, but simply an agency for a particular purpose.[4]

§ 6. **Distinguished from Mortgages.**— The enactment in many of the states of statutes prohibiting preferences in general assignments has afforded a ground of attack on partial assignments with

release; and on the part of the creditors to release the debtor, provided he could convey for certain uses. Both instruments were taken together as constituting one transaction, and as amounting to a trust for creditors.

[1] De Ruyter v. St. Peter's Church, 3 N. Y. 238, 242. See Crawford v. Kirksey, 55 Ala. 282.

[2] Taylor v. Davis, 110 U. S. 334; 4 S. Ct. Rep. 147.

[3] Beans v. Bullitt, 57 Pa. St. 221; Henderson's Appeal, 31 id. 502; Griffin v. Rogers, 38 id. 382. But see Watson v. Bagaley, 12 id. 164, and Wallace v. Wainwright, 87 id. 263; McHose v. Dutton, 55 Iowa, 728; Murphy v. Caldwell, 50 Ala. 461, where, by consent of his creditors, a failing debtor was allowed to continue his business under the supervision of a committee of the creditors for a limited time, and a cashier or clerk was also appointed to receive and pay out money, the business to be done in the debtor's name, as before, until the state of affairs could be ascertained, and the property of the debtor never came into the possession of the committee, who merely acted in an advisory manner, and the cashier as a clerk, it was *held* that the committee and cashier were not trustees as to the property of the debtor for the benefit of creditors, and consequently were not liable to such creditors. Hall v. Crane Co., 87 Ill. 283.

[4] Banning v. Sibley, 3 Minn. 389.

preferences sometimes successfully resorted to by non-preferred creditors, where the claims of other creditors are satisfied by the debtor with mortgages or other conveyances. A mortgage resembles an assignment more closely in the leading features of being a security or provision for debt and in involving a resulting interest to the grantor on a certain contingency. An assignment is more than a security for the payment of debts; it is an absolute appropriation of property to their payment.[1] It does not create a lien in favor of creditors upon property which in equity is still regarded as the assignor's, but it passes both the legal and the equitable title to the property absolutely beyond the control of the assignor. There remains, therefore, no equity of redemption in the property,[2] and the trust which results to the assignor in the unemployed balance does not indicate such an equity.[3] In the case

---

[1] State v. Benoist, 37 Mo. 500; Fromme v. Jones, 13 Iowa, 480; Vallance v. Miners' Life Ins. Co., 42 Pa. St. 441; McBroom & Wood's Appeal, 44 id. 92; Lawrence v. Nuff, 41 Cal. 566; Dana v. Standfords, 10 Cal. 269; Dunham v. Whitehead, 21 N. Y. 131; McClelland v. Remsen, 3 Abb. Dec. (N. Y.) 74; Van Buskirk v. Warren, 4 id. 457. The text is quoted with approval in Crow v. Beardsley, 68 Mo. 435; also in Bartlett v. Teah, 1 McCrary, 176. In State Bank v. Chapelle, 40 Mich. 447, Campbell, C. J., says: "We do not think the questions applicable to general assignments have any bearing on a security which is only intended to secure a single debt on specific property." This is equally true when the security is in favor of several creditors but is on a portion only of the debtor's property. Palmer v. Mason, 42 Mich. 146. See Parsell v. Thayer, 39 id. 467; Warner v. Littlefield, 89 Mich. 329; 50 N. W. Rep. 221.

[2] "If this were otherwise, and if the estate of the trustee were regarded as in the nature of a lien, and subsequent conveyances, mortgages or judgments against the assignor were considered analogous to conveyances of or liens upon an equity of redemption, it would follow that the trustees could not convey an irredeemable title to the lands assigned until they had foreclosed the rights of subsequent parties. This is not the effect of a valid trust to sell lands. For the purpose of sale in execution of the trust, the grantor of the trust and those holding derivative titles under him are entirely disregarded, and their interests are subject to the execution of the trust, not in the sense in which a junior mortgage is subject to a prior one, but absolutely. These parties have no rights, legal or equitable, until the purposes of the trust are satisfied." Mr. Justice Denio, in Briggs v. Davis, 21 N. Y. 576.

[3] Quoted with approval, Crow v. Beardsley, 68 Mo. 435; Martin v. Hauseman, 14 Fed. Rep. 160; Clapp v. Ditmar, 21 id. 15; Perry v. Colby, id. 737; Kerbs v. Ewing, id. 693; Weber v. Mick, 131 Ill. 521; 23 N. E. Rep. 646, *supra;* Hershiser v. Higman, 31 Neb. 533; 48 N. W. Rep. 272. A conveyance which contains no condition of defeasance, and which passes the property absolutely to another to be administered by him according to its terms, first to pay a preferred debt from the proceeds of the property and to appropriate the balance to the satisfaction of other debts, cannot be regarded as a mortgage, but must be treated as an assignment. Johnson v. Roberson, 68 Tex. 899; s. c., 3 S. W. Rep. 625. Chattel mortgages covering substantially all of the mortgagor's property and aggregating all that the property is really worth, do not amount, in effect, to an assignment for the benefit of creditors, with preferences, even though they provide that the mortgagees shall take immediate possession and sell the goods, unless

of Tompkins v. Wheeler,[1] in the supreme court of the United States, the conveyance,[2] which was directly to creditors of certain classes in trust to pay debts, is called a general "assignment or *mortgage.*" In the case of Leitch v. Hollister,[3] in the court of appeals of New York, an assignment of a chose in action to certain creditors for the purpose of securing their demands was considered as, in legal effect, a mortgage. In the later case of Curtis v. Leavitt,[4] in the same court, deeds of trust executed by a banking company to trustees for the purpose of obtaining money upon certain bonds issued by the company were considered by the court as, in fact, mortgages given to secure the payment of money.[5] The vital distinction between an assignment for the benefit of creditors and a mortgage is clearly pointed out in the case of Briggs v. Davis,[6] in the same court. In Ohio a chattel mortgage executed in contemplation of insolvency to a particular creditor for the purpose of preferring him was held to be an assignment of property in trust, and the mortgagee was deemed a trustee for all the creditors.[7]

§ 7. **Distinguished from Mortgages — Illustrations.**— The distinction between voluntary assignments in trust for creditors

---

the mortgagor regards the transaction as a complete disposition of his property. Van Patten v. Thompson, 73 Iowa, 103: s. c., 34 N. W. Rep. 763. See Carson v. Byres, 67 Iowa, 606; s. c., 25 N. W. Rep. 826. It was accordingly held by a majority of the court, Taylor, J., dissenting, in the case of Winner v. Hoyt, 66 Wis. 22; s. c., 28 N. W. Rep. 380; 57 Am. Rep. 257, that where insolvent debtors transferred their entire property by chattel mortgages and made assignments to certain of their creditors, with intent that one of such creditors for himself, and as agent of and trustee for the others, should take immediate possession and convert such property into money and divide the same *pro rata* among such favored creditors, such conveyances were in effect a general assignment with preferences which is void as to the other creditors. See Shirly v. Teal, 67 Ala. 449; Box v. Goodbar, 54 Ark. 6; 18 S. W. Rep. 925; Watts v. Eufaula Nat. Bank, 76 Ala. 474; Hoey v. Pierron, 67 Wis. 262; s. c., 30 N. W. Rep. 692. See Foreman v. Burnette, 83 Tex. 396; 18 S. W. Rep. 756; Bank of Montreal v. Salt & Lumber Co., 90 Mich. 345; 50 N. W. Rep. 512; Warren v. Dwyer, 91 Mich. 414; 51 N. W. Rep. 1062.

[1] 16 Pet. 106.

[2] 4 N. Y. 211. Gardner, J., speaking of the assignment in this case, observes as follows: "The conveyance, whatever may be its form, is in effect a mortgage of the property transferred. A trust as to the surplus results from the nature of the security, and is not the object, or one of the objects, of the assignment. Whether expressed in the instrument or left to implication is immaterial. The assignee does not acquire the legal and equitable interest in the property conveyed, subject to the trust, but a specific lien upon it." Id. 216.

[3] 15 N. Y. (1 Smith), 9.

[4] Brown, J., id. 143. Paige, J., id. 206, 207. Comstock, J., seems to have taken a different view. Id. 126.

[5] 21 N. Y. 574; s. c., 20 N. Y. 15.

[6] Bloom v. Noggle, 4 Ohio St. 45; Harkrader v. Leiby, id. 602.

[7] Brown v. Webb, 20 Ohio (Lawr.), 389.

and mortgagees has been declared in several adjudged cases. Thus, in Pennsylvania, mortgages to secure debts have been held not to be within the act of March 24, 1818, requiring deeds of assignment to be recorded within thirty days.[1] In the same state it has been held that a mortgage limited to a trustee, with power to sell for the payment of the debt secured by it, was not a voluntary assignment for the benefit of a creditor or creditors, such as must be recorded within the period prescribed by the statute provided for such a case.[2] In Massachusetts, instruments called bills of sale, but which in reality were mortgages, have been held not to be conveyances in trust for creditors under the statute of 1836, chapter 238.[3] In the same state a mortgage, in the form of a deed with a defeasance, has been held not to be an assignment in trust for creditors.[4] In New Hampshire a mortgage by the debtor of all his property to secure the payment of a part of his debts, leaving others unprovided for, was held to be not an assignment within the meaning of the statute of July 5, 1834, entitled "An act for the equal distribution of property assigned for the benefit of creditors."[5] In Connecticut a mortgage, by a debtor, of real estate to

---

[1] Ridgway v. Stewart, 4 Watts & Serg. 383, 391. The mortgage in this case contained words expressive of a trust, and was held by the court below to be an assignment for the benefit of creditors. But their judgment was, on appeal, reversed; the supreme court (Kennedy, J.) holding that the assignments required by the act of 1818 to be recorded were those *absolute* transfers made by debtors in embarrassed or insolvent circumstances of their estates to trustees for the benefit of their creditors, that is, for the purpose of being turned into money, and applied by the trustee to the payment of the debts owing by the assignors. See Lill v. Brant, 6 Ill. App. (Bradw.) 366; Stiles v. Hill, 62 Tex. 429; Martin v. Hauseman, 14 Fed. Rep. 160; Carter v. Rewry, 62 Wis. 552.

[2] Manufacturers' & Mechanics' Bank v. Bank of Pennsylvania, 7 Watts & Serg. 335. The conveyance in this case was contended to be not a mortgage, but an assignment in trust to pay a particular creditor. But the court observed: "It is clearly a mortgage limited to a trustee in fee with a power to sell, and the statute has regard not to a conditional conveyance which may revest the property in the debtor, but to an absolute assignment to sell and pay at all events." Gibson, C. J., id. 343. In Johnson's Appeal, 103 Pa. St. 373, it was held that no particular form of words is necessary to constitute an assignment under the statute of June 14, 1836, but the transaction must be in substance an absolute transfer of property by the assignor in trust for the benefit of creditors. A mortgage executed by the assignor to a trustee for creditors in consideration of an extension of time for the payment of the assignee's debts, being a mere security, cannot be treated as an assignment for the benefit of creditors under said act. A mortgage was distinguished from a trust deed in the case of Hewitt v. Hullins, 11 Pa. St. 27. See, also, McBroom & Wood's Appeal, 44 id. 92; Vallance v. Miners' Life Ins. Co., 42 id. 441; Diesbach v. Becker, 34 id. 152; Claflin v. Maglaughlin, 65 id. 492.

[3] Henshaw v. Sumner, 23 Pick. 446.

[4] Marden v. Babcock, 2 Metc. 99.

[5] Barker v. Hall, 13 N. H. 298. And see Low v. Wyman, 8 id. 536; Danford v. Denny, 25 id. 155.

certain creditors, to secure them for indorsements, was held to be neither an assignment nor a conveyance, nor in trust for creditors, within the meaning of the statute of 1828.[1] In Vermont a transfer by a debtor of all his property directly to certain creditors for their benefit was held to be not a general assignment in trust, under the act of November 1, 1843, but a mortgage or pledge of the property.[2] In Georgia a mortgage given to secure a just debt was recently held to be not within the statute of 1838 "to prevent assignments," etc.[3] In Iowa it is held to be a question of the intention of the parties whether a conveyance by an insolvent is to be regarded as an assignment or a mortgage.[4] In Virginia, where a conveyance of real estate was made to a creditor in trust to satisfy his own demand, it was held that such a conveyance was not to be considered as a deed of trust, but as a mortgage, to which the right of redemption was incident.[5] And in a case in the court of chancery of New York[6] a voluntary assignment was distinguished both from a sale to a creditor and a pledge of property in the nature of a mortgage.[7]

In Ohio a mortgage given to a creditor to secure the debt of any other creditor besides himself has been held to be an assignment within the provisions of the act of 1838 relating to assignments by insolvent debtors, and the mortgagee to be a trustee for

---

[1] Bates v. Coe, 10 Conn. 280.

[2] Peck v. Merrill, 26 Vt. 686; McGregor v. Chase, 37 id. 225. See Gage v. Chesebro, 49 Wis. 486, where an instrument is held to be a chattel mortgage rather than an assignment; and Dessar v. Field, 99 Ind. 548; Jaffray v. Greenbaum, 64 Iowa, 492.

[3] Lavender v. Thomas, 18 Ga. 668, 675, and cases cited ibid.; Solomon v. Sparks, 27 Ga. 385. See Code of Ga. (1873). § 1954.

[4] Cadwell's Bank v. Crittenden, 66 Iowa, 237. In this case the defendant had for some time been promised security by the debtor. Just after the burning of the debtor's store the defendant, for no consideration paid, but only as trustee, took from some of the other creditors an assignment of their claims against the debtor, and then applied to him for security, not only for his own claims but also for the claims which he thus held in trust. Thereupon the debtor executed to the defendant a bill of sale covering all his property. It was at the same time orally agreed that if any proceeds of the property remained after satisfying the claims thus held by the defendant, it should be paid back to the debtor. It was held that the instrument was intended as a mortgage only and should be treated as such, and not as an assignment for the benefit of creditors. See, also, Wheeler v. Kerkendall, 67 Iowa, 602; Kohn v. Clement, 58 Iowa, 589.

[5] Showning v. Cox, 1 Rand. 306.

[6] Dias v. Bouchaud, 10 Paige, 445, 448, 461. And see Briggs v. Davis, 21 N. Y. 574; S. C., 20 N. Y. 15; Dunham v. Whitehead, 21 N. Y. 131; McClelland v. Remsen, 3 Abb. Dec. (N. Y.) 74; Van Buskirk v. Warren, 4 id. 457.

[7] In the case of Perry Ins. Co. v. Foster, 58 Ala. 502, a conveyance with resulting trust to the grantors was held to be technically an assignment and the text cited. And see Crawford v. Kirksey, 55 id. 282; Shirley v. Teale, 67 id. 449; Danner v. Brewer, 69 id. 191; Otis v. Maguire, 76 id. 295.

all the creditors.¹ In the same state a chattel mortgage executed in contemplation of insolvency to a particular creditor, for the purpose of preferring him, was held to be an assignment of property in trust, and the mortgagee was deemed a trustee for all the creditors.²

In Michigan three consecutive chattel mortgages made to secure existing debts were held to be not an assignment.³ So in Mississippi a conveyance by an officer to a trustee to indemnify his sureties against any possible loss on an official bond, though embracing all the grantor's property, was held to be not an assignment but a mortgage.⁴ In Montana it was held that where the effect of an instrument conveying personal property was to transfer the debtor's property to a creditor, with power to make an immediate sale of the same and render the overplus, after satisfying the debt therein described, to the debtor, which debt was made due at once, the transaction, though under the form and name of a chattel mortgage, will be regarded as an assignment.⁵ In Wisconsin three mortgages of debtor's stock of goods, to secure three several claims, were executed on the same day and delivered to the attorney of the mortgagees; and on the next day the goods were turned over to said attorney, either in satisfaction of all the mortgages or in payment of the claim of the third mortgagee with the understanding that he would pay the two prior mortgages; held that in either case, as no trustee was appointed or trust created, the transaction did not constitute an assignment for the benefit of creditors within the meaning of section 1694, Revised Statutes.⁶

§ 8. **Distinguished from Deeds of Trust in the Nature of Mortgage.**— Still more similar in form are deeds of trust to secure the payment of particular debts.⁷ Such instruments are, both in law and equity, substantially the same as mortgages, and the radical distinction between them and assignments for the benefit of

¹ Bloom v. Noggle, 4 Ohio St. 45; Hardraker v. Leiby, id. 602.
² Brown v. Webb, 20 Ohio (Lawr.), 389.
³ Sheldon v. Mann, 85 Mich. 265; 48 N. W. Rep. 573. See Maxwell v. Simonton, 81 Wis. 635; 51 N. W. Rep. 869.
⁴ State v. Hemingway, 69 Miss. 491.
⁵ Marshall v. Livingston Nat. Bank, 11 Mont. 351; 28 Pac. Rep. 312.
⁶ Michelstetter v. Weiner, 82 Wis. 298. In the case of Warner v. Littlefield, 89 Mich. 329; 50 N. W. Rep. 721, it was held that the question whether the instrument is a chattel mortgage or an assignment for the benefit of creditors must in all cases be determined as a question of law upon the contents of such instrument and not upon any outside testimony; and unless the conveyance upon its face purports to convey *all* the debtor's property to secure certain preferred creditors by an absolute title, the court is not at liberty to declare it a common-law assignment, but such outside testimony must be submitted to the jury.
⁷ Perry on Trusts, 602 *et seq.*

creditors consists, as in the case of mortgages, in the equitable interest which the grantor still retains in the assigned property.[1] Frequently, especially in the southern states, assignments for the benefit of creditors are referred to under the designation of deeds of trust. In most of these states, indeed, assignments in trust are frequently employed for a double purpose — ultimately, as modes of provision for the *payment* of debts, but intermediately, as instruments of *security* against default of payment by the debtor.[2] Hence they are, in many cases, drawn with a condition that, if the grantor pay the debt provided for within a specified time, the trustee shall reconvey to him the property,[3] or that the deed shall thereupon be void;[4] or *e converso*, that if the debtor do not pay the debt by a day named (called the "law day"),[5] the trustee shall sell the property and apply the proceeds in payment.[6] And special deeds of trust with such conditions are frequently made directly and exclusively to particular creditors, which gives them still more of the character of a mortgage.[7] They are, in fact, mortgages with the qualities of an assignment in trust superadded, or assignments to take effect at a future day.[8] The chief distinction

[1] Wilson v. Russell, 13 Md. 495; Fouke v. Fleming, 13 id. 392; Sanderson v. Stockdale, 11 id. 573; Pettie v. Johnson, 15 Ark. 60. But see Hannah v. Carrington, 18 Ark. 85; Lyons v. Field, 17 B. Mon. (Ky.) 543.

[2] They are called "deeds to secure the payment of money," in Stine v. Wilson, 10 Miss. 75.

[3] Hafner v. Irwin, 1 Ired. L. 490.

[4] Billups v. Sears, 5 Gratt. 31; Reynolds v. The Bank of Virginia, 6 id. 174; Cornish v. Dews, 18 Ark. 172.

[5] Lanier v. Driver, 24 Ala. 149. See Bates v. Coe, 10 Conn. 280.

[6] Hill v. Manser, 11 Gratt. 522; Farmers' Bank v. Douglas, 11 Smed. & M. 469; Hopkins v. Lacontre, 4 La. 64; Elmes v. Sutherland, 7 Ala. 262; and see Warren v. Lee, 32 id. 440; Magee v. Carpenter, 4 id. 469; Hemphill, J., in Crosby v. Huston, 1 Tex. 203, 241, 242; but see Dwight v. Overton, 25 Tex. 39. The text is quoted with approval in Crow v. Beardsley, 68 Mo. 435, 438, where it is said that the distinction is that an assignment is a conveyance to a trustee for the purpose of raising funds to pay a debt, while a deed of trust in the nature of a mortgage is a conveyance in trust for the purpose of securing a debt, subject to a condition of defeasance.

[7] Burgin v. Burgin, 1 Ired. L. 453; Harris v. De Graffenreid, 11 id. 89.

[8] See the observations of Pearson, J., in Stimpson v. Fries, 2 Jones' Eq. 156. These instruments, however, are not exclusively peculiar to the southern states. In Hendricks v. Robinson, 2 Johns. Ch. 283, the assignments, which were directly to certain creditors, had a proviso that, if the debts and engagements secured by them were paid within a certain time, the assignments should be void; otherwise the assignees were to sell the property and apply the proceeds. And in an English case in the court of bankruptcy, the assignment, which was of all the trader's property, directly to a creditor, contained a similar proviso, with a further stipulation that, until default in payment, the assignor should retain possession of the property assigned. Deeds of this character are spoken of by the court, in this case, as being "now of very frequent occurrence," but as seeming to have a tendency "directly opposed to the spirit and policy of the

between assignments and trust deeds in the nature of mortgage exists in the equitable interest which the grantor in a trust deed still retains in the assigned property; a defeasible title only passes to the assignee, while a general assignment for the benefit of creditors is an absolute conveyance.[1]

bankrupt laws." Ex parte Harvey, In re Collins, 1 Bankr. & Insolv. R. 194, 197. In the Ohio case of Hoffman v. Mackall, 5 Ohio St. 124, an assignment or unconditional deed of trust was distinguished from a deed of trust in the nature of a mortgage in the following terms: "There is a manifest and well-settled distinction between an *unconditional deed of trust* and a *mortgage* or *deed of trust in the nature of a mortgage*. The former is an *absolute* and *indefeasible* conveyance of the subject-matter thereof, for the purpose expressed; whereas the latter is *conditional* and *defeasible*. A mortgage is the conveyance of an estate, or pledge of property, as security for the payment of money or the performance of some other act, and conditioned to become void upon such payment or performance. A deed of trust *in the nature of a mortgage* is a conveyance in trust *by way of security*, subject to a condition of defeasance, or redeemable at any time before the sale of the property. A deed conveying land to a trustee as mere collateral *security* for the payment of a debt, with the condition that it shall become void on the payment of the debt when due, and with power to the trustee to sell the land and pay the debt in case of default on the part of the debtor, is *a deed of trust in the nature of a mortgage*. By an absolute deed of trust the grantor parts *absolutely* with the title, which vests in the grantee unconditionally for the purpose of the trust. The latter is a conveyance to a trustee for the purpose of *raising a fund to pay debts*, while the former is a conveyance in trust for the purpose of *securing a debt* subject to a condition of defeasance." Woodruff v. Robb et al., 19 Ohio St. 216; 1 Hilliard on Mortgages, 359. The court accordingly held (Bartley, J.), in this case, that "where the grantor in a deed of trust makes it in contemplation of insolvency, and authorizes the grantee, after paying the expenses of the trust, to make a *pro rata* distribution of the proceeds of the trust property among the grantor's creditors, such deed is absolute, and the conveyance is to a trustee for the purpose of raising a fund with which to *pay debts*, as distinguished from a deed of trust in the nature of a mortgage to *secure debts*."

In De Wolf v. Sprague Mfg. Co., 49 Conn. 282, the conveyance was to a trustee to secure the payment of certain notes of one of the grantors; it was to be void if the grantors should pay the notes according to their tenor and the expenses of the trust, and it empowered the trustee to sell the property and apply the proceeds to the payment of the notes, paying over the surplus to the grantors. This was held to be a deed of trust in the nature of a mortgage and not a voluntary assignment.

[1] Comer v. Constantine, 86 Ala. 402; 5 So. Rep. 773; Hargdime v. Henderson, 97 Mo. 375; 11 S. W. Rep. 218; In re Assignment of Zwang, 39 Mo. App. 356; Mills v. Williams, 31 id. 447.

CHAPTER II.

THE RIGHT TO ASSIGN—STATUTORY PROVISIONS RESTRICTING THE RIGHT TO ASSIGN AND REGULATING THE OPERATION OF ASSIGNMENTS.

§ 9. Debtor's Right to Assign.
10. Fraudulent Conveyances — Bankrupt Law.
11. Fraudulent Conveyances.
12. Classification of Assignments — Special or Partial Assignments.
13. General Assignments.
14. State Statutes.

§ 9. Debtor's Right to Assign.—"It would seem," observes Mr. Chief Justice Marshall,[1] "to be a consequence of that absolute power which a man possesses over his own property that he may make any disposition of it which does not interfere with the existing rights of others; and such disposition of it, if it be fair and real, will be valid. The limitations on this power are those only which are prescribed by law." The right to transfer is a necessary incident to the right of property itself, and rests on the same foundation with the absolute rights to acquire and enjoy;[2] and its exercise, where the subject of it is free from the claims of others, is placed under no other restriction than such as the general policy of the law has imposed.

Where, however, property has become subject to the rights and claims of others, and particularly where the relation of *debtor and creditor* has been created, it becomes just and reasonable that the general power of disposition should be so far restricted and qualified as that conveyances and assignments by the debtor, especially of the whole or greater part of his property, should not be employed as a means of preserving it for his own use or benefit, or of unduly protecting it from the remedies of his creditors.

§ 10. Fraudulent Conveyances — Bankrupt Law.— In order to effect this object, two systems have been devised in England and have, from that source, been introduced into the jurisprudence of the United States. The first consists of statutory provisions which simply declare conveyances by debtors in certain cases to be fraudulent and void, and subject the property conveyed to the claims

[1] Sexton v. Wheaton, 8 Wheat. 229, 242.
[2] 2 Kent's Com. [326], 377; Id. [328], 370; 1 Bl. Com. 138.

and remedies of creditors, as if no conveyance had been made, but interfere no further with the debtor's affairs. The other system is a body of regulations under which the whole of a debtor's property is, on the commission of certain defined acts, taken at once out of his hands by the law and disposed of for the general benefit of his creditors. The first of these comprises the provisions of those statutes which are generally known as the *statute of fraudulent conveyances*,[1] and which operate without distinction upon all persons making transfers of property; the second is the system of the *bankrupt laws*, which is more confined in its operation.

The effect of the bankruptcy laws upon the right to assign property for the benefit of creditors will be considered in a subsequent chapter.

§ 11. **Fraudulent Conveyances.**—The statutory provisions against fraudulent conveyances commenced in England as early as the reign of Edward III.,[2] but were not fully matured until the time of Queen Elizabeth, in whose reign two statutes were passed — the 13 Eliz., ch. 5, and 27 Eliz., ch. 4 — the former relating to creditors only, the latter to purchasers. The provisions of the 13 Eliz., ch. 5, to which we shall confine ourselves, and which is still in force in England, have been generally adopted throughout the United States.[3] These provisions have been considered by the highest authority[4] to be only declaratory of the common law, which, in the opinion of Lord Mansfield,[5] was so strong against fraud that it alone would have attained every end proposed by the statutes themselves. More will be said on this subject in another place.[6]

§ 12. **Classification of Assignments — Special or Partial Assignments.**— In tracing the history of the practice of assignments by debtors, we find that they are, for the most part, reducible

---

[1] Sometimes, though not with strict accuracy, called *statutes of frauds*.

[2] Stat. 50 Edw. III., ch. 6, Crabb's Hist. Eng. Law (Am. ed. 1831), 274; Stat. 3 Hen. VII., ch. 4, Crabb's Hist. 440; 2 Kent's Com. [440], 547. And see *post*, ch. XXV.

[3] 2 Kent's Com. [440], 548; 4 id. [463], 510; 1 Story's Eq. Jur., § 353. See Hamilton v. Russell, 1 Cranch, 309.

[4] Co. Litt. 76a, 290b; Lord Mansfield, in Cadogan v. Kennett, Cowp. 432, 434; Marshall, C. J., in Hamilton v. Russell, 1 Cranch, 309, 316; Story, J., in Meeker v. Wilson, 1 Gall. 419, 423; Spencer, J., in Sands v. Hildreth, 14 Johns. 493, 498; 2 Kent's Com. [440], 548, note; Garland, J., in The United States v. The Bank of the United States, 8 Rob. (La.) 262, 402.

[5] Cadogan v. Kennett, Cowp. 434e.

[6] For the statute in full, and also the statutes of the various states, see Bump on Fraudulent Conveyances, Appendix, pp. 583 *et seq.*; Roberts on Fraudulent Conveyances, pp. 2, 3. And see *post*, ch. XXV. The recent work of Mr. Wait on Fraudulent Conveyances contains much valuable information on the subject.

§ 12.] CLASSIFICATION OF ASSIGNMENTS. 21

under three principal divisions: first, transfers of some *specific* article, or one or more descriptions of property, directly to some favored creditor, and for his exclusive benefit; secondly, transfers of *all* or the greater part of the debtor's property to one or more *preferred* creditors, either directly or through the medium of a trust; and thirdly, transfers by formal deeds of trust of *all* the debtor's property, for the benefit of *all* his creditors. All these descriptions of transfers have, at one time or other, been made the subjects of judicial investigation, and have been construed, by the courts in England and the United States, with reference either to the statutes against fraudulent conveyances or to the bankrupt laws, and, in some cases, with reference to both.

Assignments of the first description just mentioned, by which a debtor transfers some specific article of property, or some part of his effects, to one or more creditors, by deed or by mere delivery, and in the way of payment or security when made by persons in solvent circumstances, and in a course of trade or dealing, are in the nature of ordinary business transactions and rarely give rise to questions of any kind. Where, however, the obligations of the debtor are large and the portion of his means thus specially appropriated is considerable, and the rights of other creditors become thereby affected, and especially where the transaction is inconsistent with the prosecution of his business, or is expressly done with reference to or in contemplation of suspension, failure or bankruptcy, questions frequently arise as to the validity of these special or partial assignments. In England they have most commonly been tested by the bankrupt laws, under which they have in some cases been upheld, but more frequently avoided, as giving undue or fraudulent preferences, contrary to the spirit and policy of that peculiar system. The same rules have, for the most part, been adopted in the United States in cases which have arisen under our bankrupt laws.[1]

In cases not within the bankrupt laws, these *special* or *partial* assignments have been construed by the English courts with ref-

[1] Under the bankrupt law (section 5128), in order to render a transfer void, it was necessary that certain facts occur. The debtor must be insolvent, the transfer must be made with a view to give a preference to the creditor, the creditor must have reasonable cause to believe the person making the transfer to be insolvent, and that it was in fraud of the bankrupt act, and the transfer must have been made within four (in cases of involuntary or compulsory bankruptcy, two, [section 5131*a*]) months before the filing of the petition by or against the bankrupt. Bump on Bankruptcy (8th ed.), 792 *et seq*. and cases cited; Clark *v.* Iselin, 11 N. B. R. 337; Kohlsaat v. Hoguet, 5 N. B. R. 159. See Mays v. Fritton, 11 N. B. R. 229; s. c., 20 Wall. 414. As to preference under the bankrupt acts of 1800 and 1841, see Ogden v. Jackson, 1 Johns. 370, 373; Locke v. Winning, 3 Mass. 325; Freeman v. Deming, 3 Sandf. Ch. 327; McAllister v. Richards, 6 Barr, 133; 2 Kent's Com. [532], 688; Jones v. Sleeper, 2 N. Y. Leg. Obs. 131.

erence to the common law, or the statute of fraudulent conveyances; and under these they have been more frequently sustained.[1] And in the United States, assignments of this class, made directly to particular creditors where no bankrupt law was in force, have been in many instances declared valid;[2] and even in those states where preferences in general assignments have been expressly prohibited by statute, the prohibition has been held not to extend to transfers of particular portions of a debtor's property, directly to a creditor in payment of a debt.[3]

§ 13. **General Assignments.**— Assignments of the second and third descriptions above mentioned (and which may be distinguished as *general* assignments),[4] by which all or substantially all the debtor's property is appropriated for the benefit either of one or more preferred creditors, or of the creditors at large, comprise such as are made by debtors in declining or insolvent circumstances; and whenever brought within the application of the bankrupt laws have almost uniformly been condemned by the English courts, on the ground of their inconsistency with the provisions or policy of those laws and their tendency to defeat their leading objects.[5]

In cases not within the English bankrupt laws, assignments of all a debtor's property, whether in favor of particular creditors or of all the creditors, have frequently been held valid.[6]

[1] Holbird v. Anderson, 5 Term R. 235; Estwick v. Caillaud, id. 420.

[2] Seymour v. Wilson, 19 N. Y. 417; Towsley v. McDonald, 32 Barb. 604; McMahon v. Morrison, 16 Ind. 172; Hessing v. McCloskey, 37 Ill. 341. In the case of Archer v. O'Brien, 7 Hun, 146, Mr. Justice Brady states the rule as follows:

"The creditor, when he discovers circumstances which would put a prudent man on inquiry, should, in the preservation of his own rights, seek the payment of his debt, the protection of his own property. Such a course is not only consistent with honesty, but is a duty which he owes to himself, the observation of which is sanctioned by the rules of law authorizing the preference which he obtains."

"To constitute a valid transfer by a debtor to his creditor, it is only necessary that three things should concur:

"1. That there was a valid subsisting indebtedness on the part of the vendor or assignor to him.

"2. That the property transferred was conveyed to secure the debt.

"3. That it was reduced to possession."

[3] The New York County Bank v. Carter, 38 Pa. St. 446; Tillou v. Britton, 4 Halst. 120; Meredith Man. Co. v. Smith, 8 N. H. 357; Brown v. Foster, 2 Metc. 152; Eastman v. McAlpin, 1 Kelly, 157; Blakey's Appeal, 7 Barr, 449; Wilcox v. Kellogg, 11 Ohio, 394. See *post*, ch. XI. Dessar v. Field, 99 Ind. 548; Boling v. Howell, 93 id. 329; Tomlinson v. Matthews, 98 Ill. 178; Carter v. Rewey, 62 Wis. 552; 22 N. W. Rep. 129; Rothell v. Grimes, 22 Neb. 526; 35 N. W. Rep. 392.

[4] As to what are general assignments, see *post*, ch. VIII.

[5] See *post*, ch. III.

[6] Ingliss v. Grant, 5 Term R. 530; Nunn v. Wilsmore, 3 id. 521; Goss v. Neale,

The general power to assign property in trust, in behalf and for the benefit of creditors, has always been recognized and approved in the fullest manner, both by the state and federal courts, as well as by the most eminent American jurists.[1] The only checks and restrictions for a long time imposed on the exercise of this power, were the general ones afforded by the provisions of the statutes of fraudulent conveyances, and the exercise of the equity powers of courts in setting aside assignments on the ground of fraud. And even these checks and restrictions were not always rigorously applied in practice. The right to prefer one creditor over another in these conveyances, by priority of payment, which amounted in many cases to the absolute exclusion of a non-preferred creditor, was universally recognized;[2] and the debtor was usually allowed a large discretion in prescribing the terms upon which such prefer-

5 J. B. Moore, 19; Meux v. Howell, 4 East, 1; Pickstock v. Lyster, 3 M. & S. 371; approved in James v. Whitbread, 20 L. J. Rep. (N. S.) C. P. 217.

[1] "Every debtor has a legal right to assign property for the security of the debts due by him, and so far from such an act being reprehended by the law, it is justified and approved." Story, J., in Brown v. Minturn, 2 Gall. 557, 559. General assignments are spoken of by the same judge as "encouraged by the common law." Halsey v. Whitney, 4 Mason, 206, 210. See, also, Bascom v. Rainwater, 30 Mo. App. 483; Bryce v. Foot, 25 S. C. 467; Hanselt v. Vilmar, 76 N. Y. 630; Barton v. Brent, 87 Va. 385; 13 S. E. Rep. 29; Hyde v. Weitzner, 45 Minn. 35. "A conveyance in trust to pay debts is a valid conveyance founded on a good consideration." Kent, C., in Dey v. Dunham, 2 Johns. Ch. 182, 189. "It is settled that an insolvent debtor may at any time before his property becomes bound by any lien assign it over to trustees for the benefit of all his creditors by an act made *bona fide*. The assignment is to be referred to an act of duty, attached to his character of debtor, to make the fund available for the whole body of the creditors." Kent, C., in Nicoll v. Mumford, 4 Johns. Ch. 522, 529. "The right of an insolvent debtor to make an assignment for the benefit of his creditors, before the property is bound by any lien, does not admit of question, provided it be *bona fide*." 2 Tucker's Com. [443], 432. "The right to make a general assignment of all a man's property results from that absolute ownership which every man claims over that which is his own." Marshall, C. J., in Brashear v. West, 7 Pet. 608, 614. Garland, J., in The United States v. The Bank of the United States, 8 Rob. (La.) 262, 404: "I think that where an assignment is for the benefit of all the creditors of the assignor equally and ratably, it must command the sanction of every enlightened tribunal. It is a practical enforcement of the maxim that equality is equity." Buckner, C., in Robins v. Embry, 1 Sm. & Marsh. Ch. 207, 258. See Malcolm v. Hall, 9 Gill, 177. And see the opinion of Bennett, J., in Hall v. Denison, 17 Vt. 310; and Ewing J., in Vernon v. Morton, 8 Dana, 247, 251. Mr. Justice Field, in Mayer v. Hellman, 13 N. B. R. 440: "Whenever such a disposition has been voluntarily made by the debtor, the courts in this country have uniformly expressed their approbation of the proceedings." Mr. Justice Buchanan, in The State v. The Bank of Maryland, 6 Gill & Johns. 217: "Equality is equity, and when a debtor makes a transfer of his property for the fair purpose of equal distribution among his creditors, he does an honest act and discharges a moral duty." See Kalkman v. McEldeny, 16 Md. 60. Mr. Justice Bailey, in Hoffman v. Mackall, 5 Ohio St. 124; Forbes v. Scannell, 13 Cal. 242.

[2] The text is quoted with approval in Crawford v. Kirksey, 55 Ala. 282.

ence, or indeed any benefit of the assignment, should be enjoyed. The same liberality was extended to the execution of the trust, after its creation by the debtor; the powers of assignees not being very rigidly limited, nor their duties very carefully defined. The whole transfer, in short, was in many cases a private transaction between the debtor and the assignee, with little of the notoriety which its avowed object would seem to require; and in its effect has, not inaptly, been characterized as "a bankrupt law made by the debtor for himself."[1] The evils growing out of this system of assignment were occasionally noticed by the courts, and the increasing abuses of the power with which it armed the debtor were at length strongly exposed in some able judicial opinions.

§ 14. **State Statutes.**— The attempt to correct these abuses has led in many states to the enactment of statutory regulations limiting, on the one hand, the debtor's power in creating these trusts, and defining, on the other, the duties of assignees in executing them; and at the same time giving to creditors a more effectual power of inspection and control over the acts and proceedings of both. It is obvious, from what has been said, that the power to make such assignments is not dependent upon these statutory provisions.[2] Assignments for the benefit of creditors are voluntary on the part of the debtor. No authority can exact them; and when made, they partake of the nature of a private contract. The assignee derives his authority entirely from the grantor, and the appointment carries with it an actual and not merely a theoretical trust and confidence. The assignee is the choice of the debtor to whom to intrust his property and his relations with his creditors. Under this view of the relation, we should not expect the legislature to go further than to regulate, direct and secure a performance of the trust.[3]

[1] Gibson, C. J., in Thomas v. Jenks, 5 Rawle, 221.
[2] Mr. Justice Sharswood, in Beck v. Parker, 65 Pa. St. 262; Cook v. Rogers, 13 N. B. R. 97; Bentley v. Thrasher, 59 N. Y. 649; s. c., 2 Supm. Ct. (T. & C.) 309; Dehner v. Helmbacher Mills, 7 Ill. App. (Brad.) 47. The right to assign existed at common law, and is not derived from any statute. Weider v. Maddox, 66 Tex. 372; 1 S. W. Rep. 168; 59 Am. Rep. 617. See King v. Glass, 73 Iowa, 205; 34 N. W. Rep. 820; Barton v. Brent, 87 Pa. 385: 13 S. E. Rep. 29; Pillsbury v. Kingon, 31 N. J. Eq. 624; Holmberg v. Dean, 21 Kan. 74.
[3] Drain v. Mickel, 8 Iowa, 438. For a digest of the statutes of the several states and territories relative to assignments, see Appendix I.

CHAPTER III.

VOLUNTARY ASSIGNMENTS CONSIDERED IN CONNECTION WITH THE BANKRUPT LAW.

§ 15. The Common Law.
16. English Statutes.
17. English Statutes — Continued.
18. English Statutes — Continued.
19. The English Doctrine.
20. Assignments with Preferences.
21. Assignments for Equal Benefit of Creditors.
22. Assignments for Equal Benefit of Creditors — English Statutes.
23. Exemption of Assignments from Operation of Act.
24. General Grounds of English Rule.
25. United States Bankrupt Acts of 1800 and 1841.
26. Provisions of the Act of 1867 Applicable to General Assignments.
27. The Power to Assign Not Suspended by Bankrupt Laws.
28. Assignments Fraudulent at Common Law, or Under 13 Eliz., or Giving Preferences.
29. Is the Making of a *Bona Fide* Assignment for Creditors Ratably an Act of Bankruptcy.
30. Cases.
31. Duty of Insolvent.
32. Insolvency and Assignment Under the Act.
33. Assent of Creditors.
34. Assignments Not Void but Voidable in Bankruptcy.
35. Avoiding Assignment by Assignee.
36. Right of Action in Assignee Exclusive.
37. Proceeding Under Voluntary Assignments — When Avoided — Protection of Voluntary Assignee.
38. Allowance of Expenses to Voluntary Assignee.
39. Bar to Discharge.
40. Composition in Bankruptcy and General Assignments.

§ 15. **The Common Law.**— The bankruptcy system introduced by statute into the jurisprudence of England, and derived from the civil law,[1] proceeds upon principles and methods in many respects dissimilar to those of the common law. While the common law rewards the diligence of creditors by distributing the estate of an insolvent debtor amongst them according to the priorities they

---

[1] The early law of Rome gave creditors the savage remedy of dividing the body of their debtor or selling him and his family into slavery. The *Lex Paetelia* (about 326 B. C.) enabled a debtor who could swear to being worth as much as he owed to save his freedom by resigning his property. And many years later the legislation of Julius Cæsar established the *cessio bonorum*, as an available remedy for all honest insolvents. See Institutes Justinian, 4, 6, 40; Sanders' Justinian (Hammond), 541.

obtain in the pursuit of it, the bankruptcy system regards the property of the debtor as of right belonging to the whole body of his creditors, to be distributed ratably among them towards the satisfaction of their claims.[1]

The common law, in the enforcement of its judgments, seizes only so much of the debtor's property as is sufficient to pay in full the individual claim of each creditor as it ripens into execution, but the bankruptcy law on the occasion of certain acts, termed acts of bankruptcy, at once sequestrates the entire estate of the debtor, and places it beyond his control and under a course of distribution in the hands of its own officers and under its own direction.[2] At common law the debtor must satisfy the claims of his creditors to obtain their voluntary releases, if he would be rid of the burden of his liabilities. The humane policy of the bankrupt law discharges the honest debtor from all his obligations, upon compliance with the conditions prescribed by the law for his discharge.[3]

Voluntary assignments for the benefit of creditors manifestly interfere with the operation of each of these systems. Apart from statutory regulations they may be said to be the creatures of courts of equity.[4] But although they withdrew the property of the debtor from the legal pursuit of creditors, they are not, when honestly made, regarded as in contravention of the common law.[5]

Inasmuch, however, as the method they provide for the payment of the debts of an insolvent is that ordained by the debtor himself, and that method may be at variance with the provisions of the bankruptcy system, they are, whenever brought within the jurisdiction of that system, "subjected to the sharpest scrutiny;"[6] and they have not unfrequently been regarded, even when made for the equal benefit of all creditors, as wholly repugnant to the spirit and provisions of the bankrupt act. A brief review of the bankruptcy legislation as affecting voluntary assignments is essential to a clear apprehension of the questions which have arisen under the administration of the bankrupt law.

§ 16. **English Statutes.**— The first introduction of a bankrupt law in England was by the statutes of 34 and 35 Hen. VIII., ch. 4.[7] This statute was very imperfect. It empowered the lord chancel-

[1] Robson's Law of Bankruptcy (2d ed.), p. 1.
[2] McClure v. Campbell, 71 Wis. 350.
[3] After the bankrupt's debts are paid the original title of the surplus reverts to him by operation of law. Saunders v. Mitchell, 61 Miss. 321.
[4] Carlton v. Baldwin, 22 Tex. 724.
[5] See *ante*, p. 24. Lord Ellenborough, in Pickstock v. Lyster, 3 M. & S. 372.
[6] Mr. Justice Swain, in Farren v. Crawford, 2 N. B. R. 602.
[7] 2 Bl. Com. 474.

lor and other high officers, upon petition of a creditor, to seize and distribute the estates of bankrupts ratably among their creditors. But the grounds of the application were confined within no definite limits.[1] This statute was enlarged[2] and almost totally altered by 13 Eliz., ch. 7. By the statute of Elizabeth the law of bankruptcy was restricted to traders, and certain acts of bankruptcy were prescribed, upon the commission of which a trader became liable to be adjudged bankrupt. But it does not appear that a voluntary assignment for creditors, or that even fraudulent conveyances, such as those included within the statute of fraudulent conveyances[3] enacted in the same year, were regarded as acts of bankruptcy. The statute of 1 Jac. I., ch. 15, sec. 2, made it an act of bankruptcy for a debtor to "make, or cause to be made, any fraudulent grant or conveyance of his, her or their lands, tenements, goods or chattels, to the intent or whereby his, her or their creditors, being subjects born as aforesaid, shall, or may be, defeated or delayed for the recovery of their just and true debts."[4]

Numerous statutes[5] relating to bankruptcy were thereafter from time to time enacted, the most important of which were 21 Jac. I., ch. 19, and 5 Geo. II., ch. 30. By the latter statute the creditors were empowered for the first time to make choice of an assignee.

§ 17. **English Statutes — Continued.**— All these statutes were repealed by that of 6 Geo. IV., ch. 16, which consolidated the different regulations on this subject into one act. In this act the language in reference to fraudulent conveyances was changed, and it was made an act of bankruptcy for a debtor to make, or cause to be made, any fraudulent gift, delivery or transfer of any of his goods or chattels with intent to defeat or delay his creditors in the recovery of their debts.[6] This language remained substantially unaltered in the English bankrupt acts down to 1869, when the words "with the intent to defeat and delay," etc., were omitted.

By the act of Geo. IV. an important exception was made in favor of conveyances of all a debtor's property to a trustee for the benefit

---

[1] This statute was, as we learn from the preamble, directed against debtors "who, craftily obtaining into their hands great substance of other men's goods, do suddenly flee to parts unknown, or keep their houses, not minding to pay, or return to pay, any of their creditors their debts and duties, but at their own will and pleasure consume the substance obtained by credit from other men for their own pleasure and delicate living, against all reason, equity and good conscience."
[2] Sir J. Jekyll, in Small v. Oudley, 3 P. Wms. 427.
[3] 13 Eliz., ch. 5.
[4] Mr. Justice Cadwalader, in Barnes v. Rettew, 8 Phila. 135.
[5] Bl. Com. 474. No provision was made for the discharge of the bankrupt from his debts until 4 Anne, ch. 17, § 10; Ibid., ch. 15.
[6] Mr. Justice Cadwalader, in Barnes v. Rettew, 8 Phila. 135.

of all his creditors. By the fourth section of this act, such a conveyance executed in the manner prescribed, by the trustee, duly attested and given publicity by published notice, was declared not to be an act of bankruptcy unless a commission issued within six months thereafter.[1] This act was followed by numerous others,[2] to which no particular allusion is here required.

In the year 1849 a most important statute, known as "the bankrupt law consolidation act, 1849,"[3] was passed for the amendment and consolidation of the bankruptcty laws.

By the sixty-eighth section of that act it was provided that if any trader amenable to the act should execute any conveyance or assignment by deed of all his estate and effects to a trustee or trustees for the benefit of all his creditors, the execution of such deed should not be deemed an act of bankruptcy, unless a petition for an adjudication of bankruptcy should be filed within three months from the execution thereof, provided the deed were executed by the assignee, attested, and notice thereof given as prescribed.[4]

It was further provided by the twenty-fourth section of the act, and the sections immediately following, that deeds of arrangement entered into between a debtor and his creditors, and executed by six-sevenths in number and value of the creditors whose debts amounted to £10 and upwards, should be binding upon all creditors, and provision was made for completing such arrangements.

The construction put upon these provisions by the case of Tetley v. Taylor[5] defeated to a large extent the benefits which were expected to result from deeds of arrangement, by requiring in every case a complete surrender of the entire estate of the debtor, thus destroying one important element in such arrangements, namely, the continuance of the debtor's business.[6]

By the bankrupt act of 1861[7] the bankruptcy system was extended to non-traders as well as traders, and still more liberal provision was made for carrying out amicable arrangements and settlements between debtors and their creditors.

Under the one hundred and ninety-second section of that act, deeds of trust entered into between a debtor and his creditors, or

---

[1] Botcherly v. Lancaster, 3 N. & M. 384; Lord Abinger, in Siebert v. Spooner, 1 M. & W. 714.

[2] 1 & 2 Wm. IV., ch. 56; 2 & 3 Wm. IV., ch. 114; 5 & 6 Wm. IV., ch. 29; 7 & 8 Vict., ch. 70; 7 & 8 Vict., ch. 96; 10 & 11 Vict., ch. 102.

[3] 12 & 13 Vict., ch. 106.

[4] 12 & 13 Vict., ch. 106, § 68; Chitty's Stat., vol. I, p. 277.

[5] 1 El. & Bl. 521; S. C., 21 L. J. Rep. (N. S.) Q. B. 346.

[6] See Lord Chan. Westbury, in Ex parte Morgan, In re Woodhouse, 32 L. J. Rep. Bank. 15.

[7] 24 & 25 Vict., ch. 134.

any of them, or a trustee on their behalf, were declared valid, effectual and binding on all the creditors of such debtor, as if they were parties to it, providing a majority in number, representing three-fourths in value of the creditors of such debtors whose debts, respectively, amounted to £10 and upwards, should assent to or approve of such deed, and provided such deed should be accepted by the assignee, be attested, registered, stamped, and notice thereof given in compliance with the requirements of the act.

§ 18. **English Statutes — Continued.**— No material changes were thereafter made in the English bankruptcy laws as affecting voluntary assignments for the benefit of creditors previous to the date of the passage by congress of the bankrupt act of March 2, 1867. Very important alterations, however, have been effected in the English system by the bankruptcy act of 1869.[1] By the sixth section of that act it is expressly declared to be an act of bankruptcy, "that the debtor has, in England or elsewhere, made a conveyance or assignment of his property to a trustee or trustees for the benefit of his creditors generally;" and by the ninety-second section preferences fraudulent in bankruptcy may be avoided by the assignee.

By the bankruptcy act of 1883, an act passed to amend and consolidate the law of bankruptcy, 46 & 47 Vict., ch. 52, the English bankruptcy law was materially changed.[2] The provisions of this act are comprehensive and specific and it repeals as to England the bankruptcy act of 1869, 32 & 33 Vict., ch. 71, the absconding debtors act of 1870, 33 & 34 Vict., ch. 76, and amends the statutes of Westminster the second, Edw. I., ch. 18, the debtors act of 1869, 32 & 33 Vict., ch. 62, the bankruptcy repeal and insolvent court act of 1869, 32 & 33 Vict., ch. 83, the bankruptcy disqualification act of 1871, 34 & 35 Vict., ch. 50, and the supreme court judicature act of 1875, 38 & 39 Vict., ch. 77.

Inasmuch as the existing bankrupt law in this country was modeled largely upon the English statutes of 1849 and 1861, in connection with the insolvent law of Massachusetts,[3] an examination of the construction placed upon the English statutes as affecting voluntary assignments for creditors will not be out of place.

§ 19. **The English Doctrine.**— It should, in the first place, be observed that at no time previous to the act of 1869[4] has any

---
[1] 32 & 33 Vict., ch. 71. This act is said to have been modeled upon the Scotch system as contained in the 19 & 20 Vict., ch. 79. See Robson's Law Bank. (2d ed.), p. 10.
[2] Crook v. Morley, 1 Ap. Ca. 316.
[3] Mr. Justice Cadwalader, in Barnes v. Rettew, 8 Phila. 135.
[4] 32 & 33 Vict. 71, §§ 6, 92.

English statute expressly declared the giving of a preference or the assignment of the whole or any part of a debtor's estate, either directly to creditors or in trust for them, to be an act of bankruptcy or avoidable by an assignee in bankruptcy.

The rules of law relating to these subjects have arisen entirely from judicial construction [1] of the language of the statute of fraudulent conveyances introduced into 1 Jac. I., ch. 15,[2] and retained in a somewhat modified form in 6 Geo. IV., ch. 16,[3] interpreted in the light of the policy and object of the bankruptcy system. The words made use of are, in substance, the same as those employed in the statute of fraudulent conveyances, 13 Eliz., ch. 5, and as construed in the bankruptcy acts have always been understood as comprehending conveyances void at common law or under the statute of 13 Eliz., ch. 5.[4] Their interpretation in the bankrupt law has, however, been greatly extended by the courts.

§ 20. **Assignments with Preferences.**— As early as the year 1758, Lord Mansfield, in the case of Worseley v. De Mattos,[5] very clearly and emphatically announced the doctrine which has ever since been regarded a ssettled law, that a conveyance by an insolvent debtor of his entire estate to a particular creditor is an act of bankruptcy. He said: "An equal distribution among creditors who equally give a general personal credit to the bankrupt is anxiously provided for ever since the act of 21 Jac. I., ch. 19."

The same opinion was expressed by him in the cases of Wilson v. Day,[6] Compton v. Moore,[7] and Hooper v. Smith.[8] Some years later Lord Ellenborough, in the case of Newton v. Chandler,[9] said: "As a general proposition it cannot be disputed that a conveyance by deed by a trader of all his property to a particular creditor in prejudice to the rest is an act of bankruptcy." [10]

[1] The doctrine of fraudulent preference described by Lord Ellenborough as an excrescence on the bankrupt act (2 Camp. 168) is entirely of judicial creation and is generally considered to have been introduced by Lord Mansfield. Alderson v. Temple, 4 Burr. 2235; s. c., 1 W. Bl. 660; Harman v. Fisher, Cowp. 117; Rust v. Cooper, Cowp. 629; Martin v. Pewtress, 4 Burr. 2477; Robson's Law of Bank. (2d ed.) 125.

[2] See *ante*, § 16.
[3] See *ante*, § 17.
[4] Eden on Bankruptcy, p. 17.
[5] 1 Burr. 567.
[6] 1 Burr. 827.
[7] 1 Wm. Bl. 361.
[8] 1 Wm. Bl. 441.
[9] 7 East, 143 (1806); and see Lord Abinger, in Siebert v. Spooner, 1 M. & W. 714; The Oriental Banking Co. v. Coleman, 3 Gif. 11.
[10] See, also, Linden v. Sharpe, 6 M. & G. 875; Siebert v. Spooner, 1 M. & W. 714; Whitwell v. Thompson, 1 Esp. 72; Hutton v. Crutwell, 1 El. & Bl. 15; Lomax v. Buxton, L. R. 6 C. P. 107.

§ 20.]   ASSIGNMENTS WITH PREFERENCES.   31

And the same conclusion is reached where the conveyance is of all a debtor's property except some specified.[1] These decisions appear to have been placed upon two distinct grounds: First, the manifest effect of such conveyances in defeating the great object of the bankrupt law, to wit, an equal distribution of the estate of a debtor; and second, the fact that such conveyances, by divesting a trader of his entire property, render it impossible for him to carry on his trade.

It has sometimes been said that the reason why a conveyance of a debtor's entire estate is an act of bankruptcy is because it amounts to a declaration of insolvency,[2] or, as Lord Mansfield is reported to have said, because it is "an assignment of his solvency."[3] But, clearly, a man may be insolvent without being a bankrupt, and an act which simply amounts to a declaration of insolvency, or which renders a debtor insolvent, is not necessarily an act of bankruptcy. And Lord Mansfield, subsequently admitting this to be the rule of law, observed that the remark above quoted was incorrectly reported, and "that the reason why a man becomes a bankrupt who conveys away all his property is that he thereby becomes totally incapable of trading."[4] We shall have occasion to refer to this topic again.

But where there is a substantial exception out of the debtor's property, such an exception as ought possibly to enable him to carry on his trade with advantage, a conveyance of his property is not necessarily and by force of law, without reference to extrinsic circumstances showing fraud, an act of bankruptcy.[5] And where the conveyance is of the whole property, not merely for an antecedent debt, but also for a present advance of which the debtor really has advantage, and which he can apply to the purchase of stock or otherwise for his use, it is not necessarily and *per se* an act of bankruptcy.[6] It should be further remarked, under the law as it existed previous to 1869, two things were held necessary to constitute a fraudulent preference: first, the transaction was required to be the voluntary and spontaneous act of the debtor from which

---

[1] Pulling v. Tucker, 4 B. & A. 382; Gaynor's Case, cited in Worseley v. De Mattos, 1 Burr. 479; and also in Butcher v. Easto, 1 Doug. 294; and see 2 Cowp. 633.

[2] Worseley v. De Mattos, 1 Burr. 827; Haswell v. Simpson, 1 Doug. 91.

[3] Hooper v. Smith, 1 W. Bl. 441; Compton v. Bedford, id. 362.

[4] See Reporter's Note to Law v. Skinner, 2 W. Bl. 996.

[5] Lomax v. Buxton, L. R. 6 C. P. 107. See Robinson's Law of Bankr. (2d ed.) p. 124, and cases cited.

[6] Whitwell v. Thompson, 1 Esp. 72; Hutton v. Crutwell, 1 El. & Bl. 15; Brittlestone v. Cook, 6 id. 296; s. c., 2 Jur. (N. S.) 758; Harris v. Rickett, 4 H. & W. 1; s. c., 28 L. J. Exch. 197. See, also, Frazer v. Thompson, 5 Jur. (N. S.) 669; also, s. c. on appeal, 4 De G. & J. 659.

the desire to prefer was inferred;[1] and secondly, it was required to be done in contemplation of bankruptcy.[2] It is therefore clear that a general voluntary assignment by an insolvent debtor, permitting preferences, is, and always has been, regarded as an act of bankruptcy, unless it be assented to by all the creditors.

§ 21. **Assignments for Equal Benefit of Creditors.**— Where, however, no preference is given, and the assignment is honestly made for the equal benefit of all the creditors, a more difficult question arises. The English cases have gone to the full extent of declaring such conveyances fraudulent in bankruptcy. "This doctrine," says Lord Henley, "has occasionally met with disapprobation, and the reasons upon which it is founded are by no means satisfactory."[3]

The first case in which the point was judicially determined was Kettle v. Hammond,[4] before Lord Mansfield at *nisi prius*, which was an assignment by a trader to two of his creditors in trust for all the rest. A few years later, in the case of Eckhardt v. Wilson,[5] the general doctrine was considered so clear that it was not argued, and in the early case of Tappenden v. Burgess,[6] Mr. Justice Grose, in delivering the opinion of the court, said: "Here the bankrupts have done an act to divest them of all their property, which by all the cases is an act of bankruptcy." And the court relied upon the authority of Bamford v. Baron.[7] A little later Lord Eldon, in Ex parte Bourne,[8] went somewhat more into the question. He said: "I recollect cases in which it was settled upon a single ground, that an assignment of all the property is an act of bankruptcy, though the direct and immediate object is not to delay but to satisfy the creditors; but it was held that a trader had not a right by deed to place his property under a distribution different from that

---

[1] Brown v. Kempton, 19 L. J. C. P. 169; Edwards v. Glyn, 2 El. & Bl. 20; s. c., 5 Jur. (N. S.) 1397. See, also, Smith v. Timms, 1 H. & C. 849; s. c., 9 Jur. (N. S.) 1285; 32 L. J. Exch. 215; Morgan v. Brundrett, 5 B. & Ad. 296; Pennell v. Heading, 2 F. & F. 744; Graham v. Candy, 3 id. 206; Kennear v. Johnson, 2 F. & F. 753; Davidson v. Robinson, 3 Jur. (N. S.) 791; Bills v. Smith, 34 L. J. Q. B. 68; Robson's Law of Bankr. (2d ed.) p. 127.

[2] Morgan v. Brundrett, 5 B. & Ad. 296; Atkinson v. Brindall, 2 Bing. N. C. 225; Abbot v. Burbage, 2 Scott, 656; Strachan v. Barton, 11 Exch. 647; Gilson v. Boutts, 4 M. & G. 169; s. c., 3 Scott, 229; Gibson v. Muskett, 4 M. & G. 160; s. c., 3 Scott (N. R.), 427; Poland v. Glyn, 4 Bing. 22, n.; Ex parte Simpson, De G. 9; Aldred v. Constable, 4 Q. B. 374; s. c., 7 Jur. 509; Robson's Law of Bankruptcy (2d ed.), p. 128.

[3] Eden on Bankruptcy, p. 28.
[4] Cooke Bank. Law, 100; Eden on Bankruptcy, 29.
[5] 8 Term R. 140.
[6] 4 East, 220 (1803).
[7] 2 Term R. 594.
[8] 16 Ves. 148 (1809).

ordained by the bankrupt law; and it was carried to this extravagant length, that though the assignment was intended for the benefit of all the creditors, including that one, yet it was an act of bankruptcy." In a previous case, Ex parte Richardson,[1] Lord Eldon, without passing upon the question, directly assumed the assignment to be an act of bankruptcy, and in later cases[2] he adhered to the authority by which he had declared himself bound in Ex parte Bourne. The rule thus established has been frequently applied[3] by the British courts, and although attempts have been made on the part of the legislature to relax it,[4] none have fully succeeded,[5] and it has now become an integral part of the English bankrupt law.[6] The reasons adduced in support of this doctrine are substantially as follows:

First, that announced by Lord Eldon, that a debtor has no right to place his property under a distribution different from that ordained by the bankrupt law. This objection lies not against the ultimate distribution effected by the assignment, but against the means employed in effecting it, assuming that the creditors have a legal right in cases of insolvency to the privileges and methods provided by the bankrupt act and to the assistance and protection of the bankrupt court in the distribution of the insolvent's estate.

The second is that advanced by Lord Mansfield, that by such a disposition of his property a trader deprives himself of the power of carrying on his trade.

§ 22. **Assignment for Equal Benefit of Creditors — English Statutes.**— This doctrine, as we have seen, arose from judicial construction of the language of the statute 1 Jac. I., ch. 17.[7] When the words of that statute were altered by 6 Geo. IV., ch. 16, from these, "with intent, or whereby his creditors may be defeated, etc.," to these, "with intent to defeat or delay his creditors, etc.," making the phraseology of the statute conform more nearly to that of 13 Eliz., ch. 5, it was contended, in the case of Stewart v.

---

[1] 14 Ves. 184 (1087).
[2] Ex parte Smith, 1 Ves. & B. 518 (1813); Dutton v. Morrison, 17 Ves. 199; Ex parte Cawkwell, 19 Ves. 234.
[3] Linden v. Sharpe, 6 M. & G. 895; Stewart v. Moody, 1 C., M. & R. 777; Ex parte Wensley, 1 De G., J. & S. 273; Turner v. Hardcastle, 11 C. B. 704; Botcherly v. Lancaster, 3 N. & M. 383; Smith v. Timms, 7 Jur. (N. S.) 1015; Sperritt v. Willows, 13 W. R. 329; Ex parte Zwelchenbart, 3 M., D. & D. 671; Porter v. Walker, 1 M. & G. 686; Smith v. Cannan, 2 El. & Bl. 35.
[4] See Lord Henley, Eden on Bankruptcy, p. 81.
[5] Lord Chan. Westbury, in Ex parte Morgan, In re Woodhouse, 32 L. J. Bank. 15.
[6] Bankrupt Act, 1869, 32 and 33 Vict. 71, § 6.
[7] Mr. Justice Montague Smith, in Lomax v. Buxton, L. R. 6 C. P. 115.

Moody,[1] that though the former act might warrant the construction put upon it in cases where creditors were in fact delayed, though such was not the intention of the parties, yet in the latter act it was open to contend that the intent to defeat or delay the creditors was requisite and material to constitute an act of bankruptcy. To this Baron Parke replied that the latter statute was the same in effect as the former, only more concise, and that the latter act was not intended to alter the former law; and, he adds, "it has been clearly settled that if the necessary consequence of a man's acts is to delay his creditors, he must be taken to intend it;" but this answer hardly meets the force of the contention.

It has been well settled under 12 Eliz., ch. 5, that a general assignment for the equal benefit of all creditors, honestly made, does not delay or defraud creditors within the meaning of that statute,[2] and as a consequence no fraudulent intent on the part of the debtor could be presumed from the execution of such a conveyance. When the language of the bankrupt act, therefore, was made to conform to that of 13 Eliz., ch. 5, why should a fraudulent intent be assumed under the language of the bankrupt act when no such intent could be assumed under similar language in the statute of Elizabeth? No satisfactory answer to this question was then given, nor has any since been suggested.[3]

§ 23. **Exemption of Assignments from Operation of Act.**— The provisions of the acts of 1849 and 1861, protecting general assignments for the benefit of creditors from the operation of those acts, upon compliance with the statutory regulations, have not been considered as altering the law making such assignments fraudulent within the policy of the bankruptcy system, except upon strict compliance with the terms imposed.[4]

[1] 1 C., M. & R. 777.
[2] Pickstock v. Lyster, 3 M. & S. 375. And see *ante*, p. 22.
[3] Lord Justice Melish, in Ex parte Luckes, In re Wood, 36 L. T. Chan. 117, in commenting upon the express reference to voluntary assignments contained in the sixth section of the act of 1869, observes: "Now I agree that the reason why that particular act of bankruptcy has been separated from the act of bankruptcy respecting fraudulent conveyances and transfers, in which it is included in all former acts, is this, that although it was an undoubted rule of law that such a transfer or conveyance was to be deemed to be fraudulent, *yet it was really absurd to call it fraudulent*. It had no taint of fraud at all about it in the great majority of cases, and therefore it was for the sake of making the language of the act rational, and not for the sake of altering the law — for it left the law exactly as it was — that the act of bankruptcy comprised in the first subsection of the sixth section has been separated from the other acts of bankruptcy with which it was formerly joined, namely, from the fraudulent conveyances and transfers, and therefore the words 'with intent to defeat or delay his creditors' have been left out."
[4] Ex parte Alsop, In re Rees, 1 De G., J. & J. 289; Ex parte Morgan, In re Wood-

When the bankruptcy system was extended to non-traders as well as traders, the argument that an assignment by a trader of all his estate was an act of bankruptcy because it prevented him from carrying on his trade was applicable to a part only of those persons amenable to the act, for it might well be that an insolvent non-trader might be able to carry on his avocation, although he had executed such an assignment.[1]

The special provisions of these acts referred to were undoubtedly intended to relax the severity of the rule in reference to the execution of assignments by creditors ratably.

Lord Westbury, in commenting upon these provisions, remarked, "it was the object of the legislature in passing the one hundred and ninety-second section of the bankruptcy act of 1861, and the seven or eight subsequent sections, to establish and give security to a private administration of an insolvent estate against process at common law, and also against proceedings in bankruptcy." [2]

§ 24. **General Grounds of English Rule.**— At the time of the passage by congress of the bankrupt act of March 2, 1867, the making of a general assignment, although for the equal benefit of all creditors, was, as we have seen, subject to the restrictions above stated, regarded by the English courts as an act of bankruptcy, and such a conveyance was therefore void in bankruptcy, unless assented to by all the creditors. The grounds of this doctrine, uncertain at first, had not been strengthened by the lapse of time. The rule so established had rested upon an extended construction of the words of the statute 13 Eliz., ch. 5, incorporated into the bankrupt act, and that construction was not in harmony with the interpretation already placed upon these words.[3]

Lord Eldon's declaration that a debtor had no right to place his property under a course of distribution different from that ordained by the bankrupt law proceeded upon the theory that creditors had the right to the management of the estate of an insolvent previous to the commission of an act of bankruptcy, and that an interference with this right was itself an act of bankruptcy. And this was so held, while it was fully admitted that the mere fact of insolvency conferred no legal rights upon creditors before the debtor had come under the operation of the bankrupt law. The notion that a trader may not terminate his trade by a general assignment, rather than to wait for creditors to secure their prefer-

house, 32 L. J. Bank. 15; Ex parte Rawlings, id. 27; Ex parte Godden, In re Shettle, id. 37; Ex parte Spyer, id. 63; Dell v. King, 33 L. J. Exch. 47.

[1] See Ex parte Luckes, 26 L. T. (N. S.) 113; In re Wood, 7 L. J. Ch. 302.
[2] Ex parte Morgan, In re Woodhouse, *supra.*
[3] See *ante*, § 19 and note. See Globe Ins. Co. v. Cleveland Ins. Co., 14 N. B. R. 322.

ences by law, or to break him up by an adjudication in bankruptcy, is based ultimately upon the same theory that the debtor's right to manage his property ceases with his solvency. The unsatisfactory grounds upon which the general doctrine rests, together with the alterations effected by the acts of 1849 and 1861, and the intent of those alterations, as defined by Lord Westbury, may well create a very serious doubt as to whether congress, in enacting the present bankrupt law, intended to adopt the English rule in reference to general assignments for the equal benefit of all creditors, as established under the general bankruptcy system.

§ 25. **United States Bankrupt Acts of 1800 and 1841.**— Under the constitutional power conferred upon congress "to establish uniform laws upon the subject of bankruptcies throughout the United States," three bankrupt laws have been enacted — one under the act of congress of April 4, 1800,[1] which was repealed by the act of December 19, 1803;[2] one under the act of August 19, 1841,[3] which was repealed by the act of March 3, 1843;[4] and one under the act of March 2, 1867,[5] which was repealed in 1878.[6]

The two statutes first referred to were modeled, to a large degree, upon the English statutes existing at the time of their enactment respectively, but neither of them remained upon the statute book for a sufficient length of time to acquire a settled interpretation upon the points here discussed.

Under the act of 1800 no cases are reported touching upon the effect of general assignments. The act of 1841 had no provision directed against assignments more specific than the general enactment making "any fraudulent conveyance, assignment, sale, gift or other transfer of lands, tenements, goods or chattels, credits or evidences of debt," an act of bankruptcy.[7] Preferential payments and transfers made in contemplation of bankruptcy were, however, declared void and a fraud upon the act, and the assignee was empowered to claim the property so conveyed.[8] In accordance with established principle, a general assignment for the benefit of preferred creditors was under this statute deemed an act of bankruptcy, even if made without moral fraud and under the importunity of creditors.[9]

[1] U. S. Stat. at Large, vol. II, ch. 19, p. 19.
[2] Ibid., p. 248.
[3] U. S. Stat. at Large, vol. V, p. 440.
[4] Ibid., p. 614.
[5] R. S. U. S., title LXI, p. 969.
[6] U. S. Stat. 1877, 1878, ch. 160.
[7] U. S. Stat. at Large, vol. II, ch. 19, p. 19, § 2.
[8] Ibid.
[9] Ex parte Brenneman, Crabbe, 456; Freeman v. Deming, 3 Sandf. Ch. 327;

Where, however, the assignments were free from objectionable preferences, the cases under this statute were not uniform as to their being acts of bankruptcy. Thus, in the case of Ex parte Potts & Garwood,[1] in the eastern district of Pennsylvania, where a petition for an adjudication was based on an alleged act of bankruptcy in the making of an assignment of property, and it was shown that the assignment was made on a parol trust for the benefit of all the creditors ratably, Mr. Justice Randall, in refusing the adjudication, said: "An assignment for the benefit of creditors is made on good and sufficient consideration, and is perfectly valid, both at common law and under the statute; while to make it void under the second section of the bankrupt law, it must be made not only in contemplation of bankruptcy, but also for the purpose of giving a creditor, indorser, surety or other person a preference or priority over the general creditors of the bankrupt; but when the object is, as the evidence shows it to have been here, to prevent such a preference or priority, I cannot consider the transfer as a fraud." But in the cases of McLean v. Johnson[2] and McLean v. Meline,[3] in the district of Ohio, Mr. Justice McLean was of the opinion that such assignments were acts of bankruptcy, as having been made in contemplation of a state of insolvency. The reported decisions on this point were few, and remained in conflict at the time of the repeal of the act.[4]

§ 26. **Provisions of the Act of 1867 Applicable to General Assignments.**— The provisions of the act of 1867 to which it is necessary here to refer relate to what conveyances are regarded as acts of bankruptcy, what bar the bankrupt's discharge, and what are voidable by the assignee in bankruptcy. Section 5021, Revised Statutes of the United States, recites all the acts which subject a person to involuntary bankruptcy. Among the acts which constitute a man a bankrupt are those of giving preference to creditors in contemplation of bankruptcy, or the making of any assignment,

McAllister v. Richards, 6 Pa. St. 133; Cornwell's Appeal, 7 W. & S. 405. For an able note on the bankruptcy acts of 1800 and 1841, and the effect of the latter on voluntary assignments for benefit of creditors with preferences, see Philips on Evidence (4th ed.), vol. III, p. 628, note 1118. See, also, Hutchins v. Taylor, 5 Law Rep. 289, Story, J.: Jones v. Sleeper, 2 N. Y. Leg. Obs. 131; Arnold v. Maynard, 2 Story, 349; Morse v. Cohannet Bank, 3 id. 364; Everett v. Stone, id. 446.
[1] Crabbe, 469.
[2] 3 McLean, 202.
[3] 3 McLean, 199. And see Carr v. Hilton, 1 Curtis C. C. R. 230.
[4] Mr. Justice Emmons, in Globe Ins. Co. v. Cleveland Ins. Co., 14 N. B. R. 316, remarks that, under the act of 1841, "few doctrines were more generally acquiesced in than that general assignments for the benefit of creditors had become unlawful." He cites, however, only the cases referred to in the text.

gift, sale, conveyance or transfer of his estate, property, rights or credits, either within the United States or elsewhere, with intent to delay, defraud or hinder his creditors, or the making when bankrupt or insolvent, or in contemplation of bankruptcy or insolvency, of any gift, grant, sale, conveyance or transfer of money or other property, estate, rights or credits with the intent, by such disposition of his property, to defeat or delay the operation of the act.

By an amendment to this section[1] it is provided: "That no voluntary assignment by a debtor or debtors of all his or their property, heretofore or hereafter made in good faith for the benefit of all his or their creditors, ratably and without creating any preference, and valid according to the law of the state where made, shall of itself, in the event of his or their being subsequently adjudicated bankrupts in a proceeding of involuntary bankruptcy, be a bar to the discharge of such debtor or debtors."

By section 5110 it is provided that no discharge shall be granted, or, if granted, shall be valid, in the following cases, among others: When the bankrupt has given any fraudulent preference contrary to the provisions of the bankrupt act, or has made any fraudulent payment, gift, transfer, conveyance or assignment of any part of his property; or if, in contemplation of becoming bankrupt, he has made any pledge, payment, transfer, assignment or conveyance of any part of his property, directly or indirectly, absolutely or conditionally, for the purpose of preferring any creditor or person having a claim against him, or who is or may be under liability for him, or for the purpose of preventing the property from coming into the hands of the assignee or of being distributed in satisfaction of his debts.

By sections 5128 and 5129 certain transfers are prohibited and declared void, and the assignee is empowered to recover the property so transferred.

By the former section all dispositions of property made by one who is insolvent or in contemplation of insolvency within four months[2] before the filing of the petition by or against him to any creditor or person having a claim against the bankrupt, or who is under any liability for him, and who has reasonable cause to believe that such disposition of property is made by an insolvent and in fraud of the provisions of the bankrupt act, is declared void. By the latter section it is provided that if any person, being insolv-

---

[1] Approved July 26, 1876 (19 Stat. at L. 102; Supp. to R. S., vol. I, 232). This is an amendment to section 12 (corresponding to section 5021, R. S. U. S.) of the amendatory act of June 22, 1874. The words quoted in the text are inserted after the word "committed," in line forty-four.

[2] R. S. U. S., § 5130a. In cases of voluntary bankruptcy the time is limited to two months.

ent, or in contemplation of insolvency or bankruptcy, within six months [1] before the filing of the petition by or against him, makes any payment, sale, assignment, transfer, conveyance or other disposition of any part of his property to any person who then has reasonable cause to believe him to be insolvent, or to be acting in contemplation of insolvency, and knowing that such payment, sale, assignment, transfer or other conveyance is made with a view to prevent his property from coming to his assignee in bankruptcy, or to prevent the same from being distributed under this title, or to defeat the object of, or in any way impair, hinder, impede or delay the operation and effect of, or to evade any of the provisions of this title, the sale, assignment, transfer or conveyance shall be void, and the assignee may recover the property, or the value thereof, as assets of the bankrupt.

The phrase "fiduciary character" in section 5117 applies only to technical trusts.

By section 5128 it is provided that the fact that such a payment, pledge, sale, assignment, conveyance, or other disposition of a debtor's property as is described in the two preceding sections, is not made in the usual and ordinary course of business of the debtor, shall be *prima facie* evidence of fraud.

§ 27. **The Power to Assign Not Suspended by Bankrupt Laws.** Before discussing these provisions more in detail, it is important to observe that, while the existence of a bankrupt law established by congress under its constitutional powers *ipso facto* suspends and supersedes the operation of state insolvent laws,[2] in so far at least as they are in conflict with such laws,[3] yet this principle has no

[1] In cases of involuntary bankruptcy four months. Ibid.; Maxwell v. Evans, 90 Ind. 596; 46 Am. Rep. 234; citing Palmer v. Hussey, 87 N. Y. 303; Scott v. Porter, 93 Pa. St. 38; 39 Am. Rep. 719, and other cases.

[2] Sturgis v. Crowninshield, 4 Wheat. 122; Ogden v. Saunders, 12 Wheat. 213; Hyde v. Zacharie, 6 Pet. 638; Ex parte Eames, 2 Story, 322; In re Reynolds, 9 N. B. R. 50; Torrens v. Hammond, 4 Hughes, 596; Day v. Bardwell, 97 Mass. 246. See Boedefeld v. Reed, 55 Cal. 299; Lewis v. County Clerk, id. 604; Seattle Coal Co. v. Thomas, 57 id. 197; Rowe v. Page, 54 N. H. 190; Sadler v. Immel, 15 Nev. 265. In Lyman v. Bond, 130 Mass. 291, it is held that if the effect of the New Hampshire statute of 1867, chapter 126, was a bar in an action upon a creditor's claim, it was an insolvent law, the operation of which was suspended by the bankrupt act; and in Lothrop v. Highland Foundry Co., 128 Mass. 120, it was held that a conveyance by way of preference, made contrary to the insolvent law, while the bankrupt act was in force, is sufficient cause for instituting proceedings in insolvency after the repeal of the bankrupt act. In Tua v. Carriere, 117 U. S. 201. It was held that the insolvent laws of Louisiana revived on the repeal of the bankruptcy act of 1867.

[3] Ex parte John Zergenfuss, 24 N. C. 463; Shryock v. Bashore, 13 N. B. R. 481; reversed on error, 15 id. 283; s. c., 82 Pa. St. 159; Maltbie v. Hotchkiss, 38 Conn. 80; Geery's Appeal, 43 id. 289; s. c., 17 N. B. R. 196; Beck v. Barker, 65 Pa. St. 262; Barber v. Rogers, 71 id. 362.

application to general voluntary assignments for the benefit of creditors.[1] The right to make such assignments exists independent of any statute,[2] and the various state statutes regulating the execution of such assignments and the procedure under them are in no sense insolvent laws. There is no proper analogy between insolvent law, correctly so called, and those principles of the common law which allow and sanction the conveyance of his property by a debtor for the equal benefit of all his creditors, and no resemblance or relation as to warrant the conclusion that, if the existence of a bankrupt law suspends the first, it must also suspend the last.[3]

[1] Cook v. Rogers, 31 Mich. 391; 18 N. B. R. 97; Thrasher v. Bentley, 59 N. Y. 649; s. c. below, 2 Sup. Ct. R. 399; Ebersole v. Adams, 13 N. B. R. 141; Hawkins' Appeal, 34 Conn. 548; s. c., 2 N. B. R. 378; Maltbie v. Hotchkiss, 38 Conn. 80; Barnes v. Rettew, 8 Phila. 133; Mayer v. Hellman, 13 N. B. R. 440. See Re Kimball, 16 N. B. R. 188; Dolson v. Kerr, id. 405. Voluntary assignments under the state laws are valid, unless proceedings in bankruptcy are instituted within six months thereafter. Geery's Appeal, 43 Conn. 289; s. c., 17 N. B. R. 196. But an assignment, under a law of New Jersey, which "imposes restraint upon the rights to participate in the distribution of an assigned estate," inconsistent with the bankrupt act, and changing the course of administration under the act, is a conveyance in violation thereof, within the scope of section 5129. Matter of Troth, 1 Fed. Rep. 405. Where all the creditors of a bankrupt are secured to the same extent and in the same manner, so that no one has a preference over the others — as by an assignment — the provisions of the bankrupt act, discriminating between secured and unsecured creditors, have no application. Matter of Backer, 2 Abb. N. C. 379. The mere existence of the bankrupt law does not *ipso facto* render a common-law assignment void. Sadler v. Immel, 15 Nev. 265. Same ruling, provided no proceedings in bankruptcy have been instituted, Bostwick v. Burnett, 74 N. Y. 317. Nor are the rights of the assignee affected by the subsequent bankruptcy of the debtor. Bigler v. Nat. Bank of Newburgh, 26 Hun, 520.

[2] Cook v. Rogers, *supra;* Thrasher v. Bentley, *supra.* See Sadler v. Immel, 15 Nev. 265; Boese v. King, 78 N. Y. 471; affirmed, 108 U. S. 379.

[3] Mr. Chief Justice Graves, in Cook v. Rogers, 31 Mich. 396. In the case of Globe Ins. Co. v. Cleveland Ins. Co., 14 N. B. R. 316, 320, Mr. Justice Emmons has expressed a contrary view of the law. This point was, however, necessarily before the supreme court of the United States in the case of Mayer v. Hellman, *supra,* and was there distinctly ruled upon. Mr. Justice Field, after considering the Ohio statute regulating voluntary assignments, which does not vary in its character materially from the statutes of other states on the same subject, remarked: "There is nothing in the act resembling an insolvent law," and it was held that the assignment, irrespective of the statute, was valid and binding at common law, although the bankrupt act was in force. In Boese v. King, 78 N. Y. 471, it was held that although part of a state statute (New Jersey) is in the nature of a bankrupt law, and consequently suspended by the United States bankrupt act, yet that fact does not affect the validity of the remainder of the law, or its effect upon the assignment; and it was further held that even if the whole of the state statute was suspended by the bankrupt act, the right of a debtor to make an equal distribution of his property among his creditors by means of a voluntary assignment still existed.

This case was affirmed on writ of error by the United States supreme court in 108 U. S. 379.

§ 28. Assignments Fraudulent at Common Law, or Under 13 Eliz., or Giving Preferences.

—Where the assignment is fraudulent at common law,[1] or under the statutes of the state where it is made,[2] or where it attempts to create a preference[3] among cred-

[1] Farrin v. Crawford, 2 N. B. R. 602.
[2] Hyde v. Sontag, 8 N. B. R. 225; Bean v. Amsink, Blatchford, J., id. 235; In re Randall & Sunderland, 3 N. B. R. 26.
[3] Jackson v. McCullough, 13 N. B. R. 283; Stobaugh v. Mills, 8 N. B. R. 361. See Harris v. Exchange Nat. Bank, 4 Dillon, 133. An assignment being valid until proceedings in bankruptcy are instituted, it is not void as against a subsequent execution creditor, although it gives preferences. Bostwick v. Burnett, 74 N. Y. 317. More than two months before the filing of a creditors' petition, the bankrupt transferred parts of his property to several creditors in satisfaction of their claims, he being then insolvent to the knowledge of said creditors, and he and they knowing that the transfers were intended for the purpose of preferring them over other creditors to whom he was indebted, as indorser for his son, who was also insolvent. *Held*, that the transfers could not be impeached as preferences under section 5128. Van Kleeck v. Miller, 19 N. B. R. 484. See Matthews v. Stewart, 44 Mich. 209. See, also, Talcott v. Harder, 119 N. Y. 536; 23 N. E. Rep. 1056. U. S. Rev. Stats., § 5128, construed, Chadwick v. Carson, 78 Ala. 116. The assignee in bankruptcy, though he represents all the creditors of the bankrupts, acquires only the title of the bankrupts, except as he is also invested with the right of creditors to assail fraudulent transfers, and with title to property conveyed to the bankrupts contrary to the provisions of the bankrupt act. With these exceptions, his title is subject to all liens existing upon the property, legal or equitable, at the time of the commencement of the proceedings in equity. Where an assignment, fraudulent at common law, because made with the intent to hinder and delay creditors, was set aside at the suit of the assignee in bankruptcy, it was held that the latter took the assigned property subject to the liens of judgment creditors which had attached subsequent to the assignment. Johnson v. Rogers, 15 N. B. R. 1. If, however, a creditor, by reason of exceptional circumstances, is precluded from assailing the assignment, as to him it is as valid as it is to the assignors and to the assignees who have accepted it. Thus when creditors have concurred in the execution of the assignment, they cannot be heard to allege that it was fraudulent because of facts of which they were fully informed when they gave assent; they cannot impeach a transaction for fraud in which they participated as parties. Steel v. Brown, 1 Taunt. 381; Philips v. Wooster, 36 N. Y. 412; Johnson v. Rogers, *supra*. Where the assignment was held void as against an assignee in bankruptcy because regarded as repugnant to the bankrupt law, although otherwise valid, *held*, that an execution creditor, under a judgment obtained after the assignment took effect and before the filing of the petition in bankruptcy, secured a preference over the title of the assignee in bankruptcy. Macdonald v. Moore, 1 Abb. N. Cas. 53; s. c., 15 N. B. R. 26. See Dolson v. Kerr, 16 id. 405; Re Beadle, 5 Sawyer, 351. It is said, however, that Johnson v. Rogers, and Macdonald v. Moore, are in conflict (Re Beisenthal, 14 Blatch. 146; s. c., 15 N. B. R. 228), where the former of the two cases followed. A voluntary assignment was made, and the assignee accepted and qualified. Afterward a creditor recovered judgment, and the sheriff seized the property. After that an assignee in bankruptcy was appointed. *Held*, that the judgment creditors had no lien upon or right in the assigned property, so as to be let in to intercept, and take precedence of, the right of the assignee in bankruptcy to the property when he exercised his right to avoid the assignment and to recover the property. Re Beisenthal, *supra*; Linder v. Lewis, 19 N. B. R. 455; s. c., 10 Ben. 49; Re Walker, 18 id. 56; Belden v. Smith, 16 N. B. R. 302, Reed v. McIntyre, 98 U. S. 570.

itors, it is clearly repugnant to the bankrupt act. The execution of such an assignment is unquestionably an act of bankruptcy, and it may be avoided by the assignee in bankruptcy.

§ 29. **Is the Making of a Bona Fide Assignment for Creditors Ratably an Act of Bankruptcy?**—Among the earliest cases in which the question whether the execution of an assignment honestly made for the equal benefit of all creditors is an act of bankruptcy was that of In re Wm. H. Langley,[1] in the southern district of Ohio. The facts were that Langley, being in failing circumstances, and judgments being about to be recovered against him, executed an assignment of all his estate for the equal benefit of his creditors, in compliance with the various statutory requirements of the Ohio statute in reference to such assignments. Within a month thereafter Perry filed a petition against him in the district court, setting forth the assignment, and claiming that it was made with the intent to hinder and delay him in the collection of his debt, and also with intent, by such disposition, to defeat and delay the operation of the bankrupt law, and that it was therefore an act of bankruptcy.

The district court (Mr. Justice Leavitt) regarded the assignment as in contravention of the spirit and policy of the bankrupt law, although admitted to be made in good faith, and rested its decisions on the English cases and upon the decisions in McLean v. Meline,[2] McLean v. Johnson,[3] and Shawhan v. Wherritt,[4] and upon the further ground that the particular creditor was hindered and delayed in the collection of his debt. The case was taken to the circuit court, where Mr. Justice Swayne delivered an opinion which unfortunately is not reported in full.[5] From the abstract given he appears to have decided:

"That where a creditor is about to recover a judgment against his debtor in Ohio, and the debtor makes a general assignment of all his property for the benefit of all his creditors before the judgment is rendered, such conveyance is not necessarily a conveyance with the intent to hinder, defraud or delay creditors. And where such assignment is made under like circumstances, with intent to secure an equal distribution of all the debtor's property among all his creditors, it is not necessarily a conveyance of property with intent to defeat or delay the operation of the bankrupt act. To make such an assignment an act of bankruptcy it must be made

---

[1] 1 N. B. R. 559; s. c. on appeal, 2 N. B. R. 596.
[2] 3 McLean, 190.
[3] 3 McLean, 202.
[4] 7 How. 627.
[5] Reported *sub nom.* Langley v. Perry, 2 N. B. R. 596.

with intent to delay, defraud or hinder creditors within the meaning of 13 Elizabeth, or with intent to defeat or delay the operation of the bankrupt act. It becomes a question of fact. The innocence or guilt of the act depends upon the mind of him who did it, and it is not a fraud within the meaning of the bankrupt law unless it was meant to be so."[1]

The opinion thus expressed was subsequently reviewed and approved by the same learned judge, in the case of Farrin v. Crawford,[2] where he said: "Now while I have held, and still emphatically hold, that an assignment such as this purports to be (made for the equal benefit of all creditors) is valid and proper when made in good faith, it is yet to be subjected to the sharpest scrutiny, and any badge of fraud that attaches itself in the light of extraneous circumstances will, unless fully and satisfactorily explained, be fatal to its validity, and the arm of the bankrupt law will sweep it away and subject the person and estate to its own provisions." It was consequently held in that case that where the assignor had reserved to himself a sum of money largely in excess of the amount exempt, this fact, taken in connection with other suspicious circumstances, was such a badge of fraud as to render the assignment fraudulent and create an act of bankruptcy. In harmony with these opinions is that expressed by Mr. Justice Nelson, in the case of Sedgwick v. Place,[3] in the circuit court for the southern district of New York. In that case, where an assignment untainted with fraud had been duly executed, and the requirements of the statute of the state of New York regulating such assignments had been complied with, and the assignees in bankruptcy, under a subsequent voluntary assignment, filed their bill in equity seeking to have such assignment set aside, and in the meantime applied for an injunction restraining the voluntary assignees from proceeding with the administration of the trust, the circuit judge, in denying the application for an injunction, said: "Assuming the assignment in question to be untainted with fraud, either against creditors or against the bankrupt act, which is the present position of the case, we find nothing in the provisions of the law which would authorize us to take this property out of the

---

[1] This opinion has been criticised as not having been necessary to the determination of the case (see Emmons, J., in Globe Ins. Co. v. Cleveland Ins. Co., 14 N. B. R. 314; Cadwalader, J., in Barnes v. Rettew, 8 Phila. 141). The assignment under which the question arose appears to have been recorded under the laws of Ohio five days before the bankrupt act took effect, and the opinion of the court below, that the statute was retroactive, might have been a sufficient ground of reversal.
[2] 2 N. B. R. 602.
[3] 1 N. B. R. 673.

hands of the assignee under the state law, and turn it over to the assignee in bankruptcy."

§ 30. Cases.— While these cases have in some instances been followed and approved,[1] yet their authority has been frequently questioned and in the majority of instances entirely dissented from.[2] The question, however, may still be regarded as open and undetermined.

The leading cases which uphold the doctrine that such assignments are acts of bankruptcy are Barnes v. Rettew[3] and the late case of Globe Ins. Co. v. Cleveland Ins. Co.[4]

In the former of these cases, decided in the circuit court for the eastern district of Pennsylvania, Mr. Justice Cadwalader delivered an able and careful opinion,[5] in which he looked into the English cases and reviewed the subject on principle and on authority. Advancing upon the theory that the judicial interpretation of an act forms a part of it, and that congress in enacting the law of March 2, 1867, modeling it to a large degree upon the English bankruptcy law, adopted the approved construction of that law in its relation to general assignments,[6] he proceeds to show that under the English system general assignments, though made for the equal benefit of all creditors, were regarded as acts of bankruptcy, and that the reason for that rule was that by such an act the debtor attempted to put his estate into a course of distribution different from that prescribed by the bankrupt act, which had been the substance of the language of Lords Mansfield, Eldon and Wensleydale, and which are words of like import of those employed in the statute, to wit: "with intent to delay or defeat the operation of this act."

In addition he emphasizes the inconvenience which would arise from permitting general assignments under the various state acts

---

[1] In re Kintzing, 3 N. B. R. 217; In re Charles J. Marter, 12 N. B. R. 185; Smith v. Teutonia Ins. Co., 4 C. L. N. 130. And see In re George H. Arledge, 1 N. B. R. 648; In re George A. Hawkins, 2 N. B. R. 378; In re Alfred L. Wells, Jr, 1 N. B. R. 171. See, also, Mayer v. Hellman, 13 N. B. R. 440.

[2] In re Randall & Sunderland, 3 N. B. R. 18; s. c., Deady, 527; In re Smith, 3 N. B. R. 377; s. c., 4 Ben. 1; s. c., 1 L. T. R. 147; In re Spicer & Peckham, 3 N. B. R. 512; Rettew v. Barnes, 8 Phila. 133; In re Burt, 1 Dillon, 439; Hobson v. Markson, id. 421. And see In re Goldschmidt, 3 N. B. R. 164; Burkholder v. Stump, 8 Phil. 172; In re The Union Pacific R. R. Co., 10 N. B. R. 178; In re Brodhead, 2 N. B. R. 278; In re Stubbs, 4 N. B. R. 376; In re Mendelsohn, 12 N. B. R. 533; Globe Ins. Co. v. Cleveland Ins. Co., 14 N. B. R. 311.

[3] *Supra*.

[4] *Supra*.

[5] Concurred in by Mr. Joseph McKennan.

[6] See Globe Ins. Co. v. Cleveland Ins. Co., 14 N. B. R. 324.

to be made *pari passu* with the bankrupt act, and attempts to distinguish the cases of Langley v. Perry[1] and Sedgwick v. Place.[2]

In the case of Globe Ins. Co. v. Cleveland Ins. Co.[3] in the circuit court for the northern district of Ohio, Mr. Justice Emmons considered the question very fully. In addition to the grounds of decision adopted by Mr. Justice Cadwalader, he argues at length to show that the principle which underlies the doctrine that state insolvent laws are suspended by the operation of the bankrupt act, necessarily involves the determination that general assignments are in conflict with that act and are prohibited by it.[4] The opinion reviews the English and American cases, and is an important and instructive discussion of the question, reversing the rule formerly prevailing in that circuit.

In the case of Randall and Sunderland,[5] in the district of Oregon, Mr. Justice Deady placed his decision upon the ground that the necessary consequence of the assignment would be to prevent the assignor's property from coming to the assignee in bankruptcy, and from being distributed among his creditors under the bankrupt act, and thus the operation of the act would be defeated; and since every person is presumed to intend the natural and probable consequences of his own act, the intent of the assignor must have been to defeat the operation of the bankrupt act. The assignment in that case was a clear act of bankruptcy, inasmuch as it appears to have been invalid and fraudulent upon its face. In the northern district of New York the question was presented in the case of In re Wells, Jr.,[6] but was not deemed essential to a determination of the case. In the later case, in the same district, of In re Smith,[7] an assignment was declared an act of bankruptcy because it defeats the operation of the bankrupt act in depriving the creditors of the right to select an assignee, and in taking from the bankrupt court the supervision of the assignee and the administration of the estate. In Goldschmidt's[8] case, in the southern district of New York, where a debtor who was insolvent, and while actions were pending against him, and more than six months before the commencement of proceedings in bankruptcy, made a general assignment, it was held that the inference from these facts was that the assignment was made with the intent to hinder and delay creditors, and was therefore a bar to the bankrupt's discharge. The question

[1] 2 N. B. R. 596.
[2] 2 N. B. R. 28.
[3] 14 N. B. R. 311.
[4] See *ante*, § 27 and notes.
[5] 3 N. B. R. 18.
[6] 1 N. B. R. 171.
[7] 3 id. 377.
[8] 3 id. 164.

was raised in the case of the Union Pacific Railroad Company,[1] in the district of Massachusetts, and although the decision turned upon another point, yet Mr. Justice Lowell made these observations: "I consider the better opinion under our bankrupt law to be the same (as the English doctrine), that it forbids such a distribution by means of a private trust created by the debtor, unless all his creditors consent. Various reasons are given, the substance of which is that if an estate is to be wound up by trustees, they should be appointed by and be subject to the order of the courts having jurisdiction of the subject-matter, and that the creditors should have a voice in their appointment. Putting a person into bankruptcy who has undertaken to have his affairs wound up in this way is scarcely more than a specific performance of the trusts he has himself created. The only general proposition that can safely be laid down is one which I mentioned before, that one who is not only insolvent, but who undertakes to make a final distribution of his assets, must do it through the bankrupt court." And in a late case[2] in the district of California, it was remarked that the weight of authority is decided that even a fair general assignment for the benefit of creditors is an act of bankruptcy, because it necessarily defeats the operation of the act, and hinders and delays creditors.

Quite recently the question was discussed before the supreme court of the United States,[3] and Mr. Justice Field, in delivering the opinion of the court, made these observations: "The counsel for the defendants have filed an elaborate argument to show that assignments for the benefit of creditors generally are not opposed to the bankrupt act, though made within six months previous to the filing of the petition. Their argument is that such an assignment is only a voluntary execution of what the bankrupt court would compel; and as it is not a proceeding in itself fraudulent as against creditors, and does not give a preference to one creditor over another, it conflicts with no positive inhibition of the statute. There is much force in the position of counsel, and it has the support of a decision of the late Mr. Justice Nelson, in the circuit court of New York, in Sedgwick v. Place, 1 N. B. R. 673, and of Mr. Justice Swayne, in the circuit court of Ohio, in Langley v. Perry, 2 N. B. R. 596. Certain it is that such an assignment is not absolutely void; and if avoidable it must be because it may be deemed perhaps necessary, for the efficiency of the bankrupt act, that the administration of an insolvent's estate shall be intrusted to the direction of the district court, and not left under the control of the appointee

[1] 10 N. B. R. 178.
[2] In re Mendelsohn, 12 N. B. R. 533.
[3] Mayer v. Hellman, 13 N. B. R. 440.

of the insolvent. It is unnecessary to express any decided opinion upon this head, for the decision of the question is not required for the disposition of the case."

The ultimate rule to be deduced from the cases which hold that such assignments are acts of bankruptcy is well expressed in the language of Mr. Justice Lowell, "that one who is insolvent, and who undertakes to make a final distribution of his assets, must do it through the bankrupt courts,"[1] a rule which is adduced from no affirmative mandate of the statute, but which arises, if at all, by implication from judicial determination, that every other method of distribution must necessarily either delay and defraud creditors or hinder and defeat the operation of the bankrupt act.

§ 31. **Duty of Insolvent.**— It is proper here to refer to a proposition which has been frequently maintained and applied, to wit, that there is a legal duty imposed upon an insolvent by the exist-

[1] Mr. Justice Lowell, In re The Union Pacific R. R. Co., 10 N. B. R. 178. In Platt v. Preston, 10 N. B. R. 241, Choate, J., says: "The great weight of authority at present is, that a general assignment for the benefit of creditors without preferences is necessarily a fraud under the bankrupt law, defeating the operation of the law, because it provides for the administration of the estate in a different way from that provided by the bankrupt law, and by an assignee selected by the bankrupt himself." Re Beisenthal, 14 Blatch. 146; s. c., 15 N. B. R. 228; Harding v. Crosby, 17 Blatch. 348; Re Croughwell, 17 N. B. R. 337; Linder v. Lewis, 19 N. B. R. 445; s. c., Ben. 49; Re Temple, 17 id. 345; Re Skoll, 16 id. 175; Re Croft, 17 id. 324; Re Frisbee, 14 Blatch. 185. The intent to have the debtor's estate wound up and distributed under a general assignment constitutes an intent to prevent the property from coming to the assignee in bankruptcy and of being distributed under the bankrupt law. Re Kraft, 4 Fed. Rep. 523. See Re Seeley, 19 N. B. R. 1; Re Kasson, 18 id. 379. The defective execution of a voluntary assignment does not prevent it being an act of bankruptcy. Re Lawrence, 18 N. B. R. 516. A general assignment, though under a state law without preferences, is void as against an assignee in bankruptcy if the petition in bankruptcy is filed in season. Macdonald v. Moore (U. S. Dist. Ct. S. Dist. of N. Y.), 1 Abb. N. Cas. 53; s. c., 15 N. B. R. 56. Where a debtor executed an assignment, valid under the laws of the state of New York, and without preferences, on the 9th day of January, 1872, and on the 18th day of May, 1872, was adjudged bankrupt, in an action brought by the assignee in bankruptcy to obtain possession of the assigned property, held, that the assignment did not contravene any of the provisions of the bankrupt act. Miller, J. : "In Tiffany v. Lucas, 15 Wall. (U. S.) 410, 412, it was held that two things must concur to bring an assignment within the jurisdiction of the bankrupt act, viz., the fraudulent design of the bankrupt and the knowledge of it on the part of the assignee. Neither of these features characterizes the case at bar. The admission and proof established that there was no such design or knowledge; in fact, that all the parties acted in entire good faith and with no intent to violate the provisions of the act. The principle is settled in this court (New York court of appeals), that where the debtor has not been proceeded against, or taken any proceedings in the bankrupt court, an assignment for the benefit of the creditors is not an instrument void *per se* in hostility to the bankrupt act." Haas v. O'Brien, 1 Abb. N. Cas. 173; s. c., 66 N. Y. 507; 16 N. B. R. 508; Von Hein v. Elkus, 15 N. B. R. 194; Coates v. First Nat. Bank, 47 N. Y. Super. Ct. 322.

ence of the bankrupt act to avail himself of its provisions for the benefit of his creditors. This doctrine has found expression in the dicta of many able judges and was made the foundation of a course of decision in a very important class of cases.

Thus, it has been said, "strictly and truthfully speaking an insolvent has no property, and therefore he has no natural right to dispose of his property in his possession otherwise than with the consent of the real owners — his creditors."[1] Again, "at the date of the assignment Holloman was insolvent and he knew it. It was his duty to go into bankruptcy;"[2] and in the case of Wilson v. The City Bank,[3] and other analogous cases,[4] it was for the time maintained that the silent acquiescence of the debtor without invoking the protecting shield of the bankrupt act in permitting a creditor to obtain judgment and secure a lien when the debtor was insolvent and known so to be by the creditor was a fraud upon the bankrupt act. This doctrine, however, failed to meet the approval of the supreme court of the United States.[5]

Mr. Justice Miller, in delivering the opinion of that court in the case of Wilson v. City Bank, on appeal said:[6] "It is said, however, that the grand feature of that law (the bankrupt law) is to secure equality of distribution among creditors in all cases of insolvency, and to secure this it is the legal duty of the insolvent, when sued by one creditor in an ordinary proceeding likely to end in judgment and seizure of property, to file himself a voluntary bankrupt, and that this duty is one to be inferred from the spirit of the law and is essential to its successful operation. The argument is not without force and has received the assent of a large number of the district judges to whom the administration of the bankrupt law is more immediately confided. We are, nevertheless, not satisfied of its soundness.

"We have already said there is no moral obligation on the part of the insolvent to do this unless the statute requires it, and then only because it is a duty imposed by the law. It is equally clear that there is no such duty imposed by that act in express terms. It is therefore an argument solely of implication. This implication is said to arise from the supposed purpose of the statute to secure equality of distribution in *all* cases of insolvency, and, to

---

[1] Mr. Justice Deady, In re Silverman, 1 Saw. 416.
[2] Mr. Justice Woods, in Jackson v. McCulloch, 13 N. B. R. 285. And see remarks of Mr. Justice Blatchford, in Hardy v. Clarke, 3 N. B. R. 392.
[3] 5 N. B. R. 270.
[4] Warren v. Tenth Nat. Bank, 7 N. B. R. 481; Smith v. Buchanan, 8 Blatch. 153; Haskell v. Ingalls, 5 N. B. R. 205; Catlin v. Hoffman, 2 Sawyer, 486. See Rogers v. Palmer, 102 U. S. 263.
[5] Wilson v. City Bank, 17 Wall. 473.
[6] Ibid. 484, 485.

make the argument complete, it is further necessary to hold that this can only be done in bankruptcy proceedings under that statute. Does the statute justify so broad a proposition? Does it, in effect, forbid all proceedings to collect debts in cases of insolvency in other courts and in all other modes than by bankruptcy? We do not think that its purpose of securing equality of distribution is to be carried so far."

§ 32. **Insolvency and Assignment Under the Act.**— Inasmuch, then, as there is no legal duty imposed upon an insolvent by the mere fact of insolvency to resort to bankruptcy, and since no legal rights are acquired by creditors to their debtor's property solely by his insolvency, it would appear that an insolvent debtor may make any disposition of his property not prohibited by law,[1] but a general assignment for the benefit of all his creditors equally is not prohibited by law; on the contrary, " whenever such a disposition has been voluntarily made by a debtor, the courts in this country have uniformly expressed their approbation of the proceeding." [2]

The only provisions of the bankrupt act under which it has been or can be claimed that an assignment honestly made for the equal benefit of all creditors is an act of bankruptcy are the clauses of section 5021 respecting fraudulent conveyaces, to wit, assignments, etc., made by a debtor, with the intent to delay, defraud or hinder his creditors, and the subsequent clause of the same section in reference to conveyances by an insolvent made with the intent to defeat or delay the operation of the act.[3] For the bankruptcy courts to declare such an assignment as has been described a fraudulent conveyance, under the former of these clauses, would be to disregard the authority of courts of law and equity in this country upon the construction of the words employed from the earliest time, and no decision of the bankruptcy courts in this country has ever gone fully to this length.[4] The opinions adverse to such assignments have, for the most part, been rested upon the latter clause of the section. The words " with intent to defeat or delay the operation of the act " appear for the first time in the bankrupt act of 1867, and they have not acquired a distinct and definite interpretation. It is difficult to perceive how any act of a debtor can be said to defeat or delay the operation of a law in the abstract. The words

---

[1] Mr. Justice Baldwin, in Davis v. Turner, 4 Gratt. 426. See, also, Stewart v. Platt, 101 U. S. 731.
[2] Mr. Justice Field, in Mayer v. Hellman, 13 N. B. R. 442.
[3] See *ante*, § 26.
[4] See remarks of Mellish, L. J., in Ex parte Luckes, In re Wood, 36 L. T. Chan. 117, quoted *ante*, § 22, note; Field, J., in Mayer v. Hellman, 13 N. B. R. 442.

have ordinarily been regarded as referring to the rights of creditors secured under or by the operation of the act. But to say that an assignment honestly made for the equal benefit of all creditors is an act of bankruptcy because it defeats or delays the operation of the act by depriving creditors of the right to administer the estate of an insolvent is to say that it is an act of bankruptcy because it deprives them of a right which they have not yet acquired, and which they cannot acquire except by an appeal to the court in certain numbers and under peculiar circumstances, and the mere insolvency of their debtor is not one of those circumstances.

But if it be said that the rights of creditors protected by this clause are prospective rights which will spring into existence when the insolvent shall be brought under the operation of the act, then every interference by a debtor with his property after his insolvency is equally an act of bankruptcy, since every such interference, to the extent to which it goes, as effectually prevents the property of the insolvent from coming into the hands of the assignee in bankruptcy and from distribution under the act as does a general conveyance of his entire estate. Such a proposition is tantamount to affirming that insolvency itself is an act of bankruptcy.

When it is asserted that the clause under consideration was inserted into the act from the English decisions, and is equivalent to the language of Lord Eldon, "puts his property under a course of distribution different from that ordained by the bankrupt law,"[1] it may well enough be replied, that, admitting the analogy between the phrases (although not entirely apparent), still no intent on the part of the legislature to adopt the English rule on this subject can be gathered from the discussion of the act during its progress through congress; and it is not to be presumed that a rule of law which was declared by the eminent chancellor who first formulated it, to have been placed on a "singular ground," and to have been "carried to an extravagant length,"[2] and the force of which has been materially affected by the amendments to the bankrupt acts in existence at the time of the passage of the act of 1867, was incorporated into that law without more pointed reference to it either in the act itself or in the extended discussion which the passage of the act evoked.

If assignments honestly made for the equal benefit of all creditors and carrying out the beneficial design of the bankrupt law were regarded by congress as antagonistic to that law, it is somewhat surprising that conveyances so familiar to the law of this country should have been referred to only under the indirect phraseology employed.

[1] See *ante*, § 22.
[2] Lord Eldon, in Ex parte Bourne, 16 Ves. 148.

§ 33. Assent of Creditors.

—Under the English decisions it has been uniformly held that a creditor who has either executed, or been privy to, or acted under, a deed of assignment, cannot afterwards set it up as an act of bankruptcy.[1] And so a creditor who, by standing by and not objecting, assents to the execution by the debtor of the assignment, cannot afterwards rely on its execution as an act of bankruptcy.[2] And this rule is believed to prevail in this country, though perhaps not to the same extent. Thus where a debtor caused his property to be transferred to trustees for the payment of certain specified debts, and was subsequently adjudged bankrupt, it was held that the creditors secured by the assignment might dissent therefrom and prove their debts; but in the absence of an actual dissent, creditors preferred under an assignment will be deemed to assent to its provisions and cannot prove their claims without surrendering their preference.[3]

But where an application for an adjudication of bankruptcy was made against the debtor, and the acts of bankruptcy alleged were that the debtor, being a merchant, had suspended payment of his commercial paper, and had not resumed within a period of fourteen days, and it appeared that, before the expiration of the fourteen days, the debtor had made an assignment for the benefit of creditors under the Ohio statute, it was held that the assignment did not prevent the running of the fourteen days; held, also, that the fact that the state court had acquired jurisdiction of the debtor's estate did not prevent the bankrupt court from proceeding under the bankrupt law, no fraud having been shown in the assignment.[4]

§ 34. Assignment Not Void but Avoidable in Bankruptcy.

—In the absence of actual fraud, the assignment, even though constructively fraudulent, is not void, but voidable, in bankruptcy, and is voidable only at the suit of the assignee;[5] but transfers void

---

[1] Bamford v. Baron, 2 Term R. 594, note; Ex parte Cawkwell, 1 Rose, 313.

[2] Ex parte Stray, L. R. 2 Ch. 374; Marshall v. Barkworth, 4 B. & Adol. 508; Jackson v. Irvine, 2 Camp. 49; Oliver v. King, 25 L. J. Ch. 427; Ex parte Strang, L. R. 2 Ch. App. 374. See Bradley, J., Barings v. Dabney, 19 Wall. 9.

[3] In re W. A. Sanders, 13 N. B. R. 164. And where the petitioning creditor applied to the state court to have the security of the voluntary assignee increased, this was not such an assent to the proceedings as to estop him from claiming that the assignment was an act of bankruptcy. In re William H. Langley, 1 N. B. R. 559.

[4] In re Laner, 9 N. B. R. 494.

[5] In re George H. Arledge, 1 N. B. R. 644; McGready v. Harris, 9 N. B. R. 135; Mayer v. Hellman, 13 N. B. R. 440; Cadwalader, J., In re Pierce & Holbrook, 3 N. B. R. 258. And see Barnes v. Rettew, 8 Phila. 133; Ostrander v. Meunch, 2 McCrary, 267; Belden v. Smith, 16 N. B. R. 302; Reed v. McIntyre, 98 U. S. 507; Re Temple, 17 N. B. R. 345. In Shryock v. Bashore, 82 Pa. St. 159; s. c.,

under the law of the state where the transfer is made, or fraudulent at common law, may be avoided by the assignee in bankruptcy, though made more than six months prior to proceedings in bankruptcy.¹ Conveyances and transfers, however, which are fraudulent by virtue of sections 5128 and 5129, can be impeached only when proceedings in bankruptcy are commenced within the time limited by section 5130a.²

The pleadings may be so framed as to assail the instrument, both because fraudulent under the bankrupt act and under the common law or under the statute of the state.³

§ 35. **Avoiding Assignment by Assignee.**— The bankrupt law (sec. 5046, R. S. U. S.) declares that all the property conveyed by a bankrupt in fraud of his creditors shall, by virtue of adjudication of bankruptcy, and the appointment of his assignee, but subject to the exceptions stated in the previous section, be at once vested in such assignee.⁴

The assignee, therefore, not only succeeds to the rights and liabilities of the bankrupt, but he also represents the rights of the creditors,⁵ and, as such representative, may maintain and defend proceedings which, on the ground of public policy or otherwise, the latter would not be allowed to.⁶ He has the rights which an

---

15 N. B. R. 283, the assignees of an insolvent bank brought an action against the maker of a note to the bank. *Held*, that he could not be permitted to set up as a defense that the assignment was void as being contrary to the bankrupt act. Where the voluntary assignee sues to recover money due the assignor, and the assignee in bankruptcy is brought in by interpleader, the latter, in order to recover, must establish that the voluntary assignment was not merely void at his election, but so absolutely void that the plaintiff's title under it can be assailed and defeated collaterally; this position is not tenable. The voluntary assignment is not void *ab initio* even as against the assignee in bankruptcy, but voidable at his election, and he must elect to treat the assignment as void *in toto* or not at all. Wehl v. Wald, 18 Blatch. 163.

¹ Massey v. Allen, 17 Wall. 351; s. c., 7 N. B. R. 401; Bean v. Amsinck, 8 N. B. R. 235; Hyde v. Sontag, 8 N. B. R. 225; Bean v. Brookmire, 1 Dillon, 151; s. c., 4 N. B. R. 57; Knowlton v. Mosely, 105 Mass. 136; Bradshaw v. Klein, 1 N. B. R. 542; s. c., 1 L. T. R. 72; s. c., 7 A. L. Reg. 505; Cragin v. Carmichael, 11 N. B. R. 511. See Olney v. Tanner, 19 N. B. R. 178; Mann v. Flower, 25 Minn. 500.

² Mayer v. Hellman, 13 N. B. R. 440; In re George H. Arledge, 1 N. B. R. 644; Seaver v. Spink, 8 N. B. R. 218; Geery's Appeal, 43 Conn. 289; s. c., 17 N. B. R. 196; Maltbie v. Hotchkiss, 38 Conn. 80; Re Temple, 19 N. B. R. 345; Barnewell v. Dunn, 14 N. B. R. 278.

³ Cragin v. Carmichael, 11 N. B. R. 511.

⁴ Vanslyke v. Shryer, 98 Ind. 126; Johnson v. Rogers, 15 N. B. R. 1.

⁵ Bolling v. Munchus, 59 Ala. 482.

⁶ In re The St. Helen's Mills Co., 10 N. B. R. 418; In re Wynne, 4 N. B. R. 23; Allen v. Massey, 8 N. B. R. 401; s. c. on appeal, 17 Wall. 351; Carr v. Hilton, 2 Story, 231; Black v. Terrin, 2 N. B. R. 643. An action may be maintained by the assignee in bankruptcy against a voluntary assignee and intervening cred-

attaching creditor would have.[1] He may attack an assignment on the same grounds on which a creditor, having obtained judgment, might attack it.[2] "He may," says Mr. Justice Woodruff, "impeach any conveyance and recover any property which, were there no bankrupt law, the creditors (having first obtained judgment) might impeach and recover on the ground that it was conveyed, or transferred, to defraud them." [3]

But he may also attack an assignment upon grounds upon which a judgment creditor could not, as giving a preference or being fraudulent under the provisions of the bankrupt act.[4] But in that event he is restricted in his right of maintaining his action by the time in which the proceedings in bankruptcy were commenced after the fraudulent act complained of, and if the proceedings were not instituted within the time limited his right of action is lost.[5] And when the action is brought to avoid a transaction as fraudulent under the provisions of the bankrupt act, it may be brought in a state court.[6]

itors to avoid the assignment and recover of such creditors the avails of the property levied upon and sold by them. Linder v. Lewis, 19 N. B. R. 455; s. c., 10 Ben. 49. See Adams v. Hyams, 19 Blatch. 487. The bankrupt cannot set up in defense to the claim of the assignee the title of a prior assignee under a voluntary assignment, merely for the purpose of retaining property in his own possession. Matter of Moses, 1 Fed. Rep. 845. An assignee stands upon the right of the bankrupt and may be opposed by the same defenses as if the suit were in his name. Cady v. Sanford, 53 Vt. 632. See Burgett v. Paxton, 99 Ill. 288; also Jenkins v. Pierce, 98 Ill. 646. But *it seems* that the assignee is not bound to take possession of all property conveyed by the bankrupt in fraud of the bankrupt law. Nash v. Simpson, 78 Me. 142; 3 Am. Rep. 53. Specific liens existing at the time of adjudication are preserved. Broach v. Powell, 79 Ga. 86; 3 S. E. Rep. 763.

[1] Cragin v. Carmichael, 11 N. B. R. 511.
[2] Farrin v. Crawford, 2 N. B. R. 602; In re Randall & Sunderland, 3 N. B. R. 18; Massey v. Allen, 17 Wall. 351; Bean v. Amsinck, 8 N. B. R. 235; Knowlton v. Moseley, 105 Mass. 136; In re Wynne, 4 N. B. R. 23; s. c., 9 A. L. Reg. 627; Bradshaw v. Kline, 1 N. B. R. 542; s. c., 2 Biss. 20; In re Metzger, 2 N. B. R. 353; In re Meyers, 1 N. B. R. 581; s. c., 2 Ben. 424; Boone v. Hall, 7 Bush, 66; Pratt v. Curtiss, 6 N. B. R. 139; Carr v. Gale, 3 W. & M. 38; s. c., 2 Ware, 330; Carr v. Hilton, 1 Curt. 230; Ashley v. Robinson, 29 Ala. 112.
[3] Smith v. Ely, 10 N. B. R. 554. Where a general assignment was held void as against the assignee in bankruptcy, it was also held that his title related back to the date of the general assignment, and cut off the lien of a creditor whose execution was levied on goods subsequently thereto, and before the filing of the creditors' petition. Waring v. Buchanan, 19 N. B. R. 502. See cases cited with Re Beisenthal, in note 3 of § 28.
[4] Jackson v. McCulloch, 3 N. B. R. 283. See *ante*, § 28. All the persons uniting in a common design to effect a fraudulent disposition of the bankrupt's property may be joined as defendants in one suit brought by the assignee, although the relief sought against them respectively relates to different parts of the estate. Van Kleeck v. Miller, 19 N. B. R. 484.
[5] Seaver v. Spink, 8 N. B. R. 218; Mann v. Flower, 25 Minn. 500; Tappan v. Whittemore, 15 Blatch. 440; Coates v. First Nat. Bank, 47 N. Y. Super. Ct. 322.
[6] A state court has jurisdiction of an action by an assignee in bankruptcy to

§ 36. **Right of Action in Assignee Exclusive.**— After the commencement of proceedings in bankruptcy, no one but the assignee can bring or maintain an action to set aside a fraudulent conveyance made by the bankrupt.[1] The right of action to set aside such a conveyance is, after an adjudication in bankruptcy, exclusively in the assignee,[2] and the judgment creditor cannot maintain an action thereon; and this is true even when the creditor had no notice of the proceedings in bankruptcy, and when his debt was not included in the schedules.[3] And when a trustee, claiming under an assignment, filed a bill to recover assets belonging to the estate, the assignee in bankruptcy was permitted to intervene by supplementary bill.[4]

And a creditor cannot disregard the assignment and levy upon the property transferred by it, although it is void under the bankrupt law, for it is void only as to persons claiming in virtue of proceedings under the statute.[5]

Nor can the voluntary assignee claim that the assignment is void under the bankrupt law, without showing that the property has been recovered from him by the assignee in bankruptcy.[6]

recover a debt due the bankrupt (Kidder v. Horrobin, 72 N. Y. 159; Mann v. Fowler, 25 Minn. 500), or to avoid transactions which constitute a fraud on the bankrupt act (Ansley v. Patterson, 77 N. Y. 156; Olcott v. MacLean, 73 id. 223; Thompson v. Sweet, id. 622; Goodrich v. Wilson, 119 Mass. 429; Tyler v. Wing, 19 Hun, 622; Wente v. Young, 12 id. 220. See Claflin v. Houseman, 93 U. S. 130; Cook v. Whipple, 55 N. Y. 150. But see Bingham v. Claflin, 7 N. B. R. 412; Voorhees v. Frisbie, 8 id. 152; Cornwell's Appeal, 7 W. & S. 305; Seavey v. Maples, 94 Ind. 205), and on the refusal of the assignee, creditors may bring such an action in a state court (Bates v. Bradley, 24 Hun, 84, distinguishing Glenny v. Langdon, 98 U. S. 20); but state courts have no jurisdiction of an action against the assignee to reach the bankrupt's assets in his hands. Griswold v. Watkins, 20 Hun, 114. The jurisdiction of the bankrupt court is not affected by the fact that an assignment for the benefit of creditors under the state law has been made prior to the adjudication. Pool v. McDonald, 15 N. B. R. 560. Nor is the jurisdiction of the court defeated by the fact that the complainant or cross-complainant is declared a bankrupt while proceedings are pending on his complaint or cross-complaint. Anderson v. Wilson, 100 Ind. 402.

[1] In re Meyers, 1 N. B. R. 581; s. c., 2 Ben. 424; Stewart v. Isidor, 1 N. B. R. 485; s. c., 5 Abb. Pr. (N. S.) 68; Goodwin v. Sharkey, 3 N. B. R. 485; s. c., 5 Abb. Pr. (N. S.) 64; Allen v. Montgomery, 10 N. B. R. 503.

[2] Gayle v. Randall, 71 Ala. 469; Lane v. Nickerson, 99 Ill. 284; Thatcher v Rockwell, 4 Colo. 375.

[3] Thurmond v. Andrews, 13 N. B. R. 157. A receiver in supplementary proceedings cannot bring such an action. Olney v. Tanner, 21 Blatch. 540. The law will not compel an assignee in bankruptcy to accept property of the bankrupt which is onerous and will yield nothing towards payment of his debts. Glenn v. Howard & Savage, 65 Md. 4. Nor when the property is incumbered for its full value. Slinkard v. State ex rel., 87 Ind. 188. Leasehold estates, see White v. Griffin, 44 Conn. 437.

[4] Collateral Bank v. Fowler, 12 N. B. R. 289. See Freeman v. Deering, 3 Sandf. Ch. 327; Wehl v. Wald, 18 Blatch. 163.

[5] Dodge v. Sheldon, 6 Hill, 9.

[6] Seaman v. Stoughton, 3 Barb. Ch. 344. See Re Manahan, 19 N. B. R. 65.

§ 37. Proceedings Under Voluntary Assignments, When Avoided — Protection of Voluntary Assignee. — Where the assignment is set aside the bankrupt court will sometimes, to facilitate the administration of the estate, recognize the voluntary assignee, and refuse to interfere with him pending certain transactions which are deemed to be of advantage to the estate.[1] In the case of In re Pierce & Holbrook,[2] Mr. Justice Cadwalader, referring to this subject, remarked: "Even when the assignment has been the sole foundation of the proceedings in bankruptcy, I have considered it not a void act, but an act voidable by the assignee in bankruptcy under a bill in equity filed for the purpose of avoiding it, and have sustained acts done under it previously in good faith. In one case I refused an injunction under such a bill because the injunction would have prevented the working out of an equity beneficial to the creditors. In another case I suspended granting an injunction and appointing a receiver until the completion of a beneficial sale by the assignee under a previous deed. In the third case, of a very suspicious kind, where a sale had apparently been forced by the assignee under the previous deed, at a sacrifice, and the bill was at the suit of the petitioning creditor before the appointment of an assignee in bankruptcy, as the previous assignee was of questionable solvency, and might be liable for the full value of what had been sacrificed, I made a qualified and guarded order for a receiver." And where, previous to the commencement of an action on the part of the assignee in bankruptcy to obtain possession of the assigned property, the voluntary assignee sold the property assigned to him, and distributed the proceeds under the orders of the state court, acting in good faith and deriving no interest or benefit therefrom himself, the United States circuit court for Iowa held the voluntary assignee free from liability in an action subsequently brought by the assignee in bankruptcy to recover the value of the assigned property.[3]

§ 38. Allowance of Expenses to Voluntary Assignee. — The assignee claiming under a voluntary assignment is not chargeable with the value of property in good faith turned over to creditors, or payments made to creditors in accordance with the terms of the assignment before proceedings in bankruptcy were instituted; but he is liable for the balance which shall appear to be in his hands

---

[1] Burkholder v. Stump, 8 Phila. 172; s. c., 4 N. B. R. 597.
[2] 3 N. B. R. 258.
[3] Cragin v. Thompson, 12 N. B. R. 81. But in this case Mr. Justice Dillon said: "If the present action were against the creditors who received dividends under the assignment, there could, as it now seems to me, be little or no doubt as to their liability." See Neill v. Jackson, 8 Fed. Rep. 144; Wehl v. Wald, 18 Blatch. 163; Wald v. Wehl, id. 495.

upon a proper accounting with the assignee in bankruptcy, after deducting such payments.[1]

The expenses of converting the property into money may be allowed to a trustee under an assignment,[2] and in the case of Burkholder v. Stump [3] the court directed an allowance to be made to the voluntary assignee for his necessary and reasonable charges and expenses; but it was said that no allowance could be made of a future settlement of the trustee's account in the court of a state under its laws relating to assignments.

But where the debtors had made an assignment under the laws of the state of Maine, and were within a month thereafter adjudged bankrupt, and the voluntary assignee surrendered to the assignee in bankruptcy all the property of the debtors which had come into his hands, reserving only enough to cover the expenses and commissions to which he was entitled under the state law, it was held, in a proceeding to compel him to pay over the balance, that he was not entitled to the deductions claimed, for the reason that the proceedings under the state law were in fraud of the bankrupt act, and that the bankrupt court would not allow the expenses incurred in an attempt to defeat the operation of the act.[4] It is usual and proper, when the assignment is set aside, for the decree to contain a direction for a reconveyance by the trustee to the assignee in bankruptcy.[5]

§ 39. **Bar to Discharge.**— Previous to the recent amendment [6] to the bankrupt act, the authorities were in conflict as to whether

[1] Jones v. Kinney, 4 N. B. R. 649.

[2] In re J. S. Cohen, 6 N. B. R. 379; Stobaugh v. Mills, 8 N. B. R. 361; s. c., 5 C. L. N. 526.

[3] 4 N. B. R. 597; s. c., 8 Phila. 172. Upon setting aside the assignment under the state law in bankruptcy, the assignee will be allowed his disbursements, and for his own services and those of his counsel. Macdonald v. Moore, 1 Abb. N. Cas. 53; Wald v. Wehl, 18 Blatch. 495. But the assignee will be allowed no compensation for his own services unless the court can see clearly that the estate will not be subjected to a duplication of charges. Re Kurth, 17 N. B. R. 573. As to compensation and attorney's fees, the voluntary assignee is not entitled to priority of payment, but as to such items stands in the same position as other creditors, and must prove his claim. Re Lains, 16 N. B. R. 168. As to the allowance of expenses to a creditor who brings suit, see Re Dumahaut, 17 N. B. R. 517; affirmed by Waite, C. J., 15 Blatch. 20. See, also, Re Dumahaut, 19 N. B. R. 393.

[4] In re Stubbs, 4 N. B. R. 376. See Clark v. Marx, 6 Ben. 275.

[5] Burkholder v. Stump, *supra*.

[6] Act of July 26, 1876, ch. 234; 19 Stat. L. 102; Supp. to R. S., vol. I, 232 (see *ante*, p. 38). "This amendment alters the law only in involuntary cases, and in them only in the single particular that such an assignment (*i. e.*, one in good faith, without preferences, and valid by state law), of itself, is no longer a bar to a discharge. In voluntary cases it is a bar, and in all cases it is an act of bankruptcy, and is void as against the assignee." Re Beisenthal, 15 N. B. R., 248, per Johnson, J.

the execution of an assignment for the equal benefit of all creditors was a bar to the debtor's discharge in case of a subsequent adjudication of bankruptcy.[1] And the question may be still regarded as being open in a case where voluntary proceedings in bankruptcy are instituted. Where, however, the debtors are adjudicated bankrupt in a proceeding of involuntary bankruptcy, no voluntary assignment for the benefit of all creditors ratably and without preference, and valid according to the laws of the state where made, will be a bar to a discharge, and this applies to assignments heretofore or hereafter made.

§ 40. **Compositions in Bankruptcy and General Assignments.**— Under the provisions for composition[2] in the bankrupt act, creditors may resolve that a composition proposed by the debtor shall be accepted in satisfaction of their claims. It has been decided that the making of an assignment prior to the commencement of proceedings in bankruptcy does not preclude the confirmation of the composition;[3] nor where a debtor has made a general assignment in good faith are the rights of the assignee to the property affected by the subsequent bankruptcy of the debtor and his discharge under a composition in bankruptcy.[4] The creditors' right to an accounting by the assignee under a general assignment is not divested by the mere fact of a composition in bankruptcy, unless this right is relinquished by the creditors;[5] nor will an order of the bankruptcy court, made in composition proceedings to which the assignee is not a party, directing him to hand over the assigned property to the assignor, protect the assignee from the necessity of an accounting on the petition of a creditor who did not personally assent to the composition, although his name was duly entered on the list of creditors.[6]

[1] An assignment was regarded as a bar to a discharge in the cases of In re Goldschmidt, 3 N. B. R. 165; s. c., 3 Ben. 379; In re Brodhead, 2 N. B. R. 278; s. c., 3 Ben. 106; but the contrary doctrine was sustained in In re Pierce & Holbrook, 3 N. B. R. 258; s. c., 16 Pitts. L. J. 204; In re John M. Quackenboss, 1 N. Y. Leg. Obs. 146; Smith v. Ely, 1 id. 343. Where an assignment was made for the purpose of preventing some portion of the firm assets from being distributed to satisfy the firm debts, it was held that the court would not grant a discharge. Re Croft, 8 Bissell, 188.

[2] Act of June 22, 1874, ch. 390, sec. 17; 18 Stat. L. 178; adding to R. S., § 5103. A composition with creditors is authorized to be made only in cases pending in court, and has no validity until confirmed by the court, and then it is binding on all creditors who were named and made parties. Bidwell v. Bidwell, 92 Pa. St. 61; Clay v. Severance, 55 Vt. 300.

[3] Pool v. McDonald, 15 N. B. R. 560

[4] Bigler v. National Bank, 26 Hun, 520; Matter of Stowell, id. 258. See Matter of Backer, 2 Abb. N. C. 379.

[5] Matter of Allen, 24 Hun, 408; Matter of Herman, 53 How. Pr. 377. See Re Dumahaut, 15 Blatch. 20; affirming 17 N. B. R. 517; 19 id. 393; Matter of Straus, 9 Abb. N. C. 131; Matter of Stowell, 46 Hun, 342.

[6] Matter of Stowell, 26 Hun, 258. See Matter of Stowell, 16 Abb. N. C. 90.

CHAPTER IV.

WHO MAY MAKE AN ASSIGNMENT.

§ 41. Who May Assign.
42. Insolvency, When Important.
43. Insolvency, What.
44. Insolvency, What — Continued.
45. Corporation — Right to Assign.
46. Restrictions on the Right.
47. Power of Partners to Assign.
48. Power of Partners to Assign — Review of Cases.
49. Review of Cases — Continued.
50. Review of Cases — Preferences.
51. Review of Cases — Preferences — Continued.
52. Power of Partners to Assign — Summary.
53. Power of Partner to Assign — Summary of Authorities.
54. Power of Each Partner to Assign His Interest.
55. Surviving Partners.
56. Limited Partnership.

§ 41. Who May Assign.— Assignments for the benefit of creditors are most commonly made by persons engaged in business as merchants, traders, manufacturers, mechanics, and the like, either individually or as *copartners*. Any person, however, of sound mind, and not laboring under legal disability,[1] may make such a disposition of his or her property. A general assignment may be made by an agent or attorney in fact, properly authorized thereto.[2]

[1] It was held in the case of Fox v. Heath, 21 How. Pr. 384, that an assignment executed by partners, one of whom was an infant, was void for the reason that the instrument being voidable by the infant the conveyance was not absolute and irrevocable, and was consequently fraudulent as to creditors. In the late case of Yates v. Lyon, 61 N. Y. 344, this doctrine was disapproved, and it was there held that the defense of infancy must be made, if at all, by the infant himself; and it seems that the most he could claim would be that he should not be held personally for debts beyond what the assets of the firm are able to pay. In Soper v. Fry, 37 Mich. 237, it is held that an infant's assignment is not void, but only voidable, and that only by the infant or some one in his right. In an assignment by a partnership to pay a firm debt the fact that one of the partners was an infant cannot be set up by a third person, for the reason that infancy is a personal privilege, and no one but the infant can take advantage thereof. Avery v. Fisher, 28 Hun, 508; citing Slocum v. Hooker, 13 Barb. 537. And see Foot v. Goldman, 68 Miss. 529; 10 S. Rep. 62. A married woman having a separate estate and engaged in a separate business may make an assignment for the benefit of creditors. Third Nat. Bank v. Guenther, 123 N. Y. 568; 25 N. E. Rep. 986. In Maryland a married woman may make an assignment of her property, the same as any other person. Schumann v. Peddicord, 50 Md. 560.

[2] Gouldy v. Metcalf, 75 Tex. 455; 12 S. W. Rep. 830; citing McKee v. Coffin, 66 Tex. 307; 1 S. W. Rep. 276.

The power of corporations to assign their property for the benefit of creditors has frequently been discussed, and important restrictions have in some instances been imposed upon the exercise of this right by corporate bodies. The authority of partners to make such disposition of the partnership effects has likewise given rise to judicial discussion and legislative enactment. The questions thus presented will be considered in the course of the present chapter. But, before entering upon this division of the subject, it will be proper to devote some attention to the meaning of a term which is constantly used, not only as descriptive of that condition of affairs in which assignments usually originate, but as a test of the validity of the instruments themselves, namely, *insolvency.*

§ 42. **Insolvency, When Important.**— As we have already seen, many of the state statutes, which have been enacted for the purpose of restraining the right of making assignments and regulating their operation, are confined by their terms to assignments made by debtors who are insolvent or acting in contemplation of insolvency.[1] When, therefore, the attempt is made to bring an assignment within the operation of these acts, either for the purpose of having it declared fraudulent and void or for the purpose of compelling an administration of the assigned property in accordance with its provisions,[2] it becomes essential to establish primarily the fact that the instrument was made by a debtor in insolvency or in view of insolvency;[3] and when the deed purports on its face to be made by a solvent debtor, proof may be given of his insolvency, and if that is established it will then be governed by the same principles as if the insolvency appeared on its face.[4]

The question of insolvency also frequently becomes of importance in considering the validity of assignments executed by corporations, the restrictions upon their right to make such conveyances depending in some instances upon their financial condition and outlook at the time of the execution of the instrument.[5]

Independent of statutory regulations, it has been thought that the right to make an assignment for the benefit of creditors belonged exclusively to debtors who were insolvent or who honestly believed themselves to be so, and that the execution of such an instrument by a solvent debtor was conclusive evidence of an intent

---

[1] See *ante*, ch. II.
[2] Hampton v. Morris, 2 Met. (Ky.) 336.
[3] Morgentham v. Harris, 12 Cal. 245.
[4] Hardy v. Skinner, 9 Ind. 191; Hardy v. Simpson, 13 Ind. 132; Green v. Banks, 24 Tex. 508; Pearson v. Maxfield, 51 Iowa, 76; Joiner v. Van Alstyne, 22 Neb. 172; 34 N. W. Rep. 366; Driggs & Co.'s Bank v. Norwood, 50 Ark. 42; 6 S. W. Rep. 323.
[5] See *post*, § 46.

to hinder, delay and defraud creditors.[1] This doctrine no longer prevails to the same extent.[2] "The solvency of the debtor," says Mr. Justice Comstock, in the case of Ogden v. Peters,[3] "in his own estimation or in fact, does not invalidate his assignment of all or any portion of his property for the payment of his debts." The solvency of the debtor, taken in connection with other suspicious circumstances, may be evidence of a fraudulent intent of the debtor to delay and defraud creditors which will invalidate the assignment.[4]

[1] "Where a man," it was said in the case of Planck v. Schermerhorn, 3 Barb. Ch. 344, "has ample means to pay all his debts in cash as they become due, there seems to be no reason for making a general assignment and giving preferences, except for the purpose of delaying the creditors in the assertion of their legal rights." See Van Nest v. Yoe, 1 Sandf. Ch. 4, 9; Kellogg v. Slawson, 15 Barb. 56; Mason, J., in Rathbun v. Platner, 17 id. 272, 275. "Some of the cases have decided that where a debtor was perfectly solvent, having funds immediately available for the satisfaction of his debts, and knew that he was so, an assignment of all his property to pay his debts must necessarily be to delay his creditors in the collection of their debts, and must be designed for his own advantage, and was therefore void under the statute." Strong, J., in Ogden v. Peters, 15 Barb. 560, 563; disapproved in s. c., 21 N. Y. 23. And see the observations of Roosevelt, J., in Ely v. Cook, 18 id. 612, 614. See London v. Parsley, 7 Jones' L. (N. C.) 313; Malvin v. West, 19 Fed. Rep. 721. In Munson v. Ellis, 38 Mich. 331, it was held that an assignment by a solvent person is valid unless creditors can show that it was made with the fraudulent intent of hindering them.

[2] Ogden v. Peters, 21 N. Y. 23; Angell v. Rosenbury, 12 Mich. 241. But see Bates v. Ableman, 13 Wis. 644.

[3] 21 N. Y. 23.

[4] Baldwin v. Buckland, 11 Mich. 389. And see Northrup v. Livermore, 44 N. Y. 109, where Mr. Justice Leonard said: "Where the assets are clearly in excess of the liabilities of the debtor to a large extent, it may raise a presumption of an intent to hinder and delay creditors in the collection of their just demands and amount to a *prima facie* case of fraud." In Knapp v. McGowan, 96 N. Y. 75, it was held that a conveyance by a solvent debtor to trustees of a part of his property for the benefit of part of his creditors, with a provision for a return of the surplus to the debtor, was not, as matter of law, fraudulent and void as to creditors not provided for, nor did the statutes relating to voluntary assignments apply, they having reference only to general assignments by insolvent debtors for the benefit of all their creditors. And in the case of Pillsbury v. Kingon, 31 N. J. Eq. 624; 36 Am. Rep. 556, it was held that a solvent debtor may make an assignment. See Munson v. Ellis, 58 Mich. 332. So long as a debtor remains solvent, no sale, mortgage or assignment by him can be held to have been made in contemplation of insolvency unless actual fraud be alleged and proved. Griffith v. Cox, 79 Ky. 562. In Maryland the fact that a petitioner under the insolvent laws of the state is not actually insolvent does not preclude him from his discharge nor his right to the surplus in hands of the trustee. Weaver v. Leiman, 52 Md. 708. In Holmberg v. Dean, 21 Kan. 73, it is said: "The law does not permit a debtor who, believing himself fully solvent and actually having resources sufficient, either of cash or of property, to satisfy all his creditors in full, to assign his property and thereby withdraw it from attachments and execution of creditors, with the motive to obtain a compromise or to procure an extension of time, so as to save a larger surplus to himself." Seibert v. Thompson, 8 Kan. 65; Gardner v. Commercial Nat. Bank, 95 Ill. 298; First Nat. Bank v. Hughes, 10 Mo. App. 7.

§ 43.] INSOLVENCY, WHAT.

§ 43. Insolvency, What.— Insolvency literally imports *inability to pay;* but the term cannot be adequately defined without reference to the two important circumstances of *manner* and *time.*

Absolute insolvency may be described as that condition of a debtor's affairs in which the whole mass of his means, including property of every description, falls short of satisfying his existing engagements, and cannot, by any possibility, or in any event, be made adequate to their entire liquidation. There can be no question as to the competency of a debtor so circumstanced to make a general assignment of his property, or as to the validity of the transfer itself, in this particular.

On the other hand, where a debtor is able to meet all his engagements as they become due, in the ordinary way, that is, to satisfy them in money or its equivalent, without resorting to the general mass of his property or disturbing the course of his business, he is clearly solvent. But between these two conditions of absolute and irreparable insolvency at one extreme, and perfect ability to pay at the other, there is an extensive middle ground, representing that condition of a debtor's affairs which — in itself of various shades and degrees of difficulty — is described by a corresponding variety of expressions in daily use; such as "involved," and "embarrassed circumstances," "declining" and "failing circumstances." How far the conditions thus described amount to insolvency now remains to be considered.

Insolvency has been defined, "inability to pay one's debts out of one's own means,"[1] and "inadequacy of a man's funds to the payment of his debts,"[2] and "inability to pay debts as they become due in the ordinary course of business."[3] Other definitions are given in the books,[4] but these describe insolvency in the primary and ordinary sense of the term,[5] and are the only definitions which are important to be considered under the present head.

Insolvency, then, is the inadequacy of a debtor's means, that is, of his whole means or resources (including not only money or its equivalent, but property in its most extensive sense), for the pay-

---

[1] Cowen, J., in Herrick v. Borst, 4 Hill (N. Y.), 650, 652; Paige, J., in Curtis v. Leavitt, 15 N. Y. 200.
[2] Bell's Com. 162, cited by Brown, J., in Curtis v. Leavitt, 15 N. Y. 141.
[3] Anderson's Dic. of Law, p. 552. See Millard v. Webster, 54 Conn. 415; 8 Atl. Rep. 470.
[4] Bayly v. Schofield, 1 M. & S. 338; Shone v. Lucas, 3 D. & R. 218, cited by Cowen, J., in Herrick v. Borst, 4 Hill, 653; De Tastet v. Le Tavernier, 1 Keen, 161, 171; Ingraham on Insolvency (ed. 1827), 9; Brown, J., in Curtis v. Leavitt, 15 N. Y. 141; Paige, J., id. 201.
[5] Cowen, J., in Herrick v. Borst, 4 Hill, 652.

ment of all his debts.[1] Debts are paid with property;[2] and so long as a debtor is in possession of means of *any* kind with which, or out of which, he can himself at once discharge all his liabilities in full, or out of which his creditors can collect all their debts by legal process, it is hardly necessary to say he cannot be considered insolvent in the sense now under consideration.[3] However deficient in cash resources, if he can without any doubt satisfy all his creditors in full, either by directly distributing his property among them, or by converting it into money for the purpose of payment, though (it may be) for less than its real value, and even with the result of absorbing all his means, he is not insolvent to that degree which would justify the making of an assignment.[4]

[1] Gardner, J., in Leitch v. Hollister, 4 N. Y. 215. "The term insolvency," said Mr. Justice Field, in Toof v. Martin, 13 Wall. 40, "is not always used in the same sense. It is sometimes used to denote the insufficiency of the entire property and assets of an individual to pay his debts. This is its general and popular meaning. But it is also used in a more restricted sense to express the inability of a party to pay his debts as they become due in the ordinary course of business. It is in this latter sense that the term is used when traders and merchants are said to be insolvent; and as applied to them, it is the sense intended by the act of congress." The latter is the sense in which the term is used in the bankrupt act. See In re Randall & Sunderland, 3 N. B. R. 18; Bump's Bankruptcy (8th ed.), 397, 793 *et seq.*, and cases cited. See, also, Leon v. Welborne, 58 Tex. 157; Malvin v. West, 19 Fed. Rep. 721. The term has been construed variously in its application to debtors making assignments. Thus, in the case of McArthur v. Chase, 13 Gratt. 683, Mr. Justice Daniel, in discussing the construction of the term insolvency, as employed in the statutes prohibiting preferences by limited partnerships when insolvent, remarks: "To declare that open and notorious bankruptcy is the true and only test of insolvency would defeat in most cases the design of the law, inasmuch as the desire of the firm in failing circumstances to sustain itself, as also to prefer its special friends, would generally result in sales and assignments of most of its property, made to insure those ends, before such bankruptcy would occur. To say, on the other hand, that the firm should be held to be insolvent whenever from any cause it may fail to meet its engagements in the usual course of business, would seem to be harsh, and might tend greatly to discourage the formation of such partnerships." And he applied as a test the question whether the partnership property at the time of the assignment was sufficient to pay its debts. But in the case of Blow v. Gage, 44 Ill. 208, where the solvency of the debtors was relied upon as a badge of fraud, the fact that the debtor firm, if wound up, would be unable to pay all its liabilities, was not regarded as evidence of insolvency. In Wheelock v. Kost, 77 id. 296, it is held that to prove the insolvency of a banking corporation no better evidence need be produced than a return of *nulla bona* to executions. So, also, when the debtor's property is insufficient to satisfy his debts under process of law. Ackers v. Rowan, 33 S. C. 451; 12 S. E. Rep. 165. Yet insolvency may be proved in other ways. Postlewait v. Howes, 3 Iowa, 365; Gordon v. Worthley, 48 id. 429.

[2] Cowen, J., in Herrick v. Borst, 4 Hill, 652.

[3] Ibid. Under the provisions of the civil code of California relating to voluntary assignments, a debtor is insolvent when he is unable to pay his debts from his own means as they become due. Title 3, part II, p. 54, § 3450.

[4] McArthur v. Chase, 13 Gratt. 683. See Rokenbaugh v. Hubbell, 5 Law Rep.

§ 44.]   INSOLVENCY, WHAT.   63

It often happens that parties owning large property, much more than sufficient to pay all demands against them in the ordinary course of business, have not property enough for the purpose if all their creditors should at once press for payment. They are clearly not insolvent.[1]

§ 44. Insolvency, What — Continued.— In addition to the circumstance of the *mode* of payment (including the character of the means employed by the debtor), that of the *time* of payment constitutes an important element in the idea and definition of insolvency. In strictness the term imports *present*[2] inability to pay; it is descriptive of a present, not a future, condition of affairs. It is true that present inability to pay, though a clear matter of fact, may be consistent with ability to pay at a future day. Owing to peculiar circumstances the debtor's assets, though in ordinary times ample, may prove unavailable, because inconvertible into money. Indulgence in point of time on the part of creditors may enable the debtor to satisfy all his engagements in full; and the prospect of such a result in such a case may be morally certain. But according to a writer of high authority,[3] whose definition of insolvency has been adopted by the courts,[4] "a person in this state is truly insolvent; and it does not follow that he is not insolvent because in the end his affairs may come round, and he may ultimately have a surplus on winding them up."[5]

In what has just been said the present inadequacy of the debtor's means to satisfy his engagements has been assumed as a known fact, even in connection with the probable fact of ultimate solvency. But it may happen that this fundamental fact, instead of being apparent, is itself a matter of uncertainty, being dependent upon contingencies of various kinds which cannot be foreseen or estimated. This state of things frequently occurs in the affairs of embarrassed debtors; and it is a condition which justifies, equally with the one last mentioned, the course of making a general assignment. "Where the property of a debtor," it has been said, "is of

---

(N. S.) 95, 96; cited by Strong, J., in Ogden v. Peters, 15 Barb. 563, 564. And see Shakelford v. P. & M. Bank of Mobile, 22 Ala. 238, 242, *arg.*

[1] Millard v. Webster, 54 Conn. 417; 8 Atl. Rep. 470.

[2] The statement in the assignment that the debtor "is indebted to divers persons in considerable sums of money which he is at present unable to pay in full" is a declaration of his insolvency. Cunningham v. Norton, 125 U. S. 90; 8 S. Ct. Rep. 804. See Peabody v. Knapp, 153 Mass. 242; s. c., 26 N. E. Rep. 696; Bridges v. Miles, 152 Mass. 249; 25 N. E. Rep. 461.

[3] 2 Bell's Com. 162.

[4] Cowen, J., in Herrick v. Borst, 4 Hill, 652; Brown, J., in Curtis v. Leavitt, 15 N. Y. (1 Smith), 141; Paige, J., id. 201.

[5] Blow v. Gage, 44 Ill. 208; Savery v. Spaulding, 8 Iowa, 239; Baldwin v. Buckland, 11 Mich. 389.

a doubtful character, and may or not, according to circumstances, be sufficient to discharge his debts in full, and his primary object and influencing motive is to distribute it equitably and fairly, an assignment in such case, instead of violating the policy of the law or the rights of creditors, would be in harmony with both."[1] The possibility even of a surplus resulting in such a case to the debtor himself would form no objection to such an arrangement.

It seems reasonable, therefore, to distinguish between mere *supposition* or even belief, on the part of a debtor, at the time of making an assignment, that he is solvent, and actual *knowledge* of that fact.[2]

A mere supposition on the part of a debtor at the time of making an assignment to secure preferred creditors that he is solvent is not necessarily a badge of fraud; and an assignment will not be rendered invalid by proof of the mere supposition or belief of the debtor at the time of making it that he was solvent, when in fact he had not sufficient property to pay his debts.[3]

§ 45. **Corporation — Right to Assign.**—"A corporate body as well as a private individual," observes Chancellor Kent in his Commentaries, "when in failing circumstances and unable to redeem its paper, may without any statute provision, and upon general principles of equity, assign its property to a trustee in trust to collect its debts and pay debts and distribute as directed. It has unlimited power over its property to pay its debts."[4] "It appears to be settled," remarked Chancellor Walworth in a case before him,[5] "by a weight of authority which is irresistible, that a corporation has the right to make an assignment in trust for its creditors; and may exercise that right to the same extent and in the same manner as a natural person unless restricted by its charter or some statutory provision."[6] A corporation may conse-

---

[1] Roosevelt, J., in Ely v. Cook, 13 Barb. 612, 614. See, also, the observations of Strong, J., in Ogden v. Peters, 15 Barb. 564, 565.

[2] Kellogg v. Slawson, 15 Barb. 56 (Onondaga General Term, October 4, 1852). This was decided on the authority of Van Nest v. Yoe, 1 Sandf. Ch. 4, in which it was further said that if the assignor was in truth insolvent at the time it would make no difference as to the conclusion.

[3] Morganthem v. Harris, 12 Cal. 245; Quinnebaug Bank v. Brewster, 30 Conn. 539. But see Bates v. Ableman, 13 Wis. 644. A corporation may be insolvent under the law and yet its stock be worth par or more. Alden v. Wright, 47 Minn. 225; 49 N. W. Rep. 767.

[4] 2 Kent's Com. (10th ed.), p. 398 and note.

[5] De Ruyter v. The Trustees of St. Peter's Church, 3 Barb. Ch. 119, 124; affirmed on appeal, 3 N. Y. 238.

[6] See Catlin v. The Eagle Bank of New Haven, 6 Conn. 233; Pope v. Brandon, 2 Stew. (Ala.) 401; State v. Bank of Maryland, 6 Gill & J. 205; Union Bank of Tennessee v. Ellicott, id. 363; Warner v. Mower, 11 Vt. 385; Flint v. The

quently make an assignment with preferences to particular creditors where such transfers are permitted.¹ It has been objected to the power of a corporation to make such an assignment, that, on the happening of its insolvency, the corporation and its agents became trustees for the creditors, who were entitled to a ratable payment out of the trust fund in proportion to the amount of their debts.² This position, however, has not been sustained, and apart from statutory provisions no distinction exists between an individual and a corporation in regard to the exercise of the power of conferring preferences.³

It has also been contended, and in some instances successfully, that a general assignment of corporate property, since it practically works a dissolution of the corporation, is an act outside of the corporate powers of the officers of the company.⁴ The better opinion, and the one sustained by authority, however, is that an assignment of all the corporate property does not affect the corporate franchises and does not dissolve the corporation.⁵

Clinton Co., 12 N. H. 431; Buell v. Buckingham, 16 Iowa, 285; McCallie v. Walton, 37 Ga. 611; Dobbin v. Walton, id. 614; Rengo v. Real Estate Bank, 13 Ark. 563; Dana v. The Bank of United States, 5 Watts & Serg. 223; United States v. Bank of United States, 8 Rob. (La.) 262; Ex parte Conway, 4 Ark. 304; Hopkins v. Gallatin Co., 4 Humph. (Tenn.) 403; Bank of United States v. Huth, 4 B. Mon. 428, 429; Robins v. Embry, 1 S. & M. Ch. 207; Montgomery v. Commercial Bank of Rodney, id. 632, 644; Arthur v. Commercial Bank of Vicksburg, 9 id. 394; Ingraham v. Grig, 13 id. 22; Town v. Bank of River Raisin, 2 Doug. (Mich.) 520. But see Coners v. Bank of Brest, Harr. (Mich.) 106; Haxum v. Bishop, 3 Wend. 13; Hill v. Reed, 16 Barb. 280; Ang. & A. on Corp. (10th ed.), § 191; Bun's Ex'r v. MacDonald, 3 Gratt. 215; Hurlbut v. Carter, 21 Barb. 221; Shultz v. Sutter, 3 Mo. App. 137; Lionberger v. Broadway Savings Bank, 10 id. 499; Covert v. Rogers, 38 Mich. 363; Seav v. Bank of Rome, 66 Ga. 609; Shockley v. Fisher, 75 Mo. 498; Chew v. Ellingwood, 86 id. 260; Lamb v. Cecil, 25 W. Va. 288; Harvey v. Cubbedge, 75 Ga. 792; Bankmay-Fouche v. Brower, 74 id. 251; Cartwright v. Dickinson, 88 Tenn. 478; 12 S. W. Rep. 1030; 17 Am. St. Rep. 910.

¹ Ringo v. Real Estate Bank, 13 Ark. 563; Dana v. Bank of United States, 5 Watts & Serg. 223; State v. Bank of Maryland, 6 Gill & J. 205; Union Bank of Tennessee v. Ellicott, 6 id. 363.

² Catlin v. Eagle Bank of New Haven, 6 Conn. 233.

³ Id. 242. See review of cases in Lamb v. Laughlin, 25 W. Va. 300; **Bissell** v. Besson, 47 N. J. Eq. 580; 22 Atl. Rep. 1077. Directors of an insolvent bank in making an assignment may in good faith prefer themselves if they be creditors. Planters' Bank v. Whittle, 78 Va. 737; Kendall v. Bishop, 76 Mich. 634; 43 N. W. Rep. 643.

⁴ Smith v. New York Consolidated Stage Co., 18 Abb. Pr. 419. See Abbot v. Am. Hard Rubber Co., 33 Barb. 578; Com'rs v. Bank of Brest, Har. Ch. (Mich.) 106. See argument in Buell v. Buckingham, 16 Iowa, 284. Mr. Justice Story dissenting in Beaston v. Farmers' Bank of Delaware, 12 Pet. 138.

⁵ State v. Bank of Maryland, 6 Gill & J. 205; Union Bank of Tennessee v. Ellicott, id. 363; Hurlbut v. Carter, 21 Barb. 221, 224; Ringo v. Real Estate Bank, 13 Ark. 563; Ohio Life & Trust Co. v. Merchants' Ins. & Trust Co., 11 Humph. 1; Craig's Appeal, 92 Pa. St. 396; Ahl v. Rhoads, 84 id. 319; Shryock v. Bashore,

The right of assignment is not affected by a provision in the charter that the stockholders shall be individually liable for the corporate debts.[1] The power may be exercised by a quorum of a board of directors of a corporation at a meeting at which a bare quorum is present.[2]

The president of a corporation has not the power on his own authority to execute a general assignment,[3] but the power may be exercised by a quorum of the board of directors at a meeting at which a bare quorum is present, provided the absent members had legal notice of the meeting.[4] And this authority may be conferred by the directors upon one or more of the officers.

§ 46. Restrictions on the Right.—In some cases the general power of alienation is restrained, either by the particular act creating the corporation or by general statute.

In New York conveyances by an insolvent corporation, its officers or directors, to any of the officers, directors or stockholders, in payment of existing debts, are void. Preferences by such corporations, and assignments of stock in contemplation of insolvency, are prohibited. Every director or officer who violates this statute thereby becomes personally liable for the resulting loss.[5]

82 id. 159; Ang. & A. on Corp., § 191; Southern L. Rev., vol. III (N. S.), 553. See *post*, ch. XXII.

[1] Pope v. Brandon, 2 Stew. 401. The assignee may be authorized by the assignment to collect unpaid subscriptions of stock. Chamberlain v. Bromberg, 83 Ala. 576; 3 S. Rep. 434; Eppright v. Nickerson, 78 Mo. 482; Shockley v. Fisher, 73 id. 498.

[2] Buell v. Buckingham, 16 Iowa, 284. In Milliken v. Steiner, 56 Ga. 251, it was held that the president and cashier of a bank were the proper officers to execute an assignment. And in Assignment of the Union Banking Co., 12 Phila. 214, 469, that the stockholders of a bank have the right to select an assignee subject to the approval of the court, and having done so, a receiver appointed by the court pending litigation will be ordered to pay over to the assignee when duly qualified. In Lamb v. Cecil, 25 W. Va. 288, it was held that the common seal of the corporation, and due proof of the signature of the proper officer, is *prima facie* evidence of due execution, the presumption being that the officer did not exceed his authority. In Eppright v. Nickerson, 78 Mo. 482, it was held that the assignment, if made by the board of directors without the consent of the stockholders, is *ultra vires* and void, but only as against the stockholders. A creditor of the corporation cannot make the objection. But in the later case of Descombes v. Wood, 91 Mo. 196, the same court held that the board of directors of an insolvent banking corporation, acting in good faith, have the authority to make an assignment of all its property for the benefit of its creditors without first obtaining the consent of the stockholders to the assignment. See Hutchinson v. Green, 91 Mo. 367; 1 S. W. Rep. 853; Chew v. Ellingwood, 86 id. 260; 56 Am. Rep. 429.

[3] Richardson v. Rogers, 45 Mich, 591; 8 N. W. Rep. 526.

[4] Chase v. Tuttle, 55 Conn. 455; 12 Atl. Rep. 874; 2 Bl. Com. 480; 3 Pars. Contr. 465, 489; Simon v. Sevier Ass'n, 54 Ark. 58.

[5] R. S., part I, ch. 18, title 4, § 4 (8th ed.), p. 1729; Birdseye's ed., p. 679; L. 1890, ch. 564, § 48; also L. 1892, ch. 688, § 48. See Throop v. Hatch Lithographic Co., 125

In Missouri it is held that an insurance company cannot, even with the consent of stockholders, make a valid voluntary assignment, and thus withdraw itself and its property from the control of the insurance department of the state, after it has violated the laws made for the regulation of insurance companies. Such an assignment would be in fraud of those laws.[1]

Another special restriction imposed by statute on the right of moneyed corporations to make assignments in the state of New York is to the effect that the assignment must be authorized by the board of directors by a previous resolution when the property assigned exceeds $1,000.[2]

§ 47. **Power of Partners to Assign.**— The power of partnership firms to make general assignments for the benefit of creditors has been repeatedly recognized by the courts under unsettled restrictions regarding preferences and other special provisions. And this power may be exercised in the name of the firm by a single partner, by the authority or with the consent of his copartners, with the same effect as if made by all.[3]

The right of a partnership to assign the firm property without including the individual property of each member of the firm had been questioned,[4] but the later cases generally concur in holding such assignments valid, the right of the creditor to proceed against such individual property not being affected thereby.[5] But to what extent one partner may bind the firm by an assignment of the partnership property, in the name of the firm, *without the knowledge or consent* of his copartners, does not seem to be settled.[6] It is well established that where an assignment has been executed by one of

N. Y. 530; 58 Hun, 149; Braem v. Merchants' Nat. Bank, 127 N. Y. 508; National B'way Bank v. Wessell Metal Co., 59 Hun, 470; Keiley v. Mechanics' & Traders' Bank, 39 St. Rep. 438; Paulding v. Chrome Steel Co., 94 N. Y. 334.

[1] Relfe v. Commercial Ins. Co., 5 Mo. App. 123.

[2] R. S., part I, ch. 18, title 4, § 4 (8th ed.), p. 1729; Birdseye's ed., p. 679; L. 1890, ch. 564, § 48; L. 1892, ch. 688, § 48.

[3] Baldwin v. Tynes, 19 Abb. Pr. 32; Welles v. March, 30 N. Y. 244; Ely v. Hair, 16 B. Mon. 230; Paul v. Cullum, 132 U. S. 539. Oral assent is sufficient. Hooker v. Baillie, 118 N. Y. 413.

[4] Still v. Focke, 66 Tex. 715; 2 S. W. Rep. 59; Donaho v. Fish, 58 Tex. 164; following Coffin v. Douglass, 61 id. 406; Shropshire v. Behrens, 77 id. 275; 13 S. W. Rep. 1043; Focke v. Blum, 82 Tex. 436; 17 S. W. Rep. 770; National Bank v. Scriven, 63 Hun, 375; Blank, etc. Co. v. Walker, 46 Mo. App. 484.

[5] Bradley v. Bischel, 81 Iowa, 80; 46 N. W. Rep. 755; McFarland v. Bate, 45 Kan. 1; 25 Pac. Rep. 238; Ex parte Hopkins, 104 Ind. 157; 2 N. E. Rep. 587; Auley v. Osterman, 65 Wis. 118; 25 N. W. Rep. 657; 26 N. W. Rep. 568; Drucker v. Wellhouse, 82 Ga. 129; 8 S. E. Rep. 40, citing Harris v. Visher, 57 Ga. 229.

[6] Coleman v. Darling, 66 Wis. 155; 28 N. W. Rep. 367; 57 Am. Rep. 253; Klump v. Gardner, 114 N. Y. 153; 21 N. E. Rep. 99; Adee v. Cornell, 93 N. Y. 572. Not invalidated by being ratified on Sunday. Farwell v. Webster, 71 Wis. 485; 37 N. W. Rep. 431.

the partners, which is inoperative for the reason that the other partners did not join in or consent to its execution, it may become valid by their subsequently ratifying it; but not against liens acquired in the meantime by assailing creditors.[1] It is clear that one partner may so assign *portions* of the partnership effects, in payment of partnership debts, or by way of security for antecedent debts, or debts thereafter to be contracted on account of the firm.[2] And in this way he may give a preference to one creditor or to several.[3] Assignments of this description are frequently made in the course of trade, for the purpose of sustaining the credit of a firm, or with a view to the continuance of the partnership.[4] So a single partner may sell[5] or mortgage[6] all the partnership effects — his power to bind the firm to this extent being an implied power, arising out of the nature of the partnership relation.[7] But whether one partner or any number less than all the partners may, without the knowledge or consent of his copartners, make a general assignment of all the funds and effects of the partnership, especially in trust for the benefit of creditors, has been doubted;[8] and the question, as a general one in American law, is not yet conclusively settled.

[1] Mayer v. Bernstein, 69 Miss. 17.

[2] Harrison v. Sterry, 5 Cranch, 589; Anderson v. Tompkins, 1 Brock. 456; Parker, C. J., in Hodges v. Harris, 6 Pick. 360, 361, 362; Tapley v. Butterfield, 1 Metc. 515, 518; Walworth, C., in Havens v. Hussey, 5 Paige, 30, 31; Farnsworth, C., in Kirby v. Ingersoll, 1 Harr. (Mich.) 172, 187, 191; Hoffman, A. V. C., in Hitchcock v. St. John, Hoff. Ch. 511; Story on Partn., § 101; Collyer on Partn., § 395 (Perkins' ed. 1848). In Fox v. Hanbury, Cowp. 445, Lord Mansfield decided that, even after an act of bankruptcy committed by one partner, an assignment *bona fide* of partnership effects, by the solvent partner, to a creditor of the firm, in payment of his debt, was binding on the firm. In Hodges v. Harris, 6 Pick. 360, it was held that one partner may assign goods at sea to pay a partnership debt. In Mills v. Barber, 4 Day, 428, the assignment of a debt due the firm, made by a single partner without the knowledge of his copartner, was held valid. In Everit v. Strong, 7 Hill (N. Y.), 485, it was held to be no objection to an assignment of an account due to several partners that it was made by only one of them. See 5 Hill, 163; Roger Wheel Co. v. Fielding, 101 N. Y. 504. The power of one partner to *sell* the partnership effects, without the knowledge or consent of his copartners, in payment of debts, is well settled. Lamb v. Durant, 12 Mass. 54; Anderson v. Tompkins, 1 Brock. 456; Forkner v. Stuart, 6 Gratt. 197; McClelland v. Remsen, 3 Abb. Dec. (N. Y.) 74; Mowson v. Mendenhall, 18 Minn. 232; Young v. Keighley, 15 Ves. 557.

[3] Story on Partn., § 101.

[4] Harrison v. Sterry, 5 Cranch, 289.

[5] Anderson v. Tompkins, 1 Brock. 456; Arnold v. Brown, 24 Pick. 89; Whitton v. Smith, 1 Freeman (Miss.), 231; Mabbett v. White, 12 N. Y. 442; Graser v. Stellwagon, 25 N. Y. 315; Collumb v. Bloodgood, 15 Ala. 34; Boswell v. Green, 1 Dutch. (N. J.) 390. See McNutt v. Strayhow, 39 Pa. 269.

[6] Tapley v. Butterfield, 1 Metc. 518.

[7] Story on Partn., § 101; 3 Kent's Com. [44, 46], 47, 49; Parsons on Partnership, 167.

[8] Story on Partn., *ubi sup.;* 3 Kent's Com., *ubi sup.*

§ 48. Power of Partners to Assign — Review of Cases.— The earliest reported American case in which the question appears to have arisen is that of Dickinson v. Legare,[1] in the court of chancery of South Carolina. In that case an assignment of all the partnership effects had been made by an absent partner, without the knowledge or consent of his copartner, to pay the debt of a particular creditor. The court decided the assignment to be invalid, on the general ground of the want of power in one partner to assign the partnership property in this manner, without the consent of his copartner. The assignment appears to have been made directly to the creditor; but it was executed under very peculiar circumstances, which are supposed to have materially influenced the decision. The company, during the revolutionary war, were doing business in this country; and while one of the partners was on a voyage to France, he was taken by a British ship of war and carried as a prisoner to England, where he was prevailed upon by a creditor residing there to give him a general assignment of all the partnership funds, which funds were then in this country, to secure the payment of his particular debt against the firm. It is remarked by Chancellor Walworth, in reviewing this case in Egberts v. Wood,[2] that "although the decision was put upon the general ground that one partner had not the right to assign the partnership funds in this manner without the consent of his copartner, there is no doubt that the particular circumstances under which that assignment took place had a very considerable influence in bringing the mind of the chancellor to that result. The assignment in that case being made by a citizen of one of the United States during the existence of the war to an alien enemy and in an enemy's country was probably void by the laws of war, so far at least as to prevent its being carried into effect by any of the courts of this country. And certainly it could not be considered as made according to any mercantile usage." The decision itself was considered to have been overruled by the court of appeals of South Carolina in the case of Robinson v. Crowder,[3] which will be mentioned on a succeeding page.

§ 49. Review of Cases — Continued.— In the case of Harrison v. Sterry[4] the question as to a partner's power of assignment first came before the supreme court of the United States. In that case an assignment of a large amount of partnership property[5] had

[1] 1 Dessaus. 537.
[2] 3 Paige, 517.
[3] 4 McCord's Law, 519. See Parsons on Partnership, p. 167, n.; Kimball v. Hamilton Fire Ins. Co., 8 Bosw. (N. Y.) 495.
[4] 5 Cranch, 289.
[5] It does not appear to have been of *all.*

been made by a partner of a London house residing in New York to a trustee for the benefit of certain creditors, but without the knowledge or consent of the other partners. The assignment itself, which was under seal, professed to be made for the purpose of raising funds in aid and support of the credit of the firm, and with reference to a continuation of the business; and the partner making it had a power of attorney from the others, which, however, did not authorize him to execute deeds in their names generally. It was objected to the assignment that one partner was not authorized to make it, because it was not a transaction within the usual course of trade. But the court (Marshall, C. J.) were of opinion that it was such a transaction, and laid stress on the circumstances under which it was executed. "The whole commercial business of the company in the United States," it was said, "was necessarily committed to Robert Bird (the partner by whom the assignment was executed), the only partner residing in this country. He had the command of their funds in America, and could collect or transfer the debts due to them. The assignment under consideration is an act of this character, and is within the power usually exercised by a managing partner. In such a transaction he had the power to sign the names of both firms, and his act is the act of all the partners." The assignment, however, was adjudged to be void on another ground, namely, that of being a fraud on the bankrupt laws.

§ 49a. **Review of Cases — Continued.** — In the case of Mills v. Barber,[1] in the supreme court of Connecticut, the assignment was not a general one, the subject of it being a debt due the company, which was assigned directly to a particular creditor (with a power to collect and apply the avails) by one of the partners without the knowledge of his copartner. The court in sustaining the assignment recognized the general principle that one partner has the absolute power of disposing of all the partnership property where the act done has relation to the joint trade or business; and that, with regard to all personal property, both in possession and in action, each partner necessarily has the same power and control over it that any individual has over his own.[2]

In the case of Pearpoint v. Graham,[3] which came before Mr. Justice Washington, in the circuit court of the United States for the district of Pennsylvania, the assignment was a general one of all the partnership estate, and was executed by one of two partners

[1] 4 Day, 428.
[2] Id. 430, Brainard, J.
[3] 4 Wash. C. C. 232; sometimes inaccurately cited as "Pearpoint v. Lord." Usually cited as "Pierpont v. Graham."

to a trustee for the benefit of such of the creditors as should, within a specified time, execute in favor of the partners a full release of all demands. The executing partner resided in Philadelphia, the others in Charleston, the business being conducted in both places, under different firms. The assignment was contended to have been made without the assent of the copartner; and was objected to as invalid, on the ground that one partner could not dispose of the whole of the partnership effects, and thus by his own act dissolve the partnership, contrary to the terms of the association, without the assent of his copartners. The principle of the objection seems to have been acknowledged by the learned judge, who, in the course of delivering his opinion, remarked as follows: "It may admit of serious doubt whether one partner can, without the consent of his associates, assign the whole of the partnership effects (otherwise than in the course of the trade in which the firm is engaged) in such manner as to terminate the partnership. An assignment of all the effects to trustees for the benefit of the creditors of the concern would seem emphatically to be of this character. Such is its obvious design, and such must be its necessary consequence."[1] The learned judge, however, thought that in the case before him the assignment had been ratified by the other partner, and so became the act of the firm; and on that ground it was sustained.

§ 49b. Review of Cases — Continued.— In the case of Robinson v. Crowder,[2] in the court of appeals of South Carolina, the assignment was of all the partnership property to a trustee for the benefit of all the creditors ratably, and was executed by two of three partners, who resided in Liverpool, the remaining partner residing in Charleston, South Carolina, and having the partnership effects conveyed in his possession. The court considered it to be no objection to the assignment that it was not executed by the partner in this country; and Mr. Justice Johnson, who delivered the opinion, after referring to the case of Harrison v. Sterry as having decided "on very sound principles" that an assignment of funds for the payment of debts was in the course of trade, went on to remark as follows: "Indeed, every partial application of funds to the payment of debts, whether it consists of cash or goods, or anything else, is in effect an assignment for that purpose, and binds the firm. And if, in the course of things, a general assignment becomes necessary, there can be no reason why it should not be equally binding. The principle is the same whether it be partial

[1] 4 Wash. C. C. 234.
[2] 4 McCord's Law, 519.

or total, and it follows that, in either case, one may bind the whole."[1] The decision, however, was against the assignment on other grounds.

In the case of Egberts v. Wood,[2] in the court of chancery of New York, an assignment of all the partnership effects had been made by one of two surviving copartners, to trustees, to pay certainp referred creditors, without the assent of the other or of the representative of the deceased partner (though this was denied). The non-executing partner does not appear to have been absent; but it is said he was a dormant partner, and the execution of the assignment by him was for that reason not considered necessary to its validity. It was held by the chancellor to be "the better opinion that one of the partners, at any time during the existence of the partnership, may assign the partnership effects, in the name of the firm, for the payment of the debts of the company, although by such assignment a preference is given to one set of creditors over another."[3] The cases of Dickinson v. Legare, Robinson v. Crowder, Pearpoint v. Graham, Mills v. Barber and Harrison v. Sterry[4] were reviewed, and considered as authorizing this conclusion. The chancellor declined, however, expressing any opinion "in favor of the validity of such an assignment of the partnership effects to a *trustee* by one partner against the known wishes of his copartner, and in fraud of his right to participate in the distribution of the partnership funds among the creditors; or in the decision of the question which of the creditors should have a preference in payment out of the effects of an insolvent concern."[5]

§ 49c. **Review of Cases — Continued.** — In the case of Havens v. Hussey,[6] in the same court, an assignment of all the partnership property and effects had been made by one of two copartners — without the consent of the other, and against the known wishes of her attorney, who was present and attending to her interests — to trustees, to pay certain preferred creditors. The point mentioned and passed over in Egberts v. Wood, without an opinion, was here distinctly presented; and it was decided that such an assignment was illegal and inequitable and could not be sustained. The chancellor explained his conclusion in Egberts v. Wood to have been, "that from the nature of the contract of copartnership one of the partners, during the continuance of the partnership, might make

---

[1] 4 McCord's Law, 537.
[2] 3 Paige, 517.
[3] 3 Paige, 523.
[4] The case of Anderson v. Tompkins was not noticed.
[5] 3 Paige, 525.
[6] 5 Paige, 30.

a valid assignment of the partnership effects, or so much thereof as was necessary for that purpose, in the name of the firm, *directly* to one or more of the creditors, in payment of his or their debts, although the effect of such an assignment was to give a preference to one set of creditors over another."[1]

In the case of McCullough v. Somerville,[2] in the court of appeals of Virginia, the assignment was executed by one of two partners to trustees for the payment of creditors in a certain order, and included all the private property of the assignor and all the property of the firm. It appeared that the partner executing the assignment had the whole management of the concern, the other partner residing in another state (Pennsylvania). The court (Carr, J.) thought the deed effectual to convey the absent copartner's interest, on the grounds that the whole of the partnership property was personal, that the assignor was the sole managing partner, and that the purpose for which the effects were conveyed was the payment of *bona fide* creditors. The case of Anderson v. Tompkins was considered as fully in point and as decisive of the case. "Following this high authority," observed Carr, J., "I conclude that a partner has a right to convey the social effects (save real estate) to trustees to pay specified creditors of the firm, and this without the consent of his copartner, where (as here) that copartner resides out of the state, and the grantor is sole manager of the concern."[3] And Cabell, J., observed: "That one partner living in this state, and having the management of all the business of the company (the other partner residing out of the state), has the power to deliver over and assign the goods and choses in action of the company to the creditors of the company in discharge of the partnership debts, is a position too clear, in my opinion, to require either argument or authority. If he can do this directly, I think it equally clear that he may indirectly, by delivering or assigning them to an agent or trustee to be applied in payment of the partnership debts. And if he may do this as to all the creditors he may do it as to any one or more of them; and hence he may give a preference to a particular creditor or to a class of creditors, although the consequence of such preference may, in case of a deficiency of funds, defeat the claims of the postponed creditors."[4]

§ 49d. Review of Cases — Continued.— In the case of Deckard v. Case,[5] in the supreme court of Pennsylvania, the assignment

[1] 5 Paige, 31.
[2] 8 Leigh, 415.
[3] 8 Leigh, 415, 433.
[4] Id. 436.
[5] 5 Watts, 22. Sometimes inaccurately cited as "Deckard's Case."

was of the whole stock in trade of the firm directly to certain creditors in payment of debts. It was made by one of two partners, without the assent of the other; but it appeared that the nonassenting partner had left the country. The court sustained the assignment on the general ground of the implied power of a partner to dispose of the whole partnership interest, as held in Mills v. Barber and other cases; though the peculiar facts of the case were also urged as strengthening such a conclusion.

In the case of Hennessy v. The Western Bank,[1] in the same court, the principle maintained in Deckard v. Case was applied to the case of a general assignment of partnership effects to trustees executed by two of three copartners, the assignment being held to be binding on the third.

The case of Deckert v. Filbert,[2] in the same court, involved the same general question, though under some new circumstances. In this case two assignments had been made of all the partnership effects in trust for creditors: one by one of the partners with preferences, and the other shortly after by the other partner without preferences. The court below was of opinion that the facts in evidence proved the express dissent of each partner to the assignment made by the other, and that therefore neither assignment had validity. On appeal to the supreme court the judgment was affirmed.

§ 49e. Review of Cases — Continued.— In the case of Kirby v. Ingersoll,[3] in the court of chancery of Michigan, an assignment of all the partnership effects had been made by one partner to a trustee, who was also a creditor, with preferences to particular creditors, without the knowledge or consent of the other, *who was present*, and without any previous consultation with him. The court not only held the assignment to be void, but went the further length of declaring that one partner could not make a general assignment of the partnership effects to a trustee, for the benefit of the creditors of the firm (even without preferences), without the knowledge or consent of his copartner, where the latter is on the spot, and *might be consulted.* The chancellor, in the course of delivering his opinion, observed that "a partner may transfer a portion of the assets or obligations for the purpose of paying or securing debts, or to raise money to carry on the concern; but that the power of divesting entirely one partner of his interest, appointing a trustee for both and breaking up the concern, is not one of the powers either contemplated or implied by the contract of copart-

---

[1] 6 Watts & Serg. 300; Rogers, J., id. 310.
[2] 3 Watts & Serg. 454.
[3] 1 Harr. (Mich.) 172; s. c. on appeal, 1 Doug. 477.

nership."[1] The New York case of Havens v. Hussey was cited and relied on; and the principle upon which assignments of this kind have been declared void was stated to be that one partner has no authority to make a general assignment of the partnership effects in fraud of the rights of his copartner to participate in the distribution of them among the creditors.[2]

In the Missouri cases of Hughes v. Ellison,[3] Drake v. Rogers,[4] and Hook v. Stone,[5] it has also been decided that one partner has no authority to make a general assignment to a trustee for creditors.

§ 49f. Review of Cases — Continued.— In the case of Dana v. Lull,[6] in the supreme court of Vermont, the assignment was of all the partnership effects to a trustee for the benefit of preferred creditors, and was made by one of two partners without the authority or assent of the other. It appeared that the partners resided in different parts of the state, and that the partner who made the assignment had the superintendence and care of the business. The court held the assignment to be void as not being within the implied power of the partner, as agent of the firm; and that such power extended only to such acts as are incidental to the carrying on of the business of the firm, and not to the appointment of a trustee to close up the business and distribute the proceeds of the partnership effects in unequal proportions among the creditors, and thereby exclude the other partners from participating in the distribution, or in the decision of the question in regard to what creditors should have a preference, if any.[7] The cases principally relied on by the court were those of Hitchcock v. St. John, and Havens v. Hussey.

§ 49g. Review of Cases — Continued.— In the case of Hayes v. Heyer,[8] in the court of chancery of New York for the first circuit, the question whether one partner could make a general assignment of the partnership effects, even without preferences, where his copartner *was present* attending to business as usual, came up incidentally and was noticed by the court as being one of importance and difficulty, but was not further considered, the point not being

[1] 1 Harr. 187.
[2] Id. 191.
[3] 5 Mo. 463.
[4] 6 id. 317.
[5] 34 id. 329.
[6] 17 Vt. 390.
[7] 17 Vt. 394.
[8] 4 Sandf. Ch. 485.

before the court for decision. The case was subsequently transferred to the superior court of the city of New York, where it was decided against the validity of the assignment, as will be seen below.

§ 49h. Review of Cases — Continued.— In the case of Deming v. Colt,[1] in the superior court of the city of New York, a general assignment had been made of all the partnership property by one of two partners to a trustee in trust for the benefit of the creditors of the firm without any preferences; and it was made without the consent or assent of the other partner and without consulting him, although he was at the time actively engaged in the business. The court held the assignment to be void on the principle that one partner cannot of his own exclusive authority appoint a trustee to dispose of the partnership effects in behalf of all the copartners; and that it is not incident to the right of one partner thus to select an agent and clothe him with all the authority of the firm for the disposal and application of its property. The rule in this case was laid down by the court without hesitation, "that a partner can *in no case* make a general assignment to a trustee for the benefit of creditors against the consent or without the acquiescence of his copartner; *the latter being present* or capable of acting in the matter."[2]

In the case of Hayes v. Heyer,[3] in the same court, and reported with the last case, the same question arose under somewhat different circumstances. This was a case of an assignment made by one of the general partners in a limited partnership, with the consent of the special partner, but without the knowledge or assent of the other general partner, who was present and might have been consulted. The assignment was a general one of all the partnership effects to a trustee for the benefit of all the creditors ratably. The court adopted the views and conclusion of the court in Deming v. Colt, and declared the assignment void, holding that the power to appoint a trustee, and transfer to him the entire partnership effects, was not an implied power which one partner might exercise without the knowledge or consent of the others.[4]

[1] 3 Sandf. S. C. 284.
[2] Id. 392.
[3] Id. 284, 293.
[4] In the case of Everson v. Gehrman, decided at the New York general term of the supreme court, February, 1855, it was held that the confession of a judgment to a particular creditor, by one of two partners, against the known wishes of his copartner, was void; the court holding it to be more objectionable than even an assignment to a trustee. The cases of Havens v. Hussey, Deming v. Colt, and Hayes v. Heyer, were cited and approved.

§ 49i. Review of Cases — Continued.— In the case of Kemp v. Carnley,[1] in the same court, an assignment had been made by one of two partners of all the partnership property to a trustee, giving a preference to a mortgage creditor of the firm. It appeared that the non-executing partner had absconded. The court held the assignment valid. The doctrine of Deming v. Colt and Hayes v. Heyer was recognized as the established rule of the court.

In the case of Fisher v. Murray,[2] in the New York court of common pleas, it was held that to support an assignment of the whole of the partnership property to a trustee for the payment of debts, by one partner, or any number short of the whole, even without preferences, it must be shown that it was made under circumstances that rendered it impossible to consult the other partners; or from their acts or declarations, either before or subsequent thereto, it must appear that it was executed with their assent or by their authority.

§ 49j. Review of Cases — Continued.— In the case of Forbes v. Scannell,[3] in the district court of California for the fourth judicial district, an assignment had been made by one of three partners doing business in Canton, China, in the absence of the others, of all the partnership property to trustees for the equal benefit of all the creditors. One of the absent partners was residing and doing business at Shanghai, about nine hundred miles from Canton; but it appeared that after the assignment he had denied that he was a partner at the time of the failure, asserting that he had previously withdrawn from the firm. The other partner was a salaried partner, not sharing in the profits and losses, and at the time of the assignment was absent from China on a trip to Calcutta. The court held the assignment valid.

§ 49k. Review of Cases — Continued.— In the case of Robinson v. McIntosh,[4] in the New York common pleas, a copartnership assignment to trustees for the benefit of creditors, in all respects equitable and just to all parties, made in a condition of insolvency by the general and managing partners of a limited copartnership, was sustained. Mr. Justice Woodruff observed: " Whatever doubts there may be in ordinary cases of the power of some of the members of a firm to make such a disposition of the property, while other members are present and equally entitled to a voice in the disposition, I do not doubt that we ought to sustain an assignment

---
[1] 3 Duer, 1.
[2] 1 E. D. Smith (N. Y.), 341.
[3] 13 Cal. 242.
[4] 4 E. D. Smith, 221.

in all respects equitable and just to all parties, made in a condition of hopeless insolvency by all of those who, by the terms of the actual arrangement between the members, are the active managing partners in the business."

§ 49l. Review of Cases — Continued.— In the case of McGregor v. Ellis,[1] in the superior court of Cincinnati, where the non-assigning partner was present and dissented, the court (Storer, J.), in an opinion reviewing the cases, expressed itself very strongly in favor of the doctrine that a transfer of the partnership property in trust for creditors by one partner was obligatory upon the others. And the same doctrine was applied in the case of Graves v. Hull,[2] in the supreme court of Texas.

§ 49m. Review of Cases — Continued.— Robinson v. Gregory,[3] in the supreme court of New York, and affirmed at the court of appeals, is an important case. The firm consisted of three partners, one of whom was residing in Paris. The partnership affairs having become embarrassed, the two resident partners executed a general assignment of individual and partnership property, with preferences. The assignment was adjudged invalid in the court of last resort, but the opinion of the court is not reported. The court below placed its decision upon the ground that a partner who went abroad immediately granted a power, in cases of emergency, to the remaining partners to act for him. This view of the law was regarded as incorrect by the appellate court.

In Pettee v. Orser,[4] in the superior court of New York, where an assignment was executed by two of four partners, the others of whom were absent temporarily on business, the conveyance was adjudged void.

§ 49n. Review of Cases — Continued.— In the case of Wells v. March [5] one of the partners had absconded, leaving a letter addressed to his copartner, saying, among other things, "Take charge of everything in our business — close it up speedily," etc. The remaining partner thereupon executed a general assignment of the

---

[1] 2 Disn. (Ohio), 386.
[2] 33 Tex. 665.
[3] 29 Barb. 560, referred to in Welles v. March, 30 N. Y. 344. Wright, J., observed: "Our judgment proceeded upon the ground that it was not competent for the two partners, without the consent or authority of the third, to make a general assignment of the partnership property of a trustee. Our opinion was that no such power could be implied from the partnership relation."
[4] 6 Bosw. (N. Y.) 123; affirmed in court of appeals. See Ingraham, J., in Palmer v. Myers, 43 Barb. 509 (1860).
[5] 30 N. Y. 344.

partnership property, which was assailed by judgment creditors as being fraudulent in fact, and not the act of the partners. The court were of opinion that the conduct and declaration of the absconding partner were such as to empower his copartner to execute the assignment. Mr. Justice Wright, who delivered the opinion of the court, said: " A general assignment to a trustee of all the funds and effects of the partnership for the benefit of creditors is the exercise of a power without the scope of the partnership enterprise, and amounts of itself to a suspension or dissolution of the partnership itself. It is no part of the ordinary business of the copartnership, but outside and subversive of it. No such authority as that can be implied from the partnership relation.[1] The assignment in the present case was without preference, but the principle of law to be applied to it is not affected by that circumstance." The case of Kelly v. Bader, where the facts were very similar, was rested on substantially the principle adopted in this case.

In the case of Palmer v. Myers,[2] where it appeared that one of the partners had absconded, and ineffectual efforts had been made to consult with him and obtain his consent to the execution of an assignment, it was held that evidence of these facts was admissible to sustain an assignment executed by the remaining partners. The court relied upon Kemp v. Carnley,[3] Deckard v. Case,[4] and Kelly v. Baker,[5] and with this agrees the case of National Bank v. Sackett.[6]

The case of Coope v. Bowles[7] was substantially the same in its facts as Robinson v. Gregory,[8] and a similar conclusion was reached. Where it was provided in the copartnership agreement that either partner might dissolve or close up the copartnership upon the failure of the other partner to contribute his proportion of the capital, this was deemed a sufficient authority to enable one partner to execute a general assignment without the consent of his copartner.[9]

In the case of Stein v. La Dow,[10] in the supreme court of Minnesota, the rule was stated to be that under ordinary circumstances one partner may not, without the assent of the other, assign the firm property to a trustee for the benefit of the creditors, yet, if an extraordinary emergency occurs in the affairs of the partnership, and the non-assigning partner cannot be consulted on account

---

[1] Johnson, J., concurred upon the ground of an express authority. See p. 353.
[2] 43 Barb. 509.
[3] 3 Duer, 1.
[4] 5 Watts, 22.
[5] 2 Hilt. 536.
[6] 2 Daly, 395.
[7] 42 Barb. 87; S. C., 18 Abb. Pr. 442; 28 How. Pr. 10.
[8] 29 Barb. 560; reversed in court of appeals. See Welles v. March, 30 N. Y. 344.
[9] Roberts v. Shepherd, 2 Daly, 110.
[10] 13 Minn. 412; Williams v. Frost, 27 Minn. 255.

of his absence under circumstances which furnish reasonable ground for inferring that he intended to confer upon the assigning partner authority to do any act for the firm which could be done with his concurrence if he were present, such an assignment, if fairly made, will be presumed, *prima facie*, to be valid. The temporary absence of one partner from the state was not regarded as sufficient to empower the remaining partner to execute an assignment of firm property.

§ 49o. Review of Cases — Continued.— In Ohio[1] it was held that one of the members of an insolvent firm cannot, either before or after dissolution of the partnership, make a valid assignment of all its effects for the benefit of creditors, against the will of a copartner, or without his assent, when he is present or accessible. The same point and like conclusions were had in Adams v. Thornton.[2]

In the case of Loeb v. Pierpont[3] the court, after reviewing the authorities, said: "We think the American cases are almost unanimous in holding that one partner has not the authority to execute an assignment of the property of the firm unless his copartner be absent, so that he cannot be consulted, or is incapable, from some cause, of expressing either assent or dissent." Temporary insanity of one partner does not authorize the other to make a general assignment.[4]

In the case of Rumery v. McCulloch[5] the assignment was made without preferences, and in every respect regular, except that it was made by one partner only. The facts were that the other partner had abandoned the business and permanently located in Canada. The assignment was held to be valid.

In the case of Chadwick v. Burrows,[6] a firm being insolvent and one of the partners having absconded, the remaining partner made an assignment upon the recommendation of all the creditors except one who attacked the assignment. Held, that the assignment was a valid conveyance.

§ 49p. Review of Cases — Continued.— A partner who has in fact withdrawn from the firm, so that as between himself and the other partners he has no authority or control over the property or business of the firm (although as between himself and creditors he

[1] Holland v. Drake, 29 Ohio St. 441.
[2] 82 Ala. 261; 56 Am. Rep. 49; 3 S. Rep. 20.
[3] 58 Iowa, 469; 43 Am. Rep. 122, citing the text. Anderson v. Thompson, 1 Brock. 456, distinguished.
[4] Stadhman v. Loehr, 47 Hun, 327.
[5] 54 Wis. 565; 12 N. W. Rep. 65.
[6] 42 Hun, 39.

may still be liable for its debts), need not join in an assignment by such firm for the benefit of its creditors.[1]

In the case of Johnson v. Robinson[2] the court held: "It is generally held that one partner cannot, without the authority or consent of his copartner, make a general assignment. An exception is recognized when one partner has the entire management of the business or the other is absent, so as to be beyond the reach of prompt communication." In this case the partner who did not sign the assignment was absent from the state at the time, and the assignment was made to secure a firm debt. The court decided that under these circumstances the assignment was a valid conveyance.

In the case of Coleman v. Darling,[3] R., N. and H. were partners doing business under a firm name at Unity in the state of Wisconsin The assignment was made by R. alone, at Wausau, in the same state, on the 22d of June, 1885. The other partners were at that time at their place of business, and knew nothing of the assignment until the 23d of June, at which time N. assented to it. H. did not then assent, but after a garnishee process had been served in this case he did consent to the assignment and ratify the same. Held, the assignment was void when made.

§ 49q. **Review of Cases — Continued.**— In the case of Anderson v. Tompkins,[4] before Chief Justice Marshall, in the circuit court for the district of Virginia, the question of a partner's power of assignment was distinctly presented, and very fully considered by the court. In this case an assignment had been made by one of two partners of an American firm during the absence of the other on a voyage to England, and (as was alleged) without his knowledge or consent. It was an assignment of all the effects, personal and real, of the company (the house having stopped payment) to trustees, for the payment, first, of certain creditors named in the deed, and then of those who should exhibit their claims within certain specified periods. The general doctrine as to the power of each partner of a firm to dispose of the whole of the partnership effects was not controverted on the argument; but it was contended that it did not authorize the deed in that case because, first, it was not an act in the course of trade, but was a disposition of the whole subject, and a dissolution of the partnership; and secondly, because it was a preference to particular creditors, in making which the

---

[1] First Nat. Bank v. Hackett, 61 Wis. 335; 21 N. W. Rep. 280.
[2] 68 Tex. 400; 4 S. W. Rep. 625.
[3] 66 Wis. 155; 57 Am. Rep. 253; 28 N. W. Rep. 367; citing Brooks v. Sullivan, 32 Wis. 444; Rumery v. McCulloch, 54 id. 565; 12 N. W. Rep. 65, *supra*, and the text.
[4] 1 Brock. 456.

other partner ought to be consulted. The court, however (after considering these objections at length), was of opinion that the assignment, so far as it embraced the partnership effects for sale, was valid; and on this point Chief Justice Marshall expressed himself with peculiar confidence, as having "never, from the first opening of the cause, entertained a moment's doubt." He could perceive no distinction between an *assignment* of all the partnership effects to pay debts, and a *sale* of all for money or on credit, which was clearly within the power of a single partner.[1] Both were regarded as acts fairly within the course of trade,[2] and the circumstance that the goods were conveyed to *trustees* to be sold was considered not to affect the power.[3] The assignment was regarded as not necessarily dissolving the contract of partnership, though it might suspend the operations of the company.[4]

It is evident, from a perusal of this important case, that the decision of the court was placed partly on the ground of a partner's general power, and partly on that of the necessity of the case, arising from the absence of the non-executing partner; but it is difficult to ascertain which of these considerations exercise a controlling influence upon the mind of the court. Throughout his opinion the chief justice seems to place the power to *assign* on the same footing with the power to *sell;* the latter being conceded to belong absolutely to each partner, to the extent of the *whole* effects, "though the others be *within reach.*"[5] The situation of the partners in the case before the court is referred to as giving "increased force" to the reasoning by which the assignment was sustained as an act within the course of trade, but not as constituting the main ground of the opinion.[6]

§ 50. **Review of Cases — Continued — Preferences.**— And in this last cited case it is only on the point of giving a *preference to creditors* that the court expressly say that had the non-executing partner been present "he ought to have been consulted," and that "the act ought to have been a joint act."[7] *Preference of creditors*, indeed, is evidently regarded as the most important feature of the power; *conveyance to trustees* being held to be an immaterial consideration. From these expressions it might be inferred to have been the opinion of the court (though not expressed in terms) that

---

[1] 1 Brock. 460, 461.
[2] Ibid.
[3] Ibid. 461.
[4] Ibid.
[5] Ibid. 459, 461.
[6] 1 Brock. 460.
[7] Id. 462.

an assignment by one partner to trustees for the benefit of creditors, *without preferences*, would be valid, though the non-assenting partner was present or within reach. On the other hand, there are expressions in the opinion which seem to limit even the power of *sale* by one partner to cases where the other is absent, and make the consultation of a partner who is present a necessary preliminary to its exercise. Thus, it is said of the power of sale, that "it would certainly not be exercised in the presence of a partner without consulting him; and if it were so exercised, slight circumstances would be sufficient to render the transaction suspicious, and perhaps to fix on it the imputation of fraud."[1] And again, "In the absence of one of the partners, in a case of admitted and urgent necessity, the power to sell may be exercised by the partner who is present, and who must act alone, in such manner as the case requires, provided it is exercised fairly."[2]

§ 51. **Review of Cases — Continued — Preferences.**— In the case of Hitchcock v. St. John,[3] in the court of chancery of New York for the first circuit, the facts were these: One of two partners resided in the city of New York, carrying on the business there; and the other in Augusta, Georgia, conducting the business there, under the same firm. The partner residing in New York made an assignment to trustees of all the partnership property of that firm, with preferences to certain creditors, without the assent of the partner in Augusta. The assignment was declared void, the court holding that one partner, on the eve of insolvency, cannot assign all the partnership property to a trustee for the purpose of paying debts of the firm *with any preferences*. The case was held to be different where the assignment was *without preferences*, the vice-chancellor observing that "the rule seems well established that this court will sustain an assignment of the whole of the partnership funds by one partner where all the creditors are admitted to equal participation."[4] It was further held that although partnership funds might be exhausted by an immediate payment to a creditor by one partner, yet there was no implied authority, arising from the partnership relation, in one partner to appoint a trustee of all the funds, to collect and distribute them as that partner shall determine. The appointment of a trustee was regarded as an extraordinary act, in which all the members of the firm were entitled to a voice and share.[5]

[1] Id. 460.
[2] Id. 463.
[3] Hoff. Ch. 511.
[4] Hoff. Ch. 514, 515.
[5] Hoff. Ch. 518.

The facts of this case resemble, to a considerable extent, those in Pearpoint v. Graham, already noticed,[1] which, however, was not cited. The effect of the *absence* of a non-assenting partner, as qualifying the rule applicable to the case, was not adverted to; the principal test adopted by the court for determining the question being the fact whether the assignment was with or without *preferences*.

§ 52. **Power of Partners to Assign — Summary.**— It will be seen, on an examination of the cases just reviewed, that those of them which deny the partner's power to assign in trust, place such denial on different grounds, which may be reduced to the following: that such an assignment works a dissolution of the copartnership;[2] that it is an act out of the course of trade, not contemplated by the contract of partnership, and not within the implied powers incident to the partnership relation; and that it is an act in fraud of the rights of other partners to participate in the distribution of the partnership funds among the creditors, and in the decision of the question which of the creditors, if any, should have a preference in payment out of the property assigned. The cases which affirm the power place it, to some extent, on the general ground of being an implied power incident to the partnership relation, but more frequently on the ground of the relative situation of the partners, and the necessity of the case; as where it is impossible to consult the copartners, owing to their absence or other cause. The following propositions appear to be deducible from the adjudged cases on the question now under consideration, and to be sustained by the weight of authority:

I. One partner may, without the assent of his copartner, assign a portion or the whole of the partnership effects directly to creditors in payment of partnership debts.[3]

II. One partner cannot make a general assignment of the partnership effects to a trustee for the benefit of creditors, even ratably, without the consent[4] or against the known wishes of the other

---

[1] *Ante*, p. 72.

[2] On this point, the opinions of Mr. Justice Washington, in Pearpoint v. Graham, and of Chief Justice Marshall, in Anderson v. Tompkins, are in conflict. See *ante*, pp. 72, 74.

[3] Mills v. Barber, 4 Day, 428; Egberts v. Wood, 3 Paige, 517; Havens v. Hussey, 5 id. 30; Deckard v. Case, 5 Watts, 22; Mabbett v. White, 12 N. Y. 442; Graser v. Stillwagen, 25 N. Y. 315; Johnson v. Robinson, 68 Tex. 400; 4 S. W. Rep. 625.

[4] But he may, with the express consent of the other partners. Ely v. Hair, 16 B. Mon. 230; Baldwin v. Tynes, 19 Abb. Pr. (N. Y.) 32; Lowenstein v. Flauraud, 82 N. Y. 494; affirming 11 Hun, 399; Kelly v. Baker, 2 Hilt. 531; Roberts v. Shepherd, 2 Daly, 110. See Wooldridge v. Irving, 23 Fed. Rep. 676, and note.

§ 52.] POWER OF PARTNERS TO ASSIGN. 85

partners, for the reason that no such authority can be implied from the partnership relation.[1]

III. Where a partner has relinquished all control of the partnership affairs by absconding, this will be regarded as evidence of an authority to the remaining partners to make an assignment either with or without preferences.[2]

IV. But the mere absence of a partner from the country will not be regarded as conferring such a power upon the remaining partners.[3]

V. But where the absence or non-residence of the partner is coupled with other circumstances tending to show such an authority, especially where the assignment is made without preferences,[4]

But the rule requiring all the partners to unite in the assignment does not apply to those who are liable as partners to third persons, but only to those who are partners as between each other. Adee v. Cornell, 25 Hun, 78; affirmed, 93 N. Y. 572; Whitworth v. Patterson, 6 Lea (Tenn.), 119; Loeb v. Pierpont, 58 Iowa, 469; 43 Am. Rep. 123; 12 N. W. Rep. 544, *supra*, p. 80.

[1] Robinson v. Gregory, cited in Welles v. March, 30 N. Y. 344; reversing S. C., 29 Barb. 560; Palmer v. Myers, 43 Barb. 509; Pettie v. Orser, 6 Bosw. 123; affirmed in Court of Appeals; Wilcox v. Jackson, 7 Col. 521; Loeb v. Pierpont, 58 Iowa, 469; Steinhart v. Fyhrie, 5 Mont. 463. See Palmer v. Myers, 43 Barb. 509; Welles v. March, 30 N. Y. 344; Coope v. Bowles, 42 Barb. 87; Haggerty v. Granger, 15 How. 243; Paton v. Wright, id. 481; National Bank v. Sackett, 2 Abb. Pr. (N. S.) 280; Stein v. La Dow, 13 Minn. 412; Bull v. Harris, 18 B. Mon. (Ky.) 195; Dunklin v. Kimball, 50 Ala. 251; Maughlin v. Tyler, 47 Md. 545; Wetter v. Schlieper, 4 E. D. Smith (N. Y.), 917; Sloan v. Moore, 37 Pa. St. 217; Dana v. Lull, 17 Vt. 390; Hook v. Stone, 34 Mo. 329; Hughes v. Ellison, 5 id. 463; Drake v. Rogers, 6 id. 317; Kirby v. Ingersoll, Harr. Ch. (Mich.) 172; 1 Doug. 477; Bowen v. Clark, 1 Biss. 128; Cleaver v. Brenzel, 1 Luz. Leg. Reg. 228. *Contra*, Ch. J. Marshall, in Anderson v. Tompkins, 1 Brock. 456; Hitchcock v. St. John, Hoff. Ch. 511; Robinson v. Crowder, 4 McCord, 519; McGregor v. Ellis, 2 Disn. (Ohio), 286; McCullough v. Sommerville, 8 Leigh, 415; Graves v. Hall, 32 Tex. 665; Gordon v. Cannon, 18 Gratt. 387. And see Deckard v. Case, 5 Watts, 22; Hennessy v. Western Bank, 6 Watts & Serg. 300; Egberts v. Wood, 3 Paige, 517; Lassell v. Tucker, 5 Sneed (Tenn.), 1. But see Barcroft v. Snodgrass, 1 Cold. (Tenn.) 430; Hollum v. Drake, 29 Ohio St. 441; Adams v. Thornton, 82 Ala. 261; 3 S. Rep. 20; 56 Am. Rep. 49; Stadhman v. Loehr, 47 Hun, 327; Shattuck v. Chandler, 40 Kan. 516; 20 Pac. Rep. 225.

[2] Welles v. March, 30 N. Y. 344; Kemp v. Carnley, 3 Duer, 1; Palmer v. Myers, 43 Barb. 509; S. C., 29 How. Pr. 8; Deckard v. Case, 5 Watts, 22; Kelly v. Baker, 2 Hilt. 531; National Bank v. Sackett, 2 Daly, 395; Rumery v. McCulloch, 54 Wis. 565; First Nat. Bank v. Hackett, 61 id. 335; Coleman v. Rosenfeld, 28 N. W. Rep. 367; Aubrey v. Osterman, 25 id. 657, and note; S. C., 65 Wis. 118; Petition of Daniels, 14 R. I. 500; Sullivan v. Smith, 15 Neb. 476; S. C., 18 Neb. 450; 19 N. W. Rep. 620; Chadwick v. Burrows, 42 Hun, 39.

[3] Robinson v. Gregory, cited in Welles v. March, 30 N. Y. 344; reversing S. C., 29 Barb. 560; Coope v. Bowles, 42 Barb. 87; S. C., 18 Abb. Pr. 442; Pettee v. Orser, 6 Bosw. 123; Stein v. La Dow, 13 Minn. 412; Coleman v. Darling, 66 Wis. 155; 57 Am. Rep. 253; 28 N. W. Rep. 367, *supra*, p. 81.

[4] Pearpoint v. Graham, 4 Wash. C. C. 232; Hitchcock v. St. John, Hoff. Ch. 511; Dana v. Lull, 17 Vt. 390.

and in an extraordinary emergency, or where a subsequent ratification can be inferred,[1] the assignment will be sustained.[2]

The mere fact of the absence or residence of a partner out of the state does not seem to furnish the test for determining the validity of assignments by a copartner. Taken in connection with the fact that the latter is sole manager of the company's business, and the other a merely dormant or inactive partner, it would indeed be allowed its full weight, as in the case of McCullough v. Sommerville, where both facts appeared. But where the partners are equally active in the business, and especially where the business is transacted in different states, under the same firm or different firms, by partners resident at each place, the right of one to assign on the mere ground of the absence of the other would be much less readily conceded.[3]

§ 53. Power of Partner to Assign — Summary of Authorities. It remains to notice the opinions of several eminent American jurists on this question of a partner's power of assignment; and these seem to have left it in much of its original uncertainty. The inclination of Mr. Justice Story's mind seems to have been against the power to assign *all* the property of the partnership under *any* circumstances. In his Treatise on Partnership he observes: "It may well admit of some doubt whether this power extends to a general assignment of all the funds and effects of the partnership by one partner for the benefit of creditors; for such an assignment would seem to amount of itself to a suspension or dissolution of the partnership itself."[4] In a note to this passage he cites Pearpoint v. Graham, Dana v. Lull, Cullum v. Bloodgood,[5] Deming v. Colt, Kirby v. Ingersoll, and Deckert v. Filbert.[6] He then extracts

---

[1] Forbes v. Scannell, 13 Cal. 242; Stein v. La Dow, 13 Minn. 412; McGregor v. Ellis, 2 Disn. (Ohio), 286; Pearpoint v. Graham, 4 Wash. C. C. 232; McNutt v. Strayhorn, 39 Pa. St. 269; Holland v. Drake, 29 Ohio St. 441; Adee v. Cornell, 93 N. Y. 572; Petition of Daniels, 14 R. I. 500.

[2] Forbes v. Scannell, 13 Cal. 242; Stein v. La Dow, 13 Minn. 412; McCullough v. Sommerville, 8 Leigh, 415; McGregor v. Ellis, 2 Disn. (Ohio), 286; Pearpoint v. Graham, 4 Wash. C. C. 232; Harrison v. Sterry, 5 Cranch, 289; Johnson v. Robinson, 68 Tex. 400; 4 S. W. Rep. 625; Farwell v. Webster, 71 Wis. 485; 37 N. W. Rep. 437.

[3] See Pearpoint v. Graham, 4 Wash. C. C. 232; and Hitchcock v. St. John, Hoff. Ch. 511, in which the facts were as above stated.

[4] Story on Partn., § 101. The same view of the effect of such an assignment was taken by Mr. Justice Washington in Pearpoint v. Graham, and by Chancellor Walworth in Havens v. Hussey. But in Anderson v. Tompkins Chief Justice Marshall held that such an assignment did not necessarily dissolve the contract of partnership; and the same was held by the supreme court of Pennsylvania in Deckard v. Case, 5 Watts, 22.

[5] 15 Ala. 42.

[6] 3 Watts & Serg. 454.

largely from the opinions of the court in the cases of Anderson v. Tompkins, Egberts v. Wood, Havens v. Hussey, and Hitchcock v. St. John, and sums up by observing: "There is no small difficulty in supporting the doctrine, even with qualifications, that one partner may make a general assignment of all the partnership property."[1] Chancellor Kent, in his Commentaries,[2] remarks: "It is a point not quite settled whether one partner, without the knowledge or assent of his copartner, though under circumstances, may not assign over all the partnership effects and credits, in the name of the firm, to pay the debts of the firm; and where all the creditors are admitted to an equal participation, the conclusion is that he may.[3] He may give a preference to one creditor over another; though whether it might be made to a trustee for that purpose, against the known wishes of the copartner, so as to terminate the partnership, was left an unsettled point in Egberts v. Wood."[4] He then cites the case of Havens v. Hussey as settling this point, and refers to some of the other cases on the subject.[5] The passage concludes as follows: "There is no small difficulty," says Mr. Justice Story, "in supporting the doctrine, even under qualifications, that one partner may make a general assignment of all the partnership property, so as to break up its operations.[6] This I consider to be the soundest conclusion to be drawn from the conflicting authorities."[7]

Mr. Parsons, in his work on Partnership,[8] refers to the subject in the following language: "Whether one partner may assign all the property in trust to pay creditors, the firm being solvent, has

[1] Story on Partn., § 101, n. 4.
[2] 3 Kent's Com. [44], 47, n.
[3] Harrison v. Sterry, 5 Cranch, 289; Mills v. Barber, 4 Day, 428; Lamb v. Durant, 12 Mass. 54; Pothier, Traité du Con. de Soc., Nos. 67, 69, 72. 90; Robinson v. Crowder, 4 McCord (S. C.), 519; Hodges v. Harris, 6 Pick. 360; Deckard v. Case, 5 Watts, 22; Hitchcock v. St. John, Hoff. Ch. 511; Anderson v. Tompkins, 1 Brock. 456.
[4] 3 Paige, 517. Some doubt expressed in Pearpoint v. Graham, 4 Wash. C. C. 232.
[5] Hitchcock v. St. John, Hoff. Ch. 516; Kirby v. Ingersoll, Harr. Ch. (Mich.) 174; Dana v. Lull, 17 Vt. 390; Gibson, C. J., 8 Watts & Serg. 63, S. P.
[6] Story on Partn., pp. 145–150.
[7] Mr. Troubat, in his Treatise on the Law of Limited Partnership, states the rule in regard to general partners to be, that one partner may separately, at any time during the existence of the partnership, assign the effects and property of the firm, and prefer one of its creditors to another. "It is true," he adds, "that it was not without great doubt and difficulty that the courts could arrive at this conclusion, but it became *and is now the rule*, as far as such a rule can be established by the authority of the highest judicial tribunals in South Carolina, Connecticut, Massachusetts and the United States as a federal body." Law of Commandatory and Limited Partnership in the United States, p. 390, § 393 (Phila. ed., 1853).
[8] Parsons on Partnership, p. 166.

been much doubted. That he may, in good faith, assign a part of the property to pay or secure an existing debt, or a debt to be contracted, is not doubted; and we think the weight of authority sanctions his assigning the whole property in trust for all the creditors, especially if this be done without preferences of any kind; although this has been questioned on the ground that such a transfer of itself operates a dissolution; but so, in fact, would the previous and actual insolvency, in effect, though not technically."

On the whole — while the law remains thus unsettled on this point — it may be laid down as the only safe practical rule, that in making assignments of partnership property, particularly to trustees, all the partners, special as well as general, dormant as well as active, should be consulted; and the assignment should either be the joint act of all, or should be made by the express authority or with the consent or concurrence of those who do not actually execute it, or subject to ratification on their part.

It is clear, however, that the right of one partner to dispose of partnership property is confined strictly to *personal* effects, and does not extend to *real* estate owned by the partnership.[1] One partner cannot convey away the real estate of the firm without special authority.[2]

§ 54. **Power of Each Partner to Assign His Interest.** — The power of each partner over his own share or interest of the partnership property stands upon an entirely different footing from his power over the partnership property generally. No partner owns absolutely any part of the property. His interest is an interest subject to the interest of his copartners.[3] While, therefore, he cannot transfer his share of any specific partnership property, he may transfer the interest which he has in the firm property, subject to the rights of his copartners; and he may make a valid assignment of this interest to trustees for the benefit of his creditors.[4] But such an assignment will pass only so much as may re-

---

[1] Anderson v. Tompkins, 1 Brock. 456; Brainerd, J., in Mills v. Barber, 4 Day, 428, 430; Shaw, C. J., in Tapley v. Butterfield, 1 Metc. 518; Carr, J., in McCullough v. Sommerville, 8 Leigh, 415, 433; Collyer on Partn., § 394; Story on Partn., § 101; Thompson v. Bowman, 6 Wall. 316. See Collumb v. Coldwell, 16 N. Y. 484; S. C., 24 N. Y. 505; Tieman v. Molliter, 71 Mo. 512.

[2] Collyer on Partn., § 394; Story on Partn., § 101. The separate property of a partner can in no case be conveyed, unless by an instrument executed by him. In re Wilson, 4 Barr, 430. But with such authority he can convey away the real estate of the firm by an assignment under seal in the name of the firm. Rumery v. McCulloch, 34 Wis. 565; Scruggs v. Burruss, 25 W. Va. 670.

[3] Parsons on Part., p. 168.

[4] Fellows v. Greenleaf 43 N. H. 421; Horton's Appeal, 13 Pa. St. 617; Kirby v. Schoonmaker, 3 Barb. Ch. 46. But see Hagerty v. Granger, 15 How. Pr. 243. And separate assignments by each of the partners of all his property to the same

main after the payment of the firm debts and a settlement with his copartners.[1]

An assignment by one partner of all his interest in the joint property to the other partner or partners works a dissolution of the firm,[2] and the remaining partner may thereupon execute an assignment of all his property, whether belonging to the previous firm or not, in trust for the payment of his individual creditors.[3]

§ 55. **Surviving Partners.**— As to the power of *surviving* partners it has been held in South Carolina that a surviving partner, especially in case of insolvency, may assign the firm's effects to a trustee for the payment of debts.[4] The supreme court of the United States has recently held that a sole surviving partner of an insolvent firm who is himself insolvent may make a general assignment of all the firm's assets for the benefit of all joint creditors with preferences to some of them.[5]

In New York it is held that the surviving partner has no power without the consent of the representatives of the deceased partner to make an assignment to a trustee creating preferences,[6] but such an assignment cannot be attacked by creditors, although liable to

assignee convey the firm property. Boughton v. Crosby, 47 Conn. 577; Bulger v. Rosa, 119 N. Y. 459; 24 N. E. Rep. 853; Keith v. Ham, 89 Ga. 590.

[1] See Platt v. Hunter, 11 N. Y. Weekly Dig. 300; Schiele v. Healy, 61 How. Pr. 73; Fellows v. Greenleaf, 43 N. H. 421. An assignment by one partner of *his* property for the benefit of his creditors which does not purport to convey the partnership property gives the assignee no title to said property or right to its possession. Van Kleeck v. McCabe, 87 Mich. 599, 49 N. W. Rep. 872. A voluntary assignment by an insolvent partnership which devotes partnership assets to the payment of individual debts of a partner is fraudulent and void as to firm creditors. Marks v. Bradley, 69 Miss. 1.

[2] Horton's Appeal, 13 Pa. St. 617; Armstrong v. Fahnstock, 19 Md. 59; Power v. Kirk, 1 Pitts. R. 510; Clark v. Wilson, 19 Pa. 414; Parsons on Part., p. 400; Conrad v. Burke, 21 W. Va. 396; Ogden v. Arnot, 29 Hun, 146.

[3] Clark v. McClelland's Assignee, 2 Grant (Pa.), 31; Clark v. Wilson, 19 Pa. St. 414; Power v. Kirk, 1 Pitts. R. 510; Marsh v. Bennett, 5 McLean, 117; Price v. De Ford, 18 Md. 489; Dimon v. Hazard, 32 N. Y. 35; Smith v. Howard, 20 How. Pr. 266; Crane v. Rosa, 23 N. Y. Weekly Dig. 440; Gutman v. McNulty, 22 id. 241. *Contra*, Heye v. Bolles, 33 How. Pr. 266; S. C., 2 Daly, 231.

[4] White v. Union Insurance Co., 1 Nott & McCord, 556. And see in Virginia, Galt v. Callaud, 7 Leigh, 594. In Colorado he may make an assignment for the equal benefit of all the firm's creditors. Salisbury v. Ellison, 7 Col. 167. See 8 id. 157. But the rule is otherwise in Tennessee. See Bancroft v. Snodgrass, 1 Cold. (Tenn.) 430; Tiernan v. Molliter, 71 Mo. 512; Vosper v. Kramer, 31 N. J. Eq. 420. The surviving partner cannot apply the partnership assets to the satisfaction of his individual debts before fully discharging those due from the firm. Gable v. Williams, 59 Md. 46.

[5] Emerson v. Senter, 118 U. S. 3.

[6] Nelson v. Tenney, 36 Hun, 327; Egberts v. Wood, 3 Paige, 517.

be set aside at the instance of the representatives of the deceased partner.[1]

§ 56. **Limited Partnership.**— In almost if not quite all the states, restrictions have been placed by statute [2] upon the powers of limited partnerships and their members, when insolvent or in contemplation of insolvency, to make assignments. These restrictions in general prevent such partnerships and their members, under such circumstances, from giving any preferences to creditors.[3]

But although a limited partnership cannot make an assignment giving preferences, when insolvent or in contemplation of insolvency, nor can any member of such partnership make such assignment under like circumstances, yet an assignment for the benefit of creditors in all respects equitable and just to all parties, made in a condition of hopeless insolvency by all those who, by the terms of the actual arrangement between the members, are the active managing partners in the business, will be sustained.[4]

---

[1] Williams v. Whedon, 39 Hun, 98; Beste v. Burger, 17 Abb. N. C. 162, and note. See Haynes v. Brooks, id. 152. In Loeschigk v. Hatfield, 5 Robt. 26 (S. C., as Loeschigk v. Addison, 4 Abb. Pr. (N. S.) 210; affirmed, 51 N. Y. 660), the power of a surviving partner to make an assignment with preferences was sustained, but it is to be observed that the conveyances in this case were not technically a general assignment but rather a mortgage to a creditor. It would seem from Hutchinson v. Smith, 7 Paige, 26 (Walworth, Ch. id. 35, 36), that since the adoption of the Revised Statutes, the surviving member of an insolvent firm is not authorized to give a preference in payment to some creditors of the firm over others; and that a general assignment made by him of the partnership effects to a trustee for the purpose of securing a preference to some of the creditors, even with the assent of the legal representatives of the deceased partner, is invalid; but this case is of doubtful authority on this point, in view of the above decisions and the remarks of Allen, J., in Beste v. Burger, 17 Abb. N. C. 162, 169. In a case in the circuit court of the United States for the district of Michigan, it was held that by the dissolution of a partnership, provision being made in the articles of dissolution for the payment equally of all the creditors of the firm by the partner who purchases the interest of the retiring partner and continues the business, such partner is a trustee for the creditors of the firm; and a subsequent assignment by such a partner of the partnership effects, preferring certain creditors to others, and contrary to the stipulation in the articles of dissolution, is fraudulent and void. Marsh v. Bennett, 5 McLean, 117; Williams v. Whedon, 39 Hun, 98; Beste v. Burger, 17 Abb. N. C. 162; 13 Daly's Rep. 317; 110 N. Y. 644. See Haynes v. Brooks, 17 Abb. N. C. 152; 116 N. Y. 487; 42 Hun, 528. A surviving member of a firm may in making an assignment prefer a bank from which he borrowed money to pay his firm debts. Durant v. Pierson, 124 N. Y. 444; 21 Am. St. Rep. 684.

[2] See *post*, ch. X.

[3] See, on this subject, Troubat on Limited Partnership, ch. 13.

[4] Robinson v. McIntosh, 3 E. D. Smith, 221; Jackson v. Sheldon, 9 Abb. 133; Hayes v. Heyer, 3 Sandf. 293; 4 Sandf. Ch. 485; Whitewright v. Stimpson, 2 Barb. 379; Greene v. Breck, 10 Abb. 43; Darrow v. Bruff, 36 How. 479; Mills v. Argall, 6 Paige, 582; S. C., 7 Paige, 586; Van Alstyne v. Cook, 25 N. Y. 489.

§ 56.]   LIMITED PARTNERSHIP.   91

And such assignment is valid when made by the general partner only.[1] But this has been doubted, unless the express consent of the special partner is contained in the partnership agreement or can be inferred from the circumstances of the case.[2]

[1] Robinson v. McIntosh, *supra*. Under the laws of Texas an assignment by a limited partnership consisting of one general and one special partner, for the benefit of creditors, may be executed by the general partner, and such assignment need not embrace the individual property of the special partner. Tracy v. Tuffly, 134 U. S. 206; 10 S. Ct. Rep. 527.

[2] Mills v. Argall, 6 Paige, 582. See Crary's Specl. Proceedings, vol. I, p. 714. On the insolvency of a limited partnership, the partnership property becomes a trust for the benefit of creditors; and if the partners neglect to place it in the hands of a trustee for immediate distribution among all the creditors ratably, any creditor may file a bill on behalf of himself and all other creditors for distribution of the partnership funds without first obtaining a judgment at law. Innes v. Lansing, 7 Paige, 583. See Jackson v. Sheldon, 9 Abb. Pr. 127; Whitewright v. Stimpson, 2 Barb. 379; Darrow v. Bruff, 36 How. 479; McArthur v. Chase, 13 Gratt. 683. An assignment by a general partnership in which a member of a limited partnership may be also a member is not to be treated, in view of these prohibitions, as an assignment by the individual member of the limited partnership of his individual property. Fanshawe v. Lane, 16 Abb. 71.

CHAPTER V.

TO WHOM AN ASSIGNMENT MAY BE MADE—QUALIFICATIONS OF ASSIGNEES.

§ 57. Who May be Assignee.
58. Qualifications of Assignee.
59. Relative as Assignee.

§ 57. **Who May be Assignee.**— A voluntary assignment for the benefit of creditors may be made either to a person who is a creditor of the assignor or to one who is not a creditor,[1] and it may be made to a single individual or to several.[2] The persons to whom it is made are, from the usual form of the transfer, called *trustees* as well as *assignees;* the latter being the more general term by which they will be designated in the present work.

When the assignment is made to partners, it is not material whether they are designated by the firm name or their individual names, if the language used is such to indicate with certainty the

[1] Yates, J., in Wilt v. Franklin, 1 Binn. 502, 520; Lee, J., in Johnston v. Zane's Trustees, 11 Gratt. 552, 564; United States Bank v. Huth, 4 B. Mon. (Ky.) 423; Wooster v. Stanfield, 11 Iowa, 128; Frink v. Buss, 45 N. H. 325. See Layson v. Rowan, 7 Rob. (La.) 1. Creditor may be assignee. Marshall v. Livingston Nat. Bank, 11 Mont. 351; 28 Pac. Rep. 312. In Virginia, in the case of Gordon v. Cannon, 18 Gratt. 388, where the trustee was a creditor, and the trust was to secure his own demand amongst others, it was contended that the trust deed was a mortgage, and the trustee could not sell by the mere authority of the deed, and without resorting to a court of equity; the objection was not regarded as valid.

[2] Where made to several, only those who accept are required to act (Moir v. Brown, 14 Barb. 39; Douglass v. Cissna, 17 Mo. App. 44), but those who accept must all act. Brennan v. Wilson, 4 Abb. N. C. 297; 71 N. Y. 502. It may be made to a non-resident (see Backrack v. Norton, 132 U. S. 337; 10 S. Ct. Rep. 106) or to an attorney (Tucker v. Parks, 7 Colo. 62), but not to a married woman (Haydock Carriage Co. v. Pier, 74 Wis. 582), or by a corporation to an officer or stockholder. Conlee Lumber Co. v. Ripon L. & M. Co., 66 Wis. 481; 29 N. W. Rep. 285; Pope v. Brandon, 2 Stew. 401. In Covert v. Rogers, 38 Mich. 363, it was held that the fact that the assignee is or has been a stockholder of the insolvent corporation, or is insolvent himself, does not disqualify him; but the jury may consider its bearing upon the good faith of the transaction. But an officer of the court before whom the trustee is required to qualify cannot himself be assignee and qualify before his deputy. Bancroft v. Snodgrass, 1 Cold. (Tenn.) 430. In Brahmstadt v. McWhirter, 9 Neb. 6, it was held that a clerk of court might act as assignee, and his approval of his own bond did not render his acts void. Trustees are not disqualified by the fact that they are also *cestuis que trustent*. Story v. Palmer, 46 N. J. Eq. 1; 18 Am. Rep. 363; Winner v. Hoyt, 66 Wis. 227; 28 N. W. Rep. 380; 57 Am. Rep. 257.

persons who are nominated as assignees.¹ Where it is intended to make the transfer to an assignee, he must be named in the instrument.² But where the conveyance is declared by the court to be an assignment for creditors, and no trustee is named, the court will either regard the transferee as trustee³ or will name a trustee.

The power to select and appoint his own assignee is one which the common law of voluntary assignments allows to every debtor contemplating such a disposition of his property;⁴ and he is not bound to consult his creditors, or any of them, and obtain their previous consent to the appointment,⁵ but may make his selection even against their will.⁶ But this power is not to be exercised arbitrarily and without proper reference to the interests of the creditors.⁷

§ 58. **Qualifications of Assignee.**—It is an essential qualification of an assignee, not only that he should be capable from age, health and education of performing the duties of the office, but also that he should be of sufficient character and pecuniary ability to afford assurance to creditors that the fund will be safe in his hands, and that the trust will be properly administered;⁸ and the selection of incompetent assignees, in order to retain control of the property or otherwise intentionally defraud creditors, will have the effect of rendering the assignment void.⁹ Thus, where the debtor selected

---

¹ Forbes v. Scannell, 13 Cal. 242; Douglass v. Cissna, 17 Mo. App. 44.

² In the case of Reamer v. Lamberton, 59 Pa. St. 462, where an assignment for the benefit of creditors, leaving a blank for the assignee's name, was executed and acknowledged, and an execution was afterwards issued against the assignor and put into the sheriff's hands, and subsequently the assignee's name was inserted and the assignment recorded, it was held that the title to the property remained in the assignor till the assignee's name had been inserted and the assignment delivered to him, and the assignor's goods were not protected from the execution. See Park v. Glover, 23 Tex. 469.

³ See Burrows v. Lehndorff, 8 Iowa, 96.

⁴ Tilghman, C. J., in Wilt v. Franklin, 1 Binn. 502, 516; Sandford, A. V. C., in Cram v. Mitchell, 1 Sandf. Ch. 251, 253; and Jackson v. Cornell, id. 354. In Burd v. Smith, 4 Dall. 76, this right was denied. But in all the subsequent Pennsylvania cases it has been conceded.

⁵ Harris, J., in Webb v. Daggett, 2 Barb. 9, 11.

⁶ Id.

⁷ Sandford, A. V. C., in Cram v. Mitchell, 1 Sandf. Ch. 254; Roosevelt, J., in Childs v. Mouseley, N. Y. Supreme Ct., Sp. Term, Nov. 1854.

⁸ See observations of Tilghman, C. J., in Wilt v. Franklin, 1 Binn. 502, 516; Christiancy, J., in Angell v. Rosenbury, 12 Mich. 241; Flandrau, J., in Guerin v. Hunt, 6 Minn. 375; Jennings v. Prentice, 39 Mich. 421.

⁹ This will depend upon the question whether the selection was made with a fraudulent intent. In the case of Guerin v. Hunt, Mr. Justice Flandrau laid down the rule as follows: "If it appears that the selection of an incompetent as-

for assignees three relatives, one of whom was incapacitated by his residence, one by blindness, and the third by his want of education, from executing the trust, it was held to be evidence of an intent on the part of the assignor to keep the control of the property in his own hands, or to appropriate it for his own use and benefit; and the assignment was therefore declared void.[1] So, where the debtor selected as his assignee his brother, who at the time was unfit to attend to business by reason of a lingering disease which the assignor himself believed was incurable, and of which he died, the assignment was held for that cause to be fraudulent and void as against creditors; and it was considered by the court that the selection of such an assignee furnished strong presumption of an intent on the part of the assignor to keep the control and disposal of the property.[2]

The selection of a person as assignee who is known to the assignor to be insolvent has been repeatedly pronounced by the courts to be a fraud upon the rights of creditors, as evincing an intention on the part of the assignor to place his property beyond their reach, or, in the language of the statute of fraudulent conveyances, "to delay or hinder them" in the collection of their debts.[3] But the better doctrine is that based upon the presence or absence of *fraudulent intent* in the assignor. The mere fact that the assignee is a poor man and destitute of means is not a badge of fraud, but in a suit attacking an assignment for fraud it is competent to show the insolvency of the assignee.[4] But where the creditors are consulted, and consent to the assignment to a particular individual, such consent will rebut the presumption that there was any intention to commit a fraud, although the assignee was

signee was made in order to allow the assignor to control the administration of the estate, then the assignment will be declared void, because such an intent on the part of the assignor would be a fraud upon his creditors. If it should appear that the assignee was incompetent in fact from any cause, but that his selection was not made from any improper motive on the part of the assignor, then the assignee would be subject to removal at the instance of a creditor of the state and a proper person would be substituted by the court to carry out the trust." A want of capacity on the part of the assignee to act as such does not show fraudulent intent in the assignment. Conlee Lumber Co. v. Ripon L. & M. Co., 66 Wis. 481; 29 N. W. Rep. 285.

[1] Cram v. Mitchell, 1 Sandf. Ch. 251.
[2] Currie v. Hart, 2 Sandf. Ch. 353.
[3] Reed v. Emery, 8 Paige, 417; Walworth, C., id. 418; Haggarty v. Pittman, 1 id. 298; Connah v. Sedgwick, 1 Barb. 210; Browning v. Hart, 6 id. 91. But see Shryock v. Waggoner, 28 Pa. St. 430; Angell v. Rosenbury, 12 Mich. 241; Jennings v. Prentice, 39 id. 421.
[4] Chambers v. Meant, 66 Wis. 625; Pearce v. Beach, 12 How. Pr. 404; In re Paddock, 6 id. 215; Holmberg v. Dean, 21 Kan. 73; Klauber v. Charlton, 47 Wis. 564; 3 N. W. Rep. 443.

known to be destitute of property, as the creditors would have the right to repose themselves upon his honesty only.[1]

§ 59. **Relative as Assignee.**— The selection of members of the assignor's family, and of doubtful competency (such as a clerk and a journeyman boarding in his family, and both young men), as assignees, conduces, it has been held, to raise a presumption that there was a secret trust in the assignment for the benefit of the assignor.[2] And the selection of near relatives as assignees, especially where they are placed before all other creditors in the schedule of preferred debts, is a circumstance against the assignment.[3] But the relationship of the parties, though calculated to awaken suspicion, is of itself no evidence of fraud in a conveyance of property.[4] And in a case where all the parties to a deed of trust made by an insolvent debtor (viz., the debtor, the trustee, and most of the secured creditors) were related, it was held that such relationship furnished no predicate for a legal presumption or conclusion of fraud, although it was a circumstance which might go to a jury, to be considered by them in connection with the other facts of the case in determining the question of fraud in fact.[5]

In some of the states the appointment of a competent and responsible assignee is provided for by statutory enactments, and in most of them he is required to execute bonds with sureties for the faithful performance of the trust.[6]

An assignment by a religious corporation, in trust to pay debts, may be made to persons ineligible, under its charter, as general trustees of the society.[7]

It is an important preliminary to the making of an assignment that the person selected as assignee be one who will accept the ap-

[1] Walworth, C., in Reed v. Emery, 8 Paige, 417, 418. The creditors, indeed, may agree that the assignor himself shall act as trustee or agent in certain cases. Tompkins v. Wheeler, 16 Pet. 106, 120.

[2] Perkins, J., in Caldwell v. Rose, Smith (Ind.), 190; Caldwell v. Williams, 1 Ind. 405; Perkins, J., id. 408; Martin v. Kennedy, 83 Ky. 336; Sattler v. Marino, 30 La. Ann. 335.

[3] Sandford, A. V. C., in Cram v. Mitchell, 1 Sandf. Ch. 251, 255. In this case as well as in Currie v. Hart and in Connah v. Sedgwick the assignees were relatives of the assignors.

[4] Bumpas v. Dotson, 7 Humph. 310; Nesbitt v. Digby, 13 Ill. 33; Baldwin v. Buckland, 11 Mich. 389; Shultz v. Hoagland, 85 N. Y. 464; Sininger v. Herron, 18 Neb. 450; 25 N. W. Rep. 578; Collins v. Cronin, 117 Pa. St. 35; 11 Atl. Rep. 869; Archer v. Long, 32 S. C. 171; 11 S. E. Rep. 86.

[5] Montgomery's Ex'rs v. Kirksey, 26 Ala. 172. And see, on this point, Dunlap v. Bournonville, 26 Pa. St. 72; Adams v. Ryan, 61 Iowa, 733; 17 N. W. Rep. 159.

[6] This branch of the subject will be particularly considered hereafter, under a distinct head. See ch. XXXI.

[7] De Ruyter v. St. Peter's Church, 3 N. Y. 238.

pointment and undertake the trust; as his refusal to act, after the execution and delivery of the instrument, might impair its effect or interfere with its operation.[1]

A debtor, having once appointed his assignee, cannot, by the assignment, reserve the right to name another person as successor of the assignee, in case the latter wishes to resign the trust.[2]

[1] See *post*, ch. XVIII.
[2] Planck v. Schermerhorn, 3 Barb. Ch. 644; Smith v. Bowdre, 69 Miss. 692.

CHAPTER VI.

THE ASSIGNED PROPERTY—THE AMOUNT ASSIGNED—WHAT MAY BE ASSIGNED—WHAT PASSES BY THE ASSIGNMENT.

§ 60. The Amount of Property Assigned.
61. Exemptions.
62. Exception of Property Not Exempt.
63. When the Assignment Must Embrace All.
64. Proportion of Amount Assigned to Debts.
65. What May be Assigned.
66. What Passes Under General Terms.
67. Foreign Property.
68. Claims for Damages for Torts.
69. Wife's Property.
70. Leasehold Interests.
71. Interests of Devisees.
72. Interests of Heirs.
73. Rents.
74. Money in Bank.
75. Property Fraudulently Transferred by Assignor.
76. What Does Not Pass.
77. After-acquired Property.

§ 60. **The Amount of Property Assigned.**— The amount of property embraced in, or intended to be conveyed by, an assignment determines its character as being general or partial. A general assignment is understood to import, in its nature, a transfer of *all* the debtor's property for the benefit of his creditors. The nature of the relation created by insolvency usually requires that the transfer should be of this comprehensive character. "Creditors," observes Chief Justice Marshall,[1] "have an equitable claim on *all* the property of their debtor, and it is his duty, as well as his right, to devote the *whole* of it to the satisfaction of their claims." Partial assignments, however, when not within the prohibition of any statute, and where they leave the unassigned residue open to creditors, are, as we shall see, valid conveyances.[2]

In some of the states an assignment of *all* the debtor's property is expressly required by statute, and in others assignments are construed to pass all the debtor's property, real and personal, whether specified in the assignment or not. The intentional withholding from a general assignment of property included in it is

---

[1] In Brashear v. West, 7 Pet. 608.
[2] See *post*, ch. IX.

fraudulent and makes it void; but the unintentional omission of property of small value does not render it void.[1]

Apart from all statutory provisions it may be said that if there be nothing in the instrument or schedules annexed to it to limit or qualify its operation, a general assignment by a debtor of all his estate and effects will pass to the assignee everything which is in its nature assignable, except such property as may be specially exempted by law, or excepted by the terms of the deed itself, where such exception is allowed.

It is, however a leading rule in the construction of assignments by debtors, that no more property will pass to the assignee than is embraced in the terms of the instrument; and even where *all* the debtor's property is assigned in terms, if there be subsequent words of description or a reference to a schedule, as setting it forth particularly, the contents of such clause or schedule will operate to limit the general clause of transfer, and nothing will pass that is not so set forth or specified.[2]

§ 61. Exemptions.— There are, however, portions of a debtor's property which the law expressly exempts from the process of creditors; and these of course he is allowed to except and retain out of the general conveyance.[3] Provision is frequently made by

---

[1] Farrington v. Sexton, 43 Mich. 454; 5 N. W. Rep. 654, *post*, p. 543; Krug v. McGilliard, 76 Ind. 28.

[2] See *post*, ch. VIII.

[3] Heckman v. Messenger, 49 Pa. St. 465; Mulford v. Shirk, 26 Pa. St. 473; Dow v. Platner, 16 N. Y. 562; Baldwin v. Peet, 22 Tex. 708; Garner v. Frederick, 18 Ind. 507; Smith v. Mitchell, 12 Mich. 180; Brooks v. Nichols, 17 Mich. 38; Farquharson v. McDonald, 2 Heisk. (Tenn.) 404; Sugg v. Tillman, 2 Swan, 208. See Simpson v. Roberts, 35 Ga. 180; Dolson v. Kerr, 5 Hun, 643; Barber v Buffalo, 111 N. C. 206. In Michigan an assignment is not void on its face for excepting property exempt from execution without specifying it, and the assignor may select property exempt from execution after the execution of the instrument, and the assignee takes the property subject to this right of selection. Smith v. Mitchell, 12 Mich. 180; Hollister v. Loud, 2 Mich. 309, 310, 322. So in Missouri. Hartzler v. Tootle, 85 Mo. 23. But in New Jersey an assignment of all his property by a debtor divests him of the personal right to claim what is by statute exempt from execution, and does not vest it in the assignee. Moses v. Thomas, 26 N. J. L. 124; Van Waggoner v. Moses, id. 570. So where the debtor made no reservation in the instrument of the one hundred dollars exempt, he was held to have waived his right to reserve the money. Raymond's Appeal, 28 Conn. 47; Brooks v. Nichols, 17 Mich. 38. The exemption is not lost by offering the exempted property for sale, or changing the place or conditions of occupation. Rosenthal v. Scott, 41 Mich. 632. When an assignment limits the transfer to property "which might be reached or recovered by any of the creditors of the assignor," it sufficiently excludes such property as would be exempt by law. Chandler v. Jenks, 50 Mich. 151. But where a debtor executes a deed of trust of all his property for the benefit of his creditors, without reservation of his right to exemption, he is entitled to no allowance on that account out of the proceeds

statute for these exemptions. Under a general reservation of exempt property in an assignment for the benefit of creditors the debtor will be allowed such exempt articles as he may select within a reasonable time after the execution of the assignment. But his right to claim such property may be lost by undue laches.[1] A partner is not entitled to any exemption from firm property until all the firm debts are paid, and a provision in an assignment conveying partnership property excepting such articles as may be exempt by law is nugatory and inoperative.[2] In Wisconsin a reservation of the homesteads of partners in the assignment by the firm does not render such an assignment void.[3] In the Kentucky case of Hemphill v. Haas,[4] it was held that a deed of assignment for the benefit of creditors executed by the debtor alone does not divest either him or his wife of the homestead exemption. And in Ohio the court went so far as to hold that the assignor's wife was entitled to an allowance in lieu of the homestead, against the assignee, though the family dwelling-house had been burned previous to the sale by the assignee.[5]

§ 62. **Exception of Property Not Exempt.**— It has sometimes been the practice to except, in addition to such articles as were exempted by law, other portions of property for the debtor's use; and it has been held that the insertion of such a clause of exception would not vitiate the assignment. Thus, in Maine, previous to the statute of April 1, 1836, concerning assignments, where the assignor excepted from the general conveyance of his property " necessary and proper household furniture and means of paying his small debts under fifty dollars, and ordinary family expenses," it was held that as the excepted property did not pass to the as-

of the property. Carroll v. Else, 75 Md. 301; Chilcoat's Appeal, 101 Pa. St. 22. See Bank of Commerce v. Payne, 86 Ky. 446; 8 S. W. Rep. 856.

[1] Meyers v. Conway, 90 Ala. 109; 7 S. Rep. 639; Cribben v. Ellis, 69 Wis. 337; 34 N. W. Rep. 154; Bradley v. Bischel, 81 Iowa, 80; 46 N. W. Rep. 755; Bobbitt v. Rodwell, 105 N. C. 236; 11 S. E. Rep. 245; Muhr v. Pinover, 67 Md. 480; 10 Atl. Rep. 289; O'Neil v. Beck, 69 Ind. 239; Garner v. Frederick, 18 Ind. 407.

[2] McFarland v. Bate, 45 Kan. 1; 25 Pac. Rep. 238; Ex parte Hopkins, 104 Ind. 157. See, also, McNair v. Rewey, 62 Wis. 167; First Nat. Bank v. Hackett, 61 id. 335; Goll v. Hubbell, id. 293. The presumption is that the exemption was intended to be from individual property and not from firm property, so as to sustain the assignment. Wooldridge v. Irving, 23 Fed. Rep. 676. An assignment by an individual of the assets of a partnership for the purpose of holding them as his own under the exemption law is fraudulent as to firm creditors. Luce v. Barnum, 19 Mo. App. 359.

[3] Shawano County Bank v. Koeppen, 78 Wis. 533; 47 N. W. Rep. 723.

[4] 88 Ky. 492; 11 S. W. Rep. 510.

[5] Kelly v. Duffy, 31 Ohio St. 437. See, also, Hoge v. Hollister, 8 Baxter (Tenn.), 533. As to the Ohio exemption act see Close v. Sinclair, 38 Ohio St. 530; Kuhn v. Nieberg, 40 id. 631.

signee, but was left open to attachment as it was before, the exception did not vitiate the assignment.[1] But it was afterwards held in that state that an exception of property not exempted by law rendered an assignment void.[2] It is now declared by statute that assignments shall be construed to pass all the debtor's property, real and personal, whether specified in the assignment or not, which is not by law exempt from attachment.[3] In Mississippi a deed of assignment by a bank for the benefit of its creditors, which conveys all its assets and property, except certain specified portions, to trustees, has been held not void because of the reservation.[4] In Pennsylvania an assignment (stipulating for a release), excepting the household furniture of the assignors *and* property exempt from execution, is voidable; but until an election by creditors to avoid it, conveyances by the assignees for value received by them are valid.[5] But in other cases in that state it has been held that the reservation from a general assignment for the benefit of creditors of certain specified property, without any stipulation, reservation or condition, in favor of the assignor, does not render it void as to creditors.[6] And even where all the debtor's property passes under the assignment by reason of statutory enactment, the fact that a foreign tribunal will not give efficacy to the assignment, and that certain real property of the debtor situated elsewhere may not pass owing to such construction, will not invalidate the assignment.[7] And an express exception from the

[1] Canal Bank v. Cox, 6 Greenl. 395.
[2] Foster v. Libby, 24 Me. 448.
[3] See Act of March 21, 1844; Merrill v. Wilson, 29 Me. 58.
[4] Ingraham v. Grigg, 13 Sm. & M. 22. See Wooldridge v. Irving, 23 Fed. Rep. 676.
[5] Johns v. Bolton, 12 Pa. St. 339; Boker v. Crookshank, 1 Phila. 193.
[6] Knight v. Waterman, 36 Pa. 258; Heckman v. Mersenger, 49 Pa. St. 465. In Bousman's Appeal, 90 Pa. St. 178, the court say: "The general right of the assignor to except and reserve from the assignment property to the value of $300 is undoubted. He may not do so out of land to the injury of one holding a lien for the purchase-money, or a judgment lien in which the exemption from execution is waived. His claim, however, must be restricted to some property which he owned, or in which he had an interest at the time of the assignment, or, at the farthest, to the proceeds for which that property was sold. It cannot extend to money made by the assignee's care, management and use of the assigned property. Hildebrand v. Bowman, 100 Pa. St. 580; Wiley's Appeal, 90 id. 173. The proper time to claim the exemption is when the appraisers act. The assignor cannot claim the exemption when at the time of making the assignment there are judgments against him in which he has waived the benefit of the exemption laws. Shaeffer's Appeal, id. 45. Where the debtor assigned, reserving property exempt by law, and afterward a creditor recovered judgment against him on a note containing a waiver of exemption, it was held that the creditor must assert the waiver by execution or attachment against the reservation, and had no standing to claim in the distribution of the fund assigned. Myers' Appeal, 78 Pa. St. 452. See Numbers v. Shelly, id. 426.
[7] Frink v. Buss, 45 N. H. 325.

grant of a portion of the property, as, for instance, a claim against certain persons then in suit, there being no reservation of any benefit from or interest in the property actually assigned, does not invalidate an assignment;[1] nor does the insertion of the clause, "except what is by law exempt," when in fact none is exempt.[2] Considering the present general inclination of the courts against all reservations in assignments for the debtor's own benefit, the safest rule is to avoid these clauses altogether.

§ 63. **When the Assignment Must Embrace All.**— Assignments containing a stipulation for the release of the debtor (even where such stipulations are allowed) are in most of the states invalid unless they contain a transfer of *all* the debtor's property;[3] but assignments with preferences not conveying all the property are not necessarily void for that reason.[4]

In Rhode Island it has been held that an assignment which on its face purports to convey all the assignor's property, when in fact he has other property not disclosed in the assignment, is void as against creditors; but if it does not so purport, it is valid, notwithstanding property may remain in the hands of the assignor unassigned.[5] And in Massachusetts an assignment by partners, not purporting to transfer their whole property, but only their partnership property, and not purporting to transfer their separate property, nor alleging that they had no separate property (and it not appearing elsewhere that they had no separate property), and providing for a discharge from their entire partnership debts, was held to be repugnant to the insolvent laws of the state.[6]

But in Maine the provision of the act of 1844, that an assignment shall be construed to pass all property not exempt from attachment, whether specified in such assignment or not, will not bring the private property of partners within an assignment of

[1] Carpenter v. Underwood, 19 N. Y. 520. See Bates v. Ableman, 13 Wis. 644; Baldwin v. Peet, 22 Tex. 702; Foster v. Libby, 24 Me. 448; Moss v. Humphrey, 3 Greene (Iowa), 443.
[2] Dodd v. Hills, 21 Kan. 707; Hildebrand v. Bowman, 100 Pa. St. 580; Rainwater v. Stevens, 15 Mo. App. 544; Perry v. Vezina, 68 Iowa, 25; McNair v. Rewey, 62 Wis. 167; First Nat. Bank v. Hackett, 61 id. 335; Goll v. Hubbell, id. 293; Wooldridge v. Irving, 23 Fed. Rep. 676; Luckmeyer v. Seltz, 61 Md. 313; Fay v. Grant, 53 Hun, 44; N. Y. S. Rep. 910; Rothschild v. Saloman, 52 id. 486; 5 N. Y. S. Rep. 865; In re Shotwell, 43 Minn. 389; 45 N. W. Rep. 842.
[3] See *post*, ch. XI.
[4] See *post*, ch. XI.
[5] Pierce v. Jackson, 2 R. I. 35.
[6] Shaw, C. J., in Wyles v. Beals, 1 Gray, 233, 236. It has been held in Indiana that an assignment by a firm of firm property for the payment of firm debts is valid though it does not embrace individual property. Ex parte Hopkins, 104 Ind. 157.

property belonging to the copartnership.[1] In Michigan an assignment has been held void for not including[2] the assignor's real estate; but an express omission of property subject to specific claims did not necessarily invalidate an assignment.[3]

§ 64. **Proportion of Amount Assigned to Debts.**— Where an assignment is made for the benefit of *particular* creditors, the proportion which the amount of property assigned bears to the amount of debts provided for is frequently an important consideration. If a debtor in failing circumstances makes an assignment of this character, and the value of the property assigned is more than the parties could have reasonably supposed necessary to satisfy the claims of the creditor provided for, fraud may be inferred from that circumstance alone, unless a satisfactory excuse is shown for the transfer of the excess.[4] Such a transaction affords ground for the conclusion that the assignment was upon some secret or implied understanding between the parties to keep the surplus from other creditors, and for the benefit of the debtor himself.[5] But where, at the time of making the assignment, it is doubtful whether the property assigned will be sufficient to satisfy the claims of the creditors for whose benefit it was made, a mere nominal excess in the amount of the property over that of the debts will not justify a conclusion of fraud. Thus, where the debts provided for were upwards of $26,000, and the whole nominal amount of property and demands assigned, including $21,000 of outstanding claims, was short of $34,000, the court refused to pronounce the transaction fraudulent, considering it probable that there would not be any excess after making due allowance for bad debts and deducting the expenses of collection and of executing the trust.[6] The same principle has been applied to deeds of trust for the security of particular creditors, which are so common in the southern states.[7]

[1] Simmons v. Curtis, 41 Me. 373.
[2] Price v. Haynes, 37 Mich. 487.
[3] Henry v. Root, 38 Mich. 371.
[4] Beck v. Burdett, 1 Paige, 305; Stetson v. Miller, 36 Ala. 642. See Longmire v. Goode, 38 Ala. 577; Watkins v. Jenkins, 24 Ga. 431; Du Bose v. Carlisle, 51 Ala. 590; Geilinger v. Philippi, 133 U. S. 246; 10 S. Ct. Rep. 266.
[5] Butler v. Stoddard, 7 Paige, 163; Walworth, C., id. 165.
[6] Beck v. Burdett, 1 Paige, 305; Walworth, C., id. 309.
[7] Burgin v. Burgin, 1 Ired. L. 453. In this case it was remarked by the court as follows: "With respect to the amount of property it must be remembered that, as it cannot be ascertained what accidents may occur to diminish the perishable part of it, or lessen its value, or how old accounts will turn out upon collection, it is usual to convey more in mortgage or trust, by way of security, than it may be supposed will precisely meet the demand. It is indeed fair that the creditor should have ample security; and therefore it furnishes no conclusive argument of a dishonest purpose if the deed conveys property of value fully to

§ 65.] WHAT MAY BE ASSIGNED. 103

The proportion between the amount assigned and the debts provided for was also a material consideration in Massachusetts, in cases under the system of assignment which prevailed in that state prior to the regulation of assignments by statute. In those cases the proportion to be observed was between the amount of property assigned and the debts of the creditors who became parties to the assignment. If more was assigned than such debts amounted to, the surplus was open to attachment by other creditors of the assignor; but if such debts equaled or exceeded the amount of the assigned property, they had the prior and better title, and nothing remained to be reached by an attachment.[1]

§ 65. **What May be Assigned.**— An assignment for the benefit of creditors may embrace every description of property which is in its nature assignable; and, when purporting or intended to be a general disposition of the assignor's property, should be in good faith a transfer of the whole, including real [2] and personal estate, debts and choses in action. Among these [3] may be more particularly mentioned lands; interests in lands or real estate, such as the interests of a purchaser,[4] mortgagor,[5] lessor,[6] mortgagee, lessee and

cover the debts, under any and all contingencies that may be expected or reasonably apprehended. But it is equally true that, under the pretense of securing a debt, the debtor may convey much more than is necessary for that purpose, and really for securing the use to himself and baffling his other creditors. Hence the question is one of intention," etc. Id. 459. In Johnson v. Thweatt, 18 Ala. 741, where the property conveyed was of much greater value than the aggregate of the debts intended to be secured, the deed was held to be fraudulent and void on its face as against creditors. It contained, however, other objectionable provisions. In Georgia, an assignment by an insolvent debtor to his creditor of effects to an amount greater than the debt, in which it is stipulated that any surplus remaining in the hands of the assignee, after satisfying his debt and paying the expenses of reducing the effects to cash, shall be subject to the order of the assignor, is not, upon its face, void under the statute of 1818; though the excess is a badge of fraud to be considered by a jury. Banks v. Clapp, 12 Ga. 514; Walkins v. Jenks, 24 Ga. 431.

[1] Shaw, C. J., in Foster v. Saco Manufacturing Co., 12 Pick. 451, 454. See Russell v. Woodward, 10 id. 408; Hastings v. Baldwin, 17 Mass. 552; Adams v. Blodgett, 2 Woodb. & Min. 233.

[2] In Price v. Haynes, 37 Mich. 487, an assignment was held void because it did not include the assignor's real estate.

[3] Some of the rules given under this head have been established with particular reference to that class of assignments called *special* assignments, which do not always contemplate provision for creditors. But most of them appear to have an equal application to general assignments by debtors.

[4] A purchaser's right to a deed of land agreed to be conveyed is assignable. Thus, a bond for the conveyance of land is assignable. Halbert v. Deering, 4

[5] A statutory right to redeem a mortgage after the sale of an equity is assignable. Bigelow v. Wilson, 1 Pick. 458. See Reed v. Bigelow, 5 id. 281; Graves v. McFarlane, 2 Cold. (Tenn.) 167; Birdwell v. Cain, 1 Cold. (Tenn.) 301.

[6] See Demarest v. Willard, 8 Cow. 206; Willard v. Tillman, 2 Hill (N. Y.), 274.

tenants for life;[1] profits of lands;[2] goods,[3] merchandise, stock and other descriptions of personal property; debts[4] and choses in action generally,[5] including promissory notes, bills of exchange,[6]

Littell, 9; Brown v. Chambers, 12 Ala. 697; Ensign v. Kellogg, 4 Pick. 1; Rogers v. Dibrell, 6 Lea (74 Tenn.), 69. A right to call on a trustee to convey an estate in fee is an equitable interest or chose in action which may be assigned. Coverdale v. Aldrich, 19 Pick. 391, 395. The assignment of a contract to convey an interest in real estate upon the performance of certain conditions vests an equitable interest therein in the assignee, which will be protected and made available by courts of law. Dyer v. Burnham, 25 Me. 9. A vendor's lien for purchase-money is assignable. Fisher v. Johnson, 5 Ind. 492. But see Inglehart v. Armiger, 1 Bland, 519.

[1] See Outcalt v. Van Winkle, 1 Green Ch. 513; Emmons v. Cairns, 3 Barb. 243; Graham v. Newman, 21 Ala. 397. The interest of a tenant at will in real estate is not such an interest as can be assigned. Whittemore v. Gibbs, 16 N. H. 485. In Georgia an estate at will, growing out of the statute of frauds, is assignable, but if created by the acts of the parties under the common law it is not. Cody v. Quarterman, 12 Ga. 386.

[2] A growing crop of cotton may be conveyed by deed of trust. Robinson v. Mauldin, 11 Ala. 977; Bellamy v. Bellamy's Adm'r, 6 Fla. 52. So, growing crops of wheat, rye and oats. Cochran v. Paris, 11 Gratt. 348; Dance v. Seaman, id. 778; Montgomery's Ex'rs v. Kirksey, 26 Ala. 172.

[3] Goods of a debtor which are the subject of an action may be assigned. There is nothing improper in embracing in an assignment goods attached under restraining orders out of chancery, nor in making provision to procure security to obtain the release of those goods, nor in providing for the defense of the suits. Vernon v. Morton, 8 Dana, 247, 252. If goods are sold to the assignor before the assignment, and subsequently are delivered to the assignee, title vests in the assignee. McElroy v. Seery, 61 Md. 389. But the assignment of all the goods of a debtor in Cincinnati and elsewhere, and "that might hereafter be purchased," is fraudulent and void, the goods being in the hands of auctioneers. Shaw v. Lowry, Wright (Ohio Ch.), 190. By statute in Ohio mortgaged chattels pass to the assignee, though the condition of the mortgage has been broken. Ingram v. Lindeman, 12 Rep. 664. A mortgagor's equity of redemption in a chattel mortgage, after condition broken, passes to the assignee. Gimble v. Ferguson, 58 Iowa, 414.

[4] A part only of the entire debt cannot be assigned without the consent of the debtor. Gibson v. Cook, 20 Pick. 15; 2 Kent's Com. [552], 688 and n. A contingent debt may be assigned in equity. Crocker v. Whitney, 10 Mass. 316, 319. An assignment of debts due to a firm passes only the balance of a debt after setting off a claim not yet due, held by the debtor against the firm. Fry v. Boyd, 3 Gratt. 73. The plaintiff cannot assign a debt the subject of a suit during the pendency of the suit to the prejudice of a third person. Westbrook v. McDowell, Ga. Dec., part I, 133. A debtor cannot revive and transfer to his assignee a debt due to him which he has in fraud of creditors discharged. Brownell v. Curtis, 10 Paige, 210; Browning v. Hart, 6 Barb. 91, 95. It is the well settled law of this state that a contingent debt founded on an existing contract is assignable. Knevals v. Blauvelt, 82 Me. 458; 19 Atl. Rep. 818.

[5] Spring v. S. Carolina Ins. Co., 8 Wheat. 268; Dehner v. Helmbacher Mills, 7 Ill. App. (Brad.) 47. The doctrine of the common law that choses in action are

[6] But a note or bill payable wholly or partly in personal services is not assignable. Bothick v. Purdy, 3 Mo. 82; Halbert v. Deering, 4 Littell, 9; Henry v. Hughes, 1 J. J. Marsh. 454. See Ransom v. Jones, 1 Scam. 291.

§ 65.] WHAT MAY BE ASSIGNED. 105

bonds,[1] covenants to indemnify,[2] book accounts,[3] and balances of account;[4] interests in personal contracts,[5] policies of insurance [6] and all vested rights *ad rem* and *in re;* [7] possibilities coupled with

not assignable does not obtain in Iowa. Watson v. Hankins, 13 Iowa, 547. All choses in action may be assigned in equity. Dobyns v. McGovern, 15 Miss. 662; Bell v. Lond. & N. W. Railway Co., 21 Eng. L. & Eq. 566; Parsons, C. J., in Dix v. Cobb, 4 Mass. 508, 511; Sewell, C. J., in Brown v. Maine Bank, 11 id. 153, 157; Parker v. Grout, id., n.; Wheeler v. Wheeler, 9 Cow. 34; Morton, J., in Eastman v. Wright, 6 Pick. 316, 322; Welch v. Mandeville, 2 Wheat. 233, 236; Corser v. Craig, 1 Wash. C. C. 424; Smith v. N. Y. & N. H. R. R., 28 Barb. 605; Grocers' Nat. Bank v. Clark, 48 id. 26. See Williams v. Galt, 95 Ill. 172; Flickey v. Looney, 4 Bax. (51 Tenn.) 169.

[1] Bac. Abr., Assignment (A). See Minor v. Edwards, 10 Mo. 671; Knighton v. Tufli, 11 id. 531; Ensign v. Kellogg, 4 Pick. 1.

[2] A written promise of indemnity, whether under seal or not, is assignable under the statute of Indiana. Fletcher v. Piatt, 7 Blackf. 522.

[3] Dix v. Cobb, 4 Mass. 508; Norris v. Douglass, 2 South. 817; Woodbridge v. Perkins, 3 Day, 364. But see Wright v. Williamson, 2 Pa. 965; Anderson v. Tompkins, 1 Brock. 456; Newman v. Vickery, 1 Smith (Ind.), 363; Kindrick v. Glover, Ga. Dec., part I, 63; Forepaugh v. Appold, 17 B. Mon. (Ky.) 625; Walter v. Whitbeck, 9 Fla. 86. A debt for goods sold, of which the evidence rests on an account book, is assignable. Dix v. Cobb, 4 Mass. 511; Norris v. Douglass, 5 N. J. L. 817; Woodbridge v. Perkins, 3 Day, 364.

[4] Crocker v. Whitney, 10 Mass. 316, 319; Bartlett v. Pearson, 29 Me. 9; Westcott v. Potter, 40 Vt. 271.

[5] A contract for the performance of personal duties or services is not assignable. Halbert v. Deering, 4 Littell, 9, 10; Henry v. Hughes, 1 J. J. Marsh. 454; Marcum v. Hereford, 8 Dana, 1; Davenport v. Gentry's Adm'r, 9 B. Mon. 427. A covenant to pay a sum in promissory notes is assignable by statute in Kentucky. Sirlott v. Tandy, 3 Dana, 142. In Arkansas an agreement for the delivery of property may be assigned. Lafferty v. Rutherford, 5 Ark. 649. A contract is assignable only where the entire interest therein can pass by the assignment, both legal and equitable. White v. Buck, 7 B. Mon. 546. A contract on which personal representatives can sue is assignable. Seers v. Conover, 34 Barb. 330. A contract for the labor of convicts. Prindle v. Carruthers, 15 N. Y. 425. A contract for grading a street. St. Louis v. Clemens, 42 Mo. 69. See Taylor v. Palmer, 31 Cal. 240; Geist's Appeal, 104 Pa. St. 351.

[6] Spring v. S. Carolina Ins. Co., 8 Wheat. 268; Brichta v. New York Lafayette Ins. Co., 2 Hall, 372; Gourdon v. Ins. Co. of North America, 3 Yates, 327; 1 Binn. 430, n.; Cleveland v. Clap, 5 Mass. 201; Wakefield v. Martin, 3 id. 558; Nat. Bank v. Chase, 16 R. I. 37. As to the necessity of assent on the part of the insurers to the validity of the assignment, see Carroll v. Boston Marine Ins. Co., 8 Mass. 515; Lazarus v. Commonwealth Ins. Co., 5 Pick. 76; Bassett v. Parsons, 140 Mass. 169; Brichta v. New York Lafayette Ins. Co., 2 Hall, 372. And see De Rouge v. Elliott, 23 N. J. Eq. 486; Emerick v. Coakley, 35 Md. 188; Van Dine v. Willett, 38 Barb. 319; Lowery v. Clinton, 32 Hun, 267. See Bliss on Life Ins., p. 375; Dube v. Fire Ins. Co., 64 N. H. 527; 15 Atl. Rep. 141.

[7] Story, J., in Comegys v. Vasse, 1 Pet. 193. Certificates issued for sums awarded by the secretary of the treasury under the treaty with Mexico of April 11, 1839, and the acts of congress of June 12, 1840, and September 1, 1841, are legally assignable. Baldwin v. Ely, 9 How. 580. An interest created by a pledge of personal property may be assigned. Russell v. Filmore, 15 Vt. 130.

an interest,[1] contingent interests and expectancies[2] and claims growing out of and adhering to property;[3] rights of action for damages,[4] the right to use a trade-mark,[5] interests in actions pend-

---

[1] Story, J., in Comegys v. Vasse, 1 Pet. 193; Wilde, J., in Bigelow v. Wilson, 1 Pick. 485, 492, 493, citing 3 Term R. 88; Shep. Touch. 239; Nimmo v. Davis, 7 Tex. 26. By the Revised Statutes of New York, a mere possibility coupled with an interest is capable of being conveyed or assigned at law as well as in equity, in the same manner as an estate or interest in possession. 1 R. S. 725, § 35; 3 R. S. (7th ed.) p. 2178; Lawrence v. Bayard, 7 Paige, 70. See Emmons v. Cairns, 3 Barb. 243, 245. To the contrary, see First Nat. Bank v. Kimberlands, 16 Watts (W. Va.), 555.

[2] Wilde, J., in Bigelow v. Wilson, 1 Pick. 485, 493; Mitchell v. Winslow, 2 Story, 630; Ivison v. Grassiot, 27 Eng. L. & Eq. 483; Nimmo v. Davis, 7 Tex. 26; Cooper v. Douglass, 44 Barb. 409. A thing existing in expectation and not *in esse* may be assigned, as a right to a distributive share in the profits of a voyage not yet commenced. Gardner v. Hoeg, 18 Pick. 168. But see Robinson v. Macdonnell, 5 M. & S. 228, 236; McNeeley v. Hart, 10 Ired. L. 63. See Bodenhamer v. Welch, 89 N. C. 78. Courts of equity support assignments of contingent interests and expectancies, and also of things which have no present actual or potential existence, but rest in mere possibility only. Story, J., in Mitchell v. Winslow, 2 Story, 630, 639. A mere gratuity, such as an anticipated donation from the state, is not assignable. This was so held by the supreme court of New York, in Munsell v. Lewis, 4 Hill, 635, 638, in regard to an extra allowance made by the statute to contractors on a public work where it was claimed by the assignee of the original contract. But the court of errors (S. C. on error, 2 Den. 224) reversed the decision, holding such extra allowance to be not a gratuity, but rather an equitable compensation to cover extra expenses. A legacy may be assigned. Ex'rs of Luce v. Park, 17 N. J. Eq. 415; Brooks v. Brooks, 12 S. C. 422; See v. Zabriskie, 27 N. J. Eq. 422. So the right of an heir to an inheritance. Grayson v. Sandford, 12 La. Ann. 646; Fitzgerald v. Vestal, 4 Sneed (Tenn.), 258. But see McDonald v. McDonald, 5 Jones' Eq. (N. C.) 211; Needles v. Needles, 7 Ohio St. 432. The moment a man has acquired an exclusive interest in anything, though it should be but a contingent and executory interest, he may dispose of it if not forbidden by law. Graham v. Henry, 17 Tex. 164; Read v. Mosby, 87 Tenn. 759; 11 S. W. Rep. 940, citing Steele v. Frierson, 85 id. 435. The bid of a purchaser at sheriff's sale is assignable.

[3] Blount v. Davis, 2 Dev. 19; Story, J., in Comegys v. Vasse, 1 Pet. 193. The assignee can enforce a mechanic's lien. German Bank v. Schloth, 59 Iowa, 316; McDonald v. Kelly, 14 R. I. 335.

[4] Whitaker v. Gavit, 18 Conn. 522. A right of action for a mere personal tort which dies with the party and does not survive to his personal representative is not assignable. Story, J., in Comegys v. Vasse, *ub. sup.* In Gardner v. Adams, 12 Wend. 297, a right of action in trover was held to be not assignable. But see Hall v. Robinson, 2 N. Y. 293. See Pulver v. Harris, 52 N. Y. 73. In Jackson v. Losee, 4 Sandf. Ch. 381, a right of action in replevin was held to be assignable. And in McKee v. Judd, 12 N. Y. 622, it was held by the court of appeals that a right of action for the wrongful taking and conversion of personal prop-

[5] Warren v. Warren Thread Co., 134 Mass. 247; Matter of Knox, 1 Monthly Law Bulletin, 47. See Milliken v. Dart, 26 Hun, 24; Hegeman v. Hegeman, 8 Daly, 1. *Contra*, Bradley v. Norton, 33 Conn. 158. As to a patent, see Campbell v. James, 2 Fed. Rep. 338; 5 id. 806; 18 Blatch. 92; reversed in 104 U. S. 356; Wilmer v. Thomas, 74 Md. 485.

§ 65.] WHAT MAY BE ASSIGNED. 107

ing and undetermined,[1] judgments and executions,[2] and decrees in

erty is assignable; and that an assignment by a debtor of all his property and estate transfers a right of action existing in his favor for such tortious conversion. The decision in this case has been followed in the cases of Foy v. Troy & Boston R. R. Co., 24 Barb. 382, and The People v. Hudson R. R. R. Co., 4 Duer, 74. A right of action for damages for false representations passes. Moore v. McKinstry, 37 Hun, 194. In Pennsylvania it has been held that where a wrongdoer or his estate has derived a benefit from his wrong, a right of action will in general survive against them and pass by general assignment for the benefit of creditors, but personal wrongs do not. Sibbald's Estate, 18 Pa. St. 249. In Schultz v. Christman, 6 Mo. App. 338, it was held that a right of action against a director to recover for loss sustained by the assigning bank through the fraudulent sale to it of its own stock by such director, being essentially a right of property as distinguished from a personal tort, passes by the assignment to the assignee. In England the rule as to the assignability of rights of action was clearly laid down by Lord Denman, in the case of Rogers v. Spence, in the exchequer chamber (13 Mees. & W. 571, 580), which was under the bankrupt act of 6 Geo. IV., ch. 16, in the following terms: "That as the object of the law is manifestly to benefit creditors by making all the pecuniary means and property of the bankrupt available to their payment, it has in furtherance of this object been construed largely so as to pass not only what in strictness may be called the property and debts of the bankrupt, but also those rights of action to which he was entitled for the purpose of recovering *in specie* real or personal property, or damages in respect of that which has been unlawfully diminished in value, withheld or taken from him. But causes of action not falling within this description, but arising out of a wrong personal to the bankrupt, for which he would be entitled to remedy, whether his property was diminished or impaired or not, are clearly not within the letter and have never been held to be within the spirit of the enactments, even in cases where injuries of this kind may have been accompanied or followed by losses of property; and to this class, we think, the action of trespass *quare clausum fregit*, and that of trespass to the goods of the bankrupt, must be considered to belong." In Marshall v. Means, 12 Ga. 61, a mere right to file a bill in equity was held to be not assignable. And it seems generally that all such rights of action for a tort as would survive to the personal representatives may be assigned so as to pass to the assignee. Butler v. New York & Erie R. R. Co., 22 Barb. 110; Hodgman v. Western R. R. Co., 7 How. 492; Patten v. Wilson, 34 Pa. St. 299; Jordan v. Gellen, 44 N. H. 424. So a right of action against a common carrier for negligence in not delivering goods. Jordan v. Gellen, *supra*. Cause of action for malicious prosecution not assignable even after verdict. Lawrence v. Martin, 22 Cal. 174.

[1] Such as an award, report or judgment which might be obtained or recovered in a suit pending. Leitch v. Hollister, 4 N. Y. 211. A plaintiff on the record, in an action of trespass *de bonis asportatis*, may assign his interest in the damages sought by the suit. *Aliter* as to the plaintiff in an action of slander or assault and battery. North v. Turner, 9 Serg. & R. 244; Gibson, J., id. 248, 249. Goods which have been attached under restraining orders out of chancery may be assigned, where the orders authorize their restoration to the debtors upon their giving the necessary security for their return, and provision is made in the assignment for giving such security. Vernon v. Morton, 8 Dana, 247, 252.

[2] Dunn v. Snell, 15 Mass. 481; Brown v. Maine Bank, 11 id. 153; Emigrant Industrial Savings Bank v. Roche, 93 N. Y. 374; Pearson v. Talbot, 4 Littell, 435; Vanhouten v. Reily, 6 Sm. & M. 440; Becton v. Ferguson, 22 Ala. 599. In North Carolina the assignment of a judgment is held void at law, and a court at law cannot notice it. Ferebee v. Doxey, 6 Ired. L. 446. In Indiana the legal interest in a judgment is not assignable, either by the statute or com-

equity;[1] wages to be earned under an existing contract,[2] and claims against the United States.[3] Unpaid subscriptions to the stock of a corporation will pass under a general assignment.[4]

§ 66. **What Passes Under General Terms.**—These, and whatever else is capable of assignment, may be made the subject of conveyance in an assignment. Where general words are employed purporting to convey the debtor's entire estate, questions frequently arise as to what will be construed as included in the assignment, and assignees for the benefit of creditors are sometimes clothed by statute with rights in reference to the assigned property which the assignor could not himself assert, and which, therefore, he could not convey. A few particulars in reference to the subjects thus suggested remain to be noticed.

§ 67. **Foreign Property.**— As a rule, an assignment, valid where made, will pass the title to personal property wherever situated, but this general proposition is subject to limitations and qualifications hereafter to be considered. With regard to mere incorporeal rights, such as debts, the established rule seems to be that an assignment, valid where made, will operate upon them wherever due,[5] and will preclude their subsequent attachment.[6] Under a general assignment, a claim passes for indemnity against a foreign government, as for an illegal capture[7] or detention of a vessel; and such a claim will pass under the words "all debts due the grantor."[8]

mon law. Richardville v. Cummins, 5 Blackf. 48. See Moore v. Ireland, 1 Ind. 531. Money in the hands of a sheriff collected on execution passes. Reynolds v. Collins, 78 Ala. 94.

[1] Coates' Ex'r v. Muse's Adm'rs, 1 Brock. 552; Shotwell v. Webb, 23 Miss. 375; Dinsmore v. Boyd, 6 Lea (74 Tenn.), 689.

[2] Haynes v. Thompson, 80 Me. 125; 13 Atl. Rep. 276; Edwards v. Peterson, 80 id. 367; 14 id. 936; Giles v. Ash, 123 Mass. 353. But see Herbert v. Bronson, 125 id. 475; Railroad Co. v. Woodring, 116 Pa. St. 513; 9 Atl. Rep. 58.

[3] Goodman v. Niblack, 102 U. S. 556; Stanford v. Lockwood, 24 Hun, 291; 95 N. Y. 582. See Morgan v. United States, 14 Ct. of Claims, 319.

[4] Lionberger v. Broadway Savings Bank, 10 Mo. App. 499; Shultz v. Sutter, 3 id. 137; Franklin v. Menown, 10 id. 570; Menown v. Crawford, id. 574; Boeppler v. Menown, 17 id. 447; Eppright v. Nickerson, 78 Mo. 482; Yeager v. Scranton Trust Co., 14 Weekly Notes of Cas. 296; Cartwright v. Dickinson, 88 Tenn. 478; 17 Am. St. Rep. 910; Beck v. Burns, 83 Ga. 471; 10 S. E. Rep. 121.

[5] Caskie v. Webster, 2 Wall. Jr. 131; Speed v. May, 17 Pa. St. 91; Guillaudet v. Howell, 35 N. Y. 657. See Burrows v. Keays, 37 Mich. 430; Harrison v. Farmers' Bank, 9 W. Va. 424.

[6] Kerr, J., in Holmes v. Remsen, 4 Johns. Ch. 460, 487.

[7] United States v. Hunter, 5 Mason, 62. See Comegys v. Vasse, 1 Pet. 193; Couch v. Delaplaine, 2 N. Y. 397; Maitland v. Newton, 3 Leigh, 714.

[8] Griffin's Ex'r v. Macaulay's Adm'r, 7 Gratt. 476.

§ 68. Claims for Damages for Torts.— Claims growing out of mere personal torts, which die with the party and do not survive to his personal representatives, are incapable of passing by assignment.[1] But rights of action for the wrongful taking and conversion of personal property are assignable, and will pass by an assignment of all the debtor's property and estate.[2] So claims for torts to personal property may be assigned;[3] though in some states they are held not to pass unless specifically included in the assignment. Thus, in Connecticut, where a debtor, having a claim against a person for wilfully and maliciously mutilating the model of a propeller belonging to him, made an assignment under the statute of 1828, but through mistake the claim was omitted, although intended and agreed to be assigned, it was held, on a bill filed by the purchaser of such claim from the assignee, that the claim not having been included in the assignment, there was no assignment thereof in writing, pursuant to the statute, and that the complainant was not entitled to the relief sought.[4]

§ 69. Wife's Property.— Under an assignment by an insolvent debtor, whatever rights he may have in the property of his wife, acquired by virtue of his marriage, will pass to the assignee.[5] But an assignment of real estate by a debtor does not divest his wife's right of dower, unless she be a party to the assignment[6] or an accompanying deed. Nor does an assignment of all an insolvent's estate for the benefit of creditors pass a chose in action of the wife, unless specially included.[7]

In Ohio it is provided by statute[8] that in certain cases the wife of the assignor may ask the court to have the real estate sold free

[1] Comegys v. Vasse, 1 Pet. 193; Sibbald's Estate, 18 Pa. St. 249; Jordan v. Gellen, 44 N. H. 424; Lawrence v. Martin, 22 Cal. 174; Central R. Co. v. B. & W. R. R. Co., 87 Ga. 386; 13 S. W. Rep. 520; First Nat. Bank v. Hartman Co., id. 435; 13 S. E. Rep. 586; Averill v. Longfellow, 66 Me. 237; Stewart v. Railway Co., 62 Tex. 246; Francis v. Burnett, 84 Ky. 24. Torts, rights of action are not assignable, nor are judgments, even after verdict, until actual rendition. Gamble v. Railroad Co., 80 Ga. 595; 7 S. E. Rep. 315; 12 Am. St. Rep. 276.

[2] McKee v. Judd, 12 N. Y. 622; Jackson v. Losee, 4 Sandf. Ch. 381; Coffin v. McLean, 80 N. Y. 560; Patten v. Wilson, 34 Pa. St. 299; Jordon v. Gellen, 44 N. H. 424. See *ante*, p. 86, note 1.

[3] See Rogers v. Spence, 13 Mees. & W. 571, and other cases cited, *ante*, p. 106, note 1.

[4] Whitaker v. Gavit, 18 Conn. 522.

[5] Outcalt v. Van Winkle, 1 Green, Ch. 513. This was a case of assignment under an insolvent law.

[6] Helfrich v. Obermyer, 15 Pa. St. 113; Porter v. Lazear, 109 Pa. St. 84; Wright v. Gelvin, 85 Ind. 128.

[7] Eshelman v. Shuman, 13 Pa. St. 561.

[8] Laws of 1880, p. 190; amending R. S., § 6350. See Dwyer v. Garlough, 31 Ohio St. 158. As to dower, see, further, § 88.

of her contingent right of dower and to allow her a sum of money in lieu thereof. Such action on her part is equivalent to a release of her dower interest in the property sold.

Under the code of Iowa, a sale of the real estate by the assignee is such a "judicial sale" as will cut off the wife's right of dower therein.[1]

§ 70. **Leasehold Interests.**— Under the general words, "all his personal estate and effects whatever," a deed of assignment of household premises, by way of mortgage, has been held to pass.[2] So, under the general words (following the more particular description), "all other the personal estate and effects of [the assignor], whatsoever and wheresoever," it was held that the lease of a mill passed to the assignee.[3] So an assignment in favor of creditors conveying all real and personal property and estates, whatever and wheresoever situate, and all interest therein, will pass the interest of the assignee of a lease equitably assigned.[4]

§ 71. **Interests of Devisees.**— An assignment of all a debtor's estate and effects will pass the interest of the debtor as a devisee of property, even though the property may have been devised in trust, to be conveyed to the debtor for his own proper use and without being liable for his debts.[5] But where lands were devised and charged with legacies, and, by agreement among the parties, the legacies were apportioned among the devisees, and one of the devisees assigned his property for the benefit of creditors, it was held in Pennsylvania that the assignee took the land subject to the charge of the legacies so apportioned.[6] A legacy is assignable and passes the whole right of the assignor.[7]

§ 72. **Interests of Heirs.**— Where real estate was placed in the hands of a trustee to be conveyed to T.'s appointee, or, in failure of the appointment, to her heirs at law, and she died without making an appointment, and an heir of T. made a general assignment for the benefit of his creditors of all his lands, tenements and her-

---

[1] Stidger v. Evans, 64 Iowa, 91. As to Indiana, see Hall v. Harrell, 92 Ind. 498, and cases cited.
[2] West v. Steward, 14 Mees. & W. 47.
[3] Ringer v. Cann, 3 Mees. & W. 343.
[4] Astor v. Lent, 6 Bosw. 612; Powers v. Carpenter, 15 N. Y. Weekly Dig. 155; Crouse v. Frothingham, 97 N. Y. 106.
[5] Stuchert v. Harvey, 1 Miles, 247.
[6] Swoyer's Appeal, 5 Barr, 377. And see Couch v. Delaplaine, 2 N. Y. 397; Brooks v. Brooks, 12 S. C. 422.
[7] Executors of Luce v. Park, 17 N. J. Eq. 415. See Miller's Appeal, 35 Pa. St. 481; Meeker v. Felts, 49 N. J. Eq. 502; Smith & Wolf's Appeal, 104 Pa. St. 381.

editaments, goods and chattels, etc., and all his right, title and interest in and to the same, it was held that his share in the real estate in the hands of such trustees passed by the assignment.[1]

§ 73. **Rents.**— An assignment of estate passes a right to rents subsequently falling due, and the debtor cannot afterwards lease or assign the rents as against creditors.[2] And where a railroad company leased their road, with the provision that a share of the future earnings should be applied by the lessee to the payment of the lessor's debts, it was held that both the actual and potential interests passed to the assignee for the benefit of creditors, and that both the lease and the rent were capable of inventory and appraisement, under the Pennsylvania statute.[3]

§ 74. **Money in Bank.**— A general assignment of all a debtor's property passes a deposit to his credit in a bank, and carries to the assignee all the right which the depositor had in the deposit at the date of the assignment. And the bank has no lien, in such case, upon the deposit for the amount of a bill of exchange, indorsed by the depositor, and discounted by the bank, but which bill has not yet matured.[4]

§ 75. **Property Fraudulently Transferred by Assignor.**—Under the common law of assignments the assignee stands in the place of the assignor, and can assert no claim to property which the assignor might not. The assignment, therefore, does not carry with it to the trustee the title to property which the assignor has previously transferred in fraud of his creditors, for the purpose of hindering, delaying and defrauding them.[5] But under the statutes of some

[1] Coverdale v. Aldrich, 19 Pick. 391.
[2] Williamson v. Richardson, 6 Mon. 604. See Pratt v. Lovan, 1 Miles, 358. The father of the assignor bequeathed the income of certain property in trust for the benefit of the assignor and his wife during their lives. *Held*, that the assignor's share passed by the assignment. See v. Zabriskie, 28 N. J. Eq. 422.
[3] Brittenbender v. Sunbury & Erie Railroad Co., 40 Pa. St. 269.
[4] Beckwith v. Union Bank, 4 Sandf. S. C. 604; affirmed on appeal, 9 N. Y. 211. See Buckner v. Sayre, 18 B. Mon. 745; Coates v. First Nat. Bank, 47 N. Y. Super. Ct. 322; Simonton v. First Nat. Bank, 24 Minn. 216. As between the holder of a check which is an equitable assignment of a fund on deposit with a bank, and an assignee for the benefit of creditors, the former is entitled to the fund to the extent of the check. First Nat. Bank v. Coates, 12 Rep. 514; S. C., 3 McCrary, 9; Covert v. Rhodes, 48 Ohio St. 66; 27 N. E. Rep. 94; Watts v. Shipman, 21 Hun, 598. See Bank of Alexandria v. Payne, 85 Va. 890. Money laid aside by a banking firm to be returned to a general depositor, but not amounting to the latter's full credit, is covered by a subsequent general assignment of the firm if not tendered and accepted before the assignment. Coots v. Topping, 39 Mich. 742.
[5] Brownell v. Curtis, 10 Paige, 210; Browning v. Hart, 6 Barb. 91; Leach v. Kelsey, 7 Barb. 466; Van Dyke v. Christ, 7 Watts & Serg. 373; Lord Tenterden,

of the states the power of the assignees in this respect have been extended. In New York the assignee is empowered to maintain an action against any person who has received, taken, or in any manner interfered with the estate, property and effects of the debtor in fraud of his creditors.[1] So under the Connecticut statute the assignee may maintain an action to set aside a fraudulent conveyance made by the assignor.[2] But when proceedings are not commenced under the insolvent act of that state within sixty days, a conveyance, though made with the intent to defraud creditors, will not be set aside under the act, nor at common law unless the purchaser participated in the fraud.[3]

§ 76. **What Does Not Pass.**—Where the general partner (in a special partnership conducted in his name) made a general assignment of his property for the benefit of creditors, and used no language showing an intention to assign the property of the firm, it was held that the partnership property did not pass by the assignment.[4] And where one partner makes an assignment for the benefit of creditors, this gives to his assignee no control over the partnership funds or claims so as to release them.[5] The interest conveyed is only the interest in the surplus after the company's debts are paid.[6] An assignment of "all the assignor's goods and chattels, wares and merchandise, rights, credits, notes, accounts and demands" does not pass his interest in a sum of money borrowed by him, and then in the course of transmission to him from

in Jones v. Yates, 9 Barn. & Cres. 532; Van Heusen v. Radcliffe, 17 N. Y. 580; Estabrook v. Messersmith, 18 Wis. 545; Hawks v. Pritzlaff, 51 Wis. 160; Flower v. Cornish, 25 Minn. 473; Heinrichs v. Woods, 7 Mo. App. 236; Hanes v. Tiffany, 25 Ohio St. 549; Riddle v. Norris, 46 Mo. App. 512; Bouton v. Dement, 123 Ill. 142; 14 N. E. Rep. 62; Matter of Carpenter, 45 Hun, 552; Kloeckner v. Bergstrom, 68 Wis. 197; Frost v. Citizens' Nat. Bank, id. 234; 32 N. W. Rep. 110; Rouse v. Bowers, 108 N. C. 182; 12 S. E. Rep. 985; Springfield Homestead Ass'n v. Roll, 137 Ill. 205; Penn's Ex'r v. Penn, 88 Va. 361; 13 S. E. Rep. 707.

[1] L. of 1858, ch. 314; Bliss' Ann. Code (1890), p. 2279; Southard v. Benner, 72 N. Y. 424; Ball v. Slafter, 26 Hun, 353; Leonard v. Claflin, id. 288; Miller v. Halsey, 4 Abb. (N. S.) 28, 33; McMahon v. Allen, 35 N. Y. 403; S. C., 32 How. Pr. 313.

[2] Thomas v. Beck, 39 Conn. 241; Shipman v. Ætna Ins. Co., 29 Conn. 245; Palmer v. Thayer, 28 Conn. 257; Robertson v. Todd, 31 Conn. 555.

[3] Sisson v. Roath, 30 Conn. 15. See further, on this section, ch. XXXII.

[4] Merrill v. Wilson, 29 Me. 58. Property held in trust by the surviving partners of an old firm who have formed a new one will not pass to an assignee for the benefit of the individual creditors of the surviving partners and the creditors of the new firm. Tieman v. Molliter, 71 Mo. 512.

[5] Moddewell v. Keever, 8 Watts & S. 63.

[6] Fellows v. Greenleaf, 43 N. H. 421. The right of a purchaser from the assignee of an insolvent copartnership to the exclusive use of the firm name is denied in the case of Iowa Seed Co. v. Dorr, 70 Iowa, 481; 59 Am. Rep. 446; 30 N. W. Rep. 866.

the lender.¹ Nor does an assignment of "all the bills, drafts, promissory notes, negotiable securities of every name and nature belonging to" the assignor's firm and connected with the business of said firm pass a bill or note transferred to the maker of the deed by indorsement merely for purposes of collection.² But under the words "all debts due the grantor," the indebtedness of a partner of the grantor to the partnership will pass.³

Where a creditor assigned a distil-house in M. and land and wharf adjoining, "and all the rum and other liquors in the distil-house or on the wharf, or elsewhere on the premises, and all the casks, etc., and other *personal property* whatsoever, being on the premises of, or belonging to," the debtor, it was held that barrels of rum previously consigned to a commission merchant in B. for sale did not pass by the assignment.⁴ In Pennsylvania, before the act of April 11, 1848, by which all a married woman's property is exempted entirely from her husband's control, and from liability for his debts, it was held that a legacy to his wife did not pass by a voluntary assignment.⁵ And in the same state, where a person holding land in trust for another, who paid the purchase-money, conveyed the legal title to the latter, but, before the deed was recorded, made an assignment of all his property for the benefit of his creditors who should agree to release their debts on receiving their share of the estate, and a release was executed accordingly, it was held that the assignment passed no interest in such trust land, although the assignor was in possession, and the creditors had no notice of the trust until after the execution of the release.⁶

§ 77. **After-acquired Property.**—Where purchases are made by a firm some time before an assignment, but arrive subsequently, the title thereto vests in the assignee, the seller having failed to exercise the right of stoppage *in transitu;* but property, the title to which is acquired subsequent to the assignment, does not pass,⁷ nor a cause of action accruing to the assignor after the date of the

¹ Sheldon v. Dodge, 4 Den. 417.
² Worthington v. Greer, 17 B. Mon. (Ky.) 741.
³ Griffin's Ex'r v. Macaulay's Adm'r, 7 Gratt. 476.
⁴ Tucker v. Clesby, 12 Pick. 22.
⁵ Skinner's Appeal, 5 Barr, 262. As to dower and choses in action of the wife, see *ante*, p. 109.
⁶ Ludwig v. Highley, 5 Barr, 132. Property held in trust for others by a debtor does not pass to the assignee. Holmes v. Winchester, 133 Mass. 140; Low v. Welch, 139 id. 33; Watts v. Shipman, 21 Hun, 598. Nor does land conveyed by the debtor to a purchaser who has not had the deed recorded until after the debtor's assignment in insolvency. Smythe v. Sprague, 149 Mass. 310; 21 N. E. Rep. 383.
⁷ McCabe's Appeal, 22 Pa. St. 427; Haskins v. Alcott, 13 Ohio St. 210; Shipman v. Graves, 41 Mich. 675; Lorenz v. Orlady, 87 Pa. St. 228. The assignee

assignment but before its delivery.[1] The title to bank stock does not pass to the assignee until the statutory requirement has been complied with, when it is necessary that the transfer should be entered on the corporate records.[2] But an assignment of a particular claim passes all the remedies and securities which the assignor possesses, although not named or set forth in the assignment.[3]

A parol transfer of goods to arrive, as security for a pre-existing indebtedness and for advances subsequently made, is valid as against the assignee for the benefit of the creditors of the transferrer, although actual possession of such goods is not obtained by the pledgee until after the assignment for the benefit of creditors.[4]

"under chapter 80, Revised Statutes, gets no title to property in transit at the time of making the assignment, and which is not mentioned or referred to in the assignment or the required inventory, and where neither the vendor nor vendee ever intended that the title should vest in such vendee making the assignment, notwithstanding he may get the property into his actual possession." Clark v. Bartlett, 50 Wis. 543. See Lacker v. Rhoads, 51 N. Y. 641; reversing 45 Barb. 499. Where property was forfeited to the government, and the forfeiture was afterward remitted, it was held that the avails of the property would not inure to the benefit of the assignee under a general assignment made after the forfeiture and before its remission. Ward v. Webster, 9 Daly, 182.

[1] Crow v. Colton, 7 Daly, 52.
[2] Fiske v. Carr, 20 Me. 301.
[3] Mehaffy v. Share, 2 Penn. (Penr. & W.) 361; Gayden v. Tufts, 68 Miss. 69; Whitten v. Fitzwater, 129 N. Y. 626; Brower v. Goodyer, 88 Ind. 572.
[4] Gammons v. Holman, 11 Ore. 284; 3 Pac. Rep. 676.

CHAPTER VII.

FOR WHOSE BENEFIT AN ASSIGNMENT MAY BE MADE.

§ 78. Who May be Secured.
79. Sureties, Future Responsibilities, etc.
80. Future and Contingent Liabilities.
81. Secured Debts.
82. Fictitious and Fraudulent Debts.
83. Usurious Debts.
84. Other Cases.

§ 78. Who May be Secured.—Assignments may be made not only for the benefit of *creditors*, strictly so called, that is, persons to whom the assignor is actually indebted,[1] but also for the benefit of persons who have incurred *responsibilities* on his behalf, such as sureties,[2] indorsers,[3] and bail;[4] actual liabilities being as proper subjects of security by assignment as debts due.[5] This is called, by Mr. Justice Story,[6] "a clear principle." Nothing, in fact, is

---

[1] One to whom another is liable on a contract, express or implied, though contingently, is a creditor from the time the liability is entered into, within the meaning of the statute of 13 Elizabeth. Foote v. Cobb, 18 Ala. 585. A creditor may honestly obtain a security for a debt known or believed to exist, though unliquidated. Ruffin, C. J., in Dewey v. Littlejohn, 2 Ired. Eq. 495, 504.

[2] Stevens v. Bell, 6 Mass. 339; Ingram v. Kirkpatrick, 6 Ired. Eq. 463; Wiswall v. Potts, 5 Jones' Eq. (N. C.) 184; Loeschigk v. Jacobson, 26 How. Pr. 526; Dickson v. Rawson, 5 Ohio St. 218. See Lill v. Brant, 6 Ill. App. (Bradw.) 366.

[3] Griffin v. Marquardt, 21 N. Y. 121; Stoddard v. Tomlinson, 10 Ala. 824; Copeland v. Weld, 8 Me. 411; Bank v. Cox, 6 Me. 395; Keteltas v. Wilson, 36 Barb. 298; s. c., 23 How. Pr. 69; Bank v. Talcott, 22 Barb. 550; Vaughan v. Evans, 1 Hill Ch. 414; Cunningham v. Freeborn, 11 Wend. 241; s. c., 3 Paige, 537; Halsey v. Whitney, 4 Mason, 206; Duvall v. Raisin, 7 Mo. 449. Indorsers are viewed by courts as creditors, and a deed of assignment for their security is valid although no payment had been made by them at the time of the execution of the deed. In the case of Griffin v. Marquardt, *supra*, the assignee was directed to pay the amount of certain notes not yet due to the indorsers; this provision was regarded as in effect the same as if the direction had been in favor of the holders of the notes. As to future indorsers, see *post*, p. 116.

[4] Woodward v. Braynard, 6 Mart. (La.) 572. But see Wallon v. Scott, 10 Watts, 237; Price v. Moses, 10 Rich. Law, 454, 562.

[5] Canal Bank v. Cox, 6 Greenl. 395; Halsey v. Whitney, 4 Mason, 206, 231; Stevens v. Bell, 6 Mass. 339; Hendricks v. Robinson, 2 Johns. Ch. 283; Loeschigk v. Jacobson, 26 How. Pr. 526.

[6] In Halsey v. Whitney, 4 Mason, 206, 331. See, also, Dance v. Seaman, 11 Gratt. 778, 782.

more common than for debtors, on the eve of failing, to assign property for the security of indorsers, sureties on bonds in the custom-house, etc.[1]

§ 79. Sureties, Future Responsibilities, etc.— In regard to official sureties the decisions have not been uniform. In the case of Dewey v. Littlejohn,[2] it was held in North Carolina that a person who is appointed to a public office, for the faithful performance of the duties of which he is bound to give sureties, may properly indemnify such sureties by a deed of trust on his property. In this case a debtor who had executed a deed of trust for the benefit of his creditors had made provision in it for the security of the sureties in a bond given by him for the performance of his duties as clerk and master of the court of equity. The deed was objected to, in this particular, as being against good morals and public policy, especially as it included *future* as well as past breaches of duty; but the objection was overruled by the court. But in the case of Currie v. Hart,[3] in the court of chancery of New York for the first circuit, where an assignment had been made by a sheriff of official fees due and to become due, having for one of its objects an indemnity of his sureties against future misappropriation of moneys which should be collected on executions, it was held to be void.[4]

§ 80. Future and Contingent Liabilities.— Assignments for the benefit of persons who may incur liabilities for the assignor at a *future period* in the shape of advances, suretyships, and the like, will not be sustained.[5] But deeds of trust in the nature of mortgages to secure such persons do not come within this rule.[6]

---

[1] Parker, C. J., in Cushing v. Gore, 15 Mass. 69, 74. See United States v. Hoyt, 1 Blatch. C. C. 332. By the Massachusetts act of April 15, 1836 (Stat. of 1836, ch. 238), it was formally declared that the indorsers and sureties might be considered as creditors within the provisions of the act.

[2] 2 Ired. Eq. 495.

[3] 2 Sandf. Ch. 353.

[4] The assistant vice-chancellor, in this case, expressed an opinion to this effect, but waived a formal decision of the point; the assignment being held void on several other grounds. In Alabama a deed of trust executed by a defaulting guardian, to indemnify and save harmless his securities, was held valid. Hopkins v. Scott, 20 Ala. 179.

[5] Barnum v. Hempstead, 7 Paige, 570, 598; Lansing v. Woodnorth, 1 Sandf. Ch. 43. And see Griffin v. Marquardt, 21 N. Y. 121; Brainerd v. Dunning, 30 N. Y. 211; Neuffer v. Pardue, 3 Sneed (Tenn.), 191; Caruthers, J., id. 193, 194; Whallon v. Scott, 10 Watts, 237. It is said that where there is a trust for payment of debts, it extends only to debts existing at the time of its execution. 1 Madd. Ch. 433.

[6] Hendricks v. Robinson, 2 Johns. Ch. 283, 308; affirmed on error, 17 Johns. 438; United States v. Howe, 3 Cranch, 73; Marshall, C. J., Shunos v. Caig, 7 Cranch, 34.

The proposition here stated in no wise limits the right of a debtor to provide for contingent liabilities, provided the liability is based on an existing right or obligation.[1] The fact that the liability is contingent does not constitute a valid objection; for an assignment to protect a contingent liability no more hinders or delays creditors than one to pay a debt not yet due, even if the assignee is not authorized to pay such debt before its maturity, for the assignee has a right to retain sufficient funds in his hands to meet such liability and distribute the residue, and, after the liability is disposed of, distribute the balance.[2]

§ 81. **Secured Debts.**— It is no objection to a provision for creditors by an assignment that they have already been secured by judgment or mortgage.[3] But such a provision will be considered as made subject to the equity as between the creditors to have the mortgage debt paid out of the mortgaged property.[4] Where one of the creditors had obtained a lien by attachment, and in an signment subsequently executed he was preferred to the amount which should be found due in the attachment proceedings, provided they were sustained and were a lien, this provision was not considered objectionable, either as being uncertain or as giving an improper preference.[5] When the assignment is, by its terms or by operation of law, for the equal benefit of all the creditors, secured creditors will be paid their dividends on the amount which may be found due to them, after applying the security to the discharge of the debt.[6] The securities held by the debtor should be set forth in the inventory. An omission to refer to them in the assignment will not be regarded as a badge of fraud.[7]

§ 82. **Fictitious and Fraudulent Debts.**— The debts secured by the assignment must be the debts of the assignors, which are actually owing or for which a liability has been contracted. Any attempt on the part of the debtor to create a secret trust by providing for the payment of fictitious debts, or for an amount greater

---

[1] Brainerd v. Dunning, 30 N. Y. 211; Griffin v. Marquardt, 21 N. Y. 121; Read v. Worthington, 9 Bosw. (N. Y.) 617; Loeschigk v. Jacobson, 26 How. Pr. 536; s. c., 2 Robt. 645; Hawkins v. May, 12 Ala. 673; Grant v. Chapman, 38 N. Y. 293.
[2] Loeschigk v. Jacobson, 26 How. Pr. 525; Bump on Fraud. Conv. 388.
[3] Strong v. Skinner, 4 Barb. 546; Paige, J., id., 559; Perry Ins. & Trust Co. v. Foster, 58 Ala. 502.
[4] Dimon v. Delmonico, 35 Barb. 554.
[5] Grant v. Chapman, 38 N. Y. 293.
[6] Wurtz v. Hart, 13 Iowa, 515.
[7] Stern v. Fisher, 32 Barb. 198. See further, on this subject, § 393.

than that for which he is liable, will be evidence of an intent to defraud creditors.[1]

The question whether provision in the assignment for the payment of a fictitious debt will invalidate the entire assignment, or whether the instrument will be sustained for the benefit of creditors who have not participated in the fraud, has given rise to conflicting decisions. It will be seen, from the cases referred to in the notes, that the preponderance of authority seems to be in favor of the opinion that the assignment will be held good as to all debts that are *bona fide;* and this rule would undoubtedly prevail in those states where provision is made by statute for testing the validity of claims presented to the assignee for payment under the assignment.[2]

[1] In Lockhard v. Brodie, 1 Tenn. Ch. 384, it is said that the insertion of a debt as due, or intended to be secured, when in fact no such sum was due, is conclusive evidence of an intent to hinder and delay creditors, and the deed must be set aside as void; citing Peacock v. Thompkins, Meigs, 317, 329; Gibbs v. Thompson, 7 Humph. 179; Bumpas v. Dotson, 7 Humph. 310; Jacobs v. Remsen, 36 N. Y. 668. But see Kayser v. Heavenrich, 5 Kan. 324. So, in New York, it has been held that the schedules under the act of 1860 are still to be regarded as part of the assignment, and when they contain fictitious debts the assignment will be deemed fraudulent. Terry v. Butler, 43 Barb. 395. But in the case of Pinneo v. Hart, 90 Mo. 561, the fact that some of the claims in the list of preferred debts were fictitious, and that the assignee was aware of their fraudulent character, was not regarded as ground for avoiding the assignment. The duty of the trustee in such cases is to disregard the fraudulent or fictitious claims. And see Kayser v. Heavenrich, 5 Kan. 324. See Marks v. Bradley, 69 Miss. 1; Hastings Malting Co. v. Heller, 47 Minn. 71; 49 N. W. Rep. 400.

[2] In Mackintosh v. Corner, 33 Md. 607, Mr. Justice Alvey, discussing this question, says: "It by no means follows that because some of the preferred debts may be fraudulent, and therefore void, that the assignment itself, intended as it is for the benefit of all the creditors, should be declared a nullity. Some of the debts claiming priority may be founded in fraud, and still the general assignment be good as to all debts that are *bona fide.* Indeed, it is the duty of the trustee under such an assignment to resist and defeat all claims founded in fraud, and which would operate to the prejudice of *bona fide* creditors; it not being supposed that the trustee accepts such a trust except for real and *bona fide* creditors." So Mr. Justice English, in Hempstead v. Johnston, 18 Ark. 137: "If it be assumed . . . that they (the debts) were simulated, the deed of trust would nevertheless be valid as to the other beneficiaries, unless it had been shown that they were privy to the insertion of the simulated claims for fraudulent purposes." Citing Anderson v. Hook, 9 Ala. 704; Tatum v. Hunter, 14 id. 557. So, in Hardcastle v. Fisher, 24 Mo. 75, Mr. Justice Leonard observed: "We think it pretty well settled by the course of decisions in this state in reference to a voluntary assignment, that the fraud of one or more of the creditors does not defeat it altogether, and render it wholly ineffectual in favor of the others; and we are not disposed, after reconsidering the matter, to change the course of adjudication upon this subject. The courts of Virginia, North Carolina and Alabama have taken the same view. Anderson v. Hook, 9 Ala. 704; Perry Ins. & Trust Co. v. Foster, 58 Ala. 502; Sewall v. Henry, 5 Gratt. 31; Harris v. De Graffenried, 11 Ired. L. 89; Brannock v. Brannock, 10 id. 428. But in New York the old rule, void in part, void *in toto,* seems to be adhered to and applied to

But a debt is not fictitious because the statute of frauds, if interposed, would prevent its enforcement.[1] Where the deed was made to secure not only the debt of the grantor, but also of a third party, the deed was held void only to the extent of the debts of the third party.[2]

§ 83. **Usurious Debts.**—Whether an assignment for the payment of debts, which intentionally provides for the payment of notes and other securities, together with usurious premiums which are included therein, would not of itself be void under the usury laws of New York, is a question which was noticed but not decided in the case of Pratt v. Adams, in the court of chancery.[3] The chancellor said it was a question which the parties who came in to claim under the assignment could not raise. For if the assignment was void, none of them were entitled to claim a preference under it and at the same time to insist upon its illegality in respect to the claims of others whose debts, whether valid or not, the assignor intended to provide for specifically. The provision, however, in any event was held to be good only to the extent of the amount actually and honestly due from the assignor, rejecting the usurious excess. And even this benefit, it was held, could only be claimed under an assignment providing in terms for the payment of the usurious claims. A general provision for the payment of debts in an assignment would not include debts founded upon a usurious consideration. In the case of Murray v. Judson, in the court of

these transactions. Fiedler v. Day, 2 Sandf. S. C. 596.'· But in the New York case of Kavanagh v. Beckwith, 44 Barb. 195, where it appeared that certain preferred debts were named at a larger amount than the sums actually due, Mr. Justice James C. Smith said: "The overstatements of the amounts of the preferred debts do not make the assignment *necessarily* fraudulent. The assignees are not bound to pay the debts at the amounts therein specified. The provisions of the assignment upon that point are the following: The assignees are first required, in general terms, to pay 'the debts due or to grow due from the assignor, *or for which he is liable*, to the following persons.' In the schedules subsequently filed the debts were named at the actual amounts due. This was regarded as evidence of an honest intent. The fact, also, that the debts were referred to in the assignment as being *about* certain amounts, and that the books of account from which the amounts were taken had not been written up for several months, was regarded as evidence rebutting the fraudulent intent." In the case of Jacobs v. Remsen, 36 N. Y. 671, the court of appeals sustained a charge to the jury in which they were told that if any portion of the preferred claims were fictitious the assignment would be fraudulent and void. In Frazier v. Truax, 27 Hun, 587, it was held that the assignment must show on its face the creditors intended to be preferred; and that a preference to persons who were not creditors upon a trust for real creditors avoids the assignment. Talcott v. Hess, 31 Hun, 282. And see cases cited in notes, p. 165.

[1] Livermore v. Northrup, 44 N. Y. 107.
[2] Harvey's Adm'r v. Steptoe's Adm'r, 17 Gratt. 289.
[3] 7 Paige, 615, 617, 641.

appeals,[1] it was expressly held that a general assignment by an insolvent debtor of his property to a trustee for the payment of his debts is not void on account of its providing for the payment of an irregular and usurious judgment, giving it priority over other debts, if it be in other respects free from objection, and that it is not a fraud upon other creditors for a debtor to pay or provide for the payment of a usurious debt. Gardner, J., said that the question in the case was not whether a provision for a usurious debt may not in certain cases be evidence more or less cogent of a fraudulent intent on the part of the debtor, but whether the law will permit a trust for that purpose to any extent under any circumstances.

It now seems to be settled in New York that a preferred debt must be paid by the assignee though usurious.[2]

In North Carolina it has been held that a deed of trust made to secure a single usurious debt was void.[3] But in a later case where a deed of trust was given for the security of several debts due to different individuals, some of which were *bona fide* and some tainted with usury, the deed was held to be valid as to the former, but void as to the latter, there being no connection between them.[4]

In Alabama the validity of a deed of trust is not affected by the fact that one of the items of which the debt secured is composed consisted of usurious interest which the creditor had in good faith been compelled to pay to a third person for the purpose of replacing money that the grantor had borrowed from him and failed to return.[5]

In Virginia, where a deed of trust was made to secure a usurious debt and the debt was afterwards freed from its usurious character, and it was agreed that the deed should stand as security for it, the deed was sustained.[6]

§ 84. **Other Cases.**— In a case in New York where money belonging to a wife had come into the hands of her husband previous to the married woman's act and which he agreed to hold as a loan, it was held that equity would permit him to pay the loan under

---

[1] 9 N. Y. 73; Livermore v. Northrup, 44 N. Y. 167; Busby v. Firm, 1 Ohio St. 409. The assignee is not a borrower within the meaning of the usury law, and cannot maintain an action to cancel usurious notes of the assignor without paying the sums loaned, and no such right can be conferred on the assignee. Wright v. Clapp, 28 Hun, 7.

[2] Chapin v. Thompson, 89 N. Y. 270; Matter of Thompson, 30 Hun, 195; Matter of Brown, 10 Daly, 115.

[3] Shober v. Hauser, 4 Dev. & Batt. 91.

[4] Brannock v. Brannock, 10 Ired. L. 428. And see Roane v. Bank of Nashville, 1 Head (Tenn.), 526.

[5] Pennington v. Woodall, 17 Ala. 685.

[6] Martin v. Hall, 9 Gratt. 8.

§ 84.] OTHER CASES. 121

an assignment, and for that purpose to prefer her.[1] A similar doctrine prevails in Illinois.[2] Provision may also be made for the payment of a mortgage for the purpose of restoring her inchoate right of dower in the mortgaged premises discharged of the mortgage.[3]

In Pennsylvania a wife can prove her claim against the assigned estate of her husband like any other creditor, it appearing that her claim was *bona fide* and upon good consideration.[4] The holders of matured stock in a building association which has assigned are not creditors, and can only share *pro rata* with the holders of unmatured stock after the payment of the creditors of the corporation.[5]

[1] McCartney v. Welch, 44 Barb. 271; affirmed, 51 N. Y. 626; Woodworth v. Sweet, 44 Barb. 268.
[2] Tomlinson v. Matthews, 98 Ill. 178.
[3] Dimon v. Delmonico, 35 Barb. 554.
[4] Zeigler's Appeals, 84 Pa. St. 342.
[5] Criswell's Appeal, 100 Pa. St. 488. See Christian's Appeal, 102 id. 184.

CHAPTER VIII.

FORM OF THE ASSIGNMENT.

§ 85. Principal Modes of Assignment.
86. Special Assignments.
87. General Assignments.
88. Parties to the Instrument.
89. Assignees.
90. Creditors.
91. Writing, When Necessary.
92. Form of Assignment.
93. Assignment by Several Instruments.
94. Assignment by Single Instrument.
95. Simplest Form.
96. Commencement and Recital.
97. Consideration.
98. Transfer.
99. Description of Property.
100. Amount Assigned — Reference to the Schedule.
101. Amount Assigned — Reference to the Schedule — Continued.
102. Amount Assigned — Reference to the Schedule — Continued.
103. When the Schedules Should be Annexed.
104. Habendum.
105. Declaration of Trusts.
106. To Convert the Property into Money.
107. To Apply and Distribute the Proceeds.
108. To Pay the Expenses of the Trust.
109. To Retain a Reasonable Compensation to the Assignee.
110. To Pay the Debts Designated or Referred to.
111. To Pay Over the Surplus to the Assignor.
112. Power of Attorney.
113. Covenant by Assignee.
114. Concluding Clauses.
115. Schedules.
116. Assignments with Preferences.
117. Assignments with Preferences — Continued.
118. Assignments Tripartite.

§ 85. **Principal Modes of Assignment.**— There are two principal modes in which a debtor not having the means of paying his liabilities in money may make provision for creditors by the transfer and appropriation of property. He may adopt a course of making *special* transfers of specific portions of property from time to time as circumstances may require, or he may make one *general* transfer embracing the whole. The former course is usually pursued where the creditors are few or the indebtedness limited, not amounting to insolvency or involving the necessity of suspension of business. The latter is the method commonly resorted to by insolvent debtors.

§ 86. **Special Assignments.**— Again, provision by *special* or separate transfers may be either absolutely in *payment* and satisfaction of the debt provided for, or by way of security. Of the forms of security a very common one is by mortgage; another is by assignment directly to the creditor, and having the operation of the mortgage;[1] a third is by special deed of trust, which in many respects resembles a mortgage — the conveyance to the creditor, which is direct, being accompanied by a declaration of trust expressing the particular mode and time of appropriating the assigned property in case the debt so secured is not sooner paid;[2] a fourth is by deed of trust to a trustee for the creditor, which also is frequently treated as a mortgage.[3]

The appropriation of a debtor's *whole* property in payment of his debts may be either by *separate* transfers to each of the creditors provided for,[4] or by one *general* transfer of the whole for their common benefit. Where the latter form is adopted (which is most usual), it may be *directly* to the creditors themselves, without the intervention of a trustee. But the most common form of general transfer, and one the best known in the mercantile community, is a conveyance of the debtor's whole property to one or more *trustees* or assignees, whether creditors or strangers, for the benefit of the creditors provided for.[5] This is the description of conveyance which the term *voluntary assignment* has been held to import,[6] and will receive a principal share of attention in the present work. The most prominent features of these general transfers will now be noticed.

[1] See Leitch v. Hollister, 4 N. Y. 211. According to Mr. Justice Story, an assignment directly to a particular creditor for the payment of his own debts, or as a security or discharge of his own liabilities, is not properly an assignment "for the benefit of creditors." United States v. McLellan, 3 Sumn. 345, 354, 355. See the observations of Redfield, C. J., in Mussey v. Noyes, 26 Vt. 462, 471.
[2] See *ante*, p. 17.
[3] See Stimpson v. Fries, 2 Jones' Eq. 156.
[4] "In transferring every part of his property, separately, to individual creditors, in payment of their several debts, would be not only fair but laudable; it cannot be fraudulent to transfer the whole to trustees for the benefit of all." Marshall, C. J., in Brashear v. West, 7 Pet. 608, 614.
[5] In the case of Cunningham v. Freeborn, in the court of errors of New York (11 Wend. 241, 256), Mr. Justice Nelson expressed strong disapprobation of the principle of assignments to *a trustee*, and declaring his preference for assignments *directly* to the creditors themselves; leaving them to act, either each as his own trustee, or, if this were inconvenient, to appoint a trustee in their place. See, also, the observations of Redfield, C. J., in Mussey v. Noyes, 26 Vt. 462, 471. See *ante*, p. 5.
[6] Walworth, C., in Dias v. Bouchaud, 10 Paige, 445, 448, 461; *ante*, § 3.

§ 87. **General Assignments.** — A general assignment in trust for the benefit of creditors is understood to import a conveyance of *all* the debtor's property,[1] as distinguished from a *partial* assignment, the nature of which will be considered in the next chapter. An exception of a trifling amount, whether by accident or design, will not alter the character of the conveyance in this respect.[2]

A general assignment is also understood to import a provision for a considerable number of creditors, or at least for *several*, or more than one. An assignment of a debtor's property in trust for the benefit of *one* creditor was lately held, in New York, not to be a voluntary assignment for the benefit of creditors within the meaning of the act of congress of March 2, 1799, creating a priority of payment in favor of the United States.[3]

[1] Thompson, J., in United States v. Clark, 1 Paine, 629, 640. We have seen that the term *assignment*, in its application to real estate, implies of itself, and without any words of qualification or description, a transfer of the assignor's *whole* interest in the subject of assignment. See *ante*, p. 1. In mercantile language the term is daily used in the same broad sense. When it is said of a merchant that he has "made *an* assignment," it is understood, not that he has made a transfer of some specific article, or portion of property, to this or that particular creditor in payment or as security, but that he has made a *general* disposition of his property, and suspended his whole business in consequence. In the case of The United States v. Mott, 1 Paine, 188, 195, the term "voluntary assignment" was considered to mean an assignment of all the debtor's property. In the Vermont case of Mussey v. Noyes, 26 Vt. 462, 473, it was remarked by the chief justice that an assignment which includes all one's attachable property, and which is intended to close up one's business, and does so at once, is clearly a general assignment. See, also, Bishop v. Hart's Trustees, 28 Vt. 71. An assignment intended by its maker to be general — as shown by its language and mode of execution — by which a firm transfers its assets, consisting of personalty alone, to an assignee to secure all its creditors *pro rata*, will be treated as a *general* assignment in a litigation involving its validity, when all the parties have so treated it in their pleadings, although it does not on its face declare itself and does not in terms purport to convey all the assignor's property. Bank v. Noe, 2 Pick. (86 Tenn.) 21. The material and essential characteristic of a general assignment is the presence of a trust and the assignee taking the title as trustee. Brown v. Guthrie, 110 N. Y. 435; 18 N. E. Rep. 254. Whether an instrument is a *general* assignment depends on its character, and not on the name which the parties see fit to give it. Kendall v. Bishop, 76 Mich. 634; 43 N. W. Rep. 645.

[2] United States v. Hooe, 3 Cranch, 73, 91; United States v. Clark, 1 Paine, 629. See United States v. Bank of the United States, 8 Rob. (La.) 262. And see the Vermont cases of Mussey v. Noyes, 26 Vt. 462; Noyes v. Hickok, 27 id. 36; and Bishop v. Hart's Trustees, 28 id. 71. In the case of United States v. Clark, 1 Paine, 629, where a debt amounting to $7,400 had been omitted in the statement of the assignor's property, the assignment was held to be general. Krug v. McGilliard, 76 Ind. 28; Du Bose v. Carlisle, 51 Ala. 590.

[3] Bouchaud v. Dias, 1 N. Y. 291. Where a debtor assigned all the debts owing to him and his book accounts to an assignee "to collect and settle if possible," the proceeds to "go" toward paying two debts, and the balance, if any, to the assignor's wife, it was held that this was not a general assignment within the meaning of the assignment act. Tiemeyer v. Turnquist, 85 N. Y. 516. The

The transfer by a debtor of all his property does not of itself make what is termed a *general* assignment, but it must also be conveyed to trustees to be held by them *in trust* for other creditors;[1] and if the trust is not declared in the instrument itself, it may arise by implication from the character of the transaction.[2] Thus in those states[3] in which fraudulent conveyances made by an insolvent debtor inure by statute to the equal benefit of all his creditors and operate as a voluntary assignment, the trust is declared by statute, and the court carries it into effect by the appointment of a trustee.

A general assignment may consist of several separate transfers, if constituting one transaction, or having one and the same general object.[4] But ordinarily such assignments are effected by a single transfer and expressed by a single instrument of conveyance.

§ 88. Parties to the Instrument — Assignment.— Where an assignment is made by several persons jointly indebted as partners they are all of course named in the instrument as assignors.

In some of the states, as Pennsylvania,[5] Virginia[6] and Maryland,[7]

General Assignment Act of 1877 does not include or apply to a specific assignment by a debtor for the benefit of one or a portion of his creditors, and such an assignment is not void because not executed in accordance with the provisions of that act. Royer Wheel Co. v. Fielding, 101 N. Y. 504. In the Vermont case of Mussey v. Noyes it was remarked by Redfield, C. J., in delivering the opinion of the court, that "the term *general*, as applied to assignments, does not have reference, probably, so much to the proportion of creditors as to the proportion of property." 26 Vt. 472. After referring to the present work the learned chief justice adds: "We may conclude, then, that if a majority of the creditors are provided for and all the property is assigned, the assignment is still general." Id. 473. In the southern states general assignments are characterized as being absolute conveyances of the debtor's property, in contradistinction from mere deeds of trust, which are intended as security for particular debts, or to protect particular individuals, and which reserve to the grantor the right of redeeming the property by a given time. See the observations of Dargan, C. J., in Johnson v. Thweatt, 18 Ala. 741, 746, and of Chilton, C. J., in Shearer v. Loftin, 26 id. 710, 714.

[1] Isham, J., in Peck v. Merrill, 26 Vt. 696. See Noyes v. Hickok, 27 Vt. 36; Bishop v. Hart's Trustees, 28 Vt. 71; also, Robbins v. Magee, 76 Ind. 381, where a conveyance was held to be a composition agreement rather than an assignment. It would seem that there should be in a general assignment: (1) a transfer of the debtor's property; (2) a trust created; (3) for the purpose of paying debts; (4) full power given to sell any or all of the property to fully execute the trust reposed in the assignees. Ginther v. Richmond, 18 Hun, 232. See *ante*, §§ 3-8.

[2] Burrows v. Lehndorff, 8 Iowa. 96.

[3] R. S. (1889), paragraph 6343; Gen. Stats. (1887), ch. 44, art. II, paragraph 4, p. 675.

[4] See § 59.

[5] See Hennessy v. The Western Bank, 6 Watts & Serg 300.

[6] See Reynolds v. The Bank of Virginia, 6 Gratt. 174.

[7] Schumann v. Peddicord, 560 Md. 50; Reiff v. Horst, 55 id. 42; Reiff v. Eshleman, 52 id. 582.

where real estate is conveyed by assignment, the wives of the assignors are made parties to the deed; and it has been held in the first state that a voluntary assignment for the benefit of creditors by the husband alone and the subsequent sale and conveyance by his assignees does not divest the wife's right of dower in the lands assigned.[1] In New York the wife's dower is conveyed by her joining with the husband in a separate deed of the land in the ordinary form, such deed bearing even date with the assignment and accompanying it.[2]

§ 89. Assignees.— Where the assignment is to a trustee for the benefit of creditors it is usual to make the assignee or trustee a formal party to the deed of assignment; and this is necessary where it is intended that the instrument shall contain an express provision for its execution by the assignee or any covenant to be performed by him. But it has been held that where the assignment contained no such provision or covenant it was not necessary that the assignee should become a party to it by signing.[3]

Where the assignee is not thus made a party the assignment may be drawn in the first person in the form of a deed-poll. Where, however, he is made a formal party, the instrument is drawn in the form of an indenture of two parts, technically called an *indenture bipartite*.

§ 90. Creditors.— Besides the assignee or assignees, it is sometimes the practice to make the creditors themselves, for whose benefit it is intended, parties to the assignment. In general this is not necessary,[4] nor is it usual unless there is something in the assignment to which it is desirable to obtain the express written assent of the creditors so as to bind them to its provisions; as where the assignor stipulates for a release or some other advantage to himself to which he would not otherwise be entitled. It appears to be a

---

[1] Helfrich v. Obermyer, 15 Pa. St. 113. See Caldwell v. Bruggerman, 4 Minn. 270.

[2] See Darling v. Rogers, 22 Wend. 483, in which there were five of these separate and accompanying deeds.

[3] Flint v. Clinton Co., 12 N. H. 430. See further as to the execution of the assignment by the assignee, *post*, ch. XVI.

[4] By the established principles of law as held by eminent authority in this country, it is not necessary to the creation of any trust by deed in favor of any persons that the person for whose benefit the trust is created should be a party to it. Story, J., in Halsey v. Whitney, 4 Mason, 206, 214; Layson v. Rowan, 7 Rob. (La.) 1. And courts of equity generally will compel the execution of a trust for creditors though they be not at the time assenting and parties to the conveyance. Halsey v. Whitney, *ubi supra;* Nicoll v. Mumford, 4 Johns. Ch. 522, 529, 530; Brooks v. Marbury, 11 Wheat. 78; Gray v. Hill, 10 Serg. & R. 436; Kinnard v. Thompson, 12 Ala. 487; Smith v. Turrentine, 8 Ired. Eq. 185.

settled rule in our law on this subject that assignments *directly* to creditors are not valid without their assent; but that assignments to *trustees* for their benefit do not require such assent to render them valid and operative.[1] In the United States a common form of assignment (if not the prevailing form) is that of two parts, executed between the debtor or assignor of the one part, and the assignee or trustee of the other part, without any creditor becoming a party; and such an assignment, on its acceptance by the assignee, is held to be valid and effectual as a provision for creditors, creating a trust for them which they can enforce in the proper courts, and is irrevocable by the assignor.[2] A different rule prevails in England, and hence has arisen a material distinction between the forms of assignment in use in the two countries in regard to their legal qualities and effect as modes of provision for creditors.[3]

[1] Nicoll v. Mumford, 4 Johns. Ch. 522; Ward v. Lewis, 4 Pick. 518; Pingree v. Comstock, 18 id. 46; Weir v. Tannehille, 2 Yerger, 57; Robertson v. Sublett, 6 Humph. 313; Ingram v. Kirkpatrick, 6 Ired. Eq. 462; Stimpson v. Fries, 2 Jones' Eq. 156; Jones v. Dougherty, 10 Ga. 273; Bellamy v. Bellamy's Adm'r, 6 Fla. 62; Hall v. Dennison, 17 Vt. 310; 2 Kent's Com. [533], 691; Brown v. Chamberlain, 9 Fla. 464; Forbes v. Scannell, 13 Cal. 242. See *post*, ch. XX.

[2] In Fellows v. Greenleaf, 43 N. H. 421, it is said that an assignment not only does not need to contain, but should not contain, any provision for the creditors to sign it, or become parties to it, because if it is properly drawn and executed between the debtor and assignee, the assent of the creditors will be presumed; and if not so, it will be void as well to those who have assented to it as to those who have not. See Stimpson v. Fries, 2 Jones' Eq. (N. C.) 156; 2 Kent's Com. [553], 692, n. See the subject more fully considered, and the principal cases cited, in chapter XIV. See Gibson v. Rees, 50 Ill. 383.

[3] Assignments to which no creditor is a party are in England called *deeds of agency*, or voluntary deeds of agency, the nature and operation of which are thus explained by Rolfe, V. C., in the case of McKinnon v. Stuart, 20 L. J. (N. S.) Chan. 49: "The doctrine of this court as to mere deeds of agency is perfectly simple and intelligible. It is competent to any one to make another his agent or attorney, to get in his property and apply it in payment of his debts, or in any other mode he may direct. And after he has done so, he may, at his pleasure, *revoke* the authority so given, and direct any other disposition of his property which he may prefer. What was really decided in Garrard v. Lord Lauderdale, and other cases involving the same point, was only this: that in such a case the conveyance of property to the agent makes no difference as to the right of revocation in the debtor. The party in whom the property has been vested is a mere trustee for the debtor by whom it has been conveyed to him. He is still the mere agent or attorney, or in the nature of an agent or attorney, of the debtor, and must obey his directions as to the disposal of the property. On the other hand, it is abundantly clear on the authorities, that where a creditor is a party to a deed whereby his debtor conveys property to a trustee to be applied in liquidation of the deed due to that creditor, the deed is, as to the creditor, irrevocable. A valid trust is created in his favor, and the relation between the debtor and trustee is no longer that of mere principal and agent. Of course that which is true where a single creditor is the *cestui que trust* is at least equally so where there are many creditors. Nor does the creditor executing the

In some of the states assignments have been required by statute to be so drawn as to enable the creditors to become parties to them, if they choose, otherwise they were invalid as against creditors not parties. But in New York it has been expressly held to be not necessary that the creditors should be parties;[1] and the same has been held in Missouri if the assignment contains no provisions prejudicial to their interests;[2] otherwise it is of no avail until executed by them.[3]

Assignments are also sometimes expressly made for the benefit of such creditors as shall become parties to them without reference to the requirements of any statute. In these cases it is of course necessary for the creditors to become parties in order to obtain the benefit of the assignment.

deed become less a *cestui que trust* because he gives nothing to the debtor as a consideration for the trust created in his favor, or because it was the voluntary, unsolicited act of the debtor to create the trust. I never knew that any question had been raised on this subject as against creditors who had executed the deed and so made themselves *cestuis que trust*. Where they have not executed the deed, questions have often arisen how far, by having been apprised of its execution, and so, perhaps, been induced to do or abstain from doing something which may affect their interests, they may not have acquired the rights of *cestuis que trust*. This is the question referred to by Sir John Leach, in Acton v. Woodgate, 2 Myl. & K. 492, and by Sir E. Sugden, in Brown v. Cavendish, 1 J. & L. 606. But where, as in the present case, the creditors have actually executed the deed, I apprehend there is no longer any possibility of treating it as a mere voluntary deed of agency, revocable by the debtor." In the later case of Siggers v. Evans, 32 Eng. L. & Eq. 139, it was decided that the doctrine that a conveyance of property to trustees in favor of creditors operates as a mere power in the hands of mandataries or agents, revocable until communicated to or assented to by the creditors, does not apply where the trustee himself takes a beneficial interest under the deed. And according to the same case, it seems that where a deed of assignment has been executed to a stranger as trustee for creditors, a communication of the trust to a creditor, by reason of which he may not have pursued his remedy, or his position may have been altered, will render the deed irrevocable by the assignor, without any actual assent by any creditor. In Smith v. Hurst, 22 L. J. (N. S.) Chan. 286; s. c., 15 Eng. L. & Eq. 520, it was held that a deed of arrangement between a debtor and one of his creditors, conveying all the property of the debtor to the creditor, and which deed the debtor has power to revoke and alter at any time, and attempts to use as a shield to protect himself against the claims of his other creditors, is fraudulent and void against creditors whose interests are affected by the deed, notwithstanding the deed, upon the face of it, purports to be for the benefit of all the creditors. Such a deed is, in truth, a deed for the benefit of the debtor; and if a creditor accepts it, he takes it not for his own benefit, but for the purpose of carrying out the views and objects of the debtor, in fraud of the other creditors. And this rule and practice has been conformed to by a few American decisions. Carr v. Dole, 18 Me. 358; Whitney v. Kelley, 67 Me. 377.

[1] Cunningham v. Freeborn, 11 Wend. 240. So in Vermont. Hall v. Denison, 17 Vt. 310.

[2] Duval v. Raisin, 7 Mo. 440.

[3] Drake v. Rogers, 6 Mo. 317; Swearingen v. Slicer, 5 id. 240. But see Gale v. Mensing, 20 Mo. 461.

Creditors may become parties to an assignment in other ways than by actually signing the instrument; as by coming in under it and filing their claims for the purpose of obtaining a dividend.[1] The effect of thus becoming parties will be considered hereafter.[2]

§ 91. **Writing, When Necessary.**— In considering how an assignment should be made, the necessity of *writing* to its validity occurs as a preliminary and most important inquiry.[3] *Special* or particular assignments are usually evidenced by some written instrument more or less formal in its character; and in many cases a writing is expressly required by law to give them validity. In other cases, however, a mere delivery of the subject assigned is sufficient to pass the property; and in equity many assignments are held good which are not evidenced by any writing.[4]

In regard to *general* assignments, or those usually executed by insolvent debtors, a stricter rule prevails, and a writing of some kind is generally required, not only as a security against fraud and collusion, but as a necessary means of giving effect to the assignments themselves. The very nature of the transfer, especially when in the form of a trust, comprehending various descriptions of property, and accompanied by directions more or less numerous and complicated as to the mode of distribution, renders a written instrument important.[5] Where *real* property is either wholly or

[1] See Bodley v. Goodrich, 7 How. 276.
[2] See *post*, ch. XLII.
[3] An assignment, it is said, does not necessarily imply or require writing; and when alleged of any subject it should always be construed in connection with the law of transfer applicable to that particular subject-matter. Hutchings v. Low, 1 Green (N. J.), 246. Assignments are very generally made in writing, but they are by no means exclusively so made. Scott, J., in Edison v. Frazier, 4 Eng. (Ark.) 220, 221. And see further, as to the import of the term, *ante*, p. 3. n. 1.
[4] See *ante*, p. 3. In Boyden v. Moore, 11 Pick. 362, where a debtor delivered certain chattels to a creditor, saying: "Take the property, do the best you can with it, pay yourself and pay the rest to my creditors," it was considered by the court as an assignment and sustained in favor of the assignee. In Loftin v. Lyon, 22 Ala. 540, a debtor had delivered to his creditor a quantity of cotton to be sold and the proceeds appropriated, first, to the payment of his own debt, and the balance to be paid to other creditors named in extinguishment of their debts. And see Higginbottom v. Peyton, 3 Rich. Eq. 398; Gordon v. Green, 10 Ga. 534; Lockwood v. Canfield, 20 Ill. 126; Newby v. Hill, 2 Metc. (Ky.) 530. In the case of Foster v. Lowell, 4 Mass. 308, an assignment of a very simple character — being an agreement by the debtor that a third person having money belonging to him in his hands should retain it for the use of a particular creditor — was held void on the ground of its not being reduced to writing. But see the reporter's note to the case. A trust in personalty need not be in writing. Calder v. Moran, 49 Mich. 14; 12 N. W. Rep. 892; Conrad v. Marcotte, 23 Minn. 55. But see Hoopes v. Knell, 31 Md. 550.
[5] Hertle v. McDonald, 2 Md. Ch. Dec. 128. But see Dale v. Olmstead, 36 Ill. 150.

in part the subject of the assignment a writing is expressly required by statute. The provision of the English statute of frauds, requiring a writing signed by the party to give effect to transfers of estates or interests in lands, includes *assignments* as well as other conveyances;[1] and this is said to have been either expressly adopted or assumed as law throughout the United States.[2]

In many of the states it is expressly required by statute that an assignment for the benefit of creditors should be in writing, and further formalities are in some instances prescribed.[3]

§ 92. **Form of Assignment.**— In regard to the particular character of the writing by which an assignment is required to be evidenced, it may be observed that it partakes usually of the character of a *deed*, and is drawn with the same care as any other instrument of conveyance, consisting of two principal parts — a *transfer* to the assignee, which vests in him the property, and a declaration of *trust*, which directs him how to dispose of it.[4] In some cases, however, very informal writings have been pronounced sufficient as assignments.[5] Thus, where a debtor inclosed notes to one of his creditors by letter, with directions, first, to satisfy his own debt, and then those of other creditors designated by him, it was held, in South Carolina, that this was a good assignment, as against other attaching creditors, for the benefit of the creditors named.[6] So, a power

---

[1] All estates and interests in lands (except leases not exceeding three years) created, granted or *assigned* by livery and seizin only, or by parol, and not in writing, and signed by the party, were declared to have no greater force or effect than estates at will only. Stat. 19 Car. II., ch. 3, §§ 1, 2; 4 Kent's Com. [450], 491. A verbal assignment of both real and personal property is invalid. Such an attempted transfer of real estate alone would be of course be in violation of the statute of frauds; and where the agreement includes both real and personal property it will be regarded as entire, and come within the statute. Lill v. Brant, 6 Ill. App. (Bradw.) 366. An express trust in real estate can be created only by an instrument in writing. Ingham v. Burnell, 31 Kans. 333; 2 Pac. Rep. 804. But in Texas it is not made necessary by the statute of frauds that an agreement creating a trust should be in writing. James v. Fulcrod, 5 Tex. 512.

[2] Kent's Com., *ubi supra*.

[3] See Appendix, I.

[4] Sometimes, instead of combining the declaration of trust in the same instrument with the conveyance of the property, the property is conveyed absolutely by deed in the ordinary way, and the declaration of trust expressed by a separate instrument. This was the form in the cases of Schuylkill Bank v. Reigart and Reigart's Appeal, 4 Barr, 477; and in Johnson v. Whitwell, 7 Pick. 71. But this is not usual. See Danner v. Brewer, 69 Ala. 191; Bowen v. Hadden Blue Stone Co., 30 N. J. Eq., 171.

[5] Page v. Weymouth, 47 Me. 238.

[6] Shubar v. Winding, 1 Cheves' L. 218. The letter in this case contained, in fact, the elements of a conveyance in trust to pay debts. The assignment in Hall v. Marston, 17 Mass. 575, was of the same simple character. Directions to pay money already in hand present a still simpler form of the class termed *equitable*

of attorney to col'ect certain moneys and pay them to certain creditors in a prescribed order of preference has been held in Pennsylvania to be virtually an assignment.[1] In this case Chief Justice Gibson remarked that "an assignment of a chose in action or of a fund need not be by any particular form of words or particular form of instrument. . . . Any binding appropriation of it to a particular use, by any writing whatever, is an assignment, or, what is the same, a transfer of the ownership."[2] In a California case, where the assignment was in the form of a declaration made before the American consul at Canton, China, and signed and acknowl-

assignments, being resolvable into a mere declaration of trust. But these have no necessary connection with insolvency, and rather belong to the head of *special assignments.* So in the case of Brown v. Chamberlain, 9 Fla. 464, where a debtor, without any writing whatever, but verbally and by word of mouth only, assigned, transferred and delivered to three of his creditors, composing a firm, a package containing notes, drafts, etc., for nearly $30,000, in trust to collect and distribute the proceeds as far as they would go *pro rata* between the assignees and his other "Charleston creditors," this was held to be a voluntary assignment.

[1] Watson v. Bagaley, 12 Pa. St. 164. But a revocable power of attorney, without any trust for creditors, was held by the same court not an assignment for the benefit of creditors. Beans v. Bullitt, 57 Pa. St. 221. And see Kalkman v. McElderry, 16 Md. 57. But in Britton v. Lorenz, 45 N. Y. 51, a bill of sale, absolute on its face, was shown by parol to be executed in trust for the benefit of creditors, and was declard invalid as such because not acknowledged in compliance with the statute. See Truit v. Caldwell, 3 Minn. 364. See Matter of Oakley, 2 Edw. Ch. 478. A mortgage of substantially all a debtor's property for the security of a particular creditor has been held to operate as a general assignment. Shirley v. Teal, 67 Ala. 449. In the North Carolina case of Stimpson v. Fries, 2 Jones' Eq. 156, one of the trust deeds was very loosely drawn, having the form and a good deal of the language of a power of attorney, the debtor appointing the trustee his general agent and attorney to sell and dispose of all of his estate, real and personal, and to pay and satisfy the debts, etc. But it contained an express consideration of $10, and concluded with a clause of express transfer to the trustee of all the debtor's property for the purposes mentioned. On these grounds the court held it to be more than a mere power of attorney, and that it contained sufficient words of conveyance to vest the fee-simple and absolute estate in the trustee. But in a New Jersey case, where a debtor, in compliance with the request of some of his creditors, placed, by assignment, the books of account, notes, etc., of a dissolved firm in the hands of a responsible person to collect, and for no other purpose, such an assignment was held to be nothing more than a power of attorney, which did not place the property beyond the control of the debtor and created no rights between the assignee and the creditors. Brown v. Holcomb, 1 Stock. 297.

[2] No particular form of words is necessary to create a trust. Gordon v. Green, 10 Ga. 534. Where a person, being largely indebted, executed to an attorney for some of his creditors an assignment of numerous claims and judgments "in payment" of their demands, the transaction was held to be an assignment for the benefit of creditors. Wallace v. Wainwright, 87 Pa. St. 263. And see the discussion of cases upon irregular assignments in the opinion by Woodward, J. In Corn Exchange Nat. Bank v. Philadelphia Trust, etc. Co., 11 Phila. 510, it is held that, where the effect of an instrument is to transfer property beyond the reach of an execution in trust for the benefit of assenting creditors, it is within the purview of the statutes regulating voluntary assignments to creditors.

edged by the assignor, it was sustained as valid.[1] But a *judgment* given to prefer a particular creditor has been held in Pennsylvania to be not an assignment in substance or in form.[2] And it has been further held, in the same state, that the confession of a judgment by a debtor to a trustee for the payment of certain specified creditors is not an assignment for the benefit of creditors, and does not require to be recorded as required of assignments by the law of that state.[3] It would seem, however, that a judgment may be confessed in favor of the creditors at large, so as to operate as a general assignment.[4]

So in the case of Lucas v. The Sunbury & Erie R. R. Co.,[5] a lease reserving a portion of the rent for the payment of the lessor's debts was held to be an assignment for the benefit of creditors. Mr. Justice Hare said: "The means employed in each particular instance would have seemed to me immaterial if the result were a transfer in trust or a trust bottomed on a transfer; if, in short, the property ceased to be the debtor's without vesting directly and absolutely in his creditors and remained outstanding in the hands of a third person who could not be compelled to render an account or to fulfill the duties imposed upon him without a recourse to the aid of equity." And this language is referred to with approval by Mr. Justice Read in the same case on appeal.[6] In the case of Watts v. Eufaula Nat. Bank, a mortgage executed by an insolvent debtor for protection and indemnity on his official bond was declared and enforced a general assignment at the instance of his other creditors where it conveyed all his property.[7]

§ 93. **Assignment by Several Instruments.**— A general assignment, though usually made by one deed or instrument, may be made as effectually by *several* instruments relating to the same

[1] Forbes v. Scannell, 13 Cal. 242.
[2] Blakey's Appeal, 7 Barr, 449. See Worman v. Wolfersberger's Ex'rs, 19 Pa. St. 59; Lansing v. Woodworth, 1 Sandf. Ch. 43, 45.
[3] Guy v. McIlree, 26 Pa. St. 92. "There is little if any similarity," observes Knox, J., in this case, "between an assignment and a judgment. The one is an absolute transfer of its subject-matter, whilst the other is but the means whereby to enforce the payment of a debt. An assignment passes the property in real and personal estate, rights and credits, whilst a judgment of itself gives no vested estate in any of the property of the defendant, merely creating a lien upon his real estate, if any he has, at the time of its entry." Id., 94.
[4] In Meux v. Howell, 4 East, 1, the assignment was in the form of a judgment confessed to a creditor for a large sum, with a defeasance that execution should only issue for such an amount as should cover the debt of the creditor and all the other creditors among whom a ratable distribution was to be made. See Adams v. Woods, 8 Cal. 152.
[5] 32 Pa. St. 458; Bittenger v. Railroad Co., 40 Pa. St. 269.
[6] Lucas v. Railroad Co., *supra*.
[7] 76 Ala. 474.

subject-matter.[1] Thus, in Inglis v. Grant,[2] there were two deeds. The first was of three parts, between the debtor, the trustee and certain creditors, by which the latter covenanted that, if the debtor would assign to the trustee all his effects to pay creditors in a certain order, they would release him. The second deed was an assignment to the trustee, made pursuant to the foregoing. In Johnson v. Whitwell[3] the assignment was by two instruments — an absolute deed of conveyance and an indenture of three parts declaring the trust. In Blank v. German[4] there was, first, an agreement in writing by the debtor to convey the property subject to the payment of a mortgage, and also subject to a full release of certain debts; next, an agreement in writing by the creditors that if the debtor would convey to two of their number for the use of the creditors they would release him; and finally, a conveyance in the form of an ordinary deed by the debtor and his wife to the two creditors. These instruments were taken together as constituting an ordinary assignment to trustees for the use of creditors. In Mussey v. Noyes[5] the assignment was in two parts, consisting of two principal deeds referring to each other, together with other papers, all relating to the same subject-matter, executed on the same day, and to effect the same general design. The court took them together, regarding them as one transaction. In French v. Townes[6] two instruments had been executed by the debtor to a creditor on the same day; one being a power of attorney for the particular benefit of the creditor, the other a deed of trust to secure the creditors generally, with preferences. The court held that both papers were to be construed as one instrument. In Stimpson v. Fries[7] there were three deeds of trust, separated by considerable intervals; one executed in the year 1848, another in 1854 of all the debtor's property to the same trustee, and a third in 1855 of the same property to another trustee. The court upheld and gave effect to all the three deeds as parts of a general provision for creditors.

[1] Norton v. Kearney, 10 Wis. 443; Burrows v. Lehndorff, 8 Iowa, 96; Van Vleet v. Slauson, 45 Barb. 317; Bridges v. Hindes, 16 Md. 101; Berry v. Cutts, 42 Me. 445; Moody v. Paschal, 60 Tex. 483. See Schoolfield v. Johnson, 11 Fed. Rep. 297; 3 McCrary, 551; Van Cott v. Prentice, 35 Hun, 317; Tenney v. Simpson, 37 Kan. 579; Loring v. Palmer, 118 U. S. 321; 6 S. Ct. Rep. 1073.
[2] 5 Term R. 530.
[3] 7 Pick. 71.
[4] 5 Watts & Serg. 36.
[5] 26 Vt. 468, 471. In the later case of Peck & Co. v. Merrill & Trustees, id. 680, 691, there was an assignment by the debtor, and also several mortgages of real estate, executed by him about the same time. The court treated them as one instrument.
[6] 10 Gratt. 513.
[7] 2 Jones' Eq. 156.

Again, a general assignment may be made either by one instrument conveying the whole of the assignor's property, or by *several* instruments conveying several portions respectively. In this way several partial assignments, though in the form of distinct deeds, and executed at different periods, will be taken together as constituting one general assignment.

Thus, in the case of White v. Cotzhausen,[1] there were two conveyances of real estate, a bill of sale and a judgment by confession under a warrant of attorney and certain transfers of property accompanying that warrant, all made by an insolvent debtor in the state of Illinois in contemplation of insolvency, disposing of his entire estate, which were held to constitute, under the voluntary assignment act of that state prohibiting preferences, but one instrument operating as a general assignment. But in Central National Bank v. Seligman[2] an assignment executed and judgments recovered within a few minutes of each other were regarded as separate transactions, and preferential.

In the case of Downing v. Kintzing[3] there were two assignments made to different persons by an insolvent debtor, with an interval of thirty-one days between them, and together conveying the whole of the debtor's estate; the object being to evade the act of congress giving a priority to the United States. It was contended that the two deeds were to be construed each by itself. But the court held the contrary, taking them to constitute but one general assignment, and so coming within the act. The same question arose in the late case of The United States v. The Bank of the United States,[4] where three partial assignments had been made by the bank, dated June 7th and September 4th and 6th, 1841, respectively. The court below had held that all of these assignments should be considered as one, so as to give the United States their priority; and on appeal the supreme court held that decision to be correct. The rule governing these cases was laid down by the counsel for the plaintiffs in the following terms, which seem to have met the approval of the court: that, no matter how many instruments are employed to effect the same result, they all partake of the same character, and all should be considered as parts of the same whole. If the same causes which led to the execution of one of the instruments, partial when considered alone, continue to op-

---

[1] 129 U. S. 329; 9 S. Ct. Rep. 309.
[2] 138 N. Y. 435; reversing 64 Hun, 615.
[3] 2 Serg. & R. 326, 335. In the case of Dance v. Seaman, 11 Gratt. 778, there were two deeds, dated on the same day; one executed by one of two debtors, and the other by the other debtor, each conveying one moiety of the same property, with substantially the same provisions.
[4] 8 Rob. (La.) 262.

erate until every particle of the debtor's property is divested, the first instrument is to be coupled with those that follow, and the whole should be construed together.[1]

§ 94. **Assignment by Single Instrument.**— But assignments in trust for the benefit of creditors are usually made by formal instruments having all the requisites of a deed. They may be drawn in either of the following varieties of form, viz.: First, by the debtor to the assignee, in the form of a *deed-poll*, without making the latter a party;[2] secondly, between the debtor and the assignee, the latter being made a formal party, and this is called an assignment *bipartite*, or of two parts; and thirdly, between the assignor, assignee and creditors, the latter being also made formal parties,

[1] Holt v. Bancroft, 30 Ala. 195; Danner v. Brewer, 69 id. 191; Burrows v. Lehndorff, 8 Iowa, 96; Van Vleet v. Slauson, 45 Barb. 317. Where a firm, just before making an assignment, executed warrants of attorney to confess judgment to certain creditors who were merely passive participants in the transaction, it was held that the warrants of attorney and the assignment were but parts of the same transaction, and together constituted a general assignment within the meaning of the statute. Preston v. Spaulding, 18 Ill. App. 341. Similar in Missouri. See Clapp v. Nordemeyer, 25 Fed. Rep. 71; Freund v. Yaegerman, 26 id. 812. As to Michigan, see Rollins v. Van Baalen, 23 N. W. Rep. 332. Where two conveyances operating as an assignment were executed at the same time and between the same parties and relating to the same subject-matter, they should be construed together as forming parts of a single conveyance. The argument that the assignor had no interest to assign after having executed the recorded deed was considered of no weight. Kruse v. Prindle, 8 Oreg. 158. A defendant executed chattel mortgages for the benefit of certain creditors, and immediately thereafter and on the same day executed a deed of general assignment. It was held that, the instruments being executed together, it was really but one transaction constituting a general assignment, which was invalidated by the preference. Van Patten v. Burr, 52 Iowa, 518; Van Horn v. Smith, 59 id. 142; Perry v. Vezina, 63 id. 25. See, also, Winner v. Hoyt, 28 N. W. Rep. 380 (Wis.); Kellogg v. Root, 23 Fed. Rep. 525 (Mich.). Where the mortgages were in good faith, for a valuable consideration, and duly filed, and on the next day an assignment was executed, it was held that each was valid as a separate transaction. Bailey v. Kansas Mfg. Co., 32 Kan. 73. See, also, Nelson v. Garey, 15 Neb. 531. The transfer by an insolvent of all his property, in parcels, by deeds and mortgages, to several of his creditors, in satisfaction or security of their claims, does not constitute an assignment for the benefit of creditors, though all done at one time and as one transaction. Aulman v. Aulman, 71 Iowa, 124; 32 N. W. Rep. 240. See Garret v. Burlington Plow Co., 70 id. 697; 29 N. W. Rep. 295. But where several deeds are made at the same time and as part of the same transaction, with an assignment for the benefit of creditors, they will be considered as together constituting one assignment. Moore v. Church, 70 Iowa, 208; 30 N. W. Rep. 855; 59 Am. Rep. 439. A transfer, by verbal arrangement, of both real and personal property, to secure a surety, the real estate being afterward conveyed by warranty deed to the surety, is an assignment and not a mortgage. Lill v. Brant, 6 Ill. App. (Bradw.) 366.

[2] This appears to be the ordinary form in Connecticut, where assignments are required to conform to the statute. Strong v. Carrier, 17 Conn. 319. See Whittaker v. Williams, 20 id. 98. But see G. S. 1888, § 501 *et seq.*

and this is termed an indenture *tripartite,* or of three parts. The two last constitute the species of form in most general use. There is also a fourth variety, of *quadripartite* assignments, in which the parties are arranged in four parts,[1] but these are rarely adopted.

§ 95. **Simplest Form.**— The essential features of an instrument of assignment may be conveniently illustrated by taking up the simplest variety in common use, which is the assignment bipartite, considering it as divested of all special clauses, and examining in succession its formal parts. These consist of the following: 1, the commencement; 2, the recital; 3, the consideration; 4, the transfer; 5, the description of the property assigned; 6, the *habendum;* 7, the declaration of the trusts or directions to the assignee; 8, the reservation to the assignor; 9, power of attorney to the assignee; 10, covenant by the assignee; and 11, the concluding clause. To the assignment are usually appended two *schedules*, which are marked and referred to in the body of the instrument, and are taken as a part of it — first, a schedule of the property assigned; and secondly, a schedule of the assignor's creditors, or of the debts to which the property is to be appropriated. The forms in the appendix to this work may be consulted with advantage in connection with the following explanations.

§ 96. **Commencement and Recital.**— The date of the instrument and the names of the parties are first inserted.

The assignment next proceeds to recite the indebtedness of the assignor to his creditors in divers sums, which, by reason of losses, etc., he is unable to pay; and his agreement to transfer to assignees all his property in trust for their benefit. The indebtedness is usually stated in this part of the instrument in general terms, the particular debts being afterwards specified in a schedule. But sometimes, as where the creditors are few in number, the debts are described in the recital in lieu of a schedule. It is better that no language should be employed which can raise a question as to the fact of the assignor's insolvency.[2]

A false recital of losses as the occasion of the debtor's failure has been held not to affect the rights of creditors under an assignment.[3] Nor will a misdescription in the recital of debts described as the consideration of the assignment affect the validity of the deed.[4] And a trust deed to secure creditors, reciting the amount

[1] This was the form of assignment in Foster v. Saco Manufacturing Company, 12 Pick. 451.

[2] See Kellogg v. Slauson, 15 Barb. 56; Allen, J., id. 57, 58; s. c. on appeal, 11 N. Y. 302; Parker, J., id. 304, 305; Van Nest v. Yoe, 1 Sandf. Ch. 4.

[3] Reinhard v. Bank of Kentucky, 6 B. Mon. 252.

[4] Graham v. Lockhart, 8 Ala. 9.

of the debts due to the different creditors, is not conclusive even as against the grantor and his administrator of the amount of the respective debts.[1]

It has sometimes been the practice to recite in this part of the assignment the reasons which led to the making of it, the object contemplated by it, and even the circumstances under which it was made.[2] This, while not strictly necessary, may in certain cases be hazardous, as the language of recitals is sometimes relied on to show a fraudulent intent on the part of the assignor where the assignment is assailed on that ground.[3] In a case in New York where the assignment was declared to be made for the purpose of carrying into effect the assignor's intention of "applying his property and estate to the payment of his debts in a fair and equitable manner and without *sacrifice*," it was held to be no evidence of an intent to hinder or delay creditors, although the terms used were admitted to be not happily selected.[4] In a case in Alabama where a deed of trust recited that some of the grantor's creditors were urging the collection of their debts at a time when there was a great pressure in the money market, and that his property if sold at a more favorable period would be more than enough to pay off all his debts, it was held that this was but a statement of the reasons which induced him to make the deed, and did not render it fraudulent on its face.[5]

§ 97. **Consideration.**— Next follows the statement of the consideration of the assignment, which usually is — "of the premises and of one dollar," or some nominal sum, paid to the assignor; and of the covenants on the part of the assignee. It is always best to express the consideration on the face of the deed, although it will be held to import one.[6]

In deeds of trust the amount of the debts intended to be secured is something specifically recited as the consideration. In such cases the recital should correspond with the actual indebtedness. The recital of fictitious consideration as the ground of the deed will be evidence of an intention to hinder and delay creditors.[7] In a case in Tennessee a deed of trust purporting to be for a debt

[1] Griffin's Ex'r v. Macaulay's Adm'r, 7 Gratt. 476.
[2] See Brigham v. Tillinghast, 15 Barb. 618; Shackelford v. P. & M. Bank of Mobile, 22 Ala. 238.
[3] Ward v. Trotter, 3 Mon. 1; Vernon v. Morton, 8 Dana, 247.
[4] Brigham v. Tillinghast, 15 Barb. 618; Allen, J., id. 620. The judgment in this case was afterwards reversed on another ground. 13 N. Y. 215.
[5] Shackelford v. P. & M. Bank of Mobile, 22 Ala. 238.
[6] See *post*, ch. XII.
[7] Nueffer v. Pardue, 3 Sneed, 190, 194; Lockhard v. Browdie, 1 Tenn. Ch. (Cooper), 384.

then due of $2,500, when only $304 were in fact due, was held to be upon a false and fictitious consideration calculated to deceive creditors.[1]

§ 98. **Transfer.**— Next follows the clause of transfer, by which the assignor grants, bargains, conveys, assigns, transfers and sets over to the assignee, his heirs, executors, administrators and assigns, all his estate, real and personal, describing it by sufficient words.

§ 99. **Description of Property.**— The property intended to be assigned is described either in this part of the instrument or in a schedule annexed, to which reference is here made; the latter being the usual method, where the property is considerable in amount, or consists of a variety of particulars. In either case the description should be sufficiently explicit to enable the assignee to take possession.[2] A mere imperfection in the description will not, however, have the effect of invalidating the instrument, unless there is a failure to comply with some express statute provision; and a description in general terms has frequently been held unobjectionable. Thus, in a case in Massachusetts, where the property assigned was described as the cargoes of certain vessels named, without invoices, bills of lading or valuations; and real estate lying in Boston, Charlestown and Maine, without a particular description of each parcel, it was held that, as the description could be made certain by the references given, it was sufficient.[3] And in another case in the same state, where the property was described as "quantities of leather and stock, designed for the manufacture of boots and shoes, and also of boots and shoes already made or partly made," in the hands of divers persons named, this was held to be a sufficient specification of the property and the place where it was to be found.[4] And even a description of the real estate of the debtor as "all his lands, tenements and hereditaments" was held.

---

[1] Nueffer v. Pardue, *supra*.

[2] In a case in Missouri, where the property assigned was described as "one bundle of orders, one bundle of fee bills, two bundles of notes, two bundles of accounts and one of receipts," it was held to be void for uncertainty. Crow v. Ruby, 5 Mo. 484. And in the case of The State v. Keeler, 49 Mo. 548, it was said by Adams, J.: "It may be assumed as a proposition of universal acceptance that the absolute owner of property has the right to transfer the same by any description which, together with parol evidence, may ascertain the property conveyed." Clark v. Few, 62 Ala. 243. See note 2, p. 144; Nave v. Britton, 61 Tex. 572; Cunningham v. Norton, 125 U. S. 77; 8 S. Ct. Rep. 804; Bock v. Perkins, 139 U. S. 628; Kuefler v. Shreve, 78 Ky. 307; Scheibler v. Mundinger, 86 Tenn. 674; 9 S. W. Rep. 33.

[3] Hatch v. Smith, 5 Mass. 42.

[4] Emerson v. Knower, 8 Pick. 63; Parker, C. J., id. 65.

in a later case, sufficient to pass all his real estate without a more particular description.[1] But the words "all the goods, chattels and effects, and property of every kind, personal and mixed," do not include real estate. The words "personal and mixed" limit the assignment to the personal estate; nor can the assignee make any claim upon the proceeds after the sale and conversion of the realty by the assignor.[2] And where an assignment purported to be a conveyance of the various articles of property stated in a schedule annexed, but no schedule was in fact annexed at the time of the delivery of the assignment, it was held that even if the assignment at the time of delivery was invalid on account of uncertainty in the description of the property proposed to be assigned, the annexation of the schedule, with the consent of the parties on the day after delivery, would cure the defect; or would be considered as equivalent to a redelivery as against a creditor attaching subsequently to such annexation.[3] So, in Connecticut, where a deed of assignment was made with a view to proceedings under the statute of 1828 against fraudulent conveyances, and was a part of such proceedings, the circumstance that it was general in its terms, embracing all the assignor's estate, real and personal (except such as was by law exempt from execution), without any specification or description of such estate, was held, in the absence of any other objection, not to render the assignment invalid.[4] And in another case in the same state, where the deed purported to assign to the trustees all the real and personal property of the assignors of every description in the state except their household furniture, a schedule of which property was to be made out and annexed thereto as soon as convenient, it was held that such an assignment was not invalid as against the assignors, either because the description of property was too general or because the sched-

---

[1] Pingree v. Comstock, 18 Pick. 46; Raynor v. Raynor, 21 Hun, 36. But in a late case in Florida it was held to be essential to the conveyance of real estate that there be some description of the land. Bellamy v. Bellamy's Adm'r, 6 Fla. 62. So in the case of Ryerson v. Eldrid, 18 Mich. 12, a description of lands as follows: "14¼ lots of land in Kankakee City, Kankakee Co., Illinois, valued at $5,400, and ⅔ of 1,600 acres of land in Green Co., Illinois, at $2,500, and 120 acres of land in Chickasaw Co., Iowa, valued at $600," was regarded as too uncertain and vague to make the assignment operate as a transfer of title, at least without clear evidence that the assignor owned certain lands in the places named which might fall within the description, and that these were the only lands owned by him in such places. See Drakeley v. Deforest, 3 Conn. 272.

[2] Rhoads v. Blatt, 84 Pa. St. 31.

[3] Clap v. Smith, 16 Pick. 247. See Bates v. Simmons, 62 Wis. 69.

[4] Strong v. Carrier, 17 Conn. 317. The court, however, in this case, placed their decision on the ground that, by the provisions of the statute, two months were allowed for making an inventory after the deed was lodged for record. Church, J., id. 330.

ule referred to was not then in existence.¹ In a case in New York where the property assigned was described as "all and singular the goods and chattels, merchandise, bills, bonds, notes, book accounts, judgments, evidences of debt, and property of every name and nature whatever," without further specification and without any inventory, it was held that such omission was not conclusive evidence of fraud, but only a circumstance to be considered by the jury in connection with the other circumstances of the case.² In Pennsylvania, where an assignment of personal property described it in a vague manner, it was held that a notice given by the assignees before the right of any third person had attached to the person in whose hands the property was, that it had been conveyed to them, and requesting him to hold it subject to their order, under which was written by the assignor, "I confirm the above," amounted to a declaration identifying the property.³ In a case in Virginia where the deed conveyed, among other things, cattle, household and kitchen furniture, and debts, without specification either in the deed or by schedule accompanying it, it was held that the deed was not therefore fraudulent.⁴ So in Alabama it has been held that a deed of assignment is not void on account of an imperfect description of some of the chattels conveyed by it,⁵ and that the omission to specify the property assigned does not render it fraudulent on its face, but is a circumstance merely to be weighed by a jury in determining the question of fraudulent intent.⁶ In Mississippi, where in an assignment by a bank the property was described as "all the estate of the corporation, whether real, personal or mixed, and all the stock, goods, wares, merchandise, bills receivable, bonds, notes, book accounts, claims, demands, judgments, and choses in action," without any schedule, it was held to be a sufficient general description of the property to give precise information of its nature and extent by reference and inquiry.⁷ It seems that a less accurate description will be sufficient where a statute provides for the filing of a schedule or where the assignee had no difficulty in finding the property.⁸ And in the

---

[1] Clarke v. Mix, 15 Conn. 152.
[2] Kellogg v. Slauson, 15 Barb. 56, 58, 59: affirmed on appeal, 11 N. Y. 302.
[3] Passmore v. Eldridge, 12 Serg. & Rawle, 198.
[4] Kevan v. Branch, 1 Gratt. 274.
[5] Tarver v. Roffe, 7 Ala. 873. See Robinson v. Rapelye, 2 Stew. 86; Pope v. Brandon, id. 401.
[6] Brown v. Lyon, 17 Ala. 659.
[7] Robins v. Embry, 1 Sm. & M. Ch. 207, 208, 273, 274; Wickham v. Green, 61 Miss. 463.
[8] Lininger v. Raymond, 9 Neb. 40; Walker v. Newlin, 22 Kan. 106. See Farwell v. Gundry, 52 Wis. 268. In the absence of any statute on the subject, a schedule is not necessary if the property is described with reasonable certainty. Smith v. Stokes, 8 Col. 286.

case of Brashear v. West,[1] in the supreme court of the United States, an objection that the assignment was in general terms and that no schedule was annexed was overruled by the court. And even an erroneous description of the property assigned will not prevent its passing to the assignee. Thus where a party assigned his right to certain insurance money, describing it as then in the hands of a person named, when in fact it had not been paid to such person, the assignment was held to pass his right to the money.[2] And in the case of Walker v. Newlin[3] a deed of assignment describing the property as "my stock of goods now on hand in store in the building on Main street, in Council Grove, Morris county, state of Kansas; and in the frame store building on Main street, in Winfield, Cowley county, state of Kansas, where I do business," is not void because of uncertainty in the description of the property assigned, and especially not where the assignee had no difficulty in finding the property.

§ 100. **Amount Assigned — Reference to the Schedule.** — Where the assignment is intended as a general one it should convey in terms *all* the debtor's property of every kind, except such as may be exempted by law; and under this head particular reference should be had to the statute law of the state in which the assignment is drawn.[4] In New York an omission of assets from the schedule does not,[5] *ipso facto*, make the assignment void, and in New Jersey it has been held that an inventory required by statute is not conclusive as to the *quantum* of the debtor's estate.[6]

Where it is intended to assign all the property, care should be taken not to restrict the description by words of reference to the schedule annexed, unless the schedule itself actually contains all.

Greater particularity is requisite in the description of the property in the schedule annexed to a general assignment than in the body of the assignment itself. The office of the schedule is to aid the more general description in the body of the deed and thereby

---

[1] 7 Pet. 608, 614. See Sadler v. Immel, 15 Nev. 219.
[2] Sanford v. Conant, 2 Sandf. S. C. 143.
[3] 22 Kan. 106.
[4] See *ante*, ch. VI.
[5] Shultz v. Hoagland, 85 N. Y. 464. But the inclusion in the schedule of debts which have been paid is fraudulent (Talcott v. Hess, 31 Hun, 282), and the intentional omission of valuable property is sufficient to establish fraudulent intent. Bagley v. Bowe, 50 N. Y. Super. Ct. 100; White v. Fagan, 18 N. Y. Weekly Dig. 358. In a case arising in Arkansas, the supreme court of the United States held that the intentional omission by the grantor of assets from the schedule, and the applying of them to his own use, without the knowledge of the assignee or the beneficiaries, did not invalidate the assignment. Emerson v. Senter, 118 U. S. 3.
[6] Hays v. Doane, 11 N. J. Eq. 84. See Merrill v. Wilson, 29 Me. 58; Hasseld v. Seyforth, 105 Ind. 534.

furnish such particular, definite and detailed information of the property conveyed as will, on the one hand, give adequate knowledge to the assignee and creditors of their rights, and, on the other hand, to guard against the assignor's fraud.[1]

Thus, in the case of The United States v. Howland,[2] in the supreme court of the United States, where the property was described as "all and singular the estate and effects which is contained in a schedule hereunto annexed, marked A," and the caption of the schedule was, "Schedule of property assigned by [the debtors] to [the creditors]," it was held by the court (Marshall, C. J.) that the deed conveyed only the property contained in the schedule; and the schedule did not purport to contain all the property of the parties who made it; and that, in such a case, the presumption must be that there was property not contained in the deed, unless the contrary appeared. In accordance with this decision it was held by Mr. Justice Story, in a case in the circuit court of Massachusetts,[3] where the assignment was of all the debtor's property in a schedule referred to, which enumerated only specific property, and did not purport to contain all, that no presumption arose that the property assigned was all the debtor's property, or that the assignment was a general one. So, in a case in Maryland, where the assignment was of all the debtor's "goods, chattels, promissory notes, debts, wares, merchandise, securities and vouchers for, and affecting, etc., and property of every name and nature whatsoever of or belonging to him, and which are more particularly and fully enumerated in the schedule hereto annexed, marked Schedule A," a sum of money not mentioned in the Schedule A, annexed to the deed of assignment, did not pass to the assignee, for the reason that the general words of the deed were restrained and limited by the reference to the schedule.[4]

§ 101. **Amount Assigned — Reference to the Schedule — Continued.**— So in New Hampshire, where a debtor assigned "all and all manner of goods, chattels, debts, demands, moneys, and other things of him, the said D., whatsoever, as well real as personal, of what kind, or nature, or quality whatsoever, in the schedule hereto annexed, and particularly mentioned and expressed," it was held that the latter words were restrictive, and that nothing would pass

[1] Scheibler v. Mundinger, 86 Tenn. 674; 9 S. W. Rep. 33.
[2] 4 Wheat. 108.
[3] United States v. Langton, 5 Mason, 280.
[4] Mims v. Armstrong, 31 Md. 87, citing Wood v. Radcliffe, 5 Eng. L. & Eq. 471; Wilkes v. Ferris, 5 Johns. 335, and this treatise. And see Guerin v. Hunt, 6 Minn. 375. Similarly in Tennessee, Belding v. Franckland, 8 Lea, 67; and Iowa, Bock v. Perkins, 28 Fed. Rep. 123. And so if the specification follows the words of grant in the instrument. Price v. Haynes, 37 Mich. 487.

by the assignment unless it was specified in the schedule.¹ And in the same state, where an assignment was made by an individual of "all his property, real and personal, in the schedule annexed particularly mentioned," to be paid out to the several persons named in the schedule, where all the names of the creditors were not mentioned, it was held that the assignment was invalid under the statute of July 5, 1834, as not showing either an assignment of all the property or as made to all the creditors.² So in Massachusetts, where the debtors assigned "all their books, stock in trade, printing apparatus and machinery, books of account, book debts, notes and demands, and all their other property of every name and nature, except such as is exempt from attachment, most of the same being now at their place of business, a schedule of which is annexed;" and it was expressed that other and fuller schedules of the property assigned should be annexed as soon as the same could conveniently be made; and the schedule annexed to the assignment contained three items, viz.: stock of books in store, printing presses and materials, notes and demands, etc.,— it was held that the words of the assignment, though broad enough in themselves to comprise furniture of one of the partners, were restricted by the schedule; that the furniture was not included in the schedule, as originally made, the "etc." being applicable to things *ejusdem generis;* and that parol evidence that the assignment was intended to embrace the furniture was inadmissible because it would vary the written instrument.³ And in a case in England, where a bill of sale purported to assign to G. R. "all the household goods and furniture of every kind and description whatsoever, in the house No. 2 Meadow Place, more particularly mentioned and set forth in an inventory or schedule of even date, and given up to the said G. R. on the execution thereof," but the inventory did not specify all the goods and furniture in the house, it was held that the bill of sale only operated as an assignment of the goods and furniture specified in the inventory.⁴

§ 102. **Amount Assigned — Reference to the Schedule — Continued.**— In the earlier cases in New York this doctrine was applied,⁵ but in the later cases the principle of construction, prohibiting a false or erroneous addition from vitiating what had been previously sufficiently and fully described as a portion of the subject-

---

¹ Rundlett v. Dole, 10 N. H. 458.
² Beard v. Kimball, 11 N. H. 471.
³ Driscoll v. Fiske, 21 Pick. 503.
⁴ Wood v. Rowcliffe, 20 L. J. (N. S.) Exch. 285; 5 Eng. L. & Eq. 471.
⁵ Wilkes v. Ferris, 5 Johns. 335; Moir v. Brown, 14 Barb. 39. See Keep v. Sanderson, 2 Wis. 42; Crawford, J., id. 60, 61.

matter intended to be transferred by the instrument, has been regarded as the correct rule of construction in such cases. Thus, in the case of Turner v. Jaycox,[1] where the transfer was of "all and singular the lands, tenements and hereditaments situate, lying and being in the state of New York, and all the goods, chattels, merchandise, bills, bonds, notes, book accounts, claims, demands, choses in action, judgments, evidences of debt, and property of every name and nature whatsoever of the said parties of the first part, more particularly enumerated and described in the schedule hereto annexed, marked Schedule A," and no allusion was made in the schedule to any of the tangible personal property of the assignors, it was held that such property passed under the previous general description.[2]

An assignment of a greater amount of property than is sufficient to pay the debts thereby to be secured is not, of course, fraudulent; but if the excess be great it will be presumptive evidence of fraud.[3]

§ 103. **When the Schedules Should be Annexed.**—Where schedules are intended to be prepared and are referred to in the assignment they should, in strictness, be prepared before the assignment is drawn; or at any rate be in readiness so as to be annexed to the instrument before it is executed. In some cases, however, where time has not been allowed for the preparation of schedules, particularly those of the property assigned, an assignment executed without schedules, and only referring to them as "to be made out

[1] 40 N. Y. 470; s. c., 40 Barb. 164; Burghard v. Sondheim, 50 N. Y. Super. Ct. 116. But see Kircheis v. Schloss, 49 How. 284; Hotop v. Neidig, 17 Abb. Pr. 332; Birchell v. Strauss, 28 Barb. 293.

[2] See comments of Selden, J., on Wilkes v. Ferris, *supra*, in Platt v. Lott, 17 N. Y. 481. In Clark v. Few, 62 Ala. 243, the terms of the assignment were very broad, and included "all the property, real, personal and mixed," of the assignor. Schedules of the property, *so far as remembered*, were annexed, and any property omitted was expressly declared to be nevertheless conveyed. It was held that "the generality of the description of the property intended to be conveyed by the assignment for the benefit of creditors does not affect its validity when, by the aid of parol evidence, a definite application of the terms may be made." Though the schedule does not embrace the demand (in this case a judgment sought to be reached by garnishment), and though it embraced certain choses in action and credits of the assignor, if the demand is the property of the assignor it passes. In Knefler v. Shreve, 78 Ky. (1 Rodm.) 297, under similar provisions, the income of property held in trust for the benefit of the debtor, although not mentioned in the schedule, was held to pass to the assignee. An insufficient description in the schedule is not remedied by an offer made therein to furnish "more full" and complete description of the property, "if required." Scheibler v. Mundinger, 86 Tenn. 674; 9 S. W. Rep. 33; *ante*, p. 142.

[3] Hastings v. Baldwin, 17 Mass. 552; Burlingame v. Bell, 16 id. 318. And see further, on this head, *ante*, § 64.

and annexed" at a future time, has been adjudged valid. Thus in Connecticut, where the property assigned was described as "all the real and personal property of the assignors of every description in this state, except their household furniture," a schedule of which property was to be made out and annexed thereto as soon as convenient, it was held that the assignment was not invalid because the schedule referred to was not in existence.[1] So in Massachusetts where an assignment described the property in general terms, and provided that a schedule of the property should be prepared and made a part of the instrument when completed, it was held that the annexation of the schedule was not a condition precedent to the operation of the assignment.[2] So in New York, where an absolute assignment of all the assignor's property and choses in action contained a provision that the assignor would, with all convenient speed, make out an inventory of such property and choses in action, and which inventory, when made out, was to be considered a part of the assignment, it was held that the assignment conveyed a present interest to the assignee, and that its taking effect did not depend upon the making out of the inventory.[3] And in England a deed referring to a schedule as annexed, which was not in fact annexed until after its execution, was held valid.[4] But in a case in New York where the property assigned was described as "all and singular the lands, tenements, etc., situate, etc., and all the goods, chattels, etc., and property of every name and nature whatever of the said parties of the first part, more particularly enumerated and described in the schedule *hereto annexed* marked Schedule A," but Schedule A was not annexed until after the assignment had been executed and recorded, it was held that such schedule was a necessary part of the assignment as showing what property passed by it, and that without it the assignment was insensible, imperfect and inoperative, and, as against creditors, did not convey the property to the assignees.[5] More will be said on this subject in considering the schedule as a part of the assignment.[6]

§ 104. Habendum.— After the description of the property intended to be assigned follows the *habendum* or formal clause

[1] Clark v. Mix, 15 Conn. 152.
[2] Woodward v. Marshall, 22 Pick. 468; Stamp v. Case, 41 Mich. 267.
[3] Keyes v. Brush, 2 Paige, 311.
[4] West v. Steward, 14 Mees. & W. 47.
[5] Moir v. Brown, 14 Barb. 39; Dodd v. Martin, 25 Fed. Rep. 338; Barkman v. Simmons, 23 Ark. 1. See *post*, p. 151, note 3. In the case of Kellogg v. Slauson, in the same court, and decided about the same time (15 Barb. 56), in which it was held that the omission of a schedule of the property would not avoid the assignment, there was no reference to a schedule as annexed. And see Kircheis v. Schloss, 49 How. Pr. 284.
[6] See *post*, pp. 150 *et seq*.

expressing the legal estate[1] which the assignee is to have in it: "To have and to hold the same to [the assignee, naming him], his heirs, executors, administrators and assigns" [or, if there be more than one assignee, "to [the assignees], and the survivors and survivor of them, their and his heirs," etc.].[2] Where there are several assignees, and especially where the assignment conveys real estate, it is advisable to use words expressive of survivorship, so as to avoid all ground of question as to the estate taken by them, whether it be a joint tenancy or tenancy in common;[3] although in New York every estate vested in trustees is declared by statute to be held in joint tenancy.[4]

§ 105. **Declaration of Trusts.**— Immediately following the *habendum*, and in fact constituting a part of it, is that portion of the instrument (commencing with the words "in trust" or "upon trust") which declares the *trusts* upon which the assigned property is to be held, in the form of *directions* to the assignee what disposition to make of it. These trusts may be ranked under two general heads: first, to reduce the property into a form in which it may be distributed; and secondly, to distribute it.

§ 106. **To Convert the Property into Money.**— In order to reduce the property into a form for distribution, the trusts or directions in this part of the assignment are, first, to take possession of the property assigned; second, to sell and dispose of it to the best advantage and with the least delay;[5] and third, to collect and recover the debts due to the assignor.

---

[1] A deed of trust to secure debts must convey the legal as well as the equitable title. Rossett v. Fisher, 11 Gratt. 492.

[2] The technical meaning of the word "premises" is everything which precedes the *habendum*, and it is in the premises of a deed that the thing is really granted. Farquharson v. Eichelberger, 15 Md. 63. Under a deed of trust to sell and pay debts the fee may pass by necessary implication without the word "heirs." Farquharson v. Eichelberger, *supra*. A conveyance to the assignee, "his heirs, executors, administrators and assigns," is not fraudulent. These words describe the quality of the estate conveyed and not the class of persons taking. Flagler v. Schœffel, 40 Hun, 178; Bates v. Simmons, 62 Wis. 69. Nor is a conveyance to the assignee, "his successors and assigns," fraudulent. Hess v. Blakeslee, 1 N. Y. State Rep. 309.

[3] A question of this kind arose in the case of Benedict v. Morse, 10 Metc. 223. The court, however, held it unnecessary to be decided in the case, because, *quacunque via data*, the defendant could not avail himself of the legal difference between the two estates. Hubbard, J., id. 228.

[4] 3 R. S. (7th ed.) p. 2179, § 44.

[5] A power to sell and convey is necessarily implied by a conveyance of property for the payment of debts. Williams v. Otey, 8 Humph. 653; Hager, J., in Forbes v. Scannell, 13 Cal. 326. But it is always the practice to give the power or declare the trust for this purpose in express terms. As to special provisions respecting the sale, see *post*, ch. XI. But it seems that an assignment of "goods,

§ 107. To Apply and Distribute the Proceeds.— The trusts or directions under this head comprise the following: first, to pay the expenses of the trust, including a reasonable compensation to the assignee or assignees for his or their services;[1] secondly, to pay out of the residue all the creditors of the assignor named in the assignment or in a schedule annexed and referred to in full, or in proportion to their respective demands; and, after payment of the said creditors, and all the creditors, in full, thirdly, to pay over the residue to the assignor, his executors, administrators or assigns. These several trusts will now be considered more in detail.

§ 108. To Pay the Expenses of the Trust.— These expenses include costs of suits and of defenses necessarily incurred by the assignee in collecting the debts and claims and obtaining or retaining possession of the property assigned. They are sometimes provided for specifically in the assignment.[2] But although the deed contains no such provision, the law authorizes the retention by the assignee of all reasonable charges and expenses.[3]

§ 109. To Retain a Reasonable Compensation to the Assignee. Sometimes the amount to be allowed the assignee for his services is fixed and specified in the assignment as a gross sum named,[4] or so much yearly. A stipulation that salaries shall be paid to the trustees out of the trust property has been expressly held to be not improper.[5] And even large salaries so stipulated to be paid do not make the deed fraudulent upon its face.[6] But where the trustees were to receive each $8,000 per annum, the assignment was for this and other reasons held void as against creditors not parties.[7]

chattels, book accounts, stock debts, and all other estate and effects," does not give the assignee power of sale over real estate without express words. Boker v. Crookshank, 1 Phila. 193. And see In the Matter of the Assigned Estate of Gallagher, 5 Phila. 83.

[1] Canal Bank v. Cox, 5 Greenl. 395; Andrews v. Ludlow, 5 Pick. 28.

[2] A debtor may provide in an assignment for payment of present and prospective costs of suits going on, relating to some of the assigned property. Lentilhon v. Moffatt, 1 Edw. Ch. 451. A direction to the assignee to pay first of all the just and reasonable expenses, costs and charges, and commissions of executing and carrying into effect the assignment, and all reasonable and proper charges for attorney and counsel fees respecting the trust, does not render the assignment invalid. Butt v. Peck, 1 Daly (N. Y.) 83; Iselin v. Dalrymple, 27 How. Pr. 137.

[3] Blow v. Gage, 44 Ill. 208; Moody v. Carroll, 71 Tex. 143; 8 S. W. Rep. 510.

[4] Andrews v. Ludlow, 5 Pick. 28.

[5] Vernon v. Morton, 8 Dana, 247.

[6] Ingraham v. Grigg, 13 Sm. & M. 22.

[7] Bodley v. Goodrich, 7 How. 276. Compensation to the assignee at a fixed sum, provided it should not exceed what the laws of the state allow to executors or administrators, and if it should exceed that amount, then at the rate so prescribed for executors and administrators, limits and does not enlarge their legal claims, and is unobjectionable. Keteltas v. Wilson, 36 Barb. 298.

In New York it is held that the debtor cannot provide for the trustees a higher rate of compensation than is allowed to executors, administrators and guardians for similar services.[1] A trustee is entitled to commission as compensation for his labor in managing the trust committed to him, though no provision be made for it in the deed of trust.[2]

§ 110. To Pay the Debts Designated or Referred to.— Where the debts to be paid are few, it is frequently the practice to specify them in this part of the assignment. But where they are numerous, the more usual course is to refer to them as set forth in a *schedule* annexed. In both cases they should be described with sufficient certainty, in order that the assignee may not be at a loss, either as to the person or amount to be paid.[3] It has been held that a debt, to secure which a deed of trust has been executed, may be described by the name of the debtor, and its amount be left to be ascertained.[4] And parol evidence has been held admissible to show that a particular bill of exchange was intended to be secured by a deed of trust, though generally or improperly de-

---

[1] Barney v. Griffin, 2 N. Y. 365; Meacham v. Stevens, 9 Paige, 398. In the case of Duffy v. Duncan, 35 N. Y. 187, where the referee allowed the assignee the commissions payable to executors, Mr. Justice Leonard said that "had he found the commissions at the rate allowed to trustees by the Revised Statutes, when they are appointed in proceedings in relation to concealed and absconding debtors, I think his judgment would have remained undisturbed." In Wynkoop v. Shardlow, 44 Barb. 84, a commission of twenty per cent. for the collection of assigned accounts, consisting of small bills of account which cause much trouble and loss of time in their collection, was not considered unreasonable. And see Campbell v. Woodworth, 24 N. Y. 304; Eyre v. Beebe, 28 How. Pr. 333.

[2] Sherrill v. Shuford, 6 Ired. Eq. 228; Blow v. Gage, 44 Ill. 208. And see, further, as to compensation to the assignee, *post*, ch. XXXVI.

[3] In Canton v. Mosely, 25 Tex. 374, when the assignment recited that the assignor was indebted to sundry persons, but did not name them nor specify the amount of the assignor's indebtedness, but directed the assignee to hold said property and dispose of the same as soon as he could do so to the best advantage for the benefit of any creditors, generally, the assignment was held invalid for uncertainty in not furnishing some certain means of ascertaining who were the creditors. But in many of the states a method of ascertaining the debts to be paid is provided, and this objection would not in these states be of the same force.

[4] Platt v. Hodge, 8 Iowa, 386; Van Hook v. Walton, 28 Tex. 59; England v. Reynolds, 38 Ala. 370; Brown v. Knox, 6 Mo. 302; U. S. Bank v. Huth, 4 B. Mon. 423; Butt v. Peck, 1 Daly, 83; Halsey v. Whitney, 4 Mason, 206; Layson v. Rowan, 7 Rob. (La.) 1. In Hudson v. Ravett, 5 Bing. 368; 2 M. & P. 66°, where a blank was left in the deed for one of the principal debts, the precise amount of which was not ascertained until after its execution by the debtor, when it was inserted in his presence and with his assent, it was held that by reason of such assent the deed was valid from that time; but the court laid it down clearly that it was not a complete deed until then. West v. Steward, 14 Mees. & W. 48, 49, *arg*.

scribed in the deed.[1] But where a debt intended to be secured is not correctly described in the deed, though the creditor by identifying it may recover it out of the trust fund, while that remains, yet if the trustee has *bona fide* paid out the trust fund to discharge other debts, without any notice of the mistake by the creditor to the trustee, the creditor cannot make the trustee personally responsible.[2] In a case in Pennsylvania, where a debt due a creditor was put down in the assignment as "*about eleven* thousand dollars," which was, in fact, upwards of *thirteen* thousand dollars, it was held that the trust included the latter sum.[3] So in Massachusetts, where a debt was described as "about $4,500," and the creditor proved claims to the amount of $5,867, it was held that he was entitled to a dividend on the latter sum.[4] But in a case in Kentucky, where a debt due to a creditor on a note was put down, by mistake, as $1,150 instead of $1,282, it was held that the mistake could not be corrected to the prejudice of other creditors; and that such creditors had a right to insist on the distribution of the fund according to the proportions recognized upon the face of the deed. If, however, there should be a surplus of the trust fund after paying these debts, the mistake might be corrected and the surplus applied accordingly.[5] If a deed of trust is intentionally made to secure to the creditor a larger amount than is justly due to him, it renders the deed void; but a miscalculation, mistake or unintentional error will not vitiate it.[6]

It may happen, however, that a debtor is unable to state the names of all the creditors for whom he is desirous of providing in consequence of ignorance of the extent of his indebtedness. In such a case a direction to the assignee to give public notice to creditors to present their claims at a reasonable time and place, and to pay those who shall comply with such notice, would be proper.[7] In a case in New York it was held that a provision in an assign-

[1] Posey v. Decatur Bank, 12 Ala. 802; Platt v. Hodge, 8 Iowa, 386.
[2] Allemand v. Russell, 5 Ired. Eq. 183.
[3] Brown v. Wier, 5 S. & R. 401; Canaday v. Paschall, 3 Ired. Eq. (N. C.) 178. So where the date of the debt was erroneously stated the error was corrected. Miller v. Cherry, 3 Jones' Eq. (N. C.) 24. So an error in the name of the payee. Gardner v. Pike, id. 306.
[4] Dedham Bank v. Richards, 2 Metc. 105.
[5] Miles v. Bacon, 4 J. J. Marsh. 458, 465. The opinion in this case was delivered by Underwood, J. But it is said that the chief justice was of opinion that the deed secured to the creditor the full amount of his note, and that the error as to the amount in the description of the note did not essentially affect the construction of the deed. Id. 465.
[6] Pennington v. Woodall, 17 Ala. 685. See *ante*, p. 118.
[7] Ward v. Tingley, 4 Sandf. Ch. 476. In this case it was decided that a direction to the assignee to pay as a third class, and before other creditors, such as should comply with a notice of this kind, was valid.

ment directing the assignees, out of the net proceeds and avails of the assigned property, to pay the laborers and workmen of the assignors, residing in Albany and Buffalo, the amounts due to them respectively for work and labor done for the assignors, would not avoid the assignment, although the names of those creditors, with their places of residence and the respective amounts due to each, were not mentioned.[1]

§ 111. **To Pay Over the Surplus to the Assignor.**— It is usual to provide for the disposition of any ultimate surplus that may remain in the assignee's hands after payment of all the assignor's debts, by a trust or direction of this kind, although, as we shall see, such a trust would result in favor of the assignor by the mere operation of law.[2] It will hereafter be shown under what circumstances reservations of this kind will avoid the assignment.[3]

§ 112. **Power of Attorney.**— After the particular trusts and directions which have just been described follows a general power of attorney to the assignee, which must be irrevocable, to receive and recover the property and debts, to give receipts and acquittances, to collect by suit, etc.

§ 113. **Covenant by Assignee.**— Next follows the covenant, on the part of the assignee or trustee, by which he formally accepts the trust, and undertakes to execute it faithfully, to the best of his ability, according to the true intent and meaning of the assignment. It is usual, in this covenant, for the assignee to undertake to be responsible only for his own defaults or moneys actually received by him; and where there are several, each assignee covenants for himself to be responsible only for his own acts and defaults and not for those of his co-assignees. Under this head it has been held that a provision that the trustee shall be responsible only for his own defaults must, on its face, be understood to import that he shall not be liable for the acts of such agents as are necessary to enable him to execute the trust, selected in good faith, with a due regard to their fitness and with a proper supervision exercised over them.[4] But clauses intended to limit the assignee's responsibility have sometimes an injurious effect upon the assignment;[5] and in many of the forms in use covenants on the part of the assignee are wholly dispensed with.[6]

[1] Bank of Silver Creek v. Talcott, 22 Barb. 550.
[2] See *post*, ch. XXXVIII.
[3] See *post*, ch. XI.
[4] Ashurst v. Martin, 9 Port. 556. See Jacobs v. Allen, 18 Barb. 549.
[5] See Litchfield v. White, 3 Sand. S. C. 545. And see *post*, ch. XI.
[6] See Cunningham v. Freeborn, 1 Edw. Ch. 256; s. c. on appeal, 11 Wend. 240.

§ 114. Concluding Clauses.— The assignment concludes with the usual *in testimonium* clause: "In witness," etc.

§ 115. Schedules.— Appended to the assignment are the *schedules* of the property assigned, and of the debts or creditors provided for (or, as they are sometimes termed, schedules of assets and of liabilities), which constitute an important part of the instrument. Usually there is but one schedule of each kind, but sometimes several are employed. If possible, these schedules should be completed and annexed to the assignment before execution, but this is sometimes dispensed with. The general rule on this subject appears to be this: that the mere omission to annex the usual schedules is not in itself sufficient to avoid the assignment; and it has been so laid down in New Hampshire,[1] Massachusetts,[2] New York,[3] Colorado,[4] North Carolina,[5] Connecticut,[6] Missouri,[7] Minnesota,[8] Mississippi,[9]

---

[1] Rundlett v. Dole, 10 N. H. 438.
[2] Stevens v. Bell, 6 Mass. 339; Halsey v. Whitney, 4 Mason, 206; Emerson v. Knower, 8 Pick. 63.
[3] Cunningham v. Freeborn, 1 Edw. Ch. 256, 264; affirmed on appeal, 3 Paige, 557; affirmed, 11 Wend. 240. See Keyes v. Brush, 2 Paige, 311; Kellogg v. Slauson, 15 Barb. 56; Mathews v. Poultney, 33 id. 127; Terry v. Butler, 43 id. 395; Hotop v. Neidig, 17 Abb. Pr. 332; Turner v. Jaycox, 40 N. Y. 470; Platt v. Lott, 17 N. Y. 478. But see the qualification of this rule in Averill v. Loucks, 6 Barb. 470. And see Kercheis v. Schloss, 49 How. Pr. 284; Moir v. Brown, 14 Barb. 39, cited *ante*, p. 145. In this last case it was held that where the schedule was made a part of the conveyance and is referred to as conveying a specification of property conveyed and intended to be annexed, it must be annexed at the time of execution, not only as a description and specification of the property, but as necessary by the very terms of the instrument to complete the conveyance or transfer. Hand, J., id. 46, 48, 50. Under the act of 1860 as amended (Laws of 1874, ch. 600), a failure to make and deliver the inventory and schedule required by the act did not invalidate the assignment. Previous to the amendment the decisions were in conflict. See, also, Hardman v. Bowen, 39 N. Y. 196; Juliand v. Rathbone, 39 N. Y. 369; s. c., 39 Barb. 97; Van Vleet v. Slauson, 45 Barb. 317; Evans v Chapin, 12 Abb. Pr. 161; s. c., 20 How. Pr. 289; Barbour v. Everson, 16 Abb. Pr. 366; Read v. Worthington, 9 Bosw. 617; Camp v. Marshall, 2 Abb. Pr. (N. S.) 373; Fairchild v. Gwynne, 16 Abb. Pr. 23; s. c., 14 id. 121. Under the present law (Laws of 1877, ch. 466; Laws of 1878, ch. 318; 3 R. S. (7th ed.), p. 2277), the debtor is required to make and deliver an inventory or schedule; but if he does not the assignee must do so or show cause why he should not be removed.
[4] Smith v. Stoker, 8 Colo. 286.
[5] Means v. Montgomery, 23 Fed. Rep. 421.
[6] Clark v. Mix, 15 Conn. 152. See Laws of 1880, ch. 52; Laws of 1882, ch. 13.
[7] Duvall v. Raisin, 7 Mo. 449; Deaver v. Savage, 3 id. [180], 252; Hardcastle v. Fisher, 24 id. 70; Winne v. Madden, 18 Mo. App. 261.
[8] Strong v. Lynn, 38 Minn. 315; 37 N. W. Rep. 448.
[9] Robins v. Embry, 1 Sm. & M. Ch. 207. Creditors omitted in a first schedule may be named in a second schedule. Armstrong, etc. v. Guenther, 67 Miss. 693; 7 S. Rep. 499.

Alabama,[1] Michigan,[2] New Mexico,[3] Virginia,[4] Kentucky,[5] California,[6] Colorado,[7] Oregon,[8] Iowa,[9] Texas,[10] Wisconsin,[11] and by the supreme court of the United States.[12] In some instances, and when taken in connection with other circumstances, this fact of omission may be considered a badge of fraud.[13] But the inference of fraud may be repelled by various circumstances.

Thus, in Massachusetts, where the assignment itself contained a provision that schedules were to be made out as soon as might be, the presumption of fraud was held to be removed.[14] So, in New York, where full schedules were presented to the court in answer to a bill filed by a judgment creditor, the inference of fraud was held to be repelled.[15] So if the property be described in the assignment with sufficient certainty to enable the assignee to take possession of it, the omission to annex a schedule, although provided for in the deed, will not render the assignment void.[16] And if pos-

[1] Shackelford v. P. & M. Bank of Mobile, 22 Ala. 238; Brown v. Lyon, 17 id. 659.
[2] Hollister v. Loud, 2 Mich. 310, 322; Nye v. Van Husan, 6 id. 329; Stamp v. Case, 41 id. 267; Coots v. Chamberlain, 39 id. 565; Re Kimball, 16 N. B. R. 188.
[3] Leitensdorfer v. Webb, 1 N. Mex. 34.
[4] Lewis v. Caperton's Ex'r, 8 Gratt. 148; Gordon v. Cannon, 18 id. 388.
[5] Ely v. Hair, 16 B. Mon. 230.
[6] Forbes v. Scannel, 13 Cal. 242; Poehlmann v. Kennedy, 48 Cal. 201.
[7] Raynolds v. Ray, 12 Colo. 108; 20 Pac. Rep. 4. See Smith v. Stoker, 8 Colo. 286; 7 Pac. Rep. 10.
[8] Dawson v. Crossen, 10 Or. 41.
[9] Meeker v. Saunders, 6 Iowa, 61.
[10] Linn v. Wright, 18 Tex. 317.
[11] Bates v. Ableman, 13 Wis. 644; Ball v. Bowe, 49 id. 495; Steinlein v. Halstead, 52 id. 289.
[12] Brashear v. West, 7 Pet. 608, 614.
[13] McCoun, V. C., in Cunningham v. Freeborn, 1 Edw. Ch. 264; Sandford, A. V. C., in Van Nest v. Yoe, 1 Sandf. Ch. 4, 7; Allen, J., in Kellogg v. Slauson, 15 Barb. 56; Stevens v. Bell, 6 Mass. 339; Pearpoint v. Graham, 4 Wash. C. C. 232; Wilt v. Franklin, 1 Binn. 502, 514; Burd v. Smith, 4 Dall. 76. See Hower v. Geesaman, 17 Serg. & R. 251; Haven v. Richardson, 5 N. H. 113; Drakeley v. De Forest, 3 Conn. 272; Moir v. Brown, 14 Barb. 39; Brown v. Lyon, 17 Ala. 659; Pine v. Rickert, 21 Barb. 469; Young v. Gillespie, 12 Heisk. (Tenn.) 239.
[14] Stevens v. Bell, 6 Mass. 339. See Halsey v. Whitney, 4 Mason, 206.
[15] Cunningham v. Freeborn, 1 Edw. Ch. 264. But in another case in that state, where the schedule of the property assigned was referred to as annexed, but was not annexed until after the assignment had been executed and recorded and after the commencement of a suit by purchasers of the property from the assignees against the sheriff, who had levied upon the property under a creditor's execution, it was held that such subsequent annexation did not remove the objection to the validity of the assignment. Moir v. Brown, 14 Barb. 39; Hand, J., id. 48. In this case there was no evidence that the schedule was annexed by the authority of the parties or with their knowledge. Id. See Spring v. Strauss, 3 Bosw. (N. Y.) 607; Kercheis v. Schloss, 49 How. Pr. 284.
[16] Emerson v. Knower, 8 Pick. 63. See Robins v. Embury, 1 Sm. & M. Ch. 207; Smith v. Stoker, 8 Colo. 286; Means v. Montgomery, 23 Fed. Rep. 421.

session accompany the transfer, and the transaction be in all other respects fair, the mere want of a schedule will not render it fraudulent.[1] Want of a schedule is less suspicious where the whole of the assignor's property is conveyed for the benefit of all the creditors than where part of it is conveyed for particular creditors.[2] And in New York the schedules required to be delivered and filed under the act are still regarded as part of the assignment, and where they contain fictitious debts the assignment was deemed void.[3]

It has also been held that the annexation of a schedule, even where it is provided by the assignment that a schedule shall be made out and annexed as soon as may be, is not a condition precedent to the operation of the assignment.[4] If the assignor neglect to furnish a schedule the assignee may file a bill of discovery against him, and also to obtain a delivery of the books, etc.[5] And it has been decided in England that the fact that there is no schedule to regulate the trust does not prevent the property from passing, unless the schedule be expected to show what passed by the deed.[6] In assignments giving preferences the actual annexation of schedules of creditors is a matter of more importance.[7]

In some of the states schedules are expressly required by statute to be annexed to the assignment.

In regard to the form of the schedules it may be observed that the items composing them should be stated with as much accuracy as possible.[8] But as entire correctness in this respect is not always attainable, it is sometimes the practice to insert a provision in the assignment that corrections may be made in the schedules, and such items and amounts be afterwards inserted as shall conform to

[1] Pearpoint v. Graham, 4 Wash. C. C. 232. See, also, Deaver v. Savage, 3 Mo. 252.
[2] Wilt v. Franklin, 1 Binn. 514, 523.
[3] Terry v. Butler, 43 Barb. 395. And when verified by the assignor is competent evidence against the assignee and those representing him. Sibley v. Killom, 19 N. Y. Weekly Dig. 190. But in Indiana the schedules are not a part of the assignment and need not be recorded. Black v. Weathers, 26 Ind. 242.
[4] Emerson v. Knower, 8 Pick. 63; Woodward v. Marshall, 22 id. 468; Keyes v. Brush, 2 Paige, 311. See Cunningham v. Freeborn, 3 id. 557, 561; Kellogg v. Slauson, 15 Barb. 56; affirmed on appeal, 11 N. Y. 302. In Emerson v. Knower the court remarked that the property passed and was intended to pass before any schedule should be taken.
[5] Keyes v. Brush, 2 Paige, 311.
[6] West v. Steward, 14 Mees. & W. 47. In Weeks v. Maillardet, 14 East, 568, the schedule was material to show what passed. This case was relied on by the court in Moir v. Brown, 14 Barb. 49, 50.
[7] See *post*, p. 154.
[8] As to the headings and contents of the schedules and the inferences deducible from them, see United States v. Clark, 1 Paine, 629, 631, 641.

the actual state of facts.[1] Where in a schedule of the property assigned sums were set against the different articles as the value of the property, it was held that the mere fact that these sums were entered in the schedule was not even *prima facie* evidence of the value of the property.[2] But in a case where the schedule of creditors contained only a list of the preferred creditors without specifying the amount of their several claims, it was held that such omission would not invalidate the deed, if it were in other respects unexceptionable.[3]

Having thus presented an outline of the simplest form of an assignment in trust for creditors, it remains to notice the peculiarities of the principal variations from this form, as they are exhibited in assignments with preferences and assignments tripartite.

§ 116. **Assignments with Preferences.** — In assignments of this character the preferences intended to be given are declared in that part of the instrument which specifies the particular debts to be paid immediately after providing for the expenses of the trust. These preferences, as we have seen, must be distinctly declared, and the order of payment fixed by the assignment itself or by the schedules annexed to it, and not be left open to future alteration either by the assignor or assignee. Where the creditors are few this part of the instrument may be expressed substantially as follows: "First, to pay and discharge a certain debt (describing it); secondly, to pay and take up a certain note (describing it); thirdly, after full payment of the said debt and note out of the residue, if any, to pay all the other creditors of the said party of the first part, in proportion to their respective demands." But where the creditors are numerous and arranged in classes, it is usual to name them in the schedule of creditors as "class number one," "class number two," etc., referring to them in the assignment substantially in this form: "First, to pay in full the creditors named and designated in Schedule A, hereto annexed, as class number one; secondly, to pay the creditors named in said schedule as class number two," etc. Sometimes a separate schedule is employed for each class, and the reference is then to the schedules in their order.

§ 117. **Assignments with Preferences — Continued.** — Where a preference is intended to be indicated by a schedule, it must be distinctly shown by some separation of the debt intended to be

[1] See Dedham Bank v. Richards, 2 Metc. 105; Halsey v. Whitney, 4 Mason, 206, 208; Re Wilson, 1 Monthly L. Bul. 5.
[2] Savings Bank v. Ela, 11 N. H. 335.
[3] Brown v. Knox, 6 Mo. 302.

preferred from the other debts specified. The mere placing of a debt at the head of a schedule is not sufficient.[1] And where an assignment refers to one or more schedules as fixing the order in which certain preferred creditors shall be paid, it is essential that they should be annexed to the assignment previous to its execution, unless the assignment itself prescribe what debts shall be inserted in them, and in what order. Accordingly, where an assignment directed the assignees to pay the debts specified in the schedules annexed thereto, according to the priority of the several schedules, and provided that such schedules should be made within sixty days, and be annexed to and form a part of the assignment, but did not prescribe what debts should be inserted in the respective schedules, or in what order they should be arranged therein, the preparation of such schedules being left entirely to the discretion of the assignors; and it appeared that such schedules had not been made out and annexed to the assignment previous to its execution, but that they were prepared by the assignors and annexed at some subsequent time, it was held by the supreme court of New York that the assignment was fraudulent and void.[2]

§ 118. **Assignments Tripartite.**— In these assignments the parties are arranged in three parts; the debtor being the party of the first part, the assignee of the second part, and the creditors of the third part.[3] Their principal peculiarities are the covenants which they contain on the part of the several parties, and which the form of the instrument admits to a great extent. Thus, the debtor covenants that he will aid the assignee in the receipt and collection of the debts and property, will ratify and confirm all his lawful acts under the assignment, and will do all further acts necessary in the execution of the trust. The assignee covenants to execute the trust, to account with the creditors, and make just distribution among them. And the creditors formally accept the provisions of the assignment, in full payment of their respective debts, and release and discharge the debtor from all claims and demands. There are also frequently inserted a variety of clauses giving spe-

---

[1] Winslow v. Assignees of Ancrum, 1 McCord's Ch. 100. See Colgin v. Redman, 20 Ala. 650; Frazier v. Truax, 27 Hun, 587, *ante*, p. 118.

[2] Averill v. Loucks, 6 Barb. (S. C.) 470. See Kercheis v. Schloss, 49 How. Pr. 284; Wolf v. O'Conner, 88 Mich. 124; 50 N. W. Rep. 118.

[3] This is the proper form of an assignment according to the English practice, as illustrated in several important cases. See Estwick v. Caillaud, 4 Term R. 420; Inglis v. Grant, id. 530; Bowker v. Burdekin, 11 Mees. & W. 128; West v. Steward, 14 id. 47; Janes v. Whitbread, 20 L. J. C. P. (N. S.) 217. It has also been the prevailing form in Massachusetts, and still is in Maine and other New England states.

cial powers to the assignee, and marking out, in considerable detail, the course of his proceedings in the execution of the trust.

In the execution of these instruments it is usual to employ counterparts, so that the transfer may be made complete by a delivery to the assignee, in case the assignment is retained by the debtor for any purpose, as to procure the signatures of creditors.[1]

[1] Marston v. Coburn, 17 Mass. 454, 457.

CHAPTER IX.

PARTIAL ASSIGNMENTS.

§ 119. Partial, Special and General Assignments Distinguished.
120. Stipulations for Releases.
121. Preferences.
122. Priority to United States.

§ 119. **Partial, Special and General Assignments Distinguished.**— A partial assignment is an assignment of a portion of a debtor's property, in trust, for the benefit of his creditors,[1] and is distinguished, on the one hand, from a *special* or particular assignment, which is made directly to the creditor, in payment or as security; and, on the other, from a *general* assignment, the nature of which has already been explained.[2] A general assignment, with an express exception of part of the debtor's property, is, in effect, a partial assignment, and has been so treated.[3] An assignment of

---

[1] The term *partial* has been occasionally applied to assignments in another sense, namely, as descriptive of the disposition made of the assigned property by the assignor, where he prefers one or more creditors to others. Thus, in Riggs v. Murray, 2 Johns. Ch. 565, 577, assignments with preferences are called *partial* assignments.

[2] If an assignment in trust does not, on its face, purport to be of all the assignor's property, it will be treated as a partial assignment. See Seaving v. Brinkerhoff, 5 Johns. Ch. 329; Lentilhon v. Moffatt, 1 Edw. Ch. 451; Halsey v. Whitney, 4 Mason, 206. A voluntary assignment by a partnership firm of partnership property exclusively is, upon its face, *partial* and not general. May v. Walker, 35 Minn. 195; 28 N. W. Rep. 252. An assignment which, on its face, purports to be but a partial assignment is so to be regarded and treated until the contrary is shown. Redfield, C. J., in Mussey v. Noyes, 26 Vt. 462, 474. But in a case where an assignment in terms conveyed all the property which the assignors owned in certain towns named, and it did not appear either upon the face of the assignment or from the evidence that they owned any property which was situated elsewhere, it was held in Vermont that the court would infer that *all* the property which the assignors owned was thereby conveyed. Dana v. Lull, 17 Vt. 390. So in Maryland, an assignment for the benefit of creditors stipulating for releases must, on its face and by its terms, convey all the property of the grantor, and unless it does so it is void, no matter whether it does in fact convey all his property or not. Rosenberg v. Moore, 11 Md. 376; Barnitz v. Rice, 14 id. 24; Malcolm v. Hodges, 8 id. 418.

[3] Ingraham v. Grigg, 13 Sm. & M. 22. An assignment which, on its face, purports to convey all the assignor's property, when in fact he has other property not disclosed in the assignment, is void as against creditors; but if it does not so purport, it is valid, notwithstanding property may remain in the hands of the assignor unassigned. Pearce v. Jackson, 2 R. I. 35. And where the assignor had real estate not conveyed to the assignee (the assignment gave preferences

partnership effects is a partial one, whenever the debtor has separate property which is not conveyed.[1] There may be cases where a debtor may find it expedient to provide for creditors by a partial assignment, but transfers of this kind are comparatively rare in practice, and when made are usually preliminary, either to further transfers of the same kind,[2] or to a general assignment.[3] If the appropriation of part of the debtor's property be found sufficient to liquidate all claims against him, it is usually made in a different and more direct form; and if it be insufficient, an assignment of such portion, without any further transfer, is of little value, the unassigned residue being open to the remedies of creditors, the same as if it had not been made.

§ 120. **Stipulations for Releases.**— It is true that assignments of this description have sometimes been made with a stipulation for a full release by the creditor as the condition of receiving the benefit of them; and in the important case of Halsey v. Whitney,[4] Mr. Justice Story gave effect to such a condition in a partial assignment. But it is remarked by Chancellor Kent, in commenting on the decision in this case, that the learned judge's own judgment was not satisfied with the authorities under which he acted,

but did not stipulate for releases), this did not render the assignment void. Bates v. Ableman, 13 Wis. 644. In that case Mr. Justice Paine said the answer to this objection is, that if the property is not conveyed it is left as it was before, liable to seizure. See State v. Benoist, 37 Mo. 500; Carpenter v. Underwood, 19 N. Y. 520; Knight v. Waterman, 36 Pa. St. 258; Baldwin v. Peet, 22 Tex. 708; Henry v. Root, 38 Mich. 371.

[1] Gibson, C. J., in Thomas v. Jenks, 5 Rawle, 221.

[2] This was the case in The United States v. The Bank of the United States, 8 Rob. (La.) 262.

[3] This was the case in Johnson v. Whitwell, 7 Pick. 71. In Nicholson v. Leavitt, 4 Sandf. S. C. 252, the debtor's property was transferred by several partial assignments, followed by a general assignment. In Johnson v. Whitwell, a partial assignment had been made, as a temporary arrangement, for the benefit of three creditors, with the understanding and expectation that a general assignment should afterwards be made for the benefit of all the creditors. The partial assignment was in fact canceled, and the general assignment made in the same form. But the first deed was held void, as intended to cover the property and intercept attachments. So in the case of Holt v. Bancroft, 30 Ala. 195, where a partial assignment was made eight days previous to the execution of a general assignment, and it appeared that the intention to make the general assignment existed at the time the first instrument was executed, and the same trustee appointed in both, the entire transaction was taken together and deemed void as giving preferences.

[4] 4 Mason, 206. The assignment in this case did not, on its face, purport to convey all the debtor's estate. It was, however, suggested at the bar, that in point of fact the debtor had no other property. Story, J., id. 218. In the reporter's statement of the case the assignment is said to have been of all the debtor's property. Id. 207. See the observations of Curtis, J., in Stewart v. Spencer, 1 Curt. 157, 164.

and that partial assignments with such a condition ought not to be tolerated.[1] It appears, indeed, to be now the settled rule in New York, that an assignment to a trustee of part of the debtor's property, upon condition of a full release, is void;[2] such a condition being regarded as oppressive, coercive, and unjust as against creditors.[3] The same rule has been adopted, and for similar reasons, in Pennsylvania,[4] Maryland,[5] Virginia,[6] Mississippi,[7] Indiana [8] and Minnesota.[9] On this principle it was held by the supreme court of Pennsylvania, that an assignment by partners of the partnership effects, and not of their separate property also, if it contain a condition that the creditors shall release their claims against the assignors individually and as copartners, is fraudulent and void.[10]

[1] 2 Kent's Com. [534], 695, note a.
[2] Seaving v. Brinkerhoff, 5 Johns. Ch. 329; Lentilhon v. Moffatt, 1 Edw. Ch. 451; Grover v. Wakeman, 11 Wend. 187; Berry v. Riley, 2 Barb. S. C. 307. See the observations of Clayton, J., in Ingraham v. Grigg, 13 Sm. & M. 22, 30; Austin v. Bell, 20 Johns. 442. See Selden, J., in Dunham v. Waterman, 17 N. Y. 9.
[3] Kent, C., in Seaving v. Brinkerhoff, 5 Johns. Ch. 332. The chancellor said in this case, "A partial assignment upon such a condition is pernicious in its tendency, if it be not (as I rather apprehend it to be) fraudulent in its design." Id.
[4] Thomas v. Jenks, 5 Rawle, 221; Hennessy v. The Western Bank, 6 W. & S. 300; In re Wilson, 4 Barr, 430. In the last case, Rogers, J., speaking of the former decisions, observed: "It was ruled that such an assignment was against the policy of law; that the condition was oppressive, without the color of justice, and evinced on the face of the instrument a fraudulent design; that it was taking an unfair advantage of the situation of the creditor to impose the condition of a release unless on the terms of the surrender of all the debtor's property. We thought so then, and, notwithstanding all that has been so pertinaciously and strenuously urged to the contrary, we are of the same opinion still." Id. 448, 449. In Wiener v. Davis, 13 Pa. St. 331, it was held that, since the act of 1843, an assignment by a debtor of part of his property to some of his creditors, they stipulating to give a release, is not necessarily void. See opinion of Agnew, J., in Miners' National Bank Appeal, 57 Pa. St. 193, reviewing the history of legislation and decision in Pennsylvania.
[5] An assignment for the benefit of creditors, exacting releases as the condition on which they may participate in the fund, must transfer *all* the debtor's estate. Green v. Trieber, 3 Md. 11. See Sangston v. Gaither, id. 40; Rosenberg v. Moore, 11 Md. 376; Barnitz v. Rice, 14 id. 178; Bridges v. Wood, 16 id. 102; Whidbee v. Stewart, 40 id. 414.
[6] Skipwith's Ex'r v. Cunningham, 8 Leigh, 271, 291; Gordon v. Cannon, 18 Gratt. 387; 2 Tuck. Com. [442], 431.
[7] Ingraham v. Grigg, 13 Sm. & M. 22. In this case Clayton, J., observed: "A debtor in failing circumstances cannot devote a part of his property to the payment of his debts, reserve a part, and say to his creditors that they shall not touch the part so devoted unless upon surrendering all claims to that which is reserved. In other words, a debtor cannot keep any part of his property from his creditors except that which the law secures to him; and any attempt to do so amounts to a fraud." Id. 30.
[8] Henderson v. Bliss, 8 Ind. 100.
[9] May v. Walker, 28 N. W. Rep. 252.
[10] Thomas v. Jenks, 5 Rawle, 221.

And where an assignment by the members of a firm purported to convey merely the partnership goods and effects, with certain specified real estate, in trust for certain preferred creditors, and then in trust for such as should execute a release, but contained no words of conveyance of the private or individual estate of either member of the firm, and did not even purport to convey all the real estate of the firm, it was held by the same court to be invalid.[1]

§ 121. **Preferences.**— In some of the states assignments for the benefit of creditors are required to convey all the debtor's estate, and in some such assignments will be construed to pass all the estate, whether purporting to or not; but, independently of statute, partial assignments, when they leave the unassigned residue open to the claims of creditors, are valid conveyances,[2] and they have been so held in England.[3] In some instances, also, where preferences have been prohibited in general assignments, they may still be made in partial assignments,[4] or by means of such conveyances. But in other states, even where preferences are allowed in general assignments, they will not be sustained in transfers for the benefit of creditors of less than the entire estate.[5]

§ 122. **Priority to United States.**— Partial assignments are not within the provisions of the act of congress of March 2, 1799, giv-

[1] Weber v. Samuel, 7 Barr, 499. Whether an insolvent debtor who assigns but a part of his property for the benefit of all his creditors can stipulate for a release in Rhode Island, see Stewart v. Spencer, 1 Curt. 157, 160. And see Le Prince v. Guillemot, 1 Rich. Eq. 187.

[2] Fisher v. Dinwiddie, 12 B. Mon. (Ky.) 208; Ingraham v. Grigg, 13 Sm. & M. 22; Du Bose v. Carlisle, 51 Ala. 590; Leitensdorfer v. Webb, 1 N. Mex. 34; Pearce v. Jackson, 2 R. I. 35; State v. Benoist, 37 Mo. 500.

[3] Estwick v. Caillaud, 5 Term R. 420; Goss v. Neal, 5 J. B. Moore, 19.

[4] Thus in New York an insolvent debtor may assign a part of his property in trust for a part of his creditors. Matter of Gordon, 49 Hun, 370; 3 N. Y. S. Rep. 589. And in Iowa, where preferences in general assignments invalidate the conveyance, "it is still competent," says Mr. Justice Cole, in Samson v. Arnold, 19 Iowa, 480, "for any debtor to pay a part of his creditors in full, to secure another part by mortgage or deed of trust upon a part of his property, to make a partial assignment of still other property for the benefit of certain other creditors, with or without preference, and afterward to make a general assignment." And see Fromme v. Jones, 13 Iowa, 474; Davis v. Gibson, 24 id. 257; Farewell v. Howard, 26 id. 381. So in Indiana. Grubbs v. Morris, 103 Ind. 166. So in Alabama, where preferences are not permitted in general assignments, the right of preferring creditors by partial assignments is untouched. Holt v. Bancroft, 30 Ala. 195; Stetson v. Miller, 36 id. 642. So in Missouri. Johnson v. McAllister's Assignee, 30 Mo. 327; State v. Benoist, 37 id. 500; Shapleigh v. Baird, 26 id. 322; Woods v. Timmerman, 27 id. 107; Many v. Logan, 31 id. 91. These decisions were mainly under the act of 1855. But compare Stat. of Mo. (Wagner), ch. 9, p. 150. So in Michigan. Newman v. Mineral Co., 57 Mich. 97; 23 N. W. Rep. 600.

[5] See *post*, ch. X.

ing priority of payment to the United States in cases of insolvency; nor are they within those of the act of March 3, 1797, giving similar priority of payment out of the property of an insolvent who had made a voluntary assignment for the benefit of his creditors; such priority existing only in cases of *general* assignments by debtors.[1] But if only a trifling portion of the assignor's estate be reserved, especially for the purpose of evading the law, such reservation will not make the assignment a partial one.[2] And a party cannot, by assigning all his property by different acts, defeat the priority of the United States under the pretext of the assignments being partial.[3]

[1] United States v. Hooe, 3 Cranch, 73; Conard v. Atlantic Ins. Co., 1 Pet. 386; Story, J., id. 439; United States v. Clark, 1 Paine, 629; United States v. McLellan, 3 Sumn. 345; United States v. Bank of the United States, 8 Rob. (La.) 262.
[2] United States v. Hooe, 3 Cranch, 91; United States v. McLellan, 3 Sumn. 345. See Dias v. Bouchaud, 10 Paige, 435, 448, 461.
[3] United States v. Bank of the United States, 8 Rob. (La.) 262. In United States v. Griswold, 8 Fed. Rep. 496, it was held that a debtor of the United States may assign his property, within the meaning of the statute, by means of judgments confessed in favor of various persons, for amounts equal in the aggregate to the value thereof, and the priority of the United States will thereupon attach to the property and prevail against the judgments, but subject to all prior liens thereon.

CHAPTER X.

ASSIGNMENTS WITH PREFERENCES.

§ 123. Preferences, how Regarded.
124. Right of a Debtor to Prefer a Creditor.
125. Methods of Giving Preference.
126. Preferences by Direct Transfer.
127. Preferences in Assignments to Trustee.
128. Preferences in Assignments to Trustee — Continued.
129. Restrictions on the Right to Prefer.
130. Preferences Regarded with Disfavor.
131. Preferences in Special Instances.
132. Preferences in Special Instances — Continued.
133. Preferences in Partial Assignments.
134. Restrictions on the Right to Prefer.
135. Restrictions on the Right of Limited Partnerships to Prefer.
136. Restrictions on the Right of Corporations to Prefer.
137. Restrictions on the Right of Corporations to Prefer —" Insolvency."
138. Restrictions on the Right of Corporations to Prefer — In New Jersey.
139. Subjects of Preferences in Assignments.
140. Personal Preferences.
141. Modes of Giving Preferences in Assignments.
142. Preferences Absolute or Conditional.
143. Future Preferences.
144. Preferences by Implication.
145. Illegal and Fraudulent Preferences.

§ 123. **Preferences, how Regarded.**— Assignments in trust for the benefit of creditors, giving preferences to certain creditors or certain classes of creditors over others, though here treated for the sake of convenience as exceptional forms, have in fact constituted until recently one of the most common descriptions of this species of transfer in use in this country. They present the form which an assignment seems in most instances to have naturally taken wherever a debtor has been allowed to be the distributor of his property among his creditors, as distinguished from the equal distribution provided by law, through the medium of systems of bankruptcy and insolvency; but they have always been a subject of criticism, objection, or open condemnation, as founded on an unjust and erroneous principle. In the courts where their principle, policy and practical operation have been daily investigated and discussed, they have been viewed, especially of late, with a growing sentiment of jealousy and disfavor; and the continued use of them has finally led to most of the legislative interposition by which an

§ 124.] RIGHT TO PREFER A CREDITOR. 163

insolvent debtor's power of assignment has been controlled and its exercise regulated by specific provisions.[1]

§ 124. **Right of a Debtor to Prefer a Creditor.**— It has long been a settled rule in England and American law (subject to qualifications which will be considered) that a debtor in failing circumstances[2] may not only dispose of his property in trust for the use and benefit of his creditors generally, but may by such a conveyance give a preference in payment to one creditor before another, or to one class of creditors before another class.[3]

This rule may be viewed as the result of a gradual expansion of the acknowledged principle that a debtor owing several creditors, and not having the means of paying them all, may *pay* one in preference to another, or some in preference to others;[4] in other words, that he has the right of *selection* in this mode of satisfying their demands; and that a payment thus made to one creditor in good faith cannot be questioned or interfered with by another.[5] This

---

[1] See Appendix, I.

[2] See *ante*, p. 22.

[3] 2 Kent's Com. [532], 689; 1 Tucker's Com. [335], 325; 2 id. [443], 432; Marshall, C. J., in Brashear v. West, 7 Pet. 608, 614; Mackie v. Cairns, 1 Hopk. 278; Sutherland, J., in Grover v. Wakeman, 11 Wend. 187, 194; Gaston, J., in Hafner v. Irwin, 1 Ired. L. 490, 496; Harris, J., in Webb v. Daggett, 2 Barb. 9, 11; Gamble, J., in Richards v. Levin, 16 Mo. 596, 598, 599; Totten v. Brady, 54 Md. 170; Hanscom v. Buffum, 66 Me. 246; Sheldon v. Mann, 85 Mich. 265; 48 N. W. Rep. 573; Kendall B. & S. Co. v. Bain, 46 Mo. App. 581; Nat. Bank v. Morris (1892), A. C. 287; P. & H. Manuf. Co. v. Caldwell, 136 Ill. 163; 26 N. E. Rep. 599.

[4] Sandford, C., in Mackie v. Cairns, 1 Hopk. Ch. 373, 406; Curtis, J., in Stewart v. Spenser, 1 Curt. 161, 162.

[5] In the case of Tillou v. Britton, in the supreme court of New Jersey (4 Halst. 120, 136), Mr. Justice Ford, in delivering his opinion, observed as follows: "The law contains no such principle as that a man in failing circumstances may not pay any just debt first which will best relieve his circumstances. If, while a man retains his property in his own hands, the right of giving preferences should be denied, he would so far lose the dominion over his own that he could not pay *anybody*, because whoever he paid would receive a preference. He could only pay ratably, which is never incumbent till after he has taken the benefit of the insolvent laws, or has assigned his property to trustees for the benefit of creditors, and so put the dominion over it into other hands. Accordingly it was decided by this court in the case of Hendricks v. Mount, 2 South. 743, that the making of such preferences was *every day done, was every day sustained in our courts of justice, and is legal.*" In the case of Blakey's Appeal, in the supreme court of Pennsylvania (7 Barr, 449, 451), Coulter, J., observed: "It is only when a man loses dominion over his property and transfers that dominion to another that the right of creditors to a *pro rata* dividend attaches. Whilst a man retains dominion of his property he may incumber and convey it as he pleases, if not directly forbidden by law, and prefer such creditors by payment or transfer as he chooses. And if it were not so, an individual could not get along in his business." And see Uhler v. Maulfair, 23 Pa. St. 481; Hopkins v. Beebe, 26 id. 85. "It is settled," says

principle has been admitted in England, even under the stringent system of the bankrupt law;[1] and it has been broadly laid down by the supreme court of the United States that a debtor may pre-

Walworth, Chancellor, in Wakeman v. Grover, 4 Paige, 23, 36, "that the insolvent has the right, while his property remains in his own hands, to apply the same to the payment of one creditor in preference to another, notwithstanding the principle of this court that equality among creditors is equity." See the observations of Nelson, J., in Cunningham v. Freeborn, 11 Wend. 256; of Wright, J., in Atkinson v. Jordan, 5 Ohio, 178; and of Wheeler, J., in Edrington v. Rogers, 15 Tex. 188. And see Kuykendall v. McDonald, 15 Mo. 416; Gassett v. Wilson, 3 Fla. 235; Gorham v. Innis, 115 N. Y. 87; 21 N. E. Rep. 722; Barton v. Brent, 87 Va. 385; Farwell v. Nilsoon, 133 Ill. 45; Hanford Oil Co. v. First National Bank of Chicago, 126 Ill. 584; 21 N. E. Rep. 483; Maack v. Maack, 49 Hun, 507; 2 N. Y. S. Rep. 506; Dwight v. Lumber Co., 67 Mich. 507; Whipple v. Stebbin, 35 N. W. Rep. 94; Goar v. McCauless, 60 Miss. 244; King v. Gustafson, 80 Iowa, 207; 45 N. W. Rep. 565; Carnahan v. Schwab, 127 Ind. 507; 26 N. E. Rep. 67; Sutton v. Dana, 15 Colo. 98; 25 Pac. Rep. 90; Bank v. Newton, 13 id. 245; Britton v. Boyer, 27 Neb. 526; 43 N. W. Rep. 356; Carter v. Rewey, 62 Wis. 552; 22 N. W. Rep. 129. An insolvent corporation has a right to prefer one creditor over another. Bissell v. Besson, 47 N. J. Eq. 580. Upon an accounting in bankruptcy or insolvency a trust creditor is not entitled to preference over general creditors of the insolvent merely on the ground of the nature of the claim. To authorize such a preference, some specific recognized equity founded on some agreement or relation of the debt to the assigned property must be shown. Cavin v. Gleason, 105 N. Y. 256; 11 N. E. Rep. 504. In Surget v. Boyd, 57 Miss. 485, it was held that a deed of trust made by a debtor against whom a suit for a large amount is pending, just before judgment, to secure pre-existing debts due his relatives and friends, is valid. Unless such security is a sham, never to be enforced, other creditors can vacate it only by showing that the secured debts are simulated, or that some benefit is reserved to the grantor. The fact that an assignment for the benefit of creditors, made by a married woman having a separate estate and engaged in a separate business, contained a preference to her husband for salary agreed to be paid to him by the wife for his services as agent in managing said business, did not render it fraudulent and void as to her creditors as a matter of law. Third Nat. Bank v. Guenther, 123 N. Y. 568; 25 N. E. Rep. 986; 20 Am. St. Rep. 780. But see Nichols v. Wellings, 61 Hun, 601.

[1] In the early case of Hopkins v. Gray, 7 Mod. 139, it was held by Lord Holt that if a banker or goldsmith who has many people's money refuse payment, yet keep his shop open, and as often as he is arrested give bail, he may by that means give preference of payment to his friends; and when he has done, if he runs away, yet such payment shall stand against a commission of bankruptcy; and his lordship cited the case of Sheppard the banker in confirmation of this doctrine. In the case of Cock v. Goodfellow, 10 Mod. 489, 497, Lord Chancellor Parker said: "A man that knows he must be a bankrupt may by law pay off any of his creditors." The modern English cases establish the principle that a preference given to a creditor by payment is not fraudulent unless it appears to have been voluntary, without pressure by the creditor, and with the view of giving a fraudulent preference in contemplation of bankruptcy. Cook v. Pritchard, 6 Scott N. R. 34; 5 Mann. & Gr. 329; Green v. Bradfield, 1 Carr. & K. 449; Ogden v. Stone, 11 Mees. & W. 494; Kynaston v. Crouch, 14 id. 266; Brown v. Kempton, 19 L. J. C. P. (N. S.) 169; Hale v. Allnutt, 36 Eng. L. & Eq. 383. But see the bankrupt act of 1869, 32 and 33 Vict., ch. 71. Fraudulent preference has now for the first time been defined by the legislature. The whole law of bankruptcy is to be found in the bankruptcy act of 1869, and the whole law of fraud-

§ 124.] RIGHT TO PREFER A CREDITOR. 165

fer one creditor, pay him fully, and exhaust his whole property, leaving nothing for others equally meritorious.[1] The same principle has been affirmed by the state courts.[2] Even in Massachusetts, where a system of insolvency has been established partaking of the character of a bankrupt law, a payment in money, by an insolvent debtor, of a debt due to a particular creditor, has been held valid.[3] And in Louisiana, where the fundamental law of the state

ulent preferences in section 92 of that statute. See Ex parte Mathew, In re Cherry, 19 W. R. 1005; s. c. on appeal, Ex parte Boland, L. R. 7 Ch. Ap. 24; Ex parte Craven, L. R. 10 Eq. 648; s. c. on appeal, Ex parte Tempest, L. R. 5 Ch. Ap. 70. So it has been held, under the United States bankrupt law of 1800, that if a person on the eve and even in contemplation of bankruptcy pay money, give security or assign property to a creditor, it will be valid if the effect of measures taken by the creditor, or if done at the creditor's instance and on his application; but if done voluntarily, without solicitation or compulsion, and merely to prefer one creditor to another, it will be fraudulent and void. Ogden v. Jackson, 1 Johns. 370, 373; Phœnix v. Ingraham's Assignees, 5 id. 412. And see, under the act of 1841, Ex parte Garwood and Ex parte Potts, Crabbe, 516; Atkinson v. The Farmers' Bank, id. 529. As to what will constitute a fraudulent preference under the act of 1867, see Bump on Bank. (8th ed.), pp. 792 et seq. and cases cited. See Mays v. Fritten, 20 Wall. 414; Wilson v. City Bank, 17 Wall. 473.

[1] Clark v. White, 12 Pet. 178. See Tompkins v. Wheeler, 16 id. 106.

[2] Buffum v. Green, 5 N. H. 71; Tillou v. Britton, 4 Halst. 120; Stover v. Herrington, 7 Ala. 142; Ford v. Williams, 3 B. Mon. 550; Ex parte Conway, 4 Ark. 302; Powles v. Dilley, 2 Md. Ch. Dec. 119; Edrington v. Rogers, 15 Tex. 188, 195; Sibley v. Hood, 3 Mo. [206], 290; Richards v. Levin, 16 id. 596; Sedgwick, J., in Hatch v. Smith, 5 Mass. 42, 49; Parsons, C. J., in Widgery v. Haskell, id. 144, 157; Wilde, J., in Johnson v. Whitwell, 7 Pick. 71, 73; Dewey, J., in Nostrand v. Atwood, 19 id. 281, 284; Wing, P. J., in Hollister v. Loud, 2 Mich. 309, 315; Hauseli v. Vilmar, 43 N. Y. Super. Ct. 574; s. c., 2 Abb. N. C. 222; affirmed, 76 N. Y. 630. Where a debtor owes two parties, one of them may accept payment of his debt in anything of value he can get, though he knows that the debtor owes the other party and cannot pay both. Hopkins v. Beebe, 26 Pa. St. 85; Archer v. O'Brien, 7 Hun, 146; Lampson v. Arnold, 19 Iowa, 480; The York County Bank v. Carter, 38 Pa. St. 446.

[3] Wall v. Lakin, 13 Metc. 167. The decision in this case was placed on the ground that the case of payment, in money, of an existing debt by an insolvent debtor is not among the cases embraced within the provisions of section 3 of the statute of 1841, chapter 124. The following remarks of Mr. Justice Dewey have an important bearing on the principle considered in the text: "It was strongly urged upon us at the argument that it was against the whole policy of the insolvent laws thus to allow a payment to an individual creditor to be retained by him to his own use. If we look merely at the principle of equitable distribution of the whole assets among all the creditors *pro rata*, it would seem to be in derogation of that principle. But there are other considerations favoring the construction we have given. A different rule might be found to operate with great practical inconvenience in its application to payments made in the usual course of business. Many cases occur of traders and other persons who do business while there is a strong public impression that if their debts were at once all demanded there might not be assets sufficient to pay them, yet who continue to pay such debts as are most strongly pressed, hoping to survive their embarrassments, and by better success in business eventually to discharge their entire in-

declares all the property of the debtor to be the common pledge of his creditors, and the courts have always been jealous of any conveyance or transaction calculated to defraud creditors, or give an unjust preference to one class over another, payments on the eve of insolvency in the ordinary course of business have been sustained.[1]

§ 125. **Methods of Giving Preference.**— But an insolvent debtor may exercise this right of preference not only in the form of the actual *payment of money* to a particular creditor, but also in the form of the assignment or appropriation of *property*.[2] And this again may be done by either of the following methods: first, by the transfer of property *directly* to the creditor, either (1) absolutely, in lieu of payment and as a satisfaction of the debt so preferred;[3] or (2) conditionally or by way of security, as by bond,

---

debtedness. Whether it would be sound policy to disturb such payments may certainly be somewhat questionable." 13 Metc. 171, 172. This rule has since been changed by statute. See Appendix, I.

[1] Garland, J., in The United States v. The Bank of the United States, 8 Rob. (La.) 262, 404. See Kallman v. Creditors, 39 La. Ann. 1089; 3 S. Rep. 382.

[2] Garr v. Hill, 1 Stock. 210; Curtis, J., in Heydock v. Stanhope, 1 Curt. 474; Uhler v. Maulfair, 23 Pa. St. 481; Glen v. Grover, 3 Md. 212; Powles v. Dilley, 2 Md. Ch. Dec. 119; Cooper v. McClun, 16 Ill. 435; Wright v. Linn, 16 Tex. 34; Gassett v. Wilson, 3 Fla. 235. A debtor in failing circumstances may give a preference to one or more of his creditors to the exclusion of others; and such disposition of his effects is not impeachable on the ground of fraud even, though it embraces all his property. Cason v. Murray, 3 Mo. 378. A debtor in failing circumstances may convey all his property to a *bona fide* creditor at an adequate price, even though the known effect of such sale and conveyance may be to delay or defeat his other creditors. Young v. Dumas, 29 Ala. 60. See Pulliam v. Newberry, 41 id. 168; Harkins v. Bailey, 48 id. 377.

[3] Parsons, C. J., in Widgery v. Haskell, 5 Mass. 144, 153; Dewey, J., in Nostrand v. Atwood, 19 Pick. 281, 284; Sandford, C., in Mackie v. Cairns, Hopk. Ch. 373, 406. He may assign all or any part of his effects in satisfaction of a *bona fide* debt in exclusion of all other creditors. Tilghman, C. J., in The United States v. King, Wall. Sr. 13, 21; Lawrence v. Davis, 2 McLean, 177; Ford v. Williams, 3 B. Mon. 550; Bennett, J., in Hall v. Denison, 17 Vt. 310, 315; Stover v. Herrington, 7 Ala. 142; Bruce's Adm'rs v. Smith, 3 Harr. & J. 499; Hickley v. The Farmers' & Merchants' Bank, 5 Gill & J. 377; Eastman v. McAlpin, 1 Kelly, 157; King v. Trice, 3 Ired. Eq. 568; Gaston, J., in Hafner v. Irwin, 1 Ired. L. 490; Powers v. Green, 14 Ill. 38; Little v. Eddy, 14 Mo. 160; Kuykendall v. McDonald, 15 id. 416; Edrington v. Rogers, 15 Tex. 188; Hancock v. Horan, id. 507; Paige, J., in Curtis v. Leavitt, 15 N. Y. 197. A conveyance of land by an insolvent debtor to a creditor to pay an existing debt, though the parties intend thereby that the claims of other creditors shall be defeated, is not fraudulent. Covanhovan v. Hart, 21 Pa. St. 495. See Lloyd v. Williams, id. 327. A debtor in possession of his property and having the right to dispose of it in payment of his debts may lawfully transfer to a creditor any of his property in satisfaction of his debt, or make any other arrangement which would render its appropriation upon the debt certain and secure. Stanley v. Nat. Union Bank, 115 N. Y. 122; 22 N. E. Rep. 29. See Dessar v. Field, 99 Ind. 548; Boling v. Howell, 93

pledge or mortgage;[1] secondly, by consenting to a transfer by operation of *law*, as by voluntarily confessing a judgment;[2] and thirdly, by transferring property to a third person *in trust*, to hold

id. 329; Oppenheimer v. Holff, 68 Tex. 409. But an insolvent cannot give away his property to defeat creditors. Buckley v. Dunn, 67 Miss. 710. "A debtor in failing circumstances has the right to prefer one creditor to another; and if he takes his property and pays one of his creditors with it, designing at the time and knowing that the effect of such payment to the particular creditor will be to prevent some other creditor or creditors from taking his property upon their executions, this will not affect the title of the creditor to whom he has delivered the property." Marvin, J., in Hall v. Arnold, 15 Barb. 599, 600. But see, as to the good faith of the transaction, the observations of Nelson, C. J., in Birdseye v. Ray, 4 Hill, 158, 163. And see Garr v. Hill, 1 Stock. 210, 215; Hancock v. Horan, 15 Tex. 507; Reehling v. Byers, 94 Pa. St. 316; Stamets v. Quinn, 27 N. J. Eq. 383. While a preference must necessarily, to some extent, operate to defer, hinder or delay other creditors, the mere knowledge of the preferred creditor that such will be its effect, and the debtor intended it should have that effect, will not be sufficient to avoid the transaction as to a creditor not preferred. But if it further appears "that the preferred creditor was not acting from an honest purpose to secure the payment of his own debt, but from a desire to aid the debtor in defeating other creditors, or in covering up his property, or in giving him a secret interest therein, or in locking it up in any way for the debtor's own use and benefit, he will not be protected, and the sale (to preferred creditors) would be fraudulent as to other creditors, because, in such cases, the fraud of the debtor becomes the fraud of the preferred creditor because of his participating therein." Shelley v. Boothe, 73 Mo. 74; Frazer v. Thatcher, 49 Tex. 26.

[1] Stevens v. Bell, 6 Mass. 339; Wilde, J., in Johnson v. Whitwell, 7 Pick. 71, 73; Dewey, J., in Nostrand v. Atwood, 19 id. 284; Bates v. Coe, 10 Conn. 280; Pomeroy v. Manin, 2 Paine, 476; Waters v. Comly, 3 Har. (Del.) 117; Anderson v. Tydings, 3 Md. Ch. Dec. 167; Davis v. Anderson, 1 Kelly, 176; Nelson, C. J., in Birdseye v. Ray, 4 Hill, 158, 163; Paige, J., in Curtis v. Leavitt, 15 N. Y. 197; Redfield, C. J., in Mussey v. Noyes, 26 Vt. 462, 471; Tootle v. Caldwell, 30 Kan. 125; Giddings v. Sears, 115 Mass. 505; Isham, J., in Peck v. Merrill, id. 686, 693; Leitch v. Hollister, 4 N. Y. 211; Livermore v. McNair, 34 N. J. Eq. 478 (see the case under § 129). A creditor has a right to secure himself by obtaining a lien on the property of a failing debtor, and if done fairly he may thus obtain a preference over other creditors. Caldwell, J., in Fassett v. Traber, 20 Ohio, 540, 545. See Wiley v. Knight, 27 Ala. 336. The fact that pending a contemplated assignment a mortgage was executed in good faith to secure a pre-existing debt, which mortgage had long previously been promised by the debtor, does not show that the assignment was executed with the intention of hindering, delaying and defrauding creditors, nor does it render the assignment void. Dodd v. Hills, 21 Kan. 707. See Sweetzer v. Higby, 63 Mich. 13; 29 N. W. Rep. 506; Root v. Hare, 62 Mich. 420; 29 N. W. Rep. 29; Stix v. Sadler, 109 Ind. 254. But this right has been abridged by statute in some of the states. See Appendix, I.

[2] Williams v. Brown, 4 Johns. Ch. 682; Wilder v. Winne, 6 Cow. 284; Blakey's Appeal, 7 Barr, 449; Guy v. McIlree, 26 Pa. St. 92. See Livermore v. McNair, 34 N. J. Eq. 478. See the case under § 129. In the English case of Holbird v. Anderson, 5 Term R. 235, where a debtor preferred a creditor by confessing a judgment to him under which execution was issued and levied even after judgment obtained and execution issued by another creditor, the preference was held to be not fraudulent under the statute of 13 Eliz., ch. 5. A failing debtor may prefer one creditor to the exclusion of others, and it is immaterial whether the preference be given by payment, conveyancing, mortgage, by delivery of

and dispose of for the benefit of the creditor.¹ By this gradation we reach that common form of voluntary assignment by which a debtor transfers the *whole* of his property to a trustee to be applied for the benefit of certain creditors, or in which he classifies his creditors and directs his trustee to pay them in a certain prescribed *order*.

§ 126. **Preferences by Direct Transfer.**— The right of a debtor in embarrassed or failing circumstances to provide for particular creditors by appropriations out of property of which he himself retains the dominion, or, in other words, the right to prefer by the *direct transfer* of property to the creditor preferred, rests in a great degree on the necessities of mercantile business,² and is conceded even in those judicial opinions which deny or condemn the exercise of the right in the indirect form of a trust.³ The mere preference thus given is nothing more than what the law itself constantly allows and secures to one creditor over another as the reward of superior vigilance and diligence in the prosecution and enforcement of his remedies. The priority everywhere given to a creditor who obtains a *judgment* over other creditors equally meritorious is a familiar example of this preference by law. On the same ground rested the priority given in New York to creditors proceeding under the "act to abolish imprisonment for debt and to punish fraudulent debtors,"⁴ and in other states to attaching creditors, and in all these cases the preference is one which cannot be divested by the debtor, even by an assignment of all his property for the benefit of all his creditors.⁵ The exercise of the right to prefer in this direct form, especially where the appropriations made by it are limited and partial, leaving the residue of the debtor's

---

goods, by confession of judgment, or by suffering an attachment. Claflin v. Sylvester, 99 Mo. 276; 12 S. W. Rep. 508. See Nichols v. Ellis, 98 id. 344; 11 S. W. Rep. 741; Smith v. Whitfield, 67 Tex. 121; 2 S. W. Rep. 822; Schroeder v. Babbitt, 108 Mo. 289; Breneman's Estate, 150 Pa. St. 494; 24 Atl. Rep. 633. But see Rochester v. Armour, 92 Ala. 432; 8 S. Rep. 780.

¹ Stevens v. Bell, 6 Mass. 339; Dewey, J., in Nostrand v. Atwood, 19 Pick. 284.

² See the observations of Coulter, J., in Blakey's Appeal, 7 Barr, 449, 451, and of Ford, J., in Tillou v. Britton, 4 Halst. 128, 136.

³ See the opinion of Nelson, J., in Cunningham v. Freeborn, 11 Wend. 240, 256, and of Sutherland, J., in Grover v. Wakeman, id. 194, 201. In Atkinson v. Jordan, 5 Ohio, 178, Wright, J., observed: "It seems admitted that a debtor in failing circumstances may, in good faith, pay one creditor in money or goods in preference to another, but the frequent abuses practiced in transfers to effect a preference by means of *trusts* instead of actual payment has led many to doubt the policy of holding such transfers valid."

⁴ This act is now repealed.

⁵ Wood v. Bolard, 8 Paige, 556; Spear v. Wardell, 1 N. Y. 144. See Hall v. Kellogg, 12 N. Y. 325; Wilde, J., in Johnson v. Whitwell, 7 Pick. 71, 75; Story, J., in Halsey v. Whitney, 4 Mason, 206, 213.

property open to the legal pursuit of his creditors, does not affect the right of unpreferred creditors to proceed against such residue, nor does it necessarily hinder or delay them in the prosecution of their legal remedies. Hence we find it admitted in the jurisprudence of those states where preferences by general assignments in trust are expressly or in effect prohibited by statute, as in New Hampshire,[1] Connecticut,[2] New Jersey,[3] Pennsylvania,[4] Iowa,[5] Alabama,[6] Missouri,[7] California[8] and Ohio.[9]

§ 127. **Preferences in Assignments to Trustee.**— But where an insolvent debtor, instead of retaining the dominion of his property, divests himself of it by a general assignment *to a trustee* with directions to the latter to apply it in satisfaction of certain specified debts to the exclusion or postponement of others, he places the rights of unpreferred creditors on quite a different and much less favorable footing. Deprived by such a transfer of all remedy against the property except where the assignment can be avoided as fraudulent or illegal, they are compelled to await the uncertain result of the execution of the trust in its due course with all the delays necessarily attendant on the processes of collection, sale and distribution by the assignee, and are effectually turned over to the

---

[1] Meredith Manuf. Co. v. Smith, 8 N. H. 347; Law v. Wyman, id. 536; Barker v. Hall, 13 id. 298. So formerly in Massachusetts. Henshaw v. Sumner, 23 Pick. 446; Brown v. Foster, 2 Metc. 152; Danforth v. Denny, 25 N. H. 155. But see the statutes of 1838, 1841 and 1856, referred to *post*, p. 177 n. '7.

[2] Bates v. Coe, 10 Conn. 280; Pomeroy v. Manin, 2 Paine, 476. But see the act of 1853. Rev. Stat. (ed. 1875), p. 378.

[3] Tillou v. Britton, 4 Halst. 120, 121; Garr v. Hill, 1 Stock. 210, 215.

[4] Blakey's Appeal, 7 Barr, 449; Worman v. Wolfersberger's Ex'rs, 19 Pa. St. 59; Uhler v. Maulfair, 23 id. 481; York Co. Bank v. Carter, 38 id. 446; Guy v. McIlree, 26 id. 92. See Wilson v. Berg, 88 id. 167; Hutchinson v. McClure, 20 Pa. St. 63. And see as to partial assignment in trust, Miners' Nat. Bank Appeal, 57 Pa. St. 193.

[5] Fromme v. Jones, 13 Iowa, 474; Davis v. Gibson, 24 id. 257; Farwell v. Howard, 26 id. 381; Lampson v. Arnold, 19 id. 480. In Van Patten v. Burr, 52 id. 518, it was held that an assignment giving preferences was none the less invalid because it consisted of several instruments. The statute does not prevent the insolvent at the time he executes the assignment from paying certain creditors while he retains the *jus disponendi* of his property, but simply limits his right to prefer where he makes a general assignment.

[6] Young v. Dumas, 29 Ala. 60; Pulham v. Newberry, 41 id. 168; Harkins v. Bailey, 48 id. 377.

[7] Cason v. Murray, 15 Mo. 378; Johnson v. McAllister's Assignee, 30 id. 327; State v. Benoist, 37 id. 500.

[8] Civil Code of California, §§ 34, 51, expressly provides that the provisions of the act shall not affect the power of a person, although insolvent, to transfer property to a particular creditor for the purpose of paying or securing the whole or a part of a debt owing to such creditor, whether in his own right or otherwise.

[9] Wilcox v. Kellogg, 11 Ohio, 394; Hulls v. Jeffrey, 8 id. 390.

remote chances of sharing in a possible surplus remaining after full satisfaction of the claims preferred. The temptations were to the abuse or inequitable exercise of the right of preference itself in this form and the facilities for reserving undue advantages to the debtor, through the services of a friendly trustee, or other evils attending the unrestricted allowance of the right to favor one creditor at the expense of another through the medium of this description of conveyance.[1] Hence, the policy of the rule allowing preferences in general assignments to trustees has frequently been questioned by high authority in this country, as conferring a power which may be easily abused and rendered subservient to fraud, and the practice itself has been pointedly condemned as calculated to create confusion, uncertainty and collusion.[2]

[1] Quoted with approval in Grubbs v. Morris, 103 Ind. 166.
[2] In the case of Riggs v. Murray, 2 Johns. Ch. 565, 577, Chancellor Kent described the operation of the rule in the following terms: "As we have no bankrupt system, the right of the insolvent to select one creditor and to exclude another is applied to every case, and the consequences of such partial payments are extensively felt and deeply deplored. Creditors out of view and who reside abroad or at a distance are usually neglected. This checks confidence in dealing and hurts the credit and character of the country. These partial assignments are no doubt founded in certain cases upon meritorious considerations, yet the temptation leads strongly to abuse and to the indulgence of improper motives." In Cunningham v. Freeborn, 11 Wend. 240, 256, Mr. Justice Nelson expressed his disapprobation in still stronger language: "The root of the vice in all these cases of voluntary assignments lies in the principle of *preference*. It affords the pretense for putting the property into the possession of a friendly trustee, and thereby may substantially secure to the debtor the control of it for a long time after the law presumes it to have passed from him, and when his own possession would be incompatible with its security." In Burd v. Smith, 4 Dall. 76, decided when preferences were allowed in Pennsylvania, though the court admitted the right, Mr. Justice Breckenridge condemned the practice in the following terms: "The right has been allowed, perhaps on a principle of humanity, or in favor of just debts, to exclude debts in law not strictly *ex debito justitæ*. But I do not think that the practice should be encouraged. It is calculated to create confusion, uncertainty and collusion." Id. 88. In Pingree v. Comstock, 18 Pick. 46, 51, decided before preferences were prohibited in Massachusetts, Mr. Justice Wilde observed: "It is to be regretted that an insolvent debtor has the power to make any preferences. It is a power which may be grossly abused and ought not to be extended or encouraged." In Atkinson v. Jordan, 5 Ohio, 178, Mr. Justice Wright described the operation of the rule in Ohio, while preferences were allowed in that state, as follows: "The practice among speculating traders of shattered and desperate circumstances of accumulating property upon credit with a desire of securing the means of satisfying the claims of confidential creditors, who contribute in various ways to keep up the credit upon which the property has been procured, and then passing these effects so procured into the hands of trustees to be protected from legal process and to be exhausted in satisfying those preferred claims, leaving all creditors without a farthing, can hardly be justified on any sound moral or legal principle. Instances are frequent of merchandise procured from an honest trader on credit being handed over in bulk to trustees to secure indorsers and other confidential creditors. Equity delights in equality, and it is becoming a grave question whether courts of justice should

§ 128. **Preferences in Assignments to Trustee — Continued.**—
Notwithstanding these objections, however, the right to give preferences to creditors in deeds of assignment to trustees has in cases not within the bankrupt law been freely admitted, nay justified, by the courts in England,[1] and repeatedly recognized by the federal and state courts of the United States. So that it may be laid down as a general rule that, in the absence of any statutory prohibition and of a bankrupt law, a debtor may, at any time before liens have attached upon his property, make a general or partial assignment to a trustee for the benefit of his creditors with preferences; which assignment will be valid as against the process of creditors from the time of the execution of the deed.[2] "He may," observed

longer countenance a sinking debtor in preferring one creditor to another in the distribution of his effects." Id. See, also, the observations of Hinman, J., in Beers v. Lyon, 21 Conn. 610; of Woods, J., in Barker v. Hall, 13 N. H. 301; of Isham, J., in Peck v. Merrill, 26 Vt. 686, 692; and of Pratt, J., in Pierson v. Manning, 2 Mich. 445, 448. The preamble to the Georgia statute of December 19, 1818, prohibiting preferences in general assignments, is in the following words: "Whereas, a practice of selecting particular creditors by assignment and transfers of property made by persons indebted, and thereby excluding or defrauding other *bona fide* creditors of their just claims on the estate of insolvent debtors, is *contrary to the first principles of equity and justice;* to prevent the mischief thereof, be it enacted," etc. See, also, the observations of Roosevelt, J., in Nichols v. McEwen, 17 N. Y. 22; of Fairchild, J., in Hull v. Roane, 22 Ark. 184.

[1] In the case of Estwick v. Caillaud, 5 Term R. 420, where a debtor had assigned a portion of his property in trust for the benefit of certain creditors, Lord Kenyon, in sustaining this conveyance, observed that "it was neither illegal nor immoral to prefer one set of creditors to another;" and that even under the bankrupt law a trader might by partial assignment give a preference in some respects to his creditors. Id. 423. In the same case, Ashurst, J., said: "Where the bankrupt laws do not interfere, a debtor may give a preference to particular creditors." Id. 425. And in Nunn v. Wilsmore, 8 Term R. 521, where the debtor had conveyed all his effects in trust for the benefit of creditors, Lord Kenyon, in pronouncing the assignment good, remarked that "putting the bankrupt law out of the case, a debtor may assign all his effects for the benefit of particular creditors." Id. 425. And such preference by a creditor has not only been conceded, but in some of the older cases justified. Thus, it was said by the master of the rolls, in Small v. Oudley, 2 P. Wms. 427: "There may be just reason for a sinking trader to give a preference to one creditor before another; to one that has been a faithful friend, and for a just debt lent him in extremity, when the rest of his debts might be due from him as a dealer in trade, wherein his creditors may have been the gainers; whereas the other may be not only a just debt but all that such a creditor has in the world to subsist upon; in this case (I say), and so circumstanced, the trader honestly may, nay *ought*, to give the preference." Id. 429. Similar views were taken by Lord Chancellor Parker in Cock v. Goodfellow, 10 Mod. 489. So in the United States, in Burd v. Smith, 4 Dal. 76, 86, Smith, J., observed that cases may be easily conceived in which the giving of a preference "would be a *duty*." And in Murray v. Riggs, 15 Johns. 571, 585, Thompson, C. J., said: "I think I may assume it as a settled and unshaken principle, both at law and in equity, that a failing debtor has a *just*, legal and *moral* right to prefer, in payment, one creditor or set of creditors to another."

[2] American Leading Cases (Hare & Wallace's notes), 95 [65, ed. 1857]; 2 Kent's

Mr. Justice Sutherland, in Grover v. Wakeman,[1] assign the whole of his property for the benefit of a single creditor, in exclusion of all others, or he may distribute it in unequal proportions either

Com. [532], 689; Marbury v. Brooks, 7 Wheat. 556; Spring v. S. Carolina Ins. Co., 8 id. 268; Brooks v. Marbury, 11 id. 78; Brashear v. West, 7 Pet. 608, 614; Clark v. White, 12 id. 178; Tompkins v. Wheeler, 16 id. 106; Pearpoint v. Graham, 4 Wash. C. C. 232; United States v. King, Wall. Sr. 13, 21; Halsey v. Whitney, 4 Mason, 206, 212, 213; Lawrence v. Davis, 3 McLean, 177; Curtis, J., in Stewart v. Spencer, 1 Curt. 157, 162; Kent, C., in Hendricks v. Robinson, 2 Johns. Ch. 283, 306; Van Ness, J., in McMenomy v. Ferrers, 3 Johns. 71, 84; Wilkes v. Ferris, 5 id. 335; Van Ness, J., in Hyslop v. Clarke, 14 id. 458, 463; Thompson, C. J., in Murray v. Riggs, 15 id. 571, 583; Mackie v. Cairns, 5 Cow. 547; Wintringham v. Lafoy, 7 id. 735; Grover v. Wakeman, 11 Wend. 187; Jacobs v. Remsen, 36 N. Y. 668; Putnam v. Hubbell, 42 N. Y. 106; Webb v. Daggett, 2 Barb. S. C. 9; Brigham v. Tillinghast, 15 id. 618; Burd v. Smith, 4 Dall. 85, n.; Smith, J., id. 86; Wilt v. Franklin, 1 Binn. 502, 514; Lippincott v. Barker, 2 id. 174; Cameron v. Montgomery, 13 Serg. & Rawle, 128; Wilson v. Berg, 88 Pa. St. 167; De Forest v. Bacon, 2 Conn. 633; Ingraham v. Wheeler, 6 id. 277; Hatch v. Smith, 5 Mass. 42; Widgery v. Haskell, id. 144, 153; Russell v. Woodward, 10 Pick. 407; Foster v. Saco Manufacturing Co., 12 id. 451; Nostrand v. Atwood, 19 id. 281; Pierce v. Jackson, 2 R. I. 35; Beckwith v. Brown, id. 311; Dockray v. Dockray, id. 547; Nightingale v. Harris, 6 id. 321; Allen v. Gardner, 7 id. 22; Buffum v. Green, 5 N. H. 71; Haven v. Richardson, id. 113; Hall v. Denison, 17 Vt. 310; Redfield, C. J., in Mussey v. Noyes, 26 Vt. 462, 471; Canal Bank v. Cox, 6 Greenl. 395; Tillou v. Britton, 4 Halst. 120; Atkinson v. Jordan, 5 Ohio, 178; Hickley v. The Farmers' and Merchants' Bank, 5 Gill & J. 377; State of Maryland v. Bank of Maryland, 6 id. 205; Cole v. Albers, 1 Gill, 412; McCall v. Hinckley, 4 id. 128; Beatty v. Davis, 9 Gill, 211; Sangston v. Gaither, 3 Md. 40; Maennel v. Murdock, 13 id. 164; McColgan v. Hopkins, 17 id. 395; McCullough v. Somerville, 8 Leigh, 415; Skipwith's Ex'r v. Cunningham, id. 271; Phippen v. Durham, 8 Gratt. 457; Dance v. Seaman, 11 id. 778; Gordon v. Cannon, 18 Gratt. 388; Moffat v. McDowall, 1 McCord's Ch. 434; Moore v. Collins, 3 Dever. 126; Hafner v. Irwin, 1 Ired. L. 490; Allemand v. Russell, 5 Ired. Eq. 183; Smith v. Campbell, Rice, 353; Niolon v. Douglass, 2 Hill's Ch. 443; Eastman v. McAlpin, 1 Kelly, 167; Cameron v. Scudder, id. 204; Bellamy v. Bellamy's Adm'r, 6 Fla. 62; Holbrook v. Allen, 4 Fla. 87, 92; Robinson v. Rapelye, 2 Stew. 86; Richards v. Hazard, 1 Stew. & Port. 139; Williams v. Jones, 2 Ala. 314; Hindman v. Dill, 11 id. 689; Rankin v. Loder, 21 id. 380; Sharkey, C. J., in Brown v. Bartee, 10 Sm. & M. 268, 274; Layson v. Rowan, 7 Rob. (La.) 1; McQuinnay v. Hitchcock, 8 Tex. 33; Edrington v. Rogers, 15 id. 188, 195; Wright v. Linn, 16 id. 34, 42; Vernon v. Morton, 8 Dana, 247; Pearson v. Rockhill, 4 B. Mon. 296; Marshall v. Hutchinson, 5 id. 305; Ramsdell v. Sigerson, 2 Gilm. 73; Cross v. Bryant, 2 Scam. 37; Howell v. Edgar, 3 id. 417; How v. Camp, Walk. 427; Hollister v. Loud, 2 Mich. 309, 314; Bell v. Thompson, 3 Mo. [61], 84; Sibley v. Hood, id. [206], 290; Cason v. Murray, 15 id. 378; Gamble, J., in Richards v. Levin, 16 id. 596, 598, 599; Ex parte Conway, 12 Ark. 302; Hoff v. Roane, 22 id. 184; Hempstead v. Johnson, 18 id. 123; Bailey v. Mills, 27 Tex. 434; Rowland v. Coleman, 45 Ga. 204; Lay v. Seago, 47 id. 82; Tomlinson v. Matthews, 98 Ill. 178; Reed v. McIntyre, 98 U. S. 507; Hauselt v. Vilmar, 76 N. Y. 630; aff'g 43 Super. Ct. 574; s. c., 2 Abb. N. C. 222; Mayer v. Hellman, 91 U. S. 496. The cases above cited embrace the decisions of the highest courts in almost every state of the Union. It will be seen, however, from the text, that in some of these states the right to prefer has latterly been either wholly taken away or more or less modified by statute.

[1] 11 Wend. 187, 194, 197.

among a part or the whole of his creditors. No matter how or upon what principles the distribution is made, if the debtor devotes the whole of his property to the payment of just debts, neither law nor equity inquires whether the objects of his preference are more or less meritorious than those for whom he has made no provision. The right to prefer may originally have been sustained, in part, upon the supposition that just and proper grounds of preference did in most cases exist and would be duly regarded by the debtor; but whatever may have been the reason or foundation of the rule, it is one of that numerous class of cases in which the rule has become absolute, without any regard to the fact whether the reason on which it was founded exists or not in the particular cases. It is now too late to agitate the question whether these assignments, either partial or general, are sustained by considerations of true wisdom and policy. Reflecting men have differed upon that subject; but the better opinion seems to be that, in the absence of a general bankrupt system, the interests of a commercial community require that they should be sustained. They have accordingly grown into use, and have been sanctioned by judicial decisions in most of the states of the Union. They have become thoroughly incorporated into our system; and all that it is now competent for our courts to do is to see that they fairly appropriate all the insolvent's property, or such portion of it as he undertakes to assign, to the payment of his just debts, and are not made the instruments of placing it beyond the reach of his creditors, and for the benefit, either immediate or remote, of the insolvent himself."[1] "It is now entirely settled in this state," observed Mr. Justice Harris, in the case of Webb v. Daggett,[2] "that a debtor in failing circumstances may assign his property in trust for his creditors, and give such preference among them as he may choose." It is true, also, that assignments of this character have heretofore been in constant use, and as constantly sustained in most of the United States, and that, at common law, the right to prefer cannot be questioned.[3]

§ 129. **Restrictions on the Right to Prefer.**— Of late, however, the tendency has been toward a restriction of the exercise of this right on the part of insolvent debtors; and in several of the states

[1] And see, to the same effect, the observations of Gaston, J., in Hafner v. Irwin, 1 Ired. L. 490; of Allan, P., in Dance v. Seaman, 11 Gratt. 780, 781; and of Wing, P. J., in Hollister v. Loud, 2 Mich. 309, 315.
[2] 2 Barb. S. C. 9. And see the observations of Duer, J., in Nicholson v. Leavitt, 4 Sandf. S. C. 252, 482.
[3] Tilghman, C. J., in United States v. King, Wall. Sr. 13, 21; Lawrence v. Davis, 3 McLean, 177; Beatty v. Davis, 9 Gill, 211; Redfield, C. J., in Mussey v. Noyes, 26 Vt. 462, 471.

statutes have been passed declaring assignments with preferences, or such as provide for an unequal distribution of the debtor's property, to be either absolutely void, or to inure to the equal benefit of all the creditors.[1]

§ 130. **Preferences Regarded with Disfavor.**— In New York, particularly, the inclination of the courts against assignments with preferences has been becoming stronger and its expression more pointed and emphatic ever since the case of Riggs v. Murray,[2] in the court of chancery in 1817. In that case Chancellor Kent, while admitting the legality of the rule allowing preferences, observed that its application was "always to be watched with jealousy;" and that the court was not "required by any reasons of expediency or justice to enlarge the rule by giving it a new and dangerous facility."[3] In the leading case of Grover v. Wakeman,[4] in the court of errors in 1833, it was decided that a debtor in failing circumstances may prefer one creditor or set of creditors by assigning his property for their benefit in exclusion of his other creditors; *provided* that he devote the whole of the property assigned to the payment of his just debts; that the assignment be absolute and unconditional; that it contains no reservation or condition for his benefit, and does not extort from the fears or apprehensions of his creditors an absolute discharge as a consideration for a partial dividend.[5] In the case of Boardman v. Halliday,[6] in the court of chancery (1843), Chancellor Walworth characterized the principle of preference as "an erroneous principle, as injurious to the just rights of creditors as it is dangerous to the morals of the community,"[7] and refused to sanction its extension beyond what must be considered as the settled law of the land. In the case of Goodrich v. Downs,[8] in the supreme court (1844), Mr. Justice Bronson observed that "the courts have found great difficulty in upholding assignments which give a preference among creditors; and such transfers have only been allowed to stand where the debtor makes an unconditional surrender of his effects for the benefit of those to

[1] See Appendix, I.
[2] 2 Johns. Ch. 565.
[3] 2 Johns. Ch. 579.
[4] 11 Wend. 187.
[5] See the opinion of Mr. Justice Sutherland in this case (11 Wend. 192), from which an extract has already been made (*ante*, p. 172).
[6] 10 Paige, 223.
[7] The chancellor also referred to the opinions of Judge Holman of the district court of the United States for Indiana; of Judge Judson of Connecticut, and of Judges Story and Baldwin of the supreme court of the United States, as strongly adverse to the principle.
[8] 6 Hill, 438, 439.

whom they rightfully belong." In the later case of Webb v. Daggett,[1] in the same court (1847), it was said that assignments giving preferences have not ceased to be regarded with jealousy, and that they are rather tolerated than favored.[2] In the case of Barney v. Griffin,[3] in the court of appeals (1849), it was remarked by Bronson, J., that "the courts have very reluctantly upheld general assignments by an insolvent debtor which give a preference among creditors; and they can only be supported when they make a full and unconditional surrender of the property to the payment of debts. The debtor can neither make terms nor reserve anything to himself until after all the creditors have been satisfied." The same determination to confine these assignments within the narrowest limits and to scan every provision they contain without favor has been still more strongly exhibited in the later case of Nicholson v. Leavitt,[4] in the same court (1852), on appeal from the superior court of the city of New York.

So in the case of Dunham v. Waterman,[5] Mr. Justice Selden said: "The true principle applicable to all such cases is that a debtor who makes a voluntary assignment for the benefit of his creditors may direct, in general terms, a sale of the property and collection of the dues assigned, and may also direct upon what debts and in what order the proceeds shall be applied, but beyond this can prescribe no conditions whatever as to the management or disposition of the assigned property." And in a still later case it was remarked by Mr. Justice Davis that "it is needless to cite authorities to show that by the law of this state preferential assignments are not for that reason fraudulent and void."[6]

In North Carolina it was decided by the supreme court, in the case of Hafner v. Irwin,[7] that though a debtor has a right, by the

[1] 2 Barb. S. C. 9, 11.
[2] And see, to the same effect, the observation of Sandford, V. C., in Cram v. Mitchell, 1 Sandf. Ch. 251, 253; of Duer, J., in Nicholson v. Leavitt, 4 Sandf. S. C. 252, 280, 281; and of Allen, J., in Brigham v. Tillinghast, 15 Barb. 618.
[3] 2 N. Y. 365, 371.
[4] 6 N. Y. 510.
[5] 17 N. Y. 9.
[6] Jacobs v. Remsen, 36 N. Y. 668; Hauselt v. Vilmar, 76 N. Y. 630; affirming 43 Super. Ct. 574. See Dana v. Lull, 54 id. 646. In Haydock v. Coope, 53 id. 68, it is held that the right to prefer cannot be exercised so as to secure directly or indirectly to the debtor the future control of any part of the assigned estate.
[7] 1 Ired. L. 490. The observations of Gaston, J., in this case are very much in the strain of those of Sutherland, J., in Grover v. Wakeman, the principle of which is adopted. The following quotation may be added to what is said in the text: "It is enough, perhaps more than enough, for human infirmity, that the debtor shall be allowed, under these distressing circumstances, to select, according to his unbribed judgment, among his creditors, for those who merit a preference, and to make a simple and unconditional appropriation of his property to

laws of the state, by a deed of trust, to convey all his property for the purpose of paying certain creditors in preference, yet there must be no condition, direct or indirect, controlling this application. Such a deed must be *bona fide* for the purpose it professes to have in view. In South Carolina it was held in Smith v. Henry,[1] that the law allows a debtor to give a preference to one creditor over another, but it will not allow him to secure an advantage to himself, at the expense of creditors, as the price of such preference. In Tennessee it was held in Galt v. Dibrell,[2] that though a debtor may, by a deed of trust, prefer one creditor to another, yet he cannot thereby contract for his own benefit, and secure to himself the use and enjoyment of the property; if he does so, the transaction is fraudulent and void as to other creditors. Similar views have been expressed by the supreme court of Alabama.[3] In Maryland, it was held, in American Exchange Bank v. Inloes,[4] that although at common law a debtor may secure one creditor to the exclusion of others, yet such a provision in a deed of trust is only permitted by a court of equity, and if followed by other provisions equally suspicious, the court will have little difficulty in discovering sufficient fraud to vacate the deed.[5] In Mississippi it was held, in the case of Richardson v. Marqueze, that preferential assignments should, *per se*, be judged favorably by the same principles of law as those which are *pro rata*, but they are subject to a jealous scrutiny of the facts.[6]

§ 131. **Preferences in Special Instances.**—It is observed, however, that even in some of those states where preferences in assignments have been either actually prohibited by being declared void by

the payment of their claims. But to allow him to negotiate for terms with them, to seek out those who will be most favorable to him, either in the way of profit or commerce, direct or indirect, to stipulate, openly or covertly, with regard to the property conveyed, other than its appropriation to the purposes of the conveyance, would be injurious to the best interests of the community." Id., 499, 500.

[1] 1 Hill (S. C.), 16.
[2] 10 Yerg. 146. And see Lockhard v. Brodie, 1 Tenn. Ch. (Cooper), 384.
[3] Rankin v. Lodor, 21 Ala. 380.
[4] 7 Md. 380.
[5] The learned editor of the first volume of the "American Leading Cases," in concluding his notes to the cases of Thomas v. Jenks and Grover v. Wakeman, remarks that "the view now generally adopted appears to be this: that since the claims of creditors may be meritorious in unequal degrees, and since particular creditors have it in their power to obtain a priority by legal proceedings, the preference of creditors is an allowed object or *result* of a debtor's assignment, but that it is not permitted to be used as a *means* of accomplishing ends which are not the legitimate object of a debtor's efforts." 1 Am. Lead. Cases, 102 [75, ed. 1857].
[6] 59 Miss. 80; 42 Am. Rep. 353. See Turnipseed v. Schaefer, 76 Ga. 109.

statute, or virtually prohibited by being rendered inoperative, the prohibition has been confined by the courts to cases of *general* assignments, where the preferences are given by the *assignment itself*, or by some instrument or act so connected with it as to be deemed in law part of the same transaction, and has been held not to extend to distinct *special* transfers of property in payment or security of some particular debt. Thus in New Hampshire it has been held[1] that the statute of July 5, 1834, entitled "An act for the equal distribution of property assigned for the benefit of creditors," does not apply to an assignment made by a debtor of some particular part of his property, merely for the purpose of paying some particular debt or debts, nor to a pledge of all his attachable property to secure a particular debt or debts,[2] nor to a mortgage of all his property to secure a portion of his debts.[3] So formerly in Massachusetts, the statute of 1836, chapter 238, was held not to impair the debtor's right of securing a particular creditor to the prejudice of other creditors, unless when attempted to be exercised by or in connection with a conveyance by the debtor to assignees in trust for the use of any of his creditors.[4] Preferences given in this way, by mortgage,[5] and by the delivery to the creditor of promissory notes, immediately before executing an assignment under this statute,[6] were held not to avoid it.[7]

[1] Meredith Manufacturing Co. v. Smith, 8 N. H. 347.
[2] Low v. Wyman, 8 N. H. 536; Danforth v. Denny, 25 N. H. 155.
[3] Barker v. Hall, 13 N. H. 298.
[4] Henshaw v. Sumner, 23 Pick. 446. See Fairbanks v. Haynes, id. 323.
[5] Ibid.
[6] Brown v. Foster, 2 Met. 152.
[7] But in that state the right to prefer by the direct transfer of property has been greatly abridged by statutory enactments (being parts of a system of insolvency). The provisions of the act are as follows (Pub. Stat. (1882), pp. 894, 895):

§ 89. If a person being insolvent, or in contemplation of insolvency, within six months before the filing of the petition by or against him, with a view to give a preference to a creditor or person who has a claim against him, or is under any liability for him, procures any part of his property to be attached, sequestered or seized on execution, or makes any payment, pledge, assignment, transfer or conveyance of any part of his property, either directly or indirectly, absolutely or conditionally, the person receiving such payment, pledge, assignment, transfer or conveyance, or to be benefited thereby, having reasonable cause to believe such person is insolvent, or in contemplation of insolvency, and that such payment, pledge, assignment or conveyance is made in fraud of the laws relating to insolvency, the same shall be void, and the assignees may recover the property or the value of it from the person so receiving it or so to be benefited.

§ 91. If a person being insolvent, or in contemplation of insolvency, within six months before the filing of the petition by or against him, makes a sale, assignment, transfer, or other conveyance of any description, of any part of his property to a person who then has reasonable cause to believe him to be insolvent, or in contemplation of insolvency, and that such sale, assignment, transfer

§ 132. **Preferences in Special Instances — Continued.**— So, in Connecticut, where a debtor in failing circumstances, and with a view to his insolvency, executed a mortgage of his estate to certain of his creditors, and afterwards, on the same day, made a general assignment of his property, including the mortgaged premises, in trust for all his creditors, under the statute of 1828, chapter 3, it was held that the mortgage and assignment were not to be deemed parts of the same transaction, and that the preference given by the former was not within the prohibition of the statute; the court holding that the object of the statute was merely to provide a responsible trustee to receive property when assigned for the benefit of creditors, and to cause it to be distributed proportionally among them; "but not at all to interfere with the long-established principle of a debtor giving a preference voluntarily."[1] So in New Jersey it has been held[2] that the act "to secure creditors an equal and just division of the estate of debtors who convey to assignees for the benefit of creditors," does not extend to a solitary transfer of an individual item of property to a creditor in payment of a debt; and the operation of the act must be confined, if not to cases where a trust is created, at least to cases where there is something like universality in the assignment. Mortgages and judgments, also, are expressly excepted, but judgments confessed for the purpose of preferring creditors are within the act.[3] In Pennsylvania preferences by direct transfers of property to the creditors preferred are not within the act of April 17, 1843, concerning preferences in assignments.[4] Nor are judgments confessed to secure creditors such preferences as are avoided by the act, although an assignment for creditors may be intended and be

or other conveyance is made with a view to prevent the property from coming to his assignee in insolvency, or to prevent the same from being distributed under the laws relating to insolvency, or to defeat the object of, or in any way impair, hinder, impede or delay the operation and effect of, or to evade any of said provisions, the sale, assignment, transfer or conveyance shall be void, and the assignee may recover the property or the value thereof as assets of the insolvency; and if such sale, assignment, transfer or conveyance is not made in the usual and ordinary course of business of the debtor, that fact shall be *prima facie* evidence of such cause of belief. See Bush v. Moore, 133 Mass. 198.

[1] Bates v. Coe, 10 Conn. 230; Daggett, C. J., id. 295. But see the act of 1853, Gen. St. (Rev. of 1888), § 501.
[2] Tillou v. Britton, 4 Halst. 120; Garr v. Hill, 1 Stock. 210, 215; Moses v. Thomas, 26 N. J. L. 124; Van Waggoner v. Moses, id. 570; Garretson v. Brown, 26 id. 425.
[3] See Rev. of N. J. (1878), p. 36.
[4] Worman v. Wolfersberger's Ex'rs. 19 Pa. St. 59; Uhler v. Maulfair, 23 id. 481; Hopkins v. Beebe, 26 id. 85; Hutchinson v. McClure, 20 id. 63; Morgan's Appeal, id. 152; Griffin v. Rogers, 38 id. 382; Mellon's Appeal, 1 Grant, 212; York Co. Bank v. Carter, 38 Pa. St. 446. But it applies to partial assignments for the benefit of particular creditors. Miners' Bank Appeal, 57 Pa. St. 193.

shortly afterwards executed.[1] In Ohio an absolute conveyance to a creditor, in payment of his debt, does not come within the provisions of the act of February 23, 1835, relating to fraudulent assignments,[2] nor was it affected by the later statutes of 1838, 1853 and 1859.[3] And the rule is the same in the case of a mortgage to a creditor, unless where it is for the benefit of some other creditor besides the mortgagee.[4] And in Georgia an absolute conveyance of property by a debtor, who is in fact insolvent, to a creditor in payment of his debt, without any reservation for the benefit of the debtor, is not fraudulent as to the other creditors under the statute of 1818, "to prevent assignments," etc.[5] Nor is a mortgage given to secure a just debt within such statute.[6] But in Louisiana, if a debtor shall, within three months next preceding his failure, have sold, engaged or mortgaged any of his goods and effects, or shall have otherwise disposed of the same in order to give an unjust preference to one or more of his creditors over the others, such deed or act is required to be declared null and void.[7]

So in Iowa it has been repeatedly held that the statute prohibiting preferences does not limit or affect the right of an insolvent debtor to sell or mortgage *bona fide* a part or all of his property to one or more of his creditors in payment or security of a particular debt.[8]

§ 133. **Preferences in Partial Assignments.** — It has been thought that an assignment giving preferences to certain creditors or classes of creditors is not valid unless it contains a transfer of *all* the debtor's property; and expressions may be found in the opinions of the court in several important cases which go the

[1] See *ante*, p. 169, note 4.
[2] Wilcox v. Kellogg, 11 Ohio, 394; Wood, J., id. 399.
[3] Hulls v. Jeffrey, 8 Ohio, 390; Lane, J., id. 391. See Doremus v. O'Hara, 1 Ohio St. 45.
[4] Bloom v. Nagle, 4 Ohio St. 45; Harkrader v. Leiby, id. 602; Atkinson v. Tomlinson, 1 id. 237; Justice v. Uhl, 10 id. 170; Dickson v. Rawson, 5 id. 218. See Mitchell v. Gazzam, 12 Ohio, 315; overruled in Atkinson v. Tomlinson, *supra*.
[5] Eastman v. McAlpin, 1 Kelly (Ga.), 157; Cameron v. Scudder, id. 204; McWhorter v. Wright, 5 Ga. 555; Starnes, J., in Miller v. Conklin, 17 Ga. 430, 433; Brown v. Lee, 7 Ga. 267; Ezekiel v. Dixon, 3 Kelly (Ga.), 146. See Code of Ga. (ed. 1873), § 1953; and see the proviso in the statute.
[6] Davis v. Anderson, 1 Kelly, 176; Lee v. Brown, 7 Ga. 276; Lavender v. Thomas, 18 Ga. 668, 675.
[7] Rev. St. of La. (ed. 1870), p. 359, §§ 28, 1801.
[8] Lambson v. Arnold, 19 Iowa, 479; Cole v. Dealman, 13 id. 551; Gray v. McCallister, 50 id. 497; Johnson v. McGrew, 11 id. 151; Fromme v. Jones, 13 id. 457; Whitaker v. Lindley, 14 id. 598; Buell v. Buckingham, 16 id. 284; Davis v. Gibbon, 24 id. 257; Farrall v. Howard, 26 id. 381; Graves v. Alden, 13 id. 573.

length of establishing such a doctrine. Thus, in Goodrich v. Downs,[1] in the supreme court of this state, Bronson, J., in delivering the opinion of the court, observes: " Such transfers have only been allowed to stand where the debtor makes an unconditional surrender of his effects for the benefit of those to whom they rightfully belong."[2] " They can only be supported," says the same learned judge, in Barney v. Griffin, in the court of appeals,[3] " when they make a full and unconditional surrender of the property to the payment of debts." In Burdick v. Post,[4] Barculo, J., more explicitly says: " As we understand the settled law in this state, derived from an examination of all the decisions, assignments preferring certain creditors are only tolerated when they are absolute and unconditional; when they devote *the whole of the assignor's property* to the immediate and unqualified payment of his debts," etc.[5] In Rathbun v. Platner,[6] Mason, J., observes: " The law only tolerates them when honestly made for the purpose of giving the preference, and devoting *the whole property of the debtor* to the payment of the debts." Similar expressions may be found in decisions made in the courts of other states.[7] But in the leading case of Grover v. Wakeman,[8] upon which the New York decisions above referred to either professedly or actually, for the most part, rest, the opinion of the court, instead of declaring partial assignments with preferences void, expressly admits their validity. " It is now too late," observes Mr. Justice Sutherland in this case, " to agitate the question whether these assignments, *either partial or general*, are sustained by considerations of true wisdom and policy. . . . They have become thoroughly incorporated into our system; and all that it is now competent for our courts to do is to see that they fairly appropriate all the insolvent's property, *or such portion of it as he undertakes to assign*, to the payment of his just debts."[9] The true doctrine is here stated with great clearness and discrimination. It has been further laid down, in a work of authority,[10] as

[1] 6 Hill, 438.
[2] Ibid. 439.
[3] 2 N. Y. 365, 371.
[4] 12 Barb. 168.
[5] Ibid. 175
[6] 18 Barb. 272, 275. See, also, the observations of Comstock, J., in Curtis v. Leavitt, 15 N. Y. 132.
[7] Sangston v. Gaither, 3 Md. 40; Phelan, J., in Rankin v. Lodor, 21 Ala. 380, 389; Goldthwaite, J., in Shackelford v. P. & M. Bank of Mobile, 22 id. 238, 245.
[8] 11 Wend. 187.
[9] 11 Wend. 195.
[10] American Leading Cases (Hare & Wall. notes), 65 (ed. 1857). In Vermont, prior to the statute prohibiting preferences, partial assignments with preferences were held to be valid. Hall v. Dennison, 17 Vt. 310. And see Cole v. Dealman, 13 Iowa, 551, and cases cited *ante*, p. 171. In Gray v. McCallister, 50 Iowa, 497,

the general American rule on this point, that in the absence of statutory prohibitions and of a bankrupt law, partial as well as general assignments may be made with preferences to creditors. In the case of Wilson v. Forsyth,[1] in the supreme court of this state, the question as to the validity of a partial assignment with preferences was distinctly raised and argued; and the court (Gould, J.), after reviewing the cases, came to the conclusion that an assignment giving preferences among creditors, and not embracing *all* the debtor's property, is not void for those reasons. In Maryland[2] it is held that an assignment creating preferences and exacting releases is void, unless it appears on its face to convey all the property of the debtor, and where it is executed by partners it must so appear to convey both their partnership effects and their individual estate.

§ 134. Restrictions on the Right to Prefer.—The right to prefer one or more creditors to others in assignments by debtors is sometimes either restrained or entirely taken away by statute. Where a bankrupt law exists the right is also considered as taken away, its exercise having always been regarded as inconsistent with the policy and objects of such a system.[3] And the insolvent laws of a state sometimes create a restriction in this respect by depriving an insolvent debtor who attempts to exercise the right of the benefit of a discharge under them.[4] But such provisions do not avoid *bona fide* assignments by debtors merely because of preferences given to some creditors over others.[5] So in South Carolina, assignments by debtors giving undue preferences to creditors have

---

a transaction was held "to be nothing more than a partial assignment of the debtor's property in good faith, preferring certain of his creditors. Such an assignment is not invalid." Partial assignments with preferences which do not exact releases are valid in Maryland. Price v. Ford, 18 Md. 489. In Indiana, where the statute prevents preferences in general assignments, the debtor may prefer by a partial assignment. Grubbs v. Morris, 103 Ind. 166. But in the Michigan case of Smith v. Mitchell, 12 Mich. 180, it was said that the assignment was void if it did not fairly, *bona fide*, assign all of the assignor's property liable for the payment of his debts. See Carpenter v. Underwood, 9 N. Y. 520; McClelland v. Remsen, 36 Barb. 622; affirmed, 33 How. 618; Roller Wheel Co. v. Fielding, 101 N. Y. 504. The right to prefer is unqualified except that the debtor must not reserve the surplus for his own benefit or that of any favored creditor, to the exclusion of other creditors. McFerran v. Davis, 70 Ga. 661; The Princeton Mfg. Co. v. White, 68 id. 96.

[1] 22 Barb. 105, 122–127.
[2] Maughlin v. Tyler, 47 Md. 545; Loney v. Bayly, 45 id. 447.
[3] 2 Kent's Com. [532], 688. See Ex parte Breneman, Crabbe, 456; Caryl v. Russell, 13 N. Y. 194.
[4] Egberts v. Wood, 3 Paige, 517, 521.
[5] McColgan v. Hopkins, 17 Md. 395.

the effect of debarring such debtors from the benefit of the insolvent or "prison bounds" act.[1] But in North Carolina a deed of trust to satisfy certain creditors, conveying an amount of property greater in value than the amount of debts secured by the deed, is no bar to the debtor's taking the insolvent act, if he sets forth the deed in his schedule and surrenders all his resulting interest.[2]

In New York the power to make an assignment, with or without preferences, is entirely denied to a debtor against whom proceedings have been instituted by a creditor under the "act to abolish imprisonment for debt and to punish fraudulent debtors."[3]

§ 135. Restrictions on the Right of Limited Partnerships to Prefer.— The right of giving preferences to creditors is also, in many of the states, denied to *limited partnerships*, even where preferences by other partnerships are allowed. Thus, in New York, every sale, assignment or transfer of any of the property or effects of a limited partnership, made by such partnership when insolvent or in contemplation of insolvency, or after or in contemplation of the insolvency of any partner, with the intent of giving a preference to any creditor of such partnership or insolvent partner over other creditors of such partnership, and every judgment confessed, lien created or security given by such partnership, under the like circumstances and with the like intent, are by statute declared void as against the creditors of such partnership.[4] Similar preferences given by any general or special partner are also declared void.[5] Similar provisions have been enacted in Arkansas,[6] Delaware,[7] Idaho,[8] Iowa,[9] Kentucky,[10] Maryland,[11] Minnesota,[12] Nebraska,[13] Nevada,[14] New Jersey,[15] New Mexico,[16] North Dakota,[17]

---

[1] McKenzie v. Garrison, 10 Rich. L. 234. And see Brandon v. Rogers, id. 9.
[2] Adams v. Alexander, 1 Ired. L. 501.
[3] Spear v. Wardell, 1 N. Y. 144; Wood v. Bolard, 8 Paige, 556, 557.
[4] R. S. (8th ed.), p. 2495.
[5] Ibid. See Mills v. Argall, 6 Paige, 576; Whitcomb v. Fowle, 7 Abb. N. C. 275. See *ante*, p. 90.
[6] Mansf. Dig. (1884), §§ 4843, 4844.
[7] Rev. Code (1874), p. 358.
[8] R. S. (1887), § 3281.
[9] McClain's Am. Code (1888), § 3351.
[10] Gen. Stats. (1887), ch. 82, § 10, p. 977.
[11] Pub. Gen. Stats. (1888), p. 1076, § 15.
[12] R. S. (1881), p. 327, § 17.
[13] G. S. (1891), ch. 653, § 20.
[14] G. S. (1885), §§ 9, 10.
[15] R. S. (1877), p. 808.
[16] Act 89, ch. 36, § 15.
[17] Comp. Laws (1887), § 4089.

Rhode Island,[1] Pennsylvania,[2] South Carolina,[3] South Dakota,[4] Tennessee,[5] Texas,[6] Virginia,[7] West Virginia,[8] Wisconsin,[9] Wyoming.[10]

§ 136. **Restrictions on the Right of Corporations to Prefer.**— A corporation, like an individual, may prefer its creditors in or by an assignment of its property;[11] but in some of the states this right has been subjected to material restrictions by statute.[12] Thus in New York, where an individual debtor's right to give preference is unquestioned, it has been provided by statute on the subject of moneyed corporations, after declaring that no conveyance, assignment or transfer, not authorized by a previous resolution of its board of directors, shall be made by any such corporation of any of its real estate, or of any of its effects exceeding the value of one thousand dollars,[13] "that no such conveyance, assignment or transfer, nor any payment made, judgment suffered, lien created or security given by any such corporation when insolvent or in contemplation of insolvency, with the intent of giving a preference to any particular creditor over other creditors of the company, shall be valid in law; and every person receiving by means of any such conveyance, assignment, transfer, lien, security or payment any of the effects of the corporation shall be bound to account therefor to its creditors or stockholders or their trustees, as the case shall require."[14]

§ 137. **Restrictions on the Right of Corporations to Prefer — "Insolvency."**— The language of the ninth section of the statute, just cited, has been made the subject of much discussion in several cases in the courts of this state.[15] In the case of Gillet v. Phillips,[16] in the court of appeals, it was said that " when a moneyed corpo-

[1] P. S. (1882), ch. 136, § 10.
[2] Purd. Dig. (1883), p. 1072, §§ 22, 23.
[3] G. S. (1881), § 1306.
[4] Comp. Laws, § 4084.
[5] M. & V. Code (1884), §§ 2418, 2419.
[6] Sayles' S. C. (1888), art. 3461.
[7] Code (1887), § 2874.
[8] Code (1891), pp. 720, 721.
[9] S. & B., C. & S. (1889), §§ 1719, 1720.
[10] R. S. (1887), § 4085.
[11] Blalock v. Kernersville Mfg. Co., 110 N. C. 99; 14 S. E. Rep. 501. And may prefer its officers. Id.
[12] See Appendix, I.
[13] 2 Rev. Stat. (7th ed.), p. 1366, § 8.
[14] 2 Rev. Stat. (7th ed.), p. 1366, § 9.
[15] See Bowery Bank Case, 5 Abb. 415; s. c., 16 How. Pr. 56; Matter of Empire City Bank, 10 How. Pr. 498; Brouwer v. Harbeck, 9 N. Y. 589; Curtis v. Leavitt, 15 N. Y. 9; Gillet v. Phillips, 13 N. Y. 114; Johnson v. Bush, 3 Barb. Ch. 207.
[16] 13 N. Y. 114.

ration was insolvent, in such a sense that all its debts cannot probably be discharged from its assets, the payment of any one creditor in full is a preference within the meaning of the statute."[1] But it was in the later case of Curtis v. Leavitt,[2] in the same court, that the language of the same section received the fullest consideration, and the meaning of the terms "insolvency," "contemplation of insolvency" and "intent of giving a preference" was considered at much length in the course of the opinions delivered. "The term insolvency," it was said, "can mean nothing less than the inability of the company and the inadequacy of its property to pay its debts, and not a present inability to pay in cash or its equivalent."[3] "The insolvency intended by the statute was an actual or absolute insolvency, by which is meant an inability of the company to pay all its debts from its own property."[4] "A contemplation of insolvency is where the debtor, having full knowledge of his embarrassed circumstances, has no hope or expectation of relief, and anticipates an entire failure in business and absolute insolvency; or when his circumstances are such that any prudent man, taking a reasonable view of his situation and of the surrounding circumstances, might at the time fairly expect insolvency to follow."[5] The result arrived at by the court was that "notwithstanding the fact of insolvency, according to any definition of the term, a conveyance by a moneyed corporation is not within the said ninth section unless made with *intent* to prefer a particular creditor over others. The intent to prefer is a fundamental fact which must be alleged and proved."[6] "From this it must follow," said Comstock, J., "that so long as the debtor corporation, notwithstanding the pressure of great embarrassments, entertains an honest expectation, in the exercise of a reasonable intelligence, of going on with its business and paying all its debts, its acts cannot be brought within the operation of this statute. While this expectation is entertained in sincerity and good faith it may lawfully secure a particular creditor or sell or pledge a portion of its assets to raise money to meet its necessities."[7] "The intent to give a preference," said Paige, J., "and either an actual insolvency or a contemplation of insolvency, must be proved as facts. The intent and the contemplation of insolvency may be proved either by direct evidence or

[1] Gardiner, C. J., id. 119, cited by Brown and Paige, JJ., in the case, *infra*.
[2] 15 N. Y. 9.
[3] Brown, J., id. 150. The learned judge cites 2 Bell's Com. 162, and Gillet v. Phillips, cited *supra*.
[4] Paige, J., id. 200. The learned judge goes into a critical examination of the meaning of the term, and gives various definitions.
[5] Paige, J., id. 203, citing Gibson v. Muskett, 8 M. & G. 158, 168.
[6] 15 N. Y. 10.
[7] 15 N. Y. 109. See the observations, Brown, J., id. 139.

inferred as the necessary consequence of other facts clearly proved. If insolvency is relied upon to defeat the securities, knowledge of the insolvency by directors of the company, or a belief by them that it existed at the time the securities were made, must be proved; for an intent to give a preference to particular creditors in fraud of all other creditors of the company cannot be conceived except as connected with a knowledge or belief that the company is insolvent or with a contemplation of its insolvency." [1]

It has been decided by the supreme court of this state that insurance companies are within the provision of the statute prohibiting preferences.[2]

§ 138. Restrictions on the Right of Corporations to Prefer — In New Jersey.—"Since the repeal of the 'Act to Prevent Frauds by Incorporated Companies,' and the failure to re-enact the provision of its second section in the present 'Revision' (of 1878), there exists no statutory prohibition against the preference of creditors by an insolvent corporation, except a preference by way of confessed judgment under the provision of section 80 of the act concerning corporations." In the case of Wilkinson v. Bauerle,[3] the New Jersey court of error and appeals uses the identical language above set forth, adding, however, that corporations and their officers may not divert the corporate property from the payment of debts, and that when such diversion charged is by a sale of corporate property to one of the directors taking part in the transaction as buyer and seller, it devolves on the directors to establish the good faith of the transaction, and that the sale produced the full value of the property. If not made in good faith, or if it did not produce the full value of the property, the directors taking part in the sales will be answerable to creditors for what was thus lost. This case is cited in Vanderpoel v. Gorman,[4] where such an assignment by a New Jersey corporation made in the state of New York was upheld, the learned judge stating that "under the law of New Jersey, in which state the corporation was created, its right to make an assignment of this nature seems to be established."

§ 139. Subjects of Preferences in Assignments. — In those states where preferences are not prohibited by statute it is well

---

[1] 15 N. Y. 198.
[2] Hill v. Reed, 16 Barb. 280; Hurlbut v. Carter, 21 id. 221.
[3] Wilkinson v. Bauerle, 14 Stewart, 635.
[4] Vanderpoel v. Gorman, Sheriff, New York Court of Appeals, January 7, 1894, Peckham, J.

settled that not only actual *creditors*, but *sureties* and *indorsers*, may be preferred by debtors in making assignments of their property.[1] Drawers and indorsers of what is termed "accommodation paper," being considered entitled to peculiar favor, are frequently provided for in this way. A debtor is also allowed to secure a creditor for future advances and responsibilities, as well as for existing claims and engagements, by an assignment to him in preference to other creditors.[2] Sureties liable on existing or even future responsibilities are as much entitled to indemnity and preference as creditors in the more strict sense of that term.[3] And a deed of assignment for the security of indorsers is valid, though no payments have been made by them at the time of its execution.[4] It seems that a wife's claim for dower may be preferred.[5]

In some of the states claims of various classes of employees for wages or salary are preferred by force of special statute.[6]

§ 140. **Personal Preferences.**—A preference also may not only be *personal*, but may be extended so as to cover particular demands, *whoever* may be the holder. Thus, where, among the preferred demands contained in a schedule annexed to an indenture of assignment, was "S. & T.'s draft (accepted by the debtors), for which they hold a mortgage of B. W.," etc., it was held that the trust was not personal to S. & T., but that the holders of the draft, to whom it had been indorsed before the making of the indenture, were entitled to the benefit of the trust.[7]

A debtor making an assignment may also include among preferred debts such as have been previously secured by either judg-

---

[1] Hendricks v. Robinson, 2 Johns. Ch. 283; affirmed on error, 17 Johns. 438; Cunningham v. Freeborn, 11 Wend. 240; Lansing v. Woodworth, 1 Sandf. Ch. 43; Duval v. Raisin, 7 Mo. 449.

[2] Hendricks v. Robinson, 2 Johns. Ch. 283. See Barnum v. Hempstead, 7 Paige, 568: *ante*, pp. 115, 116.

[3] Cunningham v. Freeborn, 11 Wend. 240.

[4] Duval v. Raisin, 7 Mo. 449.

[5] Miller v. Crawford, 32 Gratt. 277; Reiff v. Horst, 55 Ind. 42. See Reiff v. Eshleman, 52 id. 582.

[6] In New York, for instance, by Laws of 1884, ch. 328; Laws of 1886, ch. 283. See on the construction of these statutes, Richardson v. Herron, 39 Hun, 537; Burley v. Hartson, 40 id. 131; Blackington v. Goldsmith, 3 How. Pr. (N. S.) 77; Smith v. Hartwell, 1 N. Y. State Rep. 241. Such a statute exists in Pennsylvania. Act of April 22, 1854; Assigned Estate of Gitt, 13 Phil. 494; Re Sackett, 1 Luz Leg. Rep. 243. And in Wisconsin. Laws of 1883, ch. 349; Laws of 1885, ch. 48; Lang v. Simmons, 64 Wis. 525; Campfield v. Lang, 25 Fed. Rep. 128; Conlee Lumber Co. v. Ripon Lumber Co., 29 N. W. Rep. 285. As to other states, see Appendix, *post*.

[7] Ward v. Lewis, 4 Pick. 518. The court in this case say: "The parties were designating the *demands* which were to be paid in full and not the persons to whom payment was to be made," and cite Heilner v. Imbrie, 6 Serg. & R. 401.

ment or mortgage; and a provision for their payment will not render the assignment fraudulent and void.[1] But the creditors thus doubly secured are held bound in equity to resort to their previous security first, so as to give the other creditors provided for the benefit of the assigned fund.[2]

§ 141. **Modes of Giving Preferences in Assignments.**— Preferences may be given to creditors in a variety of forms; as by simply directing certain named creditors or designated debts to be first paid in full out of the proceeds of the assigned property, and the balance to be applied for the benefit of all the other creditors without distinction; or by formally dividing the creditors into numbered or designated *classes*, arranged in a certain *order*, and directing each class to be paid to the extent of the proceeds applicable for that purpose before the one immediately following.

§ 142. **Preferences, Absolute or Conditional.**— Again preferences may be given either *absolutely*, as by directing certain named creditors to be first paid, at all events; or *upon condition*, as by preferring such creditors as shall comply with certain requisitions named in the assignment. In regard to the latter species of preferences it has been said that a debtor having an unquestionable power of preference, of which he is the absolute master, may set his price upon it, provided it be not a reservation of part of the effects for himself or anything that would carry his power beyond mere preference;[3] and that a debtor may deprive the creditor who refuses to accede to the terms of his preference and postpone him to all other creditors.[4] A condition of preference frequently in-

[1] Strong v. Skinner, 4 Barb. 546; Kruse v. Prindle, 8 Oregon, 158.
[2] Besley v. Lawrence, 11 Paige, 581.
[3] Gibson, C. J., in Thomas v. Jenks, 5 Rawle, 221. And see Layson v. Rowan, 7 Rob. (La.) 1. But see Jackson v. Cornell, 1 Sandf. Ch. 348, 354.
[4] 2 Kent's Com. [534], 694. See Bellows v. Patridge, 19 Barb. 176. In this case the assignment preferred, in the third class of creditors, two notes made to one H. upon condition that H. accounted for certain collaterals. If he did not account for them, however, no portion of the assigned property was to be applied on those notes until all the residuary creditors were paid except B. The notes were then to be paid, and B.'s claim was to follow. In any event B. was to be paid last. It was held by the court that these provisions were nothing more than the exercise of the assignor's undoubted right to direct preferences, and to prescribe the order in which his debts should be paid, and did not render the assignment void. In the case of Spaulding v. Strong, 37 N. Y. 135; s. c., 38 N. Y. 9, preferences were given to such of the creditors as had already executed a conditional release on receiving fifty per cent. of their claims. If the preference had been conditioned on the release, the assignment would have been invalid under the decisions in Grover v. Wakeman, 11 Wend. 201; Hyslop v. Clarke, 14 Johns. 458. See also, to the same effect, Low v. Graydon, 50 Barb. 414; Powers v. Graydon, 10 Bosw. (N. Y.) 630. See Palmer v. Giles, 5 Jones' Eq. (N. C.)

serted in assignments is that which requires the creditors to exhibit their demands to the assignee within a specified period; and a condition of this kind has been sustained in New York.[1] Another condition of constant occurrence has been that which requires the creditors to *release* or agree to release their claims against the debtor, by becoming parties to the assignment itself where it contains a release, or by the execution of a separate instrument to that effect. Assignments containing both these species of condition have been adjudged to be valid in Rhode Island.[2] But the coercive power which such a condition obviously gives to the debtor has subjected it to much question, and where it is not regarded as illegal it is now usually viewed with disfavor.[3] A provision in an assignment postponing the payment of those creditors who should have made any cost or expense upon their claims until all the other creditors should be paid in full has been held to be fraudulent and void.[4] And as to conditions of preference generally, the inclination of the courts in most of the states is against them, as has already been shown in this chapter.

§ 143. **Future Preferences.**— It is a further rule on the subject of preferences that the debtor must declare such preferences *in the assignment* at the *time of executing it*, and he cannot reserve to himself or transfer to his assignee the right to declare future preferences, or to change the order of the preferences already given, or to give preferences at the assignee's discretion.[5] Assignments containing provisions to this effect have been repeatedly held fraudulent and void.[6] Thus, where an assignment contained a provision

---

75. In the case of Grant v. Chapman, 38 N. Y. 293, a provision preferring the amount found due in certain attachment proceedings, provided they were sustained and were a lien, was not regarded as rendering the assignment invalid, as being conditional or giving an illegal preference. See Haydock v. Coope, 53 N. Y. 68, 74.

[1] Ward v. Tingley, 4 Sandf. Ch. 476.

[2] Pearce v. Jackson, 2 R. I. 35. See Nightingale v. Harris, 6 R. I. 321; Sadlier v. Fallon, 4 id. 490; Allen v. Gardner, 7 id. 22.

[3] In Pennsylvania, by the act of April 16, 1849, a condition in an assignment for the payment of those creditors only who shall execute a release is declared to be a preference in favor of creditors and to be void. Laws of 1849, p. 664; Purdon's Dig., p. 22, pl. 3. The subject of stipulations for a lease, as a general condition in assignments, will be more fully considered in chapter XI.

[4] Marsh v. Bennett, 5 McLean, 117, 123.

[5] Sutherland, J., in Grover v. Wakeman, 11 Wend. 187; Boardman v. Halliday, 10 Paige, 223, 228; Sandford, A. V. C., in Van Nest v. Roe, 1 Sandf. Ch. 4; 2 Kent's Com. [532], 691, note; Van Vorst, J., in Kercheis v. Schloss, 49 How. 288.

[6] Barnum v. Hempstead, 7 Paige, 568; Boardman v. Halliday, 10 id. 223; Sheldon v. Dodge, 4 Denio, 217; Strong v. Skinner, 4 Barb. S. C. 546; Averill v. Loucks, 6 id. 470; Mitchell v. Stiles, 13 Pa. St. 306; Gazzam v. Poyntz, 4 Ala.

giving to the assignee a discretionary power to pay off or discharge a certain class of claims against the assignor, or certain small debts due from the latter, in preference to other debts provided for in the assignment, it was held void as against the creditors of the assignor, as being calculated to injure, delay and hinder creditors in the collection of their just debts.[1] So, where a debtor in failing circumstances made an assignment of all his property to trustees in trust, to apply the proceeds to the payment of certain preferred creditors, so far as should be necessary, and to apply the residue of the proceeds to the payment of his other creditors in such order of priority as the trustees should think proper, and if the fund was insufficient to pay all such debts, then to apply the same in payment of such part of such debts as the trustees should judge most just and equitable, it was held that the assignor could not legally delegate to the trustees the power to give preferences at their discretion, and that the assignment was fraudulent and void as to creditors who did not assent to the same.[2] So where an assignment providing for the payment of the debts of the assignor, according to several classes of preference, contained a provision that if any of the debts in the sixth class should become pressing, and the trustees should thereupon assume them, the debts so assumed should be preferred over similar debts in the prior classes, the assignment was held void as to non-assenting creditors.[3] And it is immaterial whether the right thus to declare or alter preferences is reserved by the express terms of the assignment, or only in effect and in substance; as through the medium of a power to the assignees to compound with certain creditors,[4] or a right to annex schedules at a future period. Accordingly, where an assignment directed the assignees to pay the debts specified in the schedules annexed thereto, according to the priority of the several schedules, and provided that such schedules should be made within sixty days and be annexed to and form part of the assignment, but did not prescribe what debts should be inserted in the respective schedules, or in what order they should be arranged therein, the preparation of such schedules being left entirely to the discretion of the assignors; and it appeared that such schedules had not been made out and annexed to the assignment previous to its execution, but that they were prepared by the assignors and annexed at some

---

374. An assignment which attempts to confer on the assignee power to declare future preferences, as to non-preferred creditors, in his discretion, is void. Moody v. Paschal, 60 Tex. 483.

[1] Barnum v. Hempstead, 7 Paige, 568, 571. See Morse v. Slason, 13 Vt. 296.
[2] Boardman v. Halliday, 10 Paige, 223.
[3] Sheldon v. Dodge, 4 Denio, 217.
[4] Wakeman v. Grover, 4 Paige, 23, 41.

subsequent time, it was held that the assignment was fraudulent and void.[1] But where an assignment providing for the payment of creditors in certain classes directed the assignee to pay as a third class such creditors as should present their claims within a certain time after notice to be given by him, it was held that this was not giving to the assignee a discretion as to performances, within the meaning of the rule established by the preceding cases.[2]

§ 144. **Preferences by Implication.**— A deed of trust for the benefit of creditors may have the effect of preferring certain debts by *implication* without any express words. Thus, where such a deed was made to secure certain creditors, for some of whose debts sureties were bound, and the deed directed the trustee so to dispose of the trust property that no surety in the said debts should suffer or be injured on account thereof, it was held that the debts for which sureties were bound were preferred debts, and to be first satisfied.[3]

§ 145. **Illegal and Fraudulent Preferences.**— Where a preference is privately given to one or more creditors over others, contrary to the principle and professed object of the deed of assignment itself, it is clearly fraudulent and void. This happens more frequently in cases of *deeds of composition* between a debtor and his creditors, in which the parties always profess to deal upon equal terms and are supposed to stand in the same situation.[4] In regard to these instruments, the rule has been established in England by numerous cases, that the secret or separate agreement between the debtor and one or more of the creditors, by which a greater advantage is secured to them than the others would have under the deed,[5] whether in the form of payment or security of the balance of their debts,[6] or of a greater sum than the deed purports to secure to all,[7] or of additional security, though for no great sum,[8] is a fraud upon the other creditors,[9] and is void not only in

---

[1] Averill v. Loucks, 6 Barb. S. C. 470; Kercheis v. Schloss, 49 How. Pr. 284.
[2] Ward v. Tingley, 4 Sandf. Ch. 476, 479.
[3] Miller v. Holcombe's Ex'r, 9 Gratt. 665.
[4] Best, C. J., in Britton v. Hughes, 5 Bing. 465.
[5] Mawson v. Stock, 6 Ves. Jr. 300.
[6] Spurrett v. Spiller, 1 Atk. 105; Middleton v. Lord Onslow, 1 P. Wms. 768; Jackson v. Mitchell, 13 Ves. Jr. 561; Jackson v. Lomas, 4 Term R. 166.
[7] Chesterfield v. Janssen, 2 Ves. 125; Lord Hardwicke, id. 156.
[8] Ex parte Sadler & Jackson, 15 Ves. Jr. 52; Leicester v. Rose, 3 East, 371.
[9] It is said to be a fraud both upon the debtor and the other creditors. Ex parte Sadler & Jackson, *ubi supra*. And see Jackson v. Mitchell, 13 Ves. Jr. 581. In Hagen's Appeal, 11 Weekly Notes of Cas. 86, it is held that where a creditor who has become a party to a composition deed, whereby he agrees in common with the other creditors to take the notes of the common debtor, payable at a future

equity but at law.[1] And the rule is the same whether tne agreement be voluntary on the part of the debtor, with the object of inducing the creditor preferred [2] or other creditors to agree to the composition; [3] or whether the preference be extorted by the creditor by holding out a threat of refusal to sign.[4] And in a case where a creditor refused to accede to the proposed composition until the debtor's brother agreed to supply him with coal equal in value to the residue of the debt, which agreement was unknown to the other creditors and was fully performed by the brother, it was held that the creditor could not recover upon the note given him for the amount of the composition.[5] The doctrine established by the preceding cases has also received the sanction of the courts in this country.[6]

The same rule against secret preferences has been applied in England [7] and the United States [8] to cases of deeds of trust for the benefit of creditors ratably where the creditors become parties or agree to release the debtor on receiving their proportion of the trust fund.[9]

day, for the amount of his claim, subsequently gives up said notes to the debtor and receives from him other and better security in lieu thereof, such action will not be deemed fraudulent as against the other creditors unless in pursuance of an agreement entered into with the debtor prior to or contemporaneous with the execution of the composition deed.

Where creditors have entered into a composition with their debtor after a general assignment for their benefit the assignment is thereby vacated and the property restored to the debtor. The assignee cannot thereafter seize such property. Where such creditors receive from the debtor an amount in excess of their share under the composition deed, it is no fraud upon subsequent creditors, and under a subsequent assignment they are entitled to their dividend on a new debt without accounting to subsequent creditors for the excess so received on their first debt. Guggenheimer v. Groeschel, 23 S. C. 274.

[1] Jackson v. Mitchell, *ubi supra;* Cockshott v. Bennett, 2 Term R. 763.
[2] Chesterfield v. Janssen, 2 Ves. 125.
[3] Buller, J., in Jackson v. Lomas, 4 Term R. 166; Bennett v. Ellison, 23 Minn. 242.
[4] Spurrett v. Spiller, 1 Atk. 105; Cockshott v. Bennett, 2 Term R. 763; O'Shea v. Tne Collier White Lead & Oil Co., 42 Mo. 397.
[5] Knight v. Hunt, 5 Bing. 432.
[6] Russell v. Rogers, 10 Wend. 473, 499; Breck v. Cole, 4 Sandf. S. C. 79. The latter case contains a good summary of the doctrines on this point. See Jaffray v. Steedman, 35 S. C. 33; 14 S. E. Rep. 632; Thompkins v. Hunter, 65 Hun, 441.
[7] Cockshott v. Bennett, 2 Term R. 763; Jackson v. Lomas, 4 id. 166.
[8] Smith v. Stone, 4 Gill & J. 310; Case v. Gerrish, 15 Pick. 49; Clark v. White, 12 Pet. 178; O'Shea v. The Collier White Lead & Oil Co., 42 Mo. 397. See Claflin v. Iseman, 23 S. C. 416, a; Dansby v. Frieberg. 76 Tex. 463; 13 S. W. Rep. 331; Carey v. Hess, 112 Ind. 398; 14 N. E. Rep. 235; Crossley v. Moore, 40 N. J. Law, 27; Laird v. Campbell. 92 Pa. St. 470; Nichols v. Wellings, 61 Hun. 601.
[9] The rule against secret preferences has been applied to cases of the direct transfer of property to the creditor preferred. Edrington v. Rogers, 15 Tex. 188; Hancock v. Horan, id. 507.

A secret agreement to prefer the creditor in case of insolvency of the debtor is fraudulent,[1] as is also a preference to a dormant partner.[2] An agreement to prefer one creditor, made after the signing of the composition, violates the spirit of the composition deed, and is a fraud upon the other signers thereof as much as if made before the signing.[3] Any unlawful consideration moving from the preferred creditor to induce the performance, or a consideration founded upon a *nudum pactum*,[4] may avoid the deed which gives it.[5]

[1] Smith v. Craft, 11 Biss. 340. See Assignment of Guyer, 69 Iowa, 585; 29 N. W. Rep. 876; Farwell v. Jones, 63 id. 316; Nat. Park Bank v. Whitmore, 104 N. Y. 297; 10 N. E. Rep. 524; 40 Hun, 499; O'Brien v. Greenbaum, 92 Cal. 104; 28 Pac. Rep. 214.

[2] Claflin v. Hirsch, 19 N. Y. Weekly Dig. 248.

[3] Zoebisch v. Von Minden, 47 Hun, 213; Foakes v. Beer, 9 App. Cas. 605.

[4] Marshall, C. J., in Marbury v. Brook, 7 Wheat. 856.

[5] Where under a composition agreement with the debtor all the creditors signed to the amount of about $4,000, except one whose claim was only $250, the court held that "The agreement was substantially and legally complied with, and the deed made in pursuance of it must be upheld." Fahey v. Clarke, 80 Ky. 613.

CHAPTER XI.

ASSIGNMENTS WITH SPECIAL PROVISIONS.

§ 146. Special Provisions — Use and Effect of.
147. Special Provisions Should be Avoided.

I. STIPULATIONS FOR THE RELEASE OF THE DEBTOR AS A CONDITION OF THE ASSIGNMENT.

148. Assignments with Releases, how Drawn.
149. Rule in England.
150. Rule in the United States.
151. Releases in Several of the States.
152. Releases — Alabama.
153. Releases — Arkansas.
154. Releases — Colorado.
155. Releases — Maine.
156. Releases — Maryland.
157. Releases — Massachusetts.
158. Releases — New York.
159. Releases — Pennsylvania.
160. Releases — Rhode Island.
161. Releases — Virginia — West Virginia — South Carolina — Vermont — New Hampshire.
162. Releases in Other States.
163. Stipulations for Release — Summary.
164. Stipulations for Release, Excluding Non-releasing Creditors.
165. Obligations to Stipulations for Releases.
166. Stipulations for Releases in Partial Assignments.

II. RESERVATIONS OF BENEFIT TO THE DEBTOR.

167. Reservations — General Rule as to.
168. Reservations of Property.
169. Trusts for the Assignor.
170. What Reservations Are Allowed.
171. Reservations or Exceptions of Property.
172. Stipulations for the Use of Property.
173. Stipulations for the Use of Property — Continued.
174. Reservations in Mortgages and Deeds of Trust.
175. Reservations of Surplus Moneys or Property.
176. Reservations of Surplus Moneys or Property in Preferential Assignments.
177. Resulting Trusts for Assignor.
178. Reservation with Stipulations for Releases, and Other Conditions.

III. APPROPRIATION OF ASSETS IN ASSIGNMENTS BY FIRMS AND THEIR MEMBERS.

179. Preference of Individual Creditors.
180. Preference of Firm Creditors.

IV. STIPULATIONS FOR THE CONTINUANCE OF ASSIGNOR'S BUSINESS.

§ 181. Assignor's Business May be Continued, When.
182. Assignor's Business May be Continued, When — Illustrations.

V. PROVISIONS RESPECTING THE TIME FOR EXECUTING THE TRUST.

183. Reasonable Time Allowed for Executing the Trust.
184. Reasonable Time, What.
185. Indefinite Postponement.

VI. LIMITATION OF TIME FOR CREDITORS TO BECOME PARTIES OR ASSENT.

186. Limitation Must be Reasonable — Illustrations.

VII. PROVISIONS RESPECTING THE SALE OF THE PROPERTY ASSIGNED.

187. Time of Sale.
188. Time of Sale — Discretion of Assignee.
189. Mode of Sale.
190. Terms of Sale — Power to Sell on Credit.
191. Prohibiting Sale on Credit.
192. Sale at Retail.
193. Implied Power to Sell on Credit.
194. Implied Power to Sell on Credit — Cases.

VIII. SPECIAL POWERS AND DIRECTIONS TO ASSIGNEES.

195. Power to Mortgage and Lease.
196. Power to Pay Insurance, Interest and Incumbrances.
197. Power to Employ Agents.
198. Power to Compound and Compromise Debts.
199. Notice to Creditors by Assignee.
200. Power to Defend Suits.

IX. STIPULATIONS FOR THE BENEFIT OF ASSIGNEES.

201. Assignee Liable for Misconduct of Others, When.
202. Provisions for Expenses and Services of Assignees.

X. RESERVATIONS OF POWERS TO ASSIGNORS.

203. Reservation of Power to Assignor Invalidates the Assignment.
204. Reservation of Power to Assignor Over Preferences.
205. Reservation of Power to Assignor Over Sales.

§ 146. Special Provisions — Use and Effect of.— Allusion has already been made to the simplest form of a deed of assignment for the benefit of creditors as being that where the debtor's property is unconditionally and unreservedly transferred to the assignee, with a general authority to the latter to receive, hold and dispose of it for the equal benefit of all the creditors. It has been a common practice, however, to introduce into these instruments *special clauses* of various kinds, tending to limit or modify their usual operation, such as conditions on which creditors are to have the benefit of them; reservations for the benefit of the assignor; provisions as to the time and mode of disposing of the property;

§ 147.] SPECIAL PROVISIONS SHOULD BE AVOIDED 195

and special directions to the assignee as to the manner of executing the trust. Some of these clauses are entirely within the admitted scope of the power which the law allows an assignor of directing the disposition of the property assigned; and are useful in practice as more clearly expressing the objects of the trust, and as defining for the greater convenience of the assignee the course of his proceedings, and the nature and extent of his duties and powers. Others are either of doubtful utility, or decidedly objectionable, as tending to give rise to questions affecting the validity or operation of the instrument; and, if not to be avoided, are at least to be inserted with care and caution. Others, again, have almost uniformly the effect of invalidating the assignment and defeating its object.

§ 147. **Special Provisions Should be Avoided.**— As a general rule it is not advisable to multiply special clauses of any description. If unusual, they always excite suspicion.[1] And even those of an ordinary character are to be inserted with great care, particularly in assignments which give preferences. "Every provision in a voluntary assignment," observed Sergeant, J., in Whallon v. Scott,[2] in allusion to this class of conveyances, "ought to be narrowly scanned and closely watched;" and the courts now almost uniformly act upon this principle. Even clauses directing an assignee to do what is *prima facie* his duty to do without them, sometimes give rise to suspicions.[3] And so many instances have occurred of

[1] Clauses which are unusual ought on that account alone to excite suspicion. Gaston, J., in Cannon v. Peebles, 2 Ired. L. 449, 455.
[2] 10 Watts, 237, 244.
[3] This was strongly illustrated in a New York case. It had been decided in this state that an *authority* expressly given to an assignee to *sell* the assigned property *on credit* avoided the assignment which contained it. Barney v. Griffin, 2 N. Y. 365; Whitney v. Krows, 11 Barb. 198. In Van Rossum v. Walker, 11 Barb. 237, the assignment contained a clause (framed, perhaps, with reference to the previous decision) expressly *prohibiting* the assignee from selling on credit. The assignment was assailed on this very ground as furnishing evidence of fraud, and the court so far regarded the objection as to hold that such a provision was not *per se* evidence of fraud. The following remarks of Edwards, J., explain the ground of the decision: "It is well settled that, as a general rule, it is the duty of the assignee to dispose of the assigned property at once; and that when it can be done consistently with the interests of the parties it should be sold for cash. The question then arises whether a specific direction to the assignee to do what is *prima facie* his duty is *per se* evidence of fraud. It may be that such a provision is an unwise one and one that ought not to be countenanced, and where there are any circumstances which go to show that a forced sale was intended, to the injury of the creditors, it ought to be taken into consideration as an important item of evidence, which, in connection with the other circumstances, would justify this court in setting aside the assignment. But it seems to me that this is all the effect which should be given to such a provision." And see Whitney v. Krows, *ubi supra*. It has since been determined that such

assignments being declared fraudulent and void on account of a single provision, supposed by the draughtsman to be, at most, of a harmless character, that the drawing of a valid assignment has come to be regarded by some as a matter of no small difficulty and hazard. This difficulty was dwelt upon by counsel in the argument of the case of Litchfield v. White,[1] in the superior court of the city of New York, and the remarks of Mr. Justice Sandford in reply so well explained the grounds of it and how it may be avoided, that they are inserted here as an apt conclusion to the prefatory observations which have just been made. "The whole difficulty consists in the insertion of clauses beyond or varying the necessary provisions for transferring the debtor's property and appropriating it to the payment of his debts. We have never heard of a case, nor do we believe there has ever been one decided in this state, in which an assignment has been held fraudulent which simply vested the debtor's estate in trustees, and directed them to convert it into money and apply it absolutely and without reserve to the payment of his debts, whether equally among all the creditors or with preferences. But so long as failing debtors will make assignments containing provisions directly or indirectly for their own benefit, to the detriment of their creditors, or vesting in assignees the power of giving preferences, or excluding creditors who will not release the debtor, or exempting the assignee from his proper legal responsibility to those for whom he is to act, or otherwise deviating from the direct appropriation of the assets to the payment of debts, so far as they can be reasonably secured and applied — so long it will be the duty of the courts to pronounce such assignments fraudulent whenever they are presented for adjudication."[2]

The most important of these special provisions, together with their effect, as exemplified by cases decided in the courts, will now be considered.

a clause does not invalidate the assignment. Grant v. Chapman, 38 N. Y. 293; Carpenter v. Underwood, 9 N. Y. 520. See Work v. Ellis, 50 Barb. 512.

[1] 3 Sandf. S. C. 545.

[2] 3 Sandf. S. C. 554, 555. In the case of Ogden v. Peters, 21 N. Y. 23, Mr. Justice Comstock made the following observations: "An assignment drawn precisely as it ought to be will not undertake to speak to the assignee in regard to his duties under the trust. Those duties, unless the creditors themselves direct otherwise, are simply to convert the estate and pay the debts in the order and with the preferences indicated in the instrument. A trustee is always bound by any restrictions contained in the writing which creates the trust, and if these are inconsistent with the rights of creditors the trust itself must fall to the ground." And see remarks of Mr. Justice Selden to the same effect in Dunham v. Waterman, 17 N. Y. 9.

I. STIPULATIONS FOR THE RELEASE OF THE DEBTOR AS A CONDITION OF THE ASSIGNMENT.

§ 148. Assignments with Releases, how Drawn.— Assignments are sometimes drawn with a stipulation for a *release of the debtor* as the condition of receiving the benefit of the deed; or, in other words, making it a condition that the creditors shall accept the provision made for them in full satisfaction and discharge of their demands. Such a stipulation is in some cases introduced as a condition of receiving *any* benefit under the assignment, non-releasing creditors being wholly excluded; in others, as a condition of *preference* over other creditors provided for; and in others as a condition of sharing in the *surplus* remaining after payment of creditors who are preferred absolutely; and it is sometimes united with a provision expressly reserving the shares of non-releasing creditors to the assignor himself.[1]

§ 149. Rule in England.— In England a stipulation in an assignment for the release of the debtor, as a condition of receiving the benefit of the deed, has been held valid even against a claim of the crown,[2] and such stipulations continue to be inserted in the forms now in use.[3] In the case of Jackson v. Lomas[4] there was a proviso to the assignment that in case any creditor should not execute the trust deed, which contained among other things a release of the debts by a given day, he should not be entitled to the benefit of it, and his share was to be paid back to the debtor. "It seems to have been assumed throughout that case," observes Chancellor Kent, "that such a provision would not affect the validity of the assignment."[5] It was, in fact, held void on another ground.

§ 150. Rule in the United States.— In the United States there is no uniform rule on the subject. In some of the states assignments with stipulations for a release have been sustained to the full length of wholly excluding non-releasing creditors; in others they have been adjudged valid only so far as they operate to postpone non-releasing creditors to others. In other states they have been pronounced void under all circumstances.

§ 151. Releases in Several of the States.— The rulings in the different states upon the law of releases in assignments have been

[1] On the question discussed under this subdivision, see Bump on Fraudulent Conveyances, ch. XV.
[2] King v. Watson, 3 Price (Exch.), 6.
[3] See the case of Janes v. Whitebread, 20 L. J. C. P. (N. S.) 217; s. c., 5 Eng. L. & Eq. 431; Forbes v. Limond, 4 De G., M. & G. 298.
[4] 4 Term R. 166.
[5] 2 Kent's Com. [534], 693.

so frequently conflicting that for the use of the practitioner a summary of most of the leading cases is given in the following sections.

§ 152. Releases—Alabama.— In Alabama they were at one time held valid to the extent of excluding non-releasing creditors,[1] but in later cases this principle has been strongly condemned;[2] and more recently a stipulation for a release, coupled with an express reservation of the residue to the grantor in case of non-release, has been held to render the assignment fraudulent and void.[3] But if the debtor assigns all his property and retains no control over it, and stipulates for no share of the proceeds to result to himself, such a stipulation will be sustained.[4]

§ 153. Releases — Arkansas.— In Arkansas, in the case of Clayton v. Johnson,[5] it was held that a stipulation for a full release from the accepting creditors was not fraudulent, the assignment being of all the property, and no statute interfering. But in the late case of Collier v. Davis a contrary doctrine was established and Clayton v. Johnson expressly overruled.[6]

§ 154. Releases — Colorado.— In Colorado[7] a condition in the assignment requiring creditors to release the assignor from all claims before receiving any benefits under the assignment, and the surplus returning to the debtor and not to the non-releasing creditors, renders the deed fraudulent and void.

§ 155. Releases — Maine.— In Maine before the act of April 1, 1836, stipulations for a release in assignments were judged valid.[8]

[1] Robinson v. Rapelye, 2 Stew. 85.
[2] Ashurst v. Martin, 9 Port. 566; Gazzam v. Poyntz, 4 Ala. 374; Wiswall v. Ticknor, 6 id. 179; Smith v. Leavitts, 10 id. 92.
[3] Grimshaw v. Walker, 12 Ala. 101. See West v. Snodgrass, 17 id. 549. In this case the assignment provided that the preferred creditors were not to enjoy its benefit unless they accepted of its provisions in full satisfaction of their debts; and if any of them should refuse to accept they should be excluded, and the *pro rata* share to which they would have been entitled, had they accepted, should be paid to another specified creditor. It made no provision as to the disposition of any surplus that might remain, in the event that all the preferred creditors should refuse to accept, after paying the debt of the residuary creditor. It was held by the court to be fraudulent and void upon its face.
[4] Rankin v. Lodor. 21 Ala. 380. This is laid down by Phelan, J., as a "settled legal proposition in this state." Id. 389.
[5] 36 Ark. 406, citing numerous cases; Dodd v. Martin, 15 Fed. Rep. 338.
[6] 47 Ark. 397; 58 Am. Rep. 758; 1 S. W. Rep. 684.
[7] Duggan v. Bliss, 4 Colo. 223. See Rasmussen v. State Nat. Bank, 11 Colo. 301; 18 Pac. Rep. 28.
[8] Fox v. Adams, 6 Greenl. 245; Canal Bank v. Cox, 6 id. 395; Todd v. Buckman, 2 Fairf. 41.

But under that act it was decided that assignments containing such stipulations were illegal.[1] And it was further held that a clause of release embodied in an assignment was inoperative and void; and that a creditor who had executed the assignment was not precluded from repudiating it, though he might have received several partial payments under the assignment.[2] In the United States district court of Maine, an assignment with a stipulation for a release as a condition of participating in the fund, the surplus resulting to the assignor, was held fraudulent.[3] But under the act of March 21, 1844, chapter 112, amending that of 1836, and now the law of the state, a debtor may require a release from creditors who become parties to the assignment and shall forever discharge him from their claims on his making oath that he has assigned all his estate, real and personal, for their benefit.

§ 156. Releases — Maryland.— In Maryland, under statute, stipulations for a release, in assignments of all the debtor's property, as conditions of preference, have been sustained.[4] But the assignment must, on its face and by its terms, convey all the property of the grantor, and unless it does so it is void, no matter whether it does in fact convey all his property or not.[5] And when it is made by partners it must convey all their property, as well their individual estate as their partnership effects.[6] The whole estate must be surrendered for the benefit of the creditors, and a direction to the assignee to pay over to the grantor the balance remaining after satisfying creditors who execute releases will invalidate the assignment;[7] and a failure to provide in express terms for the

[1] Pearson v. Crosby, 23 Me. 261; Wheeler v. Evans, 26 id. 133.
[2] Vose v. Holcombe, 31 Me. 407.
[3] The Brig Watchman, Ware, 232.
[4] McCall v. Hinckley, 4 Gill, 128. The trusts in this case were, first, to pay in full certain creditors absolutely; second, to appropriate the residue among such of the creditors as should within ninety days assent to the assignment and execute a full release; third, out of the residue, if any, to pay all the other creditors; with a reservation of the ultimate surplus to the grantors. And see Kettlewell v. Stewart, 8 Gill, 472, where the assignment was of a similar character. In Hollins v. Mayer, 3 Md. Ch. Dec. 343, a trust deed directing the shares of non-releasing creditors to be held subject to the future order and control of the grantor was held valid. But see Peters v. Cunningham, 10 Md. 554.
[5] Rosenberg v. Moore, 11 Md. 376; Barnitz v. Rice, 14 id. 24; Farquharson v. Eichelberger, 15 id. 63; Green v. Trieber, 3 id. 11; Sangston v. Gaither, 3 id. 40; Coakley v. Weil, 47 id. 277; Maennel v. Murdock, 13 id. 164. But a reservation of the surplus to the grantor after the payment of releasing creditors makes the deed void on its face. O'Connell v. Ackerman, 62 id. 337.
[6] Insurance Co. v. Wallis, 23 Md. 173; Maughlin v. Tyler, 47 id. 545; **Loney v.** Bayly, 45 id. 447; Malcolm v. Hodges, 8 id. 418.
[7] Bridges v. Woods, 16 Md. 101; Green v. Trieber, 3 id. 11; Hollins v. **Mayer,** 3 Md. Ch. 343.

disposition of this surplus among the non-releasing creditors will be equally fatal.[1]

§ 157. Releases — Massachusetts. — In Massachusetts there have been several cases before the supreme court where the assignments contained stipulations for a release of the debtor; but there seems to have been no decision made in that court fully to the point upon the abstract question of the validity of such stipulations. In the case of Halsey v. Whitney,[2] in the circuit court of the United States, Mr. Justice Story observed that the point appeared not to have met with any direct decision; and so far as the cases examined by him went, they were considered as leaving the question *in equilibrio*.[3] The learned judge, in deciding the case before him, in which he upheld such a stipulation, expressed himself as yielding to what he considered to be the weight of general authority in its favor, though the inclination of his own mind, had the question been new, would have been the other way. In Borden v. Sumner,[4] Parker, C. J., spoke of the question as not then having been decided in the supreme court of the state; and in several subsequent cases in which questions arose upon assignments containing stipulations for a release this question was not raised.[5] In the case of Nostrand v. Atwood,[6] however, the point was expressly made, the assignment being objected to on the ground that it contained such a stipulation, which, it was said, operated compulsorily upon the creditors, and prescribed such conditions for the benefit of the assignors as would render the whole assignment fraudulent and void in law. The assignment was sustained by the court, the stipulation being regarded as wholly immaterial to the rights of the plaintiffs in the case, as there was no property transferred for their benefit. But Dewey, J., who delivered the opinion, observed that it was wholly unnecessary "to pronounce any opinion upon the abstract question of the effect of the introduction into an assignment of a stipulation for a release by the creditors who become parties to it, in a case where such a stipulation might be prejudicial to a creditor

---

[1] Whedbee v. Stewart, 40 Md. 414; Malcolm v. Hughes, 8 id. 418. See Nat. Bank v. Lanahan, 60 id. 479.

[2] 4 Mason, 206, 229.

[3] The cases of Widgery v. Haskell, 5 Mass. 144; Ingraham v. Geyer, 13 id. 146; and Harris v. Sumner, 2 Pick. 129, were considered as inclining against the validity of the stipulation; and those of Hatch v. Smith, 5 Mass. 42, and Hastings v. Baldwin, 17 id. 552, as going in its support.

[4] 4 Pick. 265.

[5] Andrews v. Ludlow, 5 Pick. 28; Lupton v. Cutter, 8 id. 298; Gloucester Bank v. Worcester, 10 id. 529; American Bank v. Doolittle, 14 id. 123. As late as the cases of the Brig Watchman, Ware, 232, and Grover v. Wakeman, 11 Wend. 187, the question was regarded out of the state as an open one.

[6] 19 Pick. 281.

indisposed to assent thereto, and who might thus be deprived of receiving his share of the fruits of the assignment."[1] It is to be observed that the opinion in this case was adapted to the state of the law when the assignment was executed, which was prior to the statute of 1836.

§ 158. Releases — New York.— In New York the law is to be considered as definitely settled against the validity of assignments containing a stipulation for the release of the debtor, whether as a condition of receiving *any* benefit under the assignment or only as a condition of *preference*. The following is a brief review of the cases:

In Hyslop v. Clarke[2] the assignment was in trust, first, to satisfy a debt due to a particular creditor; second, to pay all the other creditors ratably on condition of their discharging the assignors from all liability to them; and in case the creditors, or any of them, should refuse to give such discharge, then the last-mentioned trust was to cease and the trustees were directed not to execute it; third, in case of such refusal of the creditors, or any of them, to give such discharge, then in trust (after paying the first-mentioned creditor) to pay the whole of the avails of the property to *such of the creditors as the assignors should appoint* as soon as such refusal should be known; fourth, to pay the surplus, in any event, to the assignors. The assignment was held by the supreme court to be void; the stipulation for a discharge being considered coercive in its character, and the provision reserving to the assignors the right to declare a new trust being viewed as an attempt to retain the power to give future preferences, and, until such new trust should be declared, creating in effect a trust for the assignors themselves.[3]

In Austin v. Bell[4] the assignment was in trust[5] to pay all the debts of the grantors specified in a schedule annexed, in which the creditors were arranged in six classes, giving preferences according to the classes; provided that the said several creditors should, before a day specified, become parties to the assignment (which contained a

---

[1] 19 Pick. 284. The rule established by the decisions in Massachusetts is considered by the learned authors of the Notes to American Leading Cases as favoring the validity of these stipulations. 1 Am. Lead. Cas. (Hare & Wall. Notes), 100 [72, ed. 1857].
[2] 14 Johns. 458.
[3] See the opinion of Van Ness, J., 14 Johns. 462, 463.
[4] 20 Johns. 442.
[5] The assignment, before declaring this trust, contained certain reservations of moneys for the support of one of the assignors and his family for a limited time, and which, on the authority of Murray v. Riggs, 17 Johns. 571, was adjudged valid; though on this point, as we shall see hereafter, the decision of the court has since been overruled.

release of all their demands) by executing the same; and upon the further trust that in case any of the said creditors should not, within the time limited, become parties to the assignment, then the grantees (or assignees) should *pay to the grantors* the proportion of such of the creditors as should neglect or refuse to execute the assignment. The court declared the assignment invalid; considering it to be a stronger case of legal fraud than that of Hyslop v. Clarke, as it gave to the assignors themselves the absolute disposal of the shares of those creditors who should refuse to execute the assignment, to apply them to their own use or to pay to their creditors, as they pleased. It was pronounced to be "not only an attempt to coerce creditors, and to place the property beyond their reach on execution," but to be "the reservation of property which ought to have been devoted to the payment of their debts to their own private benefit and use."[1]

In Seaving v. Brinkerhoff,[2] in the court of chancery, the assignment was of certain real estate in trust for the benefit of all the creditors who should prove their debts, but upon condition that each creditor "should seal and deliver a full and complete discharge of his demand." The chancellor held this provision to be rigorous, coercive and unjust; on the ground, however, that it was an assignment of only a part of the debtor's property. This case will be referred to again in the course of this chapter.

In Wakeman v. Grover,[3] in the same court, the assignment was in trust, first, to pay certain preferred creditors of the first class; secondly, to pay to such creditors of the second class as should, within a specified time, agree in writing to receive such proportion of their debts as could be paid out of the surplus avails of the assigned property, after paying the preferred creditors, in full discharge of their debts; thirdly, to apply the residue to the payment of the creditors of the third class, and all other debts of the assignors; and lastly, to pay the residue, if any there should be, to the assignors. The court held the assignment to be fraudulent and void; and, on error to the court of errors,[4] the decision of the chancellor was sustained. It will be seen that this case goes farther than any of the previous cases, laying down the rule broadly, that the requirement of a release from any of the creditors, and as a consideration of preference merely, without any direct reservation of the share of the non-releasing creditors to the assignor himself, avoids the assignment.

[1] Spencer, C. J., 20 Johns. 450.
[2] 5 Johns. Ch. 329.
[3] 4 Paige, 23.
[4] Grover v. Wakeman, 11 Wend. 187.

In Armstrong v. Byrne,[1] in the same court for the first circuit, the trust of the assignment was to divide the proceeds of the assigned property among the creditors ratably, on condition of their releasing the balance of their debts; excluding non-releasing creditors from all benefits, and directing the shares of the latter to be equally divided among such of the creditors as should accept of the composition. The vice-chancellor declared the assignment void for fraud upon the face of it; pronouncing it to be an attempt to coerce creditors into the debtor's own terms, which was against the policy of the law, and vitiated the assignment entirely.[2]

In Lentilhon v. Moffatt,[3] in the same court, the assignment was of part of the debtor's property in trust for all his creditors, and to be paid to them ratably, as they should respectfully execute under their hands and seals a full release and discharge of their respective debts, claims and demands against him, with a proviso that unless all the creditors should accept of the assignment within sixty days, the debtor should have power to appoint so much of the proceeds as might not be accepted by the creditors to be paid to *such creditors as he might think proper;* and that the said appointment should take effect and go into operation either at the expiration of the said sixty days, or as soon as such nonacceptance could be ascertained. The vice-chancellor held the assignment to be void, as being an attempt to place the debtor's property beyond the reach of his creditors unless they should agree to accept of it upon the terms proposed; and so, in effect, hindering and delaying creditors.

In the subsequent case of Mills v. Levy,[4] in the same court, the trusts of the assignment were first, to sell, collect debts, etc.; second, to pay certain preferred debts in full; third, to pay ratably, as far as the proceeds would go, certain debts specified, and all other creditors who should, within six months, agree to release the debtors; fourth, out of the residue to pay ratably such creditors as might not within the six months agree to release. And, in case none of the creditors referred to in the third and fourth trusts should agree to give such release within the period limited, then the assignees were to apply the proceeds which might remain after satisfying the first and second trusts to the payment, so far as they would extend, of all the creditors ratably. On a bill filed to overthrow the assignment as fraudulent, on the ground of its trust tending to delay, hinder or defraud creditors, the vice-chancellor decided against its validity, principally on the authority of the case

[1] 1 Edw. Ch. 70.
[2] 1 Edw. Ch. 80.
[3] Id. 451.
[4] 2 Edw. Ch. 183.

of Burrall v. Leslie,[1] then lately decided by the chancellor, in which an assignment containing similar trusts was held fraudulent and void.[2]

But where certain creditors had executed a conditional release on payment of fifty per cent. of their claims, and the debtors failed to comply with the terms of the release, and afterwards executed a general assignment by which they preferred, first, certain confidential creditors; secondly, the creditors who had executed the conditional release, and then directed that the residue of the creditors be paid, this assignment was not regarded as coming within the rule of Wakeman v. Grover, inasmuch as the preference to the releasing creditors was absolute, and there were no terms to be agreed to, and no conditions to be fulfilled.[3] The creditors were not to be paid *if* they would consent to the compromise, but because they *had* agreed to it.

§ 159. Releases — Pennsylvania. — In Pennsylvania the law was at one time settled in favor of the validity of these stipulations to their fullest extent. In the early case of Burd v. Smith,[4] in the

---

[1] Reported in 6 Paige, 445; but the point of the invalidity of the assignment is not noticed in the report. It appears, however, from a copy of the chancellor's order, given in the note to Mills v. Levy, 2 Edw. Ch. 187. The case of Grover v. Wakeman was relied on in the argument before the vice-chancellor, but was not examined by the court, the report of the case not having then been published.

[2] And see the observations of Sandford, A. V. C., in Jackson v. Cornell, 1 Sandf. Ch. 348, 354; and of Selden, J., in Dunham v. Waterman, 17 N. Y. 9. But a release may be stipulated for in a different form. Thus where, by an arrangement between a debtor and a portion of his creditors, the former assigned his property to trustees in trust for his creditors generally, and the trustees, in consideration of the assignment, and pursuant to the arrangement, personally bound themselves to the debtor to procure for him a release and discharge from all his creditors, except certain ones who were specified, it was held that the assignment was not conditional or partial, or liable to the objection of being intended to coerce a release from the creditors. Hastings v. Belknap, 1 Den. 190. Mr. Justice Parker, in the case of Strang v. Spaulding, 38 N. Y. 12, remarks: "The law is undoubtedly well settled that such assignments (in which creditors are preferred *on condition* of their subsequently executing releases of their respective demands) are *mala fide* on their face, and void as against creditors." And see Mr. Justice Fullerton, to the same effect, in the same case, 37 N. Y. 139; and Mr. Justice Monell, in Powers v. Graydon, 10 Bosw. 659. See, also, Chadwick v. Burrows, 42 Hun, 39.

[3] Spaulding v. Strang, 37 N. Y. 135; s. c., 38 N. Y. 9; rev'g s. c., 36 Barb. 310; s. c., 32 Barb. 235; Low v. Graydon, 50 id. 414; Powers v. Graydon, 39 id. 548; s. c., 25 How. Pr. 512; Renard v. Graydon, 39 Barb. 548; s. c., 25 How. Pr. 178. See remarks of Savage, C. J., in Hone v. Henriquez, 13 Wend. 243.

[4] 4 Dall. 76, sometimes cited as "Burd v. Fitzsimmons." This case is generally considered to have involved the point of a release of the debtor. Walworth, C., in Wakeman v. Grover, 4 Paige, 23, 39. But one of the justices, in delivering his opinion, said there was no stipulation in the deed for a release in favor of the grantor. Coxe, J., 4 Dall. 92.

high court of errors and appeals, the trustees of the assignment were to dispose of the property and distribute the proceeds ratably among such creditors as should agree, in writing, to accept the same within nine months, and to pay to the assignor the proportion of all such creditors as should not signify their acceptance within the time. The court (two judges dissenting) declared the assignment invalid. But in Lippincott v. Barker,[1] where the assignment was of the debtor's property to trustees for the benefit of such creditors as should, within four months, execute a general release of all demands, after elaborate argument the deed was held valid.[2] In Pearpoint v. Graham,[3] where the same question arose, it was held by Mr. Justice Washington, in affirmance of the same doctrine, that an assignment in trust for the benefit of such creditors as should release their debts was founded upon a sufficient consideration in law. So in the cases of Cheever v. Imlay,[4] Wilson v. Kneppley,[5] Sheepshanks v. Cohen,[6] Bayne v. Wylie,[7] and Mechanics' Bank v. Gorman,[8] assignments containing stipulations for a release were adjudged valid. In the case of Brashear v. West[9] the supreme court of the United States considered the decisions in Lippincott v. Barker and Pearpoint v. Graham as embodying the settled construction of the Pennsylvania statute of frauds on the subject of assignments, and, in accordance with those decisions, pronounced an assignment valid which excluded all creditors from participating in its benefits who should not, within ninety days from its date, execute a release of all claims and demands. In Livingston v. Bell[10] an assignment in trust for the payment of debts

[1] 2 Binn. 174. It is to be observed that in this case the assignment was first submitted to the creditors of the assignors at a general meeting, which all but one or two attended, and was accepted by them. A doubt was raised in the case whether assignments made without the privity of creditors, and excluding all who do not execute releases, are valid on general principles.
[2] In Wakeman v. Grover, 4 Paige, 23, 39, Walworth, C., after citing the case of Burd v. Fitzsimmons [Smith], said it was not intended to be overruled by Lippincott v. Barker. But the Pennsylvania judges have held otherwise. See In re Wilson, 4 Barr, 430, 441, Coulter, J. And see the explanation given by Tilghman, C. J., and Yeates, J., in Wilt v. Franklin, 1 Binn. 515, 522. In Austin v. Bell, 20 Johns. 442, 450, Spencer, C. J., pronounced the case of Burd v. Smith to be expressly in point.
[3] 4 Wash. C. C. 232. See Brockley v. Brockley, 122 Pa. St. 1; s. c., 15 Atl. Rep. 646.
[4] 7 Serg. & R. 510.
[5] 10 Serg. & R. 439.
[6] 14 Serg. & R. 35.
[7] 10 Watts, 309.
[8] 8 Watts & S. 304.
[9] 7 Pet. 608.
[10] 3 Watts, 198.

was held good, although it contained a provision excluding all creditors who should not execute a release, and directing the payment to the assignor of the surplus that might remain after satisfying the creditors provided for. In the later case of Lee's Appeal[1] it was held that the right to stipulate for a release was not taken away by the Pennsylvania act of April 17, 1843, "to prevent preferences in assignments," and that under that act non-releasing creditors were not entitled to dividends under an assignment in trust for such creditors as should release.[2] But, to make the assignment good in any of these cases, it was uniformly held that it must be of *all* the debtor's property and effects, without reserving, either expressly or by the effect of the assignment, any portion of the effects for the debtor.[3] According to the present law of Pennsylvania, as established by the act of April 16, 1849, section 4, any condition in an assignment of property made by debtors to trustees, on account of inability at the time of the assignment to pay their debts, within the meaning of the act of April 17, 1843, for the payment of the creditors only who shall execute a release, is required to be taken as a preference in favor of such creditors, and is declared void, and the assignment is to be held and construed to inure to the benefit of all the creditors in proportion to their respective demands.

§ 160. Releases — Rhode Island. — In Rhode Island stipulations in general assignments, as conditions of preference, have always been allowed.[4] And it has been further held that an assignment of all the debtor's property for the benefit of creditors, with preferences in favor of certain creditors, and with a provision that no creditor shall receive any dividend or profit from the assignment except upon the condition that he execute a discharge in full of all his claims, and that the dividends of the creditors who refuse such a discharge shall result to the assignor, is valid.[5] But this is al-

---

[1] 9 Barr, 504.
[2] But in the case of Seal v. Duffy, 4 Barr, 274, it was said in argument, and allowed by the court, that clauses for a release were, in effect, expunged by the act of 1843. See the observations of Gibson, C. J., id. 275. In the case of In re Wilson, 4 Barr, 430, however, the assignment contained such a stipulation, to which no objection was made, though it was held void on other grounds.
[3] Thomas v. Jenks, 5 Rawle, 221; Hennessy v. The Western Bank, 6 Watts & S. 300; In re Wilson, 4 Barr, 430; Fassitt v. Phillips, 4 Whart. (Pa.) 399. See *ante*, p. 159, note 4.
[4] See Angell on Assignments, 112.
[5] Dockray v. Dockray, 2 R. I. 547; Haydock v. Stanhope, 1 Curt. 471; Nightingale v. Harris, 6 R. I. 321; Sadlier v. Fallon, 40 id. 490; Allen v. Gardner, 7 id. 22. See Beckwith v. Brown, 2 R. I. 311. An assignment provided that the

lowed only in cases free from fraud. In a case in the United States circuit court for the Rhode Island district,[1] an assignment made by a debtor who had absconded to a foreign country, carrying with him a large sum of money, and which contained a stipulation for a release as a condition of obtaining a preference under the assignment, was held to be fraudulent and void as to creditors.

§ 161. Releases — Virginia — West Virginia — South Carolina — Vermont — New Hampshire. — In Virginia assignments containing stipulations for a release of the debtor, and wholly excluding non-releasing creditors from the benefit of the trust, have been held valid.[2] And the same doctrine has been maintained in West Virginia[3] and South Carolina.[4] In the latter state, however, it has been held that an express reservation of the surplus to the grantor would be fraudulent.[5] In Vermont, before the act of November 1, 1843, prohibiting general assignments, stipulations for a release as conditions of preference were held valid.[6] So in New Hampshire before the act of July 5, 1834, conditions of release were valid.[7] But since that act, which provides for an equal distribution of assigned property, they are considered fraudulent.[8]

§ 162. Releases in Other States. — In Ohio,[9] North Carolina,[10]

dividends of such creditors as did not execute a release within three months from the date of the assignment should be paid to the assignors. Certain creditors exhausted their remedy at law against the assignors and filed a bill to establish a lien on the dividends of such non-releasing creditors in the hands of the assignee. Held, that they were entitled to the relief claimed. Smith v. Millett, 12 R. I. 59. See s. c., 11 id. 528.

[1] Stewart v. Spencer, 1 Curt. 157.
[2] Skipwith's Ex'r v. Cunningham, 8 Leigh, 271; Kevan v. Branch, 1 Gratt. 274; Pearpoint v. Graham, 4 Wash. C. C. 232. But this is only where all the debtor's property is conveyed. But this need not appear on the face of the deed. Gordon v. Cannon, 18 Gratt. 387. And where two or three partners conveyed all the effects of the firm and their individual property and the third had none, a stipulation requiring a release, both of the firm and all the members, by the creditors who accepted the deed was sustained. Gordon v. Cannon, *supra*. And see 2 Tuck. Com. [442], 431. See Phippen v. Durham, 8 Gratt. 457.
[3] Clark v. Figgins, 27 W. Va. 654.
[4] Aiken v. Price, Dudley, 50; Niolon v. Douglas, 2 Hill Ch. 443; Le Prince v. Guillemot, 1 Rich. Eq. 187; Pfeifer v. Dargan, 14 S. C. 44.
[5] Niolon v. Douglas, 2 Hill Ch. 443; Jacot v. Corbett, 1 Cheves' Ch. 71; Claflin v. Iseman, 23 S. C. 416.
[6] Hall v. Denison, 17 Vt. 410. But see the act of November 14, 1855, requiring all assignments to be for the benefit of all the creditors in proportion to their respective claims. Laws of 1855, p. 15.
[7] Havens v. Richardson, 5 N. H. 113.
[8] Hurd v. Silsby, 10 N. H. 108.
[9] Atkinson v. Jordan, 5 Ohio, 178; 5 Ham. 293; Woolsey v. Urner, Wright N. Pri. (Ohio), 606; Barrett v. Reids, id. 701.
[10] Hafner v. Irwin, 1 Ired. L. 490.

Mississippi,[1] Missouri,[2] Georgia,[3] Texas,[4] Tennessee[5] and Florida,[6] the courts have adopted the principle established by the New York decisions.[7]

In Connecticut[8] and Illinois[9] the requirement of a release as a condition of participation in the fund assigned, the surplus resulting to the assignor, has been held to be fraudulent and to avoid the deed; but the cases in these states have not decided the question whether a release being made a condition of preference merely is fraudulent.[10] In Indiana a stipulation for a release in an assignment not embracing all the debtor's property has been held to avoid the assignment.[11] In the same case the court expressed a

---

[1] Robins v. Embry, 1 Sm. & M. Ch. 208; Mayer v. Shields, 12 Rep. 759. See Seale v. Vaiden, 10 id. 831. In Mayer v. Shields, 59 Miss. 107, it is held that whether an assignment which exacts from creditors releases in full as a condition of receiving dividends is valid or not, one which fixes no time within which they must make their election is void.

[2] Brown v. Knox, 6 Mo. 302; Drake v. Rogers, id. 317. An assignment professing to be for the benefit of all the creditors whether named or not, although reciting by way of consideration the release of some of the creditors, but containing no stipulation that those only who release shall share in the benefits of the assignment, does not fall within the rule which avoids assignments containing stipulations for the release of the debtor. Jeffries v. Bleckman, 86 Mo. 350.

[3] Miller v. Conklin, 17 Ga. 430. In this case an assignment by a firm in insolvent circumstances of all their assets, for the use and benefit of such creditors as should within ninety days file their claims with the assignee and release the firm from all liability therefor, was held to be illegal and void as against objecting creditors. See McBride v. Bohanan, 50 Ga. 527; Lay v. Seago, 47 id. 82; Johnson v. Farnam, 56 Ga. 144; Francis v. Herz, 55 id. 249; Cohen v. Summers, 54 id. 501.

[4] Carlton v. Baldwin, 22 Tex. 724; Baldwin v. Peet, 22 id. 708: Bayne v. Denny, 1 Tex. App. Civ. Cas. 460; s. c., 13 Rep. 542; Boyd v. Haynie, 83 Tex. 7; 1 S. W. Rep. 156; Turner v. Douglass, 77 id. 619; 14 S. W. Rep. 221; Baylor County v. Craig, 69 id. 330; 6 S. W. Rep. 305.

[5] Wilde v. Rawlings, 1 Head (Tenn.), 34.

[6] Greeley v. Dixon, 21 Fla. 412; Sperry v. Gallagher, 77 Iowa, 107; 14 N. W. Rep. 586.

[7] 1 Am. Lead. Cases (Hare & Wall. Notes), 100 [72, ed. 1867]. See the argument of counsel in Livermore v. Jenckes, 21 How. (U. S.) 133, 143.

[8] Ingraham v. Wheeler, 6 Conn. 277. This was before the changes introduced by the statute of 1853.

[9] Howell v. Edgar, 2 Scam. 417; Ramsell v. Sigerson, 2 Ill. 78. In the case of Conklin v. Carson, 11 Ill. 503, where the assignment required creditors who should come in and receive dividends to release their demands, this provision was considered fraudulent, but an amendment of the obnoxious clause having been made by the parties and creditors the objection was removed. See Hardin v. Osborne, 60 Ill. 93.

[10] 1 Am. Lead. Cas., *ubi sup.*

[11] Henderson v. Bliss, 8 Ind. 100. So an assignment which required each creditor, upon payment of his *pro rata* share of the proceeds, to release his entire debt, was held fraudulent and void. Butler v. Jaffray, 12 Ind. 504. And see McFarland v. Birdsall. 14 id. 126.

strong inclination against the validity of these stipulations in general, but waived a decision of that question. In Michigan the question has been settled in accordance with the New York decisions.[1]

§ 163. **Stipulations for Release — Summary.**— It has been considered[2] that the weight of American authority was in favor of the validity of these stipulations upon general principles, and the decision in Halsey v. Whitney has been relied on as establishing such a proposition.[3] The only American authorities examined in that case were the decisions of the courts in Massachusetts, New York and Pennsylvania. The decisions in Massachusetts were admitted by the learned judge who delivered the opinion of the court to leave the question *in equilibrio*,[4] and the law was deemed to be settled in that state only by professional opinion, usage and practice.[5] The New York decisions were considered as inapplicable on the ground that they did not "turn upon the naked point of a release, but upon that as incorporated into a peculiar trust;"[6] and, so far as authority was concerned, the case appears to have been decided on the strength of the Pennsylvania case of Lippincott v. Barker,[7] the case of Pierpont v. Lord,[8] in the circuit court, and the English exchequer case of The King v. Watson.[9]

In Lippincott v. Barker it will be seen that the assignment had been formally accepted by the great majority of the creditors before it was acted upon, and Chief Justice Tilghman, in delivering

[1] Hubbard v. McNaughton, 43 Mich. 220. See the remarks of McLean, J., in Marsh v. Bennett, 5 McLean, 117, 128, 129. In this case an assignment containing a provision postponing the payment of such creditors as should commence or have commenced any legal proceedings for the recovery of their claims, until all the other creditors should have been paid in full, was held to be fraudulent and void as being made with an intent to coerce the creditors into a settlement on the debtor's own terms by embarrassing and delaying their remedy.
[2] Angell on Assignments, 114. Mr. Angell remarks that the general practice and the general current of authority in England are decidedly in favor of introducing such clauses into assignments, and refers to the principal books of precedents in conveyancing. See Bump on Fraud. Con., p. 433.
[3] Angell on Assignments, 105.
[4] 4 Mason, 230.
[5] "When we take into consideration the great length of time during which stipulations of this nature have prevailed in this state without objection, there is much reason to believe that the profession have deemed the law settled in favor of the debtor on this point." 4 Mason, 230. See the observations of Ware, J., in Lord v. The Brig Watchman, Ware, 232; of Sutherland, J., in Grover v. Wakeman, 11 Wend. 199, 200; and of Wright, J., in Atkinson v. Jordan, 5 Ohio, 178.
[6] 4 Mason, 230.
[7] 2 Binn. 174.
[8] 4 Wash. C. C. 232. So cited, the correct title being "Pearpoint v. Graham."
[9] 3 Price (Exch.), 6.

his opinion, expressly confined it to the circumstances of that particular case, observing that there were "many and strong objections to deeds of assignment made without the privity of the creditors and excluding all who do not execute releases."[1] The remaining American case of Pierpont v. Lord [or Graham] does not appear to have been very closely examined, and is in fact pronounced to be "not in point, but probably decided on the general principle." The English exchequer case of The King v. Watson was held to be decisive.

The weight of Mr. Justice Story's decision in Halsey v. Whitney is considerably affected by his own free admission that if the question had been new, and many estates had not been passed upon the faith of such assignments, the strong inclination of his own mind would have been against their validity.[2] The decision itself has been critically examined and its soundness upon principle questioned in several American cases.[3]

In the New York case of Grover v. Wakeman,[4] where the decision was fully discussed, and the English and American decisions reviewed, Mr. Justice Sutherland considered it doubtful on which side the preponderance of authority lay; but the decision in that case, and in the subsequent cases in the same state, already noticed, have clearly settled the rule against the validity of the stipulations in question; and the decisions in Ohio, Missouri, Alabama, Mississippi and Georgia have thrown great weight into the same scale.

In Brashear v. West,[5] it is true, the supreme court of the United States sustained an assignment containing a stipulation for a release; but this was done with marked reluctance,[6] and only because

---

[1] 2 Binn. 182. There was also a strong dissenting opinion by Breckenridge, J., in this case. See opinion of Walworth, C., in Wakeman v. Grover, 4 Paige, 23, 39, in which he quotes and relies on the earlier case of Burd v. Smith, 4 Dall. 76, as not intended to be overruled by Lippincott v. Barker. And see the opinion of Wright, J., in Atkinson v. Jordan, 5 Ohio, 178. But the Pennsylvania courts have held the contrary opinion. In re Wilson, 4 Barr, 430.

[2] 4 Mason, 230.

[3] See McCall v. Hinckley, 4 Gill (Md.), 228; Lord v. Brig Watchman. Ware, 232; Miller v. Conklin, 17 Ga. 430. And see White v. Winn, 7 Gill, 446.

[4] 11 Wend. 187.

[5] 7 Pet. 608; Marshall, C. J., id. 614; followed in Clayton v. Johnson, 36 Ark. 406.

[6] The objection that the deed excluded all creditors who should not within ninety days execute a release of all claims and demands was considered the most serious one in the case. The court admitted that the release was not a voluntary one, but was induced by the necessity arising from the certainty of being postponed to all those creditors who should accept the terms by giving the release. And of the objection to the deed on this ground, they say it "is certainly powerful in its tendency to delay creditors. If there be a surplus, this surplus is placed, in some degree, out of the reach of those who do not sign the release and thereby entitle themselves under the deed. The weight of this argument is felt."

the court felt itself bound by the construction which had been previously given by the courts of Pennsylvania to the statute of that state.[1] The assignment on which the question arose had been executed in Pennsylvania by a citizen of that state, and the court observe that its validity appears never to have been questioned there. But the inclination of the court is pretty clearly indicated by the expression of Chief Justice Marshall: "We are far from being satisfied that upon general principles such a deed ought to be sustained."

In the case of Marsh v. Bennett,[2] in the circuit court of the United States for the district of Michigan (June, 1850), the question as to the validity of these stipulations was not formally presented, but the court made use of the reasoning of the adverse cases in condemning a coercive stipulation of another kind. The opinion of Chief Justice Marshall in Brashear v. West was quoted, and the ground upon which the decision was placed referred to, with the observation that "the argument and expressed opinion of the chief justice on the point considered is adverse to the decision pronounced." After remarking that the question was still an open one in Michigan, the court proceed to quote the opinion and decision of Mr. Justice Story in Halsey v. Whitney, and seem to adopt his conclusion that the weight of authority was in favor of these stipulations, at least as law for the case when the question should arise.[3]

In the case of Stewart v. Spencer,[4] in the circuit court for the district of Rhode Island (June, 1852), the assignment contained a stipulation for a release as a condition of preference, but it had been made by a debtor who afterwards absconded to a foreign country, carrying with him a large sum of money. On this latter ground, and this only, the assignment was held fraudulent and void as to creditors. The court, following the law of Rhode Island, assumed to be settled law for the case, that a debtor might stipulate for a release by which his future earnings would be discharged; and cited Brashear v. West and Halsey v. Whitney; although, if such a stipulation was designed to be an instrument of fraud, it would avoid the deed.[5]

In his Commentaries on Equity Jurisprudence,[6] Mr. Justice Story appears to have still inclined in favor of his conclusion in Halsey v. Whitney; but his language is not more confident than

[1] Lippincott v. Barker and Pearpoint v. Graham were relied on.
[2] 5 McLean, 117.
[3] 5 McLean, 128, 129.
[4] 1 Curt. 157.
[5] 1 Curt. 162, 163.
[6] Vol. ii, ch. 28, § 1036.

in that case,[1] and the authorities cited are few.[2] Taking into consideration the opinion expressed by Chief Justice Marshall in Brashear v. West,[3] it seems probable that should a case be brought before the supreme court of the United States which could be decided on general principles and free from the controlling influence of state construction, the decision would be against the right to stipulate.[4]

§ 164. **Stipulations for Release, Excluding Non-releasing Creditors.**— So far as stipulations for a release are coupled with provisions cutting off from *all* participation in the assignment those creditors who refuse to accede to its terms, by reserving to the debtor himself the shares to which such creditors, had they agreed to release, would have been entitled, the weight of American authority may now be fairly pronounced to be against their validity.[5] And where, after opposition by creditors, a condition of release is sustained, equity will decree the surplus to the creditors who have not acceded to the deed.[6] But the rule is not so clearly settled against the validity of these stipulations, as conditions of *prefer-*

---

[1] "Even a stipulation on the part of the debtor, in such an assignment, that the creditors taking under it shall release and discharge him from all their further claims beyond the property assigned, will (it seems) be valid and binding on such creditors.

[2] Halsey v. Whitney, 4 Mason, 206; Spring v. South Carolina Ins. Co., 8 Wheat. 268; Pearpoint v. Graham, 4 Wash. C. C. 232; Brashear v. West, 7 Pet. 608; and Wheeler v. Sumner, 4 Mason, 183. But in Spring v. South Carolina Ins. Co. the point does not appear to have been made; and in Wheeler v. Sumner it is expressly said that the assignment contained no such stipulation. McClure v. Campbell, 71 Wis. 350; 37 N. W. Rep. 343, citing Nat. Bank v. Lanahan, 60 Md. 477.

[3] 7 Pet. 608.

[4] In the case of Livermore v. Jenckes, 21 How. (U. S.) 126 (1859), the supreme court of the United States sustained an assignment executed in Rhode Island, between citizens of that state, stipulating for releases; but the case went upon the point that the complainant's judgment creditors had not acquired a lien upon the property, the judgment having been obtained and execution issued in New York subsequent to the removal of the property from that state.

[5] 2 Kent's Com. [534], 693, 694, and note. See, also, Miller v. Conklin, 17 Ga. 430; Henderson v. Bliss, 8 Ind. 100; Sangston v. Gaither, 3 Md. 11; Bridges v. Wood, 16 id. 10 , Whedbee v. Stewart, 40 id. 414; Farrow v. Hayes, 51 id. 498; Malcolm v. Hodges, 8 id. 418; Hollins v. Mayer, 3 Md. Ch. Dec. 343; Wilde v. Rowlings, 1 Head (Tenn.), 34; Conkling v. Carson, 11 Ill. 503; Butler v. Jaffray, 12 Ind. 504; Carlton v. Baldwin, 22 Tex. 724; Baldwin v. Peet, 22 id. 708; Reavis v. Garner, 12 Ala. 661. But see Dockray v. Dockray, 2 R. I. 547; Heydock v. Stanhope, 1 Curt. 471; Gordon v. Cannon, 18 Gratt. 388; Nightingale v. Harris, 6 R. I. 321; Allen v. Gardner, 7 id. 22. And see Collier v. Davis, 47 Ark. 397; 1 S. W. Rep. 684; 58 Am. Rep. 758, *supra.*

[6] Brashear v. West, 7 Pet. 608; Vaughan v. Evans, 1 Hill Ch. 414; Vernon v. Morton, 8 Dana, 247; Skipwith's Ex'r v. Cunningham, 8 Leigh, 271, 275. But see Hollins v. Mayer, 3 Md. Ch. Dec. 343.

ence only, where the non-releasing creditors are left by the assignment to share in any surplus which may remain after the satisfaction of the others. In New York the decisions have indeed established the rule to this extent, but these have not yet been supported by the prevailing current of decisions in other states; and the general rule, as laid down by Chancellor Kent,[1] is in favor of the right of the debtor to prefer some of his creditors to others, through the medium and by the effect of such a stipulation.

§ 165. **Objections to Stipulations for Releases.**— The objections to the allowance of these stipulations in assignments to trustees are, first, that they operate by way of *coercing the creditors* into a relinquishment of part of their demands. "The debtor," observes Mr. Justice Story,[2] "surrenders nothing, except upon his own terms. He attempts to coerce his creditors by withholding from them all his property unless they are willing to take what he pleases to give, or is able to give, in discharge of their debts. This is certainly a delay, and, if the assignment be valid, to some extent a defeating of their rights." "If he can be allowed," says Vice-Chancellor McCoun,[3] "to lock up his property by means of such an assignment until the creditors comply with his terms, he can successfully delay, hinder and defraud his creditors." The force of this objection lies not in the mere circumstance of stipulating for terms with a creditor, but in so stipulating when the debtor's property is no longer accessible to the debtor's remedies. "If a debtor with his property in his own hands," observes Mr. Justice Sutherland,[4] "and open to the legal pursuit of his creditors, can satisfy them that it is for their interest, or the interest of any of them, to accept 2s. 6d. in the pound, and give him an absolute discharge, there is no legal objection to it; they treat upon equal terms; the ordinary legal remedies of the creditor are not obstructed. But the case is materially changed when the debtor first places his property beyond the reach of his creditors, and then proposes to them terms of accommodation."[5]

Another objection to assignments containing such a stipulation is that they operate to reserve to the *debtor himself* a material and substantial benefit as the direct result of the transfer; namely, an absolute discharge from his debts.[6] "The debtor," observes Vice-

[1] 2 Kent's Com. [534], 693, 694; Id. [536], 696, 697, note.
[2] In Halsey v. Whitney, 4 Mason, 206, 228.
[3] In Armstrong v. Byrne, 1 Edw. Ch. 79, 81.
[4] In Grover v. Wakeman, 11 Wend. 187, 201.
[5] And see, to the same effect, the observations of Assistant Vice-Chancellor Sandford, in Jackson v. Cornell, 1 Sandf. Ch. 338, 354. See, also, White v. Winn 8 Gill, 499.
[6] See the observations of Sutherland, J., in Grover v. Wakeman, 11 Wend. 187 201.

Chancellor McCoun,[1] "does not benefit himself by merely creating a preference of payment amongst his creditors; because he remains liable to the others until all his debts are paid; but if he stipulates for an absolute discharge before a creditor shall have the benefit of the property, he thereby assumes to himself a power over the creditors for his own personal advantage, namely, of being discharged from his debts by a payment of a part only."

A third objection to assignments of this character, not less forcible than either of the preceding, is that they are expressly designed to effect for the debtor a discharge from his liabilities on *better terms* to himself than *insolvent laws* allow to debtors who apply for their benefit. "The law of this state," observes Chancellor Walworth,[2] "does not recognize any right on the part of an insolvent debtor to an absolute discharge from his debts, although he may honestly and fairly make a cession of all his property to his creditors, to be applied to the payment of his debts equally or ratably. Much less does it recognize the right or the justice of such a discharge where he has singled out favorite creditors and devoted the mass of his property to the payment of the whole of their debts, leaving the rest of his creditors to come in for a share of the residue. In such a case he is barred from all relief under our insolvent laws, even if two-thirds of his creditors consent to his discharge. And without such consent his future earnings are, in all cases, liable for the payment of the balance of the debts, after his property has been fairly distributed among the creditors." Assignments of this character, indeed, secure to the assignor the full result of a *bankrupt law* in the absolute character of the discharge for which they stipulate, while at the same time they avoid complying with the essential requisite to a bankrupt discharge, namely, an entire and unconditional surrender of property; the debtor thus making, in the language of Chief Justice Parsons,[3] "a bankrupt law for himself."

§ 166. **Stipulations for Releases in Partial Assignments.**—What has been said thus far as to the validity of stipulations for a release in assignments by debtors is to be understood as applying exclusively to *general* assignments. In regard to *partial* assignments there is much more uniformity in the decisions, it being held, almost without exception,[4] that such a stipulation in an as-

---

[1] In Armstrong v. Byrne, 1 Edw. Ch. 79, 81.
[2] In Wakeman v. Grover, 4 Paige, 23, 38.
[3] In Widgery v. Haskell, 5 Mass. 144, 152. And see Thomas v. Jenks, 5 Rawle, 221, Gibson, C. J.; Miller v. Conklin, 17 Ga. 430, 432, 434, Starnes, J.; Henderson v. Bliss, 8 Ind. 100, 103, 104, Perkins, J.
[4] The rule in Massachusetts is considered to be an exception. 1 Am. Lead.

§ 166.] STIPULATIONS FOR RELEASES IN PARTIAL ASSIGNMENTS. 215

signment of part of the debtor's property is fraudulent.[1] The rule, to this extent, has been laid down in no state more strongly than in Pennsylvania, where such stipulations in general assignments were, previous to the statute, invariably sustained. Thus, in Thomas v. Jenks,[2] it was held that an assignment by partners of the partnership effects, and not of their separate property also, if it contain a condition that the creditors shall release ther claims against the assignors, individually and as copartners, is fraudulent and void. In Hennessy v. The Western Bank[3] it was held that an assignment by copartners, stipulating for a release, was not valid without containing a transfer of the separate property of each of the partners, though it might not appear affirmatively that a partner who omitted to execute the deed had separate property. In the subsequent case of In re Wilson[4] it was decided that a general assignment by two partners, stipulating for a release to themselves and a third partner, was fraudulent on its face, though the non-assenting partner had no estate but such as passed to the assignee. The opinion of the court was expressed by Mr. Justice Rogers in language peculiarly strong and emphatic.[5] In the still

Cases, 94, citing Nostrand v. Atwood, 19 Pick. 281. In the case of Stewart v. Spencer, 1 Curt. 157, Mr. Justice Curtis seems to have inclined to the opinion that an assignment of part of a debtor's property for the benefit of all his creditors, stipulating for a release, was not void by the law of Rhode Island. The language of the learned judge, after citing the New York and Pennsylvania cases, is as follows: "Although it is difficult to resist the force of some of the reasoning in these cases, I am not prepared to say that such a deed is necessarily fraudulent on its face. If the property not conveyed by the assignment is left within the reach of creditors, if no actual fraudulent intent by the debtor existed, and upon the whole case it appears that the instrument was not designed to aid any fraud, and could not so operate, because in point of fact no fraud was either practiced or intended, perhaps it would be going too far to say that under the laws of Rhode Island such an instrument would be void." Id. 166. The learned judge further expressed his opinion that "the only possible question as to the soundness of these decisions arises from the fact that they hold the presumption of fraud to be conclusive and refuse to look beyond the instrument." Id.

[1] Seaving v. Brinkerhoff, 5 Johns. Ch. 329; Skipwith's Ex'r v. Cunningham, 8 Leigh, 271; Green v. Trieber, 3 Md. 11; Sangston v. Gaither, id. 40; Clayton v. Johnson, 36 Ark. 406; Dodd v. Martin, 15 Fed. Rep. 338. And see *ante*, ch. X. The act of April 17, 1843, applies to partial as well as general assignments, and such assignments inure to the equal benefit of all creditors. Miner's National Bank Appeal, 57 Pa. St. 193.
[2] 5 Rawle, 221. And see Henderson v. Bliss, 8 Ind. 100.
[3] 6 W. & S. 300.
[4] 4 Barr, 430.
[5] See *ante*, p. 159, note 4. It was further said in this case (4 Barr, 449) that Thomas v. Jenks and Hennessy v. Western Bank introduced no new principle, but were nothing more than a correct application of a principle already settled in McAllister v. Marshall, 6 Binn. 338; Passmore v. Eldridge, 12 S. & R. 201; Adlum v. Yard, 1 Rawle, 173; Johnston's Heirs v. Harvey, 2 Pa. 92; and McClurg v. Lecky, 3 Pa. 83.

later case of Weber v. Samuel[1] the preceding cases were relied on; and it was held that an assignment by the members of a firm, purporting to convey merely the partnership goods and effects, with certain specific real estate, in trust for certain preferred creditors, and then in trust for such as should execute a release, while it contained no words of conveyance of the private or individual estate of either member of the firm, and did not even purport to convey all the real estate of the firm, was invalid.[2]

In Maryland the rule is established that an assignment for the benefit of creditors, exacting releases as the condition on which they may participate in the fund, must transfer all the debtor's estate, and this must appear affirmatively upon the face of the deed.[3]

In South Carolina an assignment of part of the debtor's property to such creditors as should release, the surplus to be divided among the creditors generally, where the existence of a residue was concealed by the debtor, has been considered to be fraudulent in fact;[4] and a reservation to the grantor of the surplus, after paying to releasing creditors forty per cent., if the estate would yield as much, was decided to be fraudulent.[5]

But in a case in Rhode Island, where the grantor preferred certain creditors by giving one class thirty per cent. and another fifteen, and turning the balance over to the general creditors, when it was plain that no interest would result to the grantor, the assignment was sustained.[6]

As regards the *manner* of stipulating, it is effected, on the part of the creditors, either by executing an assignment containing a release, or by executing a separate agreement to release.[7] The former is the usual practice. The particular form of the release to be given is sometimes prescribed in the assignment, and such a

[1] 7 Barr, 449.
[2] The objections to *conditional* assignments, in general, have been very forcibly expressed in Sutherland, J., in Grover v. Wakeman, and Gibson, C. J., in Thomas v. Jenks. The eminent judge last named observed in the case referred to: "It is difficult, at a glance, to reconcile the mind to the decisions in support of these conditional assignments in any case, or comprehend how a conveyance which puts the debtor's property beyond his creditor's reach, except on terms prescribed by himself, can be anything else than an act to 'delay, hinder and defraud,' within the purview of the 13 Elizabeth." And see the opinion of Gaston, J., in Hafner v. Irwin, 1 Ired. L. 490, 499, 500.
[3] Sangston v. Gaither, 3 Md. 40; Green v. Trieber, id. 11; Rosenberg v. Moore, 11 id. 371; Barnitz v. Rice, 14 id. 24; Farquharson v. Eichelberger, 15 id. 63; Insurance Co. v. Wallace, 23 id. 173; Coakley v. Weil, 47 id. 277; Maennel v. Murdock, 13 id. 164; Maughlin v. Tyler, 47 id. 545; Loney v. Bayly, 45 id. 447.
[4] Le Prince v. Guillemot, 1 Rich. Eq. 187.
[5] Jacot v. Corbet, 1 Cheves' Ch. 71; Claflin v. Iseman, 24 S. C. 416.
[6] Nightingale v. Harris, 6 R. I. 321.
[7] This was the form in Ludwig v. Highley, 5 Barr, 132.

provision has been held valid.[1] It is necessary, also, to specify a time within which the release is to be executed;[2] and this period must be a reasonable one,[3] neither too long[4] nor too short;[5] otherwise the assignment will be considered fraudulent.[6]

The deed should in such cases give to the creditors all the information in the power of the debtor as to the nature and value of the property conveyed, and the amount of the debts intended to be provided for, in order to enable the creditors to determine whether they will accept or reject the assignment.[7]

II. RESERVATIONS OF BENEFIT TO THE DEBTOR.

§ 167. **Reservations — General Rule as to.** — In the largest sense of the term "reservation," comprehending any benefit secured to the debtor, immediately or ultimately, by implication or in express terms of the instrument, this division may be considered to include not only the previous head of "stipulations for a release," but most of the provisions which form the subject of the present chapter. But the reservations now proposed to be considered are those which are directly made to the debtor by express provisions for the purpose.

"When a debtor fails," it has been well observed,[8] "his property, in moral justice, belongs to his creditors." Assignments of his property, therefore, considered as modes of provision for creditors, should in all cases be, actually and to the full extent, what (as usually designated) they profess to be — for the *benefit of the creditors*, and not for the benefit of the *debtor himself*, at their expense. Hence, it is a settled general rule in American law, that a clause or provision in an assignment by which any benefit or advantage is reserved to the debtor at the expense of the creditors, whether such benefit be temporary or permanent, whether it be in the shape of payment of a gross or annual sum, employment at a compensation or otherwise, and whether reserved to the debtor himself or

---

[1] Bayne v. Wylie, 10 Watts, 309.
[2] Pearpoint v. Graham, 4 Wash. C. C. 232; Henderson v. Bliss, 8 Ind. 100; 2 Kent's Com. [533], 693.
[3] In Halsey v. Whitney six months was held not to be an unreasonable time. Nine months has been considered too long. Burd v. Smith, 4 Dall. 76. The unreasonableness of the period of limitation will depend on circumstances. 2 Kent's Com. [533] 693, note *a*. Ninety days is a common period.
[4] Pearpoint v. Graham, 4 Wash. C. C. 232.
[5] Fox v. Adams, 5 Greenl. 245; Ashurst v. Martin, 9 Porter, 566.
[6] 2 Kent's Com. [533], 693. And see *post*, V, in this chapter.
[7] Gordon v. Cannon, 18 Gratt. 387.
[8] Savage, C. J., in Mackie v. Cairns, 5 Cow. 547, 580.

for the support of his family, is a fraud in law, and vitiates and avoids the whole assignment.[1]

§ 168. Reservations of Property.— Thus, in the case of Means v. Dowd,[2] it was held that an insolvent debtor making an assignment cannot reserve to himself the beneficial interest in the property assigned, or interpose any delay or make any provision which would hinder or delay creditors.

In Massachusetts, where the assignment contained a reservation to the debtor, in the form of an agreement that the trustees might pay the sum of $1,000, or a certain proportion of it, in a certain event, it was held void on this account.[3] So, in New York, where several assignments had been made, all subject to the trust to pay to the assignor, for the support of himself and family, at the rate of $2,000 per annum for a limited time, they were held void *in toto* as being a fraud upon creditors.[4] And in the same state it was held that retention of money, amounting to about one per cent. of the total assets, by a firm for living expenses prior to making an assignment, is not conclusive evidence of fraud.[5] But in another case[6] it was held that where unusually large sums were drawn out by one of the assignors for household expenses, other large sums were paid out of the firm assets to several of the assignors, and to the wife of the first-named assignor, and falsely charged on the

---

[1] Rogers, J., in McClurg v. Lecky, 3 Penr. & W. (Pa.) 83, 91, 93; Ingraham v. Grigg, 13 S. & M. 22, 27; Claflin v. Iseman, 23 S. C. 416; Mackie v. Cairns, 5 Cow. 547; Harris v. Sumner, 2 Pick. 129; Richards v. Hazard, 1 Stew. & P. 139; Bronson, J., in Goodrich v. Downs, 6 Hill (N. Y.), 438, 439. "To say that an insolvent debtor can put any portion of his property not exempt by law beyond the reach of creditors for his own benefit is a monstrous proposition." Id. And see Gazzam v. Poyntz, 4 Ala. 374. A debtor cannot stipulate in the deed for any benefit to himself. He has no right to make such a reservation at the expense of his creditors and with intent to defraud them. Stokes v. Jones, 18 id. 734, 737. And see Sheppards v. Turpin, 3 Gratt. 373; Leadman v. Harris, 3 Dev. 144; Byrd v. Bradley, 2 B. Mon. 239; Henderson v. Downing, 24 Miss. 106; Green v. Trieber, 3 Md. 11; Waldron v. Wilcox, 13 R. I. 518. In Cheatham v. Hawkins, 76 N. C. 335, it is said: "An assignment cannot cover up and preserve the property for the debtor's use or protect it from the remedies and demands of the creditors. Here is not only a retention of possession by the assignor, which is presumptive evidence of fraud, but there is the further power to dispose of it for the debtor's benefit, and still more, the exercise of that power annihilates the thing itself. We have, then, one of the strongest cases of presumptive fraud."

[2] 128 U. S. 173; 9 S. Ct. 793.

[3] Harris v. Sumner, 2 Pick. 129.

[4] Mackie v. Cairns, Hopk. Ch. 373; 5 Cow. 547. So a *sale* of land by one indebted at the time, in consideration of supporting his family, is fraudulent and void as to creditors. Jackson v. Parker, 9 Cow. 73.

[5] Fay v. Grant, 53 Hun, 44; 5 N. Y. S. Rep. 910.

[6] Rothschild v. Salomon, 52 Hun, 486; 5 N. Y. S. Rep. 865.

books as a loan returned to her, the assignment and whole proceeding were void.

So, in Pennsylvania, where a debtor conveyed his property to his sons, in trust to pay off certain judgments, and then to maintain the grantor and his wife as long as they should live, and the rest of his family until they should be able to maintain themselves, the deed was held to be fraudulent and void as against creditors.[1] And it is immaterial whether such reservation for the debtor or his family be expressed on the face of the assignment or not, or whether it is made in a direct or indirect form. Thus, in Pennsylvania, an assignment of all the debtor's property, with an understanding that part of the property assigned should be reconveyed to trustees for the benefit of the debtor's family, was held, so far as respected that part of the property, to be fraudulent and void as to all creditors who did not assent to the arrangement, though the assenting creditors' claims might exceed the amount of the property assigned; and the dissenting creditors might take it in execution.[2] And where a debtor executed an assignment of all his estate and effects (being a certain factory and machinery, etc.), and an agreement was entered into between him and his assignees, by which they agreed to employ him as agent in conducting the business, and to allow one-third of the profits for his support and that of his family; and it was further agreed that in case of the death of the assignor, or of his being otherwise prevented from managing the factory, another agent was to be employed by the assignees, who was to be paid a reasonable salary out of the third of the profits allowed to the assignor, it was held in the same state that the stipulation rendered the assignment fraudulent and void.[3]

So, in Tennessee, it was held that a trust deed giving preferences to certain creditors, and stipulating that the business of merchandising is to be carried on for two years and three months, that the stock of goods is to be replenished from the proceeds of sale of the goods, and that the assignee is to be retained to assist in the management of the business, is void on its face.[4] So, in New York, an understanding, though not expressed in the assignment, that the assignee should allow to the assignor a weekly sum for his services,

[1] Johnston's Heirs v. Harvey, 2 Penr. & W. (Pa.) 82.
[2] McAllister v. Marshall, 6 Binn. 338.
[3] McClurg v. Lecky, 3 Penr. & W. (Pa.) 83. But where a debtor made an assignment of his personal property to a creditor, and at the same time made a distinct agreement with the creditor for the employment of his apprentices, whose wages were to be paid to the debtor, it was held that, as the contract was collateral to the assignment, and afforded the only mode by which the wages of the apprentices could be reached on execution, the assignment was not on that account void. Faunce v. Lesley, 6 Barr, 121.
[4] Lowenstein v. Love, 16 Lea (Tenn.), 658.

the same being nominal, was held to be evidence of fraud.[1] In North Carolina, where a debtor, upon being applied to by a *bona fide* creditor to secure him by a deed of trust on his property, refused to secure any part of the debt unless the creditor would transfer one-half to a trustee for the benefit of the debtor's wife and children; and that the half so transferred should also be secured by such deed; and the creditor, though reluctantly, consented, it was held that this was tantamount to a reservation by the debtor himself of so much of his property for the use of his wife and children, and was therefore fraudulent and void as against other creditors.[2]

In Minnesota,[3] where the debtors (partners), on the eve of assignment, each took $600 from the firm's moneys for the support of their families, it was held not to show a fraudulent intent.

But in Maine[4] it was decided that a debtor's conveyance of all his property to secure the maintenance of himself and wife was fraudulent as against existing creditors.

In Virginia, where an assignment contained a stipulation that the debtor should be allowed to have possession of the assigned property for sixteen months, and should be considered the agent of the trustee, with full power and authority to sell or dispose of any of it, it was, for this and other reasons, held fraudulent on its face.[5] And in Mississippi, where a deed, besides extending the time of payment for five years, contained a stipulation that the family expenses of the grantors should be paid out of the product of the property conveyed before payment of any part of the debts, it was held to be void upon its face.[6]

So, in Kansas, where the assignment made provision for the payment of a claim in which, by previous arrangement, the assignor

---

[1] Currie v. Hart, 2 Sandf. Ch. 353.

[2] Kissam v. Edmonston, 1 Ired. Eq. 190. The reason of the doctrine on this point is well expressed by Ruffin, C. J., who delivered the opinion of the court in this case. A creditor may, out of a debt due to him, or any property belonging to him, give a bounty to the family of his debtor, or to the debtor himself; but it must be a voluntary act, not coerced by the debtor, nor made the price of any favor or preference by the debtor towards such creditor. It must be independent of any arrangement between the debtor and creditor at the time or as a part of the contract to convey the property. Id. 183.

[3] In re Shotwell, 43 Minn. 389; s. c., 45 N. W. Rep. 842.

[4] Graves v. Blondwell, 10 Me. 190.

[5] Spence v. Bagwell, 6 Gratt. 444. But in the later case of Dance v. Seaman, in the same state (11 Gratt. 778), where a deed of trust was not to be enforced for two years, and the profits were in the meantime reserved to the grantor, the possession also remaining with him, it was held to be not fraudulent *per se*, though made without the knowledge of the creditors. See the observations on the case of Spence v. Bagwell, by Allen, P., 11 Gratt. 783.

[6] Henderson v. Downing, 24 Miss. 106, 117. And see Johnson v. Thweatt, 18 Ala. 741; Montgomery v. Goodbar, 69 Miss. 333.

had an interest, this was such a secret reservation for the benefit of the assignor as to render the assignment void.¹ And in another case in the same state, where the assignment by its terms reserved to the assignors $800 worth of the property assigned, to be afterwards selected by the assignors themselves, was held to be void upon its face.²

But the fact that an assignment contemplates that the planting operations of the debtors shall be continued for the current year under their supervision, and that future advances to continue such operations shall be made by a creditor, is not inconsistent with an absolute unconditional appropriation of the property to the payment of debts; nor is it, in effect, a reservation for the use of the debtor.³

§ 169. **Trusts for the Assignor.**— The general rule on the subject of these reservations for the benefit of assignors (and which is one of the most important in the whole law of voluntary assignments) may be very comprehensively expressed in the language of the decision in Mackie v. Cairns,⁴ viz.: that an insolvent debtor can make no assignment of any part of his property *in trust for himself*.⁵ And this rule is so rigidly enforced in New York that an assignment containing such a trust is held void, not only for the portion reserved, but for the whole.⁶ And even a distinct security, such as a judgment, intended to come in aid of an assignment which contains such a provision, is, by the effect of such connection, rendered void also.⁷ And in Goodrich v. Downs⁸ it was held

---

¹ Kayser v. Heavenrich, 5 Kan. 324. Same doctrine confirmed, Grocery Co. v. Records, 40 Kan. 119; 19 Pac. Rep. 346.

² Clark v. Robbins, 8 Kan. 574.

³ Perry Ins. & Trust Co. v. Foster, 58 Ala. 502. See Commercial Bank v. Brewer, 71 id. 574.

⁴ 5 Cow. 547, 548. See Kingman, C. J., in Kayser v. Heavenrich, *supra;* Roosevelt, J., in Nichols v. McEwen, 17 N. Y. 22; Selden, J., in Jessup v. Hulse, 21 N. Y. 168.

⁵ Id.; Goodrich v. Downs, 8 Hill (N. Y.), 438; Shaffer v. Watkins, 7 W. & S. 219; Greed v. Trieber, 3 Md. 11; Hoopes v. Knell, 31 id. 550; Banks v. Clapp, 12 Ga. 514; Wheeler, J., in Wright v. Linn, 16 Texas, 34, 42. And see *post,* ch. XXV.

⁶ Mackie v. Cairns, 5 Cow. 547.

⁷ Mackie v. Cairns, 5 Cow. 547; reversing on this point the decision of the court below. D'Ivernois v. Leavitt, 23 Barb. 63, 64. Where the debtor authorized the assignees to use a judgment previously confessed by him, to secure them against contingent liabilities as his sureties, for the purpose of perfecting title to his real estate, declaring all that should be realized from the real estate should be assets in the hands of the trustees to be distributed according to the terms of the assignment, but he did not assign his statutory right of redeeming the land from a sale on the judgment, or his right to the rents and profits before the expiration of the period of redemption, held, that this was not such a reservation of property as vitiated the assignment. Dow v. Platner, 16 N. Y. 563.

⁸ 6 Hill (N. Y.), 438. But see Curtis v. Leavitt, cited *infra*.

that where, on a trial before a jury, an assignment shows *on its face* that it was made in trust for the use of the assignor, either in whole or in part, the court is bound to pronounce the transaction void, without submitting the question to the jury. So in Pennsylvania a fraudulent trust of this kind avoids the assignment *in toto*, and the property which is made the subject of it is held to remain in the debtor, liable to the execution of those creditors who have not assented to the assignment.[1]

In New York it has been expressly provided by statute that "all deeds of gift, all conveyances, and all transfers or assignments, verbal or written, of goods, chattels, or things in action, made in trust for the use of the person making the same, shall be void as against the creditors, existing or subsequent, of such person."[2] And similar provisions have been enacted in other states.[3] The New York statute (which has been recently termed "the statute of personal uses," and "the personal statute of uses")[4] was expressly relied on in the case of Goodrich v. Downs as the ground of the decision. But in the case of Curtis v. Leavitt,[5] in the New York court of appeals, it was held that this statute applied only to conveyances wholly or primarily for the use of the grantor, and not to instruments for other and active purposes, such as to secure debts or procure money on loan, where the reservations are incidental and partial only; and the case of Goodrich v. Downs, so far as it maintains the contrary, was overruled. It was further held that if the statute could be applied to the latter description of cases, it avoids only so much of the grant as is not sustained by the valid purposes for which it was made; it does not avoid the entire instrument which contains the invalid use. But so far as the case of Goodrich v. Downs applies to ordinary assignments by insolvent debtors, its principle seems to have been clearly recognized, the court holding that if an assignment is made by a debtor, when in failing circumstances, which looks to a final liquidation, and implies an inability to meet his engagements, it will be invalid unless it is an unqualified devotion of the assets assigned to the payment of all his debts, without any reservation of an interest therein to the prejudice of his creditors.[6]

[1] McClurg v. Lecky, 3 P. & W. 83. See McAllister v. Marshall, 6 Binn. 338.
[2] 3 R. S. (7th ed.), p. 2327, § 1.
[3] Indiana — Statutes of Indiana, vol. I, p. 353, § 18; R. S. of Indiana (1881), § 4921. Georgia — Code (1882), § 1952. Michigan — Compiled Laws (ed. 1871), vol. II, p. 1456. Minnesota — Statutes at Large (ed. 1873), vol. I, p. 692, § 14; Stat. of Minn. (1878), p. 543. New Jersey — R. S., p. 499, § 1; Rev. of N. J. (1878), p. 446; Nixon's Digest (ed. 1868), p. 355, § 1. And in other states. See *post*, ch. XXV.
[4] Curtis v. Leavitt, 15 N. Y. 119, 147, 149.
[5] 15 N. Y. 9.
[6] Paige, J., 15 N. Y. 208; Comstock, J., id. 132. In Collomb v. Caldwell, 16 N.

§ 170. **What Reservations Are Allowed.**— But the rule against the reservation of benefits to the assignor, in deeds of assignment, has not always been inflexibly applied by the courts, without regard to amount or circumstances.[1] Thus, in Virginia, where the grantor reserved the sum of $350 to his individual use and disposition, for the purpose of paying some small claims due from him of high honorary obligation, which were not then liquidated or specifically ascertained, it was held that such reservation did not of itself avoid the deed.[2] And in a Maryland case[3] the court held that if the assignor applied a part of the proceeds of the sale of his stock to the support of his family and himself, it could hardly be said that he had made a fraudulent application of it, or that he intended by thus selling his property to benefit himself and defraud his creditors. And clauses in assignments, giving the trustees power, *if they think proper*, to employ the debtor as agent or manager of the property for a limited time, and in subordination to the objects of the assignment, have been held valid. Thus, in Alabama, a deed conveying a plantation to trustees for the benefit of creditors was held not to be void on account of a provision that the trustees might, if they thought proper, permit the grantor to have the management of it, under their supervision, until the growing crop was sold.[4] And in England assignments are constantly drawn with clauses enabling the trustees to employ the debtor in winding up his affairs, and in collecting and getting in

Y. 484, Mr. Justice Comstock made use of the following language: Goodrich v. Downs, so far as it may have been understood to have turned upon the statute (2 R. S. 135, § 1) relating to conveyances "in trust for the use of the person making the same, has been overruled by this court (Curtis v. Leavitt, 15 N. Y. 9). But in overruling the decision in that respect, we by no means called in question the doctrine that an assignment by an insolvent is void for actual fraud, if, while he provides for only a part of his creditors, he makes the attempt in the instrument to reserve any portion of the fund to himself. In this view of the question, Goodrich v. Downs was well enough decided, and the decision depending on this principle was approved in Barney v. Griffin, 2 N. Y. 365." See McClelland v. Remsen, 36 Barb. 622.

[1] 1 Am. Lead. Cases (Hare & Wall. Notes), 98 (70, ed. 1857).
[2] Skipwith's Ex'r v. Cunningham, 8 Leigh, 271. And see Dance v. Seaman, 11 Gratt. 778; Shattuck v. Knight, 25 W. Va. 590. In a case in England, where the assignment provided that the trustees might make the debtor such allowance, or return to him such part of his household furniture or effects, not exceeding the value of 20*l.*, as they might deem expedient, it was sustained. Coate v. Williams, 21 Law J. Exch. (N. S.) 176; 9 Eng. L. & Eq. 481.
[3] Luckemeyer v. Seltz, 61 Md. 313.
[4] Planters' & Merchants' Bank of Mobile v. Clarke, 7 Ala. 765; Rindskoff v. Guggenheim, 3 Cold. (Tenn.) 284. But in Constantine v. Twelves, 29 Ala. 607, where the debtor reserved the possession of a stock of goods assigned, with the right to carry on the business and sell the goods, accounting only for the proceeds, this was held to create a presumption of fraud, which, unless rebutted, would render the deed void.

his estate and effects, and in carrying on his trade; and to allow him, out of the trust estate, such sum as they may deem proper.[1]

Such employment of the debtor by the trustees of their own accord is usually less objectionable in itself, and has been frequently sustained, as will be more fully shown under a future head. But if he be permitted as their agent to use and control the assigned effects in a manner wholly inconsistent with the purposes of the trust, and as his own, it will be evidence that the assignment was not made in good faith.[2] And in a case in Alabama, where, on the same day with the execution of a deed of trust by the debtor, a power was executed by the trustees to him, by which they appointed him their agent to sell the goods, collect the debts, compound with the creditors of the concern, etc., vesting in him the most ample powers, the court say: "If these deeds can be considered as one act, we should be strongly inclined to think it would of itself be conclusive evidence of a fraudulent intent, as it would, in effect, be the same thing as if this power had been reserved in the deed itself."[3]

§ 171. **Reservations or Exceptions of Property.**[4]— There seems to be a distinction between provisions in assignments excepting from the operation of the conveyance itself a certain portion of the property for the use of the debtor, and reservations of a benefit out of the property after it has been assigned; and the former have in some cases been held not to vitiate the assignment.[5] But as exceptions of this kind are usually inoperative and sometimes fatal, they are of very questionable propriety, and ought to be avoided.

The reservation of such property as is exempt by law from levy and sale under execution is consistent with the rights of creditors.

§ 172. **Stipulations for the Use of Property.**— Stipulations that the debtor making the assignment may *retain*, for a time, *possession* of the assigned property, so as to have the *use* of it, appear to

---

[1] See Janes v. Whitbread, 20 Law J. C. P. (N. S.) 217; 5 Eng. L. & Eq. 431; Coate v. Williams, *ubi supra*. The deeds in these cases are said by the court to be "the ordinary printed forms,"—"stereotyped deeds to be had at any law stationer's in London." Coate v. Williams, *ubi sup.*
[2] Smith v. Leavitts, 10 Ala. 92.
[3] Ormond, J., in Smith v. Leavitts, 10 Ala. 92, 105.
[4] See *post*, § 252.
[5] Thus, property incumbered beyond its value (Fassett v. Phillips, 4 Wheat. 399), or of small value (Phippin v. Durham, 8 Gratt. 457; Skipwith's Ex'r v. Cunningham, 8 Leigh, 271); so a claim in suit against certain persons, there being no reservation to the assignor. Carpenter v. Underwood, 9 N. Y. 520. *Contra*, Baker v. Crookshank, 1 Phila. 193. See Knight v. Waterman, 36 Pa. St. 258; Hickman v. Messenger, 49 id. 465.

fall under the head of reservations for the debtor's benefit, though in some instances such stipulations have been sustained. Thus, in Massachusetts, prior to the changes introduced by statute, a covenant in a general assignment that the assignor should be permitted to use and occupy the property, committing no waste thereon until it should be sold or disposed of in the due execution of the trust, was held to be not *per se* fraudulent (though possession might be evidence of fraud) as against creditors not parties to the assignment.[1] So in Virginia, a provision that the grantor should remain in possession for six months was held not to be fraudulent.[2] But where a deed of trust contained a stipulation that the debtor should be permitted to remain in possession of the property and to use the same and enjoy the profits thereof for sixteen months, and that he should be considered the agent of the trustee with full power and authority to sell or dispose of any of the property conveyed at private or public sale for cash, and to give title thereto, and to collect the proceeds of sale upon condition that he should immediately pay over the same to the trustee, and provided also that any creditors intended to be secured by the deed, who should during that time proceed by suit or by any legal process whatever against the debtor for the recovery of their respective debts, should be debarred from any right or benefit under the deed, the deed was held in the same state to be fraudulent upon its face.[3] In North Carolina a stipulation in the deed for possession by the debtor for a long time has been distinguished from a mere retention of possession by the sufferance of the trustee and creditors, it being an express trust for the debtor, which might lead to great abuses if tolerated, and must be *prima facie* fraudulent unless the period should be so short as to leave it indifferent whether it was for the convenience of the trustee or the benefit of the estate on the one hand, or, on the other, for the benefit of the debtor.[4]

In Alabama a deed of trust providing for the security of creditors designated in the deed, but providing also that the debtor

---

[1] Baxter v. Wheeler, 9 Pick. 21. In Russell v. Woodward, 10 Pick. 448, the assignment contained a similar stipulation, which was made a formal ground of objection to it on the argument, but the court took no notice of the objection.

[2] Kevan v. Branch, 1 Gratt. 274.

[3] Spence v. Bagwell, 6 Gratt. 444, 450. See Dance v. Seaman, 11 id. 778, where this case was commented on. As the practice in Virginia, in cases of deeds to trustees for the purpose of selling and paying debts, is for the debtor to remain in possession until a sale can be made, a mere stipulation to that effect in the deed seems not objectionable. See 1 Tuck. Com. [338, 340], 328, 330; Sipe v. Earman, 26 Gratt. 563.

[4] Ruffin, C. J., in Hardy v. Skinner, 9 Ired. L. 195. For the rule in Tennessee, see Galt v. Dibrell, 10 Yerg. 146.

should retain the use of the property until a day subsequent to that when the debts were due, was held to be invalid as a conveyance without the assent of all the beneficiaries, the contrary not being expressed in the deed.¹ And in another case it was further held that until such assent the property conveyed is liable to execution against the grantor.² And where a debtor conveys property in trust as security for certain creditors, reserving the use of perishable effects which might be consumed in the use, it was held in the same state that any other creditor might, notwithstanding, have all the debtor's estate reduced at once to its money value over and above the amount of the debts secured.³ It has also been held that an assignment which, after empowering the trustee to expose the property to sale on the best terms practicable, either at private sale or public auction, for cash or on credit, as should in his opinion most comport with the interest of all parties concerned, required him, if the property was not sold within six months, to sell it at public auction, etc., was not rendered fraudulent on its face by a provision that the debtor should retain possession of some of the property conveyed until a favorable opportunity for the sale of it should offer, such possession being expressly limited to the time for the sale at public auction.⁴ And in another case a deed of trust for the benefit of creditors, conveying all the debtor's estate, was held not to be rendered fraudulent upon its face by a stipulation contained in it that the grantor should retain the possession of his dwelling-house and the slaves conveyed until the trustees, in the exercise of the discretion conferred upon them, should think proper to sell.⁵ And in another case a deed of trust was held not to be fraudulent on its face which was made without the knowledge of the preferred creditor, whose debt was past due, and which reserved to the grantor the use of the property until the creditor ordered a sale.⁶ But where a deed of trust executed by an insolvent debtor conveyed all his property in trust to secure the payment of a portion of his debt, then past due, leaving other creditors unprovided for, and stipulated that the grantor should retain the possession of all the property until the law-day of the deed, and for such longer period as the sale might be postponed by the secured creditors, and that the surplus, after paying the secured debts and expenses, should be refunded to him, it was

---

¹ Lockhart v. Wyatt, 10 Ala. 231.
² Hodge v. Wyatt, 10 Ala. 271.
³ Graham v. Lockhart, 8 Ala. 9.
⁴ Abercrombie v. Bradford, 16 Ala. 560.
⁵ Shackelford v. P. & M. Bank of Mobile, 22 Ala. 238. See **Commercial Bank v. Brewer,** 71 id. 574.
⁶ Lanier v. Driver, 24 Ala. 149.

held to be fraudulent and void in law as against the unsecured creditors.[1]

And in a later case a deed of trust which was made by an insolvent debtor to his partner to secure moneys advanced by the debtor's wife, and which authorized possession of the property by the grantor, and delayed the sale for three years, and instructed the trustee to wind up the business if creditors should attempt to subject the property to the payment of their debts, was adjudged void.[2]

§ 173. **Stipulations for the Use of Property — Continued.**— In Missouri it has been held that a deed conveying to a trustee a stock of goods for the benefit of creditors, but providing that the grantor may continue to have possession, sell and dispose of the same in the regular or usual course of his business until default be made in the payment of some of the notes intended to be secured, is void as matter of law.[3]

In North Carolina, where an assignor was much embarrassed financially, and owed debts other than those secured by his assignment, and the deed contained a clause providing that he should remain on the assigned premises for two years and retain the rents and profits for his own benefit, reserving also his homestead and personal property exemptions, it was held that such conveyance raised a strong presumption that it was in fraud of creditors, and, nothing to the contrary appearing, should be declared void.[4]

In Pennsylvania[5] and New Jersey[6] a stipulation in an assign-

[1] Montgomery's Ex'rs v. Kirksey, 26 Ala. 172. Chief Justice Chilton, in delivering the opinion of the court in this case, observes: "It is not permissible for any one thus to avail himself of a part of his indebtedness to tie up all his property and exempt it from liability for his other debts, while he has the temporary benefit of the use of it, and a contingent residuum. Such assignments, when these facts appeared on their face, have uniformly been declared fraudulent in law. That the facts do not appear on their face only puts the party upon whom the burden of proving fraud is devolved to the necessity of otherwise establishing their existence, and of showing that the beneficiaries were cognizant of them. Several adjudged cases of this court show that such deeds cannot be upheld." Id. 185. The learned judge cites Gazzam v. Poyntz, 4 Ala. 382; Hindman v. Dill, 11 id. 689; Planters' & Merchants' Bank v. Clark, 7 id. 776; Wiswall v. Ticknor, 6 id. 178; Grimshaw v. Walker, 12 id. 102; Cummings v McCullough, 5 id. 324; and Rugeley v. Harrison, 10 id. 731.

[2] King v. Kenan, 38 Ala. 63. See Reynolds v. Cook, 31 id. 634.

[3] Brooks v. Wimer, 20 Mo. 502; Stanley v. Bunce, 27 id. 269; Reed v. Pellestier, 28 id. 173; Billingsley's Adm'r v. Bunce, 28 id. 547; Hatcher v. Winters, 71 id. 30.

[4] Booth v. Grant, 107 N. C. 395.

[5] Klapp's Assignees v. Shirk, 13 Pa. St. 579. But the mere circumstance of the property being left in the assignor's possession after the assignment will not in this state avoid it. Id. The subject of delivery of possession of the assigned property will be fully considered hereafter under a distinct head. See ch. XIX.

[6] Knight v. Packer, 12 N. J. Eq. 214.

ment for the retention by the assignor of the possession of the property assigned avoids the deed. And in New York and other states where actual and immediate delivery of possession to the assignee is essential to the validity of the transfer, such a stipulation would of course be fatal. And on the whole, clauses of this character, like all those which have just been considered under the present head of reservations for the debtor's benefit, should always be avoided as tending at best to give rise to questions as to their validity, and in this way to embarrass or perhaps defeat the operation and object of the whole assignment.

§ 174. **Reservations in Mortgages and Deeds of Trust.**— Reservations and provisions beneficial to the debtor and which would be fatal to a general assignment for the benefit of creditors are frequently inserted and sustained in mortgages and deeds of trust in the nature of mortgages. In these instruments the debtor may reserve the possession and use of the assigned property,[1] subject to the qualifications that the sale of the property shall not be unreasonably delayed,[2] and that the property be of such a nature that it will not be consumed or lost in the use.[3] Provisions have also been sustained in such instruments by which the property vests in the assignee until the profits pay the debts and then reverts to the assignor.[4] The distinction is to be found in these cases in the right of redemption.[5] When it exists, the contingent and residual interest of the debtor in the property still remains open to the pursuit of creditors.

§ 175. **Reservations of Surplus Moneys or Property.**— Assignments are sometimes drawn with a provision stipulating for the repayment to the assignor of the surplus moneys remaining after distribution among the creditors provided for, or for the reconveyance to him, by the assignee, of such property as may not have been converted into money. Such a stipulation is sometimes innoxious in its consequences, while, in other cases, it has the effect of invalidating the whole assignment; its validity depending upon the consideration whether or not it be a reservation of a benefit to the debtor at his creditors' expense. Thus, a reservation to the

[1] Hempstead v. Johnson, 18 Ark. 123; Marks v. Hill, 15 Gratt. 400; Sipe v. Earman, 26 id. 563.
[2] Hafner v. Irwin, 1 Ired. L. 496; Hardy v. Skinner, 9 id. 191; Hempstead v. Johnson, 18 Ark. 123.
[3] Elmes v. Sutherland, 7 Ala. 267; Darwin v. Hundley, 3 Yerg. 503; Hempstead v. Johnson, 18 Ark. 123.
[4] Balt. & Ohio R. R. Co. v. Glenn, 28 Md. 287. This was a deed made in Virginia and construed under the laws of that state. Robins v. Embry, 1 Sm. & M. 207. And see Arthur v. Commercial Bank, 9 Sm. & M. 394; Fellows v. Commercial Bank, 6 Rob. (La.) 246.
[5] Hannah v. Carrington, 18 Ark. 85; Briggs v. Davis, 21 N. Y. 574.

assignor of the surplus remaining after payment of *all* the creditors is not fraudulent, for it is no more than the law itself would imply.[1] So, a provision in an assignment by copartners of all the partnership effects, for the payment of *all* the partnership debts, directing the surplus of the assigned property, if any, to be paid to the assignors, will not render the assignment fraudulent against creditors of the individual partners.[2] But where the estate assigned consists in part of the individual property of the members of the firm (as where it consists in part of real estate owned by them as tenants in common), a reservation to the assignors of the surplus remaining after payment of the partnership debts, without providing for the payment of the debts of the individual partners, will avoid the assignment.[3]

§ 176. **Reservations of Surplus Moneys or Property in Preferential Assignments.**— Whether an assignment providing for only a part of the creditors, and without making provision for the rest, directing the assignee to pay back or re-assign to the assignor the surplus which may remain after satisfying the debts provided for, will be sustained, has given rise to much conflict of opinion. The weight of authority is in favor of the validity of such an assignment.[4] The contrary rule, however, prevails in New York[5]

[1] Wintringham v. Lafoy, 7 Cow. 735; Savage, C. J., id. 738; Story, J., in Halsey v. Whitney, 4 Mason, 206, 222; Hall v. Denison, 17 Vt. 310; Bennett J., id. 318; Burgin v. Burgin, 1 Ired. L. 453; Ruffin, C. J., id. 458; Gamble, J., in Richards v. Levin, 16 Mo. 596; Ring v. Ring, 12 Mo. App. 88; Douglas v. Cissna, 17 id. 44; Wing, P. J., in Hollister v. Loud, 2 Mich. 309, 322; Van Rossum v. Walker, 11 Barb. S. C. 237; Ely v. Cook, 18 id. 612; Comstock, J., in Curtis v. Leavitt, 15 N. Y. 120; Brown, J., id. 146; Paige, J., id. 206. See Wilkes v. Ferris, 2 Johns. 335; Finlay v. Dickerson, 29 Ill. 9; Estate of Potter v. Paige, 54 Pa. St. 465; Van Hook v. Walton, 28 Tex. 59; Farquharson v. McDonald, 2 Heisk. 404; Liniger v. Raymond, 9 Neb. 40; Hays v. Hostetter, 125 Ind. 60; 25 N. E. Rep. 134.

[2] Bogert v. Haight, 9 Paige, 297; Walworth, C., id. 302.

[3] Collomb v. Caldwell, 16 N. Y. 484. This case was again before the court of appeals (24 N. Y. 505), and it having then been shown that the real estate so conveyed was copartnership property, and so applicable in the first instance to the payment of partnership debts, it was held to have been lawfully included in the assignment to a trustee for the payment of such debts. In this case the individual property of the partners was not conveyed, and no provision was made for the payment of their individual debts.

[4] Miller v. Stetson, 32 Ala. 161; Brown v. Lyon, 17 id. 659; Hindman v. Dill,

[5] Goodrich v. Downs, 6 Hill, 438; Strong v. Skinner, 4 Barb. S. C. 546; Lansing v. Woodworth, 1 Sandf. Ch. 43; Barney v. Griffin, 4 id. 552; affirmed on appeal, 2 N. Y. 365; Leitch v. Hollister, 4 id. 211; Collomb v. Caldwell, 16 id. 484; Sutherland v. Bradner, 39 Hun, 134. See Jacobs v. Remsen, 35 Barb. 384; s. c., 36 N. Y. 668. But a conveyance by a solvent debtor of part of his property in this way is not as matter of law fraudulent. Knapp v. McGowan, 96 N. Y. 75.

and in some other states,[1] and in these states it has been held to make no difference whether the surplus be large or small, or whether there be any at all.[2] And even if there be no express reservation of the surplus to the assignor, it has been held in Vermont and Michigan that an assignment of all the debtor's property for the benefit of a portion of his creditors, without a provision that the surplus shall be distributed among all the creditors, is fraudulent, by reason of the *resulting trust* of the surplus,[3] even (in Vermont) if it turns out that there is no surplus.[4]

§ 177. Resulting Trusts for Assignor.—In regard to resulting trusts for the debtor, it has been held in New York that where such a trust arises on an assignment of part of the debtor's property for the benefit of certain specified creditors, the assignment

11 id. 689; Conklin v. Carson, 11 Ill. 503; Finlay v. Dickerson, 29 id. 9; New Albany & Salem R. R. Co. v. Huff, 19 Ind. 444; McFarland v. Birdsall, 14 id. 126; Burgin v. Burgin, 1 Ired. L. 453; Ely v. Hair, 16 B. Mon. (Ky.) 230; Bigelow v. Stringer, 40 Mo. 195; Johnson v. McAllister's Assignee, 30 id. 327; Richards v. Levin, 16 id. 596; Bailey v. Mills, 27 Tex. 434; Kneeland v. Cowles, 4 Chand. (Wis.) 49; Livingston v. Bell, 3 Watts, 198; Mechanics' Bank v. Gorman, 8 W. & S. 304; Skipwith's Ex'r v. Cunningham, 8 Leigh, 271; Phippen v. Durham, 8 Gratt. 457; Dance v. Seaman, 11 id. 778; Morgan v. Bogue, 7 Neb. 429; Floyd v. Smith, 9 Ohio St. 546. In the last case cited, the cases of Hoffman v. Mackall, 5 Ohio St. 134, and Dickinson v. Rawson, id. 224, are discussed, and held that so far as they follow Goodrich v. Downs, 6 Hill, 438, and Barney v. Griffin, 2 N. Y. 365, they do not apply under the Ohio act of 1853. The reason upon which these decisions rest is that such a reservation results by operation of law, and is simply an incident to the trust, and not an express trust for the debtor, and that creditors are not defeated or unlawfully delayed in their remedies against the debtor in following the surplus of the estate, either in his hands or those of his trustees. The English case of Estwick v. Caillaud, 5 Term R. 420, has been much relied on for the principle that an express reservation to the debtor, where the assignment is of a portion only of his property, is not necessarily fraudulent. See the observations of Putnam, J., in Harris v. Sumner, 2 Pick. 129, 134.

[1] Dana v. Lull, 17 Vt. 390; Goddard v. Hapgood, 25 id. 351; Therasson v. Hickok, 37 id. 454; Truitt v. Caldwell, 3 Minn. 364; Banning v. Sibley, 3 id. 389; Green v. Trieber, 3 Md. 11; Pierson v. Manning, 2 Mich. 445; Seiz v. Evans, 6 Ill. App. (Bradw.) 466; Lill v. Brant, id. 366; Thompson v. Parker, 83 Ind. 96.

[2] Barney v. Griffin, 2 N. Y. 365; Leitch v. Hollister, 4 id. 211. But in Beck v. Burdett, 1 Paige, 305, it was held that a mere hypothetical reservation of the surplus to the assignor would not vitiate the deed. And in Richards v. Levin, 16 Mo. 596, Gamble, J., in delivering the opinion of the court, remarked that "where the parties have agreed that the whole amount assigned is insufficient to pay the preferred debts, the idea that the reservation of a surplus to the grantor will render the deed fraudulent is a mere mistake." Id. 595, 599.

[3] Dana v. Lull, 17 Vt. 390; Redfield, C. J., in Merrill v. Englesby, 28 id. 155; Pierson v. Manning, 2 Mich. 445; Pratt, J., id. 449; Palmer v. Mason, 42 id. 150. See Burd v. Smith, 4 Dall. 76; West v. Snodgrass, 17 Ala. 549.

[4] Dana v. Lull, *ubi supra*. But in Merrill v. Englesby the assignment in such a case is declared to be merely defective, and such as may be remedied by a new assignment, or by a new declaration of trust in favor of all the creditors. 28 Vt. 150.

is not void unless it were merely colorable, and made for the sake of *the resulting trust;*[1] and that where the assignment does not purport to convey all the assignor's property, and it does not appear on its face that there are other creditors not provided for, or that the value of the assigned property exceeds the amount of the preferred debts, the mere omission of the assignor to direct that any contingent surplus which may remain after the payment of the preferred creditors shall be applied in payment of his other creditors will not render the assignment void on its face.[2] But if it can be shown that the assigned property exceeds in value the amount of the debts preferred, or that the assignor, at the time of the execution of the assignment, contemplated a surplus which would revert to him after the payment of the preferred debts, the assignment will be fraudulent and void.[3]

In Illinois it was held that although an assignment of a property right be made upon a valuable and ample consideration, without any intention to defraud any one, yet if there be a secret trust reserved, not disclosed by the writing, the law will treat the transaction as lacking the element of good faith and conclusively infer fraud.[4]

§ 178. **Reservations with Stipulations for Releases, and Other Conditions.**— A reservation of the surplus to the assignor, where it is made to depend upon certain conditions to be complied with by the creditors, and particularly upon the condition of releasing the debtor, will also avoid the assignment. This rule may now be

---

[1] Wilkes v. Ferris, 5 Johns. 335; Oliver Lee & Co. Bank v. Talcott, 19 N. Y. 146.

[2] In the case of Spies v. Joel, in the superior court (1 Duer, 669), the assignment, which was of all the debtor's property, contained no provision relative to the disposition to be made by the assignee of any surplus that might remain after the satisfaction of the debts specified. But it was conclusively shown that the preferred debts largely exceeded in amount the whole value of the property assigned, and that this was known to the parties when the assignment was made. The court held that the omission only raised a presumption of fraud, which might be repelled, and that such a presumption was in fact repelled by the evidence in the case. And where an assignment was made by a debtor of all his property in trust to pay two creditors, and the instrument was silent as to the surplus, but it appeared that there was not enough property to pay the debts provided for, this was not regarded as an unlawful reservation to the debtor. Bishop v. Halsey, 3 Abb. Pr. 400.

[3] Doremus v. Lewis, 8 Barb. S. C. 124. In the case of Hooper v. Tuckerman, 3 Sandf. S. C. 311, it was held that an assignment which transfers to a trustee in trust for creditors a larger amount of property than the assignee is empowered to distribute among the creditors is void upon its face; the legal effect being to create a resulting trust to the assignor after the trust for creditors is satisfied. Moore v. Collins, 3 Dev. 126; Beck v. Burdett, 1 Paige, 305; Hastings v. Baldwin, 17 Mass. 552; Rahn v. McElrath, 6 Watts, 151.

[4] Beidler v. Crane, 135 Ill. 92; 25 N. E. Rep. 655; 25 Am. St. Rep. 349.

considered to be established by a preponderance of authority, though in some of the states it does not prevail.¹ This statement of the rule has been expressly approved in Indiana,² and in Pennsylvania an assignment of property in trust for the payment of such creditors as should agree to accept the same within a specified time, and to pay the assignor the proportion of all such creditors as should not within such time signify their acceptance, was held fraudulent and void against a creditor who had obtained judgment.³ So, in New York, where an assignment contained a proviso that if any of the creditors named should not become parties to it within a time limited, their shares should be paid by the assignees to the assignor himself, the assignment (which contained a release of the debtor) was held fraudulent and void, and the property in the assignees' hands liable to the execution of a judgment creditor before the expiration of the time limited for creditors to execute the assignment.⁴ So where an assignment was made of part of the debtor's property for the benefit of such creditors only as should become parties to it, containing provisions highly favorable to the assignor, and reserving to him the surplus which should remain after payment of such creditors, it was held to be coercive and void as against creditors.⁵ So, in Maryland, the reservation to the grantor of the surplus that may remain after paying the assenting creditors has been held to have the effect of avoiding the assignment.⁶ So, in Alabama, an assignment of all the debtor's

---

¹ In the Virginia case of Phippen v. Durham, 8 Gratt. 457, Moncure, J., remarked as follows: 'If the question were *res integra*, whether a deed of trust conveying all the property of a debtor for the benefit of such of his creditors as may within a specified time release him from all further claims, and providing that the surplus of the trust fund after satisfying the accepting creditors should be paid to the debtor, is valid against the creditors who do not accept, I would be inclined to answer it in the negative. While the many cases on this subject are conflicting, I think the preponderance is against the validity of such deed." The case of Skipwith's Ex'r v. Cunningham, 8 Leigh, 271, was, however, considered to have settled the rule the other way in that state. Id. 464. See *post*, p. 233.

² McFarland v. Birdsall, 14 Ind. 126.
³ Burd v. Smith, 4 Dall. 76.
⁴ Austin v. Bell, 20 Johns. 442.
⁵ Berry v. Riley, 2 Barb. S. C. 307.
⁶ Green v. Trieber, 3 Md. 11; Barnitz v. Rice, 14 id. 24; Rosenberg v. Moore, 11 id. 376; Whedbee v. Stewart, 40 id. 414. In Sangston v. Gaither, 3 Md. 40, the assignment was held fraudulent and void where it provided in express terms that the balance, after paying the releasing creditors, should be paid to the assignors; and in Malcolm v. Hodges, 8 id. 418, it was further held that an implied reservation in such a case avoids the deed equally with an express reservation. This ruling was affirmed in Bridges v. Hindes, 16 id. 101. The decision in McCall v. Hinckley, 4 Gill, 128, affirmed the judgment of the court below on an equal division of the court of appeals. The case is doubtless overruled on the point under discussion by the decision in Sangston v. Gaither, *supra*.

property, in trust, first to pay certain preferred creditors, the surplus, if any, to be appropriated to the other creditors ratably who should within a specified time execute a release of their claims, and the ultimate surplus to be paid over to the assignor, was held to contain such a stipulation for the benefit of the debtor as rendered the deed fraudulent and void.[1] So, in South Carolina, a reservation to the grantor of the surplus after paying to releasing creditors forty per cent., if the estate would yield as much, was decided to be fraudulent.[2]

In Tennessee also it is held that an assignment exacting releases and reserving a surplus to the assignor is void.[3]

On the other hand, in Pennsylvania[4] and Virginia,[5] a reservation to the debtor, in an assignment of all his property, of the surplus remaining after satisfying such of the creditors as should agree to release him, has been held not to invalidate the deed containing it. The same was held in Halsey v. Whitney,[6] in the case of a partial assignment; and under the insolvent law of Minnesota an assignment is not invalidated by a stipulation therein that any surplus which may remain in the hands of the assignee after payment of the releasing creditors shall be returned to the assignor.[7]

The effect of certain special conditions which have been passed upon by the courts may be referred to in this connection though releases were not exacted.

In Alabama an assignment appropriating the property unconditionally to the payment of certain preferred creditors, and the residue *pari passu* to all other creditors who should within six months execute the deed, was held not to be vitiated by the implied reservation of such residue to the grantor, in the event the latter class of creditors should fail or refuse to comply with the conditions prescribed.[8] In Illinois and Indiana a clause in an assignment authorizing the payment to the assignor of the surplus that might remain after the satisfaction of the debts of such creditors as should

[1] Grimshaw v. Walker, 12 Ala. 101. See Seavis v. Garner, id. 661.
[2] Jacot v. Corbet, 1 Cheves' Ch. 71. An assignment preferring creditors who should accept and release, but making no provision for non-accepting creditors, and directing the assignee to pay over the surplus, if any, to the assignor, after paying creditors who accepted, is null and void. Claflin v. Iseman, 23 S. C. 416.
[3] Wilde v. Rawlings, 1 Head (Tenn.), 34.
[4] Livingston v. Bell, 3 Watts, 198; Mechanics' Bank v. Gorman, 3 W. & S. 304. But as to stipulations for a release in this state, see *ante*, pp. 204, 205.
[5] Skipwith's Ex'r v. Cunningham, 8 Leigh, 271. In Phippen v. Durham, 8 Gratt. 437, this case was considered as of binding authority, though the principle of it was disapproved.
[6] 4 Mason, 206. As to this case, see *ante*, pp. 158, 210, 212.
[7] In re Mann, 32 Minn. 60. But this statute does not apply to partial assignments. May v. Walker, 28 N. W. Rep. 252.
[8] Brown v. Lyon, 17 Ala. 659.

become parties to it does not invalidate the assignment, as creditors not parties can pursue their remedies against the debtor, following the surplus either in his hands or those of the trustee.[1] And in Missouri it has been held that a provision in an assignment that the assignees should pay the surplus, if any, after paying all the debts, exclusive of cost of suits commenced or to be commenced, to the assignor, did not avoid the assignment.[2]

In New York it has been held by the court of appeals that the rule prohibiting the reservation of a surplus to the assignor does not apply to assignments made directly to creditors themselves for the purpose of securing their particular demands.[3]

An assignment of goods for the payment of a debt due to the assignee is not rendered fraudulent in law by a parol agreement for the payment of the surplus to the assignor. If the value of the property assigned be out of proportion with the debt, this may be evidence of fraud in fact, which is for a jury to pass upon, and is not a subject of legal direction.[4] But a secret reservation of the surplus, upon a conveyance absolute upon its face, is admitted to be a fraud.[5]

III. APPROPRIATION OF ASSETS IN ASSIGNMENTS BY FIRMS AND THEIR MEMBERS.

§ 179. **Preference of Individual Creditors.**— Assignments may be made by copartners of the partnership property for the payment of the partnership debts, and by individuals of their interest in the copartnership, for the benefit of their creditors; but assignments are also frequently made in which firm and individual property[6] is assigned for the payment of firm and individual debts, and in such

---

[1] Conkling v. Carson, 11 Ill. 503; Finlay v. Dickerson, 29 Ill. 9; New Albany & Salem R. R. Co. v. Huff, 19 Ind. 444; McFarland v. Birdsall, 14 Ind. 126.
[2] Gates v. Labeaume, 19 Mo. 17. See Johnson v. McAllister, 30 id. 327.
[3] Leitch v. Hollister, 4 N. Y. 211.
[4] Rahn v. McElrath, 6 Watts, 151.
[5] McCullough v. Hutchinson, 7 Watts, 434; Smith v. Lowell, 6 N. H. 67; Smith v. Smith, 11 id. 459.
[6] Whether the conveyance is of individual as well as firm property will depend upon the intention of the parties as shown by the terms employed by them in the instrument. Thus where the assignment was by W. A. & E. A. P. of all *their* property, this was held broad enough to include the separate property of each of the partners as well as the common property of both. Coggill v. Botsford, 29 Conn. 439; Von Wettberg v. Carson, 44 id. 287; Coffin v. Douglas, 61 Tex. 406. An assignment of firm property for the payment of firm debts is valid, although it does not embrace the individual property of any of the partners. Ex parte Hopkins, 104 Ind. 157; Auley v. Osterman, 65 Wis. 118. Such an assignment, however, is not contemplated or authorized by the Minnesota statute. May v. Walker, 28 N. W. Rep. 252.

§ 179.] PREFERENCE OF INDIVIDUAL CREDITORS. 235

cases the priorities of the different classes of creditors have given rise to some conflict of decision.

When the law marshals and distributes the individual and copartnership assets of the different members of a firm, it has respect to the several equities of the creditors of the firm and its individual members respectively. In that case the copartnership assets are in the first place applied to the payment of the firm debts, and the individual funds of the several copartners to the payment of their respective individual debts.[1] But, remarks Chancellor Walworth in the case of Kirby v. Schoonmaker,[2] where the copartners are administering their own funds, the copartnership creditors have no lien upon the joint funds; nor have the individual creditors any lien or priority of claim upon the separate property of the debtors. Such being the case, the copartners may assign their joint property for the payment of their joint creditors, with such preferences as they may see fit. And the same principle would apply to dispositions of their individual property by the individual members of the firm. The case is entirely different, however, where copartners who are insolvent and unable to pay the debts of the firm, either out of their copartnership effects or of their individual property, have made an assignment of the property of both to pay the individual debt of one of the copartners only.[3]

[1] Mr. Justice Allen in O'Neill v. Salmon, 25 How. Pr. 251; Parsons on Partnership, 347, 480. A partnership made an assignment, and each of the partners a separate one. It was held that the firm creditors were not entitled, after exhausting the firm assets, to resort to the individual assets until after the individual creditors' claims had been satisfied. Davis v. Howell, 33 N. J. Eq. 72 (citing many cases). See Schiele v. Healy, 10 Daly, 42.

[2] 3 Barb. Ch. 49; Smith v. Howard, 21 How. Pr. 124. In Maine it was held that where two debtors are in insolvency as a firm and also individually, and one has assets exceeding his own private indebtedness, a firm creditor is interested in the private estate of the insolvent partner, and may contest the allowance of claims against such estate presented by other creditors. Chadbourne v. Harding, 80 Me. 580; 16 Atl. Rep. 248. When an assignment for the benefit of partnership and individual creditors includes all the property of the grantors as partners and individually, it should be construed distributively, partnership assets being applied to the payment of partnership debts and individual assets to individual liabilities. Peters v. Bain, 133 U. S. 670; 10 S. Ct. Rep. 354. But a voluntary assignment by a firm doing business in the names of the individual partners, treating all their property as firm property and all their debts as firm debts, is not fraudulent as to creditors, although they did not know of the copartnership. Severson v. Porter, 73 Wis. 70; 40 N. W. Rep. 577.

[3] Kirby v. Schoonmaker, 3 Barb. Ch. 51; Wilson v. Robertson, 21 N. Y. 592. A. and B., partners, gave a joint and several bond and warrant of attorney to a creditor for a firm debt; judgment was entered and execution issued; soon afterward A. and B. assigned, B. being also individually insolvent. The judgment being only partly satisfied, and A. having made an assignment, it was held that the creditor may, under A.'s assignment, share equally the personal effects of A., and is not to be subordinated to his individual creditors. Howard v. Teel, 29 N.

This would, in effect, be a gift from the firm to the partner — a reservation for the benefit of such partner or his creditors, to the direct injury of the firm creditors.[1] Having such an effect, it has been frequently decided that such an appropriation of the assigned fund is a fraud upon copartnership creditors.[2] And in such a case the proportion of the capital contributed by each partner is an immaterial consideration.[3]

§ 180. **Preference of Firm Creditors.**—What has been said of an assignment by copartners preferring their individual debts has been held to be equally true of assignments in which partnership creditors are preferred to individual creditors in the distribution of individual property.[4] This rule, however, has been doubted. Thus it has been said that neither the reason nor the rule applies to an appropriation of individual property to the payment of firm debts. Copartners are individually liable for the firm debts; the firm, however, is in no sense liable for individual debts of the partners. Individual creditors have no equitable claim upon the individual

---

J. Eq. 490. A general assignment transferring the property of the firm for the purpose of paying the individual debts of the partners, as well as the firm debts, is wholly void as to the firm creditors, and must be set aside. It cannot be sustained in so far as it transfers the firm property to pay firm debts and set aside as to that portion which provides for the payment of individual debts. Nat. Bank v. Cohn, 42 Hun, 381. See Newell v. Martin, 81 Iowa, 238; 46 N. W. Rep. 120; Sherwood v. His Creditors, 42 La. Ann. 103; Boos v. Marion, 129 N. Y. 536; 29 N. E. Rep. 832.

[1] Wilson v. Robertson, 21 N. Y. 592; s. c., 19 How. Pr. 350. See Davis, J., in Hurlbert v. Dean, 2 Abb. Ct. App. Dec. 432. In Stratton v. Tabb, 8 Ill. App. (Bradw.) 225, it was held that a partner cannot prove a claim against the joint estate in competition with the creditors of the firm, and thereby take part of the fund, to the prejudice of those who are not only creditors of the firm but of himself. A preference to a dormant partner avoids the assignment. Claflin v. Hirsch, 19 N. Y. Weekly Dig. 248; Whitney v. Hirsch, 39 Hun, 325. But the rule avoiding an assignment which prefers the debts of a partner in the firm does not apply where the debts preferred are those of a firm composed of a portion of the members of the firm assigning. Such an assignment is not fraudulent against creditors. Peckham v. Mattison, 15 Abb. N. C. 367; Welsh v. Britton, 55 Tex. 118.

[2] Wilson v. Robertson, *supra;* Knauth v. Bassett, 34 Barb. 31; Cox v. Platt, 32 id. 126; s. c., 19 How. Pr. 121; Keith v. Fink, 47 Ill. 272; Heye v. Bolles, 33 How. Pr. 266; s. c., 2 Daly, 231; Kirby v. Schoonmaker, 3 Barb. Ch. 46; Lester v. Abbott, 28 How. Pr. 488; s. c., 3 Robt. 691; Schiele v. Healy, 61 How. Pr. 73; Friend v. Michaelis, 15 Abb. N. C. 354; Platt v. Hunter, 11 N. Y. Weekly Dig. 300; Vernon v. Upson, 60 Wis. 418; Willis v. Bremner, id. 622; Henderson v. Hadden, 12 Rich. Eq. (S. C.) 393; French v. Lovejoy, 12 N. H. 458; Thomas v. Penrich, 28 Ohio St. 55. Only firm creditors suing as such can raise the objection. Haynes v. Brooks, 17 Abb. N. C. 152.

[3] Wilson v. Robertson, 21 N. Y. 591.

[4] Jackson v. Cornell, 1 Sandf. Ch. 348; Smith v. Howard, 20 How. Pr. 121; Lord v. Devendorf, 54 Wis. 491.

property, except to see that the firm property is primarily applied to the payment of firm debts.[1]

Hence, an application by one partner of his individual property primarily to the payment of partnership debts would be a payment by him of debts for which he was liable, and although it would create a preference yet it would not be unlawful.[2]

In Jackson v. Cornell,[3] in the court of chancery for the first circuit, the subject was extensively considered, and the cases bearing upon it reviewed; and the assistant vice-chancellor held that a general assignment of his separate property, made by an insolvent copartner, which preferred the creditors of the firm, to the exclusion of his own, was fraudulent and void as to the latter. The converse of the rule was also considered as established, viz.: that an assignment by a copartnership, preferring the creditors of the individual copartners to those of the firm, was invalid against the latter, on the same principles. The decision was rested essentially on the rule of equity (which was held to be uniform and stringent) that the property of a copartnership must all be applied to the partnership debts, to the exclusion of the creditors of the individual member of the firm; and that the creditors of the latter are to be first paid out of the separate effects of their debtor before the partnership creditors can claim anything.[4] But in the later case of Kirby v. Schoonmaker,[5] before the chancellor, it was held that the rule relied on in the last case applied only where a partnership

---

[1] O'Neill v. Salmon, 34 How. Pr. 252, Allen, J.; Eyre v. Beebe, 28 id. 333; Kirby v. Schoonmaker, 3 Barb. Ch. 46; Van Rossum v. Walker, 11 Barb. 240; Gadsden v. Carson, 9 Rich. Eq. (S. C.) 351; Newman v. Bagley, 15 Pick. 517. But this objection cannot be made by a partnership creditor who is preferred. Fox v. Heath, 16 Abb. Pr. 168; Scott v. Guthrie, 25 How. Pr. 512. It seems to have been assumed by Mr. Justice Robertson, in Scott v. Guthrie, 25 How. Pr. 512, that such a disposition of the individual property would be void as against individual creditors, under the decisions in Collomb v. Caldwell, 16 N. Y. 484, and Wilson v. Robertson, 21 N. Y. 587.

[2] And so where a firm has made a general assignment for the benefit of its creditors, a conveyance by one of its members of his individual property to the assignee, to be disposed of and applied, in accordance with the terms of the assignment, to the payment of the partnership debts, is not *per se* fraudulent or unlawful and void. None but individual creditors can object to the transfer. Royer Wheel Co. v. Fielding, 101 N. Y. 504. See Saunders v. Reilly, 105 N. Y. 12; 12 N. E. Rep. 170; 59 Am. Rep. 472; Schisster v. Rader, 13 Colo. 329; 22 Pac. Rep. 505.

[3] 1 Sandf. Ch. 348. This case is cited with approval in 3 Kent's Com. [65], 78, note *b*. But see Whiteley v. May, in the Virginia circuit court, where a contrary doctrine is strenuously maintained. U. S. Law Mag., May, 1850, p. 442; Editor's note (4) to 3 Kent's Com. (7th ed.) 78.

[4] Sandford, A. V. C., 1 Sandf. Ch. 350; citing Wilder v. Keeler, 3 Paige, 167; Egberts v. Wood, id. 517; Payne v. Matthews, 6 id. 19; Hutchinson v. Smith, 7 id. 26; 1 Story's Eq. Jur. 625, § 675.

[5] 3 Barb. Ch. 46. See Newman v. Bagley, 16 Pick. 570.

was dissolved by the death of one of the copartners, or where one or both of the copartners had become bankrupt or were discharged under the insolvent acts, so that their property was placed in the hands of the assignees appointed by *law* to make distribution; and that the rule did not go so far as to deprive the partners themselves of the power, while they have the legal control of their property, of distributing it among all their creditors in such a manner as they might see fit, provided no injustice was done to any of them. It was accordingly decided that copartners may assign their individual property as well as their partnership property to pay the joint debts of the firm; thereby giving the creditors of the firm a preference in payment out of the separate estate of the assignors over the separate creditors.[1] It was further held that each copartner, with the assent of the others, has the corresponding right to give his individual creditors a preference in payment out of the share of the effects of the firm, which, as between him and his copartners, and without reference to the debts for which they are all jointly liable, is legally his own property. And that copartners may make an assignment of their respective interests in the partnership property to trustees, giving a preference in payment to the individual creditors of each copartner out of his share of the partnership funds. But that a partner who is insolvent and unable to pay the debts of the firm has no right to assign his share of the partnership effects to pay the individual debts of his copartner, for which neither he nor his property is legally or equitably liable.

The general doctrine established by the case last cited is that there is an equity existing between the members of an insolvent copartnership, by virtue of which any of them may insist that the copartnership effects shall be applied to the payment of the debts of the firm in preference to the payment of the private debts of the individual partners; and this gives to the creditors of the firm a *quasi*-equitable lien, to be worked out through the medium of the equity of the copartners as between themselves and with their assent, or at least with the assent of one of them;[2] but that this equity of the members of the firm, as between themselves, does not deprive them of the right to apply the partnership effects to the payment of their joint and separate debts as they please, provided no injustice is done to any of their creditors.[3]

In the case of Nicholson v. Leavitt,[4] in the superior court of the city of New York, the court (Duer, J.) gave to the equitable rule

[1] Van Rossum v. Walker, 11 Barb. S. C. 237, acc.
[2] Walworth, C., 3 Barb. Ch. 49, citing Story on Part., §§ 97, 326, 360. And see 3 Kent's Com. [65], 78.
[3] 3 Barb. Ch. 47.
[4] 4 Sandf. S. C. 252.

of distribution in the case of insolvent copartnerships the same application as the assistant vice-chancellor had given in Jackson v. Cornell; and in an elaborate opinion held that a preference given in an assignment of partnership property to the creditors of one of the partners over the creditors of the firm was invalid; and that the partnership creditors might avoid it by a suit brought for the benefit of all such creditors. It was held, however, that such preference did not render the whole assignment fraudulent or void, as decided in Jackson v. Cornell, which was considered as overruled on that point by Kirby v. Schoonmaker.[1] The preference violated a rule of equity, but not any statutory prohibition.[2]

The views of the court in Jackson v. Cornell, and Nicholson v. Leavitt, in regard to the applicability of the equitable rule of distribution to cases of voluntary assignments by copartners, are in accordance with those of the court of appeals of Virginia, in the case of McCullough v. Sommerville,[3] and of the supreme court of the United States, in the case of Merrill v. Neill.[4]

But an assignment of the individual property for the payment of partnership debts, reserving the surplus to the grantors, without any provision for the individual creditors where there are such, is fraudulent and void as against an individual creditor. This is illustrated by the case of Collomb v. Caldwell,[5] where partners holding certain real estate as tenants in common assigned it with other property for the payment of the firm debts, reserving the surplus. This case was again before the court of appeals,[6] and it having been shown that the real estate assigned was partnership property,

[1] 3 Barb. Ch. 46.
[2] The distinction was taken in this case between an assignment of partnership property, giving a preference to debts due from the partners individually, but containing a general trust for the partnership creditors, and such an assignment devoting the whole property to the exclusive payment of separate debts. In the former case the security and equal distribution of the fund would be at once attained, by holding the trust to be valid, and the preference only to be void; but in the latter, the illegality running through all its provisions would of necessity vitiate the entire instrument. But in this case the suit for setting aside the assignment must be brought in behalf of all the partnership creditors. Id. 301. See, also, Kemp v. Carnley, 3 Duer, 1. In Jones v. Bartlett, 50 Wis. 589, it was held that a claim for work on stock in trade of B., who afterward entered into partnership with H.,— the latter agreeing to assume half of the "debts owing the stock," — is payable out of the assigned estate of the firm.
[3] 8 Leigh, 415.
[4] 8 How. 414. And see the case of Andress v. Miller, in the supreme court of Pennsylvania (15 Pa. St. 316).
[5] 16 N. Y. 484.
[6] 24 N. Y. 505, *sub nom.* Collomb v. Read. In the case of Scott v. Guthrie, 25 How. Pr. 512, where the assignment provided for applying the property of one of the partners to the payment of the partnership debts, it was held that the assignment was not void as against partnership creditors who were preferred. But see Smith v. Howard, 20 How. Pr. 121; O'Neill v. Salmon, 25 id. 254.

the assignment was sustained. It will be observed that this is a distinct question from that which arises where the individual property of one partner is applied to the payment of the individual debts of his copartners, for in such case the creditors benefited have plainly no claim in law or equity upon the fund out of which payment is provided for them.[1]

In the absence of an express provision directing an unlawful appropriation of the funds the law will interpret the instrument according to the rights of the parties and the respective equities of the creditors.[2] Proof has been admitted to show that the assignment included sufficient individual property of each partner to pay his individual debts directed to be paid by the assignee.[3] Evidence may also be given to show that there are no individual debts, but the burden is on the part of those supporting the assignment, and if the proof fails the assignment must be declared invalid.[4] But where it is apparent that such an unlawful disposition of the firm proceeds has been attempted, this will invalidate the entire

[1] Wilson v. Robertson, 21 N. Y. 587; Smith v. Howard, 20 How. Pr. 121; Morrison v. Atwell, 9 Bosw. 503; Eyre v. Beebe, 28 How. Pr. 340; O'Neill v. Salmon, 25 id. 254.

[2] Forbes v. Scannell, 13 Cal. 242; Farquharson v. Eichelberger, 15 Md. 63; Heckman v. Messinger, 49 Pa. St. 465; Black's Appeal, 44 id. 503; Andress v. Miller, 15 id. 316; Eyre v. Beebe, 28 How. Pr. 340; Matter of Duncan, 10 Daly, 95. An assignment by partners of all their property directed the assignee, after paying certain preferred creditors and all firm liabilities, to apply the remainder, if any, to the payment of the individual debts of the partners in full, if the remainder was sufficient. If it was not sufficient to pay the said individual debts in full, then such remainder was directed to " be applied *pro rata*, share and share alike, to the payment of said debts, demands and liabilities, according to their respective amounts." The partners owned individually different amounts of property, and their individual debts differed in amount. It was held that the individual creditors of one partner would be defrauded by allowing the individual estates of all the partners to be treated as a joint fund for the payment of all their debts, and that this illegal direction could be set up by a firm creditor. Crook v. Rindskopf, 34 Hun, 457.

[3] Knauth v. Bassett, 34 Barb. 31; Van Nest v. Yoe, 1 Sandf. Ch. 4; Hollister v. Loud, 2 Mich. 309. See Smith v. Howard, 20 How. Pr. 121; Lester v. Abbott, 28 id. 488; s. c., 3 Robt. 691.

[4] In Hurlbert v. Dean, 2 Abb. Ct. App. Dec. 428; 2 Keyes, 97, the court of appeals held that the burden of showing the non-existence of individual debts, where an assignment of partnership property on its face provided for the payment of such debts, rested on the parties claiming under the assignment. And in the later case of Turner v. Jaycox, 40 N. Y. 470, where the assignment directed the assignee to pay the individual debts of the members of the firm out of the surplus remaining after the partnership debts should be discharged, to rebut any presumption of fraud which might arise from the fact that it did not appear from the face of the instrument that the individual creditors were entitled to share equally in this surplus, each of the assignors testified that he owed no individual debts and owned no individual property, and this was deemed sufficient to rebut the presumption of fraud.

instrument,[1] though in several cases this has been doubted and the instrument has been sustained, while the illegal provision has been set aside.[2]

Where, however, one of the copartners has in good faith parted with his interest in the firm effects, and the remaining partners assign the firm property, including that in which the retiring partner was interested, for the payment of their debts, to the exclusion of the creditors of the former copartnership, no injustice is done, for the rights of the retiring partner in the property have ceased and the equities of the firm creditors are lost.[3] Indeed, the assignment of the new firm property for the payment of the indebtedness of the former partners would be a violation of the rights of existing creditors and the application of the property to the payment of the debts of strangers.[4]

If the executor of a deceased partner consents to the surviving partners continuing the business with the assets of the firm, his lien on property thereafter acquired will be postposed to that of creditors, when a case arises for an equitable marshaling of assets, as where the surviving partners make a general assignment for the benefit of creditors.[5]

[1] Wilson v. Robertson, 21 N. Y. 587; Keith v. Fink, 47 Ill. 272; Smith v. Howard, 20 How. Pr. 121. In Wilson v. Robertson, *supra*, Mr. Justice Wright remarks: "It seems very plain that the insertion of such a provision in an assignment of the partnership effects of an insolvent firm is a violation of the statute in respect to fraudulent conveyances, and furnishes conclusive evidence of a fraudulent intent on the part of the assignors."

[2] McCullough v. Sommerville, 8 Leigh, 415; Read v. Baylis, 18 Pick. 497; Kemp v. Carnley, 3 Duer, 1; Nye v. Van Husan, 6 Mich. 329; Lassel v. Tucker, 5 Sneed, 1; Gordon v. Cannon, 18 Gratt. 387. See Eyre v. Beebe, 28 How. Pr. 383. See remarks of Hogeboom, J., in Cox v. Platt, 32 Barb. 126. In Morrison v. Atwell, 9 Bosw. 503, where the assignment provided that after all partnership creditors were paid in full the individual creditors of both partners should be paid out of the residue of the partnership fund, share and share alike, without making any provision for the application of the fund to the payment of such creditors, in accordance with the right and interest of each partner in the fund, it was held that this was good ground for an individual creditor to avoid the assignment, but was not a ground of complaint as to partnership creditors.

[3] Dimon v. Hazzard, 32 N. Y. 65; Smith v. Howard, 20 How. Pr. 121; Crane v. Roosa, 40 Hun, 455; Gutman v. McNulty, 22 N. Y. Weekly Dig. 241; Price v. Ford, 18 Md. 489; Miller v. Ewtell, 5 Ohio St. 508; Mandel v. Peay, 20 Ark. 325; Whitworth v. Benbow, 56 Ind. 194; Vosper v. Kramer, 31 N. J. Eq. 420. See Matison v. Demarest, 4 Robt. 161; Cox v. Platt, 32 Barb. 126; Heye v. Bolles, 2 Daly, 231; Paton v. Wright, 15 How. Pr. 481; Lester v. Pollock, 3 Robt. 691; Phelps v. McNeely, 66 Mo. 554; Case v. Beauregard, 99 U. S. 119; Fitzpatrick v. Flannagan, 106 id. 648.

[4] Lester v. Abbott, 28 How. Pr. 488; Smith v. Howard, 20 id. 121.

[5] Hoyt v. Sprague, 103 U. S. 613.

IV. STIPULATIONS FOR THE CONTINUANCE OF ASSIGNOR'S BUSINESS.

§ 181. **Assignor's Business May be Continued, When.**— Assignments are sometimes drawn with stipulations for the continuance of the debtor's business, either by the assignees or by the debtor himself under their direction; and where this is done as ancillary to winding up the debtor's affairs, and with the view of more effectually promoting the interests of the creditors, they will be sustained as valid.[1] But in a case in New York,[2] where the property assigned was an iron foundry, and the assignees were authorized to continue the business for the purpose of completing the manufacture of any of the assigned property, or fitting it for sale and working up materials, etc., so as to realize the greatest possible amount of money therefrom, as in their judgment should seem most advisable; and were expressly directed to pay out of the proceeds of the property all such sums of money as they might find proper and expedient in and about such business and manufacture, it was held that the assignment was thereby rendered absolutely void on its face, thus reversing on this point the previous decision of the court of errors in the important case of Cunningham v. Freeborn.[3] Mr. Justice Selden, in delivering the opinion of the court of appeals, makes use of the following language: "The true

---

[1] This has been decided in England in James v. Whitbread, 20 L. J. C. P. (N. S.) 217; 5 Eng. L. & Eq. 431. But in Owen v. Body, 5 Ad. & E. 28, where one of the express purposes of the trust was to carry on the trade, the deed was held to be invalid. The English forms have for a long time been drawn with clauses authorizing the trustees to carry on the business if they think fit. Nunn v. Wilsmore, 8 Term R. 521, 522; Coate v. Williams, 21 L. J. Exch. (N. S.) 176; s. c., 9 Eng. L. & Eq. 481. And by what is called "a deed of arrangement" a debtor may make an assignment of his property to carry on his business, and to divide the profits ratably among such of his creditors as shall execute the deed, with a provision that as soon as the debts of all the creditors are satisfied the trustees shall hold the residue of the trust property in trust for the assignor. Hickman v. Cox, 36 Eng. L. & Eq. 400. In this case the creditors executing the deed were held to be partners *quoad* third persons.

[2] Dunham v. Waterman, 17 N. Y. 9; reversing s. c., 3 Duer, 166. But an authority to the assignee to finish incomplete work on buildings, if it should be necessary to the better performance of the trust, does not render the assignment fraudulent, as it gives the assignee no additional right beyond what the law imposes in all cases of trust. Watson v. Butcher, 37 Hun, 391. Where an assignment contained a provision that "should it be necessary to the better performance of the trust" the assignee shall have power "to finish such work as is unfinished," paying the necessary expenses before paying the debts provided for in the assignment, it was held that no power to determine as to the necessity was vested in the assignee by the instrument, and as therefore he could not act except under order of the court, that the provision did not vitiate the assignment. Robbins v. Butcher, 104 N. Y. 575; 11 N. E. Rep. 272.

[3] 1 Edw. Ch. 256; s. c. on appeal, 11 Wend. 240. Compare Perry Ins. & Trust Co. v. Foster, 58 Ala. 502, given below.

principle applicable to all such cases is that a debtor who makes a voluntary assignment for the benefit of his creditors may direct in general terms a sale of the property and collection of the dues assigned, and may also direct upon what debts and in what order the proceeds shall be applied, but beyond this can prescribe *no conditions whatever as to the management or disposition of the assigned property.* In all other respects the assignee must be left to act under the ordinary rules and principles which apply to trustees in analogous cases."

Where, by an assignment, the whole of the debtor's real and personal property was conveyed to trustees upon trust, "to manage and improve, sell, etc., and convert into money all the assigned property," etc., and it appeared that the real estate was heavily incumbered with mortgages, some of which were about to be foreclosed, it was held by the supreme court of New York that the power "*to manage and improve*" did not invalidate the assignment; the construction given to the clause in question being that it was not intended to embrace any act that could delay the avowed object of the assignment—"to provide for the payment of the debts."[1]

§ 182. Assignor's Business May be Continued, When — Illustrations.

In Connecticut an assignment of the contents of a country store and raw materials of a factory, empowering the assignees to dispose of the property and apply the avails as directed, also to carry on the business of the factory, and to purchase such additional articles as should be necessary, until all the raw materials on hand at the time of the assignment should be worked up, was held valid.[2]

So in Massachusetts, where in an assignment by a manufacturing company it was stipulated that, until default of payment of debts mentioned, the trustees should permit the assignors to remain in possession of all the property, and to sell and dispose of the personal property according to the usual course of their business, unless the trustees should be of opinion that the safety of creditors would require them to take immediate possession, in which case they should have the right to do so; and that they

---

[1] Hitchcock v. Cadmus, 2 Barb. 381. But was held to render the assignment void in Schlussel v. Willett, 34 id. 615; s. c., 12 Abb. Pr. 397; 22 How. Pr. 15. And see Renton v. Kelly, 49 Barb. 536; affirmed, 51 N. Y. 633.

[2] De Forest v. Bacon, 2 Conn. 633; s. p., Kendall v. New England Carpet Co., 11 id. 383. If the provision for carrying on the business is merely ancillary to winding up the debtor's affairs and made with the view of more effectually protecting the interests of creditors it is valid, but not if made for the benefit of the debtor, or with the intention of hindering and delaying creditors. De Wolf v. Swayne Manuf. Co., 49 Conn. 282, 326.

should also have the right to take possession of subsequently acquired property and apply it to the payment of subsequently contracted debts, the transaction was held to be lawful.[1] And in a subsequent case in the same state, a clause in an assignment made under the statute of 1836, chapter 238, empowering the assignees to work up unwrought stock was held not to invalidate it.[2] So in Alabama a deed of trust conveying land, slaves, mules, plantation utensils, etc., also corn, fodder and bacon, giving to the trustee the management of the plantation during the current year, and devoting the proceeds thereof to the payment of the debts to secure which the deed was made, was decided to be not fraudulent *per se*.[3] In Maryland a clause in an assignment authorizing the assignee to conduct the business " for such time as in his judgment it shall be beneficial to do so," etc., was held to avoid the deed,—the certain effect of the clause being to hinder and delay creditors; and evidence that the assignor intended that the discretion vested in the assignee should be exercised for the exclusive benefit of the creditors is inadmissible.[4]

Similar principles are applied, though the assignment provides

---

[1] Foster v. Saco Manufacturing Co., 12 Pick. 451. This was before the statute of 1836. The court in this case remark that "this assignment, as to the personal estate, was inoperative and void against any creditor who should have attached before the trustees took possession. The stipulation that the vendors should remain in possession and have the use of the property would have rendered it void against creditors. But it was a good executory contract, and when the possession was actually taken in pursuance of its terms the sale became complete." Shaw, C. J., 12 Pick. 454. In the case of Bull v. Loveland, 10 Pick. 9, an assignment was given in evidence, having the same feature of a stipulation that the assignor should continue the business under the direction of the assignees, who were creditors, but no question arose upon it.

[2] Woodward v. Marshall, 22 Pick. 468.

[3] Ravisies v. Alston, 5 Ala. 297. And see Planters' & Merchants' Bank of Mobile v. Clarke, 7 id. 765. The fact that the assignment contemplates that the planting operations of the debtors shall be continued for the current year under their supervision, and that future advances shall be made by the creditor for their successful operation, is not inconsistent with an absolute unconditional appropriation of the property to the payment of the enumerated debts, nor is it in effect a reservation for the use of the debtor. If it appears that a stipulation for continuing the business is made, "not for the interest and benefit of the debtor, and to the prejudice of unsecured creditors, but to promote the interests of the creditors who are preferred, they (assignments) are sustained. . . . If the assignment contemplated the indefinite continuance of planting operations it could not be sustained. But when the provision is simply for the temporary use profitably to the creditor of the property conveyed until a sale can be effected judiciously, it is difficult to perceive any substantial objection to it." Perry Ins. & Trust Co. v. Foster, 58 Ala. 502; Price v. Mazange, 31 id. 701. See Commercial Bank v. Brewer, 71 id. 574. But see Hill v. Agnew, 12 Fed. Rep. 230. See 21 Alb. L. J. 24.

[4] Jones v. Syer, 52 Md. 211; Malcolm v. Hodges, 8 id. 418; **Price v. Pitzer**, 44 id. 521; Webb v. Armisted, 26 Fed. Rep. 70.

that the power of the assignee to carry on the business shall cease whenever a majority of the creditors so desire.[1] Where stipulations of this kind are intended chiefly for the benefit of the assignor, or are coupled with provisions of an onerous or coercive character towards creditors, they will have the effect of avoiding the assignment. Thus, where there was a provision in the assignment that the assignor should be at liberty to continue his business for the term of six months without any proceedings being taken against him, either at law or in equity, and that in case any suit or proceeding should be commenced against him he should be at liberty to plead the assignment in discharge and acquittance thereof, such assignment was for this and other reasons held to be coercive and void as against creditors.[2]

V. PROVISIONS RESPECTING THE TIME FOR EXECUTING THE TRUST.

§ 183. Reasonable Time Allowed for Executing the Trust.—It is sometimes the practice to stipulate in assignments that the trust shall be executed by sale of the assigned property and distribution of the proceeds within a specified time. If the period fixed be a reasonable one such a stipulation will be valid.[3] But care should be taken that it be not on the one hand too short, and on the other so long as to be liable to the charge of hindering or delaying creditors, which would render the assignment fraudulent and void at law.[4] Postponing to an unreasonable time the period of sale and payment will avoid the assignment; and the reasonableness of the delay depends on the character of the property and the circumstances of the case.[5] An interval of three years before the

[1] Gardner v. Commercial Bank, 95 Ill. 298; Peters v. Light, 76 Pa. St. 289.
[2] King v. Kenan, 38 Ala. 63. And see Doyle v. Smith, 1 Cold. (Tenn.) 674; Furman v. Fisher, 4 id. 626; Rindskoff v. Guggenheim, 3 id. 284; Inloes v. American Ex. Bank, 11 Md. 173; Marks v. Hill, 5 Gratt. 400; Berry v. Riley, 2 Barb. S. C. 307. The assignment in this case was of a portion of the debtor's property for the benefit of such creditors only as should become parties, and reserved to the assignor the surplus which should remain after payment of such creditors. In Holmes v. Marshall, 78 N. C. 262, it is held that the presumption of fraud arising from the provision that the trustor "shall have the privilege of continuing his business for one year" is not rebutted by proof that the insolvency of the trustor was unknown to the trustee and *cestui que trust* at the time of the execution of the deed. An authority to the assignee to make such small purchase of goods as will better enable him to sell the stock on hand to the best advantage of creditors will not render the assignment void on its face. Mattison v. Judd, 59 Miss. 99.
[3] Rundlett v. Dole, 10 N. H. 458.
[4] Ruffin, C. J., in Hardy v. Skinner, 9 Ired. L. 191, 195; Phelps v. Curts, 80 Ill. 109.
[5] Hafner v. Irwin, 1 Ired. L. 490; Rundlett v. Dole, 10 N. H. 458; Hardy v. Skinner, 9 Ired. L. 191; Grover v. Wakeman, 11 Wend. 187; Robins v. Embry,

sale of real estate assigned has been held, in Pennsylvania and Tennessee, to be unreasonably long.¹ But in North Carolina, where a deed of trust contained a stipulation that a sale should not take place for three years, and that in the meantime the grantor should remain in possession of the property, consisting of lands, negroes, etc., it was held that the deed could not be regarded by the *court* as fraudulent in *law* upon its face; the opposing creditor having admitted that it was not fraudulent in *fact*.² So, in Alabama, a deed of trust to secure certain creditors, which postponed a sale of the property for nearly three years from the date of the deed, providing also that the grantor should in the meantime retain possession of the property, but devoted all the property as well as the profits to the payment of the debts, was sustained by the court.³ And in Virginia a deed of trust conveying land, slaves, crops, etc., and which was not to be enforced till the end of two years from its date, the profits being in the meantime reserved to the grantor, was held to be not fraudulent as to creditors.⁴ A year's suspension of proceedings, where the expressed object of the conveyance was to prevent a sacrifice of the property, was decided in Kentucky to be fraudulent.⁵ But twelve months to collect the debts and sell the property of an insolvent company was considered, in Mississippi, not unreasonable, the debts being numerous and widely scattered, and the creditors residing at a distance.⁶ The same period has been adopted in Pennsylvania as the proper limit beyond which a delay will not be allowed. Thus, where an assignment contained a provision allowing the assignees to delay payment of the creditors provided for for more than a year from the date of the assignment, it was held to render it absolutely void as to non-

---

¹ Sm. & M. 207; Arthur v. Commercial & Railroad Bank of Vicksburg, 9 id. 396; Farmers' Bank v. Douglass, 11 id. 469; Henderson v. Downing, 24 Miss. 106; Mitchell v. Beal, 8 Yerg. 134; Bennett v. Union Bank, 5 Humph. 612; Hempstead v. Johnson, 18 Ark. 123; Knight v. Packer, 12 N. J. Eq. 214; Perry Ins. & Trust Co. v. Foster, 58 Ala. 502.

¹ Adlum v. Yard, 1 Rawle, 163; Mitchell v. Beal, 8 Yerg. 134; Young v. Hail, 6 Lea (Tenn.), 175, where the delay was four years and six months. See Lowenstein v. Love, 16 Lea, 658; *ante*, p. 219.

² Hardy v. Skinner, 9 Ired. L. 191. Chief Justice Ruffin, who delivered the opinion of the court, admitted this to be "a singular and extremely suspicious transaction," and spoke of the provision as "a very extraordinary one," which might justify a jury in finding it to be fraudulent in fact; but said that the creditor, by admitting that there was no fraud in fact, had given up the case.

³ Elmes v. Sutherland, 7 Ala. 262; commented on and approved in Johnson v. Thweatt, 18 id. 741, 746.

⁴ Dance v. Seaman, 11 Gratt. 778. And see Cochran v. Paris, id. 348; Lewis v Caperton's Ex'r, 8 id. 148; Shattuck v. Knight, 25 W. Va. 597.

⁵ Ward v. Trotter, 3 Monr. (Ky.) 1.

⁶ Robins v. Embry, 1 S. & M. Ch. 207.

assenting creditors.[1] But in a later case it was decided that a proviso in an assignment that the trust should be closed within two years, and, if not then closed, that the assignees should, within six months, sell remaining assets sufficient to pay the debts preferred, but stipulating also for payment and distribution among the preferred creditors, from time to time, as often as there should be moneys in hand, did not postpone the liability of the assignees to account, or protect them from being cited after a year, and was therefore no objection to the validity of the assignment.[2] In Kentucky three months' delay of payment, for the purpose of maturing a crop and fattening stock, was held to be not unreasonable.[3] And in Alabama a provision in the deed delaying a sale for two months was held not to invalidate it.[4] In Arkansas it is provided by statute that the assignee must sell within one hundred and twenty days after the execution of his bond, and must give thirty days' notice of the time and place of sale.[5]

§ 184. Reasonable Time, What.— In the Mississippi case of The Farmers' Bank of Virginia v. Douglas [6] it was said to be "difficult, indeed impossible, to lay down any precise and definite rule applicable in all cases. In general, no further indulgence should be granted than the usual time of collecting debts by due course of law.[7] Yet there may, perhaps, be circumstances in which it would not be fraudulent to stipulate for greater delay; as where the debts are very large, the property likewise large, and where the personal exertions of the debtor are also relied on as one means of payment." [8] In the later case of Henderson v. Downing,[9] in the same state, the rule was laid down in more absolute terms, the court

[1] Sheerer v. Lautzerheizer, 6 Watts, 543.
[2] Dana v. Bank of the United States, 5 W. & S. 223. A deed of land to a trustee containing power to sell in two years to pay a specified creditor, "and if any balance remain, then to pay over the same to the grantor," is valid against *subsequent* creditors. And if the power is not executed within two years, the trust remains good, and the land cannot be sold by subsequent creditors of the grantor. Phillips v. Zerbe Run, etc. Co., 25 Pa. St. 56.
[3] Christopher v. Covington, 2 B. Mon. 357. See Perry Ins. & Trust Co. v. Foster, 58 Ala. 502.
[4] Hindman v. Dill, 11 Ala. 689. And see further, subd. VI, *post*, in this chapter.
[5] Mansf. Dig. (1884), § 309.
[6] 11 S. & M. 469; Clayton, J., id. 539. A provision requiring the assignee to sell the choses in action remaining in his hands at the end of nine months does not allow him sufficient time to collect by legal process, and avoids the deed. Richardson v. Stapleton, 60 Miss. 97. Twenty-two months has been held sufficient, however. Wickham v. Green, 61 id. 463.
[7] Mitchell v. Beal, 8 Yerg. 134; 3 Humph. 180.
[8] Bennett v. The Union Bank of Tennessee, 5 Humph. 612.
[9] 24 Miss. 106, 116.

(Yerger, J.) disclaiming the exception suggested in the preceding case, as not justified by good policy or a fair construction of the statute of frauds. In this case the deed of trust contained a stipulation extending the time of payment for five years; and this was held to render it fraudulent and void as to existing creditors.

An omission to limit any time for the assignee to apply the proceeds of the assigned property has been held, in Massachusetts, to be not objectionable; because the law in such cases requires it to be done in a reasonable time.[1] In the New York case of Cunningham v. Freeborn,[2] there was no limitation of time within which the trust was to be executed. But this was not considered objectionable, especially where, from the nature of the business, it was impossible to fix a time. "All convenient dispatch," observed Mr. Justice Nelson in that case, "was the best limit; and it put the execution of the trust under the control of a court of equity, and with it the conduct and fidelity of the trustee."[3] But in another case in New York, where an assignment provided that, after paying the preferred debts, the assignees should distribute the funds realized from the assigned estate among the general creditors, "at such reasonable time or times as they in their discretion might think proper," it was held to be, on that ground, void.[4]

In Michigan, however, an assignment containing a similar provision has been held to be unobjectionable, on the ground that no time was limited by it for closing the trust.[5]

A provision that the assignee may, in his discretion, pay creditors in instalments, or retain the money until all the assets are collected and then close up the estate at once, will not avoid the assignment, though any improper delay would render the assignee liable in damages, or subject him to removal.[6]

§ 185. **Indefinite Postponement.**— But where the provisions of the assignment itself have the effect of postponing indefinitely the time for closing the trust and making distribution, the delay, unless assented to by the creditors, will be considered fraudulent. A conveyance by a debtor in failing circumstances of all his property to trustees, in trust, to retain it for an indefinite time, until, after defraying the expenses of the trust, they have, out of the profits,

---

[1] Stevens v. Bell, 6 Mass. 339. And see Hower v. Geesaman, 17 S. & R. 251; New Albany & Salem R. R. Co. v. Huff, 19 Ind. 444; Wilt v. Franklin, 1 Binn. 502.
[2] 11 Wend. 241.
[3] Id. 255, 256.
[4] D'Ivernois v. Leavitt, 23 Barb. 63. See p. 245, *ante*. But see Townsend v. Stearns, 32 N. Y. 209; *post*, p. 252.
[5] Hollister v. Loud, 2 Mich. 309, 321.
[6] Eicks v. Copeland, 53 Tex. 581.

paid all the debts of the grantor, where the property thus conveyed is to revert or be reconveyed to him, is fraudulent and void as hindering and delaying creditors.[1] Where, therefore, an incorporated railroad and banking company, being in failing circumstances, and by its charter owning in fee-simple the site of the railroad and other buildings and lots attached to it, assigned by deed all of its real and personal estate to assignees, to pay therewith, and out of the profits of the railroad when completed, it being then unfinished, a certain debt to be contracted by the assignees for the completion of the road, and all the expenses of the trust and of the corporation, and then the debts of the corporation; and no provision whatever was made for the sale of the fee-simple of the corporation in the site of the road, etc.; and the assignment of the profits of the road was indefinite in its duration, except that it was to last until the debts were paid, when the fee, with the road, was to revert to the corporation, it was held that the tendency of the assignment was to lock up the estate indefinitely, to create a perpetuity, to hinder and delay creditors unreasonably, and to secure an ultimate and permanent advantage to the corporation, and that it was therefore void.[2]

VI. LIMITATION OF TIME FOR CREDITORS TO BECOME PARTIES OR ASSENT.

§ 186. **Limitation Must be Reasonable — Illustrations.** — Assignments are sometimes drawn with a provision requiring the creditors for whose benefit they are made to become parties to them, or to assent to them within a limited time. Where this is the case the time so limited must be a reasonable one.[3] What is to be deemed a reasonable time is matter dependent upon the particular circumstances of each case, the situation of the creditors, etc. A time may be so short, or so long, as justly to raise a presumption of fraud.[4] It must neither be too long, so as thereby to improperly delay the creditors in the collection of their debts, nor so short as not to afford time for examination, and therefore be merely

---

[1] Arthur v. The Commercial and Railroad Bank of Vicksburg, 9 Sm. & M. 396.
[2] Arthur v. The Commercial, etc. Bank, *supra*. The doctrine of this case was confirmed by the supreme court of Louisiana in Fellows v. The Commercial & R. R. Bank of Vicksburg 6 Rob. 246; and by the supreme court of the United States, in Bodley v. Goodrich, 7 How. 276. The decision in the last case went chiefly on the ground that the creditors had not assented to the assignment. The same deed of assignment had been previously held good by the court of chancery of Mississippi, in Robins v. Embry, 1 Sm. & M. Ch. 207.
[3] Green v. Trieber, 3 Md. 11.
[4] Story, J., in Halsey v. Whitney, 4 Mason, 206, 225. See Pearpoint v. Graham, 4 Wash. C. C. 232; Fox v. Adams, 5 Greenl. 245.

illusory.[1] In Pennsylvania, in the case of Burd v. Smith,[2] the creditors were required to accept the assignment within nine months. The deed not having been delivered to the assignees for about two months after its date, the court held this to be too short a time, under the circumstances, for the whole of the creditors to receive notice of the deed and signify their assent within the limited time. In Massachusetts, in the case of Halsey v. Whitney,[3] six months were allowed for the creditors to come in under the assignment; and this was held to be not too long, considering the state of the affairs of the debtor. In the case of Dedham Bank v. Richards,[4] in the same state, two calendar months were limited by the assignment for creditors to become parties, with a proviso for extending it not to exceed in the whole six calendar months, to which no objection was taken. In Virginia, in the case of Phippen v. Durham,[5] in which the assignment was sustained, the creditors were required to signify their acceptance within thirty days. In Alabama, in the case of Ashurst v. Martin,[6] one hundred and fifty days after notice of the deed was held a reasonable time, the creditors being scattered over a large space. In Brown v. Lyon,[7] in the same state, the assignment required the residuary creditors to execute it within six months. In Illinois, in the case of Howell v. Edgar,[8] an assignment requiring all creditors wishing to become parties to it to affix their signatures thereto within twelve months from its date, it being stipulated that the debtor should not be held liable to pay any creditors who might sign the same any deficiency that should remain unsatisfied of their respective demands, was held to be fraudulent and void. So in a late case in the same state, where the deed of assignment relieved preferred and resident creditors from the necessity of any acceptance, but excluded from the benefit of the assignment all other creditors, some of them residing at great distances, who should not signify their acceptance within a fixed time, which under the circumstances was unreasonably short, the assignment was held void.[9] In Tennessee, a provision in a deed of assignment requiring the creditors to present their claims within a specified time — twenty months — was not thought objectionable.[10] A provision requiring creditors

[1] Ashurst v. Martin, 9 Port. 566.
[2] 4 Dall. 76.
[3] 4 Mason, 206.
[4] 2 Metc. 105.
[5] 8 Gratt. 457.
[6] 9 Port. 566.
[7] 17 Ala., 659.
[8] 3 Scam. 417.
[9] Hardin v. Osborne, 60 Ill. 93.
[10] Meyer v. Pulliam, 2 Head (Tenn.), 346.

to prove their claims before receiving a dividend is no evidence of an intent to hinder or delay them.[1] In some states provision is made by statute regulating the time within which creditors may come in and present their claims.[2] If no time be prescribed within which the conditions of the assignment are to be complied with, where it contains or stipulates for a release of the debtor, or if the time named be unreasonable, it seems that the deed will be considered fraudulent.[3]

VII. PROVISIONS RESPECTING THE SALE OF THE PROPERTY ASSIGNED.

§ 187. Time of Sale.— We have already seen that a clause unreasonably postponing the time of sale of the assigned property will avoid the assignment. If the assignee be directed to delay the sale, for the purpose of obtaining higher prices for the property, unless by the consent of the creditors, it will be considered a fraud upon them.[4] So if the sale be made conditional upon a certain event. Thus, in a case in Michigan, where the assignment contained a clause that the real estate conveyed by it should not be sold by the assignees until all the personal property and assets assigned should be exhausted, unless with the consent of the assignor, it was held to be not an unconditional assignment, and therefore fraudulent and void in law as against creditors not preferred or not provided for in the assignment.[5] So where the deed of assignment provided that the real estate assigned should be sold at private sale, at the most favorable opportunity which should occur within two

[1] U. S. Bank v. Hutte, 4 B. Mon. (Ky.) 423.
[2] See Appendix, I.
[3] Pearpoint v. Graham, 4 Wash. C. C. 232; 2 Kent's Com. [533], 693; Green v. Trieber, 3 Md. 11; Henderson v. Bliss, 8 Ind. 100, 104. In Shackelford v. P. & M. Bank of Mobile, 22 Ala. 238, it was held that when the deed conveys all the grantor's property of every description, and places all his creditors on an equality, the failure to provide any mode of giving notice to the creditors, or to make them parties to the deed, is not sufficient to render it void upon its face.
[4] Hart v. Crane, 7 Paige, 37; Phelps v. Curtis, 80 Ill. 109. Where a clause in a deed of assignment directed the sale of the assigned property "when convenient and as soon as it can be done without material sacrifice," it did not operate to render the assignment invalid. Wooster v. Stanfield, 11 Iowa, 128. A provision allowing the assignee "to retain the property to await a rise in price or a more favorable market, as they may think most advisable," avoids the assignment. Maughlin v. Tyler, 47 Md. 545. In Maennel v. Murdock, 13 id. 164, the assignees were authorized to sell "whenever they shall think proper and most conducive to the interest of the trust," and this was held not unreasonable. In Maughlin v. Tyler the court says: "But a general sound discretion like this, to be exercised in the interest of the trust, and in the exercise of which the discretion of a court of equity may be invoked, is a very different thing from an express power to retain property to await a specified event, which can only occur at some indefinite future period."
[5] Pierson v. Manning, 2 Mich. 445, 448, 449.

years, of which the assignee was to be the sole judge, and if the property could not be sold at private sale within two years without great loss, then, at the expiration of that period, it should be sold absolutely at public sale, it was adjudged that the necessary effect of this clause was to hinder, delay and defraud creditors, and that it rendered the assignment void.[1] But, in some cases, directions for delaying a sale until the happening of a certain contingency or event have never been held valid. Thus where a deed conveying all the estate of a debtor, in trust to pay debts and secure sureties and indorsers, provided that the estate should not be sold until the estates of the sureties and indorsers were levied on upon judgments obtained against them, it was held in Alabama that the deed was not objectionable as being made "to hinder, delay or defraud creditors."[2] So an assignment of a similar character was held in the same state not to be void on account of a condition that there should be no sale until the security debt was first paid.[3]

§ 188. **Time of Sale — Discretion of Assignee.**— The assignee has a discretion as to the time of sale, but it is a legal discretion, subject to the control of a court of equity,[4] and directions which simply in terms confer such a discretion, and which are entirely in harmony with the duty of the assignee as trustee, are harmless. Thus, a direction to convert the property into cash "as soon as the same may conveniently and properly be done,"[5] "to sell the same without delay,"[6] "to sell, dispose of and convey the said real estate and personal property at such time or times and in such manner as shall be most conductive to the interests of the creditors, and convert the same into money as soon as may be consistent with the interests of said creditors,"[7] and such like,[8] have been ordi-

[1] Hardin v. Osborne, 60 Ill. 98.
[2] Planters' & Merchants' Bank v. Clarke, 7 Ala. 765.
[3] Tarver v. Roffe, 7 Ala. 873.
[4] Thornton, J., in Hardin v. Osborne, 60 Ill. 98.
[5] Ogden v. Peters, 21 N. Y. 23, Comstock, J.
[6] Griffin v. Marquardt, 21 N. Y. 121.
[7] Jessups v. Hulse, 21 N. Y. 384. And see remarks of Selden, J., in this case. In Brigham v. Tillinghast, 15 Barb. 618, the assignment directed the assignees to sell "as soon as practicable and expedient for the best interests of all concerned." In Bellows v. Partridge, 19 Barb. 176, the direction was to sell "as soon as reasonably practicable, with due regard to the rightful interests of the parties concerned." In Hollister v. Loud, 2 Mich. 309, 321, the direction was to sell "within such reasonable time as to them shall seem meet." In Mussey v. Noyes, 26 Vt. 462, the direction was to sell "as soon as practicable and in the most beneficial manner."
[8] In Townsend v. Stearns, 32 N. Y. 209, the direction was "to sell and dispose of the assigned premises at such time or times and in such manner as to

narily inserted in assignments, and although sometimes questioned as tending unduly to extend the powers of the assignee to the prejudice of creditors have been generally sustained.

And even where the time of sale has been left to the option of the trustees or creditors, it has been held not to affect the validity of the assignment. Thus, in Alabama, a provision that the assigned property might remain in the trustee's possession until he might choose to sell, or be required to do so by the beneficiaries of the deed, was held to afford no inference of fraud.[1] And in the same state an assignment by the members of a mercantile company conveying land for the payment of the debts of the partnership, and requiring the trustee to sell at the instance of any creditor of the firm, was held to be founded on sufficient consideration.[2] And in a later case in the same state it has been held that a deed of trust conveying property absolutely to the trustee for the payment of certain specified debts of the grantor, imposing no condition prejudicial to the creditors or restrictive of their rights, and stipulating for no benefit to the grantor, is not fraudulent on its face, although it gives the trustee a discretion as to the time and manner of selling the property conveyed by it. Such a power, it was said, does not affect the *bona fides* of the transaction, or tend to delay the creditors in the collection of the debts secured. Were the trustee to refuse to act promptly or within a reasonable time, they might compel him in equity to do so, or have him displaced and one appointed who would faithfully execute the trust created by the deed.[3] Even the reservation to the debtor himself of the power of fixing the time of sale has under certain circumstances been permitted. Thus, in North Carolina, where a deed of trust to secure certain creditors, prescribed a time after which the property should be sold, but reserved to the debtor the power of order-

---

him (the assignee) may seem to be most for the benefit and advantage of the creditors." In all these cases the clauses in question were held to be unobjectionable. And see Wilson v. Robertson, 21 N. Y. 587; Benedict v. Huntington, 32 N. Y. 219; Meeker v. Saunders, 6 Iowa, 61. And see observations of Duer, J., in Nicholson v. Leavitt, 4 Sandf. (S. C.) 252, 297. But in Woodburn v. Mosher, 9 Barb. 255, where the assignment directed the assignees to sell "within convenient time as to them shall seem meet," it was held that this clause authorized the assignees to discharge their duties whenever it should suit their convenience, and that it rendered the assignment void as operating to hinder or delay creditors. Monson, J., id. 257. And see the general rule laid down in Brigham v. Tillinghast, 13 N. Y. 220.

[1] Dubose v. Dubose, 7 Ala. 235.
[2] Griffin v. Doe, 12 Ala. 783.
[3] Evans v. Lamar, 21 Ala. 333; Ligon, J., id. 336. The deed in this case empowered the trustee to sell, "either at private or public sale, as he might deem best, and at such times as he might deem proper, either for cash or on credit." Id. 334. See Perry Ins. Co. v. Foster, 58 Ala. 502.

ing a sale at an earlier day, it was held that such a provision did not *per se* make the deed fraudulent in law against other creditors.[1] And in a later case in the same state it has been held that a provision in a deed of trust for the postponement of the sale of property for nine months, and then to be sold on a credit for six months, is not a fraud in law, so as to require the court to declare it void on its face.[2] And in Virginia, where a deed of trust provided that the property assigned should not be sold for two years, unless with the consent of the debtor, and that after that time the trustee should sell the property on a credit, as to the land, of one and two years, it was held that the deed was not fraudulent *per se*.[3]

In the forms of general assignments now in use it has been the practice not to fix or limit a particular time for the sale of the assigned property, but to leave it to the discretion of the assignees in general terms, they being only directed to sell "with all reasonable speed," or "as soon as reasonably practicable," or "from time to time, and at such time as they may deem reasonable and proper," or the like.[4]

A provision that a trustee "may sell" was construed to mean "must sell" in Kintner v. Jones.[5]

§ 189. **Mode of Sale.**—It has been a common practice in drawing voluntary assignments to leave the *manner* as well as *time* of sale to the discretion of the assignees, authorizing them to sell "at public or private sale," as they may deem proper,[6] they hav-

---

[1] Cannon v. Peebles, 2 Ired. L. 449; s. c., 4 id. 204.
[2] Gilmer v. Earnhardt, 1 Jones' L. 559.
[3] Dance v. Seaman, 11 Gratt. 778. See, however, the observations of Allen, P., id. 780. See, also, Shattuck v. Knight, 25 W. Va. 590. With regard to the length of time for which the sale may be delayed, it has been held that forty days (Hafner v. Irwin, 1 Ired. L. 490), three months (Christopher v. Covington, 2 B. Mon. (Ky.) 357), four months (Cannon v. Peebles, 2 Ired. L. 449; s. c., 4 id. 204), nine months (Gilmer v. Earnhardt, 1 Jones' L. (N. C.) 559), eleven months (Young v. Booe, 11 Ired. L. 347), have been considered good; but one year (Sheerer v. Lautzerheizer, 6 Watts, 543; *contra*, Graham v. Lockhart, 8 Ala. 9; Farquharson v. McDonald, 2 Heisk. 404; Rindskoff v. Guggenheim, 3 Cold. (Tenn.) 284), eighteen months (Barcroft v. Snodgrass, 1 id. 430), two years (Quarles v Kerr, 14 Gratt. 48), three years (Adlum v. Yard, 1 Rawle, 103), and five years (Storm v. Davenport, 1 Sandf. Ch. 135), have been held fatal. Bump on Fraud. Con. 412, 413.
[4] See form in Illinois, Sackett v. Mansfield, 26 Ill. 21. In Ohio, Thomas v. Talmadge, 228; Abbott's Conveyancer.
[5] 122 Ind. 148; 23 N. E. Rep. 701.
[6] Sackett v. Mansfield, 26 Ill. 21; Halstead v. Gordon, 34 Barb. 422. In Work v. Ellis, 50 Barb. 512, a restriction requiring the assignee to sell at public sale was looked upon as a strange provision, and tending to confirm the idea that the assignment was made to coerce creditors into a settlement. In Farquharson v. Eichelberger, 15 Md. 63, it was said to be no valid objection to an assignment that it provides that the assignee may sell at private sale; similarly in Kyle v.

§ 190.]   TERMS OF SALE — POWER TO SELL ON CREDIT.   255

ing such a discretion in the absence of any express direction or authority contained in the instrument.[1] In some cases objections have been raised against assignments on this ground. But in Alabama a discretion of this kind, given to the trustee in a deed of trust, has repeatedly been held to be not indicative of fraud.[2] And in North Carolina a provision authorizing a trustee to sell at private sale was held, at most, to be only evidence of fraud, to be left to a jury, and was no ground for the court to pronounce the deed fraudulent *per se*.[3] In Arkansas a sale by the assignee must be at public auction, and, as before stated, within one hundred and twenty days after the execution of the assignee's bond;[4] and a provision in the assignment contrary to these requirements renders it void.[5]

The discretion given to assignees, on this point, is sometimes expressed in more general terms; the assignment empowering them to sell " in such manner as they shall consider expedient, and most for the interests of all parties."[6] And sometimes both modes of sale are designated, the assignees being authorized to sell in such manner as they may think most advisable, within a limited time (as one year), and then to close the sale at auction.[7]

§ 190. **Terms of Sale — Power to Sell on Credit.** — It has also been a common practice, in drawing assignments, to leave the *terms*, as well as the time and mode of sale, to the discretion of the assignees, authorizing them to sell " upon such terms as they shall think most expedient or advantageous;"[8] and sometimes

---

Harveys, 25 W. Va. 716. And see observations of Duer, J., in Nicholson v. Leavitt, 4 Sandf. S. C. 252; reversed, 6 N. Y. 510; North River Bank v. Schumann, 63 How. Pr. 476. The modern English forms are drawn with a similar clause. See James v. Whitbread, 20 L. J. C. P. (N. S.) 217; 5 Eng. L. & Eq. 431.

[1] Hart v. Crane, 7 Paige, 37. In Waldron v. Wilcox (R. I. Index P. 128), provisions allowing the assignee to sell at public or private sale, to buy in the premises and resell without responsibility for loss, did not invalidate the assignment as against creditors, it not appearing that any benefit accrued to the assignor at their expense from the powers given.

[2] Brock v. Headen, 13 Ala. 370; Abercrombie v. Bradford, 16 id. 560; Evans v. Lamar, 21 id. 333; Shackelford v. P. & M. Bank of Mobile, 22 id. 238.

[3] Burgin v. Burgin, 1 Ired. L. 453. It was observed by Ruffin, C. J., in this case, that a higher price may sometimes be got by private contract than by auction. Id. 458. In point of fact, a *public* sale appears to have been intended by the assignment in this case, the word "private" being inserted by the misprision of the writer. Id. 454, 458.

[4] R. S. of Ark. (1874), § 387, p. 208.

[5] Bartlett v. Teah, 1 McCrary, 176; Raleigh v. Griffith, 37 Ark. 150.

[6] Neally v. Ambrose, 21 Pick. 185. In this case it was held that under such an assignment the assignee might sell on a credit. Farquharson v. Eichelberger, 15 Md. 63; Ely v. Hair, 16 B. Mon. 230. But see Clark v. Fuller, 21 Barb. 128, *contra*.

[7] Hopkins v. Ray, 1 Metc. 79.

[8] Ashurst v. Martin, 9 Port. 566; Pierce v. Brewster, 32 Ill. 268.

more particularly empowering them to sell "for cash or upon credit,"[1] as they may deem proper or most for the advantage of parties.[2] In regard to the power to sell *on credit*, it was formerly held in New York that a clause expressly giving such a power did not vitiate the assignment on the ground of hindering and delaying creditors;[3] that the power itself was, in many instances, beneficial to the interests of creditors, and in some cases essential to the due execution of the trust;[4] and that where it was not expressly given it was usually implied in trusts for the payment of debts.[5] But the court of appeals of this state have, in several cases, determined that a clause of this kind avoids the whole assignment;[6] its tendency and effect being to "hinder, delay and

[1] When the instrument is silent, the assignee will have the power of sale for cash or on credit, in his discretion as trustee. Hoffman v. Mackall, 5 Ohio St. 124.

[2] The forms now in use in England allow the trustees to give any credit and take any security for the purchase-money. See Janes v. Whitbread, 5 Eng. L. & Eq. 431.

[3] Rogers v. De Forest, 7 Paige, 272; Nicholson v. Leavitt, 4 Sandf. S. C. 252; reversed on appeal, 6 N. Y. 510.

[4] Nicholson v. Leavitt, 4 Sandf. S. C. 252; Duer, J., id. 289, 290.

[5] Walworth, C., in Rogers v. De Forest, 7 Paige, 272; Nicholson v. Leavitt, *ubi supra*.

[6] Barney v. Griffin, 2 N. Y. 365, 371; Nicholson v. Leavitt, 6 N. Y. 510; Burdick v. Post, id. 522; Porter v. Williams, 5 N. Y. 142; Kellogg v. Slauson, 11 id. 302; Brigham v. Tillinghast, 3 id. 215. The question, having been thus repeatedly passed upon by the court of last resort, is to be considered in this state as judicially settled. But as the contrary has also been held in able and well-reasoned opinions, a brief view of the course of the decisions, with the grounds of each, may not be without value or interest to the profession in other states. The first case in which the question appears to have arisen was that of Rogers v. De Forest, which came before the court of chancery in 1838 (7 Paige, 272). In this case the assignment, which was of both real and personal property, contained an express power to the assignee to sell on credit, and also to lease and mortgage the assigned estate for the benefit of creditors. The chancellor held that the power to *sell on credit* did not render the trust invalid under the provisions of the Revised Statutes relative to uses and trusts; neither did it render the assignment fraudulent and void as against the creditors of the assignor. "The express power to sell on credit," he observed, "is a power which is usually implied in trusts of this description, and it is not a violation of the provisions of the Revised Statutes relative to uses and trusts. Neither does the creation of such a trust tend in any manner to delay or hinder the creditors of the assignor in the collection of their debts. For if the assignees do their duty they will not sell the property on credit without obtaining therefor the difference in value between a sale for cash and a sale upon credit. And the creditors, should they think proper to do so, have a right to insist that such securities should be immediately converted into money and applied towards the satisfaction of their respective debts, or as soon as they shall deem it for their interest to have it done." But as to the power or trust in the assignment *to lease or mortgage*, the chancellor held that such a trust was not authorized by the Revised Statutes, and that for that reason no estate in the real property vested in the assignees. On an appeal from the decree in this case to the court of errors (Darling v. Rogers, 22 Wend. 483), the

defraud creditors," within the meaning of the statute. The same chancellor's decision was reversed, the court holding the assignment to be so far valid as to vest the estate in the real property in the assignee. But the question as to the validity of the power to *sell on credit* was not brought before the court, nor was it noticed in the opinion delivered on the appeal. The chancellor's decision, therefore, sustaining the assignment on that point, may be considered to have been left undisturbed. In the case of Meacham v. Sternes, which came before the court of chancery in 1842 (9 Paige, 398), the assignee was directed by the assignment to sell the trust property at such reasonable times as should seem proper to him; and it was held that this did not authorize him to *sell at retail and on credit,* nor to send to agents to sell on commission. The chancellor, in the course of delivering his opinion, observed that it was a breach of duty in the assignee to *retail* the property upon *credit.* " For the creditors were entitled to have the assigned property converted into money and applied to the payment of their debts, without any unnecessary delay. And the assignment itself would have been clearly fraudulent if the assignors had in terms directed their assignees to dispose of the property in the manner in which it was disposed of by the trustee in this case; they being at the time of the assignment in failing circumstances, and making this assignment of all their partnership effects in trust to pay their debts." In the case of Barney v. Griffin, which came before the vice-chancellor of the first circuit in 1847 (4 Sandf. Ch. 552), the assignment authorized the assignees to sell the real estate assigned at public or private sale, for cash or upon credit, or partly for cash and partly upon credit, and generally upon such terms as the assignees should think most advantageous. But it also contained other and highly obnoxious clauses, especially a reservation to the assignor of the residue of the assigned property remaining after payment of certain specified creditors to the exclusion of the general creditors, upon which the vice-chancellor's decision declaring it void seems to have been essentially based, the only authority cited and relied on by the court being that of Goodrich v. Downs, in the supreme court (6 Hill, 438), in which such a clause was the principal ground of the decision. On an appeal to the chancellor the vice-chancellor's order appointing a receiver was affirmed, and the case was then carried to the court of appeals. In Barney v. Griffin, as it came before the court of appeals in 1849 (2 N. Y. 365), the principal grounds of objection to the assignment were two, namely, the clause reserving the residue, as above stated, to the assignor, and the clause authorizing a sale of the assigned property on credit. On the first point the opinion of the court was unanimous against the validity of the assignment; the point having been in fact already conclusively settled. And on the second point it was held by Bronson, J., who delivered the opinion of the court, to be an unanswerable objection to the deed that the assignees were authorized to sell the property on credit. "An insolvent debtor," he observed, "cannot, under color of providing for creditors, place his property beyond their reach, in the hands of trustees of his own selection, and take away the right of the creditors to have the property converted into money for their benefit without delay. They have the right to determine for themselves whether the property shall be sold on credit; and a conveyance which takes away that right and places it in the hands of the debtor, or in trustees of his own selection, comes within the very words of the statute: it is a conveyance to hinder and delay creditors, and cannot stand." Id. 371. The learned judge relied on the case of Meacham v. Sternes, observing that the question was considered by the chancellor in that case, and that his views fully accorded with his own. The case of Rogers v. De Forest was not noticed. In Nicholson v. Leavitt, a very important case, involving the validity of several voluntary assignments, came before the superior court of the city of New York in 1850 (4 Sandf. S. C. 252) Some of the assignments contained a clause directing a sale of the assigned property " for cash or upon credit, or partly for cash and doctrine has been recognized by the supreme courts of Vermont,[1] partly upon credit, and by and under such terms and conditions as the assignees should deem reasonable and proper;" and upon this and several other grounds the assignments were assailed as invalid. The case was fully considered by Duer, J., in a long and elaborate opinion; and the court, through him, held that a discretionary power given to the assignee in an assignment for the benefit of creditors to sell the assigned property on credit was not evidence of an intent to defraud creditors, and did not vitiate the assignment. The court adopted the opinion, and followed the ruling of the chancellor in the case of Rogers v. De Forest, which was considered to have not been disturbed either by the judgment of the court of errors in Darling v. Rogers, or by the chancellor's own remarks in Meacham v. Sternes. The decision of the court of appeals to the contrary, in Barney v. Griffin, was not considered as of binding authority; the opinion expressed by Mr. Justice Bronson in that case, on the point of an authority to sell on credit, being regarded (from the form of the reporter's note and other circumstances) merely as his own, and not that of the court. The question was considered upon principle as well as upon authority, and the analogies derived from the practice of courts of equity and the course of the legislature itself; and it was held, in accordance with the views in Rogers v. De Forest, that such a power did not necessarily hinder or delay creditors; that it more frequently facilitated the distribution of the assigned property, and increased the amount of the fund beyond what would be produced by a sale for cash only; that it was indeed in some cases essential to the due execution of the trust; that where it was not given in terms, the law would imply its existence; and that an authority which the law itself would give by implication could not be regarded as illegal and fraudulent when given in terms. An appeal was taken from the decree of the court in this case, and the cause carried to the court of appeals, the result of which will be stated below. In Burdick v. Post, 12 Barb. 168, which came before the superior court of the second district at the Kings county general term, in 1851, an assignment containing a clause conferring upon the assignee power to sell on credit, was held by a majority of the court (Brown, J., dissenting) to be void on that ground alone. The decision of the court of appeals, in Barney v. Griffin, was considered as of binding authority, and that in Nicholson v. Leavitt disapproved. The court in this case say that a clause authorizing a sale on credit vitiates an assignment on the same principle and for the same reason as would a provision directing the assignee to wait twelve months before proceeding to execute his trust. This case also was carried to the court of appeals. A decision to the same point had been previously made at the Ulster county special term in 1851. Whitney v. Krows, 11 Barb. 198. The case of Nicholson v. Leavitt, on appeal from the superior court of the city of New York as already stated, went up on the single question which forms the subject of this note, namely, whether a voluntary assignment by a debtor in failing circumstances was void by reason of its containing a clause authorizing the assignee to sell the assigned property *on credit.* The court of appeals (in 1852) reversed the judgment of the court below, holding that the assignment was fraudulent and void, for the general reason stated in the text. Nicholson v. Leavitt, 6 N. Y. 510. The court, in delivering their opinion, remark that the debtor cannot, by the creation of a trust, avoid the obligation of immediate payment or extend the period of credit without the assent of the creditor; and that the attempt to do this, however plausible may be the pretense, is in conscience and in law a fraud and nothing else. Id. 517. They further say that if the property is more than sufficient to discharge all the debts of the assignor, he has no right to delay creditors by giving credit on the sale of

---

[1] Redfield, J., in Mussey v. Noyes, 26 Vt. 462, 470; Bennett, J., in Paige v. Olcott, 28 Vt. 465, 468, 469.

Wisconsin,[1] Minnesota,[2] Michigan[3] and Illinois.[4] On the other hand it has been decided in Alabama that a provision in an assignment authorizing the trustee to sell for cash or on credit, as shall, in his opinion, most comport with the interest of all parties concerned, was not sufficient to affect the validity of the deed.[5] The court refer to the case of Ashurst v. Martin,[6] in the same state, where it was said that such a power was necessary to enable the trustee to execute the trust, but must be exercised in reference to the objects of the trust and the interest of the creditors in good faith. The power to sell for cash or on good credit, it was said, does not vary in legal effect from the power to sell on such terms as he may deem expedient; and the court refused to pronounce that the reservation of such a power within itself renders the deed void. It is the duty of the trustee to execute the trust speedily, it is true, but yet in such a manner as will best subserve the interest of the creditors. He ought to sell for cash or on such credit as will not unreasonably delay the payment of the debts. To require the sale in all instances to be for cash only may work a prejudice to all or some of the parties interested. "We think," it is finally observed, "the trustee ought to have a reasonable discretion in fixing the terms of the sale; and that he is clothed with such discretion as may benefit the creditors if discretely exercised is not sufficient within itself

the property, with a view to increase the surplus resulting to him; this would be a trust for his own benefit, and consequently void by the first section of the "act against fraudulent conveyances." 7 Paige, 37; id. 518. Finally it is remarked that the same considerations which made the legislature require an immediate sale require an immediate payment also; and that a discretion may be as judiciously exercised in postponing the time of sale of property as in postponing the time of payment. Id. 521. The ruling of the chancellor in Rogers v. De Forest was disapproved, and the decisions in Burdick v. Huntting, *post*, and Barney v. Griffin were relied on; the authority of the latter being now expressly confirmed. At a subsequent day in the same term the judgment of the supreme court, in Burdick v. Post, was unanimously affirmed, for the reasons given in Nicholson v. Leavitt. Burdick v. Post, 6 N. Y. 522. And this ruling has been recognized in several subsequent cases and may be regarded as the settled law of the state. See Gates v. Andrews, 37 N. Y. 657; Morrison v. Brand, 5 Daly, 40; Porter v. Williams, 9 N. Y. 142; s. c., 12 How. Pr. 107; Rapalee v. Stewart, 27 N. Y. 310. In Judson v. Abeel, 5 N. Y. Weekly Dig. 221, it was held that an authority to the assignee to sell the property "to the best possible advantage" did not avoid the assignment, on the ground that it allowed a sale on credit.

[1] Hutchinson v. Lord, 1 Wis. 286. See id. 312, 313; Keep v. Saunderson, 2 id. 42; s. c., 12 id. 352; Haines v. Campbell, 8 id. 187; Lord v. Devendorf, 54 id. 491.
[2] Greenleaf v. Edes, 2 Minn. 264; Truitt v. Caldwell, 2 id. 364. See Mower v. Hanford, 6 id. 535; Benton v. Snyder, 22 id 247; Bennett v. Ellison, 23 id. 242.
[3] Sutton v. Hanford, 14 Mich. 19.
[4] Pierce v. Brewster, 32 Ill. 268; Bowen v. Parkhurst, 24 id. 257; Gardner v. Commercial Nat. Bank, 95 id. 298.
[5] Abercrombie v. Bradford, 16 Ala. 560.
[6] 9 Port. 566.

to authorize us to pronounce the deed fraudulent."[1] The same doctrine has continued to be maintained in several later cases in the same state.[2] In Virginia,[3] Tennessee,[4] Maryland,[5] Mississippi,[6] Missouri,[7] Texas,[8] and Indiana,[9] also, a trust for sale on credit has been held valid. And express powers to trustees to sell for cash or on credit are of constant occurrence in deeds of trust in Virginia[10] and other southern states.[11] In a case in Ohio[12] where the question came before the supreme court and the New York cases were cited and relied on, it was held that an express power to sell on credit did not *per se* avoid an assignment. The court (Swan, J.) in delivering their opinion observe: " A sale by a trustee upon reasonable time of credit, taking the usual security, is an act of good faith, and is recognized by our laws relating to the settlement of the estates of deceased persons, and is frequently directed by the court. An absolute and inflexible rule that a trustee for the payment of debts must at all times and under all circumstances sell for cash would not be for the interest of creditors. And if this be so, a provision in the trust deed in regard to credit, not specifically requiring a credit beyond what a court would sanction in the absence of such provision, cannot, in our opinion, be deemed *per se* fraudulent."[13] In California the rule adopted by the supreme court is that a power to assignees to sell on credit is not conclusive, but only presumptive, evidence of fraud.[14]

[1] Dargan, J., 16 Ala. 565, 566.
[2] Evans v. Lamar, 21 Ala. 333; Shackelford v. P. & M. Bank of Mobile, 22 id. 238; Goldthwaite, J., id. 244; Miller v. Stetson, 32 id. 161; s. c., 36 id. 642; England v. Reynolds, 38 id. 370.
[3] Dance v. Seaman, 11 Gratt. 778, 781, and cases cited.
[4] Gunnell v. Adams, 11 Humph. 85.
[5] Farquharson v. Eichelberger, 15 Md. 63; Berry v. Matthews, 13 id. 537.
[6] Re Walker, 18 N. B. R. 56; Richardson v. Marqueze, 59 Miss. 80; Mattison v. Judd, id. 99; Anderson v. Lachs, id. 111. But where the assignment requires the assignee to convert into money, "by a sale for ready money," all the property, the assignee has no power to sell on credit. Cox v. Palmer, 60 id. 793.
[7] Johnson v. McAllister's Assignee, 30 Mo. 327; Gates v. Labeaume, 19 id. 17.
[8] Carlton v. Baldwin, 22 Tex. 724; Eicks v. Copeland, 53 id. 581.
[9] Wright v. Thomas, 1 Fed. Rep. 716; s. c., 9 Biss. 244.
[10] Johnston v. Zane's Trustees, 11 Gratt. 552; Dance v. Seaman, id. 778.
[11] Evans v. Lamar, 21 Ala. 333.
[12] Conkling v. Conrad, 6 Ohio St. 611.
[13] Conkling v. Conrad, 6 Ohio St. 620, 621. The court, after noticing the New York rule to the contrary, and citing the cases of Nicholson v. Leavitt and Burdick v. Post, continue to say: "But this seems to be law peculiar to New York; and the dissenting opinion of Brown, J., in the case of Burdick v. Post et al., above referred to, shows very conclusively to our minds that the decision of the majority cannot be sustained upon principle or authority; and we must refer to that dissenting opinion for the reasons upon which our own opinion is based." Id. And see Hoffman v. Mackall, 5 Ohio St. 124.
[14] Billings v. Billings, 2 Cal. 107, 114.

§ 191. **Prohibiting Sale on Credit.**— But though in New York it is now settled that an express authority to an assignee to sell on credit avoids an assignment, it is not advisable to *prohibit* him from selling on credit by an express provision in the deed. In a case in the supreme court an assignment was sought to be avoided on the ground, among others, that it contained such a clause; and the court held that though in the particular case it was not *per se* evidence of fraud, so as to justify them in setting the assignment aside, it might become so in connection with other circumstances showing that a forced sale was intended to the injury of the creditors;[1] but it has since been determined that such a clause does not of itself invalidate an assignment.[2]

§ 192. **Sale at Retail.**— A direction to the assignees to sell the assigned property at *retail* and on credit will render an assignment fraudulent and void.[3] And a power given to a trustee in a deed of trust to sell property "gradually, according to the terms and manner of the grantor's business," will vacate the deed as to creditors.[4]

§ 193. **Implied Power to Sell on Credit.**— Not only has it been decided in New York and elsewhere that an express authority to sell on credit vitiates an assignment, but it has been further held in some cases [5] that if such a power can be fairly inferred or implied from the language of the instrument, it will be equally fatal to its validity. It therefore becomes important to ascertain what words will be construed to confer such a power, or what amounts to a power to sell on credit.

It has already been stated [6] to be a common practice in drawing assignments to leave the terms as well as the time and manner of the sale to the discretion of the assignees; they being directed, after taking possession of the property, to sell and dispose of it "upon such terms and conditions as in their judgment they may think best and most for the interests of the parties concerned," or words of equivalent import. Such a clause has long been in use in this and other states, and will be found in the most approved collections of precedents.[7] It has recently been contended, how-

[1] Van Rossum v. Walker, 11 Barb. 237.
[2] Grant v. Chapman, 38 N. Y. 293; Carpenter v. Underwood, 19 id. 520; Stern v. Fisher, 32 Barb. 198.
[3] Meacham v. Sternes, 9 Paige, 398; Truitt v. Caldwell, 3 Minn. 364.
[4] Am. Exchange Bank v. Inloes, 7 Md. 380; Inloes v. Am. Exchange Bank, 11 id. 73.
[5] See, however, what is said by Redfield, C. J., in Mussey v. Noyes, 26 Vt. 462, 469; and see the note *in loc.*
[6] *Ante*, p. 254.
[7] Angell on Assign., 209, 215, referred to by Parker, J., in Kellogg v. Slauson, 11 N. Y. 302, 307.

ever, that it amounts to an authority to sell on credit, and is therefore good ground for avoiding the assignment containing it. The most important cases in New York in which it has been made the subject of construction by the courts will now be briefly reviewed.

§ 194. **Implied Power to Sell on Credit — Cases.** — In Lyon v. Platner,[1] where the assignment contained a clause resembling the one in question, the supreme court held that authorized a sale upon credit and was therefore void. In Moir v. Brown[2] the clause was in terms identical with the one in question, the assignees being authorized to sell and dispose of the property upon " such terms and conditions as, in their judgment, they may think best and meet [most] for the interest of the parties concerned, and convert the same into money." The court (Hand, J.) thought that this language certainly gave a " broad discretionary power sufficient in an ordinary power of attorney to sustain a sale on credit." But the point was not decided. In Schufeldt v. Abernethy,[3] however, in the superior court of the city of New York, where the assignment contained the same clause, the court held that the words, by a necessary implication, gave a discretionary power to the assignee to sell upon credit, and therefore rendered the assignment, on its face, fraudulent and void.

But in several other cases, embracing the latest decisions in the supreme court and court of appeals, such a clause has been sustained. Thus, in Whitney v. Krows,[4] it was held that it would not be construed as authorizing the assignees to sell on credit. The court further held that the fair construction of such a provision was that the trustees were to exercise their judgment as to the manner of sale, but when they did sell they were to receive the money. In Southworth v. Sheldon[5] the same view was taken;

---

[1] This case was cited by the court in Woodburn v. Mosher, 9 Barb. 255, as decided in the sixth district in 1850; but it has not been reported. The case of Woodburn v. Mosher itself has sometimes been relied on as an authority to the same point. See Murphy v. Bell, 8 How. Pr. 468. But the question in that case was rather as to the *time* than the *terms* of the sale, the assignees being directed, " within convenient time as to them shall seem meet," to convert the property into money. The court held that this clause authorized the assignees to discharge their duties whenever it should suit their convenience, and that it rendered the assignment void, as operating to hinder and delay creditors. Monson, J., 9 Barb. 257. See the observations of Parker, J., in Kellogg v. Slauson, 11 N. Y. 307.

[2] 14 Barb. 39.

[3] 2 Duer, 533.

[4] 11 Barb. 198.

[5] 7 How. Pr. 414; New York special term, Jan., 1853. This case appears to be in conflict with that of Murphy v. Bell, 8 How. Pr. 468, decided at the Mon-

§ 194.]   IMPLIED POWER TO SELL ON CREDIT.   263

the court saying that the provision merely authorized the assignees to do what the law imposed upon them as a duty. In Kellogg v. Slauson,¹ where the same question was raised, the supreme court again held that the clause did not authorize a sale upon credit, and would not therefore render the assignment void, as hindering or delaying creditors. On appeal, the court of appeals affirmed the judgment.² These cases were cited and relied on by the supreme court in Nichols v. McEwen,³ the court saying that the question was no longer open to discussion.

In Clark v. Fuller⁴ the supreme court held that a provision empowering the assignee to sell and dispose of the assigned property " in such manner as he shall deem best and most for the interest of the parties concerned, and convert the same into money," was not to be construed as authorizing a sale on credit, and therefore did not render the assignment void on its face.

In Bellows v. Partridge the assignment authorized the assignee to convert the assigned property into money, by sale either public or private, " as soon as reasonably practicable, with due regard to the rightful interests of all the parties concerned, and in such a manner as might, in the judgment of the assignee, be for the best interests of the estate." On the hearing of the case at the special term it was objected that this clause conferred a power to sell on credit,

---

roe county special term, in the same month and year. But in the latter case, as in Woodburn v. Mosher, upon which the court relied, the clause in question seems to have had reference rather to the time of the sale than the terms. The court, it is true, laid stress upon the word "securities," as implying a sale on credit; but the reasoning on this point is not satisfactory.

¹ 15 Barb. 56.

² 11 N. Y. 302. The court, in this case (Parker, J.), remarks: "It is certain that the 'terms and conditions' on which the property is to be disposed of are left entirely to the discretion of the assignees. But that discretion is to be exercised within legal limits. The law implies a restriction not inserted in express words. It will not defeat the instrument by inferring that the assignor contemplated an illegal act. There is no express authority given in the assignment to sell on credit or do any other illegal act; and there is ample room, within legal limits, for the exercise of the discretion conferred. The assignees were at liberty to sell at public or private sale — in large or small quantities — or one article, with the privilege of taking more of the same kind at the same price. They might require a certain percentage to be paid at the time of the bid, and the balance on delivery, and might prescribe the time and place for delivery in gross or in parcels. The language of the assignment can be abundantly satisfied by a construction that shall support the instrument, and in such case the rule is well settled that a construction shall not be given which shall defeat it." Id. 305.

³ 21 Barb. 65; s. c., 17 N. Y. 22.

⁴ 21 Barb. 128. But see Neally v. Ambrose, 21 Pick. 185, contra. It had been previously held in Meacham v. Sternes, 9 Paige, 398, that a provision that the property should be sold by the trustee " in such manner and at such reasonable times as should seem proper to him " did not authorize a sale at retail on credit. Rapalee v. Stewart, 27 N. Y. 311.

and consequently rendered the assignment void. But the court (Roosevelt, J.) overruled the objection, holding that, by the language of the instrument, it was only a "rightful" or "lawful" power which was intended to be given, and that if a power to sell on credit were not lawful, no such power was given. On appeal to the general term the judgment of the court was affirmed.[1]

In Mann v. Whitbeck[2] the assignment contained a clause authorizing the assignee "generally to adopt such measures in relation to the settlement of the estate as would, in his judgment, promote the true interest thereof." It was held, on the authority of Bellows v. Patridge, and Whitney v. Krows, that this clause did not invalidate the assignment.

In Brigham v. Tillinghast[3] the assignees were directed, "as soon as practicable and expedient for the best interests of all concerned and interested," to convert the property assigned "into money or available means." The supreme court held the assignment good, but on appeal the court of appeals reversed the judgment, holding the assignment void on the ground that the words "available means" conferred, by necessary implication, a power to sell on credit.[4] The court (Dean, J.), in concluding their opinion in this case, say: "The true rule to be observed is this: An insolvent debtor may make an assignment of all his estate to trustees, to pay his debts, with or without preferences; but such assignees are bound to make an immediate application of the property. And any provision contained in the assignment, which shows that the debtor, at the time of its execution, intended to prevent such immediate application, will avoid the instrument; because it shows that it was made with 'intent to hinder and delay creditors in the collection of their debts.' Such an intent, expressed in the instrument or proved *aliunde*, is fatal alike by the language of our statute and the well-settled adjudications of the English and American courts."[5]

In Wilson v. Robertson,[6] where the language employed was the same as in Kellogg v. Slauson, it was not regarded as objectionable,

---

[1] 19 Barb. 176. The case, as decided at the general term, is all that is here reported. It will be seen that the opinion of the court is not so much on the point of a power to sell on credit as on that of a delay of the sale; the court holding that the clause in dispute "implies no authority to the assignee to delay the sale longer than the ordinary time required for the efficient performance of such a duty, which depends upon the peculiar circumstances of each case and the condition in which the assignor's affairs are placed, and does not render the assignment void."
[2] 17 Barb. 388.
[3] 15 Barb. 618. See McCallie v. Walton, 37 Ga. 611.
[4] 13 N. Y. 215.
[5] 13 N. Y. 220.
[6] 21 N. Y. 587. See Jessup v. Hulse, 21 N. Y. 168.

and the rule was there laid down as being that an assignment will not be construed as conferring an authority to sell on credit when its language is consistent with a different interpretation, which will make it legal and valid. But in Rapalee v. Stewart,[1] where the direction was that the trust property be converted into cash or otherwise disposed of to the best advantage by the assignee, this was construed as conferring a power to sell on credit, and invalidated the assignment. In Benedict v. Huntington[2] the assignees were directed to sell and dispose of the property upon such terms and conditions as in their judgment might appear best and most for the interest of the parties concerned, the court sustained the assignment. Mr. Justice Potter observed, where the language of an assignment can be abundantly satisfied with a construction that will support the instrument, the well-settled rule should control that a construction should be given which will not defeat it. And in Townsend v. Stearns,[3] where the assignee was empowered to sell and dispose of the assigned premises at such time or times and in such manner as to him may seem to be most for the benefit and advantage of the creditors, the same rule of construction was applied and the assignment was sustained.

In Wisconsin the New York doctrine in regard to an implied power to sell on credit and its effects appear to have been adopted, and even extended. Thus, in Hutchinson v. Lord,[4] where the assignment empowered the assignee to sell in such manner and "upon such terms and for such prices as to him should seem advisable," it was held that this was an authority to sell on credit, which necessarily would operate to hinder and delay creditors, and rendered the assignment fraudulent and void. And in the later case of Keep v. Sanderson,[5] where the provision objected to was in the exact words of that in Kellogg v. Slauson, the court held that it conferred an authority to sell on credit, which avoided the whole assignment.

In Vermont the doctrine of an implied power to sell on credit, and its effect, does not seem to be approved, or rather the courts decline to infer such a power where none is expressly given. Thus, in Mussey v. Noyes,[6] where the assignment empowered the

[1] 27 N. Y. 311. The assignment, however, was sustained as against the plaintiff, he having assented to and ratified it.
[2] 32 N. Y. 219.
[3] 32 N. Y. 209.
[4] 1 Wis. 286. See the observations of Crawford, J., who goes into a critical examination of the meaning of the word "terms." Id. 313, 314.
[5] 2 Wis. 42; Crawford, J., id. 59, 60. The court rely upon the previous case of Hutchinson v. Lord, *supra;* s. c., 12 Wis. 352. But see Norton v. Kearney, 10 Wis. 443.
[6] 26 Vt. 462, 468, 469. And see the note, ibid.

assignees, "as soon as practicable, and in the most beneficial manner," to convert the property into money, it was objected that this conferred a power to sell on credit. But the supreme court (Redfield, C. J.) held that the words would more naturally exclude such a power, especially where it was regarded as illegal; and that the power was neither expressly nor impliedly given. In the later case of Peck & Co. v. Merrill,[1] in the same court, the point as to the effect of an implied power to sell on credit was distinctly raised and argued by counsel. But the court passed it over without notice. In the still later case of Paige v. Olcott,[2] the court (Bennett, J.) quote the case of Mussey v. Noyes as having been "decided upon a construction of the assignment, the court holding that no express power of sale was given in the instrument, and none should be intended in order to vitiate the assignment." And it may be stated as the general rule, that an authority to sell on credit will not be implied adversely to the assignment, from language susceptible of a different construction which will support the instrument.[3]

In a case[4] in Nebraska the assignment allowed the assignee to dispose of the property "*in any manner whatsoever*, as freely and lawfully as the assignor could do himself, which the said party of the second part, trustee as aforesaid, may deem advisable to do, tending, in his opinion, to convert the same into money for the benefit of all interested." It was held that this would authorize a sale on credit or an exchange, and that the deed was void on its face.

In Utah,[5] where a debtor assigned, dividing his creditors into three classes, and directed that "the times, places and terms of selling the property shall be agreed on by the trustee and the majority interested of the first and second class creditors," it was held that the words "terms of selling" embraced the power to sell on credit, and that the assignment was fraudulent and void.

VIII. SPECIAL POWERS AND DIRECTIONS TO ASSIGNEES.

§ 195. **Power to Mortgage and Lease.**— A clause in an assignment of real property, authorizing the assignees to *lease or mortgage* the property, for the benefit of the creditors at large, is in

[1] Id. 686.
[2] 28 Vt. 465, 469.
[3] Finlay v. Dickerson, 29 Ill. 9; Sackett v. Mansfield, 26 Ill. 21; Meeker v. Saunders, 6 Iowa, 61; Berry v. Hayden, 7 Iowa, 469; Booth v. McNair, 14 Mich. 19; McCallie v. Walton, 37 Ga. 611; Brahmstadt v. McWhirter, 9 Neb. 6. And see New York cases cited *ante* in the text.
[4] McCleery v. Allen, 7 Neb. 21. Compare Brahmstadt v. McWhirter, 9 id. 6.
[5] Beuss v. Shaughnessy, 2 Utah, 492.

New York void, under the statute of uses and trusts,[1] and inoperative. But it does not, of itself, avoid the whole assignment.[2] And where the trust is to sell *or* mortgage, and apply the proceeds to the payment of debts, the assignment is a valid instrument under the statute, as to the trust to *sell*, and vests the estate assigned in the assignees, notwithstanding that the trust to *mortgage* is void.[3] And even a trust to mortgage, if expressed to be for the purpose of raising funds to pay charges upon the land, such as judgments and mortgages, would, it seems, be valid.[4] In Mississippi a clause in an assignment by a bank, permitting the trustees to sell or pledge any of the property or effects conveyed, including the bank notes of the bank, in case any pressing emergency, not otherwise provided for, should render it necessary so to employ said bank notes, does not of itself vitiate the assignment, or render it fraudulent in law; and if the power be improperly exercised, it may be controlled and checked by a court of chancery.[5] In Maryland an assignment reserving to the trustee the power to mortgage the assigned property has been sustained.[6] And in Indiana it is held that trustees possess general power to lease trust property.[7] In Illinois an assignment is void if the property may be held until new debts are incurred, and then mortgaged to secure their payment or sold, and the proceeds devoted to their payment.[9] In a case[8] in Rhode Island, where part of the estate was under mortgage, and the deed authorized the assignee to sell at public or private sale, to buy in the premises, to resell without responsibility for loss, and also to mortgage, and from the proceeds to pay first the creditors secured by mortgage and then the other creditors, it was held that the assignment was valid as against creditors, for it did not appear that any benefit accrued to the assignor, at their expense, from the powers given.

§ 196. **Power to Pay Insurance, Interest and Incumbrances.**— An assignment will not be vitiated by a provision authorizing the assignees to effect an *insurance* upon a portion of the assigned property, and to keep good an insurance already existing upon an-

[1] Rogers v. De Forest, 7 Paige, 272; on appeal, *sub nom.* Darling v. Rogers, 22 Wer.'. 483; Planck v. Schermerhorn, 3 Barb. Ch. 644, 646.
[2] Darling v. Rogers, 22 Wend. 483; Sandford, A. V. C., in Van Nest v. Yoe, 1 Sandf. Ch. 4, 6.
[3] Darling v. Rogers, *ubi supra*.
[4] Ibid.
[5] Montgomery v. Galbraith, 11 Sm. & M. 555.
[6] Beatty v. Davis, 9 Gill, 211.
[7] City of Richmond v. Davis, 103 Ind. 449; 3 N. E. Rep. 130.
[8] Gardner v. Commercial Bank, 95 Ill. 298.
[9] Waldron v. Wilcox, 13 R. I. 518. See Beatty v. Davis, 9 Gill (Md.), 211; Montgomery v. Galbraith, 19 Miss. 555.

other portion of the property, so long as in their judgment it shall be necessary.[1] Neither will it be vitiated by a provision authorizing the assignees, if they shall deem it necessary, to pay the *interest* on a mortgage which is a prior lien upon the assigned property, and the principal and interest on another mortgage, if they shall deem it for the interest of the creditors to do so,[2] the assignees having, of themselves, the power to do these acts without any express authority from the assignor.[3]

§ 197. **Power to Employ Agents.** — So a power in an assignment authorizing assignees to appoint and dismiss *agents* and to pay them out of the proceeds of the assigned property is unobjectionable, they having the same authority without such provision.[4] But a trustee cannot delegate his powers calling for the exercise of judgment or discretion, except when the instrument gives him that authority.[5]

§ 198. **Power to Compound and Compromise Debts.** — But a power given to assignees to declare future *preferences*, or change the order of preferences already given, will render the assignment void.[6] So a power to assignees *to compound* with all or any of the creditors in such manner and upon such terms as they should deem proper was regarded, in a leading case in New York,[7] as peculiarly objectionable and one that it was impossible to sustain,[8] although it was expressed with a proviso that it did not interfere with the

[1] Whitney v. Krows, 11 Barb. 198.
[2] Id. So a direction to pay the rents and taxes on real estate until sold does not invalidate the assignment. Van Dine v. Willett, 38 Barb. 319; Eyre v. Beebe, 28 How. Pr. 333.
[3] 11 Barb. 198; Harris, J., id. 201, 202. See Gough v. Clift, 81 Md. 871.
[4] Vernon v. Morton, 8 Dana, 247; Henessy v. Western Bank, 6 W. & S. 300; Mann v. Whitbeck, 17 Barb. 388; Van Dine v. Willett, 38 Barb. 319; Casey v. Jones, 37 N. Y. 608; Nye v. Van Husan, 6 Mich. 329; Maennel v. Murdock, 13 Md. 164; Langdon v. Thompson, 25 Minn. 509; Richardson v. Marqueze, 59 Miss. 80. When the assignment contained a direction that the assignee should employ certain particular persons as attorneys in collecting in the estate, this direction as a badge of fraud. Carlton v. Baldwin, 22 Tex. 724. So an agreement to employ the assignor in winding up the business as part consideration for the transfer renders it illegal. Smith v. Craft, 11 Biss. 340; Burgaman v. Hickman, 115 Pa. St. 420.
[5] Cassady v. Wallace, 102 Mo. 575; 15 S. W. Rep. 138. See Patterson v. Johnson, 113 Ill. 559. Also see *post*, p. 487.
[6] Barnum v. Hempstead, 7 Paige, 568; Green v. Grieber, 3 Md. 11; Strong v. Skinner, 4 Barb. 546; Sheldon v. Dodge, 4 Denio, 217; Kercheis v. Schloss, 49 How. Pr. 284; Brown v. Guthrie, 39 Hun, 29; Moody v. Paschal, 60 Tex. 483. See Stimpson v. Fries, 2 Jones' Eq. 156.
[7] Wakeman v. Grover, 4 Paige, 24; s. c. on appeal, Grover v. Wakeman, 11 Wend. 187.
[8] Walworth, C., in Wakeman v. Grover, 4 Paige, 41; Sutherland, J., in Grover v. Wakeman, 11 Wend. 203.

order of preference established by the assignment, the effect of the provision being considered to be to perpetuate the right of giving preferences by vesting in the assignees an arbitrary power in relation to the several classes of creditors, and of compounding with any one upon such terms as they might think proper.[1] But where an assignment contained a provision that nothing contained in the instrument should be considered as restricting or preventing the assignee from liquidating or compounding with any of the creditors by making over, assigning or transferring any of the choses in action, debts or accounts due to the assignors, the court held this to be rather the reservation of a supposed existing right than the grant of a power, and declined to presume a fraudulent intent from the clause.[2]

In a late case in the same state[3] it was held that while a grant of power to the assignee to receive payment of debts by instalments did not avoid the assignment, yet a clause authorizing the assignee to "compromise with the creditors" of the assignor for all his debts and liabilities, if in the opinion of the assignee "it would be advantageous" to the creditors and the assignor, was held to render the assignment void; for its effect and intent was to delay the payment of debts and create a trust for the assignor. But in the same state it is held that an assignment is not invalidated by a provision authorizing the assignee to compound or compromise debts owing to the assignor.[4]

In Illinois[5] and Kansas[6] a clause in a general assignment authorizing the trustee to compound with the creditors renders it void. In a case in the latter state the assignment directed the assignee in the usual way to convert the assets into money, unless the indebtedness of the assignors could be paid or settled otherwise by amicable arrangement. This condition was held to render the assignment void in connection with the fact that the assets were slightly more than the liabilities, and that the plan was to induce a settlement with creditors.[7] But a clause authorizing the assignee to compound with the assignor's *debtors* has been sustained; as where the assignee was empowered "to compromise all bad and doubtful claims,"[8] or "to compound, compromise and settle the claims assigned in his discretion."[9]

[1] Walworth, C., *ubi supra;* Sutherland, J., *ubi supra.*
[2] Van Nest v. Yoe, 1 Sandf. Ch. 4, 5.
[3] McConnell v. Sherwood, 84 N. Y. 522, affirming s. c., 19 Hun, 519.
[4] Bagley v. Bowe, 105 N. Y. 171; 11 N. E. Rep. 386; 59 Am. Rep. 488.
[5] Hudson v. Maze, 3 Scam. 578.
[6] Keevil v. Donaldson, 20 Kan. 165.
[7] Keevil v. Donaldson, *supra.*
[8] Brigham v. Tillinghast, 15 Barb. 618.
[9] Bellows v. Partridge, 19 Barb. 176; White v. Monsarrat, 18 B. Mon. 809; Price

In New York it is provided by statute[1] that the county judge may authorize the assignee to compromise or compound any claim or debt belonging to the estate of the debtor. But it has been decided[2] that a clause in the assignment simply authorizing the assignee to compromise such claims as in a sound discretion the interests of the trust require does not conflict with the statute nor invalidate the assignment.

§ 199. **Notice to Creditors by Assignee.**[3] — An assignment may contain a clause directing the trustees to *give notice* before making a dividend and requiring the creditors to *prove their debts* before they should be entitled to a dividend.[4] So where preferences are allowed it has been held that an assignment may have a clause directing the assignee to give *notice* to the creditors to present their claims to him at a reasonable time and place and preferring such creditors as should comply with such notice over others.[5]

§ 200. **Power to Defend Suits.** — A power may sometimes be given to an assignee to *defend suits* brought by creditors, and to defray the costs out of the assigned property. Thus in Kentucky, where the assignment authorized the trustees to defend certain attachment suits against the debtors and to retain so much out of the proceeds of the assigned effects as would indemnify them, it was held to be no objection to its validity.[6] So in New York, where an assignment contained a power to the assignee to defend all law, equity and other proceedings which they [he] might deem necessary to the execution of the trusts, it was held to afford no marked

---

v. Ford, 18 Md. 489; Carlton v. Baldwin, 22 Tex. 724; Watkins v. Wallace, 19 Mich. 57; Murphy v. Bell, 8 How. Pr. 468. See Conklin v. Conrad, 6 Ohio St. 611; Woodburn v. Mosher, 9 Barb. 255. Where the intention of a provision that the assignee may compromise choses in action when he deems it expedient to do so is simply to give him authority to settle doubtful claims, and is restricted to that class alone, the assignment is not void on its face. Lininger v. Raymond, 9 Neb. 40. An assignment executed with the intent of thereby affecting a compromise is void. Bennett v. Ellison, 23 Minn. 242.

[1] Laws of 1877, ch. 466, § 23; Bliss' Ann. Code, 1890, p. 2280.

[2] Coyne v. Weaver, 84 N. Y. 386; Ginther v. Richmond, 18 Hun, 232. See Matter of Ransom, 8 Daly, 89; Jessup v. Herzfeld, 1 N. Y. Weekly Dig. 241; Master of Youngs, 5 Abb. N. C. 346.

[3] See ch. XXIX.

[4] Garland, J., in U. S. v. Bank of U. S., 8 Rob. (La.) 412. See Ashurst v. Martin, 9 Port. 566; U. S. Bank v. Huth, 4 B. Mon. 423. The English forms sometimes contain a clause requiring creditors to verify their debts or lose the benefit of the assignment. See Jones v. Whitbread, 20 Law J. C. P. (N. S.) 217; s. c., 5 Eng. L. & Eq. 431.

[5] Ward v. Tingley, 4 Sandf. Ch. 476.

[6] Vernon v. Morton, 8 Dana, 247; Ewing, J., id. 252, 265. Nor does the fact that the defense proved unavailing make any difference. Id.

evidence of fraud, and the court could not perceive much in it that the assignee could not have done if the whole clause had been omitted.[1] But where a debtor in an assignment giving preferences first provided for the payment of all costs and expenses necessarily incurred by the assignee in defending any suits that might be instituted against him by any creditor or other person for anything out of the assignment or in any way connected with it, it was held that the assignment was fraudulent against his creditors.[2] And if a debtor have ample property to pay all his debts, it is a fraud upon his creditors for him to assign all his property to an assignee and to authorize such assignee to employ its proceeds in defending suits which might be brought against the assignor by his creditors to recover their several debts, the effect of such assignment being to delay his creditors in the collection of their debts.[3] In Missouri, a clause providing that the assignees shall not pay costs on the debts that have accrued or that may accrue on them by suit has been held not to avoid an assignment.[4]

An assignment may have a stipulation and direction to the assignee to deliver merchandise *in specie* to certain preferred creditors at prime cost, the value to be settled by the assignee.[5] So it may have a stipulation and direction that no *interest* shall be paid out of the effects conveyed till the principal of all the debts is paid.[6]

But an assignment of a bond and mortgage payable in five years, in trust for the benefit of certain creditors, with a proviso that it should be held by the assignee until the expiration of the period it had to mature, and in no case parted with until that time; and that the assignee should then, and not before, proceed to collect the principal, was held to be fraudulent as against creditors, carrying on its face an intent to hinder and delay them.[7]

A provision empowering an assignee, "generally, to adopt such measures in relation to the settlement of the estate as will, in his judgment, promote the true interests thereof," has been held not to render an assignment fraudulent and void upon its face.[8]

[1] Sandford, A. V. C., in Van Nest v. Yoe, 1 Sandf. Ch. 4, 6.
[2] Mead v. Phillips, 1 Sandf. Ch. 83.
[3] Planck v. Schermerhorn, 3 Barb. Ch. 644. A provision in an assignment authorizing the assignee to use or employ the proceeds of the assigned estate in defending suits that might be brought against the assignor by his creditors to recover their several debts would have the effect to hinder and delay creditors, and would render the assignment void. Levy's Accounting, 1 Abb. N. Cas. 181, and cases cited.
[4] Gates v. Labeaume, 19 Mo. 17.
[5] Bayne v. Wylie, 10 Watts, 309.
[6] Ingraham v. Grigg, 13 Sm. & M. 22.
[7] Storm v. Davenport. 1 Sandf. Ch. 135.
[8] Mann v. Whitbeck, 17 Barb. 388.

An assignment containing the clause "provided, however, that the said party of the second part (the assignee) shall pay no claims unless the correctness of the same shall be established to his satisfaction," the directions extending to all claims, and not being restricted to the creditors not named, is fraudulent and void as to the creditors named, the amounts of whose claims are given.[1]

IX. Stipulations for the Benefit of Assignees.

§ 201. Assignee Liable for Misconduct of Others, When.— A clause in an assignment exempting the assignees from liability for effects that should not come to their hands, and for losses, etc., from the misconduct of agents, has been approved.[2] And where there are two or more assignees, it is usual to stipulate that each shall be liable only for his own acts and defaults, and not for those of his co-assignees. A clause in an assignment providing that the assignees shall not be answerable or accountable for the acts, receipts, neglects or defaults of any attorney or attorneys, agent or agents, that they may employ, nor for any misfortune, loss or damage which may happen without their wilful neglect, does not vitiate the assignment where it contains a clause binding the assignees to act faithfully and justly in the execution of the trust.[3] But a provision that the assignee shall not be accountable for any defalcation committed by any clerk, agent or assistant necessarily employed by the *assignors* or either of them, in the execution of the trusts of the assignment, has been considered a badge of fraud.[4] And a stipulation limiting the liability of an assignee or trustee to his own *gross negligence* or wilful misconduct exonerates him from a great portion of the responsibility which the law attaches to his office, is considered evidence of an intent to hinder, delay and defraud creditors, and has therefore been held to render the assignment void as against them.[5] So a provision that the assignee, "while acting in good faith, shall not be made or held personally

---

[1] Hill v. Agnew, 12 Fed. Rep. 230.

[2] Henessey v. The Western Bank, 6 W. & S. 300.

[3] Jacobs v. Allen, 18 Barb. 549; Baldwin v. Peet, 22 Tex. 708; Gordon v. Cannon, 18 Gratt. 387; Henessey v. The Western Bank, 6 W. & S. 300; Rankin v. Loder, 21 Ala. 380. In Missouri it has been held, where a trustee is authorized by the deed of trust to appoint agents or substitutes to assist in the management of the trust business, and he accepts the trust upon the express condition that he shall not be responsible for the negligence or misfeasance of any person except himself, should an agent or substitute appointed by him be guilty of malfeasance a court of chancery will not hold him liable. O'Fallen v. Tucker, 13 Mo. 262.

[4] Van Nest v. Yoe, 1 Sandf. Ch. 4, 6.

[5] Litchfield v. White, 3 Sandf. S. C. 545; affirmed on appeal, 7 N. Y. 438; De Wolf v. Sprague Mfg. Co., 49 Conn. 282.

liable in the premises, in any manner," is such a restriction upon the liability of the assignee as renders the assignment fraudulent and void as against creditors, the rule being that a reservation or restriction of the liability of the assignee to a degree less than that which the law imposes upon trustees renders the assignment void.[1]

The clause "being responsible only for his actual receipts or wilful defaults," annexed to the acceptance of the assignee, will not vitiate the assignment. It does not release the assignee from the exercise of due diligence in collecting the debts due the assignor.[2]

§ 202. **Provisions for Expenses and Services of Assignees.**— A provision may be made for the payment from the fund of the just and reasonable expenses, costs, charges, damages,[3] and commissions of executing and carrying the assignment into effect,[4] and may also provide for all reasonable and proper charges for attorney and counsel fees respecting the same.[5] But where the assignment provided that the assignee, who was a lawyer, should retain, over and above the expenses of the trust, a reasonable counsel fee, this was held to render the assignment void.[6]

X. Reservations of Powers to Assignors.

§ 203. **Reservations of Powers to Assignors Invalidate Assignments.**— Clauses in assignments, reserving to the assignor any power or control over the provisions of the instrument itself or the property assigned by it, or over the disposition of it by sale or the appropriation of its proceeds, are more uniformly fatal to their validity than even those which reserve to him a benefit out of the property through the assignee.

[1] Hutchinson v. Lord, 1 Wis. 286. See Keep v. Sanderson, 2 id. 42; Whipple v. Pope, 33 Ill. 334; McIntire v. Benson, 20 id. 500; Finlay v. Dickerson, 29 id. 9; True v. Congdon, 44 N. H. 48; Olmstead v. Herrick, 1 E. D. Smith, 310; Metcalf v. Van Brunt, 37 Barb. 621. A provision that the assignee shall not be accountable for property which does not actually come to his possession renders the deed void, for he is bound to use due diligence to obtain possession. McIntire v. Benson, 20 Ill. 500; Finlay v. Dickerson, 29 id. 9; True v. Congdon, 44 N. H. 48; Pitts v. Viley, 4 Bibb, 446.
[2] Thomas v. Clark, 65 Me. 296.
[3] Blow v. Gage, 44 Ill. 208.
[4] Eyre v. Beebe, 28 How. Pr. 333; Islen v. Dalrymple, 27 id. 137; s. c., 2 Robt. 142; Jacobs v. Remsen, 36 N. Y. 668; Halstead v. Gordon, 34 Barb. 422.
[5] Butt v. Peck, 1 Daly, 83. See remarks of Robinson, J., in Levy's Accounting, 1 Abb. N. Cas. 182. But the debtor cannot contract with attorneys for services after the execution of the assignment. Hill v. Agnew, 12 Fed. Rep. 330; Mattison v. Judd, 59 Miss. 99.
[6] Nichols v. McEwen, 17 N. Y. 22; Heacock v. Durand, 42 Ill. 230. But in Thompson v. Childress, 1 Tenn. Ch. (Cooper), 369, it was held that an assignee who is also a solicitor or attorney will be allowed compensation for professional services as such in matters touching the trust estate.

18

Thus a clause reserving to the assignor a general power of revocation and the declaration of other trusts renders the assignment fraudulent on its face and void.[1] Powers of this kind are, in the emphatic language of Chancellor Kent, "fatal to the instrument and poison it throughout."[2] And "the law," in the words of the same eminent judge, "is so jealous on this subject, that if the deed contains a power in any way equivalent in its effects to a power of revocation, it is fatal."[3] Thus in an early case in England[4] it was held by the king's bench that a conveyance by an insolvent debtor in trust to pay debts was fraudulent because, among other things, it had a proviso enabling the grantor to *make leases* for any term without rent, and this was considered as putting it in his power to defeat the whole settlement; for, though the consent of the trustees was necessary, yet they were trustees of his own nomination. And in Maryland it has been held that the reservation to the grantor of the power of making leases avoids an assignment.[5] So in another English case,[6] where the deed reserved to the grantor a power *to mortgage* the estate conveyed, it was held to be fraudulent because, the grantor having reserved a power to mortgage and charge the estate with what sums he thought fit, he might have charged it to the full value, which amounted in fact to a power of revocation, rendering it fraudulent against the creditors.

In a New York case where a general assignment, although completely executed and acknowledged, was not delivered and was not intended by the parties to take effect at the time, but was retained by the assignor and by him delivered to his attorney with instructions to keep it until further orders from the assignor, or until he should think it necessary for the best interests of all the creditors to file it, it was held that there is a reservation of power which renders the assignment void.[7]

§ 204. Reservation of Power to Assignor Over Preferences.—

So a clause reserving, even indirectly, to the assignor the power of *changing* the order of *preferences* expressed in the assignment will render the deed fraudulent.[8] But in North Carolina it has been

---

[1] Riggs v. Murray, 2 Johns. Ch. 565; Reichenbach v. Winkhaus, 67 How. Pr. 512; Cannon v. Peebles, 4 Ired. L. 204; 2 Tuck. Com. [442], 431; Green v. Trieber, 3 Md. 11; Price v. Pritzer, 44 id. 521.
[2] 2 Johns. Ch. 579.
[3] Id. 579, 580.
[4] Lavender v. Blackstone, 3 Lev. 146; 3 Keb. 256, pl. 11.
[5] Green v. Trieber, 3 Md. 11.
[6] Tarbuck v. Marbury, 2 Vern. 510.
[7] Reichenbach v. Winkhaus, 12 Daly, 525; 67 How. Pr. 512.
[8] Averill v. Loucks, 6 Barb. 470; *ante*, p. 190. The debtor must settle the respective rights of the creditors under the assignment at the time of the trans-

held that where the maker of the deed only reserves the privilege of adding to the number of preferred creditors others of the same class, the deed cannot be pronounced by the court fraudulent on its face, but it must be left to a jury to determine whether such provision was inserted with a fraudulent intent.[1] "It is not the mere fact," observes Chief Justice Ruffin in this case, "that the appropriation of the trust fund may be changed, or that the debtor may modify the appropriation by letting in other creditors existing at the time, that converts the power to do those acts into a fraudulent power of revocation, either literally or substantially. The true principle is that if it appears expressly to be for the benefit of the grantor — as every general power of revocation must be — or to be a contrivance designed for that end, although covered by some form with a view to conceal that end, then it is fraudulent under the statute, but otherwise there must be a purpose actually to deceive, found by the jury." [2]

A clause reserving to the debtor the power to appoint new trustees as a consequence of the power of revocation renders the assignment fraudulent and void.[3] So a clause reserving to the assignor the right to *name* the *successor* of the assignee, in case such assignee should wish to resign the trust, is good ground of objection to an assignment.[4]

An assignment of property in trust to sell part of it to pay for advances, and to *retain* part of it subject to the *future order of the assignor*, is intended only as a cover to keep off execution creditors, and has premeditated fraud upon the face of it.[5]

---

fer, and cannot reserve the power to create preferences to himself or give it to the assignee. Brown v. Guthrie, 39 Hun, 29.

[1] Cannon v. Peebles, 4 Ired. L. 204. But where the assignment directed the assignee to pay such other debts as the assignors should thereafter specify out of any surplus which might be left after paying all the claims and debts provided for in the assignment, this was held not to make the assignment void *per se.* Hall v. Wheeler, 13 Ind. 371.

[2] 4 Ired. L. 209, 210. And see Stimpson v. Fries, 2 Jones' Eq. 156.

[3] Riggs v. Murray, 2 Johns. Ch. 565.

[4] Planck v. Schermerhorn, 3 Barb. Ch. 644. But in Connecticut it has been held, even under the statute of 1853, that an assignment is not rendered void by a provision that, if the trustee therein named should decline to accept and execute the trust, the assignor should have the power of appointing another trustee in his stead although the provision would be inoperative. Vansands v. Miller, 24 Conn. 180, 184. In Wright v. Thomas, 1 Fed. Rep. 716, it was held that an assignment was not void under the statutes of Indiana because, among other things, the assignors reserved in the deed the right to instruct the trustees as to their duties, and also the right to remove one or all of the trustees with the consent of two-thirds in value of the creditors.

[5] Hart v. McFarland, 13 Pa. St. 182. A reservation of property to be subsequently selected by the assignors renders the assignment void on its face. Clark v. Robbins, 8 Kan. 574. In Burr's Ex'r v. McDonald, 3 Gratt. 215, a provision in

§ 205. Reservation of Power to Assignor Over Sales.

— A clause in a deed of trust reserving to the debtor the power of *ordering a sale* at an earlier day than that prescribed by the deed was held in North Carolina not to be objectionable.[1] But the reservation to the debtor of the power to direct the *terms and places* of the sale was considered more objectionable, and one which, if allowed as a precedent, might lead to great abuses. The court considered that the reservation of such a power was not easily reconciled with the absolute and *bona fide* appropriation by the debtor of his property to the payment of his debts.[2] The deed, however, was not held void on this ground.

In Virginia, where a deed of trust contained a provision that if the debts secured by the deed were not paid by a day designated, then the trustee, *when required by* a creditor named, or *the debtor himself*, should proceed to sell at auction as prescribed in the deed, and should first pay off the debts for which such creditor was bound, and then all others secured by the deed which the *debtor should certify* as correct, and a proper charge upon the fund, it was held, in affirmance of the judgment of the court below, that the deed was fraudulent on its face.[3] And in Michigan, where an assignment reserved to the assignor a control over the sale of the real estate assigned, by providing that it should not be sold until all the personal assets should be exhausted unless with the consent of the assignor, it was held fraudulent and void in law as against creditors not preferred or not provided for in the assignment.[4]

A conveyance by one indebted in trust to sell, the grantor reserving a power of *appointment of the proceeds*, is fraudulent as to a prior creditor recovering judgment after the grantor had appointed the proceeds to creditors.[5]

The general rule, in fine, under this head, is that the debtor must not only part with the property, but must also surrender up all power over the estate, and all power to interfere authoritatively in the appropriation of the proceeds.[6]

an assignment by a corporation that the company should have power to direct the abandonment of any part of the property conveyed was argued to be a power reserved to the grantors incompatible with the grant. But the objection was not noticed by the court. See Sipe v. Earman, 26 Gratt. 563.

[1] Cannon v. Peebles, 2 Ired. L. 449.
[2] Cannon v. Peebles, 2 Ired. L. 449; s. c., 4 id. 204.
[3] Spence v. Bagwell, 6 Gratt. 444, 450.
[4] Pierson v. Manning, 2 Mich. 445; Pratt, J., id. 449; Sipe v. Earman, 26 Gratt. 563.
[5] Mitchell v. Stiles, 13 Pa. St. 306.
[6] Whallon v. Scott, 10 Watts. 237; Sheerer v. Lautzerheizer, 6 id. 549; Coulter, J., in Mitchell v. Stiles, 13 Pa. St. 306, 309; Phelps v. Curts, 80 Ill. 109.

CHAPTER XII

CONSIDERATION OF ASSIGNMENTS.

§ 206. Sufficient Consideration, What.
207. Assent of Creditors.

§ 206. Sufficient Consideration, What.— There can be no question whether an assignment of a debtor's property to a trustee for the benefit of his creditors is for a valuable consideration or not, because the debts due to the creditors constitute a valuable consideration in the highest sense of the terms, and the obligation of the trustee to perform the trust according to the provisions of the deed is a sufficiently valuable consideration so far as he is concerned. This was the opinion of Mr. Justice Story in the case of Halsey v. Whitney,[1] and it has been repeatedly recognized by the highest authority in this country as the general American rule on the subject. In the New York case of Dey v. Dunham it was held by Chancellor Kent that "a conveyance in trust to pay debts is a valid conveyance founded on a good consideration."[2] The opinion of Mr. Justice McLean[3] was that an assignment for the benefit of creditors cannot be considered void for want of consideration. In Pennsylvania a voluntary conveyance by a debtor in failing circumstances of property not subject to any lien has always been considered as founded on sufficient consideration.[4] In New York the nominal consideration of one dollar, or the fact that the assignee was a creditor as appearing on the face of the assignment, is held sufficient to transfer the legal title to the property and vest it in him. The amount of the consideration was never material for this purpose, and it seems to be well settled that the relation of debtor

---

[1] 4 Mason, 206, 214; cited by Garland, J., in United States v. Bank of the United States, 8 Rob. (La.) 405; and followed by Bennett, J., in Hall v. Dennison, 17 Vt. 310, 316. In the latter case there was a nominal consideration specified in the deed and also a direct covenant on the part of the trustee for the faithful performance of the trust. Hudson v. Maze, 4 Ill. 678; Meeker v. Saunders, 6 Iowa, 61; Nutter v. Harris, 9 Ind. 88; Exchange Bank v. Knox, 19 Gratt. 739; Haven v. Richardson, 5 N. H. 113; United States Bank v. Huth, 4 B. Mon. 423; Feimester v. McRorie, 12 Ind. 287; Thomas v. Clark, 65 Me. 296; Marsalis v. Oglesby, 1 Tex. App. Civ. Cas. 101. See Mackintosh v. Corner, 33 Md. 598; Hoopes v. Knell, 31 id. 550.
[2] 2 Johns. Ch. 182, 189; citing Stephenson v. Hayward, Prec. in Ch. 310. And see Kellogg v. Slauson, 15 Barb. 58, Allen, J.
[3] Lawrence v. Davis, 3 McLean, 177.
[4] Burd v. Smith, 4 Dall. 76; Wilt v. Franklin, 1 Binn. 502.

and creditor between the parties and the legal consequences of the assignment constitute a sufficient consideration as between them.[1] In Missouri a deed of assignment to a trustee for the benefit of creditors is held to be for a valuable consideration.[2] In Michigan such a deed containing covenants on the part of the assignees and stipulations beneficial to the creditors is in law to be deemed and taken as founded upon a valuable consideration.[3] In Georgia an assignment to creditors for the payment of their debts or to trustees for that purpose cannot be said to be without consideration, especially if one of the trustees be himself a creditor and the conveyance purport to be founded upon a consideration however small.[4] And in Virginia the insertion of a nominal consideration (as of five dollars) in a deed of trust for creditors is no ground of objection to its validity.[5] In Mississippi it has been held that a deed of trust as security for a debt is *prima facie* valid, and a claimant under such deed is not bound to show a consideration for it in the first instance.[6] And in Kentucky, where the facts proved amount to *prima facie* evidence of the assignor's indebtedness, further proof will be dispensed with in the absence of countervailing evidence.[7]

§ 207. **Assent of Creditors.**— In Massachusetts, however, prior to the statute regulations on the subject of assignments, a different rule prevailed, growing out of the local law which required the *assent* of creditors to give them validity. The consideration of an assignment in this state was held to depend upon the circumstance whether the creditors had become parties to it or had otherwise assented to its provisions. If no creditor became a party, the deed was without consideration, or, as it was expressed, there was no *cestuis que trust*, and so no trusts, and the consideration entirely failed.[8] If the creditors elected to become parties, or to assent,

[1] Nelson, J., in Cunningham v. Freeborn, 11 Wend. 240, 250.
[2] Gates v. Labeaume, 19 Mo. 17.
[3] Hollister v. Loud, 2 Mich. 309.
[4] Jones v. Dougherty, 10 Ga. 273. The promise of the assignee to sell and divide the proceeds of the property assigned among the creditors is a sufficient consideration for the assignment. Block v. Peter, 63 Ga. 260. See Code, § 2744.
[5] Johnston v. Zane's Trustee, 11 Gratt. 552, 564. In Exchange Bank v. Knox, 19 Gratt. 789, it is said to be well settled that the trustees and beneficiaries in a deed of trust to secure *bona fide* debts are purchasers for a valuable consideration; citing Wickham v. Martin, 13 Gratt. 427; Evans v. Greenhow, 15 Gratt. 153.
[6] Brown v. Bartee, 10 Sm. & M. 268.
[7] Vernon v. Morton, 8 Dana, 247, 253.
[8] Morton, J., in Fall River Iron Works Co. v. Croade, 15 Pick. 11, 15. Assignments in trust for the benefit of creditors, the only consideration for which is the acceptance of the trust, are of no effect against creditors who do not assent to them, and who by trustee process or otherwise attach the property described in the instrument of assignment. Swan v. Crafts, 124 Mass. 453; Faulkner v. Hyman, 6 N. E. Rep. 846.

and their debts amounted to as much as the assigned property, this completed the intended consideration, rendered the conveyance effectual against other creditors, and vested the whole property in the assignees.[1] If the debts of the assenting creditors were of less amount than the property assigned they constituted a good consideration *pro tanto* and gave the assignee a right to retain to the amount of such debts.[2] In other words, it was the rule that the creditors must assent in sufficient numbers and value to cover the property assigned, otherwise the consideration might be deemed inadequate and void as to the non-assenting creditors, though good as to those assenting.[3] This was closely following the rule, as long settled in England, that to constitute a valid consideration for a conveyance to a trustee for the payment of debts, within the statute of Elizabeth, one or more creditors must have become parties to the conveyance,[4] or have agreed or assented to it, or in some manner have become privy to it.[5] This rule has already been alluded to in considering the parties to assignments and will receive further attention under a future head.

[1] 15 Pick. 16. See Everett v. Walcott, id. 94, 97; Douglass v. Simpson, 121 Mass. 281.
[2] 15 Pick. 16.
[3] Woodbury, J., in Adams v. Blodgett, 2 W. & M. 237; citing Russell v. Woodward, 10 Pick. 408.
[4] Roberts on Fraud. Conv., pp. 429, 431, 432, 434, 437.
[5] Acton v. Woodgate, 2 M. & K. 492; Smith v. Keating, 6 M., G. & S. 136. It was remarked by Mr. Justice Story, in the case of Halsey v. Whitney, 4 Mason, 206, that "as to trusts created for the benefit of creditors and to which they are not, technically speaking, parties, if *bona fide* made, they are unquestionably valid by the law of England, and pass a legal estate to the trustee." Id. 214. But the following extracts from Mr. Roberts' work, just cited, present the subject in a different view: "A general conveyance or assignment to a stranger, in trust to pay the debts of the person conveying, is clearly not a consideration sufficient even to raise a use upon a covenant to stand seized." Rob. Fraud. Conv., p. 429. "That the mere destination of the property to the object of paying the debts of the grantor is not sufficient to raise the use upon a covenant to stand seized, or bargain and sale, appears from Lord Paget's Case, 1 Leon. 194." Id. "That such a conveyance for payment of debts, to which no creditor is a party, cannot support itself, under the statutes of Elizabeth, against purchasers or discontented creditors, is a proposition flowing pretty clearly from the general analogy of the reported decisions, and deducible from the very plan and spirit of the statutes themselves." Id. 431. "But if a creditor be a *party* to such a conveyance to a trustee for payment of debts, however open the transaction may still be considered to the imputation of fraud, from concomitant circumstances, there is a clear valuable consideration to support the deed." Id. And as to the present rule in England, see further, *ante*, p. 127, note 3.

CHAPTER XIII.

TRUSTS OF ASSIGNMENTS.

§ 208. Trusts of Assignments Defined and Distinguished.
209. Trusts Must be Declared.
210. Implied Trusts.
211. Express Trusts.
212. Passive Trusts.
213. Trusts for Assignor.

§ 208. Trusts of Assignments Defined and Distinguished.— The *trusts* of an assignment for the benefit of creditors constitute a very important feature of the transfer. These trusts, in one form or other, enter into the composition of all assignments which contemplate provision or security for creditors (as distinguished from transfers in absolute and final payment and satisfaction); embracing not only such as are made to *trustees* formally appointed by the assignor, distinct from the creditors or *cestuis que trust*, but such as are made *directly* to creditors themselves.

In one sense of the word there is but a *single* trust created by any assignment for the benefit of creditors, the term being, properly, expressive of the *confidence* reposed by the assignor in the trustee or assignee to carry into effect the *entire* arrangement and disposition of the assigned property and its proceeds, as declared and directed by the assignment; and also of the *whole line of duty* devolving upon the assignee in consequence. In this general sense the assignor is said to *create* and the assignee to *execute* the trust; and the trust itself is said to be *entered upon* by the latter, and to be *closed* when all the purposes of the assignment are accomplished. But the term is also used in a more limited sense, and with reference to certain particular objects or results of the assignment, as distinguished from others. In this sense there may be *several* trusts created by or growing out of one assignment; but they are all reducible under two general heads — *express*, and *implied* or *resulting* trusts.

§ 209. Trusts Must be Declared.— The *express trusts* of an assignment are the expressions or designations by the assignor of the particular objects or purposes for which it is made, and they usually take the form of *directions*, more or less minute, to the assignee or trustee, how to dispose of the property assigned. In the great majority of cases they are expressed in the same instrument which contains the transfer; but they are sometimes embodied in a separate instrument called a *declaration of trust*, bearing even date with the absolute conveyance, and accompanying it.[1] They may even be declared by parol,[2] but this is not usual.

It may be considered as well settled that every valid assignment must declare the uses to which the property assigned is to be applied, and must settle the rights of creditors under it, and not leave to the assignee or reserve to the assignor himself the right of subsequently doing so.[3]

The trustee is always bound by any restrictions contained in the writing which creates the trust.[4] The conditions attached to the trust are regarded as a part of the transfer, and the conditions and the transfer stand or fall together.[5]

§ 210. **Implied Trusts.**— *Implied* or *resulting trusts* are such as result from the transfer by intendment and operation of law. A trust may be thus implied for the benefit of a creditor. Thus, in a recent case, where a debtor made an assignment of his property in trust, to pay any judgment which the United States might recover against him and the sureties on his official bond as collector of customs, and after the recovery of such judgment the plaintiffs in it filed a bill for an account by the trustees, and the application of the trust funds to the payment of the judgment, it was held that a trust in favor of the plaintiffs was created by the assignment by implication of law and that the bill was properly filed.[6] But resulting trusts are, properly, those which arise out of an assignment

---

[1] See *ante*, p. 130.

[2] Lord Nottingham, in Cook v. Fountain, 3 Swanst. 585; 2 Story's Eq. Jur. § 1195, note. See Boyden v. Moore, 11 Pick. 362; Thomas v. Merry, 113 Ind. 83; 15 N. E. Rep. 244. Trust in personalty may be created and proved by parol. Harris v. Bratton, 34 S. C. 259; 13 S. E. Rep. 259, 580; Hon v. Hon, 70 Ind. 135; Wright v. Gay, 101 Ill. 233. But declarations of trust in real estate are almost uniformly required to be in writing. In Britton v. Lorenz, 45 N. Y. 51 (affirming 3 Daly, 23), parol proof was introduced to show that a bill of sale, absolute on its face, was really made upon a trust to pay certain debts and distribute the residue among other creditors. The instrument, however, was held invalid as a general assignment because not acknowledged. A trust may be established by parol proof, but the evidence must be clear and cogent to establish a parol trust as to land. Lewis v. Ziegler, 105 Mo. 604; 16 S. W. Rep. 862; Ingham v. Burnell, 31 Kan. 333. See *ante*, pp. 129, 130.

[3] Averill v. Loucks, 6 Barb., 476; Sheldon v. Dodge, 4 Den. 220; Caton v. Mosely, 25 Tex. 374; Kercheis v. Schloss, 49 How. Pr. 284; Malcolm v. Hodges, 8 Md. 418.

[4] Ogden v. Peters, 21 N. Y. 23; Goodrich v. Proctor, 1 Gray, 567; Purdy v. Whitney, 20 Pick. 25; Gould v. Lamb, 11 Metc. 84.

[5] Jessup v. Hulse, 21 N. Y. 168, Selden, J.

[6] United States v. Hoyt, 1 Blatchf. C. C. 332; Field v. Flanders, 40 Ill. 470.

for the benefit of the assignor himself; and such a *result* takes place whenever there is a surplus of property or its proceeds remaining undisposed of after the execution of the express trusts,[1] whether all the creditors are paid or not.[2] If all are paid and there is no express reservation of the surplus to the assignor, it constitutes a resulting trust for his benefit by mere operation of law,[3] which he may enforce against the assignee. And so if only a portion of the creditors are paid and a surplus of property or proceeds remains with the assignee, a trust for the assignor results by the operation of the instrument; with this very material difference, however, that such a resulting trust frequently avoids the whole assignment, being held equivalent to an express reservation for the debtor's own benefit.[4]

§ 211. **Express Trusts.**— The principal express trusts of every assignment for creditors are the trusts to *collect* the property; to convert it into money by *sale*, and to *distribute* it among the creditors provided for. But these are sometimes varied by the assignor. Thus, instead of the trust to sell and pay there may be a trust to deliver certain goods *in specie* to certain creditors.[5] So the leading trusts just mentioned may be and usually are subdivided into minor trusts, or specific directions to the assignee, such as to collect the debts due the assignor; to sell in a certain way; to reserve the expense of the trust; to pay the creditors in a certain order, and the like.[6]

In some of the states the trusts of an assignment are governed by statute provisions regulating trusts generally.[7]

[1] 2 Story's Eq. Jur., § 1196a; Weaver v. Leiman, 52 Md. 708. Where there is an express trust there cannot be a resulting or implied trust. Stevenson v. Crapnell, 114 Ill. 19.

[2] See Wilkes v. Ferris, 5 Johns. 335; Dubose v. Dubose, 7 Ala. 235.

[3] Halsey v. Whitney, 4 Mason, 206; Story, J., id. 223. In the Matter of the Estate of Potter Paige, 54 Pa. St. 465. The designation of a voluntary assignment as being for the "benefit of creditors" was held to imply a conveyance to trustees for the benefit either of the creditors at large, or for some other creditors than the immediate grantees. United States v. McLellan, 3 Sum. 345, 354, 355. In the case of Corder v. Corder, 124 Ill. 239; 16 N. E. Rep. 107, it was held that the evidence to establish a resulting trust must be very clear and is always received with great caution. So in the case of Richardson v. Haney, 76 Iowa, 101, it was held that in a resulting trust resting on parol the evidence must be clear and satisfactory.

[4] Dana v. Lull, 17 Vt. 390, 397; Burd v. Smith, 4 Dal. 76; Hooper v. Tuckerman, 3 Sandf. (S. C.) 311; Malcolm v. Hodges, 8 Md. 418.

[5] Bayne v. Wylie, 10 Watts, 309.

[6] An assignment in trust for each and all creditors of the firm is sufficiently specific; such a trust under the law imposes well-defined duties. Forbes v. Scannell, 13 Cal. 242. An assignment for the payment of debts generally without any limitations or directions confers upon the trustee the right to sell. Planck v. Schermerhorn, 3 Barb. Ch. 644.

[7] See Appendix, I.

§ 212. Passive Trusts.— A mere passive trust to hold property for another's use cannot exist under the laws of New York. It must be created for one of the active objects enumerated in the statute, and every estate or interest not embraced in the trust and not otherwise disposed of reverts to the grantor as a legal estate.[1] So when the assignor conveyed property to a trustee to sell, and directed that the avails over and above the expenses should constitute a fund for the payment of his debts, "and the residue, if any, should be invested in some safe and proper manner for the grantor's use during life, or, in case of his death before the completion of the trust, paid over and distributed to his heirs at law as by statute in case of persons dying intestate," held, that what remained after the payment of the debts vested at once in the grantor, and that after a settlement by the trustee and the death of the grantor his heirs at law could not maintain an action for an accounting against the trustee.[2]

Where a trust, valid under the statute, is coupled with another trust which is invalid, as where a trust to sell land is coupled with another trust not authorized by statute, as to mortgage or incumber, this was held valid as a trust to sell, though void as a trust to mortgage, and the assignment operates as a transfer vesting a title in the assignee. But the rule, as we shall see, is different where one of the trusts is fraudulent, for in that case the fraudulent interest permeates and vitiates the whole instrument.[3]

§ 213. Trusts for Assignor.— Another important statute provision in New York and some other states is that which declares that "all conveyances, and all transfers or assignments, verbal or written, of goods, chattels or things in action, made in trust *for the use of the persons making the same*, shall be void as against the creditors, existing or subsequent, of such person."[4] Under this section of the New York statute it was held in Goodrich v. Downs[5] that where an assignment shows on its face that it was made in trust for the use of the assignor either in whole or in part, the court is bound to pronounce the transaction void. In the case of Curtis v. Leavitt,[6] in the court of appeals, the exposition and application of this statute was made the subject of very elaborate discussion both in the arguments of counsel and in the opinions of the court. And

---

[1] Kittell v. Osborn, 4 Sup. Ct. (T. & C.) 45.
[2] Ibid.
[3] Darling v. Rogers, 22 Wend. 483; reversing Rogers v. De Forest, 7 Paige, 272. See Barnum v. Hempstead, 7 id. 568.
[4] 3 Rev. Stat. (7th ed.), p. 2327, § 1; 4 R. S. (1889), p. 2590, § 1. See *post*, ch. XXV, where similar enactments in other states are noticed.
[5] 6 Hill, 438.
[6] 15 N. Y. 9 297. See Wilson v. Robertson, 21 id. 587.

it was then determined that the statute applies only to conveyances, etc., wholly or primarily for the use of the grantor, and not to such as are created for other and active purposes where the reservations are incidental and partial only.

The principal rules in regard to the trusts of an assignment, which remain to be considered, are the following: that all express trusts must be openly declared by the assignor, a secret trust being always void,[1] and when once declared cannot afterwards be revoked or altered;[2] that there must be no express trust for the use or benefit of the assignor,[3] nor any resulting trust in his favor until after payment of all the debts;[4] that the trusts declared must be coextensive with the property assigned;[5] and that there must be no trust to hinder, delay or defraud creditors.[6]

These topics have already been partially considered and will receive further illustration under the head of "Fraudulent and void assignments."

[1] Passmore v. Eldridge, 12 S. & R. 198; McAllister v. Marshall, 6 Binn. 338; McCullough v. Hutchinson, 7 Watts, 434; Russell v. Woodward, 10 Pick. 407; Foster v. Saco Manufacturing Co., 12 id. 451; Shaw, C. J., id. 453; Parker, C. J., in Hills v. Elliott, 12 Mass. 26, 31; Anderson v. Fuller, 1 McMullen, 27; Edrington v. Rogers, 15 Tex. 188; Wheeler, J., in Wright v. Linn, 16 id. 42; Caldwell v. Williams, 1 Ind. 305; Comstock, J., in Curtis v. Leavitt, 15 N. Y. 120. "There is no plainer evidence of fraud than an absolute paper transfer by an insolvent, with a secret parol trust in contravention of such conveyance." Chilton, J., in Bryant v. Young, 21 Ala. 264, 273; Nesbitt v. Digby, 11 Ill. 387; Humphries v. Freeman, 22 Tex. 45; Golden's Appeal, 110 Pa. St. 581.

[2] See *ante*, p. 252.
[3] See *ante*, p. 221.
[4] See *ante*, p. 230.
[5] See *ante*, p. 231.
[6] See *post*, ch. XXV.

CHAPTER XIV.

EXECUTION OF THE ASSIGNMENT.

§ 214. Assignment, Executed How.
215. Execution by Assignor.
216. Execution by Assignee.
217. Execution by Creditors.
218. Attestation of Execution.
219. Oath to Assignment.
220. Acknowledgment of Execution.
221. Acknowledgment of Execution Before Proper Officer.

§ 214. **Assignment, Executed How.**— The assignment having been drawn up in due form, and the necessary schedules attached, the next proceeding is the *execution* of it by the persons named as parties. In most cases the instrument is under seal, and where it conveys real estate, or contains covenants by either party, this formality should not be omitted. The schedules should be dated and executed, as well as the assignment itself.

§ 215. **Execution by Assignor.**— It is of course indispensable that the assignment should be executed by the assignor, or, if there be several, by all of them. This may, however, be done by attorney, under proper power for that purpose.[1] In cases of partner-

---

[1] A power of attorney, executed by one of several partners subsequent to the execution of the assignment by the others, authorizing the assignment of the property of the firm, but omitting all reference to the separate estate of the partner giving the power, does not amount to a sufficient execution on the part of such partner. In re Wilson, 4 Barr, 430. Where the deed of assignment offered in evidence by a plaintiff purported to have been executed by one of the assignors by attorney, and the defendants objected that there was no proof of the execution of the power, it was held that the acknowledgment of the deed in the probate bond sued on extended to everything necessary to prove the due execution of the deed, and superseded further proof of the power. Clark v. Mix, 15 Conn. 152. A power of attorney to convey or sign away real estate in payment, or to secure the payment, of debts, authorizes the attorney to make an assignment of such real estate for the benefit of creditors. Marshall v. Shibley, 11 Kan. 114. There are cases from which it seems that under the New York statute requiring assignments to be acknowledged, an assignment cannot be executed by an attorney in fact. Adams v. Houghton, 3 Abb. Pr. (N. S.) 46; Cook v. Kelly, 14 Abb. Pr. 466, affirming 12 id. 85. But this rule does not preclude the partners who remain after one of their number has absconded from executing an assignment of the assets of the firm. National Bank v. Sackett, 2 Abb. Pr. (N. S.) 286. And it seems that non-resident members of a firm are not necessarily included in the statutory requirement of a personal execution and ac-

ship we have seen that one partner may execute the assignment in behalf of the firm, if with the concurrence or by the authority of his copartners.[1] The better course is to have it executed by all. But where the assignment was executed by all the partners, it was deemed to be their joint act, and not to pass their individual property, there being no specific reference to their individual property in the body of the assignment.[2]

In Indiana [3] it is provided by statute that a surviving partner or partners of any firm doing business in that state shall have full power to make assignments under the act. Notwithstanding the rule that one partner cannot bind his copartners by *deed*, the mere circumstance that an assignment by one or more of several partners is under *seal* will not invalidate it, if the property proposed to be conveyed is of such a description as might have been conveyed without deed, or that a title to it would have passed by the mere act of delivery;[4] the rule being that, where a seal is not essential to the validity of a contract, the addition of a seal will not vitiate it.[5]

The cases in which assignments are executed by the wives of the assignors have already been noticed.[6]

In regard to schedules it has been held that schedules not dated, but referred to in the assignment as bearing even date with the assignment, will be taken to have been executed at the same time, and this fact may be proved by parol.[7]

§ 216. **Execution by Assignee.**— Where the assignee is formally named as a party to the assignment, as where it is drawn in bipartite or tripartite form, and especially where the instrument contains any provision for its execution by him, or a covenant to

knowledgment by each of the assignors. Darrow v. Bruff, 36 How. Pr. 479, distinguishing Adams v. Houghton, *supra*. But in the late case of Lowenstein v. Flauraud, 82 N. Y. 494, affirming 11 Hun, 399, it is settled that an assignment may be executed and acknowledged by attorney. See s. c., *post*, p. 290, n. 4, and Baldwin v. Tines, 19 Abb. Pr. 32.

[1] See *ante*, p. 125. In the English case of Bowker v. Burdekin, 11 Mees. & W. 128, a deed of assignment purporting to be made by three partners of a firm, but executed by one of them only, was held to operate to convey the share of the one who executed. But see Havens v. Hussey, 5 Paige, 30, *contra*.

[2] Derry Bank v. Davis, 44 N. H. 548.
[3] R. S. of Ind. (1888), § 2683.
[4] Anderson v. Tompkins, 1 Brock. 456; Tapley v. Butterfield, 1 Metc. 515, 519; Everitt v. Strong, 7 Hill (N. Y.), 585; Deckard v. Case, 5 Watts, 22; Sale v. Dishman's Ex'rs, 3 Leigh, 548; McCullough v. Sommerville, 8 id. 415. In this last case the partner did not even execute the assignment in the name of the firm, but in his own individual name; and yet it was held to be no objection.
[5] Robinson v. Crowder, 4 McCord's L. 519.
[6] *Ante*, p. 125.
[7] Dana v. Bank of the United States, 5 W. & S. 223.

be performed by him, it is necessary that he should execute it as well as the assignor. But where this is not the case, he need not become a party by signing.[1] An assignment is good if the assignee does not execute it, or enter into any covenant to perform the trusts. If it is executed by the assignor, and delivered to the assignee, and he accepts it, and enters upon the performance of the trusts, he is as much bound as if he had executed it.[2]

In some of the states assignees execute by signing and sealing a written acceptance at the foot of the deed, immediately following the signature of the assignor.[3]

§ 217. **Execution by Creditors.**— Assignments tripartite, as we have seen,[4] are drawn with express reference to their being executed by the creditors, as well as the assignor and assignee; and unless executed by some of the creditors they are inoperative.[5] It is usual, in such assignments, to limit a time within which they must be executed by the creditors, as a condition of their participating in their benefits. Where this is the case, the condition must be complied with; and creditors will not be permitted to become parties by signing after the expiration of the time limited, provided they have had seasonable notice of the assignment, or provided proper means have been taken to give the notice.[6] In some states the time for creditors to become parties is fixed by statute.

In Massachusetts, before the statute of 1836, regulating assignments, it was held that a creditor who did not execute, within the time limited, an assignment for the benefit of such creditors as should become parties within a certain time, was not entitled to become a party to it, or to have the benefit of it, although no distribution had been made before he requested permission to execute it, and although it contained no release to the debtor.[7] And where the assignment contained a release, it was held that a creditor executing the deed after the time limited did not become a party so as to release his debt.[8] But an assignment under the statute of 1836 was held not to be void, as against subsequent attaching

---

[1] Flint v. Clinton Co., 12 N. H. 430. See ch. XVIII.
[2] Cunningham v. Freeborn, 1 Edw. Ch. 256; affirmed on appeal, 11 Wend. 240.
[3] Kennedy v. Winn, 80 Ala. 185; s. c., *post*, p. 401.
[4] *Ante*, pp. 136, 155.
[5] Marston v. Coburn, 17 Mass. 454. But see Shearer v. Loftin, 26 Ala. 703; Gale v. Mensing, 20 Mo. 461.
[6] Phœnix Bank v. Sullivan, 9 Pick. 410. See Dedham Bank v. Richards, 2 Metc. 105.
[7] Phœnix Bank v. Sullivan, 9 Pick. 410. See Battles v. Forbes, 21 id. 239; Dedham Bank v. Richards, 2 Metc. 105.
[8] Battles v. Forbes, 21 Pick. 239; s. c., 2 Metc. 93.

creditors, because it was not executed by any creditor within a reasonable time.[1] A promise to a creditor to pay his demand in full, though it should not be so paid from the proceeds of the assigned property, in order to induce him to become a party to an assignment, is fraudulent and void.[2]

In Missouri it has been held that an assignment by a debtor for the benefit of certain preferred creditors, the balance to be distributed *pro rata* among the remaining creditors, provided they will release the debtor from further liability, is of no avail until executed by the creditors; and the levy of an execution before the deed is executed will prevail over it.[3] And in another case in the same state, it was held that a deed of assignment for the benefit of such creditors as should, within a given time, become parties thereto and execute a release, would be of no avail until executed by the creditors, even though such deed were not void on account of the stipulation for a release.[4] But in a much later case, where the deed required that the creditors should sign it in order to receive any benefit from it, but none signed it, it was held that this did not render the conveyance void, as matter of law.[5] And in a case in Alabama it has been held that a deed of trust which conveys property absolutely for the benefit of specified creditors, although it purports on its face to be tripartite, does not require to be signed by either the trustee or the creditors, to give it effect.[6]

As assignments intended to be executed by creditors generally contain a release of the debtor, a creditor ought to satisfy himself on this point before signing. A want of knowledge that the instrument contained a release will not, after signing, avail him.[7] In an English case, where a deed of composition with an assignment in trust for creditors was construed to include a release of a debt guarantied, it was held, in an action against the surety, to be no answer, either on legal or equitable grounds, to a plea setting out the release, that the plaintiffs executed as creditors but as trustees, and solely for the purpose of accepting and declaring the trusts, and not with the intention of releasing the debt; that they did not sign the list of creditors; and that, if the deed operated to release the debt, it was executed by mistake and in ignorance that such would be its legal effect.[8]

[1] Shattuck v. Freeman, 1 Metc. 10.
[2] Ramsdell v. Edgarton, 8 Metc. 227.
[3] Swearingen v. Slicer, 5 Mo. 241.
[4] Drake v. Rogers, 6 Mo. 317.
[5] Gale v. Mensing, 20 Mo. 461.
[6] Shearer v. Loftin, 26 Ala. 703. And see Tennant v. Stoney, 1 Rich. (S. C.) 222.
[7] See Parsons v. Gloucester Bank, 10 Pick. 533.
[8] Teed v. Johnson, 34 Eng. L. & Eq. 545.

In a case in Massachusetts, where an assignment by an insolvent debtor of a part of his property in trust for the benefit of his creditors provided for the payment, first, of certain sureties, also creditors, including the plaintiff, who was one of the assignees, in full, if the property should be sufficient, otherwise *pro rata*, and then of such other creditors as should become parties to the assignment, in full or *pro rata*, and the assignees covenanted to dispose of the property, and pay over the proceeds within one year; and the creditors becoming parties to the assignment agreed " upon being paid in manner aforesaid, to cancel and discharge their respective demands,"— it was held that the execution of the assignment by the plaintiff, and his acceptance of the trust, operated as a full and immediate discharge and satisfaction of his claims, both as surety and as creditor, so that a subsequent conveyance to him, by the debtor, of other property, as further security for those claims, was without consideration, and invalid against a creditor not a party to the assignment.[1]

§ 218. **Attestation of Execution.**— The assignment, like all other conveyances of property, should be executed before witnesses, who attest it in the usual manner. Formerly in New Hampshire it was required by statute that an assignment, embracing real estate, in order to be valid, must be attested by *two* witnesses.[2] If it was not thus attested, the title to the real estate assigned remained in the debtor, subject to attachment.[3] And where a deed was attested by one witness only, notice of the deed did not remedy the defect in the attestation.[4]

§ 219. **Oath to Assignment.**— In some of the states it has been made necessary to the validity of an assignment that it should be *sworn to* by the assignor. The oath which the assignor is required to make is generally to the effect that the assignment conveys all his property not exempt by law and is not made with the intention of delaying or defrauding his creditors.[5]

§ 220. **Acknowledgment of Execution.**— In New York the statute declares that every assignment in trust for the benefit of creditors " shall be duly acknowledged before an officer authorized to take the acknowledgment of deeds." . . . " The assent of the assignee, subscribed and acknowledged by him, shall appear in writing, embraced in or at the end of or indorsed upon the assign-

---

[1] King v. Moore, 18 Pick. 376.
[2] Gen. Laws (ed. 1878), ch. 140, p. 336, § 2. See P. S. (1891), p. 559.
[3] Barker v. Bean, 25 N. H. 412.
[4] Id.
[5] See Appendix, I.

ment before the same is recorded, and, if separate from the assignment, shall be duly acknowledged." [1]

This requirement is mandatory and not merely directory, and every assignment which does not comply with the statute in this respect is void.[2]

It has been held that the acknowledgment must be made by the debtor in person; that it cannot be made by his attorney, or proved through the medium of a witness.[3]

But it is now settled that an assignment executed in the name of the debtor and acknowledged by an attorney duly constituted for that purpose is valid under the New York statute, and effectual to vest in the assignee the title to the assigned property.[4]

Where several debtors make an assignment each must join in the acknowledgment.[5]

Where an assignment in trust for the benefit of creditors, made by a partnership firm, is executed by all the partners, the acknowledgment which the statute requires should be made by all.[6] But where there are non-resident members of a firm, they are not necessarily included in the requirement of a personal execution and acknowledgment by each of the assignors.[7]

The old rule that an assignment could not be executed by an attorney in fact did not preclude the partners who remained, after one of their number had absconded, from executing an assignment of the assets of the firm.[8]

An acknowledgment before an officer who had no previous knowledge of the parties, and who received no more evidence of their identity at the time of execution, is fatally defective, and the defect renders the assignment null and void.[9]

---

[1] R. S. (8th ed.), Part II, ch. V, n. 1a, § 2; Laws of 1877, ch. 466.

[2] Hardman v. Bowen, 39 N. Y. 196; s. c., 5 Abb. Pr. (N. S.) 332; Fairchild v. Gwinne, 16 Abb. Pr. 23; rev'g s. c., 14 Abb. Pr. 121; Britton v. Lorenz, 45 N. Y. 51; Rennie v. Bean, 24 Hun, 123. A defective acknowledgment cannot be taken advantage of in a collateral proceeding to shield the assignee from liability as such. Randall v. Dusenbury, 39 Super. Ct. (7 J. & S.) 177; affirmed, 63 N. Y. 645. Ambiguous words in the acknowledgment should be construed in the light of circumstances and as referring to the instrument to which the certificate was appended. Smith v. Boyd, 101 N. Y. 472. See Smith v. Tinn, 14 Abb. N. C. 447 and note.

[3] Adams v. Houghton, 3 Abb. Pr. (N. S.) 46.

[4] Lowenstein v. Flauraud, 82 N. Y. 494; affirming 11 Hun, 399. See, also, Baldwin v. Tynes, 19 Abb. Pr. 32. The statute referred to is Laws of 1860, ch. 340. The present statute does not seem to differ as to this point.

[5] Cook v. Kelly, 14 Abb. Pr. 466; s. c., 12 Abb. Pr. 35.

[6] Treadwell v. Sackett, 50 Barb. 440.

[7] Darrow v. Bruff, 36 How. Pr. 479. And see Baldwin v. Tynes, 19 Abb. Pr. 32.

[8] National Bank v. Sackett, 2 Abb. Pr. (N. S.) 286. See Cook v. Kelly, *supra*.

[9] Treadwell v. Sackett, 50 Barb. 440; Jones v. Beach, 48 id. 568.

§ 221. Acknowledgment of Execution Before Proper Officer.—

In some other states, also, it is necessary that the execution of the assignment should be acknowledged or proved before some proper officer, in order to entitle it to be recorded. This is expressly required by statute in some instances,[1] and it seems to be an indispensable formality, wherever a record or registry of the assignment is necessary.

[1] See Appendix, I. As to Illinois, see Zimmerman v. Willard, 14 Ill. 364; Rendleman v. Willard, 15 Mo. App. 375. Missouri, see Eppright v. Nickerson, 78 Mo. 482. Michigan, see Ryerson v. Eldred, 18 Mich. 12. Nebraska, see Heelan v. Hoagland, 10 Neb. 511. In Minnesota the notarial seal must be attached. De Graw v. King, 28 Minn. 118.

CHAPTER XV.

RECORD OR REGISTRY OF THE ASSIGNMENT.

§ 222. Requisites After Execution.
223. Record Essential.
224. Record Essential — Cases.
225. Record Essential — Cases — Continued.
226. Record Essential — Cases — Continued.
227. Notice in Lieu of Record.

§ 222. **Requisites After Execution.**— After the assignment is executed there are certain acts which remain to be done on the parts of the assignor and assignee, and sometimes on the part of the creditors, in order to render it fully operative as a transfer for the purposes intended by it, such as the *recording* or registry of the instrument, its *delivery* by the assignor to the assignee, its *acceptance* by the latter, the *delivery* of possession of the *property* assigned, and the *assent* of the *creditors* to the assignment. These subjects will be considered in the following chapters.

§ 223. **Record Essential.**— In some of the states an assignment is of no validity against creditors unless *recorded* or *registered* in some public office within a certain time after its execution.[1]

§ 224. **Record Essential — Cases.**— In Pennsylvania, by statute of March 24, 1818, section 5,[2] an assignment is void as against creditors, unless recorded within thirty days [3] after its execution in the county where the debtor resides.[4] This statute has been held to extend to assignments in trust for payment of particular creditors, as well as to those for payment of all.[5] It has been held, also, to compre-

---

[1] See Appendix, I.
[2] Purdon's Digest (Brightley, 11th ed.), p. 121, § 18.
[3] Where the assignee named in a deed of assignment for the benefit of creditors declines to accept the trust and in his stead another is appointed, the thirty days allowed by the act within which to record the deed runs from its date and not from the time of the appointment of the new trustee. Hence, when the assignee did not record the deed of assignment until after thirty days from its execution, it was as to creditors null and void, and the fund in the hands of the assignee was liable to attachment by them. Johnson v. Herring, 46 Pa. St. 415. See Lane's Appeal, 82 Pa. St. 289.
[4] Stewart v. McMinn, 5 W. & S. 100. It is not sufficient that the deed is recorded in the county in which the property is situated. Schuylkill Bank v. Reigart, 4 Barr, 477.
[5] Englebert v. Blanjot, 2 Whart. 240; reversing the judgment in 1 Miles, 224; Murphy's Assignment, 2 Pitts. R. 271.

hend instruments subsequently executed by the assignor, for the purpose of extending the provisions of the assignment to creditors not provided for by it as originally executed. Thus, where an assignment was made for the benefit of certain creditors who should release, which assignment was duly recorded, and there being a surplus in the hands of the assignee, after paying the releasing creditors, two instruments were executed under seal by the assignors, by one of which they assigned the surplus to the same assignee, in trust, to pay the same to certain creditors who had signed a letter of license; and by the other of which they also assigned the surplus to the same assignee, in trust, to pay the same to such creditors as should release within a certain time, it was held that these instruments came within the provisions of the statute, and ought to have been recorded in conformity with it.[1]

The same statute has been held to extend to assignments made in the form of absolute conveyances, with separate declarations of trust,[2] and to all instruments of transfer for the benefit of creditors, whether in the particular form of an assignment or not. Hence, a power of attorney, if virtually an assignment, must be recorded, to make it valid against the attachment of a creditor.[3]

An assignment of numerous claims and judgments "in payment" of certain creditors' demands has been held to be an assignment for the benefit of creditors; and not having been recorded within thirty days, to be void as against a subsequent attaching creditor.[4]

The same statute has been held to extend to assignments of property in another state, and for the benefit of foreign creditors. Thus, where A., residing in Philadelphia, assigned to B., also residing at that place, real and personal estate situated in New York, in trust, to pay a creditor of A. in London, and then his creditors generally, and the assignment was not recorded according to the statute, it was held that it might be avoided by the creditors of A.[5]

But the statute has been held not to apply to assignments made directly to creditors for their own benefit only, although with an understanding that any surplus should be accounted for to the debtor;[6] nor to judgments confessed by the debtor to a trustee

[1] Flanagan v. Wetherill, 5 Whart. 280.
[2] Schuylkill Bank v. Reigart, 4 Barr, 477.
[3] Watson v. Bagaley, 12 Pa. St. 164.
[4] Wallace v. Wainwright, 87 Pa. St. 263.
[5] Weber v. Samuel, 7 Barr, 499.
[6] Chaffee v. Risk, 24 Pa. St. 432; approved in Henderson's Appeal, 31 Pa. St. 502. See Lane's Appeal, 82 id. 289.

for the payment of certain specified creditors;[1] nor to mortgages in trust to secure creditors.[2]

It has been further held in Pennsylvania that an assignment of real estate must, under the general act of March 18, 1775 (declaring all deeds and conveyances of land fraudulent and void against subsequent purchasers, unless recorded within six months after execution), be recorded in the county in which the land is situated, in order to make it valid against a subsequent purchaser from the assignor, without notice of the assignment, even though it were duly recorded in the county in which the assignor resided, pursuance of the act of 1818.[3]

By the act of May 6, 1854, section 1, in all cases where lands and tenements have been or shall hereafter be conveyed to any person or persons in trust, for the use and benefit of others, by a deed of trust, the trustee or trustees, on request of any person interested, and at the cost of the party requesting it, shall cause the said deed to be recorded in the proper county where the lands and tenements are situate; and in case such deed be in the possession of any person other than a trustee, on request as aforesaid, and at the proper cost of the person requesting the same, it shall be the duty of such person, trustee or otherwise, to cause said deed to be recorded in the proper county where the lands and tenements may be situate; and in case of neglect or refusal to cause such deed to be recorded on request as aforesaid, it shall be lawful for the court of common pleas of the proper county, on the petition of any person interested, setting forth the facts of the case to issue a citation to the person or persons having such deed as aforesaid, to appear within such time as the court shall direct and show cause why he or they refuse to cause said deeds to be recorded; and on failure to appear or to show satisfactory cause, said court shall order such persons, trustees or otherwise, to cause said deed to be recorded as aforesaid, with costs against such delinquent, which said order or decree may be enforced by attachment.[4]

But though not recorded according to the statute the assignment will still remain valid as against a subsequent voluntary assignee;[5] and dissenting creditors can only avoid it *pro tanto*.[6]

[1] Guy v. McIlree, 26 Pa. St. 92.
[2] Ridgway v. Stewart, 4 Watts & Serg. 383.
[3] Dougherty v. Daraach, 15 Pa. St. 399; Follweiler v. Lutz, 102 id. 585.
[4] Laws of 1854, p. 603; Purdon's Dig. (Brightley, 11th ed.), p. 1659, § 75.
[5] Seal v. Duffey, 4 Barr, 274. Creditors, by levying on the property assigned, avoided the deed *pro tanto* only, and are estopped from availing themselves of the first assignment, to prevent the operation of a second assignment on the

[6] Ibid. And see Weber v. Samuel, 7 Barr, 499.

The deed may be taken to be recorded by any one of the creditors for whose use the conveyance was made, or any party interested in the trust.[1]

As soon as the assignment is placed by the assignor or any one interested in the office of the recorder, the beneficial interest of creditors is completely vested.[2]

By the act of May 3, 1855,[3] assignments by non-residents of property within the state may be recorded in any county where such estate, real or personal, may be, and take effect from its date; provided that no *bona fide* purchaser, mortgagee or creditor, having a lien thereon before the recording in the same county, and not having had previous actual notice thereof, shall be affected or prejudiced.[4]

§ 225. **Record Essential — Cases — Continued.** — In Connecticut it is one of the requisites of a valid assignment that it be lodged for a record in the office of the court of probate for the district where the assignor or assignees of some of them reside.[5] But no time is limited by the statute within which this must be done; and if the assignment be recorded before the lien of a creditor attaches it will avail against it.[6] Nor is such record necessary where the parties reside in another state. Thus, where an assignment made in Ohio, the assignor and assignee both residing in that state, embraced a debt due from an incorporated company in Connecticut, but was not lodged for record in the office of any court of probate in Connecticut, it was held that the assignment, being valid by the laws of Ohio was also valid in Connecticut, against the subsequent attachment of a creditor residing in Pennsylvania.[7]

The Massachusetts statute of 1836 did not require assignments

property thus levied on, and included in the first assignment. Id., ibid. But an unrecorded assignment for the benefit of a single creditor is invalid against the assignee under a subsequent recorded assignment for the benefit of all the creditors. Kern v. Powell, 98 Pa. St. 253.

[1] Read v. Robinson, 6 Watts. & Serg. 329.

[2] Mark's Appeal, 85 Pa. St. 231.

[3] Laws of 1855, p. 415; Purdon's Dig. (Brightley, 11th ed.), p. 122, § 14. See Philson v. Barnes, 50 Pa. St. 230.

[4] Evans v. Dunkelberger, 3 Grant (Pa.), 134.

[5] Gen. Stat. of Conn. (1888), § 503. In the case of copartnerships and corporations, the assignment should be recorded in the office of the court of probate for the district where such copartnership or corporation had its office or principal place of business. And where the assignment includes partnership and individual property, and the office or principal place of business of the partnership is in one district and the residence of one or more of the individual partners is in another district, it would seem that the assignment should be recorded in both districts. Coggill v. Bottsford, 29 Conn. 439.

[6] Strong v. Carrier, 17 Conn. 319.

[7] Atwood v. Protection Ins. Co., 14 Conn. 555.

made under it to be recorded, but only notice of them to be published by advertisement.[1] This was held to have been intended as a legal notice to all creditors,[2] and to have been not inconsistent with the general provisions of law as to the registry of conveyances.[3]

In Virginia all deeds of trust are declared void as to creditors until admitted to record in the county or corporation wherein the property embraced in the deed may be,[4] provided that where the property is situated within the jurisdiction of a corporation or hustings court, the record shall be made in the clerk's office of such corporation or hustings court.

In North Carolina a deed of trust must be proved and registered within six months or it will be utterly void as against a creditor; and the circumstance of the registration before a creditor has got his judgment and execution makes no difference, as notice of a deed of trust not duly registered raises no equity against a creditor.[5] Where a creditor, knowing that another creditor has taken a deed of trust, but which is not registered, takes another deed of trust on the same property to secure his own debt and procures it to be first registered, this is held to be no fraud against any person, at least at law; more especially it is not a fraud against those who do not claim under the creditor secured by the first deed.[6] In the revised code of this state it is now declared that no deed of trust shall be valid at law to pass any property as against creditors or purchasers for a valuable consideration, but from the registration of such deeds of trust in the county where the land lies, or in case of personal estate where the donor resides.[7]

In Alabama a deed of trust not delivered for registration or recorded until thirty-one days after its execution has been declared void as against judgment creditors not having actual notice of the deed.[8]

---

[1] Stat. of 1836, ch. 238, § 5.
[2] Guilford v. Childs, 22 Pick. 434; Wilde, J., id. 435, 426. See Johnson v. Whitwell, 7 Pick. 71.
[3] Wilde, J., in Guilford v. Childs, 22 Pick. 434, 435, 436.
[4] See Act of January 16, 1867, amending and re-enacting section 5 of chapter 119, Code of 1860, p. 566; Code of 1873, p. 897; Code (1887), § 2465. See, also, Blackford v. Hurst, 16 Gratt. 203; Burr's Ex'r v. McDonald, 3 id. 215; Shanks v. Lancaster, 5 id. 110. In Kirkland v. Brune, 31 Gratt. 126, it was held that an assignment of a mere chose in action as a debt or claim on another for money due need not be recorded, and will be good against a subsequent attachment.
[5] Dewey v. Littlejohn, 2 Ired. Eq. 495; Ruffin, C. J., id. 503; citing Davidson v. Cowan, 1 Dev. Eq. 470.
[6] Burgin v. Burgin, 1 Ired. L. 453.
[7] Rev. Code of N. C., ed. 1855, ch. 37, § 22, p. 245; Battle's Rev., p. 345, § 12; Code, 1883, vol. I, § 1254.
[8] Wallis v. Rhea, 12 Ala. 646.

In Kentucky all deeds of trust are required to be recorded in the offices of the county courts.[1] And the practice seems to be to record all assignments, whether of real or personal property.[2]

In Indiana the assignment must, within ten days after its execution, be filed with the recorder of the county in which the assignor resides; and until the assignment is recorded as provided, it conveys no interest in the assigned property to the assignee.[3]

§ 226. Record Essential — Continued.— In Arizona,[4] California,[5] Connecticut,[6] Colorado,[7] Florida,[8] Illinois,[9] Indiana,[10] Iowa,[11] Kansas,[12] Kentucky,[13] Maryland,[14] Mississippi,[15] Missouri,[16] Nebraska,[17] New

---

[1] Brown & Morehead's Stat. Law, vol. I, pp. 448, 449; Session Acts of 1836, 1837, p. 255; Session Acts, 1838, 1839, p. 96; Gen. Stats. of Ky. 1881, p. 256; G. S. 1887, pp. 313, 314.

[2] See Vernon v. Morton, 8 Dana, 247; Cogar v. Stewart, 78 Ky. (Rodm.) 59; Zaring v. Cox, id. 527.

[3] R. S. of Ind. 1881, § 2663. The title to the property, whether real or personal, does not pass to the assignee until the assignment has been duly recorded. New v. Reissner, 56 Ind. 118; Forkner v. Schafer, id. 120. The assignment must be recorded in each of the counties in which real estate thereby conveyed is situated. Switzer v. Miller, 58 Ind. 561. An assignment which has neither been assented to by an execution creditor nor recorded is not binding upon such creditor, even though after it was made he had verbally assented thereto, nor does any property pass until the deed has been filed or recorded. Eden v. Everson, 65 Ind. 113. A complaint by an assignee which does not allege recording is bad on demurrer (Foster v. Brown, 65 Ind. 234; Wheeler v. Hawkins, 101 id. 486), and an assignment not recorded within ten days is not admissible in evidence. Fordyce v. Pipher, 84 id. 86.

[4] R. S. 1887, § 22.

[5] Hittell's C. & S., §§ 8458, 8459.

[6] Gen. Stats. 1888, § 503.

[7] Mills' A. S. 1891, § 169.

[8] R. S. 1892, § 2309; Eldridge v. Post, 20 Fla. 579.

[9] R. S. 1889, p. 118.

[10] R. S. 1888, § 2663. See Switzer v. Miller, 58 Ind. 561; New v. Reissner, 56 id. 118.

[11] McClain's Ann. Code, § 3294. But where possession accompanies the conveyance of personal property it is not necessary that the deed should be acknowledged and recorded. Meeker v. Saunders, 6 Iowa, 61. Title passes on delivery. American & Co. v. Frank, 62 id. 202.

[12] G. S. 1889, § 342.

[13] G. S. 1887, ch. 24, § 11, ch. 109a, § 1.

[14] Pub. Gen. Laws 1888, §§ 205, 206. See Houston v. Nowland, 7 Gill & J. 480; Brooks v. Marbury, 11 Wheat. 78; Farquharson v. Eichelberger, 15 Md. 63; Hoopes v. Knell, 31 id. 550.

[15] Prewett v. Dobbs, 13 Sm. & M. 431.

[16] R. S. 1889, § 424. Rendleman v. Willard, 15 Mo. App. 375; Winn v. Madden, 18 id. 258; Hartzler v. Tootle, 85 Mo. 23.

[17] C. S. 1891, ch. 6, § 6.

Jersey,[1] New Mexico,[2] New York,[3] North Carolina,[4] North Dakota,[5] Oregon,[6] Pennsylvania,[7] South Dakota,[8] Tennessee,[9] Texas,[10] Vermont,[11] Virginia,[12] and West Virginia,[13] assignments and deeds of trust are required to be recorded. But the recording act of Mississippi does not embrace deeds of trust executed in other states, and a failure to record such deeds in that state after a removal of the property into it does not impair their validity even against *bona fide* purchasers and creditors without notice of their existence.[14]

An Arkansas[15] title vests in the assignee, not only as against the assignor, but also as against the execution creditors, without registration. By statute,[16] however, the assignee must not take possession, sell, or in any way manage or control the property assigned until he files the schedule and executes the bond.

In Nebraska an assignment must, within twenty-four hours after its execution, be filed for record in the clerk's office of the county in which the assignee resides. Within thirty days after the execution thereof it must be filed for record in every other county of the state in which it purports to convey real estate. Failure to comply with the statute avoids the assignment.[17] The recording of an unacknowledged deed is a nullity.[18]

In New York it is provided that every assignment made under the provisions of the act of 1877 shall be recorded in the clerk's office of the county in which the debtor resided or carried on his business at the date thereof.

[1] R. S. 1877, p. 37.
[2] L. 1889, ch. 71, § 1.
[3] 4 R. S. (8th ed.), post II, ch. V, t. 1*a*, § 2.
[4] Code 1883, §§ 1246, 1254.
[5] Comp. Laws, § 4660.
[6] Hill's A. L. 1887, § 3174. Laws of 1878, p. 37. Recording is not essential to the validity of the deed where possession accompanies conveyance of personal property. Dawson v. Crossen, 10 Oreg. 41.
[7] 1 Purd. Dig., ed. of 1883, p. 121.
[8] Comp. Laws, § 4660.
[9] Brevard v. Neely, 2 Sneed, 164; Simpkinson v. McGee, 4 Lea (Tenn.), 432; Code of Tenn. § 2030. See Miller v. O'Bannon, 4 Lea (Tenn.), 398.
[10] 1 Sayles' C. S. 1888, art. 65*a*, 65*s*; Act of February 5, 1840; Paschal's Dig. vol. 1, p. 833; Acts of 1879, ch. 53; R. S. 1879, Appendix, p. 5. The validity of the assignment does not depend upon the act of registering the deed. Piggott v. Schram, 64 Tex. 447.
[11] R. L. 1880, § 1886.
[12] Code 1887, 2674.
[13] Code, p. 639.
[14] Palmer v. Cross, 1 Sm. & M. 48; Dobbs v. Prescott, 13 id. 431, cited and confirmed in Presley v. Rogers, 24 Miss. 520, 524.
[15] Thatcher v. Franklin, 37 Ark. 64.
[16] R. S. of Ark. 1874, § 385; Mansf. Dig. 1884, § 305.
[17] Laws of 1883, ch. 7, § 6; G. S. 1891, p. 8; Wells v. Lamb, 19 Neb. 355.
[18] Heelan v. Hoagland, 10 Neb. 511.

An assignment by copartners must be recorded in the county where their principal place of business is situated. When real property is a part of the property assigned, and is situated in a county other than the one in which the original assignment is required to be recorded, a certified copy of such assignment must be filed and recorded in the county where such property is situated.[1] But such filing in the clerk's office is not constructive notice of the conveyance of real estate.[2] An assignment of real estate should therefore likewise be recorded in the register's office of the county where the real estate is situated. Sometimes, instead of recording the assignment itself, it has been the practice, where real estate is conveyed by it, to have a deed of the same property prepared in the ordinary form, and bearing even date, which, after being executed and acknowledged by the proper parties, is put on record like any other conveyance. An assignment by a non-resident should be recorded in the county where the property is situated.[3] Neglect to record the assignment does not render it fraudulent and the property liable to attachment as the assignment takes effect from the time of delivery, and statutory requirements subsequent to delivery are merely directory.[4] But a recording of an assignment without the written assent of the assignee, required by statute, is void against attaching creditors.[5]

§ 227. **Notice in Lieu of Record.**— The public notice of the assignment, which is usually given by the assignee on accepting the trust (and sometimes by the assignor), of which more will be said hereafter, operates in some instances with the effect of a record.[6] In Massachusetts, under the statute of 1836, chapter 238, it was held that an assignment of real estate, duly notified in a newspaper as required by the statute, was valid as against an attaching creditor, although not recorded in the registry of deeds; and this, notwithstanding the provisions of the Revised Statutes (ch. 59, § 28), as to the registry of conveyances of real estate in general.[7] In Mississippi it was held, in the case of Dixon v. Doe,[8] that creditors,

---

[1] Laws of 1877, ch. 466, § 2; 3 R. S. (7th ed.), p. 2276; Fay's Dig., p. 394; 4 R. S. 1889, p. 2536.
[2] Simon v. Kaliske, 6 Abb. Pr. (N. S.) 224; s. c., 37 How. Pr. 249; Wagner v. Hodge, 34 Hun, 524.
[3] Scott v. Guthrie, 10 Bosw. 408.
[4] Denzer v. Mundy, 5 Robt. 636; Warner v. Jaffray, 96 N. Y. 248; Pancoast v. Spowers, 52 N. Y. Superior Ct. 523; McBlain v. Spelman, 35 Hun, 263.
[5] Rennie v. Bean, 24 Hun, 123.
[6] Van Hook v. Walton, 28 Tex. 59, citing Givens v. Taylor, 6 id. 315; Bennett v. Cocks, 15 id. 67.
[7] Guilford v. Childs, 22 Pick. 434.
[8] 1 Sm. & M. 70.

equally with subsequent purchasers, were affected by notice of an unregistered deed. This case was referred to by the court in Henderson v. Downing,[1] without controverting the decision, and with no other comment than to say that it would not be extended any farther than the case there made. In North Carolina, as already mentioned, notice of a deed of trust, not duly registered, raises no equity against a creditor.[2]

[1] 24 Miss. 106; Yerger, J., id. 114, 115.
[2] Dewey v. Littlejohn, 2 Ired. Eq. 495.

CHAPTER XVI.

DELIVERY OF THE ASSIGNMENT.

§ 228. Delivery Necessary.
228. What Amounts to a Delivery.
230. Evidence of Delivery.

§ 239. **Delivery Necessary.**— In order to complete the transfer intended by the assignment it is necessary not only that the instrument should be executed with all the requisite formalities, but that it should be actually *delivered* to the assignee.[1]

Thus in Pennsylvania in a case where, among other circumstances, there was no delivery of the assignment to the assignee until several weeks after its date, the assignment was held to be fraudulent and void against a creditor who had obtained judgment.[2] And in another case in the same state, it was held to be indispensable to the effect of an assignment for the benefit of creditors as well as of other deeds, that it should be actually delivered, or put in a course of transmission beyond the grantor's control, to the assignee; otherwise an execution would be preferred.[3] So in Massachusetts where an assignment purporting to be an indenture tripartite between the debtor, the assignees and the creditors who should execute it, was executed by the debtor and assignees, and then taken by the debtor to procure its execution by his creditors, no counterpart having been made; and after some of the creditors had executed it, and before it was delivered to the trustees another creditor attached the property assigned, the attachment was held good against the assignees, the assignment being incomplete until delivery to them.[4] In Tennessee delivery is an essential incident

[1] Van Hook v. Walton, 28 Tex. 59; Brackett v. Barney, 28 N. Y. 333; Wadleigh v. Merkle, 57 Wis. 517; Truss v. Davidson, 90 Ala. 359; 7 S. Rep. 812; Thatcher v. Franklin, 37 Ark. 64; Golden's Appeal, 110 Penn. St. 581; 1 A. Rep. 660; Kingston v. Koch, 57 Hun, 12; 10 N. Y. S. Rep. 363; McIlhargy v. Chambers, 51 id. 332; 4 N. Y. S. Rep. 698. But a deed which provides for delivery "forthwith" is fraudulent. Lincoln v. Field, 54 Ark. 471; 16 S. W. Rep. 288. Also where a trust deed is actually delivered to the grantee the rights of the *cestuis que trustent* attach, and the effect of the delivery cannot be impaired by any mental reservation on the part of the grantor or oral condition repugnant to the terms of the deed attached to the delivery. Wallace v. Berdell, 97 N. Y. 13.
[2] Burd v. Smith, 4 Dall. 76.
[3] McKinney v. Rhoads, 5 Watts, 345. See Klapp's Assignees v. Shirk, 13 Pa. St. 589.
[4] Marston v. Coburn, 17 Mass. 454.

to the proper execution of a deed of trust, as well as of all other deeds.[1]

In New York it is held that the assignment takes effect from the time of its delivery.[2]

§ 229. **What Amounts to a Delivery.**— A deposit of the deed in the postoffice directed to the assignee, who resided at some distance, was held in Pennsylvania to be sufficient as against an execution which was levied between the deposit in the office and the actual delivery to the assignee.[3]

In a case in Ohio[4] it was held that the assignment took effect from the time of placing it in the postoffice, for the assignor thereby ceased to have control of the property, and the assignee, by his previous conduct in preparing the assignment and sending it to the assignor, had accepted the trust. The possession of the carrier must therefore be regarded as the possession of the assignee.

In a case in Michigan[5] the debtor assigned to a member of a firm to which he was indebted, who had previously agreed to act as assignee. The debtor delivered the assignment to an agent of the firm, who took it to the residence of the assignee. The latter was absent, but on his return accepted and set out to take possession. On the day the assignment was executed, after the agent had departed, an attachment was levied on the goods by another creditor. It was held, in view of the previous understanding and the representative character of the agent, that the assignment, being unconditional, took effect as soon as the agent started for his principal and it was beyond the assignor's control, and that it was sufficiently perfected by acceptance and delivery to defeat the levy.

The delivery of an assignment to the clerk to be recorded may be considered as a delivery to a stranger for the use of the creditors, there being no condition annexed to the assignment making it an escrow.[6] And the record of the deed amounts to *prima facie* evidence of delivery.[7] A delivery to the trustees is equivalent to a delivery to the *cestuis que trust*.[8] In Pennsylvania, where a debtor executed an assignment in M. county, and handed it to his son to

---

[1] Brevard v. Neely, 2 Sneed, 164; McKinney, J., id. 169.
[2] Warner v. Jaffray, 96 N. Y. 248; Pancoast v. Spowers, 52 N. Y. Super. Ct. 523; McBlain v. Spelman, 35 Hun, 263.
[3] McKinney v. Rhoads, 5 Watts, 345.
[4] Johnson v. Sharp, 31 Ohio St. 611.
[5] Stamp v. Case, 41 Mich. 267.
[6] Tompkins v. Wheeler, 16 Pet. 106. See Brevard v. Neely, 2 Sneed, 164. As to delivery as an escrow, see Bowker v. Burdekin, 11 Mees. & W. 128; Johnson v. Baker, 3 B. & Ald. 440; Ward v. Lewis, 4 Pick. 518.
[7] Ingraham v. Griggs, 13 Sm. & M. 22. But see Webb v. Dean, 21 Pa. St. 29.
[8] Ingraham v. Griggs, 13 Sm. & M. 22. And see Moir v. Brown, 14 Barb. 39, 44.

take to Philadelphia to a third person, who called with it on the assignee in that city, and desired him to take it, but he refused to have anything to do with it, it was held that a presumption arose, from the nature of the case, that the tender was made by authority of the grantor.[1]

The moment an assignment is placed by the assignor or any one interested in the office of the recorder of deeds, the beneficial interest of the creditors — the *cestuis que trust* — is completely vested, and it is totally immaterial when the assignee accepts the trust, or whether he ever accepts it.[2] In Tennessee it is held that a delivery, to be valid, must be such as not only deprives the grantor of the power to recall the deed, but likewise such a consummation of the formalities of execution as to make the deed effectual to transfer the title.[3]

Where the assignors duly executed and acknowledged the deed of assignment, and the assignee accepted the trust and directed the attorney of the assignors to do whatever was necessary to perfect the assignment, it was held that this constituted a delivery to the assignee and carried with it the title to the property.[4]

§ 230. **Evidence of Delivery.**— Where an assignment by an indenture of three parts was signed and sealed, and purported to have been delivered by the debtor, the trustees and some of the creditors; and one part was found in the hands of the trustees, and another, several months after the date, in the hands of the creditors, and in adjusting their claims was often referred to, as well by the trustees as by the creditors; and the debtor's property passed into the hands of one of the trustees, who appeared before the creditors in the character of trustee, and made proposals to the creditors in the name of all trustees, and it was often spoken of by him as being held under the assignment, and was sold by him for the benefit of the creditors; and the debtor, when he requested one of his creditors to execute the indenture, informed such creditor that he had assigned his property for the benefit of his creditors, it was held in Massachusetts that this was sufficient evidence of a delivery of the deed by the debtor to the trustees and to the creditors.[5]

A subsequent fraudulent sale by an assignee has no bearing upon the question of the delivery of the assignment.[6]

[1] Read v. Robinson, 6 W. & S. 329.
[2] Mark's Appeal, 85 Pa. St. 231.
[3] McKinney, J., in Brevard v. Neely, 2 Sneed, 164, 170.
[4] American & Co. v. Frank, 62 Iowa, 202. See Reichenbach v. Winkhaus, 12 Daly, 525; *supra*, p. 274.
[5] Ward v. Lewis, 4 Pick. 518. See the New York case of Moir v. Brown, 14 Barb. 39, where the evidence showed that the assignment was not delivered to one of the assignees until after a levy of execution on the property assigned.
[6] Leeds v. Commonwealth. 83 Pa. St. 453.

CHAPTER XVII.

AMENDMENTS AND ADDITIONS TO ASSIGNMENTS.

§ 231. Amendments, How Made.
232. By Consent of Parties.
233. By the Court.
234. In Other Cases.
235. Additions.

§ 231. **Amendments, How Made.**— After an assignment has been executed it may be corrected and amended if necessary by the consent of all the parties or on application to a court of equity.

§ 232. **By Consent of Parties.**— It may be amended by the consent of parties so as to purge it of any objectionable features. And where creditors have become parties by actually assenting to the assignment, or where their assent is assumed, their consent to any alteration or modification of the assignment is essential. When the deed is fraudulent there is no presumption of an assent to it on the part of the creditors,[1] and it has been held that such a conveyance is revocable until all the creditors have assented, and may be canceled, abrogated or modified at pleasure by those who are parties to it.[2] In Illinois, where the assignment was fraudulent because it empowered the assignee to sell on credit, a subsequent agreement entered into between the assignor and assignee, excluding the objectionable power, was held to purge the instrument of fraud, no rights of creditors having attached.[3] And in another case in the same state it was held that if an assignment be so modified by the

---

[1] See *post*, ch. XX
[2] Insurance Co. v. Wallis, 23 Md. 173.
[3] Pierce v. Brewster, 32 Ill. 268. The rule in Illinois seems to follow the English doctrine. See *ante*, § 170. The assent of creditors is not assumed even where the instrument is beneficial; they are not regarded as parties to it, therefore, unless they were privy to its execution or have actually assented. Mr. Justice Walker in Gibson v. Rees, 50 Ill. 383, after citing Wilson v. Pearson, 20 id. 81, and Pierce v. Brewster, 32 id. 268, and English cases, remarks: "These authorities abundantly establish the doctrine that where such a deed is made and the creditors are not parties to it, it may under proper limitations be altered, changed or canceled by the parties to the instrument." In Ryhiner v. Ruegger, 19 Ill. App. 156, an attaching creditor was also one of the assignees. He had accepted the trust and consented to the alteration of the assignment and the elimination of certain fraudulent provisions. This was held to operate as a dissolution of the attachment and so leave the attaching creditor to take his chances with the other creditors.

consent of all parties, prior to the time when any creditor is in a position to attack it, it becomes a valid assignment and the rights of the creditors in respect to the property assigned must be governed by it.[1]

But in a later case[2] it has been held that where a debtor has executed and delivered the deed to the assignee, the assignor has no power afterward to change its terms and conditions without the consent of the assignee and the creditors.

After the execution and delivery of an assignment, a schedule (previously omitted) may be annexed to it by the consent of all the parties, and it may then be redelivered with the same effect as before.[3]

In a case in Georgia,[4] where the debtor had provided in the assignment for a release, and subsequently relinquished any benefit he might be supposed to have reserved to himself therefrom, it was held that after the execution of such a relinquishment and its acceptance by the assignee, before the plaintiffs obtained judgment, the assignment would stand.

§ 233. **By the Court.**— Mistakes in assignments will also sometimes be corrected and the instruments be reformed by a court of equity in the absence of any express statute provision to the contrary on application for that purpose. In a case in Alabama, where a debtor executed a deed of trust to secure certain of his creditors and sureties, and included in it certain notes on which one of the beneficiaries was supposed to be bound as surety, describing them as notes on which said beneficiary was security, under the belief that if he was not bound, the misdescription would exclude the holder of them from any benefit under the deed — the deed was reformed in equity, upon proof of the mistake, and that the grantor intended to secure the said beneficiary only and not the notes.[5] But in a case in Connecticut the supreme court of errors refused to reform an assignment so as to include a claim which was intended and agreed by the assignor to be included in it and conveyed to the assignee, but had been, through the mistake of the draughtsman, omitted; on the ground that, as the statute of 1828 against fraudulent conveyances, expressly required the assignment to be in writing and lodged for record in the probate office, the ordinary principles which are adopted in chancery, as to the cor-

---

[1] Conkling v. Carson, 11 Ill. 503.
[2] Union Nat. Bank v. Bank of Commerce, 94 Ill. 27.
[3] Clap v. Smith, 16 Pick. 247; Hand, J., in Moir v. Brown, 14 Barb. 39, 48.
[4] Cohen v. Summers, 54 Ga. 501.
[5] Trapp v. Moore, 21 Ala. 693. See Moale v. Buchanan, 11 Gill & J. (Md.) 314.

rection and reformation of mistakes in instruments, did not apply to the case.[1] And in a later case the same court adhered to the former decision, with the distinction that, as to the assignor, if it should become necessary to reform the assignment in consequence of a mistake attending its execution, the ordinary principles on which such relief is granted by courts of equity would apply. But such relief would not be granted against his creditors for the obvious reason that, as to them, the instrument was rendered fraudulent and void.[2]

§ 234. **In Other Cases.**— Sometimes the effect of amendment has been allowed to be obtained by the mere act of the assignor by means of a new and distinct instrument. Thus, in Connecticut, it has been held that an instrument referring to a former deed of trust, which was void by reason of a clause prescribing terms to the *cestui que trust* renewing and confirming such deed, exclusive of the exceptional clause, and assigning the same property for the same purpose, and giving the same authority to the trustee, not by a specification of such property, but by terms of reference to the former deed, might have effect as a new and independent instrument of conveyance.[3] In a late case in Vermont, where an assignment was defective on account of its containing a resulting trust before providing for all the assignor's creditors, it was held by the supreme court that the defect might be supplied by a new assignment providing in terms for the payment of all the assignor's debts. The court (Redfield, C. J.) said this was not only allowable, but it was certainly commendable; and they saw no reason why it might not be done by a mere declaration of trust in favor of all the creditors, in addition to the former assignment, without making the whole paper anew.[4] It was also held in the same case that where an assignment was voidable or inoperative as to creditors under the statute on account of its generality, the defect might be cured by a new assignment, excepting some substantial portion of the estate and leaving it open to attachment.[5] But in a case in the court of appeals of New York, where an assignment was invalid by reason of its containing an authority to the assignee to sell the assigned property on credit, it was held that it could not

---

[1] Whitaker v. Gavit, 18 Conn. 522.
[2] Whitaker v. Williams, 20 Conn. 98; Storrs, J., id. 102. See Farrow v. Hayes, 51 Md. 498.
[3] Ingraham v. Wheeler, 6 Conn. 277. As to the revocation and canceling of assignments, see *post*, ch. XXVII.
[4] Merrill v. Englesby, 28 Vt. 150, 155, 156.
[5] Id.

be made valid by any new instrument directing the property to be sold for cash only, executed by the assignor after the assignee had accepted the assignment and taken possession of the assigned property. By the assignment the assignor had divested himself of all control over the property; and he could neither revoke nor alter it to the prejudice of a creditor whose lien on the property had already attached.[1]

The insertion of a provision of the assignment that schedules may be corrected if necessary has already been noticed.[2]

§ 235. **Additions.**— In regard to *additions* to assignments, it has been held that a subsequent additional assignment, to be valid, must be made with the consent of all the parties to the instrument.[3] The rights of creditors are fixed by the assignment, and without their knowledge or consent cannot be varied by any subsequent act of the assignor or assignee. Thus, in a case in New York, it was held that no subsequent agreement by the assignees to apply a portion of the property for any other purpose than that specified by the assignment could be upheld.[4] And in a case in Maine it was held that an instrument discharging such creditors as should have become parties to an assignment from the effect of their release to the debtor contained therein would not defeat an assignment made for the benefit of creditors *pro rata* as to creditors who had not become parties.[5] But the operation of an assignment may be extended by a new deed, as where it directs the appropriation of a surplus in the hands of the assignee not appropriated by the first deed.[6] And supplemental assignments are

---

[1] Porter v. Williams, 9 N. Y. 142; Willard, J., id., 152; Sutherland v. Bradner, 39 Hun, 134. And the same rule was applied where the assignment was invalid by reason of a provision unlawfully exempting the assignee from liability. Metcalf v. Van Brunt, 37 Barb. 621. And see Gates v. Andrews, 37 N. Y. 657; Haines v. Campbell, 8 Wis. 187. But when the instrument is void by statute, and not merely voidable, no title vests in the assignee, and the assignor may therefore convey the property, by a proper instrument, to the assignee or to a third party. Juliand v. Rathbone, 39 N. Y. 369. And see Brahe v. Eldridge, 17 Wis. 184. In a special term case in New York it is held that an assignment cannot be amended, even by order of court, although the schedules may be. Matter of Wilson, 1 Monthly L. Bul. 5.

[2] See *ante*, § 80; Dedham Bank v. Richards, 2 Metc. 105; Halsey v. Whitney, 4 Mason, 206.

[3] Ramsdell v. Sigerson, 2 Gilm. 78.

[4] Bell v. Holford, 1 Duer, 58, 78.

[5] Howe v. Newbegin, 34 Me. 15.

[6] Flanagan v. Wetherill, 5 Whart. 280. In this case there were two additional instruments executed by the assignors, by which they assigned the surplus to the same assignee for different purposes.

frequently made in order to include property not comprised in the first instrument or to pass a more perfect title to the property already assigned.[1]

The filing of a supplemental assignment containing property unintentionally omitted from the original assignment does not carry forward the date of its taking effect.[2]

A subsequent assignment may be made by one of two partners for the purpose of correcting the first.[3]

[1] See Conkling v. Coonrod, 6 Ohio St. 611; Metcalf v. Van Brunt, 37 Barb. 621.
[2] Krug v. McGilliard, 76 Ind. 28.
[3] Rumery v. McCulloch, 54 Wis. 565; Morrison v. Shuster, 1 Mackey (D. C.), 190.

CHAPTER XVIII.

ACCEPTANCE BY THE ASSIGNEE.

§ 236. Acceptance Necessary.
237. When and How to be Signified.
238. Effect of Acceptance.
239. Presumed Acceptance.
240. Proceedings Where Trustee Refuses to Accept.
241. Proceedings Where Assignee Renounces After Acceptance.

§ 236. Acceptance Necessary.— In order to give the assignment validity and render it operative, it is essential that there should be an *acceptance* of the instrument, and of the trust created by it, on the part of the assignee; a delivery of the instrument without acceptance is nugatory.[1]

§ 237. When and How to be Signified.— The acceptance should be signified by the assignee immediately on the delivery of the assignment, otherwise creditors may gain a priority which will not be divested. Where an assignee delayed an express acceptance of the trust, but received the deed, and executions came to the sheriff's hands, it was held that the assignee's subsequent acceptance could not deprive the creditors of their priority.[2]

---

[1] Crosby v. Hillyer, 24 Wend., 280; Lawrence v. Davis, 3 McLean, 177; Pierson v. Manning, 2 Mich. 446; Pratt, J., id. 462; Royer Wheel Co. v. Fielding, 31 Hun, 274. Both the appointment and the acceptance of the trust are necessary to make one an assignee, and when these are denied they are facts to be proved. Dougherty v. Bethune, 7 Ga. 90. The mere making a deed to a trustee does not vest him with title if he never in any form accepted the trust (Armstrong v. Morrill, 14 Wall. 120); but when created for the benefit of a third party, though without his knowledge at the time, he may affirm the trust and enforce it. Bank of Metropolis v. Guttschlick, 14 Pet. 19. The fact that an act of the legislature recites the assignment to a certain person and confirms it does not constitute him an assignee without his acceptance. Bethune v. Dougherty, 21 Ga. 257. But in the case of Furman v. Fisher, 4 Cold. (Tenn.) 626, Mr. Justice Shackelford expressed a contrary opinion. "The assent of the trustee," he observes, "is not necessary to the validity of a trust deed. He may refuse to act, be unable to comply with the statutes, or die, and in such or similar cases a court of chancery will execute it." So where the clerk of the court was named as assignee, but was incompetent to act, it was held that this in no way affected the validity of the deed. Barcroft v. Snodgrass, 1 Cold. (Tenn.) 430. In Rendleman v. Willard, 15 Mo. App. 375, it is held that "after the recording a refusal of the trust by the assignee will leave the assignment intact, while it will devolve upon the proper tribunal the duty of vitalizing the trust by appointing a trustee."

[2] Crosby v. Hillyer, 24 Wend. 280. See Pierson v. Manning, 2 Mich. 44; Siggers v. Evans, 32 Eng. Law & Eq. 139.

The acceptance must be actually signified by the assignee; the mere taking the instrument into his hands, and retaining it, amounts to nothing.[1] It may be signified verbally;[2] but it is sometimes expressed by the assignee's signing and sealing a written acceptance appended to the assignment. Such an acceptance is decisive evidence against him.[3] Entering into possession of the property assigned,[4] or the qualifying of the assignee,[5] operates as an acceptance of the trust. An assignee having previously agreed to accept can accept by an agent.[6]

In Michigan it was held in the case of Stamp v. Case that an assignment was accepted so as to defeat the levy of attachment upon the goods conveyed therein when it had passed beyond the control of the assignor and into the hands of his agent to be delivered to the assignee.

When an assignment is made by two, and one accepts and the other refuses the trust, the assignment is operative as to the assenting trustee, unless there be a condition that it shall be void if both trustees do not assent.[7]

In New York the assent of the assignee, subscribed and ac-

---

[1] Nelson, C. J., in Crosby v. Hillyer, 24 Wend. 284. In Wisconsin the assignee is required to indorse his acceptance upon the assignment filed with the clerk. R. S. of Wis. (1878), § 1696. The names of the assignees may be affixed in their presence and at their request. Scott v. Seaver, 52 Wis. 175. The mere fact that the assignee has failed to affix his certificate required by Revised Statutes, section 1697, does not invalidate the assignment. Steinlein v. Halstead, 52 Wis. 289. There is no "execution of the assignment" until it is delivered to the assignee, and he accepts the same and gives his bond. Wadleigh v. Merkle, 57 Wis. 517. In Rowland v. Hewitt, 19 Ill. App. 450, it was held that the possession of the deed of assignment by the assignee at any time after its execution will constitute a presumption of his acceptance of it from the time it was executed and rendered.

[2] Drew Glass Co. v. Baldwin, 27 Mo. App. 44. See Salter v. Salter, 80 Ga. 178; 4 S. E. Rep. 391; 13 Am. St. Rep. 249. The acceptance having been made may be shown by oral testimony. Singer v. Armstrong, 70 Iowa, 397; 42 N. W. Rep. 382; *post*, p. 311.

[3] Mead v. Phillips, 1 Sandf. Ch. 83, 85. Where a trust deed contains a provision that the trustee shall accept by signing and the deed is signed by the trustee it is accepted. Patterson v. Johnson, 113 Ill. 559.

[4] Price v. Parker, 11 Iowa, 144.

[5] Shyer v. Lockhard, 2 Tenn. Ch. (Cooper), 365. The bringing and prosecuting a suit to a final decree furnish conclusive evidence of the acceptance of the trust by a trustee in insolvency. Taylor v. Atwood, 47 Conn. 498. Acceptance of his trust by the assignee is indicated by his taking possession of the property and notifying creditors; but it is shown conclusively by his joining in the act of assignment, and recording it when executed. Commercial Nat. Bank of Detroit v. Mosser, 27 Mich. 386; 24 N. W. Rep. 115.

[6] Stamp v. Case, 41 Mich. 267. See *ante*, p. 302.

[7] Shockley v. Fisher, 75 Mo. 498; Gordon v. Coolidge, 1 Sum. 537. See King v. Donnelly, 5 Paige, 46; Moir v. Brown, 14 Barb. 39, and cases cited by Hand, J., id. 45; Matter of Stevenson, 3 Paige, 420. See *ante*, p. 92.

knowledged by him, must appear in writing embraced in or at the end of or indorsed upon the assignment.[1] After acceptance, the assignees cannot be relieved of the duties and responsibilities of their office except by the order of a court of competent jurisdiction.[2] The provisions of the statute being mandatory, an assignment recorded without the assent of the assignee subscribed and indorsed by him thereon, though he may have orally agreed to act, is void against creditors claiming under attachments against the property of the assignor,[3] and even as between the parties.[4] It seems that an agreement to act as assignee, made prior to the execution of the assignment deed, is effective as an acceptance of the assignment soon after made. For in the Iowa case of Singer v. Armstrong, before the deed of assignment was executed, the person named as assignee had orally agreed with the assignor's brother to act as assignee in case an assignment should be made. The deed was afterwards placed in the hands of K., whom the assignor and his brother had requested to act for the assignee, who was absent. K. filed the deed for record, and afterwards an attachment was levied on the property. Held, that the deed was delivered and the trust prior to the attachment. And in the same case it was held that where it becomes material to determine whether a deed of assignment was delivered prior to the levy of an attachment, it may be presumed, in the absence of any showing to the contrary, that the deed was delivered to the assignee as long a time as thirty seconds before he caused it to be filed for record.[5]

§ 238. **Effect of Acceptance.**— By the acceptance of an assignment for the benefit of creditors the assignee becomes a trustee for the creditors, and equity will compel the execution of the trust for their benefit.[6] An assignment once accepted by the assignee is vested for the benefit of creditors, and a subsequent renunciation does not affect the validity of the conveyance.[7] But an

---

[1] 3 R. S. (7th ed.), p. 2276.
[2] Brennan v. Wilson, 71 N. Y. 502; s. c., 4 Abb. N. C. 279.
[3] Rennie v. Bean, 24 Hun, 123.
[4] Schwartz v. Soutter, 41 Hun, 323; Noyes v. Wernberg, 15 Abb. N. C. 164.
[5] 77 Iowa, 397; 42 N. W. Rep. 332.
[6] Moses v. Murgatroyd, 1 Johns. Ch. 119; Shepherd v. McEvers, 4 id. 136; Nicoll v. Mumford, id. 523; Ward v. Lewis, 4 Pick. 518; New England Bank v. Lewis, 8 id. 113; Pingree v. Comstock, 18 id. 46; Weir v. Tannehille, 2 Yerg. 57; Robertson v. Sublett, 6 Humph. 313; Pearson v. Rockhill, 4 B. Mon. 296; Furman v. Fisher, 4 Cold. (Tenn.) 626; Barcroft v. Snodgrass, 1 id. 430; Thatcher v. Franklin, 37 Ark. 64; Boardman v. Willard, 73 Iowa, 20; 34 N. W. Rep. 487; Sleeper v. Iselin, 62 id. 583; 17 N. W. Rep. 922; Nailer v. Young, 7 Lea (Tenn.), 735.
[7] Seal v. Duffy, 4 Barr, 274. See Brooks v. Marbury, 11 Wheat. 78; Curtis, J.,

ceptance by an assignee who is a creditor has been held not to bind other creditors in the case of a fraudulent assignment.[1]

Where one accepts a trust by which a debtor devotes all his property to the payment of his creditors, the trustee thereby waives any specific lien he may have on the property by virtue of execution, and must take according to the stipulations of the deed of trust.[2]

§ 239. **Presumed Acceptance.**— The assent of the trustees is presumed until the contrary be shown; and if the assignment be made without their knowledge, they may, when it comes to their knowledge, affirm it, and it will be binding.[3] Where the trustee is not present his assent may be presumed for the purpose of giving operation to the deed.[4]

§ 240. **Proceedings Where Trustee Refuses to Accept.**— If the person named in the assignment as assignee or trustee refuse to accept the trust, the execution of the trust devolves upon the court of equity having jurisdiction, which may appoint one or more new trustees if necessary.[5]

in Stewart v. Spencer, 1 Curt. 157, 166; McKinney, J., in Brevard v. Neely, 2 Sneed, 164, 170; Bethune v. Dougherty, 30 Ga. 770.

[1] Cook v. Smith, 3 Sandf. Ch. 333.

[2] Harrison v. Mock, 10 Ala. 185. As to the effect of an acceptance by an assignee who is also a creditor, see King v. Moore, 18 Pick. 367; Harrison v. Mock, 16 Ala. 616.

[3] Galt v. Dibrell, 10 Yerg. 146; Nicholl v. Mumford, 4 Johns. Ch. 522, 529; Brown v. Minturn, 2 Gall. 557; Small v. Marwood, 9 B. & Cress. 300; Smith v. Wheeler, 1 Vent. 128; Marbury v. Brooks, 7 Wheat. 556; Weston v. Barker, 12 Johns. 276; 2 Kent's Com. [533] 692, note; Bank v. Holmes, 85 Pa. St. 231; Kennedy v. Winn, 80 Ala. 185. Acceptance relates back to the day of filing. National Bank v. Ridenour, 46 Kan. 718. See p. 313, note.

[4] 1 Am. Lead. Cases, 96; McKinney, J., in Brevard v. Neely, 2 Sneed, 164, 170.

[5] King v. Donnelly, 5 Paige, 46. From what was said by the court in Seal v. Duffy, 4 Barr, 274, 277 (Bell, J.), it would appear that, as the legal title does not pass until acceptance, it remains in the assignor, or at least becomes revested in him by way of remitter, so that he may select a new assignee and assign the property to him. But where interests of creditors have in the meantime attached, it has been held in Pennsylvania that a refusal, from the beginning, of a named assignee to accept the trust would not operate to divest these intermediate interests. See Read v. Robinson, 16 W. & S. 329, 332; approved by the court in Seal v. Duffy, *ubi supra.* And in a case in the same state, where an assignment of all the debtor's estate had been executed and recorded, but the assignees never acted nor were others appointed in their stead, and there was no evidence of the delivery of the assignment to either of them, it was held that, though an assignment of real estate for the benefit of creditors passes the legal title, which is not defeated by the refusal or neglect of the assignees to act, but vests in those whom the court appoint to execute the trust, yet that a trust results to the debtor by operation of law which entitles him to the possession of the property remaining unconverted. Webb v. Dean, 21 Pa. St. 29; Woodward, J., id. 32.

In Virginia the general rule of equity is recognized that a trust shall never fail for want of a trustee, and therefore, if the trustee dies or refuses to accept the trust or is incapable of performing it, a court of equity will give to the *cestuis que trust* the proper relief, either by executing the trust or appointing a trustee for that purpose.[1] The same rule is recognized in Georgia,[2] Pennsylvania,[3] Kentucky,[4] Tennessee,[5] and South Carolina.[6] But in a case in Virginia where a debtor had conveyed a large property, real and personal, in trust to secure numerous creditors, and the trustees not having signed the deed refused to act, and two of the creditors filed a bill on behalf of themselves and the other creditors secured by the deed against the grantor and the trustees, praying for the appointment of other trustees, which prayer was granted, it was held by the court to be error simply to appoint trustees in the place of those named in the deed, but that the court should have the trust administered under its own supervision and control, and that the proper course would have been to appoint commissioners to sell and administer the trust under the supervision and control of the court,[7] A disclaimer of a non-accepting trustee relates back to the date of his appointment.[8]

§ 241. Proceedings Where Assignee Renounces After Acceptance.

— After once accepting the assignment for the purposes of the trust, the assignee cannot divest himself of the legal estate (which by the acceptance became vested in him) by a mere refusal to carry the trust into execution, or withdraw from its support

---

[1] Reynolds v. The Bank of Virginia, 6 Gratt. 174.
[2] Dawson v. Dawson, Rice's Ch. 243.
[3] Webb v. Dean, 21 Pa. St. 29. In Marks' Appeal, 85 Pa. St. 231, it is held that an assignment vests title forthwith in the assignee, and it is immaterial when the assignee accepts the trust or whether he ever accepts it.
[4] Harris v. Rucker, 13 B. Mon. 564.
[5] Field v. Arrowsmith, 3 Humph. 442; Brevard v. Neely, 2 Sneed, 164. "The acceptance of the assignment is necessary to constitute the assignee a trustee for the creditors, but it may be valid though he refuse to accept. If made for the benefit of creditors, the assent of the trustee is not essential to its validity, and a court of equity on behalf of the creditors will enforce the execution of the trust." McKinney, J., id. 171; Furman v. Fisher, 4 Cold. (Tenn.) 626; Barcroft v. Snodgrass, 1 id. 430. See Young v. Cardwell, 6 Lea (Tenn.), 168; Nailer v. Young, 7 id. 735.
[6] Brooks v. Brooks, 12 S. C. 422.
[7] Reynolds v. The Bank of Virginia, 6 Gratt. 174. The reasons of this decision are given by Baldwin, J., id. 179, 186. The deed in this case was one of that class which has been before noticed, combining the qualities of a security to creditors with that of a provision for their payment, or in other words a mortgage in trust; and the court held that it should have been treated as a mortgage and commissioners appointed as in cases of that kind.
[8] Hughes v. Brown, 88 Tenn. 578; 13 S. W. Rep. 286.

without the consent of all the parties interested.¹ He is not permitted to defeat the trust in this way by his own act; and if he does so renounce or refuse to act under the assignment, it is competent to any of the parties interested in it to call upon the proper court to appoint another assignee in his place.² Such a refusal vests no right in the assignor to execute another distinct conveyance of the same property to another assignee, though substantially on the same trusts.³ In the New York case of Brennan v. Wilson,⁴ it was held that where there are several assignees and all have accepted the trust, they cannot afterwards collectively or severally renounce or repudiate the duties and responsibilities of the office, or divest themselves of the title so vested in them, save in the performance of the trust, and all must unite in a transfer of the trust property. Nor can the assignor appoint a new assignee even in pursuance of a power reserved in the assignment itself.⁵

¹ Lewin on Trusts, 464; Jones v. Stockett, 2 Bland, 409. See Strong v. Willis, 3 Fla. 124; Bethune v. Dougherty, 30 Ga. 770. This is the general doctrine in regard to trustees. Mr. Perry, in his work on Trusts (vol. II., p. 558), says: "A mere relinquishment of the trust or of the property, which does not purport to convey the property to some person authorized to receive it, does not discharge the trust," citing Dick v. Pitchford, 1 Dev. & Bat. Eq. 480; Richardson v. Cole, 2 Swan, 100; Diefendorf v. Spraker, 10 N. Y. 246; Waugh v. Wyche, 23 L. J. Ch. 333; Thatcher v. Candee, 3 Keyes, 157; Webster v. Vanderventer, 6 Gray, 429; Gilchrist v. Stevenson, 9 Barb. 9.
² Seal v. Duffy, 4 Barr, 274; Bell, J., id. 278. See Dawson v. Dawson, Rice's Ch. 243; Shyer v. Lockhard, 2 Tenn. Ch. (Cooper), 365.
³ Seal v. Duffy, 4 Barr, 274.
⁴ 71 N. Y. 502.
⁵ See Planck v. Schermerhorn, 3 Barb. Ch. 644.

CHAPTER XIX.

DELIVERY OF POSSESSION OF THE PROPERTY ASSIGNED.

§ 242. Time of Delivery of Possession.
243. When Essential.
244. The Different Rules that Prevail.
245. Delivery Indispensable.
246. Possession *Prima Facie* Evidence.
247. The Rule in New York.
248. The Rule in the United States Courts.
249. Possession Not Evidence of Fraud.
250. The Prevailing Rule and Exceptions.
251. Time and Mode of Delivery.
252. Constructive Delivery.
253. Actual and Continual Charge.
254. Retention of Part.
255. Delivery of Chattel Not in Schedule.

§ 242. **Time of Delivery of Possession.**— The acceptance of the assignment by the assignee after its execution and delivery by the assignor completes the proceedings necessary to the transfer between those parties so far as the instrument itself is concerned; but there usually remains a very important act to be done with reference to the *property* conveyed by it, and which it is now proposed to consider, namely, the *delivery of possession*.[1]

§ 243. **When Essential.**— In order to complete the transfer of the property intended to be conveyed by the assignment and to give it every quality of validity as against creditors, the execution or delivery of the instrument should be accompanied, or at least followed, as soon as practicable by delivery of *possession* of the property itself to the assignee. This is particularly desirable in regard to *personal* property; the real estate assigned passing by mere delivery of the deed.[2] As it is, however, sometimes the practice for the assignor to retain possession after the assignment, and even to stipulate for such a privilege in the deed itself, it becomes an important consideration how far a change of possession is actu-

[1] In connection with the subject of this chapter, see *post*, ch. XXX.
[2] Marshall, C. J., in Brashear v. West, 7 Pet. 608, 613. And see Phettiplace v. Sayles, 4 Mason, 312, 321. And the argument in Tompkins v. Wheeler, 16 Pet. 106, 112; Hempstead v. Johnson, 18 Ark. 123; Wooten v. Clark, 23 Miss. 75; Noble v. Coleman, 18 Ala. 77; Seuter v. Turner, 10 Iowa, 617. See Bump on Fraud. Conv., p. 161.

ally essential to the validity of the conveyance, and what is the effect upon the assignment of withholding it.

The general question whether the retention of possession by a vendor or assignor of goods sold or assigned is fraudulent *per se*, or only presumptive evidence of fraud and susceptible of explanation; or, in other words, whether fraud in such a case is an inference of *law* to be drawn by the court and resulting inevitably from the fact, or an inference of *fact* to be drawn by a jury, has been the subject of much discussion and numerous adjudications in the courts, both in England and the United States. The question has been justly termed "a very vexatious one,"[1] the decisions in both countries being marked by much fluctuation and diversity, and the preponderance of authority inclining at one time in favor of the stern rule of fraud in law, and at another in favor of the laxer rule of presumptive fraud. It is not within the scope of this work to take even a summary view of these decisions;[2] but only to notice the rules which they have tended to establish in this country, so far as relates to the particular subject under consideration.

§ 244. **The Different Rules that Prevail.**— In regard, then, to the necessity of the delivery of possession of personal property assigned, three different rules appear to have been at different times established in the United States by decision or statute: first, that such delivery is *indispensable* to the validity of the assignment, and the want of it is *conclusive* evidence of fraud; second, that the want of possession is only *presumptive* evidence of fraud, and may be explained so as to be consistent with the validity of the transfer; and third, that non-delivery of possession is *not even presumptive* evidence of fraud, but is entirely consistent with the validity and operation of the deed until the sale of the property assigned.

§ 245. **Delivery Indispensable.**— The first and most rigid of these rules formerly prevailed in the state of Pennsylvania, where the delivery of possession of personal property assigned was held to be essential to the validity of the assignment; and the retention of possession by the assignor was conclusive evidence of fraud, or was fraudulent *per se* as against creditors. This was the doctrine established in the cases of Dawes v. Cope[3] and Hower v. Geesaman.[4] In the latter case an assignment in trust for creditors was

---

[1] 2 Kent's Com. [515], 664.

[2] They may be found fully collected and ably commented on in 2 Kent's Com. [515-532], 664-668. And see 1 Smith's Lead. Cas. (Am. ed. 1852); note to Twyne's Case [9-14c], 39-46, and the very complete and elaborate note by the American editors, id. 47-85 [ed. 1855], 46-80. See, also, Bump on Fraud. Conv., chs. V and VI.

[3] 4 Binn. 258.

[4] 17 Serg. & Rawle, 251.

held void as against a judgment creditor because the grantor retained possession and held, used and disposed of the property as his own, although the creditor had notice of the assignment. Mr. Justice Todd, who delivered the opinion of the court, declared that, to make such an assignment valid in any case, the possession must accompany and follow the transfer. This, he asserted, was settled, if anything could be settled, by precedents.[1] In Carpenter v. Mayer[2] the same doctrine was sustained, the court holding that the continuance of possession of an assignor of goods was a fraud in law, and was a question for the court and not for the jury. In Young v. McClure[3] it was further held that there must be not only a delivery of the thing to the assignee at the time of the transfer, but a continuing possession; and that must be shown by the claimant. The question in such cases, it was said, ought not to be left to the jury, whether the transfer is in good faith and without design to cover the property, or to delay or hinder creditors; but it is a question of fraud in law for the court.[4]

The rule thus established, however, had been so far relaxed by the statute of June 14, 1836,[5] and the construction given to it that an assignee under a voluntary deed of assignment for the benefit of creditors might suffer the goods to remain in possession of the assignor for thirty days without subjecting them to an execution of a creditor of the assignor, such delay being given to afford time to comply with the requisitions of the statute.[6] And later decisions have now established a rule directly the reverse of that which was formerly so repeatedly considered as settled. Thus, in Fitler v. Maitland,[7] it was held to be not fraudulent for the assignor to retain possession of the property assigned when the assignment has been recorded and the other requisitions of law complied with. And in the latter case of Klapp's Assignees v. Shirk,[8] the doctrine is laid down that a voluntary assignment for the benefit of creditors, in the manner authorized by law, is not avoided by the property being left in the possession of the assignor; that, to avoid the

[1] See Clow v. Woods, 5 Serg. & Rawle, 275-278; Cunningham v. Neville, 10 id. 201; Babb v. Clemson, id. 419; Martin v. Mathiot, 14 id. 214; Coursey v. Morton, 132 N. Y. 556; 30 N. E. Rep. 231. A reasonable time, however, will be allowed the assignee to take possession. Wilt v. Franklin, 1 Binn. 502.
[2] 5 Watts, 483.
[3] 2 Watts & Serg. 147, 150.
[4] And see McBride v. Clelland, 6 Watts & Serg. 94.
[5] Purdon Dig. (Brightley, 10th ed.), p. 118.
[6] 2 Kent's Com. [522], 673, note e.
[7] 5 Watts & Serg. 307. See Dallam v. Fitler, 6 id. 223; Mitchell v. Willock, 2 id. 253; Mackintosh v. Corner, 33 Ind. 598.
[8] 13 Pa. St. 589. See, also, Dunlap v. Bournonville, 26 Pa. St. 72; Milne v. Henry, 40 id. 352. And see Smith's Lead. Cas. (Hare & Wallace's Notes, ed. 1855), 72-76.

deed, the fraud must be in the assignment itself; that, on delivery of the deed, the property in the goods vests in the assignee for the benefit of creditors, and no subsequent fraudulent dealing between the assignor and assignee can re-invest the goods in the assignor or render them liable to levy as his property.

In Vermont, where the rule has always been maintained that an absolute sale of personal chattels unaccompanied by possession is fraudulent *per se* as against the creditors of the vendor,[1] the same strict rule has been applied to assignments for the benefit of creditors. In Hall v. Parsons[2] it was held that the same change of possession which was required in case of the sale of personal property was required where personal property was assigned for the benefit of the assignee as creditor of the assignor, and, after payment of his claims, for the benefit of the creditors generally.[3] In Illinois, also, it appears to be the rule that *all* conveyances of goods and chattels, where the possession is permitted to remain with the donor or vendor, are fraudulent *per se* and void as to creditors, though an exception is made where the retention of possession is consistent with the deed.[4] And in South Carolina it has been held that leaving property assigned in the hands of the debtor raises the presumption of a secret trust between the debtor and the preferred creditor, and the deed is void so far as the rights of creditors are affected. The law in such a case raises the conclusion of fraud, incapable of being rebutted or explained.[5]

In a case in Maryland[6] where the assignment provided for the retention by the grantor of all his real estate and household goods and certain other property, and that he should pay rent to the trustee, it was held to be absolutely void as to the creditors of the grantor.

[1] See Boardman v. Keeler, 1 Aiken, 158; Mott v. McNeil, id. 162; Weeks v. Wead, 2 id. 64; Beattie v. Robins, 2 Vt. 181; Judd v. Langdon, 5 id. 231; Farnsworth v. Shepard, 6 id. 521; Wilson v. Hooper, 12 id. 653; Mills v. Warner, 19 id. 609; Walworth v. Readsboro, 24 id. 252.

[2] 17 Vt. 271. The assignment in this case was made before the act of 1843. And see Rogers v. Vail, 16 Vt. 327.

[3] See Rice v. Courtis, 32 Vt. 460; Hanford v. Paine, id. 442. See 1 Smith's Lead. Cas. (Hare & Wallace's Notes, ed. 1855), 78, 79.

[4] Thornton v Davenport, 1 Scam. 296; Rhines v. Phelps, 3 Gilm. 455. See 1 Smith's Lead. Cas. (Hare & Wallace's Notes), 55; Dexter v. Parkins, 22 Ill. 143; Ketchum v. Watson, 24 id. 591; Bay v. Cook, 31 id. 336; Corgan v. Frew, 39 id. 31; Wilson v. Pearson, 20 id. 81; Green v. Van Buskirk, 38 How. Pr. 52.

[5] Anderson v. Fuller, 1 McMul. Eq. 27, citing Smith v. Henry, 1 Hill, 22. See 2 Kent's Com. [522], 672, note *c;* 1 Smith's Lead. Cas. (Hare & Wallace's Notes), 65-67; Terry v. Belcher, 1 Bailey, 558; Smith v. Henry, 2 id. 118; Kennedy v. Rose, 2 Mills, 125; De Brodleben v. Beekman, 1 Desaus. 846.

[6] Price v. Pitzer, 44 Md. 521.

In Colorado[1] it is held that until such a change of possession as the nature of the property will reasonably admit of takes place, the title does not pass to the assignee against a *bona fide* creditor without notice.

So in Indiana it was held that where the possession of the goods is not delivered to nor taken by the assignee the assignment will not defeat the intervening liens of attaching creditors.[2]

§ 246. **Possession Prima Facie Evidence.**— Another rule in regard to the possession of assigned property is that possession by an assignor after a transfer of personal property is only *evidence* of fraud, and not fraud *per se*, or such a circumstance as of itself necessarily invalidates the transfer; or in other words, that it is only *prima facie* and not conclusive evidence of fraud; and that it may always be explained so as to show the transfer to have been *bona fide* and upon sufficient consideration.

This is the established rule in Massachusetts,[3] Connecticut,[4] New York,[5] North Carolina,[6] Indiana,[7] and Arkansas;[8] and appears to prevail also in Maine,[9] New Hampshire,[10] New Jersey,[11] Ohio,[12] Mis-

[1] Ray v. Raymond, 8 Col. 467.

[2] Woolson v. Pipher, 100 Ind. 306.

[3] Boyden v. Moore, 11 Pick. 362; Macomber v. Parker, 14 Pick. 497; Fletcher v. Willard, 14 id. 464; Allen v. Wheeler, 4 Gray, 123.

[4] Ingraham v. Wheeler, 6 Conn. 277; Osborn v. Tuller, 14 id. 530; Strong v. Carrier, 17 id. 319. See Kirtland v. Snow, 20 id. 23; 1 Smith's Lead. Cas. 76, 77 (Am. ed. 1875).

[5] See *post*, p. 320.

[6] Dewey v. Littlejohn, 2 Ired. Eq. 495; Hardy v. Skinner, 9 Ired. L. 191. But see Gaither v. Mumford, 1 N. C. Term R. 167.

[7] Caldwell v. Rose, 1 Smith, 190; Hall v. Wheeler, 13 Ind. 371; Kane v. Drake, 27 id. 29. In this state as in Illinois even a joint possession by the assignor and assignee is evidence of fraud unless explained. Id.; Caldwell v. Williams, 1 Ind. 405. And see 1 Smith's Lead. Cas. (Am. ed. 1852), 56; Id. (ed. 1855), 57.

[8] Field v. Simco, 2 Eng. 269; Cocke v. Chapman, id. 197; Stone v. Waggoner, 3 id. 204; George v. Norris, 23 Ark. 121; Danley v. Rector, 5 id. 224; Hempstead v. Johnson, 8 id. 123.

[9] The decisions in this state and those which follow are mostly in cases of sales and mortgages. Reed v. Jewett, 5 Greenl. 96; Holbrook v. Baker, id. 309; Brinley v. Springs, 7 id. 241; Ulmer v. Hills, 8 id. 326; Cutter v. Copeland, 18 Me. 127; Bartlett v. Blake, 37 id. 124; Googins v. Gilmore, 47 id. 9.

[10] Haven v. Law, 2 N. H. 13; Coburn v. Pickering, 3 id. 415; Lewis v. Whitemore, 5 id. 364; Ash v. Savage, id. 545; Kendall v. Fitts, 2 Fost. 1. See 1 Smith's Lead Cas. (Am. ed. 1855), 63, 64.

[11] Sterling v. Van Cleve, 7 Halst. 285; Hendricks v. Mount, 2 South. 738; Bank of New Brunswick v. Hassert, Saxt. 1; Cumberland Bank v. Hann, 4 Harris, 166; Miller v. Pancoast, 5 Dutch. 250. See Livermore v. McNair, 34 N. J. Eq. 478.

[12] Barr v. Hatch, 3 Ohio, 527; Shaw v. Lowry, Wright's Ch. (Ohio), 190; Hombeck v. Van Metre, 9 Ohio, 153. See 1 Smith's Lead. Cas. (Am. ed. 1852), 56; Id. (ed. 1855), 80.

souri,[1] Kentucky,[2] Tennessee,[3] Virginia,[4] Georgia,[5] Alabama,[6] Texas,[7] Mississippi,[8] Louisiana,[9] Wisconsin,[10] Michigan,[11] and Nebraska.[12]

§ 247. **The Rule in New York.**— In New York the question as to the necessity of a delivery of possession of goods sold, mortgaged or assigned to the validity of the transfer was, after much fluctuation in the decisions of the supreme court,[13] settled by the Revised Statutes, which provide that "Every sale made by a vendor of goods and chattels in his possession or under his control, and every *assignment* of goods and chattels by way of mortgage or security, or upon any condition whatever, unless the same be accompanied by an *immediate delivery*, and be followed by an *actual* and *continued change of possession* of the things sold, mortgaged or assigned, shall be *presumed* to be *fraudulent* and void as against the creditors of the vendor, or the creditors of the person making such assignment, or subsequent purchasers in good faith; and shall be *conclusive* evidence of fraud, *unless* it shall be made to appear on the part of the persons claiming under such sale or assignment that the same was made in *good faith* and without any intent to defraud such creditors or purchasers."[14] The effect of this provision

---

[1] Milburn v. Waugh, 11 Mo. 369; Kuykendall v. McDonald, 15 id. 416; Claflin v. Rosenberg, 42 id. 439; s. c., 43 id. 593; State v. Tasker, 31 id. 445; State v. Smith, 31 id. 566; State v. Evans, 38 id. 150; Howell v. Bell, 29 id. 135; Goodwin v. Kerr, 80 id. 276. See 1 Smith's Lead. Cas. 82.

[2] Vernon v. Morton, 8 Dana, 247; Christopher v. Covington, 2 B. Mon. 357. But see Gen. Stat. (ed. 1881), p. 489, § 3.

[3] Callan v. Thompson, 3 Yerg. 475; Darwin v. Handley, id. 502; Maney v. Killough, 7 id. 440; Mitchell v. Beal, 8 id. 142; 1 Smith's Lead. Cas. 81. See Ragan v. Kennedy, 1 Tenn. 91.

[4] Davis v. Turner, 4 Gratt. 422. See Curd v. Miller's Ex'rs, 7 id. 185. See Bump on Fraud. Conv., pp. 149 *et seq.*

[5] Fleming v. Townsend, 6 Ga. 103; Carter v. Stanfield, 8 id. 49; 1 Smith's Lead. Cas. 82.

[6] Noble v. Coleman, 16 Ala. 77; Dearing v. Watkins, id. 20; Millard v. Hall, 23 id. 209. See 1 Smith's Lead. Cas. 55-57; Constantine v. Twelves, 29 Ala. 607; Perry Insurance & Trust Co. v. Foster, 58 Ala. 502; Cooper v. Davidson, 86 Ala. 367; 5 South. Rep. 650.

[7] Bryant v. Kelten, 1 Tex. 415; McQuinnay v. Hitchcock, 8 id. 33; Van Hook v. Walton, 28 id. 59; Howerton v. Holt, 23 id. 51.

[8] Summers v. Rose, 43 Miss. 749; Jayne v. Dillon, 27 id. 283; Rankin v. Holloway, 3 Sm. & M. 614; Comstock v. Rayford, 1 Sm. & M. 423; s. c., 12 Sm. & M. 369.

[9] Keller v. Blanchard, 19 La. Ann. 53; Gruce v. Sanders, 21 id. 463; Haile v. Brewster, 13 id. 155. See Zacharie v. Kirk, 14 id. 433.

[10] Whitney v. Brunette, 3 Wis. 621; Smith v. Welch, 10 id. 91; Bullis v. Borden, 21 id. 135.

[11] Jackson v. Dean, 1 Doug. 519; Parsell v. Patterson, 47 Mich. 502.

[12] Morgan v. Bogue, 7 Neb. 429.

[13] See a review of the cases in Bump on Fraud. Conv., pp. 137 *et seq.* Also in 2 Kent's Com. [526-529], 679-684 and note.

[14] 4 Rev. Stat. (8th ed.), p. 2591, § 5.

is to throw upon the vendee, mortgagee or assignee of personal property, who suffers the possession to remain unchanged, the burden of destroying the presumption of fraud which the fact of withholding possession raises.[1] It is further declared that the question of fraudulent intent shall be deemed a question of *fact*, and not of *law*.[2] A number of adjudications have taken place under these provisions, the result of which has been to settle the doctrine that the whole question of fraud, in these cases, is a question of fact for a jury.[3] A court of equity, however, is competent to pronounce upon the question;[4] and a large proportion of the cases in this state in which the principle has been applied to voluntary assignments by debtors have been cases in equity without the intervention of a jury. Thus, in Butler v. Stoddard,[5] in the court of chancery, which was a case of an absolute assignment of goods and accounts to certain creditors, the assignor, after execution of the assignment, was left in possession, to sell the goods and collect the accounts for the sole benefit of the assignees, they paying him a certain compensation for his services as their agent. The assignment was declared fraudulent and void; the court holding that the nominal appointment of the assignor as agent of the assignees, without any visible change in the mode of doing business at the store, was not a change of possession within the meaning of the statute; that there must be an actual and continued change of possession, as well as a nominal and constructive change, or the transaction would be deemed fraudulent as against creditors. So in Connah v. Sedgwick,[6] where a bill was filed in the supreme court, in equity, to set aside an assignment, and for an injunction and receiver, it was held by the court that under the provisions of the statute, unless an assignment made by a debtor for the benefit of his creditors is accompanied by an immediate delivery of the assigned property, and is followed by an actual and continued change of possession, the courts are bound to presume it fraudulent and void as against creditors; and to regard it as conclusively so, unless they are satisfied that it was made in good faith, and without any

---

[1] 2 Kent's Com. [529], 681, note *a*. See Williams v. Lowdnes, 1 Hall, 579, 596.
[2] 4 R. S. (8th ed.), p. 2593, § 4.
[3] 2 Kent's Com. [529], 681–684, note, where the cases are reviewed. In Vance v. Phillips, 6 Hill. 433. it was decided that where a validity of a sale of chattels depends upon whether it was made with *intent* to defraud creditors, however clear and conclusive the evidence of fraudulent intent may be, the judge is bound to submit the case to the jury. But if the jury find against the evidence, the court will set aside the verdict and grant a new trial. See, also, Edgell v. Hart, 13 Barb. 380. And see 1 Smith's Lead. Cases (Am. ed. 1855), 68–71.
[4] See the observations of Wing, P. J., in Hollister v. Loud, 2 Mich. 309, 313.
[5] 7 Paige, 163; affirmed on appeal, 20 Wend. 507.
[6] 1 Barb. S. C. 210.

attempt to defraud. Several decisions to the same point have been made by the vice-chancellor of the first circuit.[1] The circumstances of leaving the household furniture of the assignor in his possession for eleven months, without explanation, was held to be evidence of fraud.[2] Nor will a lease of it by the assignee render the transaction valid, where the assignor continues in possession.[3] And the possession of things in action remaining in the assignor after they have been assigned for creditors requires explanation, as well as that of goods and chattels.[4] And in a case where a substantial portion of the assigned property, consisting principally of promissory notes and household furniture, was suffered to remain in the assignor's possession for three months after the execution of the assignment, it was held indispensable, in order to rebut the presumption of fraud, that the assignee should prove the existence of the indebtedness in consideration of which the assignment was ostensibly made [5]

The rule in New York may now be regarded as settled, that the fact of there being no change of possession is presumptive evidence of fraud, and conclusive, unless rebutted by affirmative evidence of good faith and the absence of an intent to defraud.[6]

Where personal property has been levied upon under an execution and is in the possession of the sheriff at the time of the assignment by the judgment debtor, the transaction is not within the above statute requiring immediate delivery.[7]

Real estate is not included in the express language of the statute. The continuance in possession of a grantor of real estate

[1] Van Nest v. Yoe, 1 Sandf. Ch. 4; Mead v. Phillips, id. 83; Cram v. Mitchell, id. 251; Einstein v. Chapman, 42 N. Y. Super. Ct. 144; Ball v. Loomis, 29 N. Y. 412; Wilson v. Forsyth, 24 Barb. 105. See, also, Hart v. Acker and Scholefield v. Hull, cited in Edwards on Receivers (ed. 1857), 408, 410; Van Buskirk v. Warren, 4 Abb. Dec. 457; Pine v. Rickert, 21 Barb. 469. And see *post*, ch. XXX.
[2] Cram v. Mitchell, *ubi supra*.
[3] Dewey v. Adams, 4 Edw. Ch. 21.
[4] Mead v. Phillips, 1 Sandf. Ch. 82. This is so held on the common-law principle that the non-delivery of a chose in action, at the time of its assignment, is a badge of fraud. Sandford, A. V. C., id. 88; Paige, P. J., in Browning v. Hart, 6 Barb. 91, 94. But the provision of the Revised Statutes (2 R. S. 136, § 5; 3 R. S. (7 ed.), p. 2328; 4 R. S. (8th ed.), p. 2591, § 5) which requires the immediate delivery, and an actual and continued change of possession of goods and chattels sold, mortgaged or assigned, has been repeatedly held not to embrace choses in action. Paige, P. J., in Browning v. Hart, *ubi supra;* Curtis v. Leavitt, 17 Barb. 309, 310. And see, as to the retention of choses in action assigned for the benefit of creditors, Tompkins v. Wheeler, 16 Pet. 106.
[5] Jacobs v. Remsen, 36 N. Y. 668. And see Terry v. Butler, 43 Barb. 395; Van Buskirk v. Warren, 39 N. Y. 119; Miller v. Lockwood, 32 id. 293; Thompson v. Blanchard, 4 id. 303.
[6] Meade v. Phillips, 1 Sandf. Ch. 83; Tate v. McCormick, 23 Hun, 218.
[7] Mumper v. Rushmore, 79 N. Y. 19; affirming 14 Hun, 591.

after the conveyance does not of itself warrant a finding as a legal conclusion that the deed was fraudulent.[1] But where the debtor was permitted to retain possession of real estate which he had assigned for a number of years, under a nominal lease to his son without paying any rent, the conveyance was declared fraudulent and void as against creditors.[2]

A failure, however, to comply with the statute is an objection which can be taken only by creditors. The fact that assignees, immediately after the acceptance of the assignment, refused to take possession of the entire property does not deprive them of their rights, nor relieve them of their obligations under it.[3]

§ 248. **The Rule in the United States Courts.**— The question of the necessity of a change of possession to the validity of a transfer of property, as against creditors, has also been discussed in the courts of the United States. In the case of Hamilton v. Russell[4] the strict rule was laid down by the supreme court that an absolute bill of sale of a personal chattel by an insolvent was fraudulent against creditors, unless possession of the property assigned or transferred accompanied or followed the deed, and that the absence of such possession was not merely evidence of fraud, but was a circumstance *per se* which made the transaction fraudulent. In the subsequent case of United States v. Hooe[5] the court held that the rule did not apply to a deed of trust of lands to trustees by way of indemnity of a surety of the grantor. In Conrad v. Atlantic Insurance Company[6] the court avoided expressing an opinion on the question whether, in any case, the want of possession of the thing sold constitutes *per se* a badge of fraud, or is only *prima facie* a presumption of fraud; Mr. Justice Story, who delivered the opinion of the court, observing that it was "a question upon which much diversity of judgment has been expressed."[7] It is to be observed, however, that the learned judge had, in an earlier case,[8] in the circuit court of Massachusetts, adopted the more

---

[1] Clute v. Newkirk, 46 N. Y. 684; Every v. Edgerton, 7 Wend. 259. See Jackson v. Cornell, 1 Sandf. Ch. 348.

[2] Bank of Orange Co. v. Fink, 7 Paige, 87. See Mead v. Phillips, 1 Sandf. Ch. 83; Dolson v. Kerr, 5 Hun, 643; Hitchcock v. St. John, Hoffm. Ch. 511; Dewey v. Adams, 4 Ed. Ch. 21.

[3] Sheldon v. Stryker, 42 Barb. 284; s. c., 27 How. Pr. 387.

[4] 1 Cranch, 309.

[5] 3 Cranch, 73.

[6] 1 Pet. 386.

[7] Id. 449.

[8] Meeker v. Wilson, 1 Gall. 419. "By the common law a grant or assignment of goods and chattels is valid between the parties without actual delivery thereof; and the property passes immediately upon the execution of the deed. But, as to creditors, the title is not considered as perfect unless possession ac-

rigid rule, and applied it to the case of a voluntary assignment by a debtor. In Brooks v. Marbury[1] the supreme court refused to apply the doctrine of Hamilton v. Russell to the case of a deed of trust for the benefit of creditors; observing that the continuance of the possession with the donor until the trust could be executed might not be so incompatible with the deed as to render it absolutely void under all circumstances. The court, however, as in Conrad v. Atlantic Insurance Company, declined expressing any opinion on this point further than to say that it was not supposed to be decided in Hamilton v. Russell.

§ 249. **Possession Not Evidence of Fraud.**— A third rule on the subject of delivery of possession of property assigned, which prevails in some states, is that retention of possession by an assignor is not even presumptive evidence of fraud, but is consistent with the validity of the assignment. This rule is constantly applied to those deeds of trusts, already mentioned as peculiar to the southern states, which are executed by way of security to creditors, and which provide for a sale of the property in case the debt secured is not paid, and in which also express provision is frequently made for the retention of possession by the debtor. The formality of a *record* or registry, which is usually necessary to the validity of these instruments as of mortgages, dispenses with the necessity of a delivery of possession; and the general principle applied is, that it is of the nature of a security, that the debtor should retain possession until the day of payment be past.[2] Thus in Virginia delivery of possession to the trustee never occurs on the execution of a deed of trust, but possession remains with the debtor until the time to sell.[3] In this state it has been decided that the inconsistency of the debtor's possession with the deed is the matter which constitutes fraud.[4] In Mississippi[5] and Alabama[6] possession by the

companies and follows the deed. The want of possession is considered, in some of the authorities as an evidence or badge of fraud to be submitted to the jury; but the more modern authorities hold it as constituting in itself, in point of law, an actual fraud, which renders the transactions, as to creditors, void." Story, J., id. 422, 423.

[1] 11 Wheat. 78.
[2] 1 Tuck. Com. [338], 327; Hempstead v. Johnson, 18 Ark. 309.
[3] 1 Tuck. Com. [340], 329; Land v. Jeffries, 5 Rand. 211, 252. And see 1 Smith's Lead. Cas. (Am. ed. 1855), 58–63.
[4] Land v. Jeffries, *ubi supra.*
[5] Layson v. Rowan, 7 Rob. (La.) 1; Comstock v. Rayford, 12 Sm. & M. 369. In this state delivery is not necessary to the completion even of a sale of personal property. The statute of frauds (29 Car. II., ch. 3) has not been re-enacted. Ingersoll v. Kendall, 13 Sm. & M. 611.
[6] Ravisies v. Alston, 5 Ala. 297. But possession *after* the sale is evidence of fraud, though capable of being rebutted by showing some sufficient reason why

debtor until the sale is not inconsistent with the deed and raises no presumption of fraud. In the last-named state it has been decided that where a deed of assignment is not fraudulent on its face the possession and use of the property by the assignor, in conformity with the express provisions of the deed, cannot render it void.[1] And it has been declared to be well settled that the retention of possession by a grantor in a deed of trust, if such possession is consistent with the terms of the deed, is not a badge of fraud, nor is it a circumstance from which an inference of fraud would necessarily arise.[2] A similar practice of retaining possession until a sale under a deed of trust prevails in North Carolina; the courts approving it as being more convenient for all parties that the possession should not be changed.[3] In Kentucky the same rule has been recognized; and in a case where one of a firm who had assigned their effects to trustees for the benefit of their creditors was retained by the trustees to aid them in executing the trust and so remained in possession of the goods conveyed, such continued possession was held to be no evidence of fraud.[4] The same rule, as already mentioned, now prevails also in Pennsylvania, the record of the assignment and a compliance with other statutory requisitions being held to dispense with the necessity of a delivery.[5] In this state, indeed, an assignment duly recorded stands upon the footing of a transfer by law; because, as the statute gives the creditors a right to have the trust that is expressed in the deed executed for their benefit by the court, the whole trust becomes vested in them in equity under the immediate administration of the court; and therefore an assignment recorded is in effect a transfer to the creditors by the act of law, and the recording gives the transaction all the publicity of a judicial proceeding.[6]

§ 250. **The Prevailing Rule and Exceptions.**— On the whole the predominant rule in the United States appears to be that possession must accompany and follow a deed of assignment by a debtor; and the possession of the assignor after the transfer, unless explained, will render the assignment void as against creditors. But this rule is limited and qualified by several *exceptions*

the possession was permitted to remain. Id.; McGee v. Carpenter, 4 id. 469. See 1 Smith's Lead. Cas. (Am. ed. 1852), 55; id. (ed. 1855), 55-57.
[1] Abercrombie v. Bradford, 16 Ala. 560.
[2] Hopkins v. Scott, 20 Ala. 179; Ligon, J., id. 184.
[3] Dewey v. Littlejohn, 2 Ired. Eq. 495, 507. See Means v. Montgomery, 23 Fed. Rep. 421.
[4] Vernon v. Morton, 8 Dana, 247. See Christopher v. Covington, 2 B. Mon. 357. But see Gen. Stats. 1881, p. 489. § 3; Gen. Stats. 1887, ch. 44, § 3.
[5] Mitchell v. Willock, 2 W. & S. 253; Klapp's Assignees v. Shirk, 13 Pa. St. 589.
[6] 1 Smith's Lead. Cas. (Am. ed. 1852), 70, 71; id. [ed. 1855], 75.

which will now be noticed. Thus the rule applies in a peculiar manner to *personal* property. The provision of the New York statute confines it, in terms, to "goods and chattels;[1] and the distinction in this respect between personal and real estate has been clearly drawn by the courts in Connecticut"[2] and Ohio.[3] The same limitation was admitted by Mr. Justice Story, in Phettiplace v. Sayles,[4] in the circuit court for the district of Massachusetts.[5]

In Widdall v. Garsed[6] the court said: "The familiar rule that an assignment to be good against the creditors of the assignor must be accompanied by the delivery of possession refers to visible, tangible property."

Another exception to the rule has been admitted where the possession of the grantor or assignor is *consistent* with the deed;[7] that is, with its general nature and object,[8] as well as its express provisions. The mere circumstance that the deed contains an express provision for the continuance of possession in the grantor will not take the case out of the rule where it is inconsistent with the character of the transfer itself.[9] This branch of the subject has already been considered under a former head.

Again the rule ceases to have application where the creditors expressly *assent* to the assignors continuing in possession. Thus, in Tompkins v. Wheeler[10] (which was a case of an assignment directly to creditors), after the assignment, the creditors for whose benefit it was made neglected to appoint an agent or trustee to execute it, and the property assigned remained in the hands of the assignor. The property consisted principally of choses in action, which the assignor went on to collect, and divided the proceeds.

---

[1] 3 Rev. Stat. (7th ed.), p. 2328, § 5; 4 R. S. (8th ed.), p. 2591, § 5. The bare fact that a grantor remains in possession of lands conveyed by him is not enough, uncorroborated by other circumstances, to subject the transaction to the imputation of fraud. Every v. Edgerton, 7 Wend. 259. In Jackson v. Cornell, 1 Sandf. Ch. 348, the possession of real estate assigned, continuing in the assignor, was considered to be evidence of fraud. It appears in this case that the assignor had collected the rents of the property assigned and retained a portion for his own use.

[2] Church, J., in Strong v. Carrier, 17 Conn. 319.

[3] Sherman, J., in Barr v. Hatch, 3 Ohio, 527.

[4] 4 Mason, 312, 321.

[5] For the reason of the distinction, see id. 321, 322; Tompkins v. Wheeler, 16 Pet. 112, arg.

[6] 125 Pa. St. 358; 17 Am. Rep. 418.

[7] Story, J., in Meeker v. Wilson, 1 Gall. 419, 423; Putnam, J., in Bartlett v. Williams, 1 Pick. 295; Marshall, C. J., in Brooks v. Marbury, 11 Wheat. 78. And see Dawes v. Cope, 4 Binn. 258; Gibson, J., in Clow v. Woods, 5 S. & R. 278, 279; Land v. Jeffries, 5 Rand. 211, 252.

[8] Lord Mansfield, in Cadogan v. Kennett, Cowp. 432, 436.

[9] 1 Tuck. Com. (338), 327; id. [341], 330.

[10] 16 Pet. 106. And see Steel v. Brown, 1 Taunt. 381.

among the creditors under the assignment. No one of the creditors was dissatisfied, and at any time they could have taken the property out of the hands of the assignor. It was held by the supreme court of the United States that leaving the property in the hands of the assignor, under these circumstances, did not affect the assignment or give a right to a creditor not preferred by it to set it aside.

Finally, the application of the rule requiring a delivery of possession of property assigned depends upon the fact whether such delivery be *possible* under the circumstances of the case. This will be more fully considered under the head immediately following.

§ 251. **Time and Mode of Delivery.**— As a general rule, in order to avoid all ground of objection to the validity of the assignment, possession of the personal property assigned should always, if practicable, *accompany* the assignment. But where, from the circumstances of the property, *immediate* possession is not within the power of the parties, as in the case of a ship or goods at sea, it will be dispensed with upon the plain ground of its impossibility; and all that will be required will be that the assignee take possession of the property within a reasonable time after it comes within his reach.[1] And even where the property assigned is in its nature capable of immediate delivery the assignee will be entitled to a reasonable time to take possession.[2] Thus in Pennsylvania, where the trustee lived at a distance and did not hear of the assignment until four days after it was made, when he assented, and the debtor continued in possession one day and part of another after the execution of the deed, the assignment was sustained by the court.[3]

In regard to the *mode* of delivery it may be observed generally that possession of lands is delivered by delivery of the deed;[4] of goods by an actual delivery of the goods themselves, or a constructive delivery where this is impracticable;[5] and of debts or choses in action by delivery of the evidences of them. Delivery of the evidence of a debt is a sufficient delivery of the possession

---

[1] Story, J., in Conard v. Atlantic Insurance Company, 1 Pet. 386, 449; Harris v. D'Wolf, 4 id. 147, 151; Meeker v. Wilson, 1 Gall. 419, 423; Wheeler v. Sumner, 4 Mason, 183; D'Wolf v. Harris, id. 515; Bholen v. Cleveland, 5 id. 174; Brown v. Minturn, 2 Gall. 557; Portland Bank v. Stacy, 4 Mass. 661; Gardner v. Howland, 2 Pick. 599; Hodges v. Harris, 9 id. 360; Dawes v. Cope, 4 Binn. 258; Carpenter v. Mayer, 5 Watts, 485; Eagle v. Eichelberger, 6 id. 29; Langdon v. Horton, 1 Hare, 23 Eng. Ch. R. (Am. ed.) 549; Bump on Fraud. Conv., p. 198.
[2] Ingraham v. Wheeler, 6 Conn. 267.
[3] Wilt v. Franklin, 1 Binn. 502.
[4] See *ante*, p. 315.
[5] See *infra*, § 250.

of it.¹ Notice to the debtor is necessary in some cases; but not in transfers of bills of exchange or notes payable to order previous to maturity; nor afterwards, but to prevent the parties bound from acquiring equities against the holder, to which they might be entitled if not notified.²

§ 252. **Constructive Delivery.**— In regard to goods or personal chattels, a *constructive* or symbolical delivery is allowed in many cases where an actual delivery is physically impracticable.³ Thus in the case of the assignment of a vessel while abroad or at sea, a delivery of the bill of sale and other documents or muniments of title will be sufficient to pass the property, if accompanied by an actual delivery of possession as soon as conveniently may be after the vessel arrives in port.⁴ In case of the assignment of goods on board an absent vessel there should be a delivery to the assignee of the bill of lading and an invoice with an assignment indorsed;⁵ and an assignment and delivery of a duplicate of the invoice alone, where there was no other paper in the hands of the assignor, has been held sufficient as a symbolical delivery of the property.⁶ It has been held that a failure to deliver to the assignee copies of bills of lading in the assignor's possession did not leave the property subject to the attachment of creditors who had no notice of the deed.⁷ And in D'Wolf v. Harris,⁸ which was a case of an assignment of goods at sea, it was held that an indorsement of the bill of lading was not indispensable to perfect the assignment, and that it was sufficient if there was a good assignment of the property by a conveyance with apt words.

A symbolical delivery is also sufficient in those cases where the goods assigned, though physically accessible, are in the possession or custody of a third person under some lawful title. Thus in a case in Massachusetts, where the goods assigned had been previously mortgaged and were at the time in the custody of an officer under an attachment, and the assignee went to the store, gave notice to the officer of the assignment and said that he took pos-

---

[1] United States v. Bank of the United States, 8 Rob. (La.) 262.
[2] Id.
[3] Parker, C. J., in Gardner v. Howland, 2 Pick. 599, 602.
[4] This is the rule in regard to sales and mortgages of vessels. 2 Kent's Com. [132, 133], 175, 176.
[5] See Gardner v. Howland, 2 Pick. 602, 603; Balderston v. Manro, 2 Cranch's C. C. 623. Where goods were shipped for a foreign port the delivery of the bills of lading and the policy of insurance was held sufficient in the first instance. Dawes v. Cope, 4 Binn. 258. Notice of the assignment is usually given to the master. See Langton v. Horton, 1 Hare, 23 Eng. Ch. R. (Am. ed.) 549.
[6] Gardner v. Howland, 2 Pick. 602, 603.
[7] Conard v. Atlantic Insurance Co., 1 Pet. 386.
[8] 4 Mason, 515.

session of the goods and did take the account books, it was held that such a symbolical delivery of possession was sufficient.[1]

A symbolical delivery, however, as of a small portion of the goods for the whole, will not be sufficient where an actual delivery is practicable.[2] Thus, in Pennsylvania in a case where possession was retained by the assignor, after such a symbolical delivery, the assignment, although accompanied by a schedule of the goods, was declared void.[3] In Massachusetts a delivery of a portion of the goods in token of a delivery of the whole was held to be a constructive delivery of goods embraced in the assignment, which were at a distance from the place where the actual delivery of the portion was made, and which were in the hands of a third person, and subject to a lien for his labor upon them.[4]

§ 253. **Actual and Continued Change.**— It is a further rule that possession of the goods assigned must not only be *actually* changed, but such change must be *continued*.[5] This is the express language of the statute in New York,[6] and was formerly the declared rule in Pennsylvania.[7] The assignee must not only take but keep possession, and there must be no redelivery to the assignor.[8]

As to the character of the possession thus delivered, it is also held that it must be an *exclusive* one. A joint possession by the assignor and assignee, of personal property assigned, is colorable, and an evidence of fraud unless explained.[9] But this rule is more or less modified by the rule allowing the assignor to be employed, on certain conditions, as the assignee's agent, and to remain in possession in that capacity.

---

[1] Mann v. Huston, 1 Gray, 250; Dewey, J., id. 253. A symbolical delivery by a transfer of the keys of the place where the goods are stored makes a valid transfer of the title. Bullis v. Montgomery, 58 N. Y. 352; citing Hollingsworth v. Napier, 3 Caines, 182, note *a*; Dunham v. Pettee, 8 N. Y. 508; Sullivan v. Smith, 15 Neb. 476. So, where the assignor secured a third person to execute to the assignee a paper in which he acknowledged the receipt of the property from the assignee, and agreed to deliver the same to him by a certain day, and in default thereof to pay him a certain sum of money, this instrument was adjudged to have the effect of a delivery bond. Leverenz v. Haines, 32 Ill. 357.

[2] Hitchcock v. St. John, 1 Hoff. Ch. 511, 522.

[3] Cunningham v. Neville, 10 Serg. & Rawle, 201. This was before the act of June 14, 1836.

[4] Legg v. Willard, 17 Pick. 140.

[5] Hatcher v. Winters, 71 Mo. 30.

[6] 3 R. S. (7th ed.), p. 2328, § 5; 4 R. S. (8th ed.), p. 2591, § 5.

[7] Young v. McClure, 2 Watts & Serg. 147.

[8] As to the effect of a lease of the property by the assignee to the assignor, see Hitchcock v. St. John, 1 Hoff. Ch. 511; Dewey v. Adams, 4 Edw. Ch. 21.

[9] This is the rule in Indiana. Caldwell v. Rose, Smith, 190; Caldwell v. Williams, 1 Ind. 405. In Vermont a concurrent possession of personal property by the vendor and vendee, after a sale, renders the sale fraudulent *per se* as to the creditors of the vendor. Hall v. Parsons, 17 Vt. 271.

Where the delivery of the property to the assignee is complete, it is not essential that the property itself should be *removed* from the place of delivery. This was decided in New York in the case of Hitchcock v. St. John.[1] The assistant vice-chancellor, in delivering his opinion in this case, after noticing the opinions of the supreme court to the contrary,[2] observed "that the sole question was whether there was an open and actual change of the possession and control, the exclusion of the assignor, and the notorious and avowed dominion of the assignee. A possession and control might be resumed by the assignor after the removal, and removal was not, therefore, conclusive evidence of fairness. The exclusion of the assignor might be as absolute and the change of control as marked, while the property was retained upon the premises, as if it was removed."[3]

§ 254. **Retention of Part.**— Where an assignment of the debtor's whole property has been made in good faith for the benefit of all the creditors, its validity will not be impaired by the assignor's withholding a portion of the property actually conveyed; for it has become the property of the assignee and he can recover it by action.[4] In Michigan it was decided that an assignment is not necessarily fraudulent and void because some small portion of the assets was withheld from the assignee. If the assignment is legal on its face, and the assignee is acting in good faith, he may by proper remedies pursue and recover anything wrongfully detained from him.[5] But in Arkansas it was held that an assignment purporting to convey all the property of the assignor except that which is exempt by law is vitiated by the intentional withholding of any part of it not exempt.[6] In a case in New York it was held that although it is a general rule that, to give full effect to an assignment of personal property, delivery of the property and a continued change of possession are requisite, and the assignor's continuing in possession of the whole or even a part of the assigned property is a badge of fraud, yet where there is no inventory of the assigned property accompanying the assignment, the assignor's retaining some property that he might have assigned, or that (being covered by the general terms of his assignment) he might have de-

[1] 1 Hoff. Ch. 511.
[2] In Randall v. Cook, 17 Wend. 56, and in Collins v. Brush, 19 id. 199. commented on by the assistant vice-chancellor in Lee v. Huntoon, Hoff. Ch. 447, 457.
[3] And see the opinion in Lee v. Huntoon, *ubi supra*. And see Hall v. Wheeler, 13 Ind. 371.
[4] Pike v. Bacon, 21 Me. 280. See Wilson v. Forsyth, 24 Barb. 105; Eicks v. Copeland, 53 Tex. 581.
[5] Parsell v. Patterson, 47 Mich. 505; 11 N. W. Rep. 291.
[6] Penzel Grocer Co. v. Williams, 53 Ark. 81; 13 S. W. Rep. 736.

livered under it, is not an act that of course makes his whole assignment void.¹

§ 255. **Delivery of Chattel Not in Schedule.**— On the other hand, a delivery of more property than has been specially conveyed, as of an article not named in the schedule annexed, will sometimes bind the assignor. Thus, in Massachusetts, where a debtor assigned property not described in a schedule, in trust for his creditors, and afterwards delivered to the assignee a chattel not included in the schedule, either knowing that it was not so included therein, or intending, whether it was so included or not, that it should be appropriated to the benefit of his creditors, it was held that the property in the chattel passed to the assignee in trust for the creditors, and that the assignor could not reclaim it.²

¹ Gould, J., in Wilson v. Forsyth, 24 Barb. 127, 128. But see Mead v. Phillips, 1 Sand. Ch. 83.
² Faxon v. Durant, 9 Metc. 339.

CHAPTER XX.

ASSENT OF CREDITORS.

§ 256. When Necessary.
257. Assent to Assignments to Trustees.
258. The Rule in Various States.
259. The English Rule.
260. Assent Provided for.
261. Assent to Assignments Directly to Creditors.
262. Assent, How and When Given.
263. Assent of How Many Creditors.
264. Assent by Attorney.
265. Assent by Partners.
266. Limitation of Time to Assent.
267. Presumption of Assent from Lapse of Time.
268. Assent to Void Assignment.

§ 256. **When Necessary.**—Where property in which one or more individuals are interested as creditors has become, from the circumstances of its owner, exposed to danger of loss, the parties so interested would seem to have an equitable right to be apprised of any arrangements for the disposition of such property; especially where such arrangements materially affect the remedies with which the law has provided them. And the professed object of assignments by insolvent or embarrassed debtors being the *benefit of their creditors*, a desire for the most effectual accomplishment of that object would seem naturally to lead a debtor, whose circumstances induce or compel him to contemplate such a disposition of his property, to acquaint his creditors with his intention and the reasons of it. This is, in some instances, actually done; the debtor not only informing his creditors, but consulting them with a view to their concurrence in the arrangements proposed; and to use the words of an eminent judge,[1] "the propriety of pursuing such a course will generally suggest it, where they can be conveniently assembled." It is nevertheless clearly unnecessary to the validity of a voluntary assignment by a debtor that the creditors should be consulted *previous* to making it;[2] and probably, in the majority of

---

[1] Marshall, C. J., in Brashear v. West, 7 Pet. 608, 613.
[2] Brashear v. West, 7 Pet. 608, 613. See Reinhard v. Bank of Kentucky, 6 B. Mon. 252; Skipwith's Ex'r v. Cunningham, 8 Leigh, 271; Phippen v. Durham, 8 Gratt. 457; Lee, J., in Johnston v. Zane's Trustees, 11 id. 552, 564; Allen, P., in Dance v. Seaman, id. 778, 781; Bank of Harlem v. Bayonne, 48 N. J. Eq. 246; 21 Atl. Rep. 478.

actual cases, creditors are not only not consulted, but not even apprised of the debtor's intention. Circumstances, indeed, often render it necessary that assignments planned on the most equitable principles should, when once determined on, be carried into effect with the least delay possible. The previous communication of the debtor's intention would tend to defeat the object or impair the efficiency of these conveyances, by stimulating some particular creditor to gain, by prompt action, that preference with which the law itself rewards superior vigilance and diligence, and thus pay himself in full out of property intended for general and equal distribution.[1]

It has sometimes been held, however, that *after* an assignment has been made, it must receive the assent, sanction or approval of the creditors in order to give it validity, and render it an operative transfer. To what extent this doctrine is correct, becomes an important consideration, which will form the subject of the present chapter.

The necessity of assent, it may be observed, depends in a material degree upon the form of the assignment itself, as being either to an assignee in trust, or directly to creditors.

§ 257. **Assent to Assignments to Trustees.**— Where the assignment is to a *trustee* for the benefit of creditors not parties to the deed, it may be laid down as a general rule in American law, that the assent of the creditors is not necessary to its validity, and the legal estate or title will pass to the assignee without such assent, so as to prevent a judgment creditor from acquiring a lien, if real, by his judgment, or if personal, by his execution, unless upon the ground of fraud.[2] This rule is said to be founded on the established principle of the common law,[3] that it is not necessary to the

---

[1] An assignment for the benefit of creditors is in no sense a contract between the debtor and his creditors, and does not depend for its validity upon their assent. Miles v. Parkhurst, 126 N. Y. 89.

[2] Nicoll v. Mumford, 4 Johns. Ch. 522, 529; Halsey v. Whitney, 4 Mason, 207, 214; Cunningham v. Freeborn, 11 Wend. 240, 248; Houston v. Nowland, 7 Gill & J. 480, 492; Garland, J., in United States v. Bank of the United States, 8 Rob. (La.) 262, 412; Reinhard v. Bank of Kentucky, 6 B. Mon. 252; Abercrombie v. Bradford, 16 Ala. 560; The Governor, use, etc. v. Campbell, 18 id. 556; Rankin v. Lodor, 21 id. 380; Jones v. Dougherty, 10 Ga. 273; Sadlier v. Fallon, 4 R. I. 490; Forbes v. Scannell, 13 Cal. 242; Valentine v. Decker, 43 Mo. 583. In Robbins v. Magee, 76 Ind. 381, a composition agreement and a voluntary assignment are held to differ in this: that the former depends for its force on the agreement of all the contracting parties, while the latter is not dependent for its validity upon the consent of creditors.

[3] But see, as to the rule in England, *post*, p. 339. And see Gibson v. Rees, 50 Ill. 383. In some of the states by statutory enactment the assent of creditors is presumed. See Iowa Code (1880), § 2116; McClain's Ann. Code (1888), § 3293; Price

creation of a trust by deed in favor of any persons that the *cestui que trust* should either be a party or assent to it. If the trust be for his benefit, the law presumes his assent to it until the contrary is shown. And it is clear that trusts may lawfully be created where there can be no present assent, for they may be in favor of persons not in existence. It is sufficient, in general, that in such cases there is a competent grantor to convey, and a competent grantee to take, the property.[1] "Deeds of trust," observes Chief Justice Marshall, " are often made for the benefit of persons who are absent,[2] and even for persons who are not in being. Whether they are for the payment of money or for any other purpose, no expression of the assent of the persons for whose benefit they are made has ever been required as preliminary to the vesting of the legal estate in the trustee. Such trusts have always been executed on the idea that the deed was complete when executed by the parties to it."[3]

From these views the rule has been deduced, and very clearly laid down by Mr. Justice Story, in the leading case of Halsey v. Whitney,[4] that in case of an assignment to a trustee for the benefit of creditors, "where the trust is for the benefit of all, and no release or other condition is stipulated for on behalf of the debtor, but the property is to be distributed equally among all the creditors *pro rata*, the assent of the creditor must be presumed, for the trust cannot be for his injury and must be for his benefit. It must always be for his benefit to receive as much of his debt as a debtor can pay. If then in such a case such an assent be necessary it may be inferred as a presumption of law until the contrary is shown." " That which purports to have been done for the benefit of creditors," observes Mr. Justice McLean in the case of Lawrence v. Davis,[5] " and which was manifestly for their advantage, will be presumed to have been done with their assent unless the contrary appear." The same rule has been approved by the supreme court of the United States,[6] and in the case of Tompkins v. Wheeler[7] was expressly applied to the case of an assignment directly to creditors, the court observing[8] that "where the deed is absolute on its face

v. Parker, 11 Iowa, 144; Derry Bank v. Davis, 44 N. H. 548; Fellows v. Greenleaf, 43 N. H. 421; Webster v. Harknes, 3 Mackey (D. C.), 220.

[1] Story, J., in Halsey v. Whitney, 4 Mason, 206, 214.

[2] The assent of absent persons to an assignment will be presumed until their dissent be expressed, if it be made for a valuable consideration and be beneficial to them. North v. Turner, 9 Serg. & R. 224.

[3] Marshall, C. J., in Brooks v. Marbury, 11 Wheat. 78, 97.

[4] 4 Mason, 206.

[5] 3 McLean, 177.

[6] Brooks v. Marbury, 11 Wheat. 78; Brashear v. West, 7 Pet. 608, 613.

[7] 16 Pet. 118.

[8] Id. 119, Thompson, J.

without any condition whatever attached to it, and for the benefit of the grantees, the presumption is, in the absence of all evidence to the contrary, that the grantees accepted the deed."

§ 258. **The Rule in Various States.**— The same rule has been adopted in several of the state courts. In New York it has long been settled that it is not necessary to the validity of an assignment in trust for the benefit of creditors that the creditors should be parties to it or signify their assent thereto;[1] and it makes no difference in this respect whether the assignment be with preferences[2] or without.[3] In North Carolina it has been held that the assent of creditors to a deed of assignment in trust is to be presumed unless the contrary be shown.[4] In Alabama there have been numerous decisions in regard to the necessity and the presumption of the assent of creditors. In the case of Rankin v. Lodor,[5] in the supreme court of the state, the general doctrine was stated by Phelan, J., who, in delivering the opinion of the court, laid it down as a "settled legal proposition" that where the provisions of a deed of assignment are clearly beneficial to a creditor his assent to the deed will be presumed without his signing it; but where it is not so his assent will not be presumed, but must be actually had.[5] The same doctrine was held in the later case of Lanier v. Driver, in the same court.[7] In the previous case of Townsend v. Harwell[8] the same doctrine was recognized,[9] but it was further said: "Such assignment will not be considered beneficial unless the deed devotes the property absolutely and under all circumstances to the payment of the debts secured,[10] nor where it provides for the delay of

---

[1] Nicoll v. Mumford, 4 Johns. Ch. 522, 529; Cunningham v. Freeborn, 11 Wend. 240, 248.

[2] Cunningham v. Freeborn, 11 Wend. 240, 248.

[3] Nicoll v. Mumford, 4 Johns. Ch. 522, 529.

[4] Ingram v. Kirkpatrick, 6 Ired. Eq. 462. Chief Justice Ruffin, in delivering the opinion of the court in this case, places it on the grounds of "the intrinsic soundness of the principle, the prevalent impression in the profession and the course of the adjudications in the United States." Id. 476. See Moore v. Hinnant, 89 N. C. 455.

[5] 21 Ala. 380.

[6] As authority for these propositions the learned judge (Id. 389, 390) cited Robinson v. Rapelye, 2 Stew. 86; Ashurst v. Martin, 9 Port. 566; Wiswall v. Ross, 4 Port. 321; Gazzam v. Poyntz, 4 Ala. 374; Kinnard v. Thompson, 12 id. 487; Governor, use, etc. v. Campbell, 17 id. 566; Brown v. Lyon, 17 id. 659; Elmes v. Sutherland, 7 id. 262; Maulden v. Armstead, 14 id. 702; Abercrombie v. Bradford, 16 id. 560; 2 Story's Eq., § 1036.

[7] 24 Ala. 149.

[8] 18 Ala. 301.

[9] Chilton, J., id. 303, citing Kinnard v. Thompson, and Gazzam v. Poyntz.

[10] Chilton, J., id., citing Dubose v. Dubose, 7 Ala. 235; Allen v. Montgomery & W. P. R. R. Co., 11 id. 437.

the creditors secured to be paid.¹ In other words, the necessity and presumption of assent are made to depend upon the character and object of the deed. The doctrine is very clearly laid down with this distinction by Ligon, J., in the case of Evans v. Lamar.² "A deed," said the learned judge, "which postpones a creditor in the collection of his debt beyond the time of its maturity is not valid as a conveyance of the property mentioned in it until it is assented to by the creditor. Until that time it is a mere power, and may be revoked by the levy of an execution by the creditor on the property intended to be conveyed by it. Neither will the assent of the creditor to such a deed be presumed.³ But where the deed is absolute in its terms, and conveys property to the trustees for the benefit of certain specified creditors who have not executed it, but whose debts are not postponed beyond their maturity, the assent of the creditors will be presumed, and the deed is not a mere power, but will be regarded as a valid and operative conveyance."⁴ In Rankin v. Lodor,⁵ Phelan, J., in delivering the opinion of the court, observed: "There is a class of deeds in trust or assignments which are not good at all without the assent of all the creditors.⁶ . . . They are generally where a man seeks to postpone the payment of his debts by conveying property in trust to secure or pay them. In such a case *all* the creditors must assent to give *any* validity to the deed, because that is the manifest intention of the grantor."⁷ The qualities requisite in a deed of assignment, in order to raise the presumption of assent by creditors, are very clearly stated in the case of Townsend v. Harwell⁸ in the following terms: "Where a deed of assignment for the payment of debts is made to a naked trustee with the intent on the part of the debtor to delay, hinder and defraud his creditors, the assent of the creditors will not be presumed, although the deed devotes the property conveyed absolutely and unconditionally to the payment of their debts, and the trustee did not participate in the fraudu-

---

¹ Chilton, J., id., citing Lockhart v. Wyatt, 10 Ala. 231; Hodges v. Wyatt, id. 271.

² 21 Ala. 333, 335.

³ The learned judge here cites Nelson v. Dunn, 15 Ala. 502; Lockwood v. Nelson, 16 id. 294; Smith v. Leavitts, 10 id. 93; Graham v. Lockwood, 8 id. 9; and Elmes v. Sutherland, 7 id. 262.

⁴ The learned judge cites Kinnard v. Thompson, 12 Ala. 487; Maulden v. Armistead, 14 id. 702; and Lockwood v. Nelson, 16 id. 295.

⁵ 21 Ala. 380, 390.

⁶ The learned judge here adds: "The class of cases to which I refer is considered, and the law applicable to them laid down, in the cases of Elmes v. Sutherland, 7 Ala. 262; Hodge v. Wyatt, 10 id. 271, and Kemp v. Porter, 7 id. 138."

⁷ The learned judge cites Elmes v. Sutherland, 7 Ala. 262.

⁸ 18 Ala. 301.

lent intent; but such assignment will be void as against creditors who have acquired a lien on the property before *actual* assent is given."[1]

A recital in an assignment declaring preferences, that "the creditors have assented to the terms herein stated," is the mere declaration of the grantor, and does not conclude any creditor who is not otherwise shown to have assented to it.[2]

In Kentucky it is not sufficient ground to invalidate a deed made for the benefit of creditors that it was made without their request or knowledge;[3] and their assent will be presumed.[4] The same rule prevails in Michigan.[5] In Georgia, where a deed is for the payment of creditors, their assent will be presumed unless their dissent be expressed.[6]

In Tennessee the cases are not entirely in accord, but in a late decision[7] which reviews all the authorities it is held that where there is no evidence upon the subject of acceptance or renunciation except that raised by the presumption that the beneficiaries accepted provisions made for their benefit, this presumption is sufficient to protect the rights of the beneficiaries against attaching creditors.

Prima facie the presumption of acceptance arises, and the filing of an attachment bill does not furnish any evidence rebutting the presumption.

The assent of creditors will always be presumed, provided all the formalities of execution essential to the validity of the deed have been complied with.[8] In Louisiana the assent of creditors is presumed, in case of an assignment for the benefit of all the creditors, where no release or other condition is stipulated for or on behalf of the debtor, but the property is to be distributed among all the creditors *pro rata*.[9] In Missouri an assignment for the benefit of

[1] Townsend v. Harwell, 18 Ala. 301. And see Benning v. Nelson, 23 id. 801; Shearer v. Loftin, 26 id. 703; Ashley v. Robinson, 29 id. 112; England v. Reynolds, 38 id. 370; Hodge v. Wyatt, 10 id. 271.
[2] Lehman v. Tallassee Mfg. Co., 64 Ala. 567.
[3] Reinhard v. Bank of Kentucky, 6 B. Mon. 252.
[4] Stewart v. Hall, 3 B. Mon. 218.
[5] Suydam v. Dequindre, Harring. Ch. 347.
[6] Jones v. Dougherty, 10 Ga. 273; McBride v. Bohanan, 50 id. 155.
[7] Washington v. Ryan, 5 Baxter (Tenn.), 622, decided mainly on the authority of Farquharson v. McDonald, 2 Heisk. 404. See Dews v. Olwill, 3 Baxter, 432; Green v. Demoss, 10 Humph. 371; Brown v. Vanlier, 7 id. 239; Field v. Arrowsmith, 3 id. 442; Saunders v. Harris, 1 Head, 185; Breedlove v. Stump, 3 Yerg. 257.
[8] Brevard v. Neely, 2 Sneed, 164; Furman v. Fisher, 4 Cold. 626. But see Mills v. Haines, 3 Head, 332; Brown v. Vanlier, 7 Humph. 239; Nailer v. Young, 7 Lea (Tenn.), 735; Truss v. Davidson, 90 Ala. 359; 7 S. Rep. 812.
[9] Fellows v. The Vicksburg Railroad & Banking Co., 6 Rob. 246.

creditors, containing no provision prejudicial to their interests, need not be signed by them; their assent thereto will be presumed in the absence of an attack upon the deed.[1]

And this is the rule in Maryland,[2] Arkansas,[3] Ohio[4] and Texas.[5] In Ohio and New Hampshire, by statutory enactment, the law presumes the assent of creditors to assignments executed for their benefit.[6] In Rhode Island[7] assignments without the assent of creditors are held valid; and, it seems, the same rule prevails in New Mexico.[8]

In Indiana[9] an assignment is valid without the consent of creditors, if made in good faith and in compliance with the statute.

In Pennsylvania it seems to be no objection to the validity of an assignment to a trustee for the benefit of creditors that it has not been expressly accepted by the creditors. Acceptance will be presumed where it is shown that the assignment was for their benefit, and there is no stipulation for a release of the debts, nor anything calculated to delay the creditors unreasonably.[10] There are some cases, however, in which the previous assent of creditors is expressly required. Thus, by a special provision, railroad and canal companies owing debts to contractors, laborers and workmen are prohibited from making any assignment so as to defeat, postpone or delay such creditors, without their *written assent first* had and obtained.[11]

In Massachusetts an assignment is invalid, as respects attaching creditors, until one or more of the creditors of the assignor has assented to it, even where it is made for the benefit of all the creditors, without preferences, and contains no stipulation that the

---

[1] Duval v. Raisin, 7 Mo. 449. And see Major v. Hill, 13 id. 247; Gale v. Mensing, 20 id. 461; Hulse v. Marshall, 9 Mo. App. 148.

[2] Kalkman v. McElderry, 16 Md. 56.

[3] Hempstead v. Johnson, 18 Ark. 123. But where the assignment is on the condition that the assignor shall be released, assent will not be presumed. McCain v. Pickens, 32 Ark. 339.

[4] Hyde v. Olds, 12 Ohio St. 591.

[5] Green v. Banks, 24 Tex. 508. See Thomas v. Chapman, 62 id. 193; Windham v. Patty, id. 490. This section of the act which requires that creditors shall make known their consent in writing does not make consent of any other character invalid. Sanborn v. Norton, 59 id. 308.

[6] See *ante*, p. 333, n. 3.

[7] Sadlier v. Fallon, 4 R. I. 490. See Daniels v. Willard, 16 Pick. 36; Smith v. Millett, 11 R. I. 528.

[8] Leitensdorfer v. Webb, 1 N. Mex. 34.

[9] Robbins v. Magee, 76 Ind. 381; Paul v. Logansport Nat. Bank, 16 id. 199; Eden v. Everson, 65 id. 113.

[10] United States v. Bank of the United States, 8 Rob. (La.) 262. See 1 Am. Lead. Cas. 95; Klapp's Assignees v. Shirk, 13 Pa. St. 589.

[11] Resolution of January 21, 1843; Laws of 1843, p. 367; Dunl. L., p. 886, ch. 572 [884, ed. 1853]; Purd. Dig. (ed. 1873), p. 90, pl. 1; Purd. Dig. (1883), p. 119, § 5.

creditors should release their demands, or take upon themselves any onerous condition; and the assent of creditors will not be presumed.[1] This rule appears to have been altered by the act of 1836,[2] since repealed.[3] Mr. Justice Wells, in a late case,[4] observes: "Independently of those laws (act of 1836), it has always been held that voluntary assignments by a debtor in trust for the payment of his debts, and without other adequate consideration, are invalid as against attachments, except so far as assented to by the creditors for whose benefit they were made. If assented to by creditors, such assignments are good at common law, and will protect the property or funds from attachment to the extent of the amount due to creditors thus assenting, unless by the conditions of the assignment it is made to take effect only upon the assent of all or a prescribed number of creditors."

The assent of creditors will not be presumed on the ground that it is apparently for their interest, but must be shown by some form of adoption or affirmative acquiescence.

Where the deed fixes a time for creditors to assent, the courts of Massachusetts have been strict in treating the time thus fixed as of the essence of the contract, and in refusing creditors the privilege of acceding to or executing the deed after such time has elapsed.[5]

§ 259. **The English Rule.**— In England it has been settled that the assent, or at least the privity, of creditors to an assignment in trust for their benefit is essential to render it operative in their behalf. In the case of Smith v. Keating,[6] in the exchequer cham-

---

[1] Russell v. Woodward, 10 Pick. 408; Pierce v. O'Brien, 129 Mass. 314; Swan v. Crafts, 124 id. 453; Widgery v. Haskell, 5 id. 144, 154; Stevens v. Bell, 6 id. 339, 342; Ingraham v. Geyer, 13 id. 146; Marston v. Coburn, 17 id. 454; Faulkner v. Hyman, 6 N. W. Rep. 846. See the opinion of Morton, J., in Fall River Iron Works Co. v. Croade, 15 Pick. 11, 15, 16; and in Everett v. Walcott, id. 94, 97. And see the opinion of Shaw, C. J., in Burlock v. Taylor, 16 id. 335, 339.

[2] Stats. of 1836, ch. 238. The reason of this rule is explained to have been the want of a court of equity to enforce the trust in behalf of the creditors, and a doubt, or at least a difficulty, as to a remedy at law. Nelson, J., in Cunningham v. Freeborn, 11 Wend. 240, 248, 249; Parsons, C. J., in Widgery v. Haskell, 5 Mass. 154, and in Stevens v. Bell, 6 id. 342. This difficulty was removed by the statute of 1836, which gave the creditors a remedy in equity against the trustee. Stat. of 1836, ch. 238, § 7. See Dewey, J., in Shattuck v. Freeman, 1 Metc. 10, 13.

[3] Nat. Mech. & Trad. Bank v. Eagle Sugar Refinery, 109 Mass. 38.

[4] May v. Wannemacher, 111 Mass. 202; Pierce v. O'Brien, 129 id. 314; Jones v. Tilton, 139 id. 418.

[5] National Union Bank v. Copeland, 141 Mass. 257; First National Bank v. Smith, 133 id. 26.

[6] 6 M., Gr. & Scott, 136.

ber, it was held that where a debtor conveys property in trust for creditors, to whom the conveyance is not communicated, and the creditors are not in any manner privy to it, the conveyance operates not as an assignment, but only as a power to the trustee, which is revocable by the debtor. The court say it is the same as if the debtor had given money to an agent to pay his creditors, to whom no communication had been made.[1] This was substantially affirming the principles of the decisions in Wallwyn v. Coutts,[2] and Garrard v. Lord Lauderdale,[3] which have been so frequently cited and commented upon in our own courts.[4] Indeed, there is a class of cases which establish the necessity of the creditors being actual parties to the deed in order to render it anything more than a mere revocable deed of agency.[5] In Smith v. Keating, already cited, the court (Parker, B.) speak with doubt as to the sufficiency of a mere privity on the part of the creditors as distinguished from actual assent.[6] But in the later case of Sigers v. Evans[7] the point seems to have been conceded. And in the same case the general doctrine that a conveyance to trustees operates as a mere power, revocable by the debtor, until communicated to or assented to by the creditors, was held not to apply to cases where the trustee himself takes a beneficial interest under the deed. In point of fact the prevailing practice seems to have hitherto been for the creditors to give a positive assent to the conveyance.[8]

§ 260. **Assent Provided for.**—Where the assignment is drawn with reference to the creditors becoming actual parties to it, as where it is in tripartite form, there must be an express assent on the part of the creditors, or some of them, in the mode prescribed; that is, by becoming parties to the deed, in order to render the in-

[1] The court rely on the case of Acton v. Woodgate, 2 Myl. & K. 492, and adopt the doctrine of Sir John Leach as there laid down.
[2] 3 Merivale, 707.
[3] 3 Simon, 1.
[4] By McCoun, V. C., in Cunningham v. Freeborn, 1 Edw. Ch. 263; by Nelson, J., in the same case on appeal (11 Wend. 249, 250); and at greater length by Ruffin, C. J., in Ingram v. Kirkpatrick, 6 Ired. Eq. 462. In the last case the doctrine of Wallwyn v. Coutts is shown to have been inconsistent with earlier decisions in the English courts. See the remarks of Nelson, J., in the late case of United States v. Hoyt, 1 Blatchf. C. C. 332, 334; and those of Pearson, J., in Stimpson v. Fries, 2 Jones' Eq. 156. Mr. Justice Walker, in Gibson v. Rees, 50 Ill. 383.
[5] See *ante*, pp. 127, 128.
[6] 6 M., Gr. & Scott, 158.
[7] 32 Eng. L. & Eq. 139. And see Acton v. Woodgate, 2 Myl. & K. 492; Paige v. Broom, 4 Russ. 6.
[8] This appears from the cases of Estwick v. Caillaud, 5 Term R. 420, and Ingliss v. Grant, id. 530.

strument complete and operative.[1] Where the creditors are named in the assignment as parties, and they are required to execute it before they can take under its provisions, they must signify their assent in that mode, otherwise they cannot take under the instrument.[2] So, where the assignment itself is upon the express condition that a majority of the creditors shall sanction it before it can take effect, such assent is necessary, and unless it be shown the assignment will be set aside.[3]

So, where there are conditions in an assignment, as, for instance, that the creditors shall release their debts, the presumption of assent does not arise because it involves a question of discretion upon which different minds may draw different conclusions.[4] So where the assignment contains clauses restricting the rights of creditors or limiting the liability of the assignee.[5]

Where an assignment is made with preferences to certain creditors, and the preferences are given unconditionally, their assent will be presumed.[6] So where the preferred creditors are to be paid in full.[7]

[1] See the opinion of Parker, C. J., in Hastings v. Baldwin, 17 Mass. 552, 556; Camp v. Mayer, 47 Ga. 414. In May v. Wannemacher, 111 Mass. 202, Mr. Justice Wells said: "In cases of assignment by tripartite instrument, it is generally necessary that creditors should execute the instrument in order to give it full effect, because such is the intent with which it is made. But when this is not required by the form of the instrument of assignment, it is only necessary that creditors should give such assent to its provisions as will recognize and affirm the acceptance and possession of the property by the assignee as made and held for their benefit and in their behalf, in accordance with the terms of the assignment," citing Russell v. Woodward, 10 Pick. 408; Everett v. Wolcott, 15 Pick. 94. And see Gale v. Mensing, 20 Mo. 461. And see *ante*, p. 155.

[2] 2 Story's Eq. Jur., § 1036*a;* Garrard v. Lord Lauderdale, 3 Sim. 1, cited id. But see *ante*, p. 127.

[3] Lawrence v. Davis, 3 McLean, 177. See the opinion of McCoun, V. C., in Cunningham v. Freeborn, 1 Edw. Ch. 262.

[4] Story, J., in Halsey v. Whitney, 4 Mason, 206, 215, Swearingen v. Slicer, 5 Mo. 241; Wakeman v. Grover, 4 Paige, 23.

[5] "No assent can be presumed when the assignment requires that the creditors shall give to the debtor a credit for the balance that remains due after the proceeds are distributed (Todd v. Bucknam, 11 Me. 41; Elmes v. Sutherland, 7 Ala. 262), or where the majority of the creditors are to have the power to fix the time for the sale of the property (Shearer v. Loftin, 26 Ala. 703), or where the assignee is disqualified (Spinney v. Portsmouth Co., 25 N. H. 9), or where the liability of the assignee is limited to actual receipts or wilful defaults (Brown v. Warren, 43 id. 430; Spinney v. Portsmouth Co., 25 id. 9), or where the assignees are not to be responsible for the neglect of each other (Spinney v. Portsmouth Co., 25 id. 9)," Bump on Fraud. Conv., p. 341.

[6] Wheeler v. Sumner, 4 Mason, 183; Ward v. Lewis, 4 Pick. 518; Brown v. Lyon, 17 Ala. 659.

[7] New England Bank v. Lewis, 8 Pick. 113, Deforest v. Bacon, 2 Conn. 633; North v. Turner, 9 S. & R. 244; Copeland v. Weld, 8 Greenl. 411; Reinhard v. Bank of Kentucky, 6 B. Mon. 252.

§ 261. Assent to Assignments Directly to Creditors.— Where the assignment is *directly* to the creditors, their assent is always required to give it validity, on the ground that it requires the agreement of two parties to make a contract.[1] In making an assignment of property, as in every other case of contract, the assent of at least two persons is necessary to its validity. A debtor cannot change his relations to his creditors by a voluntary assignment of his property to them. If, therefore, he makes an assignment and his creditors do not accept it, there is no change of property, and legal redress is open to the creditors as before the attempted assignment.[2]

§ 262. Assent, How and When Given.— The assent of the creditors may be given, either by becoming parties to and signing the instrument of assignment where it requires such signature,[3] or by signing an acceptance appended to it,[4] or by verbally assenting to it in terms,[5] or by actually receiving the benefit of it,[6] or by claiming such benefit,[7] or by taking legal measures to obtain such benefit.[8] Where signature is required it is not essential to the validity of the assignment that the creditors should sign at the time of execution by the other parties. It is sufficient, except against

---

[1] Nicoll v. Mumford, 4 Johns. Ch. 422, 529; Cunningham v. Freeborn, 11 Wend. 240, 248, 249; Jones v. Dougherty, 10 Ga. 273; Lawrence v. Davis, 3 McLean, 177; 2 Kent's Com. [533], 692, note.

[2] McLean, J., in Lawrence v. Davis, 3 McLean, 177.

[3] See *ante*, p. 127.

[4] See Bank of Bellows Falls v. Deming, 17 Vt. 366.

[5] Wiley v. Collins, 11 Me. 193; Brooks v. Marbury, 11 Wheat. 78. Mere inquiry on the part of a creditor to ascertain whether it would be profitable for him to accept an assignment as valid is not equivalent to inducing others to act upon it. Hubbard v. McNaughton, 43 Mich. 220.

[6] Brooks v. Marbury, *ubi supra*; Brown v. Minturn, 2 Gall. 557. In Scott v. Edes, 3 Minn. 387, the court said: "That the acceptance of dividends under the assignment is an assent to and confirmation of such assignment by the creditor has been uniformly held. A judgment lien creditor who accepts a dividend with other creditors under an assignment thereby affirms the deed, and cannot afterwards enforce his judgment against property embraced in the deed of assignment." Moule v. Buchanan, 11 Gill & J. 314; Lanahan v. Latrobe, 7 Md. 268. See Haskins v. Olcott, 13 Ohio St. 211; Frierson v. Branch, 30 Ark. 453; Chafee v. Fourth Nat. Bank, 71 Me. 514.

[7] Garland, J., in United States v. Bank of the United States, 8 Rob. (La.) 262, 412; May v. Wannemacher, 111 Mass. 202; Pierce v. O'Brien, 129 id. 314.

[8] See United States v. Hoyt, 1 Blatchf. C. C. 332; Zaring v. Cox, 78 Ky. (1 Rod.) 527. When a creditor proves his claim he is conclusively presumed to have assented to the assignment. Gathercole v. Bedel, 65 N. H. 211; 18 Atl. Rep. 319. So where he voluntarily submits the question of title in the assignee of the assigned property to a tribunal having supervisory control over such controversies. Sawyer v. McAdie, 70 Mich. 286; 38 N. W. Rep. 292. In the absence of fraud a creditor who files his claim in the manner prescribed by law thereby waives all objections to the regularity of the assignment and the title of the assignee to the assets. Littlejohn v. Turner, 73 Wis. 113; 40 N. W. Rep. 621.

intervening attaching creditors, if this is done afterwards,[1] and within the time limited for that purpose by statute or by the assignment itself.[2] Where a specific time is prescribed for the creditors to come in and assent to the assignment as parties thereto or otherwise, they must comply strictly with the condition or they will be excluded from the benefit of the trust; unless, indeed, by reason of absence from the country or some other cause, any creditor has not, within the time prescribed, had any knowledge of the existence of the assignment.[3]

And a creditor may lawfully qualify his assent by limiting his signature to a part of his demands and excepting the others from its operation.[4] In Alabama it has been held that a deed of assignment which devotes the property unconditionally to the payment of debts of the preferred creditors is complete and executed, as to them, immediately upon its delivery, notwithstanding it requires the rest of the grantor's creditors to execute it within six months, as a condition to their participation in the residue.[5]

In a case in Massachusetts, where a debtor, before executing a bipartite deed of assignment in trust, called on one of his creditors to prevent his being surprised that he was about assigning his property, proposed the making of such assignment and showed him a sketch of the mode in which the proceeds of the property were to be appropriated; and this sketch, so far as it regarded the creditor, was in substance made part of the deed, it was held that as against an attaching creditor this was not a sufficient assent to the assignment, although the other creditor was preferred therein.[6] In the same state, in the case of Nutter v. King,[7] it was held that under an assignment for the benefit of such of the assignor's creditors as should "verbally or in writing assent" thereto, language or conduct which reasonably interpreted shows assent is sufficient to give validity to the instrument. In a case in Arkansas, where a proposition was made by a debtor to his creditors to secure their debts by a deed of trust on time, with specified provisions; and the creditors assented, provided the provisions of the deed were satisfactorily arranged; and they required an early answer, and no answer was given, but a deed of trust was executed three months

---

[1] Halsey v. Whitney, 4 Mason, 206, 215; Wheeler v. Sumner, id. 183; Ward v. Lamson, 6 Pick. 358.

[2] Phœnix Bank v. Sullivan, 9 Pick. 410.

[3] Phœnix Bank v. Sullivan, 9 Pick. 410; De Caters v. Le Ray De Chaumont, 2 Paige, 490; Raworth v. Parker, 2 K. & J. 163; Nicholson v. Tutin, 2 id. 18. See Broadbent v. Thornton, 4 De G. & S. 65.

[4] Deering v. Cox, 6 Me. 404.

[5] Brown v. Lyon, 17 Ala. 659.

[6] Fall River Iron Works Company v. Croade, 15 Pick. 11.

[7] 152 Mass. 355; 25 N. E. Rep. 617.

afterwards, with provisions in it materially different from those proposed, it was held that the creditors were not bound to accept the deed.[1]

§ 263. Assent of How Many Creditors.— Where the assent of creditors is required by law, or by the form of the assignment itself (as where it is drawn with reference to being executed by them), it is not necessary that *all* should assent, in order to make the instrument valid and operative, unless there is some provision in the deed, or some settled collateral agreement, that it shall be void unless all assent.[2] Thus, in Massachusetts, in the case of Hastings v. Baldwin,[3] the execution of the assignment by a single creditor, and he also being the assignee, was held sufficient to render the deed complete and operative. The rule, indeed, in that state, prior to the statute of 1836, and since its repeal, was and is that the creditors must assent in sufficient numbers and value to cover the property assigned, otherwise the consideration might be deemed inadequate and void as to the non-assenting creditors, though good as to those assenting.[4] In Alabama it has been declared, as the general doctrine on this point, that where a debtor seeks to postpone the payment of his debts by conveying property in trust to secure or pay them, *all* the creditors must assent to the deed to give it validity.[5] But where the deed is beneficial to them, and does not delay them in the collection of their debts, the assent of a creditor will be sufficient to uphold the assignment for his benefit, though other creditors refuse to participate in the deed.[6]

In Nevada [7] all the creditors need not assent if the amount of the debts exceeds the value of the property. The assent of those representing debts equal to the value of the property assigned is a

[1] Rapelye v. Cummins, 11 Ark. 689.

[2] Story, J., in Halsey v. Whitney, 4 Mason, 215, 231. Where an agreement was made whereby a debtor was to convey property to a trustee for the benefit of creditors named in a schedule contained therein, the same to be signed by all the creditors in order to be binding, it was held that if one of said creditors refused to sign, the purchase of his claim by another of said creditors and the signing of the agreement by him would be equally effective. Towne v. Rublee, 51 Vt. 62. Non-assenting creditors, not present when the deed was executed, are in no way bound by the agreement of the assenting creditors to the release of a portion of their debts in an assignment made by the debtor for their benefit. Seale v. Vaiden, 10 Fed. Rep. 831; s. c., 4 Woods' C. C. 659.

[3] 17 Mass. 556.

[4] Woodward, J., in Adams v. Blodgett, 2 Woodb. & Minot, 237; Russell v. Woodward, 10 Pick. 408; Morton, J., in Fall River Iron Works Co. v. Croade, 15 id. 11, 15, 16; and in Everett v. Walcott, id. 94, 97; May v. Wannemacher, 111 Mass. 202.

[5] Rankin v. Loder, 21 Ala. 380, 390.

[6] Maulden v. Armistead, 14 Ala. 702. And see Shearer v. Loftin, 26 id. 703.

[7] Sadler v. Immel, 15 Nev. 265.

valid consideration, and gives full legal effect to an assignment; and if their debts are of less amount than the property, they constitute a good consideration *pro tanto*, and give the assignees a right to retain property to the amount of such debts.

§ 264. Assent by Attorney.— The assent of creditors to a deed of trust made by their debtor for their benefit may be given by the attorney holding their claims; and it will be presumed that where one undertakes to act as attorney, and does so act, he is duly authorized.[1] And if the act be not within the scope of his authority, it may be inferred that they sanctioned what was thus for their benefit.[2] But if an attorney, on behalf of his client, but without his authority, executes an assignment, it will bind the former but not the latter.[3] It is otherwise if the client has given an authority.[4]

§ 265. Assent by Partners.— If one of several partners who are creditors sign and seal an assignment in the name of the firm with a single seal, it is good, and binds all the partners who are present or assent to the execution. If none but the executing partner assent, it is still valid to release the debt and bind in this respect the rights of the firm.[5]

§ 266. Limitation of Time to Assent.— The assent to an assignment requiring a release cannot be given after the time limited by the assignor has expired, provided the creditor has had seasonable notice of the assignment, or provided proper means have been taken to give the notice.[6] Being thus precluded from any participation in the fund, the creditor's only claim is upon the surplus reserved to the debtor, if any should remain after satisfying the debts

---

[1] Hatch v. Smith, 5 Mass. 53.

[2] Vernon v. Morton, 8 Dana, 247.

[3] Hatch v. Smith, 5 Mass. 42, 51; Parrot v. Wells, 2 Vern. 127; Johnson v. Ogilby, 3 P. Wms. 277.

[4] Hatch v. Smith, *ubi supra*; Johnson v. Ogilby, *ubi supra*.

[5] Story, J., in Halsey v. Whitney, 4 Mason, 206, 232. See Pierson v. Hooker, 3 Johns. 68; Mackay v. Bloodgood, 9 id. 285; Bulkley v. Dayton, 14 id. 387; Bruen v. Marquand, 17 id. 53; McBride v. Hagan, 1 Wend. 326; Salmon v. Davis, 4 Binn. 375; Emerson v. Knower, 8 Pick. 63; Ball v. Dunsterville, 4 Term R. 313.

[6] Phenix Bank v. Sullivan, 9 Pick. 410. See Raworth v. Parker, 2 K. & J. 163; Dews v. Olwill, 3 Baxter (Tenn.), 432. Where an assignment provided that creditors should release within a specified time, and that the shares of those who did not release should be paid back to the assignor, it was held that the assignee could not be garnished for the share of a creditor who did not accept the terms of the assignment before the service of the writ on the assignee. Smith v. Millett, 11 R. I. 528.

of the creditors who accept their proportion of the trust fund upon the terms proposed.[1]

§ 267. **Presumption of Assent from Lapse of Time.**— The acceptance of the trust by the trustees of a debtor, and the acquiescence of the creditors for more than twenty years, has been held to afford presumptive evidence in favor of their assent,[2] at least where the question of assent is not made a subject of direct inquiry by the pleadings in an action brought in their behalf.[3]

§ 268. **Assent to Void Assignment.**— The assent of creditors will sometimes have the effect of giving validity to a void assignment. Thus in a case in Vermont it has been held that an assignment which is void or inoperative under the act of 1843, declaring certain general assignments void, will, if assented to by the creditors, become operative and binding upon them.[4] The court (Redfield, C. J.), in giving their opinion in this case, say: "It is obvious, if all the creditors assent, the defect is cured. . . . And if the assent of all makes it binding, it is difficult to see why the assent of any less number must not have the same effect as to them. And this making it binding upon these creditors it is binding upon the other creditors, if it be such a disposition of the effects as the creditor has a right to make."[5] But in Indiana it has been held that the assent of part of the creditors to an assignment of personal property which is fraudulent as between the debtor and the assignees, the creditors having an opportunity to observe the suspicious nature of the transaction, does not purge the contract of

---

[1] De Caters v. Le Ray De Chaumont, 2 Paige, 490. But acceptance may be waived by the grantor. Bank v. Partee, 99 U. S. 325.

[2] Burke's Estate, 11 Par. Sel. Cas. (Pa.) 470. When the assignment provided for the distribution of the property among such creditors as should execute it before a specified day, *held*, that where the parties assumed to act under the instrument, although it was not actually executed by the creditors, the creditors might maintain an action, after the expiration of fifteen years, to have the trust enforced. Nicholson v. Tutin, 2 K. & J. 18. But where the creditors for whose benefit an assignment was made remained inactive for eight years thereafter, and the trust was then revoked by an arrangement between the debtor and grantor and the trustee, and such creditors continued to remain inactive for nearly thirteen years after the revocation, it was held that such prolonged inaction would overcome all presumption of assent to the terms of the assignment on the part of the creditors, and the revocation of the trust will be sustained so as to preclude the creditors or their assignees from afterwards asserting any claim under the trust. Gibson v. Rees, 50 Ill. 383.

[3] Brashear v. West, 7 Pet. 608. And see Major v. Hill, 13 Mo. 247.

[4] Merrill v. Englesby, 28 Vt. 150.

[5] Merrill v. Englesby, 28 Vt. 157. See, also, White v. Banks, 21 Ala. 705; Geisse v. Beall, 3 Wis. 307.

fraud even as to them, and the fraud pervades and vitiates the whole assignment.[1] And in a case in the circuit court for the district of Rhode Island, where a fraudulent assignment had been assented to by certain creditors after attachments by other creditors, it was held that such assent could not purge the fraud nor render the deed valid as against the attachments; and that the assignment being actually, and not merely constructively fraudulent, it was wholly void, and could not be allowed to stand as a security to a third person who had assented to it, with notice of the fraud or of such facts as were sufficient to put him on inquiry and enable him to learn the existence of the fraud.[2] A fraudulent assignment for the benefit of creditors is not so absolutely void that a creditor's right to complain of it may not be lost by waiver or acquiescence; he cannot attack it until he has in some way acquired a legal standing, and he may let it alone if he chooses to do so.[3]

Where creditors have assented to an assignment by knowingly receiving payments of dividends under it, they cannot then repudiate it and attach the property assigned. And this is true where creditors elect to affirm a fraudulent assignment made under a misunderstanding of the law.[4] An exception, however, exists where an assignment is declared void by the law of the place where it is made. If it is absolutely void by such law, no assent or ratification of creditors can make it valid; but if it is only void at the election of such creditors as choose to avoid it, and they assent to it or ratify it by accepting dividends under it, then as to such assenting or ratifying creditors the assignment will be sustained.[5]

Assent of creditors to a void assignment must be actually given, however, and will not be presumed. In the case last cited Mr. Justice Curtis declared himself not prepared to hold that the assent of creditors to a void deed is to be presumed, because the whole

[1] Caldwell v. Williams, 1 Ind. 405. In Eden v. Everson, 65 id. 113, it was held that an assignment was not binding upon an execution creditor, even though after it was made he had verbally assented thereto; no property passes until the deed has been filed and recorded as required by the statute.

[2] Stewart v. Spencer, 1 Curt. 167. The learned judge cites Boyd v. Dunlop, 1 Johns. Ch. 482; Harris v. Sumner, 2 Pick. 129; Halsey v. Whitney, 4 Mason, 218.

[3] Blake v. Hubbard, 45 Mich. 1; 7 N. W. Rep. 204.

[4] Levy v. James, 49 Hun, 161; 1 N. Y. S. Rep. 604.

[5] Chafee v. Fourth Nat. Bank, 71 Me. 514. In this case the assignment was valid by the law of the place where made, and not absolutely void by the law of Maine. Non-resident creditors were there bound by it. Resident creditors might there avoid it. But if instead of electing to do so they assented and accepted payment thereby secured to them, then their right to treat the assignment as void was held to be extinguished. Similarly in Greene v. Sprague Mfg. Co., 52 Conn. 330; Thompson v. Fry, 51 Hun, 296; 4 N. Y. S. Rep. 166; Sickman v. Abernathy, 14 Colo. 174; 23 Pac. Rep. 447; Loomis v. Griffin, 78 Iowa, 487; 43 N. W. Rep. 290.

foundation for the presumption fails.[1] The law cannot deem such a deed beneficial to the third party. Upon the assumption that the deed is valid upon its face and is rendered void only by extraneous facts, the assent of creditors is still not to be presumed, because "the presumption of assent is not founded on the face of the instrument, but in the nature and circumstances of the entire case."[2] Nor will such an assent be presumed to the prejudice of the just rights of third persons; a legal fiction is not to be permitted so to operate. *In fictione juris semper æquitas existit.*

A creditor is not precluded by taking under the assignment from showing fraud and collusion as to such debts secured by the assignment as may stand in his way or prejudice him by being paid.[3]

A consent of creditors without full knowledge of all the material facts is not binding upon them so as to prevent them from bringing an action to set aside the assignment for fraud.[4]

[1] 1 Curt. 167.
[2] The learned judge quotes Hosmer, C. J., in Camp v. Camp, 5 Conn. 309.
[3] Mackintosh v. Corner, 32 Md. 598; Reiff v. Eshleman, 52 id. 582.
[4] Hairgrove v. Millington, 8 Kan. 780.

www.ingramcontent.com/pod-product-compliance
Lightning Source LLC
Chambersburg PA
CBHW020624220526
45464CB00001B/12